Essentials of Life-Span Development

Essentials of Life-Span Development

John W. Santrock

University of Texas at Dallas

 **Higher Education**

Boston   Burr Ridge, IL   Dubuque, IA   Madison, WI   New York
San Francisco   St. Louis   Bangkok   Bogotá   Caracas   Kuala Lumpur
Lisbon   London   Madrid   Mexico City   Milan   Montreal   New Delhi
Santiago   Seoul   Singapore   Sydney   Taipei   Toronto

McGraw-Hill
Higher Education

ESSENTIALS OF LIFE-SPAN DEVELOPMENT

Published by McGraw-Hill, a business unit of The McGraw-Hill Companies, Inc., 1221 Avenue of the Americas, New York, NY 10020. Copyright © 2008 by the McGraw-Hill Companies, Inc. All rights reserved. No part of this publication may be reproduced or distributed in any form or by any means, or stored in a database or retrieval system, without the prior written consent of The McGraw-Hill Companies, Inc., including, but not limited to, in any network or other electronic storage or transmission, or broadcast for distance learning.

This book is printed on acid-free paper.

Printed in China

4 5 6 7 8 9 0 CTP/CTP 0 9

ISBN: 978-0-07-340551-3
MHID: 0-07-340551-5

Editor in Chief: *Emily Barrosse*
Publisher: *Beth Mejia*
Executive Editor: *Michael Sugarman*
Director of Development: *Dawn Groundwater*
Development Editor, Supplements: *Meghan Campbell*
Executive Manager for Market Development: *Sheryl Adams*
Executive Marketing Manager: *James Headley*
Media Producer: *Alex Rohrs*
Production Editor: *Melissa Williams*
Project Manager: *Marilyn Rothenberger*
Manuscript Editor: *Beatrice Sussman*
Cover Design: *Preston Thomas*
Interior Design: *Jeanne Calabrese*
Cover Image: © *Tay Rees/The Image Bank/Getty Images*
Art Manager: *Robin Mouat*
Illustrators: *John and Judy Waller, Rennie Evans*
Photo Research: *LouAnn Wilson*
Senior Production Supervisor: *Tandra Jorgensen*

This book was set in 9.5/12 Meridian by Aptara, Inc. and printed on 45# Pub Matte Plus by CTPS

Photo and text credits can be found following the References on page C-1, an extension of the copyright page.

Library of Congress Cataloging-in-Publication Data

Santrock, John W.
    Essentials of life-span development / John W. Santrock—1st ed.
        p. cm.
        Includes bibliographical references and index.
        ISBN-13: 978-0-07-340551-3; ISBN-10: 0-07-340551-5
    1. Developmental psychology—Textbooks. I. Title

BF711.S26 2008
155--dc22

2007078788

www.mhhe.com

With special appreciation to my wife, Mary Jo

About the Author

John Santrock with his two grandsons, Alex and Luke.

John W. Santrock John Santrock received his Ph.D. from the University of Minnesota in 1973. He taught at the University of Charleston and the University of Georgia before joining the Program in Psychology and Human Development at the University of Texas at Dallas, where he currently teaches a number of undergraduate courses and was given the University's Effective Teaching Award in 2006.

John has been a member of the editorial boards of Child Development and Developmental Psychology. His research on father custody is widely cited and used in expert witness testimony to promote flexibility and alternative considerations in custody disputes. John also has authored these exceptional McGraw-Hill texts: Psychology (8th edition), Children (10th edition), Adolescence (12th edition), Life Span Development (11th edition), Topical Life-Span Development (4th edition), and Educational Psychology (3rd edition).

For many years, John was involved in tennis as a player, teaching professional, and coach of professional tennis players. He has been married for more than 35 years to his wife, Mary Jo, who is a realtor. He has two daughters—Tracy, and Jennifer, who is a medical sales specialist at Medtronic. Tracy recently completed the New York City Marathon, and Jennifer was in the top 100 ranked players on the Women's Professional Tennis Tour. He has one granddaughter, Jordan, age 15, and two grandsons, Alex, age 3, and Luke, age 1. In the last decade, John also has spent time painting expressionist art.

Contents

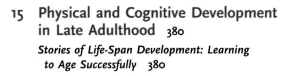

CONTENTS

xiii

Preface

Having taught life-span development every semester for the last 25 years, I found it impossible to cover everything in a comprehensive life-span development text in a single semester. Instructors from across the country have expressed similar frustrations. They wanted a streamlined text that would capture the core, essential concepts of life-span development, yet retain a strong research and applications focus. *Essentials of Life-Span Development* is written to help meet that need. *Essentials of Life-Span Development* presents the core concepts of life-span development along with applications for students in a variety of majors and career paths.

Essential Coverage

Essentials of Life-Span Development is a chronological book organized into 17 manageable chapters. It focuses on the essential topics from the prenatal period through late adulthood and death. Although brief, this text presents all of the core topics, key ideas, and most important research in life-span development that students need to know.

For every topic, I carefully examined the content to determine what could be eliminated and what needed to be included as the core material for a brief text on life-span development. Adopters, reviewers, and consultants for this extensive project provided very detailed feedback about what applications, research, and learning tools they deemed essential for a brief text on life-span development text. Their collective wisdom helped to create an essentials text that is not just a brief, cookie-cutter version of the big text. Too often essentials or brief texts are simply shorter (sometimes only minimally shorter), cut-and-paste, nonupdated versions of the big text. That is not the case for *Essentials of Life-Span Development*. The extensive rewriting, updating, and feedback from adopters, reviewers, and consultants have resulted in an essentials text that is different in many ways from its longer, more detailed counterpart.

Essential Applications

Applied examples give students a sense that the field of life-span development has personal meaning for them. Within the text are numerous applied examples. Chapter 1, for example, illustrates socioemotional processes: an infant's smile in response to her mother's touch, a young boy's aggressive attack on a playmate, a girl's development of assertiveness, an adolescent's joy at the senior prom, and the affection of an elderly couple.

In addition to applied examples within the formal text discussion, *Essentials of Life-Span Development* offers applications for students in a variety of majors and career paths.

- *How Would You...? Questions.* Recognizing that many students enrolled in the life-span course major in a variety subjects, *Essentials of Life-Span Development* provides additional applications specific to their interests. Perhaps the most prominent of these career areas are education, human development and family studies, health professions (such as nursing, pediatrics, geriatrics, and medical technology), psychology, and social work. To engage these students and ensure that this book orients them to the concepts that are key to their understanding of life-span development, I have asked instructors specializing in these fields to contribute How Would You...? questions for each chapter. Stragetically placed in the margin next to the relevant chapter content, these questions spotlight the essential ideas for these students to take away from the chapter content.

- *Careers in Life-Span Development.* A distinctive way in which applications are presented is the Careers in Life-Span Development profile. This feature personalizes life-span development by describing an individual working in a career related to the chapter's focus. Chapter 2, for example, profiles Holly Ishmael, a genetic counselor. The feature describes Ms. Ishamel's education and work setting, includes a direct quote from Ms. Ishmael about her career, discusses various employment options for genetic counselors, and provides resources for students to find out more about careers in genetic counseling.

Essential Research

A text on life-span development relies on a solid research foundation for its credibility. To fulfill this need, I have surveyed the most recent research in the field, synthesized that research for the student reader, and obtained detailed evaluations by leading experts in key areas of life-span development.

Essentials of Life-Span Development presents the latest, most contemporary research on each period of the human life span, including more than 1,000 citations from 2006 to 2008 alone. The text also includes discussion of material from research reviews in two recent major handbooks in life-span development: (1) *Handbook of Child Psychology* (2006) and (2) *Handbook of the Psychology of Aging* (2006). As a result, instructors and students can rely on *Essentials of Life-Span Development* as a scientifically based, up-to-date guide to the latest theories and findings across the field of life-span development.

Life-span development has become such an enormous, complex field that no single author can possibly be an expert in all of its many different areas. For this reason, I have sought the input of experts who provided me with detailed evaluations and recommendations in their areas of expertise. These expert research consultants evaluated my manuscript for the full-length *Life-Span Development* (11th edition) book, and much of their feedback is incorporated in *Essentials of Life-Span Development.* I am therefore pleased to give them credit in this book as well; you will find their names listed at the end of this Preface.

Essential Learning Tools for Students

To succeed as a teaching and learning tool, a text must be student-friendly—otherwise students will not read and understand it. Key ingredients in student-friendliness are the way a text is written and its pedagogy. I take very seriously the importance of communicating complex theories and research in a straightforward writing style that undergraduates can understand. At every opportunity, I incorporated examples of concepts and research that are interesting and relevant to students' lives. I also designed the following pedagogical elements to promote student understanding and retention of each chapter's content:

* *Stories of Life-Span Development.* Each chapter begins with a story, either factual or hypothetical that raises issues that will be covered in the chapter in an applied, true-to-life fashion that piques student interest. For example, Chapter 4 begins with a story of child care for 17-month-old Tom.
* *Summary.* End-of-chapter summaries, organized by section headings, provide a recap of the essential theories and concepts of each chapter.
* *Key Terms and Glossary.* Key terms appear in boldface within the formal text discussion, and their definitions appear in the margin near where they are introduced. Key terms also are listed and page-referenced at the end of each chapter and alphabetically listed, defined, and page-referenced in a comprehensive Glossary at the end of the book.

Acknowledgments

The development and writing of *Essentials of Life-Span Development* was heavily influenced by a remarkable and extensive number of consultants, reviewers, and adopters.

Application Contributors

I am especially grateful to the contributors who helped develop the *How Would You...?* questions for the various majors taking the life-span development course:

Maida Berenblatt, Suffolk Community College
Michael E. Barber, Santa Fe Community College
Susan A. Greimel, Santa Fe Community College
Russell Isabella, University of Utah
Jean Mandernach, University of Nebraska at Kearney

Expert Consultants

I owe a special gratitude to the expert consultants who provided detailed feedback about *Life-span Develoment.* They are literally a Who's Who in the field of life-span development:

EXPERT	ESSENTIALS CHAPTERS AND TOPICS
Paul Baltes *Max Planck Institute, Berlin, Germany*	Life-Span Developmental Theory and Aging Research, Chapters 1, 13, 15, and 16
Elisa Velasquez *Sonoma State University*	Culture and Diversity throughout Life-Span development
David Moore *Pitzer College and Claremont Graduate University*	Biological Beginnings, Chapter 2
Tiffany Field *University of Miami*	Prenatal Development and Birth, Chapter 2
Jean Mandler *University of California–San Diego*	Cognitive Development in Infancy, Chapter 3
Joesph Campos *University of California–Berkeley*	Socioemotional Development in Infancy, Chapter 4
Jean Berko Gleason *Boston University*	Language Development, Chapters 3, 5, and 7
Ross D. Parke *University of California–Riverside*	Socioemotional Development in Childhood, Chapters 4, 6, and 8
L. Monique Ward *University of Michigan*	Adolescent Development, Chapters 9 and 10
John Schulenberg *University of Michigan*	Early Adulthood, Chapters 11 and 12
William Hoyer *Syracuse University*	Cognitive Development in Adult Development and Aging, Chapters 13 and 15
Camille Wortman *State University of New York–Stony Brook*	Chapter 17, Death, Dying, and Grieving

General Text Reviewers

I gratefully acknowledge the extensive comments and feedback from instructors around the nation who reviewed various drafts of *Essentials of Life-Span Development* and the book's design. The following individuals should feel a special pride in helping me craft this unique text:

Reviewers

Maida Berenblatt, *Suffolk Community College*

Michael E. Barber, *Santa Fe Community College*

Gabriel Batarseh, *Francis Marion University*

Troy E. Beckert, *Utah State University*

Alda Blakeney, *Kennesaw State University*

Candice L. Branson, *Kapiolani Community College*

Margaret M. Bushong, *Liberty University*

Stewart Cohen, *University of Rhode Island*

Rock Doddridge, *Asheville Buncombe Technical*

Laura Duvall, *Heartland Community College*

Jenni Fauchier, *Metro Community College–Ft. Omaha*

Sharon Ghazarian, *University of North Carolina–Greensboro*

Dan Grangaard, *Austin Community College*

Rodney J. Grisham, *Indian River Community College*

Rea Gubler, *Southern Utah University*

Bret Heintz, *Delgado Community College*

Sandra Hellyer, *Butler University*

Randy Holley, *Liberty University*

Debra L. Hollister, *Valencia Community College*

Rosemary T. Hornack, *Meredith College*

Alycia Hund, *Illinois State University*

Rebecca Inkrott, *Sinclair Community College–Dayton*

Russell Isabella, *University of Utah*

Alisha Janowsky, *Florida Atlantic University*

Shenan Kroupa, *Indiana University Purdue University Indianapolis*

Jean Mandernach, *University of Nebraska–Kearney*

Carrie Margolin, *Evergreen State College*

Michael Jason McCoy, *Cape Fear Community College*

Ron Mossler, *Los Angeles Community College*

Bob Pasnak, *George Mason University*

Janet Reis, *University of Illinois–Urbana*

Vicki Ritts, *St. Louis Community College–Meramec*

Jeffrey Sargent, *Lee University*

Jason Scofield, *University of Alabama*

Christin E. Seifert, *Montana State University*

Peggy Skinner, *South Plains College*

Wayne Stein, *Brevard Community College–Melbourne*

Kevin Sumrall, *Montgomery College*

Barbara VanHorn, *Indian River Community College*

Laura Wasielewski, *St. Anselm College*

Lois Willoughby, *Miami Dade College–Kendall*

A. Claire Zaborowski, *San Jacinto College*

Pauline Davey Zeece, *University of Nebraska–Lincoln*

Design Reviewers

Cheryl Almeida, *Johnson and Wales University*

Candice L. Branson, *Kapiolani Community College*

Debra Hollister, *Valencia Community College*

Rosemary Hornack, *Meredith College*

Alicia Hund, *Illinois State University*

Jean Mandernach, *University of Nebraska–Kearney*

Michael Jason Scofield, *University of Alabama*

Christin Seifert, *Montana State University*

Pauline Davey Zeece, *University of Nebraska–Lincoln*

The McGraw-Hill Team

A large number of outstanding professionals at McGraw-Hill helped me to produce *Essentials of Life-Span Development*. I especially want to thank Beth Mejia; Publisher, Mike Sugarman, Executive Editor; Dawn Groundwater, Director of Development; Sheryl Adams, Executive Manager for Market Development; and Sarah Martin and James Headley, Executive Marketing Managers for the incredible vision, planning, and support they provided for this project.

Introduction

Stories of Life-Span Development: How Did Ted Kaczynski Become Ted Kaczynski and Alice Walker Become Alice Walker?

Ted Kaczynski sprinted through high school, not bothering with his junior year and making only passing efforts at social contact. Off to Harvard at age 16, Kaczynski was a loner during his college years. One of his roommates at Harvard said that he avoided people by quickly shuffling by them and slamming the door behind him. After obtaining his Ph.D. in mathematics at the University of Michigan, Kaczynski became a professor at the University of California at Berkeley. His colleagues there remember him as hiding from social

circumstances—no friends, no allies, no networking.

After several years at Berkeley, Kaczynski resigned and moved to a rural area of Montana, where he lived as a hermit in a crude shack for 25 years. Town residents described him as a bearded eccentric. Kaczynski traced his own difficulties to growing up as a genius in a kid's body and sticking out like a sore thumb in his surroundings as a child. In 1996, he was arrested and charged as the notorious Unabomber, America's most wanted killer. Over the

course of 17 years, Kaczynski had sent 16 mail bombs that left 23 people wounded or maimed, and 3 people dead. In 1998, he pleaded guilty to the offenses and was sentenced to life in prison.

A decade before Kaczynski mailed his first bomb, Alice Walker spent her days battling racism in Mississippi. She had recently won her first writing fellowship, but rather than use the money to follow her dream of moving to Senegal, Africa, she put herself into the heart and heat of the civil rights movement. Walker had grown up knowing the brutal effects of poverty and racism. Born in 1944, she was the eighth child of Georgia sharecroppers who earned $300 a year. When Walker was 8, her brother accidentally shot her in the left eye with a BB gun. By the time her parents got her to the hospital a week later (they had no car), she was blind in that eye and it had developed a disfiguring layer of scar tissue. Despite the counts against her, Walker overcame pain and anger and went on to win a Pulitzer Prize for her book *The Color Purple*. She became not only a novelist but also an essayist, a poet, a short-story writer, and a social activist.

What leads one individual, so full of promise, to commit brutal acts of violence and another to turn poverty and trauma into a rich literary harvest? If you have ever wondered why people turn out the way they do, you have asked yourself the central question we will explore in this book.

This book is a window into the journey of human development—your own and that of every other member of the human species. Every life is distinct, a new biography in the world. Examining the shape of life-span development helps us to understand it better. In this first chapter, we explore what it means to take a life-span perspective on development, examine the nature of development, and outline how science helps us to understand it. ∎

Ted Kaczynski, the convicted Unabomber, traced his difficulties to growing up as a genius in a kid's body and not fitting in when he was a child.

Alice Walker won the Pulitzer Prize for her book *The Color Purple*. Like the characters in her book, Walker overcame pain and anger to triumph and celebrate the human spirit.

The Life-Span Perspective

Each of us develops partly like all other individuals, partly like some other individuals, and partly like no other individuals. Most of the time our attention is directed to an individual's uniqueness. But as humans, we have all traveled some common paths. Each of us—Leonardo da Vinci, Joan of Arc, George Washington, Martin Luther King, Jr., and you—walked at about 1 year, engaged in fantasy play as a young child, and became more independent as a youth. Each of us, if we live long enough, will experience hearing problems and the death of family members and friends. This is the general course of our **development**, the pattern of movement or change that begins at conception and continues through the human life span.

In this section we explore what is meant by the concept of development and why the study of life-span development is important. We outline the main characteristics of the life-span perspective and discuss various sources of contextual influences. In addition, we examine some contemporary concerns in life-span development.

The Importance of Studying Life-Span Development

How might people benefit from examining life-span development? Perhaps you are, or will be, a parent or teacher. If so, responsibility for children is, or will be, a part of your everyday life. The more you learn about them, the better you can deal with them. Perhaps you hope to gain some insight about your own history—as an infant, a child, an adolescent, or a young adult. Perhaps you want to know more about what your life will be like as you grow through the adult years—as a middle-aged adult, or as an adult in old age, for example. Or perhaps you just stumbled onto this course, thinking that it sounded intriguing and that the study of the human life span might raise some provocative issues. Whatever your reasons, you will discover that the study of life-span development is intriguing and filled with information about who we are, how we came to be this way, and where our future will take us.

Most development involves growth, but it also includes decline (as in dying). In exploring development, we examine the life span from the point of conception until the time when life (at least, life as we know it) ends. You will see yourself as an infant, as a child, and as an adolescent, and be stimulated to think about how those years influenced the kind of individual you are today. And you will see yourself as a young adult, as a middle-aged adult, and as an adult in old age, and be motivated to think about how your experiences today will influence your development through the remainder of your adult years.

development The pattern of movement or change that starts at conception and continues through the human life span.

life-span perspective The perspective that development is lifelong, multidimensional, multidirectional, plastic, multidisciplinary, and contextual; involves growth, maintenance, and regulation; and is constructed through biological, sociocultural, and individual factors working together.

Characteristics of the Life–Span Perspective

Although growth and development are dramatic during the first two decades of life, development is not something that happens only to children and adolescents. The *traditional approach* to the study of development emphasizes extensive change from birth to adolescence (especially during infancy), little or no change in adulthood, and decline in old age. But a great deal of change does occur in the five or six decades after adolescence. The *life-span approach* emphasizes developmental change throughout adulthood as well as childhood (Baltes, Lindenberger, & Staudinger, 2006; Schaie, 2007).

Recent increases in human life expectancy contributed to the popularity of the life-span approach to development. The upper boundary of the *human life span* (based on the oldest age documented) is 122 years, as indicated in Figure 1.1; this maximum life span of humans has not changed since the beginning of recorded history. What has changed is *life expectancy*: the average number of years that a person born in a particular year can expect to live. In the twentieth century alone, life expectancy increased by 30 years, thanks to improvements in sanitation, nutrition, and medicine (see Figure 1.2). In 2006, the U.S. life expectancy was 78 years of age (U.S. Bureau of the Census, 2006). Today, for most individuals in developed countries, childhood and adolescence represent only about one-fourth of their lives.

The belief that development occurs throughout life is central to the life-span perspective on human development, but this perspective has other characteristics as well. According to life-span development expert Paul Baltes (1939–2006), the **life-span perspective** views

How Would You...?
As a health-care professional, how would you identify individual lifestyle choices that may enhance life expectancy?

Species (common name)	Maximum Life Span (years)
Human	122
Galápagos turtle	100+
Indian elephant	70
Chinese alligator	52
Golden eagle	46
Gorilla	39
Common toad	36
Domestic cat	27
Domestic dog	20
Vampire bat	13
House mouse	3

Figure 1.1 Maximum Recorded Life Span for Different Species Our only competitor for the maximum recorded life span is the Galápagos turtle.

Time Period	Average Life Expectancy (years)
2006, USA	78
1954, USA	70
1915, USA	54
1900, USA	47
19th century, England	41
1620, Massachusetts Bay Colony	35
Middle Ages, England	33
Ancient Greece	20
Prehistoric times	18

Figure 1.2 Human Life Expectancy at Birth from Prehistoric to Contemporary Times It took 5,000 years to extend human life expectancy from 18 to 41 years of age.

development as lifelong, multidimensional, multidirectional, plastic, multidisciplinary, and contextual, and as a process that involves growth, maintenance, and regulation of loss (Baltes, 1987, 2003; Baltes, Lindenberger, & Staudinger, 2006). In Baltes' view, it is important to understand that development is constructed through biological, sociocultural, and individual factors working together (Baltes, Reuter-Lorenz, & Rösler, 2006). Let's look at each of these characteristics.

Development Is Lifelong

In the life-span perspective, early adulthood is not the endpoint of development; rather, no age period dominates development. Researchers increasingly study the experiences and psychological orientations of adults at different points in their lives. Later in this chapter we describe the age periods of development and their characteristics.

Development Is Multidimensional

Whatever your age, your body, your mind, your emotions, and your relationships are changing and affecting each other. Consider the development of Ted Kaczynski, the bomber discussed at the opening of the chapter. When he was six months old, he was hospitalized with a severe allergic reaction, and his parents were rarely allowed to visit the baby. According to his mother, the previously happy baby was never the same. The infant became withdrawn and unresponsive. As Ted grew up, he had periodic "shutdowns" accompanied by rage. In his mother's view, a biological event in infancy warped the development of her son's mind and emotions.

Development consists of biological, cognitive, and socioemotional dimensions. Even within a dimension, there are many components—for example, attention, memory, abstract thinking, speed of processing information, and social intelligence are just a few of the components of the cognitive dimension.

Development Is Multidirectional

Throughout life, some dimensions or components of a dimension expand and others shrink. For example, when one language (such as English) is acquired early in development, the capacity for acquiring second and third languages (such as Spanish and Chinese) decreases later in development, especially after early childhood (Levelt, 1989). During adolescence, as individuals establish romantic relationships, their relationships with friends might decrease. During late adulthood, older adults might become wiser by being able to call on experience to guide their intellectual decision making, but they perform more poorly on tasks that require speed in processing information (Baltes & Kuntzman, 2007; Hartley, 2006).

Development Is Plastic

Even at 10 years old, Ted Kaczynski was extraordinarily shy. Was he destined to remain forever uncomfortable with people? Developmentalists debate how much plasticity people have in various dimensions at different points in their development.

Plasticity means the capacity for change. For example, can you still improve your intellectual skills when you are in your seventies or eighties? Or might these intellectual skills be fixed by the time you are in your thirties so that further improvement is impossible? In one research study, the reasoning abilities of older adults were improved through retraining (Willis & Schaie, 1994). However, possibly we possess less capacity for change when we become old (Baltes, Reuter-Lorenz, & Rösler, 2006). The search for plasticity and its constraints is a key element on the contemporary agenda for developmental research (Erickson & others, 2007; Kramer & Morrow, 2007).

Developmental Science Is Multidisciplinary

Psychologists, sociologists, anthropologists, neuroscientists, and medical researchers all share an interest in unlocking the mysteries of development through the life span. How do your heredity and health limit your intelligence? Do intelligence and social relationships change with age in the same way around the world? How do families and schools influence intellectual development? These are examples of research questions that cut across disciplines.

Development Is Contextual

All development occurs within a **context**, or setting. Contexts include families, schools, peer groups, churches, cities, neighborhoods, university laboratories, countries, and so on. Each of these settings is influenced by historical, economic, social, and cultural factors (Bronfenbrenner & Morris, 2006; Shirev & Levy, 2007).

Contexts, like individuals, change. Thus, individuals are changing beings in a changing world. As a result of these changes, contexts exert three types of influences (Baltes, 2003): (1) normative age-graded influences, (2) normative history-graded influences, and (3) nonnormative or highly individualized life events. Each of these types can have a biological or environmental impact on development. **Normative age-graded influences** are similar for individuals in a particular age group. These influences include biological processes such as puberty and menopause. They also include sociocultural, environmental processes such as beginning formal education (usually at about age 6 in most cultures) and retirement (which takes place in the fifties and sixties in most cultures).

Normative history-graded influences are common to people of a particular generation because of historical circumstances. For example, in their youth American baby boomers shared the experience of the Cuban missile crisis, the assassination of John F. Kennedy, and the Beatles invasion. Other examples of normative history-graded influences include economic, political, and social upheavals such as the Great Depression in the 1930s, World War II in the 1940s, the civil rights and women's rights movements of the 1960s and 1970s, the terrorist attacks of 9/11/2001, as well as the integration of computers and cell phones into everyday life during the 1990s (Elder & Shanahan, 2006). Long-term changes in the genetic and cultural makeup of a population (due to immigration or changes in fertility rates) are also part of normative historical change.

Nonnormative life events, such as Hurricane Katrina in August 2005, are unusual circumstances that have a major impact on a person's life. Here a woman and her children are shown in a Houston shelter for those left homeless by the devastating hurricane.

nonnormative life
events Unusual occurrences
that have a major impact on a
person's life. The occurrence,
pattern, and sequence of these
events are not applicable to
many individuals.

Nonnormative life events are unusual occurrences that have a major impact on the individual's life. These events do not happen to all people, and when they do occur they can influence people in different ways. Examples include the death of a parent when a child is young, pregnancy in early adolescence, a fire that destroys a home, winning the lottery, or getting an unexpected career opportunity.

How Would You...?
As a social worker, how would you explain the importance of considering nonnormative life events when working with a new client?

Development Involves Growth, Maintenance, and Regulation of Loss

Baltes and his colleagues (2006) assert that the mastery of life often involves conflicts and competition among three goals of human development: growth, maintenance, and regulation of loss. As individuals age into middle and late adulthood, the maintenance and regulation of loss in their capacities takes center stage away from growth. Thus, a 75-year-old man might aim not to improve his memory or his golf swing but to maintain his independence and to play golf at all. In Chapters 15 and 16, we will discuss these ideas about maintenance and regulation of loss in greater depth.

Development Is a Coconstruction of Biology, Culture, and the Individual

Development is a coconstruction of biological, cultural, and individual factors working together (Baltes, Reuter-Lorenz, & Rösler, 2006). For example, the brain shapes culture, but it is also shaped by culture and the experiences that individuals have or pursue. In terms of individual factors, we can go beyond what our genetic inheritance and environment give us. We can author a unique developmental path by actively choosing from the environment the things that optimize our lives (Rathunde & Csikszentmihalyi, 2006).

Some Contemporary Concerns

Pick up a newspaper or magazine and you might see headlines like these: "Political Leanings May Be Written in the Genes," "Mother Accused of Tossing Children into Bay," "Gender Gap Widens," "FDA Warns About ADHD Drug," "Heart Attack Deaths Higher in African American Patients," "Test May Predict Alzheimer Disease." Researchers using the life-span perspective are examining these and many other topics of contemporary concern. The roles that health and well-being, parenting, education, and sociocultural contexts play in life-span development, as well as how social policy is related to these issues, are a particular focus of this textbook.

Health and Well-Being

Health professionals today recognize the power of lifestyles and psychological states in health and well-being (Brown, 2007; Insel & Roth, 2008). In every chapter of this book, issues of health and well-being are integrated into our discussion.

Clinical psychologists are among the health professionals who help people improve their well-being. Read about one clinical psychologist who helps adolescents who have become juvenile delinquents or substance abusers in the Careers in Life-Span Development profile.

CAREERS IN LIFE-SPAN DEVELOPMENT
Luis Vargas, Child Clinical Psychologist

Luis Vargas (*left*) conducting a child therapy session.

Luis Vargas is Director of the Clinical Child Psychology Internship Program and a professor in the Department of Psychiatry at the University of New Mexico Health Sciences Center. He also is Director of Psychology at the University of New Mexico Children's Psychiatric Hospital.

Luis obtained an undergraduate degree in psychology from St. Edwards University in Texas, a master's degree in psychology from Trinity University in Texas, and a Ph.D. in clinical psychology from the University of Nebraska–Lincoln.

Luis' main interests are cultural issues and the assessment and treatment of children, adolescents, and families. He is motivated to find better ways to provide culturally responsive mental health services. One of his special interests is the treatment of Latino youth for delinquency and substance abuse.

Clinical psychologists like Luis Vargas seek to help people with psychological problems. They work in a variety of settings, including colleges and universities, clinics, medical schools, and private practice. Some clinical psychologists only conduct psychotherapy; others do psychological assessment and psychotherapy; some also do research. Clinical psychologists may specialize in a particular age group, such as children (child clinical psychologist) or older adults (often referred to as a geropsychologist).

Clinical psychologists, like Dr. Vargas, have either a Ph.D. (which involves clinical and research training) or a Psy.D. degree (which only involves clinical training). This graduate training usually takes five to seven years and includes courses in clinical psychology and a one-year supervised internship in an accredited setting toward the end of the training. Most states require clinical psychologists to pass a test to become state licensed and to call themselves clinical psychologists.

Parenting and Education

Can two gay men raise a healthy family? Are children harmed if both parents work outside the home? Are U.S. schools failing to teach children how to read and write and calculate adequately? We hear many questions like these related to pressures on the contemporary family and the problems of U.S. schools (Eccles, 2007; Grusec & Davidov, 2007). In later chapters, we analyze child care, the effects of divorce, parenting styles, intergenerational relationships, early childhood education, relationships between childhood poverty and education, bilingual education, new educational efforts to improve lifelong learning, and many other issues related to parenting and education.

Sociocultural Contexts and Diversity

Health, parenting, and education—like development itself—are all shaped by their sociocultural context. To analyze this context, four concepts are especially useful: culture, ethnicity, socioeconomic status, and gender.

culture The behavior patterns, beliefs, and all other products of a group that are passed on from generation to generation.

cross-cultural studies Comparisons of one culture with one or more other cultures. These provide information about the degree to which children's development is similar, or universal, across cultures, and to the degree to which it is culture-specific.

ethnicity A range of characteristics rooted in cultural heritage, including nationality, race, religion, and language.

socioeconomic status (SES) Refers to the conceptual grouping of people with similar occupational, educational, and economic characteristics.

gender The psychological and sociocultural dimensions of being female or male.

Two Korean-born children on the day they became United States citizens. Asian American and Latino children are the fastest-growing immigrant groups in the United States. *How diverse are the students in your class on life-span development that you now are taking? How are their experiences in growing up likely similar to or different from yours?*

Culture encompasses the behavior patterns, beliefs, and all other products of a particular group of people that are passed on from generation to generation. Culture results from the interaction of people over many years. A cultural group can be as large as the United States or as small as an isolated Appalachian town. Whatever its size, the group's culture influences the behavior of its members (Berry, 2007; Kagitcibasi, 2007). **Cross-cultural studies** compare aspects of two or more cultures. The comparison provides information about the degree to which development is similar, or universal, across cultures, or is instead culture-specific (Rothbaum & Trommsdorff, 2007; Takamura, 2007).

Ethnicity (the word *ethnic* comes from the Greek word for "nation") is rooted in cultural heritage, nationality, race, religion, and language. African Americans, Latinos, Asian Americans, Native Americans, European Americans, and Arab Americans are a few examples of broad ethnic groups in the United States. Diversity exists within each ethnic group (Kottak & Kozaitis, 2008).

Socioeconomic status (SES) refers to a person's position within society based on occupational, educational, and economic characteristics. Socioeconomic status implies certain inequalities. Differences in the ability to control resources and to participate in society's rewards produce unequal opportunities (Conger & Dogan, 2007).

Gender, the psychological and sociocultural dimensions of being female or male, is another important aspect of sociocultural contexts. Few aspects of our development are more central to our identity and social relationships than gender (Hyde, 2007; Leaper & Friedman, 2007). We discuss sociocultural contexts and diversity in each chapter.

The conditions in which many of the world's women live are a serious concern (UNICEF, 2007; Worell & Goodheart, 2006). Inadequate educational opportunities, violence, and lack of political access are just some of the problems faced by many women.

A recent analysis found that a higher percentage of girls than boys around the world have never had any education (UNICEF, 2004) (see Figure 1.3). The countries with the most uneducated females are in Africa. In contrast, Canada, the United States, and Russia have the highest percentages of educated women. In developing countries, 67 percent of women over the age of 25 (compared with 50 percent of men) have never been to school. At the beginning of the twenty-first century, 80 million more boys than girls were in primary and secondary educational settings around the world (United Nations, 2002).

Women in every country experience violence, often from someone close to them (Humphreys, 2007). Abuse by partners occurs in one of every six households in the United States, with the vast majority of the abuse being directed at women by men (Walker, 2006). Although most countries around the world now have shelters for battered women, beating women continues to be accepted and expected behavior in some countries (Ashy, 2004).

Gender also influences mental health. In the United States, from adolescence through adulthood, females are more likely than males to be depressed (Davison

How Would You...?
As a health-care professional, how would you explain the importance of examining cross-cultural research when searching for developmental trends in health and wellness?

& Neale, 2007). Why? Some experts believe that more women are diagnosed with depression than actually have depression (Nolen-Hoeksema, 2007). Some argue that inequities such as low pay and unequal employment opportunities have contributed to the greater incidence of depression in females than males (Whiffen, 2001). And in the view of some researchers, problems like these are likely to be addressed only when women share equal power with men (UNICEF, 2007).

Social Policy

Social policy is a government's course of action designed to promote the welfare of its citizens. Values, economics, and politics all shape a nation's social policy. Out of concern that policy makers are doing too little to protect the well-being of children and older adults, life-span researchers are increasingly undertaking studies that they hope will lead to effective social policy (Sandefur & Meier, 2007; Stagner & Zweig, 2007).

Children who grow up in poverty represent a special concern (McLoyd, Aikens, & Burton, 2006). In 2005, 17.8 percent of U.S. children were living in families below the poverty line (U.S. Bureau of the Census, 2006). As indicated in Figure 1.4, one study found that a higher percentage of children in poor families than in middle-income families were exposed to family turmoil, separation from a parent, violence, crowding, excessive noise, and poor housing (Evans & English, 2002).

In the United States, the national government, state governments, and city governments all play a role in influencing the well-being of children (Bogenschneider, 2006; Children's Defense Fund, 2007). When families fail or seriously endanger a child's well-being, governments often step in to help (Corbett, 2007). At the national and state levels, policy makers have debated for decades whether helping poor parents ends up helping their children as well. Researchers are providing some answers by examining the effects of specific policies (Ross & Kirby, 2006).

For example, the Minnesota Family Investment Program (MFIP) was designed in the 1990s primarily to influence the behavior of adults—specifically, to move adults off the welfare rolls and into paid employment. A key element of the program was that it guaranteed that adults participating in the program would receive more income if they worked than if they did not. When the adults' income rose, how did that affect their children? A study of the effects of MFIP found that increases in the incomes of working poor parents were linked with benefits for their children (Gennetian & Miller, 2002). The children's achievement in school improved, and their behavior problems decreased.

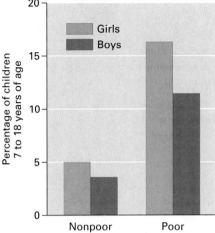

Figure 1.3 Percentage of Children 7 to 18 Years of Age Around the World Who Have Never Been to School of Any Kind When UNICEF (2004) surveyed the education that children around the world are receiving, it found that far more girls than boys receive no formal schooling at all.

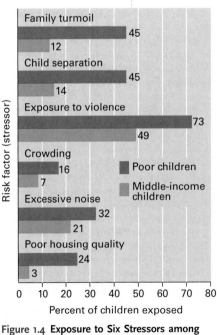

Figure 1.4 Exposure to Six Stressors among Poor and Middle-Income Children One recent study analyzed the exposure to six stressors among poor children and middle-income children (Evans & English, 2002). Poor children were much more likely to face each of these stressors.

Developmental psychologists and other researchers have examined the effects of many other government policies. They are seeking ways to help families living in poverty improve their well-being, and they have offered many suggestions for improving government policies (Coley, Lin-Grining, & Chase-Lansdale, 2006).

At the other end of the life span, the well-being of older adults also creates policy issues (Nemund & Kolland, 2007). Key concerns are escalating health-care costs and the access of older adults to adequate health care (Ferrini & Ferrini, 2008). One study found that the health-care system fails older adults in many areas (Wenger & others, 2003). For example, older adults received the recommended care for general medical conditions such as heart disease only 52 percent of the time; they received appropriate care for undernutrition and Alzheimer disease only 31 percent of the time.

These concerns about the well-being of older adults are heightened by two facts. First, the number of older adults in the United States is growing dramatically. Second, many of these older Americans are likely to need society's help. Compared with earlier decades, U.S. adults today are less likely to be married, more likely to be childless, and more likely to be living alone. As the older population continues to expand in the twenty-first century, an increasing number of older adults will be without either a spouse or children—traditionally the main sources of support for older adults (Stone, 2006). These individuals will need social relationships, networks, and supports (Asham, Ferring, & Lamura, 2007).

How Would You...?
As a health-care professional, what types of social policies would you recommend to improve healthy development of older adults?

The Nature of Development

In this section we explore what is meant by developmental processes and periods, as well as variations in the way age is conceptualized. We examine key developmental issues, how they describe development, and strategies we can use to evaluate them.

If you wanted to describe how and why Alice Walker or Ted Kaczynski developed during their lifetimes, how would you go about it? A chronicle of the events in any person's life can quickly become a confusing and tedious array of details. Two concepts help provide a framework for describing and understanding an individual's development: developmental processes and periods.

Biological, Cognitive, and Socioemotional Processes

At the beginning of this chapter, we defined *development* as the pattern of change that begins at conception and continues through the life span. The pattern is complex because it is the product of biological, cognitive, and socioemotional processes.

PEANUTS © United Features Syndicate, Inc.

Biological processes produce changes in an individual's physical nature. Genes inherited from parents, the development of the brain, height and weight gains, changes in motor skills, the hormonal changes of puberty, and cardiovascular decline are all examples of biological processes that affect development.

Cognitive processes refer to changes in the individual's thought, intelligence, and language. Watching a colorful mobile swinging above the crib, putting together a two-word sentence, memorizing a poem, imagining what it would be like to be a movie star, and solving a crossword puzzle all involve cognitive processes.

Socioemotional processes involve changes in the individual's relationships with other people, changes in emotions, and changes in personality. An infant's smile in response to a parent's touch, a toddler's aggressive attack on a playmate, a school-age child's development of assertiveness, an adolescent's joy at the senior prom, and the affection of an elderly couple all reflect the role of socioemotional processes in development.

Biological, cognitive, and socioemotional processes are inextricably intertwined (Diamond, 2007). Consider a baby smiling in response to a parent's touch. This response depends on biological processes (the physical nature of touch and responsiveness to it), cognitive processes (the ability to understand intentional acts), and socioemotional processes (the act of smiling often reflects a positive emotional feeling, and smiling helps to connect us in positive ways with other human beings).

In many instances biological, cognitive, and socioemotional processes are bidirectional. For example, biological processes can influence cognitive processes and vice versa. Thus, although usually we study the different processes of development (biological, cognitive, and socioemotional) in separate locations, keep in mind that we are talking about the development of an integrated individual with a mind and body that are interdependent.

Periods of Development

The interplay of biological, cognitive, and socioemotional processes produces the periods of the human life span. A *developmental period* refers to a time frame in a person's life that is characterized by certain features. For the purposes of organization and understanding, we commonly describe development in terms of these periods. The most widely used classification of developmental periods involves the eight-period sequence shown in Figure 1.5. Approximate age ranges are listed for the periods to provide a general idea of when a period begins and ends.

The *prenatal period* is the time from conception to birth. It involves tremendous growth—from a single cell to an organism complete with brain and behavioral capabilities—and takes place in approximately a nine-month period.

Infancy is the developmental period from birth to 18 or 24 months. Infancy is a time of extreme dependence upon adults. During this period many psychological activities—language, symbolic thought, sensorimotor coordination, and social learning, for example—are just beginning.

Early childhood is the developmental period from the end of infancy to age 5 or 6. This period is sometimes called the "preschool years." During this time, young children learn to become more self-sufficient and to care for themselves, develop

biological processes Changes in an individual's physical nature.

cognitive processes Changes in an individual's thought, intelligence, and language.

socioemotional processes Changes in an individual's relationships with other people, emotions, and personality.

Periods of Development

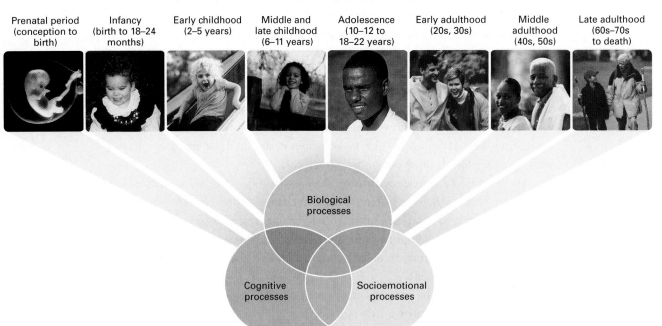

Prenatal period (conception to birth) | Infancy (birth to 18–24 months) | Early childhood (2–5 years) | Middle and late childhood (6–11 years) | Adolescence (10–12 to 18–22 years) | Early adulthood (20s, 30s) | Middle adulthood (40s, 50s) | Late adulthood (60s–70s to death)

Biological processes

Cognitive processes

Socioemotional processes

Processes of Development

Figure 1.5 Processes and Periods of Development
The unfolding of life's periods of development is influenced by the interaction of biological, cognitive, and socioemotional processes.

school readiness skills (following instructions, identifying letters), and spend many hours in play with peers. First grade typically marks the end of early childhood.

Middle and late childhood is the developmental period from about 6 to 11 years of age, approximately corresponding to the elementary school years. During this period, the fundamental skills of reading, writing, and arithmetic are mastered. The child is formally exposed to the larger world and its culture. Achievement becomes a more central theme of the child's world, and self-control increases.

Adolescence is the developmental period of transition from childhood to early adulthood, entered at approximately 10 to 12 years of age and ending at 18 to 22 years of age. Adolescence begins with rapid physical changes—dramatic gains in height and weight, changes in body contour, and the development of sexual characteristics such as enlargement of the breasts, growth of pubic and facial hair, and deepening of the voice. At this point in development, the pursuit of independence and an identity are prominent. Thought is more logical, abstract, and idealistic. More time is spent outside the family.

Early adulthood is the developmental period that begins in the late teens or early twenties and lasts through the thirties. It is a time of establishing personal and economic independence, career development, and, for many, selecting a mate, learning to live with someone in an intimate way, starting a family, and rearing children.

Middle adulthood is the developmental period from approximately 40 years of age to about 60. It is a time of expanding personal and social involvement and responsibility; of assisting the next generation in becoming competent, mature individuals; and of reaching and maintaining satisfaction in a career.

Late adulthood is the developmental period that begins in the sixties or seventies and lasts until death. It is a time of life review, retirement, and adjustment to new social roles involving decreasing strength and health.

Late adulthood has the longest span of any period of development, and as noted earlier, the number of people in this age group has been increasing dramatically. As a result, life-span developmentalists have been paying more attention to differences within late adulthood (Scheibe, Freund, & Baltes, 2007). Paul Baltes and Jacqui Smith (2003) argue that a major change takes place in older adults' lives as they become the "oldest old," on average at about 85 years of age. For example, the "young old" (classified as 65 through 84 in this analysis) have substantial potential for physical and cognitive fitness, retain much of their cognitive capacity, and can develop strategies to cope with the gains and losses of aging. In contrast, the oldest old (85 and older) show considerable loss in cognitive skills, experience an increase in chronic stress, and are more frail (Baltes & Smith, 2003). Nonetheless, as we see in later chapters, considerable variation exists in how much the oldest old retain their capabilities.

Life-span developmentalists who focus on adult development and aging increasingly describe life-span development in terms of four "ages" (Baltes, 2006):

First age: Childhood and adolescence

Second age: Prime adulthood, twenties through fifties

Third age: Approximately 60 to 79 years of age

Fourth age: Approximately 80 years and older

The major emphasis in this conceptualization is on the third and fourth ages, especially the increasing evidence that individuals in the third age are healthier and can lead more active, productive lives than their precedessors in earlier generations. However, when older adults reach their eighties, especially 85 and over (fourth age), health and well-being decline for many individuals.

Conceptions of Age

In our description of developmental periods, we linked an approximate age range with each period. But we also have noted that there are variations in the capabilities of individuals of the same age, and we have seen how age-related changes can be exaggerated. How important is age when we try to understand an individual?

According to some life-span experts, chronological age is not very relevant to understanding a person's psychological development (Botwinick, 1978). Chronological age is the number of years that have elapsed since birth. But time is a crude index of experience, and it does not cause anything. Chronological age, moreover, is not the only way of measuring age. Just as there are different domains of development, there are different ways of thinking about age.

Age has been conceptualized not just as chronological age but also as biological age, psychological age, and social age (Hoyer & Roodin, 2003). *Biological age* is a person's age in terms of biological health. Determining biological age involves knowing the functional capacities of a person's vital organs. One person's vital capacities may be better or worse than those of others of comparable age. The younger the person's biological age, the longer the person is expected to live, regardless of chronological age.

(*Top*) Dawn Russel, competing in the broad jump in a recent Senior Olympics competition in Oregon; (*bottom*) a sedentary, overweight middle-aged man. *Even if Dawn Russel's chronological age is older, might her biological age be younger than the middle-aged man's?*

How Would You...?

As a psychologist, what recommendations would you provide to an older adult to enhance their psychological age?

Psychological age is an individual's adaptive capacities compared with those of other individuals of the same chronological age. Thus, older adults who continue to learn, are flexible, are motivated, and think clearly are engaging in more adaptive behaviors than their chronological age-mates who do not do these things (Marcoen, Coleman, & O'Hanlen, 2007).

From a life-span perspective, an overall age profile of an individual involves not just chronological age but also biological age and psychological age. For example, a 70-year-old man (chronological age) might be in good physical health (biological age), but might be experiencing memory problems and having trouble coping with the demands placed on him by his wife's recent hospitalization (psychological age).

Developmental Issues

Was Ted Kaczynski born a killer, or did his life turn him into one? Kaczynski himself thought that his childhood was the root of his troubles. He grew up as a genius in a boy's body and never fit in with other children. Did his early experiences determine his later life? Is your own journey through life marked out ahead of time, or can your experiences change your path? Are the experiences you have early in your journey more important than later ones? Is your journey more like taking an elevator up a skyscraper with distinct stops along the way or more like a cruise down a river with smoother ebbs and flows? These questions point to three issues about the nature of development: the roles played by nature and nurture, stability and change, and continuity and discontinuity.

Nature and Nurture

The **nature-nurture issue** involves the extent to which development is influenced by nature and by nurture. *Nature* refers to an organism's biological inheritance, *nurture* to its environmental experiences.

How Would You...?

As an educator, how would you apply your understanding of the developmental influences of nature and nurture to create appropriate classroom strategies for students who display learning or behavioral problems?

According to those who emphasize the role of nature, just as a sunflower grows in an orderly way—unless flattened by an unfriendly environment—so too the human grows in an orderly way. An evolutionary and genetic foundation produces commonalities in growth and development (Hartwell, 2008; Lewis, 2007). We walk before we talk, speak one word before two words, grow rapidly in infancy and less so in early childhood, experience a rush of sex hormones in puberty, reach the peak of our physical strength in late adolescence and early adulthood, and then physically decline. Proponents of the importance of nature acknowledge that extreme environments—those that are psychologically barren or hostile—can depress development. However, they believe that basic growth tendencies are genetically programmed into humans (Plomin & Schalkwyk, 2007).

By contrast, other psychologists emphasize the importance of nurture, or environmental experiences, in development (Grusec & Hastings, 2007; Maccoby, 2007). Experiences run the gamut from the individual's biological environment (nutrition, medical care, drugs, and physical accidents) to the social environment (family, peers, schools, community, media, and culture).

Stability and Change

Is the shy child who hides behind the sofa when visitors arrive destined to become a wallflower at college dances, or might the child become a sociable, talkative individual? Is the fun-loving, carefree adolescent bound to have difficulty holding down a 9-to-5 job as an adult? These questions reflect the **stability-change issue**, which involves the degree to which early traits and characteristics persist through life or change.

Many developmentalists who emphasize stability in development argue that stability is the result of heredity and possibly early experiences in life. For example, many argue that if an individual is shy throughout life (as Ted Kaczynski was), this stability is due to heredity and possibly early experiences in which the infant or young child encountered considerable stress when interacting with people.

Developmentalists who emphasize change take the more optimistic view that later experiences can produce change. Recall that in the life-span perspective, plasticity, the potential for change, exists throughout the life span. Experts such as Paul Baltes (2003) argue that with increasing age and on average older adults often show less capacity for change in the sense of learning new things than younger adults. However, many older adults continue to be good at practicing what they have learned in earlier times.

The roles of early and later experience are an aspect of the stability-change issue that has long been hotly debated (Caspi & Shiner, 2006). Some argue that unless infants experience warm, nurturant caregiving in the first year or so of life, their development will never be optimal (Sroufe, 2007). The later-experience advocates see children as malleable throughout development and later sensitive caregiving as equally important to earlier sensitive caregiving (Askam, Ferring, & Lamura, 2007).

Continuity and Discontinuity

When developmental change occurs, is it gradual or abrupt? Think about your own development for a moment. Did you become the person you are gradually? Or did you experience sudden, distinct changes in your growth? For the most part, developmentalists who emphasize nurture describe development as a gradual, continuous process. Those who emphasize nature often describe development as a series of distinct stages.

The **continuity-discontinuity issue** focuses on the degree to which development involves either gradual, cumulative change (continuity) or distinct stages (discontinuity). In terms of continuity, as the oak grows from seedling to giant oak, it becomes more oak—its development is continuous. Similarly, a child's first word, though seemingly an abrupt, discontinuous event, is actually the result of weeks and months of growth and practice. Puberty might seem abrupt, but it is a gradual process that occurs over several years.

In terms of discontinuity, as an insect grows from a caterpillar to a chrysalis to a butterfly, it passes through a sequence of stages in which change is qualitatively rather than quantitatively different. Simlarly, at some point a child moves from not being able to think abstractly about the world to being able to.

stability-change issue The debate about the degree to which early traits and characteristics persist through life or change.

continuity-discontinuity issue The debate about the extent to which development involves gradual, cumulative change (continuity) or distinct stages (discontinuity).

THE NATURE OF DEVELOPMENT

This is a qualitative, discontinuous change in development rather than a quantitative, continuous change.

Evaluating the Developmental Issues

Most life-span developmentalists acknowledge that development is not all nature or all nurture, not all stability or all change, and not all continuity or all discontinuity (Gottlieb, 2007; Rutter, 2007). Nature *and* nurture, stability *and* change, continuity *and* discontinuity characterize development throughout the human life span.

Although most developmentalists do not take extreme positions on these three important issues, there is spirited debate regarding how strongly development is influenced by each of these factors (Laible & Thompson, 2007; Plomin, DeFries, & Fulker, 2007).

Theories of Development

How can we answer questions about the roles of nature and nurture, stability and change, and continuity and discontinuity in development? How can we determine, for example, whether memory declines in older adults can be prevented or whether special care can repair the harm inflicted by child neglect? The scientific method is the best tool we have to answer such questions (Smith & Davis, 2007).

The *scientific method* is essentially a four-step process: (1) conceptualize a process or problem to be studied, (2) collect research information (data), (3) analyze data, and (4) draw conclusions.

In step 1, when researchers are formulating a problem to study, they often draw on theories and develop hypotheses. A **theory** is an interrelated, coherent set of ideas that helps to explain phenomena and make predictions. It may suggest **hypotheses**, which are specific assertions and predictions that can be tested. For example, a theory on mentoring might state that sustained support and guidance from an adult makes a difference in the lives of children from impoverished backgrounds because the mentor gives the children opportunities to observe and imitate the behavior and strategies of the mentor.

This section outlines key aspects of five theoretical orientations to development: psychoanalytic, cognitive, behavioral and social cognitive, ethological, and ecological. Each contributes an important piece to the life-span development puzzle. Although the theories disagree about certain aspects of development, many of their ideas are complementary rather than contradictory. Together they let us see the total landscape of life-span development in all its richness (Newman & Newman, 2007).

Psychoanalytic Theories

Psychoanalytic theories describe development as primarily unconscious (beyond awareness) and heavily colored by emotion. Psychoanalytic theorists emphasize that behavior is merely a surface characteristic and that a true understanding of development requires analyzing the symbolic meanings of behavior and the deep inner workings of the mind. Psychoanalytic theorists also stress that early experiences with parents extensively shape development. These characteristics are highlighted in the main psychoanalytic theory, that of Sigmund Freud (1856–1939).

Freud's Theory

As Freud listened to, probed, and analyzed his patients, he became convinced that their problems were the result of experiences early in life. He thought that as children grow up, their focus of pleasure and sexual impulses shifts from the mouth to the anus and eventually to the genitals. As a result, we go through five stages of psychosexual development: oral, anal, phallic, latency, and genital (see Figure 1.6). Our adult personality, Freud (1917) claimed, is determined by the way we resolve conflicts between sources of pleasure at each stage and the demands of reality.

Freud's theory has been significantly revised by a number of psychoanalytic theorists. Many of today's psychoanalytic theorists believe that Freud overemphasized sexual instincts; they place more emphasis on cultural experiences as determinants of an individual's development. Unconscious thought remains a central theme, but thought plays a greater role than Freud envisioned. Next, we will outline the ideas of an important revisionist of Freud's ideas—Erik Erikson.

Erikson's Psychosocial Theory

Erik Erikson recognized Freud's contributions but believed that Freud misjudged some important dimensions of human development. For one thing, Erikson (1950, 1968) said we develop in *psychosocial* stages, rather than in *psychosexual* stages, as Freud maintained. According to Freud, the primary motivation for human behavior is sexual in nature; according to Erikson, it is social and reflects a desire to affiliate with other people. According to Freud, our basic personality is shaped in the first five years of life; according to Erikson, developmental change occurs throughout the life span. Thus, in terms of the early-versus-later-experience issue described earlier in the chapter, Freud viewed early experiences as far more important than later experiences, whereas Erikson emphasized the importance of both early and later experiences.

In **Erikson's theory**, eight stages of development unfold as we go through life (see Figure 1.7). At each stage, a unique developmental task confronts individuals with a crisis that must be resolved. According to Erikson, this crisis is not a catastrophe but a turning point marked by both increased vulnerability

How Would You...?
As a human development and family studies professional, how would you apply psychoanalytic theory to advise the foster family of a newly placed child who reports no history of abuse yet shows considerable violent behavior?

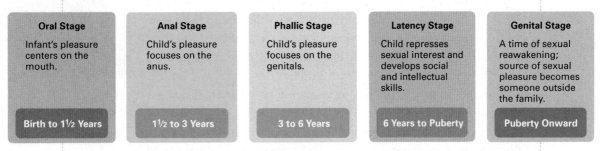

Oral Stage	Anal Stage	Phallic Stage	Latency Stage	Genital Stage
Infant's pleasure centers on the mouth.	Child's pleasure focuses on the anus.	Child's pleasure focuses on the genitals.	Child represses sexual interest and develops social and intellectual skills.	A time of sexual reawakening; source of sexual pleasure becomes someone outside the family.
Birth to 1½ Years	1½ to 3 Years	3 to 6 Years	6 Years to Puberty	Puberty Onward

Figure 1.6 Freudian Stages
Because Freud emphasized sexual motivation, his stages of development are known as *psychosexual stages*. In his view, if the need for pleasure at any stage is either undergratified or overgratified, an individual may become *fixated*, or locked in, at that stage of development.

THEORIES OF DEVELOPMENT

17

Erikson's Stages	Developmental Period
Integrity versus despair	Late adulthood (60s onward)
Generativity versus stagnation	Middle adulthood (40s, 50s)
Intimacy versus isolation	Early adulthood (20s, 30s)
Identity versus identity confusion	Adolescence (10 to 20 years)
Industry versus inferiority	Middle and late childhood (elementary school years, 6 years to puberty)
Initiative versus guilt	Early childhood (preschool years, 3 to 5 years)
Autonomy versus shame and doubt	Infancy (1 to 3 years)
Trust versus mistrust	Infancy (first year)

Figure 1.7 Erikson's Eight Life-Span Stages
Like Freud, Erikson proposed that individuals go through distinct, universal stages of development. Thus, in terms of the continuity-discontinuity issue both favor the discontinuity side of the debate. Notice that the timing of Erikson's first four stages is similar to that of Freud's stages. *What are implications of saying that people go through stages of development?*

and enhanced potential. The more successfully an individual resolves the crises, the healthier development will be.

Trust versus mistrust is Erikson's first psychosocial stage, which is experienced in the first year of life. Trust in infancy sets the stage for a lifelong expectation that the world will be a good and pleasant place to live.

Autonomy versus shame and doubt is Erikson's second stage. This stage occurs in late infancy and toddlerhood (1 to 3 years). After gaining trust in their caregivers, infants begin to discover that their behavior is their own. They start to assert their sense of independence or autonomy. They realize their *will*. If infants and toddlers are restrained too much or punished too harshly, they are likely to develop a sense of shame and doubt.

Initiative versus guilt, Erikson's third stage of development, occurs during the preschool years. As preschool children encounter a widening social world, they face new challenges that require active, purposeful, responsible behavior. Feelings of guilt may arise, though, if the child is irresponsible and is made to feel too anxious.

Industry versus inferiority is Erikson's fourth developmental stage, occurring approximately in the elementary school years. Children now need to direct their energy toward mastering knowledge and intellectual skills. The negative outcome is that the child may develop a sense of inferiority—feeling incompetent and unproductive.

During the adolescent years individuals face finding out who they are, what they are all about, and where they are going in life. This is Erikson's fifth developmental stage, *identity versus identity confusion*. If adolescents explore roles in a healthy manner and arrive at a positive path to follow in life, then they achieve a positive identity; if not, then identity confusion reigns.

Intimacy versus isolation is Erikson's sixth developmental stage, which individuals experience during the early adulthood years. At this time, individuals face the developmental task of forming intimate relationships. If young adults form healthy friendships and an intimate relationship with another, intimacy will be achieved; if not, isolation will result.

Generativity versus stagnation, Erikson's seventh developmental stage, occurs during middle adulthood. By *generativity* Erikson means primarily a concern for helping the younger generation to develop and lead useful lives. The feeling of having done nothing to help the next generation is stagnation.

Erik Erikson with his wife, Joan, an artist. Erikson generated one of the most important developmental theories of the twentieth century. *Which stage of Erikson's theory are you in? Does Erikson's description of this stage characterize you?*

Integrity versus despair is Erikson's eighth and final stage of development, which individuals experience in late adulthood. During this stage, a person reflects on the past. If the person's life review reveals a life well spent, integrity will be achieved; if not, the retrospective glances likely will yield doubt or gloom—the despair Erikson described.

Piaget's theory The theory that children construct their understanding of the world and go through four stages of cognitive development.

Evaluating Psychoanalytic Theories

Contributions of psychoanalytic theories include an emphasis on a developmental framework, family relationships, and unconscious aspects of the mind. Criticisms include a lack of scientific support, too much emphasis on sexual underpinnings, and an image of people that is too negative.

Cognitive Theories

Whereas psychoanalytic theories stress the importance of the unconscious, cognitive theories emphasize conscious thoughts. Three important cognitive theories are Piaget's cognitive developmental theory, Vygotsky's sociocultural cognitive theory, and information-processing theory.

Piaget's Cognitive Developmental Theory

Piaget's theory states that children go through four stages of cognitive development as they actively construct their understanding of the world. Two processes underlie this cognitive construction of the world: organization and adaptation. To make sense of our world, we organize our experiences. For example, we separate important ideas from less important ideas, and we connect one idea to another. In addition to organizing our observations and experiences, we *adapt*, adjusting to new environmental demands (Mooney, 2006).

Piaget (1954) also argued that we go through four stages in understanding the world (see Figure 1.8). Each stage is age-related and consists of a distinct way of thinking, a *different* way of understanding the world. Thus, according to Piaget, the child's cognition is *qualitatively* different in one stage compared with another. What are Piaget's four stages of cognitive development?

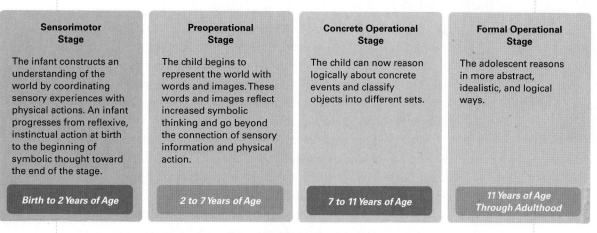

Figure 1.8 Piaget's Four Stages of Cognitive Development
According to Piaget, how a child thinks—not how much the child knows—determines the child's stage of cognitive development.

The *sensorimotor stage,* which lasts from birth to about 2 years of age, is the first Piagetian stage. In this stage, infants construct an understanding of the world by coordinating sensory experiences (such as seeing and hearing) with physical, motoric actions—hence the term *sensorimotor.*

The *preoperational stage,* which lasts from approximately 2 to 7 years of age, is Piaget's second stage. In this stage, children begin to go beyond simply connecting sensory information with physical action and represent the world with words, images, and drawings. However, according to Piaget, preschool children still lack the ability to perform what he calls *operations,* which are internalized mental actions that allow children to do mentally what they previously could only do physically. For example, if you imagine putting two sticks together to see whether they would be as long as another stick, without actually moving the sticks, you are performing a concrete operation.

The *concrete operational stage,* which lasts from approximately 7 to 11 years of age, is the third Piagetian stage. In this stage, children can perform operations that involve objects, and they can reason logically when the reasoning can be applied to specific or concrete examples. For instance, concrete operational thinkers cannot imagine the steps necessary to complete an algebraic equation, which is too abstract for thinking at this stage of development.

The *formal operational stage,* which appears between the ages of 11 and 15 and continues through adulthood, is Piaget's fourth and final stage. In this stage, individuals move beyond concrete experiences and think in abstract and more logical terms. As part of thinking more abstractly, adolescents develop images of ideal circumstances. They might think about what an ideal parent is like and compare their parents to this ideal standard. They begin to entertain possibilities for the future and are fascinated with what they can be. In solving problems, they become more systematic, developing hypotheses about why something is happening the way it is and then testing these hypotheses. We will examine Piaget's cognitive developmental theory further in Chapters 3, 5, 7, and 9.

Jean Piaget, the famous Swiss developmental psychologist, changed the way we think about the development of children's minds. *What are some key ideas in Piaget's theory?*

Vygotsky's Sociocultural Cognitive Theory

Like Piaget, the Russian developmentalist Lev Vygotsky (1896–1934) reasoned that children actively construct their knowledge. However, Vygotsky (1962) gave social interaction and culture far more important roles in cognitive development than Piaget did. **Vygotsky's theory** is a sociocultural cognitive theory that emphasizes how culture and social interaction guide cognitive development.

Lev Vygotsky was born the same year as Piaget, but he died much earlier, at the age of 37. There is considerable interest today in Vygotsky's sociocultural cognitive theory of child development. *What are some key characteristics of Vygotsky's theory?*

Vygotsky portrayed the child's development as inseparable from social and cultural activities (Cole & Gajdamaschko, 2007; Gauvain & Perez, 2007). He stressed that cognitive development involves learning to use the inventions of society, such as language, mathematical systems, and memory strategies. Thus in one culture, children might learn to count with the help of a computer; in another, they might learn by using beads. According to Vygotsky, children's social interaction with more-skilled adults and

How Would You...?
As a psychologist, how would you explain the key differences between Piaget's and Vygotsky's cognitive theories of development?

peers is indispensable to their cognitive development (Alvarez & del Rio, 2007). Through this interaction, they learn to use the tools that will help them adapt and be successful in their culture. In Chapter 5 we examine ideas about learning and teaching that are based on Vygotsky's theory.

The Information-Processing Theory

Information-processing theory emphasizes that individuals manipulate information, monitor it, and strategize about it. Unlike Piaget's theory but like Vygotsky's theory, information-processing theory does not describe development as stagelike. Instead, according to this theory, individuals develop a gradually increasing capacity for processing information, which allows them to acquire increasingly complex knowledge and skills (Munakata, 2006; Reed, 2007).

Robert Siegler (2006; Siegler & Alibali, 2005), a leading expert on children's information processing, states that thinking is information processing. In other words, when individuals perceive, encode, represent, store, and retrieve information, they are thinking. Siegler emphasizes that an important aspect of development is learning good strategies for processing information. For example, becoming a better reader might involve learning to monitor the key themes of the material being read.

Evaluating Cognitive Theories

Contributions of cognitive theories include a positive view of development and an emphasis on the active construction of understanding. Criticisms include skepticism about the pureness of Piaget's stages and too little attention to individual variations.

Behavioral and Social Cognitive Theories

Behavioral and social cognitive theories hold that development can be described in terms of behaviors learned through interactions with the environment. *Behaviorism* essentially holds that we can study scientifically only what can be directly observed and measured. Out of the behavioral tradition grew the belief that development is observable behavior that can be learned through experience with the environment (Watson & Tharp, 2007). In terms of the continuity-discontinuity issue discussed earlier in this chapter, the behavioral and social cognitive theories emphasize continuity in development and argue that development does not occur in stage-like fashion. Let's explore two versions of behaviorism: Skinner's operant conditioning and Bandura's social cognitive theory.

Skinner's Operant Conditioning

According to B. F. Skinner (1904–1990), through *operant conditioning* the consequences of a behavior produce changes in the probability of the behavior's occurrence. A behavior followed by a rewarding stimulus is more likely to recur, whereas a behavior followed by a punishing stimulus is less likely to recur. For example, when an adult smiles at a child after the child has done something, the child is more likely to engage in that behavior again than if the adult gives the child a disapproving look.

social cognitive theory The theory that behavior, environment, and person/cognitive factors are important in understanding development.

In Skinner's (1938) view, such rewards and punishments shape development. For Skinner the key aspect of development is behavior, not thoughts and feelings. He emphasized that development consists of the pattern of behavioral changes that are brought about by rewards and punishments. For example, Skinner would say that shy people learned to be shy as a result of experiences they had while growing up. It follows that modifications in an environment can help a shy person become more socially oriented.

How Would You...?
As a human development and family studies professional, how would you use operant conditioning principles to improve communication within a family?

Bandura's Social Cognitive Theory

Some psychologists agree with the behaviorists' notion that development is learned and is influenced strongly by environmental interactions. However, unlike Skinner, they also see cognition as important in understanding development (Mischel, 2004). **Social cognitive theory** holds that behavior, environment, and person/cognitive factors are the key factors in development.

American psychologist Albert Bandura (1925–) is the leading architect of social cognitive theory. Bandura (1986, 2004, 2006, 2007a, b) emphasizes that cognitive processes have important links with the environment and behavior. His early research program focused heavily on *observational learning* (also called *imitation* or *modeling*), which is learning that occurs through observing what others do. For example, a young boy might observe his father yelling in anger and treating other people with hostility; with his peers, the young boy later acts very aggressively, showing the same characteristics as his father's behavior. Social cognitive theorists stress that people acquire a wide range of behaviors, thoughts, and feelings through observing others' behavior and that these observations form an important part of life-span development.

What is *cognitive* about observational learning in Bandura's view? He proposes that people cognitively represent the behavior of others and then sometimes adopt this behavior themselves.

Bandura's (2004, 2006, 2007a, b) most recent model of learning and development includes three elements: behavior, the person/cognition, and the environment. An individual's confidence that he or she can control his or her success is an example of a person factor; strategies are an example of a cognitive factor. As shown in Figure 1.9, behavior, person/cognitive, and environmental factors operate interactively.

Albert Bandura has been one of the leading architects of social cognitive theory. *How does Bandura's theory differ from Skinner's?*

Behavior

Person/Cognitive ⟷ Environment

Figure 1.9 Bandura's Social Cognitive Model The arrows illustrate how relations between behavior, person/cognitive, and environment are reciprocal rather than one way. *Person/cognitive* refers to cognitive processes (for example, thinking and planning) and personal characteristics (for example, believing that you can control your experiences).

Evaluating Behavioral and Social Cognitive Theories

Contributions of the behavioral and social cognitive theories include an emphasis on scientific research and environmental determinants of behavior. Criticisms include too little emphasis on cognition in Skinner's view and giving inadequate attention to developmental changes.

How Would You...?
As a social worker, how would you use Bandura's model of observational learning to discuss the impact of violent television programming on children's development?

Ethological Theory

ethology An approach that stresses that behavior is strongly influenced by biology, tied to evolution, and characterized by critical or sensitive periods.

Ethology stresses that behavior is strongly influenced by biology, is tied to evolution, and is characterized by critical or sensitive periods. These are specific time frames during which, according to ethologists, the presence or absence of certain experiences has a long-lasting influence on individuals.

European zoologist Konrad Lorenz (1903–1989) helped bring ethology to prominence. In his best-known research, Lorenz (1965) studied the behavior of greylag geese, which will follow their mothers as soon as they hatch. Lorenz separated the eggs laid by one goose into two groups. One group he returned to the goose to be hatched by her. The other group was hatched in an incubator. The goslings in the first group performed as predicted. They followed their mother as soon as they hatched. However, those in the second group, which saw Lorenz when they first hatched, followed him everywhere, as though he were their mother. Lorenz marked the goslings and then placed both groups under a box. Mother goose and "mother" Lorenz stood aside as the box lifted. Each group of goslings went directly to its "mother." Lorenz called this process *imprinting*, the rapid, innate learning that involves attachment to the first moving object seen.

John Bowlby (1969, 1989) illustrated an important application of ethological theory to human development. Bowlby stressed that attachment to a caregiver over the first year of life has important consequences throughout the life span. In his view, if this attachment is positive and secure, the individual will likely develop positively in childhood and adulthood. If the attachment is negative and insecure, life-span development will likely not be optimal. In Chapter 4, we explore the concept of infant attachment in much greater detail.

In Lorenz's view, imprinting needs to take place at a certain, very early time in the life of the animal, or else it will not take place. This point in time is called a *critical period*. A related concept is that of a *sensitive period*, and an example of this is the time during infancy when, according to Bowlby, attachment should occur in order to promote optimal development of social relationships.

Another theory that emphasizes biological foundations of development—evolutionary psychology—is presented in Chapter 2, along with views on the role of heredity in development. In addition, we examine a number of biological theories of aging in Chapter 15.

Evaluating Ethological Theory

Contributions of ethological theory include a focus on the biological and evolutionary basis of development, and the use of careful observations in naturalistic settings.

Konrad Lorenz, a pioneering student of animal behavior, is followed through the water by three imprinted greylag geese. Describe Lorenz's experiment with the geese. *Do you think his experiment would have the same results with human babies? Explain.*

Criticisms include too much emphasis on biological foundations and a belief that the critical and sensitive period concepts might be too rigid.

Ecological Theory

While ethological theory stresses biological factors, ecological theory emphasizes environmental factors. One ecological theory that has important implications for understanding life-span development was created by Urie Bronfenbrenner (1917–2005).

Bronfenbrenner's ecological theory (1986, 2004; Bronfenbrenner & Morris, 1998, 2006) holds that development reflects the influence of several environmental systems. The theory identifies five environmental systems: microsystem, mesosystem, exosystem, macrosystem, and chronosystem (see Figure 1.10).

The *microsystem* is the setting in which the individual lives. These contexts include the person's family, peers, school, and neighborhood. It is in the microsystem that the most direct interactions with social agents take place—with parents, peers, and teachers, for example. The individual is not a passive recipient of experiences in these settings, but someone who helps to construct the settings.

The *mesosystem* involves relations between microsystems or connections between contexts. Examples are the relation of family experiences to school experiences, school experiences to church experiences, and family experiences to peer experiences. For example, children whose parents have rejected them may have difficulty developing positive relations with teachers.

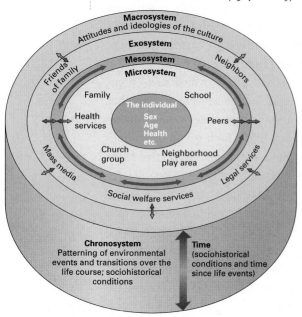

Figure 1.10 Bronfenbrenner's Ecological Theory of Development Bronfenbrenner's ecological theory consists of five environmental systems: microsystem, mesosystem, exosystem, macrosystem, and chronosystem.

The *exosystem* consists of links between a social setting in which the individual does not have an active role and the individual's immediate context. For example, a husband's or child's experience at home may be influenced by a mother's experiences at work. The mother might receive a promotion that requires more travel, which might increase conflict with the husband and change patterns of interaction with the child.

The *macrosystem* involves the culture in which individuals live. Remember from earlier in the chapter that culture refers to the behavior patterns, beliefs, and all other products of a group of people that are passed on from generation to generation. Remember also that cross-cultural studies—the comparison of one culture with one or more other cultures—provide information about the generality of development.

The *chronosystem* consists of the patterning of environmental events and transitions over the life course, as well as sociohistorical circumstances. For example, divorce is one transition. Researchers have found that the negative effects of divorce on children often peak in the first year after the divorce (Hetherington, 1993, 2006). By two years after the divorce, family interaction is

How Would You...?
As an educator, how might you explain a student's chronic failure to complete homework from the mesosystem level? from the exosystem level?

more stable. As an example of sociohistorical circumstances, consider how the opportunities for women to pursue a career have increased since the 1960s.

Bronfenbrenner (2004; Bronfenbrenner & Morris, 2006) has added biological influences to his theory and now describes it as a *bioecological* theory. Nonetheless, it is still dominated by ecological, environmental contexts (Ceci, 2000).

eclectic theoretical orientation An approach that selects and uses whatever is considered the best in many theories.

Evaluating Ecological Theory

Contributions of the theory include a systematic examination of macro and micro dimensions of environmental systems, and attention to connections between environmental systems. Criticisms include giving inadequate attention to biological factors, as well as too little emphasis on cognitive factors.

An Eclectic Theoretical Orientation

No single theory described in this chapter can explain entirely the rich complexity of life-span development, but each has contributed to our understanding of development. Psychoanalytic theory best explains the unconscious mind. Erikson's theory best describes the changes that occur in adult development. Piaget's, Vygotsky's, and the information-processing views provide the most complete description of cognitive development. The behavioral and social cognitive and ecological theories have been the most adept at examining the environmental determinants of development. The ethological theories have highlighted biology's role and the importance of sensitive periods in development.

Urie Bronfenbrenner developed ecological theory, a perspective that is receiving increased attention today. His theory emphasizes the importance of both micro and macro dimensions of the environment in which the individual lives.

In short, although theories are helpful guides, relying on a single theory to explain development is probably a mistake. This book instead takes an **eclectic theoretical orientation**, which does not follow any one theoretical approach but rather selects from each theory whatever is considered its best features. In this way, you can view the study of development as it actually exists—with different theorists making different assumptions, stressing different empirical problems, and using different strategies to discover information.

Research in Life-Span Development

If they follow an eclectic orientation, how do scholars and researchers determine that one feature of a theory is somehow better than another? The scientific method discussed earlier in this chapter provides the guide. Through scientific research, the features of theories can be tested and refined.

Generally, research in life-span development is designed to test hypotheses, which in some cases are derived from the theories just described. Through research, theories are modified to reflect new data, and occasionally new theories arise. How are data about life-span development collected? What types of research designs are used to study life-span development? And what are some ethical considerations in conducting research on life-span development?

naturalistic observation
Observation that occurs in a
real-world setting without an
attempt to manipulate the
situation.

Methods for Collecting Data

Whether we are interested in studying attachment in infants, the cognitive skills of children, or social relationships in older adults, we can choose from several ways of collecting data. Here we outline the measures most often used, beginning with observation.

Observation

Scientific observation requires an important set of skills (Graziano & Rualin, 2007; McBurney & White, 2007). For observations to be effective, they have to be systematic. We have to have some idea of what we are looking for. We have to know whom we are observing, when and where we will observe, how the observations will be made, and how they will be recorded.

Where should we make our observations? We have two choices: the laboratory and the everyday world.

When we observe scientifically, we often need to control certain factors that determine behavior but are not the focus of our inquiry (Leary, 2008). For this reason, some research in life-span development is conducted in a **laboratory**, a controlled setting where many of the complex factors of the "real world" are absent. For example, suppose you want to observe how children react when they see other people act aggressively. If you observe children in their homes or schools, you have no control over how much aggression the children observe, what kind of aggression they see, which people they see acting aggressively, or how other people treat the children. In contrast, if you observe the children in a laboratory, you can control these and other factors and therefore have more confidence about how to interpret your observations.

Laboratory research does have some drawbacks, however, including the following: (1) It is almost impossible to conduct research without the participants' knowing they are being studied. (2) The laboratory setting is unnatural and therefore can cause the participants to behave unnaturally. (3) People who are willing to come to a university laboratory may not fairly represent groups from diverse cultural backgrounds. (4) People who are unfamiliar with university settings, and with the idea of "helping science," may be intimidated by the laboratory setting.

Naturalistic observation provides insights that we sometimes cannot achieve in the laboratory (Billman, 2003). **Naturalistic observation** means observing behavior in real-world settings, making no effort to manipulate or control the situation. Life-span researchers conduct naturalistic observations at sporting events, child-care centers, work settings, malls, and other places people live in and frequent.

Naturalistic observation was used in one study that focused on conversations in a children's science museum (Crowley & others, 2001). When visiting exhibits at the science museum, parents were more than three times as likely to engage boys than girls in explanatory talk. This finding suggests a gender bias that encourages boys more than girls to be interested in science (see Figure 1.11).

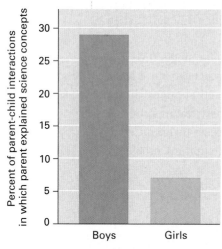

Figure 1.11 Parents' Explanations of Science to Sons and Daughters at a Science Museum In a naturalistic observation study at a children's science museum, parents were three times more likely to explain science to boys than to girls (Crowley & others, 2001). The gender difference occurred regardless of whether the father, the mother, or both parents were with the child, although the gender difference was greatest for fathers' science explanations to sons and daughters.

Survey and Interview

Sometimes the best and quickest way to get information about people is to ask them for it. One technique is to *interview* them directly. A related method is the *survey* (sometimes referred to as a questionnaire), which is especially useful when information from many people is needed. A standard set of questions is used to obtain peoples' self-reported attitudes or beliefs about a particular topic. In a good survey, the questions are clear and unbiased, allowing respondents to answer unambiguously.

Surveys and interviews can be used to study a wide range of topics from religious beliefs to sexual habits to attitudes about gun control to beliefs about how to improve schools. Surveys and interviews may be conducted in person, over the telephone, and over the Internet.

One problem with surveys and interviews is the tendency of participants to answer questions in a way that they think is socially acceptable or desirable rather than to say what they truly think or feel (Best & Kahn, 2006). For example, on a survey or in an interview some individuals might say that they do not take drugs even though they do.

Standardized Test

A **standardized test** has uniform procedures for administration and scoring. Many standardized tests allow a person's performance to be compared with that of other individuals; thus they provide information about individual differences among people (Gregory, 2007). One example is the Stanford-Binet intelligence test, which is described in Chapter 7. Your score on the Stanford-Binet test tells you how your performance compares with that of thousands of other people who have taken the test.

One criticism of standardized tests is that they assume a person's behavior is consistent and stable, yet personality and intelligence—two primary targets of standardized testing—can vary with the situation. For example, a person may perform poorly on a standardized intelligence test in an office setting but score much higher at home, where he or she is less anxious.

Case Study

A **case study** is an in-depth look at a single individual. Case studies are performed mainly by mental health professionals when, for either practical or ethical reasons, the unique aspects of an individual's life cannot be duplicated and tested in other individuals (Dattilio, 2001). A case study provides information about one person's experiences; it may focus on nearly any aspect of the subject's life that helps the researcher understand the person's mind, behavior, or other attributes. A researcher may gather information for a case study from interviews and medical records. In later chapters we discuss vivid case studies, such as that of Michael Rehbein, who had much of the left side of his brain removed at 7 years of age to end severe epileptic seizures.

A case study can provide a dramatic, in-depth portrayal of an individual's life, but we must be cautious when generalizing from this information. The subject of a case study is unique, with a genetic makeup and personal history that no one else shares. In addition, case studies involve judgments of unknown reliability. Researchers who conduct case studies rarely check to see if other professionals agree with their observations or findings.

standardized test A test that is given with uniform procedures for administration and scoring.

case study An in-depth examination of an individual.

Physiological Measures

Researchers are increasingly using physiological measures when they study development at different points in the life span. For example, as puberty unfolds, the blood levels of certain hormones increase. To determine the nature of these hormonal changes, researchers analyze blood samples from adolescent volunteers (Dorn & others, 2006).

Another physiological measure that is increasingly being used is neuroimaging, especially *functional magnetic resonance imaging (fMRI)*, in which electromagnetic waves are used to construct images of a person's brain tissue and biochemical activity (Park & Schwartz, 2007). We have much more to say about neuroimaging and other physiological measures in later chapters.

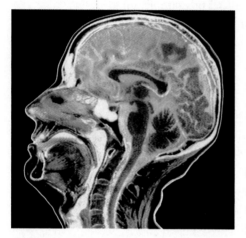

This fMRI scan of a 51-year-old male shows atrophy in the cerebral cortex of the brain, which occurs in various disorders including stroke and Alzheimer disease. The area of the upper cerebral cortex (where higher-level brain functioning such as thinking and planning occur) is colored dark red. Neuro-imaging techniques such as the fMRI are helping researchers to learn more about how the brain functions as people develop and age, as well as what happens to the brain when aging diseases such as stroke and Alzheimer disease are present.

Research Designs

In conducting research on life-span development, in addition to a method for collecting data, you also need a research design. There are three main types of research design: descriptive, correlational, and experimental.

Descriptive Research

All of the data-collection methods that we have discussed can be used in **descriptive research**, which aims to observe and record behavior. For example, a researcher might observe the extent to which people are altruistic or aggressive toward each other. By itself, descriptive research cannot prove what causes some phenomenon, but it can reveal important information about people's behavior.

Correlational Research

In contrast to descriptive research, correlational research goes beyond describing phenomena; it provides information that will help us to predict how people will behave.

In **correlational research**, the goal is to describe the strength of the relation between two or more events or characteristics. The more strongly the two events are correlated (or related or associated), the more effectively we can predict one event from the other (Mitchell & Jolley, 2007).

For example, to study if children of permissive parents have less self-control than other children, you would need to carefully record observations of parents' permissiveness and their children's self-control. You might observe that the higher a parent was in permissiveness, the lower the child was in self-control. You would then analyze these data statistically to yield a numerical measure, called a **correlation coefficient**, a number based on a statistical analysis that is used to describe the degree of association between two variables. The correlation coefficient ranges from +1.00 to −1.00. A negative number means an inverse relation. In the above example, you might find an inverse correlation between permissive parenting and children's self-control with a coefficient of, say, −.30. By contrast, you might find a positive correlation of +.30 between parental monitoring of children and children's self-control.

The higher the correlation coefficient (whether positive or negative), the stronger the association between the two variables. A correlation of 0 means that there is no association between the variables. A correlation of −.40 is stronger than a correlation of +.20 because we disregard whether the correlation is positive or negative in determining the strength of the correlation.

A caution is in order, however. Correlation does not equal causation (Howell, 2008). The correlational finding just mentioned does not mean that permissive parenting necessarily causes low self-control in children. It could mean that, but it also could mean that a child's lack of self-control caused the parents to throw up their arms in despair and give up trying to control the child. It also could mean that other factors, such as heredity or poverty, caused the correlation between permissive parenting and low self-control in children. Figure 1.12 illustrates these possible interpretations of correlational data.

Experimental Research

To study causality, researchers turn to *experimental research*. An **experiment** is a carefully regulated procedure in which one or more factors believed to influence the behavior being studied are manipulated while all other factors are held constant. If the behavior under study changes when a factor is manipulated, we say that the manipulated factor has caused the behavior to change. In other words, the experiment has demonstrated cause and effect. The cause is the factor that was manipulated. The effect is the behavior that changed because of the manipulation. Nonexperimental research methods (descriptive and correlational research) cannot establish cause and effect because they do not involve manipulating factors in a controlled way (McMillan, 2007).

Independent and Dependent Variables Experiments include two types of changeable factors, or variables: independent and dependent. An independent variable is a manipulated, influential, experimental factor. It is a potential cause. The label "independent" is used because this variable can be manipulated independently of

experiment A carefully regulated procedure in which one or more of the factors believed to influence the behavior being studied is manipulated and all other factors are held constant. Experimental research permits the determination of cause.

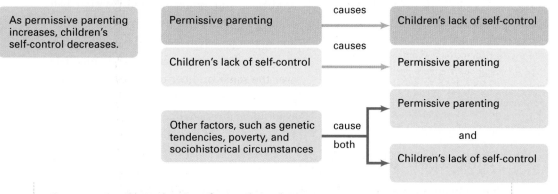

Figure 1.12 **Possible Explanations for Correlational Data**
An observed correlation between two events cannot be used to conclude that one event caused the other. Some possibilities are that the second event caused the first event or that a third, unknown event caused the correlation between the first two events.

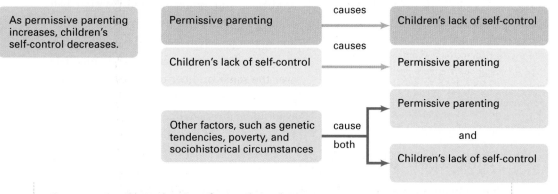
(Observed correlation: As permissive parenting increases, children's self-control decreases.
Possible explanations for this correlation:
Permissive parenting — causes → Children's lack of self-control
Children's lack of self-control — causes → Permissive parenting
Other factors, such as genetic tendencies, poverty, and sociohistorical circumstances — cause both → Permissive parenting and Children's lack of self-control)

other factors to determine its effect. An experiment may include one independent variable or several of them.

A dependent variable is a factor that can change in an experiment, in response to changes in the independent variable. As researchers manipulate the independent variable, they measure the dependent variable for any resulting effect.

For example, suppose that you conducted a study to determine whether pregnant women could change the breathing and sleeping patterns of their newborn babies by meditating during pregnancy. You might require one group of pregnant women to engage in a certain amount and type of meditation each day, while another group would not meditate; the meditation is thus the independent variable. When the infants are born, you would observe and measure their breathing and sleeping patterns. These patterns are the dependent variable, the factor that changes as the result of your manipulation.

Experimental and Control Groups Experiments can involve one or more experimental groups and one or more control groups. An experimental group is a group whose experience is manipulated. A control group is a comparison group that is as much like the experimental group as possible and that is treated in every way like the experimental group except for the manipulated factor (independent variable). The control group serves as a baseline against which the effects of the manipulated condition can be compared.

Random assignment is an important principle for deciding whether each participant will be placed in the experimental group or in the control group (Martin, 2008). Random assignment means that researchers assign participants to experimental and control groups by chance. It reduces the likelihood that the experiment's results will be due to any preexisting differences between groups (Christensen, 2007). In the example of the effects of meditation by pregnant women on the breathing and sleeping patterns of their newborns, you would randomly assign half of the pregnant women to engage in meditation over a period of weeks (the experimental group) and the other half to not meditate over the same number of weeks (the control group). Figure 1.13 illustrates the nature of experimental research.

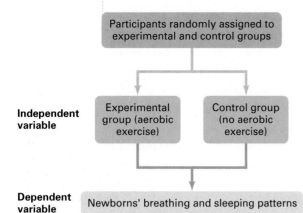

Figure 1.13 Principles of Experimental Research
Imagine that you decide to conduct an experimental study of the effects of aerobic exercise by pregnant women on their newborns' breathing and sleeping patterns. You would randomly assign pregnant women to experimental and control groups. The experimental-group women would engage in aerobic exercise over a specified number of sessions and weeks. The control group would not. Then, when the infants are born, you would assess their breathing and sleeping patterns. If the breathing and sleeping patterns of newborns whose mothers were in the experimental group are more positive than those of the control group, you would conclude that aerobic exercise caused the positive effects.

Time Span of Research

Researchers in life-span development have a special concern with studies that focus on the relation of age to some other variable. We have several options: Researchers can study different individuals of different ages and compare them or they can study the same individuals as they age over time.

Cross–Sectional Approach

The **cross-sectional approach** is a research strategy that simultane-ously compares individuals of different ages. A typical cross-sectional study might include three groups of children: 5-year-olds, 8-year-olds, and 11-year-olds. Another study might include a group of 15-year-olds, 25-year-olds, and 45-year-olds. The groups can be compared with respect to a variety of dependent variables: IQ, memory, peer rela-tions, attachment to parents, hormonal changes, and so on. All of this can be accomplished in a short time. In some studies data are collected in a single day. Even in large-scale cross-sectional studies with hundreds of subjects, data collection does not usually take longer than several months to complete.

The main advantage of the cross-sectional study is that the researcher does not have to wait for the individuals to grow up or become older. Despite its effi-ciency, though, the cross-sectional approach has its drawbacks. It gives no infor-mation about how individuals change or about the stability of their characteristics. It can obscure the increases and decreases of development—the hills and valleys of growth and development. For example, a cross-sectional study of life satisfaction might reveal average increases and decreases, but it would not show how the life satisfaction of individual adults waxed and waned over the years. It also would not tell us whether the same adults who had positive or negative perceptions of life satisfaction in early adulthood maintained their relative degree of life satisfaction as they became middle-aged or older adults.

Longitudinal Approach

The **longitudinal approach** is a research strategy in which the same individuals are studied over a period of time, usually several years or more. For example, in a longitudinal study of life satisfaction, the same adults might be assessed periodically over a 70-year time span—at the ages of 20, 35, 45, 65, and 90, for example.

Longitudinal studies provide a wealth of information about vital issues such as stability and change in development and the impor-tance of early experience for later development, but they do have drawbacks (Hofer & Sliwinski, 2006). They are expensive and time consuming. The longer the study lasts, the more participants drop out—they move, get sick, lose interest, and so forth. The partici-pants who remain may be dissimilar to those who drop out, biasing the outcome of the study. Those individuals who remain in a lon-gitudinal study over a number of years may be more responsible and conformity-oriented, for example, or they might have more stable lives.

Cohort Effects

A *cohort* is a group of people who are born at a similar point in history and share similar experiences as a result, such as living through the Vietnam war or growing up in the same city around the same time. These shared experiences may produce a range of differences among cohorts. For example, people who were teenagers

cross-sectional approach A research strategy in which individuals of different ages are compared at one time.

longitudinal approach A research strategy in which the same individuals are studied over a period of time, usually several years or more.

(a)

(b)

Cohort effects are due to a person's time of birth or generation but not to age. Think for a moment about (a) the Great Depression and (b) today. *How might your development be different depending on which of these time frames dominated your life? Your parents' lives? Your grandparents' lives?*

during the Great Depression are likely to differ from people who were teenagers during the booming 1990s in their educational opportunities and economic status, in how they were raised, and in their attitudes toward sex and religion. In life-span development research, **cohort effects** are due to a person's time of birth, era, or generation but not to actual age.

Cohort effects are important because they can powerfully affect the dependent measures in a study ostensibly concerned with age (Schaie, 2007). Researchers have shown it is especially important to be aware of cohort effects when assessing adult intelligence (Schaie, 1996). Individuals born at different points in time—such as 1920, 1940, and 1960—have had varying opportunities for education. Individuals born in earlier years had less access to education, and this fact may have a significant effect on how this cohort performs on intelligence tests.

Cross-sectional studies can show how different cohorts respond but they can confuse age changes and cohort effects. Longitudinal studies are effective in studying age changes but only within one cohort.

Conducting Ethical Research

Ethics in research may affect you personally if you ever serve as a participant in a study. In that event, you need to know your rights as a participant and the responsibilities of researchers to assure that these rights are safeguarded.

If you ever become a researcher in life-span development yourself, you will need an even deeper understanding of ethics. Even if you only carry out experimental projects in psychology courses, you must consider the rights of the participants in those projects. A student might think, "I volunteer in a home for the mentally retarded several hours per week. I can use the residents of the home in my study to see if a particular treatment helps improve their memory for everyday tasks." But without proper permissions, the most well-meaning, kind, and considerate studies still violate the rights of the participants.

Today, proposed research at colleges and universities must pass the scrutiny of a research ethics committee before the research can be initiated (Kimmel, 2007). In addition, the American Psychological Association (APA) has developed ethics guidelines for its members. The code of ethics instructs psychologists to protect their participants from mental and physical harm. The participants' best interests need to be kept foremost in the researcher's mind (McBurney & White, 2007). APA's guidelines address four important issues: (1) *Informed consent*—all participants must know what their research participation will involve and what risks might develop. Even after informed consent is given, participants must retain the right to withdraw from the study at any time and for any reason. (2) *Confidentiality*—researchers are responsible for keeping all of the data they gather on individuals completely confidential and, when possible, completely anonymous. (3) *Debriefing*—after the study has been completed, participants should be informed of its purpose and the methods that were used. In most cases, the experimenter also can inform participants in a general manner beforehand about the purpose of the research without leading participants to behave in a way they think that the experimenter is expecting. (4) *Deception*—in some circumstances, telling the participants beforehand what the research study is about substantially alters the participants' behavior and invalidates the researcher's data. In all cases of deception, however, the psychologist must ensure that the deception will not harm the participants and that the participants will be *debriefed* (told the complete nature of the study) as soon as possible after the study is completed.

Summary

The Life-Span Perspective

Development is the pattern of change that begins at conception and continues through the human life span. It includes both growth and decline. The life-span perspective includes these basic conceptions: Development is lifelong, multidimensional, multidirectional, and plastic; its study is multidisciplinary; it is embedded in contexts; it involves growth, maintenance, and regulation; and it is a coconstruction of biological, sociocultural, and individual factors. Three important sources of contextual influences are (1) normative age-graded influences, (2) normative history-graded influences, and (3) nonnormative life events. Health and well-being, parenting, education, sociocultural contexts and diversity, and social policy are all areas of contemporary concern that are closely tied to life-span development. Important dimensions of the sociocultural context include culture, ethnicity, socio-economic status, and gender.

The Nature of Development

Three key developmental processes are biological, cognitive, and socioemotional. Development is influenced by an interplay of these processes. The life span is commonly divided into these periods of development: prenatal, infancy, early childhood, middle and late childhood, adolescence, early adulthood, middle adulthood, and late adulthood. Recent interest has focused on categorizing life-span development in terms of four ages. We often think of age only in terms of chronological age, but a full evaluation of age requires consideration of biological age and psychological age. Three important developmental issues are the nature-nurture issue, the continuity-discontinuity issue, and the stability-change issue. Most developmentalists recognize that extreme positions on the nature-nurture, stability-change, and continuity-discontinuity issues are unwise.

Theories of Development

According to psychoanalytic theories, development primarily depends on the unconscious mind and is heavily couched in emotion. Two main psychoanalytic theories were proposed by Freud and Erikson. Freud believed that individuals go through five psychosexual stages. Erikson's theory emphasizes eight psychosocial stages of development. Cognitive theories emphasize thinking, reasoning, language, and other cognitive processes. Three main cognitive theories are Piaget's, Vygotsky's, and information processing. Piaget proposed a cognitive developmental theory in which children use their cognition to adapt to their world as they go through four cognitive stages. Vygotsky's sociocultural cognitive theory emphasizes how culture and social interaction guide cognitive development. The information-processing approach focuses on manipulating information, monitoring it, and strategizing about it. Two main behavioral and social cognitive theories are Skinner's operant conditioning and social cognitive theory. Bandura's social cognitive theory emphasizes reciprocal interactions

SUMMARY

33

among person/cognition, behavior, and environment. Ethology stresses that behavior is strongly influenced by biology, is tied to evolution, and is characterized by critical or sensitive periods. Ecological theory is Bronfenbrenner's view of development that proposes five environmental systems. An eclectic orientation does not follow any one theoretical approach but rather selects from each theory whatever is considered the best in it.

Research In Life-Span Development

The main methods for collecting data about life-span development are observation (in a laboratory or a naturalistic setting), survey (questionnaire) or interview, standardized test, case study, and physiological measures. Three main research designs are descriptive, correlational, and experimental. Descriptive research aims to observe and record behavior. In correlational research, the goal is to describe the strength of the relationship between two or more events or characteristics. Experimental research involves conducting an experiment, which can determine cause and effect. To examine the effects of time and age, researchers can conduct cross-sectional or longitudinal studies. Life-span researchers are especially concerned about cohort effects. Researchers' ethical responsibilities include seeking participants' informed consent, ensuring confidentiality, debriefing them about the purpose and potential personal consequences of participating, and avoiding unnecessary deception of participants.

Key Terms

development 3
life-span perspective 3
context 5
normative age-graded
 influences 5
normative history-graded
 influences 5
nonnormative life events 6
culture 8
cross-cultural studies 8
ethnicity 8
socioeconomic status
 (SES) 8
gender 8
social policy 9
biological processes 11
cognitive processes 11

socioemotional
 processes 11
nature-nurture issue 14
stability-change issue 15
continuity-discontinuity
 issue 15
theory 16
hypotheses 16
psychoanalytic theories 16
Erikson's theory 17
Piaget's theory 19
Vygotsky's theory 20
information-processing
 theory 21
behavioral and social
 cognitive theories 21
social cognitive theory 22

ethology 23
Bronfenbrenner's
 ecological theory 24
eclectic theoretical
 orientation 25
laboratory 26
naturalistic observation 26
standardized test 27
case study 27
descriptive research 28
correlational research 28
correlation coefficient 28
experiment 29
cross-sectional approach 31
longitudinal approach 31
cohort effects 32

Biological Beginnings

Stories of Life-Span Development: The Jim and Jim Twins

Jim Springer and Jim Lewis are identical twins. They were separated at 4 weeks of age and did not see each other again until they were 39 years old. Both worked as part-time deputy sheriffs, vacationed in Florida, drive Chevrolets, had dogs named Toy, and married and divorced women named Betty. One twin named his son James Allan, and the other named his son James Alan. Both liked math but not spelling, enjoyed carpentry and mechanical drawing, chewed their fingernails down to the nubs, had almost identical drinking and smoking habits, had hemorrhoids, put on 10 pounds at about the same point in development, first suffered headaches at the age of 18, and had similar sleep patterns.

Jim and Jim do have some differences. One wears his hair over his forehead, the other slicks it back and has sideburns. One expresses himself best orally; the other is more proficient in writing. But, for the most part, their profiles are remarkably similar.

Another pair of identical twins, Daphne and Barbara, are called the "giggle sisters" because, after being reunited, they were always making each other laugh. A thorough search of their adoptive families' histories revealed no gigglers. The giggle sisters ignored stress, avoided conflict and controversy whenever possible, and showed no interest in politics.

Jim and Jim and the giggle sisters were part of the Minnesota Study of Twins Reared Apart, directed by Thomas Bouchard and his colleagues. The study brings identical twins (identical genetically because they come from the same fertilized egg) and fraternal twins (who come from different fertilized eggs) from all over the world to Minneapolis

Jim Lewis (*left*) and Jim Springer (*right*).

When genetically identical twins who were separated as infants show such striking similarities in their tastes and habits and choices, can we conclude that their genes must have caused the development of those tastes and habits and choices? Other possible causes need to be considered. The twins shared not only the same genes but also some experiences. Some of the separated twins lived together for several months prior to their adoption; some of the twins had been reunited prior to testing (in some cases, many years earlier); adoption agencies often place twins in similar homes; and even strangers who spend several hours together and start comparing their lives are likely to come up with some coincidental similarities (Joseph, 2004, 2006). The Minnesota study of identical twins points to both

the importance of the genetic basis of human development and the need for further research on genetic and environmental factors (Bouchard, 1995).

The examples of Jim and Jim and the giggle sisters stimulate us to think about our genetic heritage and the biological foundations of our existence. Organisms are not like billiard balls, moved by simple, external forces to predictable positions on life's pool table. Environmental experiences and biological foundations work together to make us who we are. Our coverage of life's biological beginnings and experiences will emphasize the evolutionary perspective, genetic foundations, the interaction of heredity and environment, and charting growth from conception through the prenatal period, the birth process itself, and the postpartum period that follows birth. ▮

to investigate their lives. There the twins complete personality and intelligence tests, and they provide detailed medical histories, including information about diet and smoking, exercise habits, chest X-rays, heart stress tests, and EEGs. The twins are asked more than 15,000 questions about their family and childhood, personal interests, vocational orientation, values, and aesthetic judgments. (Bouchard & others, 1990; Lykken, 1999).

The Evolutionary Perspective

In evolutionary time, humans are relative newcomers to Earth. As our earliest ancestors left the forest to feed on the savannahs, and then to form hunting societies on the open plains, their minds and behaviors changed, and they eventually established humans as the dominant species on earth. How did this evolution come about?

Natural Selection and Adaptive Behavior

Charles Darwin (1859) described *natural selection* as the evolutionary process by which those individuals of a species that are best adapted are the ones that survive and reproduce. He reasoned that an intense, constant struggle for food, water, and resources must occur among the many young born each generation, because many of the young do not survive. Those that do survive and reproduce pass on their characteristics to the next generation. Darwin concluded that these survivors are better *adapted* to their world than are the nonsurvivors (Johnson & Losos, 2008). The best-adapted individuals survive to leave the most offspring. Over the course of many generations, organisms with the characteristics needed for survival make up an increased percentage of the population (Freeman & Herron, 2007).

Evolutionary Psychology

Although Darwin introduced the theory of evolution by natural selection in 1859, his ideas only recently have become a popular framework for explaining behavior. Psychology's newest approach, **evolutionary psychology**, emphasizes the importance of adaptation, reproduction, and "survival of the fittest" in shaping behavior.

"Fit" in this sense refers to the ability to bear offspring that survive long enough to bear offspring of their own. In this view, natural selection favors behaviors that increase reproductive success, the ability to pass your genes to the next generation (Promislow, Fedorka, & Burger, 2006).

evolutionary psychology
Emphasizes the importance of adaptation, reproduction, and "survival of the fittest" in shaping behavior.

David Buss (2008) has been especially influential in stimulating new interest in how evolution can explain human behavior. He argues that just as evolution shapes our physical features, such as body shape and height, it also pervasively influences how we make decisions, how aggressive we are, our fears, and our mating patterns. For example, assume that our ancestors were hunterers and gatherers on the plains and that men did most of the hunting and women stayed close to home gathering seeds and plants for food. If you had to walk some distance from your home in an effort to track and slay a fleeing animal, you would need not only certain physical traits but also the ability to perform certain types of spatial thinking. Men born with these traits would be more likely than men without them to survive, to bring home lots of food, and to be considered attractive mates—and thus to reproduce and pass on these characteristics to their children. In other words, these traits would provide a reproductive advantage for males and, over many generations, men with good spatial thinking skills might become more numerous in the population. Critics point out that this scenario might or might not have actually happened.

How Would You...?
As a health-care professional, how would you explain technology and medicine working against natural selection?

Developmental Evolutionary Psychology

Recently, interest has grown in using the concepts of evolutionary psychology to understand human development (Bjorklund, 2006, 2007). Following are some ideas proposed by evolutionary developmental psychologists (Bjorklund & Pellegrini, 2002).

An extended childhood period evolved because humans require time to develop a large brain and learn the complexity of human societies. Humans take longer to become reproductively mature than any other mammal (see Figure 2.1). During this extended childhood period, they develop a large brain and the experiences needed to become competent adults in a complex society.

Many evolved psychological mechanisms are domain-specific. That is, the mechanisms apply only to a specific aspect of a person's makeup. According to evolutionary psychology, information processing is one example. In this view, the mind is not a general-purpose device that can be applied equally to a vast array of problems. Instead, as our ancestors dealt with certain recurring problems such as hunting and finding shelter, specialized modules evolved that process information related to those problems. For example, a module for physical knowledge for tracking animals, a module for mathematical knowledge for trading, and a module for language.

How Would You...?
As an educator, how would you apply the idea that psychological mechanisms are domain-specific to explain how a student with a learning disability in reading may perform exceptionally well in math?

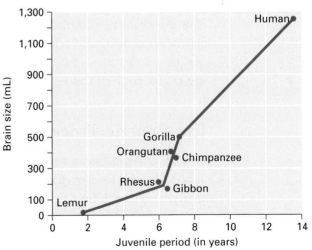

Figure 2.1 **The Brain Sizes of Various Primates and Humans in Relation to the Length of the Juvenile Period** Compared with other primates, humans have both a larger brain and a longer juvenile period. *What conclusions can you draw from the relationship indicated by this graph?*

THE EVOLUTIONARY PERSPECTIVE

Children in all cultures are interested in the tools that adults in their cultures use. For example, this 11-month-old boy from the Efe culture in the Democratic Republic of the Congo in Africa is trying to cut a papaya with an apopau (a smaller version of a machete). *Might the infant's behavior be evolutionary-based or be due to both biological and environmental conditions?*

Evolved mechanisms are not always adaptive in contemporary society. Some behaviors that were adaptive for our prehistoric ancestors may not serve us well today. For example, the food-scarce environment of our ancestors likely led to humans' propensity to gorge when food is available and to crave high-caloric foods, a trait that that might lead to an epidemic of obesity when food is plentiful.

Evaluating Evolutionary Psychology

Although the popular press gives a lot of attention to the ideas of evolutionary psychology, it remains just one theoretical approach. Like the theories described in Chapter 1, it has limitations, weaknesses, and critics (Buller, 2005). Albert Bandura (1998), whose social cognitive theory was described in Chapter 1, acknowledges the important influence of evolution on human adaptation. However, he rejects what he calls "one-sided evolutionism," which sees social behavior as the product of evolved biology. An alternative is a *bidirectional view*, in which environmental and biological conditions influence each other. In this view, evolutionary pressures created changes in biological structures that allowed the use of tools, which enabled our ancestors to manipulate the environment, constructing new environmental conditions. In turn, environmental innovations produced new selection pressures that led to the evolution of specialized biological systems for consciousness, thought, and language.

In other words, evolution gave us bodily structures and biological potentialities; it does not dictate behavior. People have used their biological capacities to produce diverse cultures—aggressive and pacific, egalitarian and autocratic. As American scientist Steven Jay Gould (1981) concluded, in most domains of human functioning, biology allows a broad range of cultural possibilities.

Genetic Foundations of Development

How are characteristics that equip a species for survival transmitted from one generation to the next? Each of us carries a "genetic code" that we inherited from our parents. Because a fertilized egg carries this human code, a fertilized human egg cannot grow into an egret, eagle, or elephant.

The Genetic Process

Each of us began life as a single cell weighing about one twenty-millionth of an ounce! This tiny piece of matter housed our entire genetic code—instructions that orchestrated growth from that single cell to a person made of trillions of cells, each containing a replica of the original code. That code is carried by our genes. What are genes and what do they do? For the answer, we need to look into our cells.

The nucleus of each human cell contains **chromosomes**, which are threadlike structures made up of deoxyribonucleic acid, or DNA. **DNA** is a complex molecule that has a double helix shape, like a spiral staircase, and contains genetic information. **Genes**, the units of hereditary information, are short segments of DNA, as you can see in Figure 2.2. They direct cells to reproduce themselves and to assemble proteins. Proteins, in turn, are the building blocks of cells as well as the regulators that direct the body's processes (Mader, 2008).

Each gene has its own location, its own designated place on a particular chromosome. Today, there is a great deal of enthusiasm about efforts to discover the specific locations of genes that are linked to certain functions (Hartwell, 2008; Plomin & Schalkwyk, 2007). An important step in this direction was accomplished when the Human Genome Project and the Celera Corporation completed a preliminary map of the human *genome*—the complete set of developmental instructions for creating proteins that initiate the making of a human organism.

One of the big surprises of the Human Genome Project was a report indicating that humans have only about 30,000 genes (U.S. Department of Energy, 2001). More recently, the number of human genes has been revised further downward to 20,000 to 25,000 (International Human Genome Sequencing Consortium, 2004). Scientists had thought that humans had as many as 100,000 or more genes. They had also believed that each gene programmed just one protein. In fact, humans appear to have far more proteins than they have genes, so there cannot be a one-to-one correspondence between genes and proteins (Commoner, 2002; Moore, 2001). Each gene is not translated, in automaton-like fashion, into one and only one protein. A gene does not act independently, as developmental psychologist David Moore (2001) emphasized by titling his book *The Dependent Gene.*

Rather than being a group of independent genes, the human genome consists of many genes that collaborate both with each other and with nongenetic factors inside and outside the body. The collaboration operates at many points. For example, the cellular machinery mixes, matches, and links small pieces of DNA to reproduce the genes and that machinery is influenced by what is going on around it.

Whether a gene is turned "on"—working to assemble proteins—is also a matter of collaboration. The activity of genes (*genetic expression*) is affected by their environment (Gottlieb, Wahlsten, & Lickliter, 2006). For example, hormones that circulate in the blood make their way into the cell where they can turn genes "on" and "off." And the flow of hormones can be affected by environmental conditions, such as light, day length, nutrition, and behavior. Numerous studies have shown that external events outside of the original cell and the person, as well as events inside the cell, can excite or inhibit gene expression (Gottlieb, 2007).

chromosomes Threadlike structures made up of deoxyribonucleic acid, or DNA.

DNA A complex molecule with a double helix shape that contains genetic information.

genes Units of hereditary information composed of DNA. Genes direct cells to reproduce themselves and manufacture the proteins that maintain life.

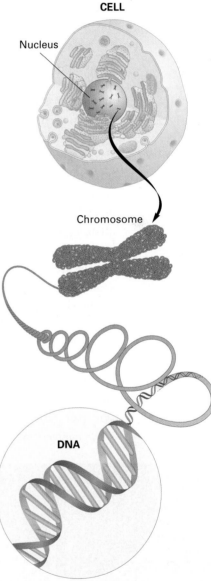

Figure 2.2 Cells, Chromosomes, DNA, and Genes (*Top*) The body contains trillions of cells. Each cell contains a central structure, the nucleus. (*Middle*) Chromosomes are threadlike structures located in the nucleus of the cell. Chromosomes are composed of DNA. (*Bottom*) DNA has the structure of a spiraled double chain. A gene is a segment of DNA.

Cellular reproduction in which the cell's nucleus duplicates itself with two new cells being formed, each containing the same DNA as the parent cell, arranged in the same 23 pairs of chromosomes.

meiosis A specialized form of cell division that occurs to form eggs and sperm (or gametes).

Genes and Chromosomes

Genes are not only collaborative; they are enduring. How do the genes manage to get passed from generation to generation and end up in all of the trillion cells in the body? Three processes explain the heart of the story: mitosis, meiosis, and fertilization.

Mitosis, Meiosis, and Fertilization

All cells in your body, except the sperm and egg, have 46 chromosomes arranged in 23 pairs. These cells reproduce by a process called **mitosis**. During mitosis, the cell's nucleus—including the chromosomes—duplicates itself and the cell divides. Two new cells are formed, each containing the same DNA as the original cell, arranged in the same 23 pairs of chromosomes.

However, a different type of cell division—**meiosis**—forms eggs and sperm (or *gametes*). During meiosis, a cell of the testes (in men) or ovaries (in women) duplicates its chromosomes but then divides *twice*, thus forming four cells, each of which has only half of the genetic material of the parent cell. By the end of meiosis, each egg or sperm has 23 *unpaired* chromosomes.

During *fertilization*, an egg and a sperm fuse to create a single cell, called a *zygote*. In the zygote, the 23 unpaired chromosomes from the egg and the 23 unpaired chromosomes from the sperm combine to form one set of 23 paired chromosomes—one chromosome of each pair from the mother's egg and the other from the father's sperm. In this manner, each parent contributes half of the offspring's genetic material.

Figure 2.3 shows 23 paired chromosomes of a male and a female. The members of each pair of chromosomes are both similar and different: Each chromosome in the pair contains varying forms of the same genes, at the same location on the chromosome. A gene for hair color, for example, is located on both members of one pair of chromosomes, in the same location on each. However, one of those chromosomes might carry the gene for blond hair; the other chromosome in the pair might carry the gene for brown hair.

Do you notice any obvious differences between the chromosomes of the male and the chromosomes of the female in Figure 2.3? The difference lies in the 23rd pair. Ordinarily, in females this pair consists of two chromosomes called *X chromosomes*; in males the 23rd pair consists of an X and a *Y chromosome*. The presence of a Y chromosome is what makes an individual male.

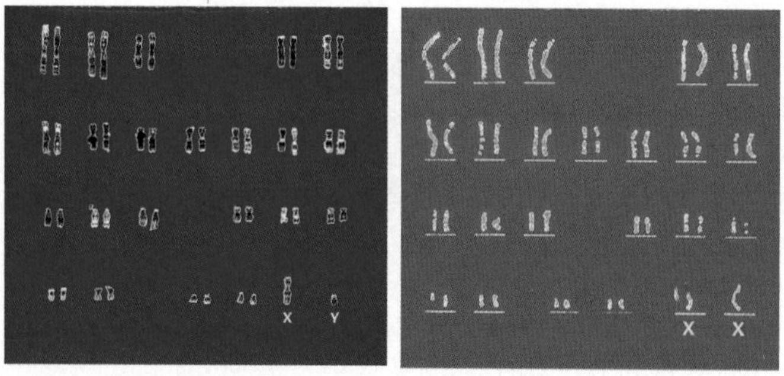

Sources of Variability

Combining the genes of two parents in offspring increases genetic variability in the population, which is valuable for a species because it provides more characteristics for natural selection to operate on (Talaro, 2008). In fact, the human genetic process creates several important sources of variability.

First, the chromosomes in the zygote are not exact copies of those in

(a)   (b)

Figure 2.3 The Genetic Difference Between Males and Females
Set (*a*) shows the chromosome structure of a male, and set (*b*) shows the chromosome structure of a female. The last pair of 23 pairs of chromosomes is in the bottom right box of each set. Notice that the Y chromosome of the male is smaller than the X chromosome of the female.

CALVIN & HOBBES, Copyright © 1991 Watterson. Reprinted with permission of Universal Press Syndicate. All Rights Reserved.

the mother's ovaries and the father's testes. During the formation of the sperm and egg in meiosis, the members of each pair of chromosomes are separated, but which chromosome in the pair goes to the gamete is a matter of chance. In addition, before the pairs separate, pieces of the two chromosomes in each pair are exchanged, creating a new combination of genes on each chromosome. Thus, when chromosomes from the mother's egg and the father's sperm are brought together in the zygote, the result is a truly unique combination of genes (Weaver, 2008).

Another source of variability comes from DNA. Chances, a mistake by cellular machinery, or damage from an environmental agent such as radiation may produce a *mutated gene,* which is a permanently altered segment of DNA (Brooker & others, 2008).

Even when their genes are identical, however, people vary. The difference between genotypes and phenotypes helps us to understand this source of variability. All of a person's genetic material makes up his or her **genotype.** However, not all of the genetic material is apparent in our observed and measurable characteristics. A **phenotype** consists of observable characteristics. Phenotypes include physical characteristics (such as height, weight, and hair color) and psychological characteristics (such as personality and intelligence).

For each genotype, a range of phenotypes can be expressed, providing another source of variability (Gottlieb, 2007). An individual can inherit the genetic potential to grow very large, for example, but good nutrition, among other things, will be essential to achieving that potential. The giggle sisters introduced in the chapter opening might have inherited the same genetic potential to be very tall, but if Daphne had grown up malnourished, she might have ended up noticeably shorter than Barbara. This principle is so widely applicable it has a name: heredity-environment interaction (or gene-environment interaction).

Genetic Principles

What determines how a genotype is expressed to create a particular phenotype? Much is unknown about the answer to this question (Dowan, 2006; Johnson, 2008). However, a number of genetic principles have been discovered, among them those of dominant-recessive genes, sex-linked genes, and polygenically determined characteristics.

Dominant–Recessive Genes Principle

In some cases, one gene of a pair always exerts its effects; it is *dominant,* overriding the potential influence of the other gene, called the

genotype A person's genetic heritage; the actual genetic material.

phenotype The way an individual's genotype is expressed in observed and measurable characteristics.

recessive gene. This is the *dominant-recessive genes principle*. A recessive gene exerts its influence only if the two genes of a pair are both recessive. If you inherit a recessive gene for a trait from each of your parents, you will show the trait. If you inherit a recessive gene from only one parent, you may never know you carry the gene. Brown hair, farsightedness, and dimples rule over blond hair, nearsightedness, and freckles in the world of dominant-recessive genes. Can two brown-haired parents have a blond-haired child? Yes, they can. Suppose that each parent has a dominant gene for brown hair and a recessive gene for blond hair. Since dominant genes override recessive genes, the parents have brown hair, but both are carriers of blondness and pass on their recessive genes for blond hair. With no dominant gene to override them, the recessive genes can make the child's hair blond.

Sex-Linked Genes

Most mutated genes are recessive. When a mutated gene is carried on the X chromosome, the result is called *X-linked inheritance*. It may have very different implications for males than females (Turner, 2006). Remember that males have only one X chromosome. Thus, if there is an altered, disease-creating gene on the X chromosome, males have no "backup" copy to counter the harmful gene and therefore may carry an X-linked disease. However, females have a second X chromosome, which is likely to be unchanged. As a result, they are not likely to have the X-linked disease. Thus, most individuals who have X-linked diseases are males. Females who have one changed copy of the X gene are known as "carriers," and they usually do not show any signs of the X-linked disease. Fragile-X syndrome, which we will discuss later in the chapter, is an example of X-linked inheritance (Raymond & Tarpey, 2006).

Polygenic Inheritance

Genetic transmission is usually more complex than the simple examples we have examined thus far (Hartwell, 2008). Few characteristics reflect the influence of only a single gene or pair of genes. Most are determined by the interaction of many different genes; they are said to be *polygenically determined*. Even a simple characteristic such as height, for example, reflects the interaction of many genes, as well as the influence of the environment.

These athletes, many of whom have Down syndrome, are participating in a Special Olympics competition. Notice the distinctive facial features of the individuals with Down syndrome, such as a round face and a flattened skull. *What causes Down syndrome?*

Chromosome and Gene-Linked Abnormalities

In some (relatively rare) cases, genetic inheritance involves an abnormality. Some of these abnormalities come from whole chromosomes that do not separate properly during meiosis. Other abnormalities are produced by defective genes.

Chromosome Abnormalities

Sometimes, when a gamete is formed, the combined sperm and ovum do not have their normal set of 23 chromosomes. The most notable examples involve Down syndrome and abnormalities of the sex chromosomes. Figure 2.4 describes some chromosome abnormalities, including their treatment and incidence.

Down Syndrome Down syndrome is one of the most common genetically linked causes of mental retardation; it is also characterized by certain physical features. An individual with Down syndrome has a round face, a flattened skull, an extra fold of skin over the eyelids, a thickened tongue, short limbs, and retardation of motor and mental abilities (Hodapp & Dykens, 2006). The syndrome is caused by the presence of an extra copy of chromosome 21. It is not known why the extra chromosome is present, but the health of the male sperm or female ovum may be involved.

Down syndrome appears approximately once in every 700 live births. Women between the ages of 16 and 34 are less likely to give birth to a child with Down syndrome than are younger or older women. African American children are rarely born with Down syndrome.

How Would You...?

As a social worker, how would you respond to a 30-year-old pregnant woman who is concerned about the risk of giving birth to a baby with Down syndrome?

Sex-Linked Chromosome Abnormalities Recall that a newborn normally has either an X and a Y chromosome, or two X chromosomes. Human embryos must possess at least one X chromosome to be viable. The most common sex-linked chromosome abnormalities involve the presence of an extra chromosome (either an X or Y) or the absence of one X chromosome in females.

Klinefelter syndrome is a genetic disorder in which males have an extra X chromosome, making them XXY instead of XY (Itti & others, 2006). Males with this disorder have undeveloped testes, and they usually have enlarged breasts and become tall. Klinefelter syndrome occurs approximately once in every 800 live male births.

Fragile X syndrome is a genetic disorder that results from an abnormality in the X chromosome, which becomes constricted and often breaks (Irwin & others, 2005). A lower level of intelligence often is an outcome and it may take the form of mental retardation, a learning disability, or a short attention span (Lewis, 2007). This disorder occurs more frequently in males than in females, possibly because the second X chromosome in females negates the effects of the other abnormal X chromosome (Fanos, Spanger, & Musci, 2006).

Name	Description	Treatment	Incidence
Down syndrome	An extra chromosome causes mild to severe retardation and physical abnormalities.	Surgery, early intervention, infant stimulation, and special learning programs	1 in 1,900 births at age 20 1 in 300 births at age 35 1 in 30 births at age 45
Klinefelter syndrome (XXY)	An extra X chromosome causes physical abnormalities.	Hormone therapy can be effective	1 in 600 male births
Fragile X syndrome	An abnormality in the X chromosome can cause mental retardation, learning disabilities, or short attention span.	Special education, speech and language therapy	More common in males than in females
Turner syndrome (XO)	A missing X chromosome in females can cause mental retardation and sexual underdevelopment.	Hormone therapy in childhood and puberty	1 in 2,500 female births
XYY syndrome	An extra Y chromosome can cause above-average height.	No special treatment required	1 in 1,000 male births

Figure 2.4 Some Gene-Linked Abnormalities

Turner syndrome is a chromosome disorder in females in which either an X chromosome is missing, making the person XO instead of XX, or part of one X chromosome is deleted (Kanaka-Gantenbein, 2006). Females with Turner syndrome are short in stature and have a webbed neck. In some cases, they are infertile. They have difficulty in mathematics but their verbal ability is often quite good. Turner syndrome occurs in approximately 1 of every 2,500 live female births.

The *XYY syndrome* is a chromosomal disorder in which the male has an extra Y chromosome (Briken & others, 2006). Early interest in this syndrome focused on the belief that the extra Y chromosome found in some males contributed to aggression and violence. However, researchers subsequently found that XYY males are no more likely to commit crimes than are XY males (Witkin & others, 1976).

Gene-Linked Abnormalities

Abnormalities can be produced not only by an uneven number of chromosomes, but also by defective genes (Brooker & others, 2008; Weaver, 2008). Figure 2.5 describes some gene-linked abnormalities, including their treatment and incidence.

Phenylketonuria (PKU) is a genetic disorder in which the individual cannot properly metabolize phenylalanine, an amino acid that naturally occurs in many food sources. It results from a recessive gene and occurs about once in every 10,000 to 20,000 live births. Today, phenylketonuria is easily detected in newborns, and it is treated by a diet that prevents an excess accumulation of phenylalanine. If phenylketonuria is left untreated, however, excess phenylalanine builds up in the child,

Name	Description	Treatment	Incidence
Cystic fibrosis	Glandular dysfunction that interferes with mucus production; breathing and digestion are hampered, resulting in a shortened life span.	Physical and oxygen therapy, synthetic enzymes, and antibiotics; most individuals live to middle age.	1 in 2,000 births
Diabetes	Body does not produce enough insulin, which causes abnormal metabolism of sugar.	Early onset can be fatal unless treated with insulin.	1 in 2,500 births
Hemophilia	Delayed blood clotting causes internal and external bleeding.	Blood transfusions/injections can reduce or prevent damage due to internal bleeding.	1 in 10,000 males
Huntington disease	Central nervous system deteriorates, producing problems in muscle coordination and mental deterioration.	Does not usually appear until age 35 or older; death likely 10 to 20 years after symptoms appear.	1 in 20,000 births
Phenylketonuria (PKU)	Metabolic disorder that, left untreated, causes mental retardation.	Special diet can result in average intelligence and normal life span.	1 in 10,000 to 1 in 20,000 births
Sickle-cell anemia	Blood disorder that limits the body's oxygen supply; it can cause joint swelling, as well as heart and kidney failure.	Penicillin, medication for pain, antibiotics, and blood transfusions.	1 in 400 African American children (lower among other groups)
Spina bifida	Neural tube disorder that causes brain and spine abnormalities.	Corrective surgery at birth, orthopedic devices, and physical/medical therapy.	2 in 1,000 births
Tay-Sachs disease	Deceleration of mental and physical development caused by an accumulation of lipids in the nervous system.	Medication and special diet are used, but death is likely by 5 years of age.	1 in 30 American Jews is a carrier.

Figure 2.5 Some Chromosome Abnormalities The treatments for these abnormalities do not necessarily erase the problem but may improve the individual's adaptive behavior and quality of life.

producing mental retardation and hyperactivity (Brosco, Mattingly, & Sanders, 2006). Phenylketonuria accounts for approximately 1 percent of institutionalized individuals who are mentally retarded, and it occurs primarily in Whites.

The story of phenylketonuria has important implications for the nature-nurture issue. Although phenylketonuria is a genetic disorder (nature), how or whether a gene's influence in phenylketonuria is played out depends on environmental influences since the disorder can be treated (nurture) (Hvas, Nexos, & Nielsen, 2006). That is, the presence of a genetic defect *does not* inevitably lead to the development of the disorder *if* the individual develops in the right environment (one free of phenylalanine). This is one example of the important principle of heredity-environment interaction (Gottlieb, 2005).

Sickle-cell anemia, which occurs most often in African Americans, is a genetic disorder that impairs the body's red blood cells. Red blood cells, which carry oxygen throughout the body, are usually shaped like a disk. In sickle-cell anemia, a recessive gene causes the red blood cell to become a hook-shaped "sickle" that cannot carry oxygen properly and dies quickly (Smith & others, 2006). As a result, the body's cells do not receive adequate oxygen, causing anemia and early death. About 1 in 400 African American babies is affected by sickle-cell anemia. One in 10 African Americans is a carrier, as is 1 in 20 Latin Americans.

Other diseases that result from genetic abnormalities include cystic fibrosis, diabetes, hemophilia, Huntington disease, spina bifida, and Tay-Sachs disease. Someday, scientists may identify why these and other genetic abnormalities occur and discover how to cure them.

Genetic counselors, usually physicians or biologists who are well-versed in the field of medical genetics, understand the kinds of diseases just described, the odds of encountering them, and helpful strategies for offseting some of their effects (Finn & Smoller, 2006). To read about the career and work of a genetic counselor, see the Careers in Life-Span Development profile.

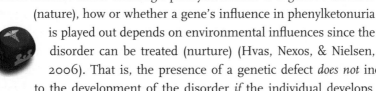

Heredity and Environment Interaction: The Nature–Nurture Debate

Is it possible to untangle the influence of heredity from that of environment and discover the role of each in producing individual differences in development? When heredity and environment interact, how does heredity influence the environment, and vice versa?

Behavior Genetics

Behavior genetics is the field that seeks to discover the influence of heredity and environment on individual differences in human traits and development (Plomin, DeFries, & Fulker, 2007; Vogler, 2006). Behavior geneticists often study either twins or adoption situations.

In a **twin study,** the behavioral similarity of identical twins (who are genetically identical) is compared with the behavioral similarity of fraternal twins. Recall that although fraternal twins share the same womb, they are no more genetically alike than brothers or sisters. By comparing groups of identical and fraternal twins,

adoption study A study in which investigators seek to discover whether, in behavior and psychological characteristics, adopted children are more like their adoptive parents, who provided a home environment, or more like their biological parents, who contributed their heredity. Another form of the adoption study is to compare adoptive and biological siblings.

behavior geneticists capitalize on this basic knowledge that identical twins are more similar genetically than are fraternal twins: If they observe that a behavioral trait is more often shared by identical twins than by fraternal twins, they can infer that the trait has a genetic basis (Bulik & others, 2006). For example, one study revealed a higher incidence of conduct problems shared among identical twins than among fraternal twins; the researchers discerned an important role for heredity in conduct problems (Scourfield & others, 2004).

However, several issues complicate interpretation of twin studies (Vogler, 2006). For example, perhaps the environments of identical twins are more similar than the environments of fraternal twins. Parents and caregivers might stress the similarities of identical twins more than those of fraternal twins, and identical twins might perceive themselves as a "set" and play together more than fraternal twins do. If so, the observed similarities between identical twins might have a significant environmental basis.

In an **adoption study**, investigators seek to discover whether the behavior and psychological characteristics of adopted children are more like those of their adoptive parents, who have provided a home environment, or more like those of their biological parents, who have contributed their heredity (Haugaard & Hazen, 2004). Another form of the adoption study compares adoptees with their adoptive siblings and their biological siblings.

CAREERS IN LIFE-SPAN DEVELOPMENT
Holly Ishmael, Genetic Counselor

Holly Ishmael is a genetic counselor at Children's Mercy Hospital in Kansas City. She obtained an undergraduate degree in psychology and then a master's degree in genetic counseling from Sarah Lawrence College.

Holly Ishmael (*left*) in a genetic counseling session.

Genetic counselors, like Holly, work as members of a health-care team, providing information and support to families with birth defects or genetic disorders. They identify families at risk by analyzing inheritance patterns and explore options with the family. Some genetic counselors, like Holly, become specialists in prenatal and pediatric genetics; others might specialize in cancer genetics or psychiatric genetic disorders.

Holly, says, "Genetic counseling is a perfect combination for people who want to do something science-oriented, but need human contact and don't want to spend all of their time in a lab or have their nose in a book" (Rizzo, 1999, p. 3).

Genetic counselors have specialized graduate degrees in the areas of medical genetics and counseling. They enter graduate school with undergraduate backgrounds from a variety of disciplines, including biology, genetics, psychology, public health, and social work. There are approximately thirty graduate genetic counseling programs in the United States. If you are interested in this profession, you can obtain further information from the National Society of Genetic Counselors at www.nsgc.org.

Heredity–Environment Correlations

The difficulties that researchers encounter when they interpet the results of twin studies and adoption studies reflect the complexities of heredity-environment interaction. Some of these interactions are *heredity-environment correlations*, which means that individuals' genes may influence the types of environments to which they are exposed. In a sense, individuals "inherit" environments that may be related or linked to genetic "propensities" (Plomin, DeFries, & Fulker, 2007). Behavior geneticist Sandra Scarr (1993) described three ways that heredity and environment are correlated:

epigenetic view Emphasizes that development is the result of an ongoing, bidirectional interchange between heredity and environment.

- *Passive genotype-environment correlations* occur because biological parents, who are genetically related to the child, provide a rearing environment for the child. For example, the parents might have a genetic predisposition to be intelligent and read skillfully. Because they read well and enjoy reading, they provide their children with books to read. The likely outcome is that their children, given their own inherited predispositions from their parents and their book-filled environment, will become skilled readers.

- *Evocative genotype-environment correlations* occur because a child's characteristics elicit certain types of environments. For example, active, smiling children receive more social stimulation than passive, quiet children do. Cooperative, attentive children evoke more pleasant and instructional responses from the adults around them than uncooperative, distractible children do.

How might heredity-environment correlations be at work in a child learning to play the piano?

- *Active (niche-picking) genotype-environment correlations* occur when children seek out environments that they find compatible and stimulating. *Niche-picking* refers to finding a setting that is suited to one's abilities. Children select from their surrounding environment some aspect that they respond to, learn about, or ignore. Their active selections of environments are related to their particular genotype. For example, outgoing children tend to seek out social contexts in which to interact with people, whereas shy children don't. Children who are musically inclined are likely to select musical environments in which they can successfully perform their skills. How these "tendencies" come about will be discussed shortly under the topic of the epigenetic view.

Notice that Scarr's view gives the preeminent role in development to heredity: her analysis describes how heredity may influence the types of environments that children experience. Critics argue that the concept of heredity-environment correlation gives heredity too much of a one-sided influence in determining development because it does not consider the role of prior environmental influences in shaping the correlation itself (Gottlieb, Wahlsten, & Lickliter, 2006).

The Epigenetic View

In line with the concept of a collaborative gene, Gilbert Gottlieb (2004, 2007; Gottlieb, Wahlsten, & Lickliter, 2006) emphasizes the **epigenetic view**, which states that development is the result of an ongoing, bidirectional interchange between heredity and the environment. Figure 2.6 compares the heredity-environment correlation and epigenetic views of development.

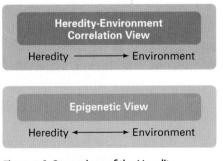

Figure 2.6 Comparison of the Heredity-Environment Correlation and Epigenic Views

How Would You...?

As a human development and family studies professional, how would you apply the epigenetic view to explain why one identical twin can develop alcoholism, while the other twin does not?

Let's look at an example that reflects the epigenetic view. A baby inherits genes from both parents at conception. During prenatal development, toxins, nutrition, and stress can influence some genes to stop functioning, while others become stronger or weaker. During infancy, environmental experiences such as toxins, nutrition, stress, learning, and encouragement continue to modify genetic activity and the activity of the nervous system that directly underlies behavior (Gottlieb, 2005). Heredity and environment operate together—or collaborate—to produce a person's intelligence, temperament, height, weight, ability to pitch a baseball, ability to read, and so on (Gottlieb, Wahlsten, & Lickliter, 2006).

Conclusions About Heredity–Environment Interaction

If an attractive, popular, intelligent girl is elected president of her high school senior class, is her success due to heredity or to environment? Of course, the answer is both.

The relative contributions of heredity and environment are not additive. That is, we can't say that such-and-such a percentage of nature and such-and-such a percentage of experience make us who we are. Nor is it accurate to say that full genetic expression happens once, around conception or birth, after which we carry our genetic legacy into the world to see how far it takes us. Genes produce proteins throughout the life span, in many different environments. Or they don't produce these proteins, depending in part on how harsh or nourishing those environments are.

The emerging view is that complex behaviors have some *genetic loading* that gives people a propensity for a particular developmental trajectory (Plomin, DeFries, & Fulker, 2007). However, the actual development requires more: an environment. And that environment is complex, just like the mixture of genes we inherit (Grusec & Hastings, 2007). Environmental influences range from the things we lump together under "nurture" (such as parenting, family dynamics, schooling, and neighborhood quality) to biological encounters (such as viruses, birth complications, and even biological events in cells) (Greenough & others, 2001).

Imagine for a moment that there is a cluster of genes somehow associated with youth violence. (This example is hypothetical because we don't know of any such combination.) The adolescent who carries this genetic mixture might experience a world of loving parents, regular nutritious meals, lots of books, and a series of competent teachers. Or the adolescent's world might include parental neglect, a neighborhood in which gunshots and crime are everyday occurrences, and inadequate schooling. In which of these environments are the adolescent's genes likely to manufacture the biological underpinnings of criminality?

Prenatal Development

Conception occurs when a single sperm cell from the male unites with an ovum (egg) in the female's fallopian tube in a process called fertilization. Over the next few months the genetic code discussed earlier directs a series of changes in the fertilized egg, but many events and hazards will influence how that egg develops and becomes a person.

The Course of Prenatal Development

Prenatal development lasts approximately 266 days, beginning with fertilization and ending with birth. It can be divided into three periods: germinal, embryonic, and fetal.

The Germinal Period

The **germinal period** is the period of prenatal development that takes place in the first two weeks after conception. It includes the creation of the fertilized egg (the *zygote*), cell division, and the attachment of the zygote to the uterine wall.

Rapid cell division by the zygote begins the germinal period. (Recall from earlier in the chapter that this cell division occurs through a process called *mitosis*.) By approximately one week after conception, the differentiation of these cells—their specialization for different tasks—has already begun. At this stage the group of cells, now called the *blastocyst*, consists of an inner mass of cells that will eventually develop into the embryo and the *trophoblast*, an outer layer of cells that later provides nutrition and support for the embryo. *Implantation*, the attachment of the zygote to the uterine wall, takes place about 10 to 14 days after conception.

The Embryonic Period

The **embryonic period** is the period of prenatal development that occurs from two to eight weeks after conception. During the embryonic period, the rate of cell differentiation intensifies, support systems for cells form, and organs appear.

This period begins as the blastocyst attaches to the uterine wall. The mass of cells is now called an *embryo*, and three layers of cells form. The embryo's *endoderm* is the inner layer of cells, which will develop into the digestive and respiratory systems. The *ectoderm* is the outermost layer, which will become the nervous system, sensory receptors (ears, nose, and eyes, for example), and skin parts (hair and nails, for example). The *mesoderm* is the middle layer, which will become the circulatory system, bones, muscles, excretory system, and reproductive system. Every body part eventually develops from these three layers. The endoderm primarily produces internal body parts, the mesoderm primarily produces parts that surround the internal areas, and the ectoderm primarily produces surface parts. **Organogenesis** is the name given to the process of organ formation during the first two months of prenatal development. While they are being formed, the organs are especially vulnerable to environmental influences.

As the embryo's three layers form, life-support systems for the embryo develop rapidly. These life-support systems include the amnion, the umbilical cord (both of which develop from the fertilized egg, not the mother's body), and the placenta. The amnion is like a bag or an envelope; it contains a clear fluid in which the developing embryo floats. The amniotic fluid provides an environment that is temperature and humidity controlled, as well as shockproof. The *umbilical cord*, which contains two arteries and one vein, connects the baby to the placenta. The *placenta*

How Would You...?

As a social worker, how would you counsel a woman who continues to drink alcohol in the early weeks of pregnancy because she believes she can't harm the baby until it has developed further?

germinal period The period of prenatal development that takes place in the first two weeks after conception. It includes the creation of the zygote, continued cell division, and the attachment of the zygote to the uterine wall.

embryonic period The period of prenatal development that occurs two to eight weeks after conception. During the embryonic period, the rate of cell differentiation intensifies, support systems for the cells form, and organs appear.

organogenesis Organ formation that takes place during the first two months of prenatal development.

49

consists of a disk-shaped group of tissues in which small blood vessels from the mother and the offspring intertwine but do not join.

Very small molecules—oxygen, water, salt, and nutrients from the mother's blood, as well as carbon dioxide and digestive wastes from the baby's blood—pass back and forth between the mother and embryo or fetus. Large molecules cannot pass through the placental wall; these include red blood cells and harmful substances, such as most bacteria, maternal wastes, and hormones. The mechanisms that govern the transfer of substances across the placental barrier are complex and are still not entirely understood (Xu, Cook, & Knipp, 2006).

The Fetal Period

The **fetal period** is the prenatal period of development that begins two months after conception and lasts for seven months, on the average. Growth and development continue their dramatic course during this time.

Three months after conception, the fetus is about 3 inches long and weighs about 3 ounces. It has become active, moving its arms and legs, opening and closing its mouth, and moving its head. The face, forehead, eyelids, nose, and chin are distinguishable, as are the upper arms, lower arms, hands, and lower limbs. The genitals can be identified as male or female. By the end of the fourth month, the fetus has grown to 6 inches in length and weighs 4 to 7 ounces. For the first time the mother can feel arm and leg movements.

By the end of the fifth month, the fetus is about 12 inches long and weighs close to a pound. Structures of the skin have formed—toenails and fingernails, for example. By the end of the sixth month, the eyes and eyelids are completely formed, and a fine layer of hair covers the head. A grasping reflex is present and irregular breathing movements occur.

By the end of the seventh month, the fetus is about 16 inches long and now weighs about 3 pounds. This is generally the time when a fetus is considered *viable*—able to survive outside the womb. But even when infants are born in the seventh month, they usually need help breathing and other forms of special care.

During the last two months of prenatal development fatty tissues develop, and the functioning of various organ systems—heart and kidneys, for example—steps up. During the eighth and ninth months, the fetus grows longer and gains substantial weight—about another 4 pounds. At birth, the average American baby weighs $7^1/_2$ pounds and is about 20 inches long.

In addition to describing prenatal development in terms of germinal, embryonic, and fetal periods, prenatal development also can be divided into equal periods of three months, called *trimesters*. Remember that the three trimesters are not the same as the three prenatal periods we have discussed. The germinal and embryonic periods occur in the first trimester. The fetal period begins toward the end of the first trimester and continues through the second and third trimesters. Viability (the chances of surviving outside the womb) occurs at the beginning of the third trimester.

Prenatal Tests

Together with her doctor, a pregnant woman will decide the extent to which she should undergo prenatal testing. A number of tests can indicate whether a fetus is developing normally; these include ultrasound sonography, chorionic villus sampling, amnocentesis, and maternal blood screening (Bromage, 2006). The decision to have a given test depends on several criteria, such as the mother's age, medical history, and genetic risk factors.

An ultrasound test is generally performed 7 weeks into a pregnancy and at various times later in pregnancy. *Ultrasound sonography* is a noninvasive prenatal medical procedure in which high-frequency sound waves are directed into the pregnant woman's abdomen (Oepkes & others, 2006). The echo from the sounds is transformed into a visual representation of the fetus's inner structures. This technique can detect many structural abnormalities in the fetus, including microencephaly, a form of mental retardation involving an abnormally small brain; it can also give clues to the baby's sex and indicate whether there is more than one fetus. Ultrasound results are available as soon as the images are read by a radiologist.

A 6-month-old infant poses with the ultrasound sonography record taken four months into the baby's prenatal development. *What is ultrasound sonography?*

At some point between the 10th and 12th weeks of pregnancy, chorionic villus sampling may be used to screen for genetic defects and chromosome abnormalities (Csaba, Bush, & Saphier, 2006). *Chorionic villus sampling* (CVS) is a prenatal medical procedure in which a tiny tissue sample from the placenta is removed and analyzed. The results are available in about 10 days.

Between the 15th and 18th weeks of pregnancy, *amniocentesis* may be performed. In this procedure, a sample of amniotic fluid is withdrawn by syringe and tested for chromosome or metabolic disorders (Chadefaux-Vekemans & others, 2006). The later in the pregnancy amniocentesis is performed, the better its diagnostic potential. However, the earlier it is performed, the more useful it is in deciding how to handle a pregnancy when the fetus is found to have a disorder (Li & others, 2006). It may take two weeks for enough cells to grow so that amniocentesis test results can be obtained.

Amniocentesis brings a small risk of miscarriage: about 1 woman in every 200 to 300 miscarries after amniocentesis. Although earlier reports indicated that chorionic villus sampling brings a slightly higher risk of pregnancy loss than

How Would You...? As a psychologist, how would you advise a 25-year-old mother who is concerned about the possibility of birth defects but has no genetic history of these types of problems?

amniocentesis, a recent U.S. study of more than 40,000 pregnancies found that loss rates for CVS decreased from 1998 to 2003 and that there is no longer a difference in pregnancy loss risk between CVS and amniocentesis (Caughey, Hopkins, & Norton, 2006).

During the 16th to 18th weeks of pregnancy, maternal blood screening may be performed. *Maternal blood screening* identifies pregnancies that have an elevated risk for birth defects such as spina bifida (a typically fatal defect in the spinal cord) and Down syndrome (Huang & others, 2005). The current blood test is called the *triple screen* because it measures three substances in the mother's blood. After an abnormal triple screen result, the next step is usually an ultrasound examination. If an ultrasound does not explain the abnormal triple screen results, amniocentesis typically is used.

Infertility and Reproductive Technology

Recent advances in biological knowledge have also opened up many choices for infertile people. Approximately 10 to 15 percent of couples in the United States experience infertility, which is defined as the inability to conceive a child after 12 months of regular intercourse without contraception. The cause of infertility can rest with the woman or the man (Amin & others, 2006). The woman may not be ovulating (releasing eggs to be fertilized), she may be producing abnormal ova, her fallopian tubes (by which ova normally reach the womb) may be blocked, or she may have a condition that prevents implantation of the embyro into the uterus. The man may produce too few sperm, the sperm may lack motility (the ability to move adequately), or he may have a blocked passageway (Kumar & others, 2006).

Surgery can correct some causes of infertility; for others, hormone-based drugs may be effective. Of the 2 million U.S. couples who seek help for infertility every year, about 40,000 try assisted reproduction technologies. *In vitro fertilization (IVF)*, the technique that produced the world's first "test tube baby" in 1978, involves eggs and sperm being combined in a laboratory dish. If any eggs are successfully fertilized, one or more of the resulting fertilized eggs is transferred into the woman's uterus.

The creation of families by means of assisted reproduction techniques raises important questions about the physical and psychological consequences for children (Ito & others, 2006). For example, one result of fertility treatments is an increase in multiple births (El-Toukhy, Khalaf, & Braude, 2006). Twenty-five to 30 percent of pregnancies achieved by fertility treatments—including in vitro fertilization—result in multiple births. Any multiple birth increases the likelihood that the babies will have life-threatening and costly problems, such as extremely low birth weight.

Hazards to Prenatal Development

For most babies, the course of prenatal development goes smoothly. Their mother's womb protects them as they develop. Despite this protection, however, the environment can affect the embryo or fetus in many well-documented ways.

General Principles

A **teratogen** is any agent that can potentially cause a birth defect or negatively alter cognitive and behavioral outcomes. The field of study that investigates the causes of birth defects is called *teratology*. Teratogens include drugs, incompatible blood types, environmental pollutants, infectious diseases, nutritional deficiencies, maternal stress, advanced maternal and paternal age, and environmental pollutants.

The dose, genetic susceptibility, and time of exposure to a particular teratogen influence both the severity of the damage to an embryo or fetus and the type of defect: (1) *Dose*—the dose effect is rather obvious—the greater the dose of an agent, such as a drug, the greater the effect. (2) *Genetic susceptibility*—the type or severity of abnormalities caused by a teratogen is linked to the genotype of the pregnant woman and the genotype of the embryo or fetus. (3) *Time of exposure*— teratogens do more damage when they occur at some points in development than at others. Damage during the germinal period may even prevent implantation. In general, the embryonic period is more vulnerable than the fetal period. The probability of a structural defect is greatest early in the embryonic period, when organs are being formed (Hill, 2007). After organogenesis is complete, teratogens are less likely to cause anatomical defects. Instead, exposure during the fetal period is more likely instead to stunt growth or to create problems in the way organs function. To examine some key teratogens and their effects, let's begin with drugs.

Prescription and Nonprescription Drugs

Prescription drugs that can function as teratogens include antibiotics, such as streptomycin and tetracycline; some antidepressants; certain hormones, such as progestin and synthetic estrogen; and Accutane (often prescribed for acne) (Berard & others, 2007). Nonprescription drugs that can be harmful include diet pills and aspirin (Norgard & others, 2006).

fetal alcohol syndrome (FAS) A cluster of abnormalities that appears in the offspring of mothers who drink alcohol heavily during pregnancy.

Psychoactive Drugs

Psychoactive drugs are drugs that act on the nervous system to alter states of consciousness, modify perceptions, and change moods. Examples include caffeine, alcohol, and nicotine, as well as illegal drugs such as cocaine, methamphetamine, marijuana, and heroin (Alvik & others, 2006).

Caffeine People often consume caffeine by drinking coffee, tea, or colas, or by eating chocolate (Bech & others, 2007). A review of studies on caffeine consumption during pregnancy concluded that a small increase in the risks for spontaneous abortion and low birth weight occurs for pregnant women consuming more than 150 milligrams of caffeine (approximately two cups of brewed coffee or two to three 12-ounce cans of cola) per day (Fernandez & others, 1998). A recent study revealed that when pregnant women consumed 300 or more milligrams of caffeine a day the risk of fetal death increased (Matijasevich & others, 2006). Taking into account such results, the Food and Drug Administration recommends that pregnant women avoid caffeine or consume it sparingly.

Alcohol Drinking by pregnant women can be devastating to their offspring (Abel, 2006; Shankaran & others, 2007). **Fetal alcohol syndrome (FAS)** is a cluster of abnormalities appearing in the offspring of mothers who drank alcohol heavily during pregnancy. The abnormalities include facial deformities and defective limbs, face, and heart. Figure 2.7 shows a child with fetal alcohol syndrome. Most of these children are below average in intelligence, and some are mentally retarded (Toga, Thompson, & Sowell, 2006). A recent study revealed that, as young adults, individuals diagnosed with FAS in infancy were characterized by intellectual disability, limited occupational options, and dependent living (Spohr, Willms, & Steinhausen, 2007). Although many mothers of FAS infants are heavy drinkers, many mothers who are heavy drinkers do not have children with FAS or have one child with FAS and other children who do not have it.

Serious malformations such as those produced by FAS are not found in infants born to mothers who are moderate drinkers, but even moderate drinking can have an effect on the offspring (Pollard, 2007). In one study, children whose mothers drank moderately (one to two drinks a day) during pregnancy were less attentive and alert, even at 4 years of age (Streissguth & others, 1984). Also, a recent study found that pregnant women who had three or more drinks a day faced an increased risk of preterm birth (Parazzini & others, 2003).

What are some guidelines for alcohol use during pregnancy? Even drinking just one or two servings of beer or wine or one serving of hard liquor a few days a week can have negative effects on the fetus, although

Figure 2.7 Fetal Alcohol Syndrome This child's wide-set eyes, flat bones, and thin upper lip are symptoms of fetal alcohol syndrome. *How much alcohol should women feel safe drinking while they are pregnant?*

it is generally agreed that this level of alcohol use will not cause fetal alcohol syndrome. The U.S. Surgeon General recommends that *no* alcohol be consumed during pregnancy. And recent research suggests that it may not be wise to consume alcohol at the time of conception. One study found that "both male and female alcohol intakes during the week of conception increased the risk of early pregnancy loss" (Henriksen & others, 2004, p. 661).

Nicotine Cigarette smoking by pregnant women can also adversely influence prenatal development, birth, and postnatal development (Noakes & others, 2007). Preterm births and low birth weights, fetal and neonatal deaths, respiratory problems and sudden infant death syndrome (SIDS, also known as crib death) are all more common among the offspring of mothers who smoked during pregnancy (Roza & others, 2007).

Prenatal exposure to heavy smoking has been linked in one study to nicotine withdrawal symptoms in newborns (Godding & others, 2004). Other studies have linked prenatal exposure to cigarette smoking during pregnancy to increased incidence of attention deficit hyperactivity disorder at 5 to 16 years of age and to an increased risk of cigarette smoking during adolescence (Porath & Fried, 2005; Thapar & others, 2003).

Cocaine Cocaine exposure during prenatal development is associated with reduced birth weight, length, and head circumference (Smith & others, 2001). In other studies, prenatal cocaine exposure has been linked to impaired motor development at 2 years of age (Arendt & others, 1999); to lower arousal, less effective self-regulation, higher excitability, and lower quality of reflexes at 1 month of age (Lester & others, 2002); to impaired language development and information processing (Beeghly & others, 2006), including attention deficits in preschool children (Noland & others, 2005); and to learning disabilities at age 7 (Morrow & others, 2006).

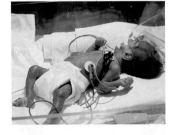

This baby was exposed to cocaine prenatally. *What are some of the possible effects on development of being exposed to cocaine prenatally?*

Some researchers argue that these findings should be interpreted cautiously (Accornero & others, 2006). Why? Because other factors in the lives of pregnant women who use cocaine (such as poverty, malnutrition, and other substance abuse) often cannot be ruled out as possible contributors to the problems found in their children (Hurt & others, 2005). For example, cocaine users are more likely than nonusers to smoke cigarettes, use marijuana, drink alcohol, and take amphetamines.

Despite these cautions, the weight of research evidence indicates that children born to mothers who use cocaine are likely to have neurological and cognitive deficits (Forrester & Mertz, 2007; Shankaran & others, 2007). Clearly, pregnant women should avoid using cocaine.

Methamphetamine Methamphetamine, like cocaine, is a stimulant, speeding up an individual's nervous system. Babies born to mothers who used methamphetamine, or "meth," during pregnancy are at risk for high infant mortality, low birth weight, and a number of developmental and behavioral problems (Thaithumyanon & others, 2006). As more young people are using meth, some experts recently concluded that meth use during pregnancy has become a greater problem in the United States than cocaine use (Elliott, 2004). A recent survey found that 5 percent of U.S. women used methamphetamine during their pregnancy (Arria & others, 2006).

Marijuana An increasing number of studies find that marijuana use by pregnant women has negative outcomes for offspring (de Moares & others, 2006; Williams & Ross, 2007). A research review concluded that marijuana use by pregnant women is related to deficits in memory and information processing in their offspring (Kalant, 2004). For example, in a longitudinal study, prenatal marijuana exposure was related to learning and memory difficulties at age 11 (Richardson & others, 2002). Another study revealed that prenatal marijuana exposure was linked with depressive symptoms at 10 years of age (Gray & others, 2005). Further, a recent study indicated that prenatal exposure to marijuana was linked to marijuana use at 14 years of age (Day, Goldschmidt, & Thomas, 2006). In sum, marijuana use is not recommended for pregnant women.

Heroin It is well documented that infants whose mothers are addicted to heroin show several behavioral difficulties (Yang & others, 2006). These include withdrawal symptoms, such as tremors, irritability, abnormal crying, disturbed sleep, and impaired motor control. Many still show behavioral problems at their first birthday, and attention deficits may appear later in development. The most common treatment for heroin addiction, methadone, is associated with very severe withdrawal symptoms in newborns.

How Would You...?

As a social worker, how would you advise women in their childbearing years who frequently abuse drugs and other psychoactive substances?

Incompatible Blood Types

Incompatibility between the mother's and father's blood type poses another risk to prenatal development. Blood types are created by differences in the surface structure of red blood cells. One type of difference in the surface of red blood cells creates the familiar blood groups—A, B, O, and AB. A second difference creates what is called Rh-positive and Rh-negative blood. If a surface marker, called the *Rh factor,* is present in an individual's red blood cells, the person is said to be Rh-positive; if the Rh marker is not present, the person is said to be Rh-negative. If a pregnant woman is Rh-negative and her partner is Rh-positive, the fetus may be Rh-positive. If the fetus' blood is Rh-positive and the mother's is Rh-negative, the mother's immune system may produce antibodies that will attack the fetus. This can result in any number of problems, including miscarriage or stillbirth, anemia, jaundice, heart defects, brain damage, or death soon after birth (Moise, 2005).

Generally, the first Rh-positive baby of an Rh-negative mother is not at risk, but with each subsequent pregnancy the risk increases. A serum (RhoGAM) may be given to the mother within three days of the child's birth to prevent her body from making antibodies that will attack future Rh-positive fetuses. Also, babies affected by Rh incompatibility can be given blood transfusions before or right after birth (Mannessier & others, 2000).

Maternal Diseases

Maternal diseases and infections can produce defects in offspring by crossing the placental barrier, or they can cause damage during birth (Avgil & Ornoy, 2006; Tappia & Gabriel, 2006). Rubella (German measles) is one disease that can cause prenatal defects. The greatest damage occurs if a mother contracts rubella in the third or fourth week of pregnancy, although infection as late as the second month can still be damaging (Kobayashi & others, 2005). A vaccine that prevents German measles is now routinely administered to children, and women who plan to have children should have a blood test before they become pregnant to determine if they are immune to the disease; if immunity is not found, they can then be vaccinated (Best, 2007).

Syphilis (a sexually transmitted disease) is more damaging later in prenatal development—four months or more after conception. Rather than affecting organogenesis, as rubella does, syphilis damages organs after they have formed. Damage includes eye lesions, which can cause blindness, and skin lesions. When syphilis is present at birth, problems can develop in the central nervous system and gastrointestinal tract (Mullick, Beksinska, & Msomi, 2005). Most states require that pregnant women be given a blood test to detect the presence of syphilis.

Another infection that has received widespread attention is genital herpes. Newborns contract this virus when they are delivered through the birth canal of a mother with an active outbreak of genital herpes (Xu & others, 2007). About one-third of babies delivered through an infected birth canal die; another one-fourth become brain damaged. If an active case of genital herpes is detected in a pregnant woman close to her delivery date, a cesarean section (in which the infant is delivered through an incision in the mother's abdomen) can be performed to keep the virus from infecting the newborn (Baker, 2007).

AIDS is a sexually transmitted syndrome that is caused by the human immunodeficiency virus (HIV), which destroys the body's immune system. An HIV-positive mother can infect her offspring with HIV in three ways: (1) during gestation across the placenta, (2) during delivery through contact with maternal blood or fluids, and (3) postpartum (after birth) through breast feeding. The transmission of AIDS through breast feeding is especially a problem in many developing countries (UNICEF, 2007). Babies born to HIV-positive mothers can be (1) infected and symptomatic (show AIDS symptoms), (2) infected but asymptomatic (not show AIDS symptoms), or (3) not infected at all. An infant who is infected and asymptomatic may still develop HIV symptoms up until 15 months of age.

Maternal Diet and Nutrition

A developing embryo or fetus depends completely on its mother for nutrition, which comes from the mother's blood (Derbyshire, 2007a, b). The nutritional status of the embryo or fetus is determined by the mother's total caloric intake, and her intake of proteins, vitamins, and minerals. Children born to malnourished mothers are more likely than other children to be malformed.

A mother's being overweight before and during pregnancy can also put the embryo or fetus at risk, and an increasing number of pregnant women in the United States are overweight (Catalano, 2007). Recent studies indicated that pre-pregnancy maternal obesity doubled the risk of stillbirth and neonatal death, and was linked with defects in the central nervous system of offspring (Anderson & others, 2005; Kristensen & others, 2005).

One aspect of maternal nutrition that is important for normal prenatal development is folic acid, a B-complex vitamin (Antony, 2007). A lack of folic acid is linked with neural tube defects in

Because the fetus depends entirely on its mother for nutrition, it is important for the pregnant woman to have good nutritional habits. In Kenya, this government clinic provides pregnant women with information about how their diet can influence the health of their fetus and offspring. *What might the information about diet be like?*

offspring, such as spina bifida, a typically fatal defect in the spinal cord (Pitkin, 2007). Orange juice and spinach are examples of foods rich in folic acid.

Eating fish is often recommended as part of a healthy diet, but pollution has made many fish a risky choice for pregnant women. Some fish contain high levels of mercury, which is released into the air both naturally and by industrial pollution (Fitzgerald & others, 2004). When mercury falls into the water it can become toxic and accumulate in large fish, such as shark, swordfish, king mackerel, and some species of large tuna. Mercury is easily transferred across the placenta, and the embryo's developing brain and nervous system are highly sensitive to the metal (Gliori & others, 2006). The U.S. Food and Drug Administration (2004) recently provided the following recommendations for women of childbearing age and young children: Don't eat shark, swordfish, king mackerel or tilefish; eat up to 12 ounces (two average meals) a week of fish and shellfish that are lower in mercury, such as shrimp, canned light tuna, salmon, pollock, and catfish.

PCB-polluted fish also pose a risk to prenatal development (Fitzgerald & others 2004). PCBs (polychlorinated biphenyls) are chemicals that were used in manufacturing until they were banned in the 1970s in the United States, but they are still present in landfills, sediments, and wildlife.

Emotional States and Stress

When a pregnant woman experiences intense fears, anxieties, and other emotions, physiological changes occur that may affect her fetus (Talge & others, 2007). For example, producing adrenaline in response to fear restricts blood flow to the uterine area and can deprive the fetus of adequate oxygen. Maternal stress may also increase the level of corticotrophin-releasing hormone (CRH) early in pregnancy (Kapoor & others, 2006). CRH, in turn, has been linked to premature delivery (Field, 2007). Women under stress are about four times more likely than their low-stress counterparts to deliver babies prematurely (Dunkel-Schetter & others, 2001). A mother's stress may also influence the fetus indirectly by increasing the likelihood that the mother will engage in unhealthy behaviors, such as taking drugs and failing to get good prenatal care.

High maternal anxiety and stress during pregnancy might have long-term consequences for the offspring (Jones & others, 2006). In a longitudinal study, high maternal anxiety during pregnancy was linked to higher levels of cortisol (a hormone secreted by the adrenal glands in response to stress) in offpsring at 10 years of age (O'Connor & others, 2005).

Maternal Age

When possible harmful effects on the fetus and infant are considered, two maternal ages are of special interest: adolescence and 35 and older (Maconochie, 2007). One recent study revealed that the rate of stillbirth was elevated for adolescent girls and women over 35 (Bateman & Simpson, 2006).

The mortality rate of infants born to adolescent mothers is double that of infants born to mothers in their twenties. Although this high rate probably reflects the immaturity of the mother's reproductive system, poor nutrition, lack of prenatal care, and low socioeconomic status may also play a role (Lenders, McElrath,

How Would You...?
As a health-care professional, how would you advise an expectant mother who is experiencing extreme psychological stress?

& Scholl, 2000). Prenatal care decreases the probability that a child born to an adolescent girl will have physical problems. However, adolescents are the least likely of women in all age groups to obtain prenatal assistance from clinics, pediatricians, and health services.

Maternal age is also linked to the risk that a child will have Down syndrome, a form of mental retardation that was discussed earlier in the chapter (Soergel & others, 2006). Women aged 16 to 34 rarely have babies with Down syndrome. However, the risk increases with maternal age so that the probability is slightly over 1 in 100 a baby born to a 40-year-old woman will have Down syndrome, and by age 50 it is almost 1 in 10.

When mothers are 35 years of age and older, risks also increase for low birth weight, for preterm delivery, and for fetal death. One study found that low birth weight delivery increased 11 percent and preterm delivery increased 14 percent in women 35 years and older (Tough & others, 2002). In another study, fetal death was low for women 30 to 34 years of age but increased progressively for women 35 to 39 and 40 to 44 years of age (Canterino & others, 2004).

We still have much to learn about the role of the mother's age in pregnancy and childbirth (Montan, 2007). As women remain active, exercise regularly, and are careful about their nutrition, their reproductive systems may remain healthier at older ages than was thought possible in the past. For example, in a recent study, two-thirds of the pregnancies of women 45 years and older in Australia were free of complications (Callaway, Lust, & McIntrye, 2005).

Paternal Factors

So far, we have discussed how characteristics of the mother—such as drug use, disease, nutrition and diet, emotional states, and age—can influence prenatal development and the development of the child. Might there also be some paternal risk factors? Indeed, there are several. Men's exposure to lead, radiation, certain pesticides, and petrochemicals before conception may cause abnormalities in sperm that lead to miscarriage or diseases such as childhood cancer (Fear & others, 2007). When fathers have a diet low in vitamin C before conception, their offspring have a higher risk of birth defects and cancer (Fraga & others, 1991). It has also been speculated that, when fathers take cocaine, it may attach itself to sperm and cause birth defects, but the evidence for this effect is not yet strong. In one study, long-term use of cocaine by men was related to impaired fertility in the form of low sperm count, low motility, and a higher number of abnormally formed sperm (Bracken & others, 1990). Cocaine-related infertility appears to be reversible if users stop taking the drug for at least one year.

The father's smoking during the mother's pregnancy can also cause problems for the offspring. In one investigation, the newborns of fathers who smoked around their wives during the pregnancy were 4 ounces lighter at birth for each pack of cigarettes smoked per day than were the newborns whose fathers did not smoke during their wives' pregnancy (Rubin & others, 1986). In another study, heavy paternal smoking was associated with the risk of early pregnancy loss (Venners & others, 2005).

The father's age also makes a difference (Maconochie & others, 2007; Yang & others, 2007). About 5 percent of children with Down

In one study, in China, the longer fathers smoked, the higher the risk that their children would develop cancer (Ji & others, 1997). *What are some other paternal factors that can influence the development of the fetus and the child?*

CHAPTER 2 BIOLOGICAL BEGINNINGS

syndrome have fathers who are 35 years or older. The offspring of older fathers are also at increased risk for other birth defects, including dwarfism and Marfan syndrome, which involves head and limb deformities.

Environmental Hazards

Many aspects of our modern industrial world can endanger the embryo or fetus. We mentioned earlier that abnormal sperm from the father's exposure to certain chemicals can put a pregnancy at risk. We also saw that the embryo or fetus may be harmed if the mother's diet includes polluted fish. Additional specific hazards to the embryo or fetus that are worth a closer look include radiation, toxic wastes, and other chemical pollutants (Kaufman & Groters, 2006).

Women and their physicians should weigh the risk of an X-ray when the woman is, or may possibly be, pregnant (Menias & others, 2007). However, a routine diagnostic X-ray of a body area other than the abdomen, with the women's abdomen protected by a lead apron, is generally considered safe (Loughlin, 2007).

Exposure to environmental pollutants and toxic wastes also poses a danger to unborn children. Among the dangerous pollutants are carbon monoxide, mercury, and lead, as well as certain fertilizers and pesticides (Yang & others, 2003).

Despite these many potential hazards during prenatal development, it is important to keep in mind that most of the time prenatal development does not go awry and development proceeds along the positive path that we described at the beginning of our discussion of prenatal development.

How Would You...?
As a human development and family studies professional, how would you justify the need for educational programming for couples planning to become pregnant?

An explosion at the Chernobyl nuclear power plant in the Ukraine produced radioactive contamination that spread to surrounding areas. Thousands of infants were born with health problems and deformities as a result of the nuclear contamination, including this boy whose arm did not form. *Other than radioactive contamination, what are some other types of environmental hazards to prenatal development?*

Prenatal Care

Information about teratogens and other prenatal hazards is one of the many benefits that expectant mothers gain from prenatal care. Although prenatal care varies enormously, it usually involves a defined schedule of visits for medical care, which typically include screening for manageable conditions and treatable diseases that can affect the baby or the mother (Kuppermann & others, 2006). In addition to medical care, prenatal programs often include comprehensive educational, social, and nutritional services (Moos, 2006; Wasserman, Bender, & Lee, 2007).

The education provided in prenatal care varies during the course of pregnancy. Those in the early stages of pregnancy, as well as couples who are anticipating a pregnancy, may participate in early prenatal classes (Davidson, London, & Ladewig, 2008). In addition to providing information on dangers to the fetus, early prenatal classes often discuss the development of the embryo and the fetus; sexuality during pregnancy; choices about the birth setting and care providers; nutrition, rest, and exercise; common discomforts of pregnancy and relief measures; psychological changes in the expectant mother and her partner; and factors that increase the risk of preterm labor and possible symptoms of preterm labor. Early classes also may include information about the advantages and disadvantages of breast feeding and bottle feeding. (Fifty to eighty percent of expectant mothers decide how they will feed their infant prior to the sixth month of pregnancy.) During the second or third trimester of pregnancy, prenatal classes focus on preparing for the birth, infant care and feeding, choices about birth, and postpartum self-care.

Research contrasting the experiences of mothers who had prenatal care and those who did not supports the significance of prenatal care (Chen & others, 2007; Daniels, Noe, & Mayberry, 2006). One study found that U.S. women who had no prenatal care, were far more likely than their counterparts who received prenatal care to have infants who had low birth weight, increased mortality, and a number of other physical problems (Herbst & others, 2003). In other recent studies, low birth weight and preterm deliveries were common among U.S. mothers who received no prenatal care, and the absence of prenatal care increased the risk for preterm birth by almost threefold in both non-Latino White and African American women (Stringer & others, 2005).

Inadequate prenatal care may help explain a disturbing fact: Rates of infant mortality and low birth weight indicate that many other nations have healthier babies than the United States (Thornton & others, 2006). In many countries that have a lower percentage of low birth weight infants than the United States, mothers receive either free or very low cost prenatal and postnatal care, and can receive paid maternity leave from work that ranges from 9 to 40 weeks. In Norway and the Netherlands, prenatal care is coordinated with a general practitioner, an obstetrician, and a midwife.

An innovative program that is rapidly expanding in the United States is CenteringPregnancy (Massey, Rising, & Ickovics, 2006; Moos, 2006). This program is relationship-centered and provides complete prenatal care in a group setting. CenteringPregnancy replaces traditional 15-minute physician visits with 90-minute peer group support settings and self-examination led by a physician or certified nurse midwife. Groups of up to 10 women (and often their partners) meet regularly beginning at 12 to 16 weeks of pregnancy. The sessions emphasize empowering women to play an active role in experiencing a positive pregnancy.

A CenteringPregnancy program. This rapidly increasing program alters routine prenatal care by bringing women out of exam rooms and into relationship-oriented groups.

Cultural Beliefs About Pregnancy

All cultures have beliefs and rituals that surround life's major events, including pregnancy. Some cultures treat pregnancy simply as a natural occurrence; others see it as a medical condition (Walsh, 2006). For most middle-income U.S. couples, it seems normal to obtain medical care and turn for help during pregnancy to doctors and other health professionals. But obtaining medical care during pregnancy may not seem important to a woman whose culture defines pregnancy as a natural condition.

How expectant mothers behave during pregnancy may depend in part on the prevalence of traditional home-care remedies and folk beliefs, the importance of indigenous healers, and the influence of health-care professionals in their culture

(Jansen, 2006). In various cultures pregnant women may turn to herbalists, faith healers, root doctors, or spiritualists for help (Mbonye, Neeman, & Magnussen, 2006). Following are some maternal health beliefs and behaviors that are common to Latino and Asian cultures (American Public Health Association, 2006):

- *Latino.* Latinas are less likely to use family planning services than non-Latino Whites and African Americans. Further, a common folk belief by Latinos is that using certain contraceptives such as birth control pills will lessen menstrual flow, causing retention of impurities and ultimately health problems. Also, many Mexican American women seek advice about their pregnancy from their mothers and older women in the community. They may call on an indigenous healer known as a *curandero*. Recent immigrant Latinas and undocumented workers tend to initiate prenatal care after the first trimester, while their counterparts who have been residing in the United States for longer periods of time are more likely to begin prenatal care earlier (Taylor, Ko, & Pan, 1999).

- *Asian.* Common among Chinese expectant mothers is the practice of listening to classical music during pregnancy because they believe it will help the offspring develop patience, wisdom, and artistic sensitivity. Many Chinese also think that a child's moral disposition is at least partially developed in the womb. As a consequence, expectant Chinese mothers may avoid contact with people they perceive to be dishonest, engage in charitable deeds, and try to avoid having negative thoughts or feelings. In some Asian countires, such as the Phillipines, many expectant mothers will not take any medication during pregnancy. Also, some immigrant Asian women return to their parents' home in their native country to deliver their baby, especially if it is their firstborn child.

When health-care professionals work with expectant mothers, cultural assessment should be an important component of their care (Laditka & others, 2005). In other words, they should identify beliefs, values, and behaviors related to childbearing. In particular, ethnic background, degree of affiliation with the ethnic group, patterns of decision making, religious preference, language, communication style, and etiquette may all affect a woman's attitudes about the care needed during pregnancy (Atiyeh & El-Mohandes, 2005). Health-care workers should assess whether a woman's beliefs or practices pose a threat to her or the fetus. If they do, health-care professionals should consider a culturally sensitive way to handle the problem (Jansen, 2006).

Birth and the Postpartum Period

Nature writes the basic script for how birth occurs, but parents make important choices about conditions surrounding birth. First, we will explore the birth process, examining variations in how it occurs and in its outcomes. Then, we will discuss the postpartum period that follows birth.

The Birth Process

What is the birth process like—its stages, its setting, the health-care professionals involved, and the available methods of childbirth? How does the baby make the transition from being a fetus to being a newborn? What are the risks when a baby is too small at birth, and what can be done to support a low birth weight baby? How does a mother bond with her new baby?

Stages of Birth

Childbirth—or labor—occurs in three stages. As the first stage begins, uterine contractions are 15 to 20 minutes apart and last up to a minute. These contractions cause the woman's cervix (the opening from the uterus into the birth canal) to stretch and open. As the first stage progresses, the contractions come closer together, appearing every two to five minutes. Their intensity increases too. By the end of the first birth stage, contractions dilate the cervix to an opening of about 4 inches, so that the baby can move from the uterus to the birth canal. The first stage is the longest of the three stages; it typically lasts 12 to 24 hours for a woman having her first child. For later births, the first stage lasts an average of 8 hours.

The second birth stage begins when the baby's head starts to move through the cervix into the birth canal. It terminates when the baby completely emerges from the mother's body. During this stage, contractions become more rapid, culminating in a frequency of almost one per minute. With each contraction, the mother bears down hard to push the baby out of her body. For a first birth, the second stage lasts approximately $1\frac{1}{2}$ hours, and for later births it averages 45 minutes in length.

Afterbirth is the third stage, at which time the placenta, umbilical cord, and other membranes are detached and expelled. This final stage is the shortest of the three birth stages, lasting only a few minutes.

Childbirth Setting and Attendants

In the United States, 99 percent of births take place in hospitals (Ventura & others, 1997). Some women with good medical histories and low risk for problems may choose a delivery at home or in a freestanding birth center, which is usually staffed by nurse-midwives (Marsh-Prelenik, 2006). Births at home are far more common in many other countries. This is true not only in non-Western cultures, but in developed countries as well; for example, in the Netherlands, 35 percent of the babies are born at home.

Who helps a mother during birth varies dramatically across cultures (Wood & Atkins, 2006). In the United States, most obstetricians are male, and it has become the norm for fathers or birth coaches to be with the mother throughout labor and delivery. In the East African Nigoni culture, in contrast, men are completely excluded from the childbirth process. When a woman is ready to give birth, female relatives move into the woman's hut and the husband leaves, taking his belongings (clothes, tools, weapons, and so on) with him. He is not permitted to return until after the baby is born. In some cultures, childbirth is an open, community affair. For example, in the Pukapukan culture in the Pacific Islands, women give birth in a shelter that is open for villagers to observe.

Midwifery is the norm throughout most of the world. In Holland, more than 40 percent of babies are delivered by midwives rather than doctors (Treffers & others, 1990). But more than 90 percent of U.S. births are attended by physicians, and only 6 percent of mothers who deliver a baby in the United States are attended by a midwife (Tritten, 2004). In the United States, most midwives are nurses who have been specially trained in delivering babies (Marsh-Prelesnik, 2006).

In many countries, a doula attends a childbearing woman (Dundek, 2006). *Doula* is a Greek word that means "a woman who helps." A *doula* is a caregiver who provides continuous physical, emotional, and educational support for the mother before, during, and after childbirth. Doulas remain with the mother throughout labor, assessing and responding to her needs. Researchers have found positive effects when a doula is present at the birth of a child (Stein, Kennell, & Fulcher, 2004). In a recent study, low-income pregnant women who were given doula support spent a shorter time in labor, and their newborn had a higher health rating at one and five minutes after birth than their low-income counterparts who did not receive doula support (Campbell & others, 2006).

In the United States, most doulas work as independent providers hired by the expectant mother. Doulas typically function as part of a "birthing team," serving as an adjunct to the midwife or the hospital's obstetric staff (Dundek, 2006). Managed care organizations are increasingly offering doula support as a part of regular obstetric care.

A doula assisting a birth. *What types of support do doulas provide?*

Methods of Childbirth

U.S. hospitals often allow the mother and her obstetrician a range of options regarding their method of delivery. Key choices involve the use of medication, whether to use any of a number of nonmedicated techniques to reduce pain, and when to resort to a cesarean delivery.

Medication Three basic kinds of drugs that are used for labor are analgesia, anesthesia, and oxytocics.

Analgesia is used to relieve pain. Analgesics include tranquilizers, barbiturates, and narcotics (such as Demerol).

Anesthesia is used in late first-stage labor and during expulsion of the baby to block sensation in an area of the body or to block consciousness. There is a trend against using general anesthesia, which blocks consciousness, in normal births because a general anesthesia can be transmitted through the placenta to the fetus and impair the baby's alertness (Lieberman & others, 2005). An *epidural block* is regional anesthesia that numbs the woman's body from the waist down. Even this drug, thought to be relatively safe, has come under recent criticism because it is associated with fever, extended labor, and increased risk for cesarean delivery (Glantz, 2005).

Oxytocics are synthetic hormones that are used to stimulate contractions. Pitocin is the most commonly used oxytocic. One recent large-scale Swedish study revealed that pregnant women who were given oxytocin during childbirth were more likely to have newborns with lower health ratings than pregnant women who were not given oxytocin during childbirth (Oscarsson & others, 2006).

Predicting how a drug will affect an individual woman and her fetus is difficult (Briggs & Wan, 2006). A particular drug might have only a minimal effect on one fetus yet have a much stronger effect on another. The drug's dosage also is a factor. Stronger doses of tranquilizers and narcotics given to decrease the mother's pain

natural childbirth This method attempts to reduce the mother's pain by decreasing her fear through education about childbirth and relaxation techniques during delivery.

prepared childbirth Developed by French obstetrician Ferdinand Lamaze, this childbirth strategy is similar to natural childbirth but includes a special breathing technique to control pushing in the final stages of labor and a more detailed anatomy and physiology course.

have a potentially more negative effect on the fetus than mild doses. It is important for the mother to assess her level of pain and have a voice in the decision of whether she should receive medication.

Natural and Prepared Childbirth In the 1970s and 80s, the idea of avoiding all medication during childbirth gained favor in the United States. Instead, many women chose to reduce the pain of childbirth through techniques known as natural childbirth and prepared childbirth became popular. Today, at least some medication is used in the typical childbirth, but elements of natural childbirth and prepared childbirth remain popular (Davidson, London, & Ladewig, 2008; Hogan & others, 2007).

Natural childbirth is the method that aims to reduce the mother's pain by decreasing her fear through education about childbirth and by teaching her to use breathing methods and relaxation techniques during labor (Sandiford, 2006). French obstetrician Ferdinand Lamaze developed a method similar to natural childbirth that is known as **prepared childbirth**, or the Lamaze method. It includes a special breathing technique to control pushing in the final stages of labor. The Lamaze method has become very popular in the United States. The pregnant woman's partner usually serves as a coach, who attends childbirth classes with her and helps her with her breathing and relaxation during delivery.

Other Nonmedicated Techniques to Reduce Pain The effort to reduce stress and control pain during labor has recently led to an increase in the use of some older and some newer nonmedicated techniques (Field, 2007; Simkin & Bolding, 2004). These include waterbirth, massage, and acupuncture.

- *Waterbirth* involves giving birth in a tub of warm water. Some women go through labor in the water and get out for delivery, others remain in the water

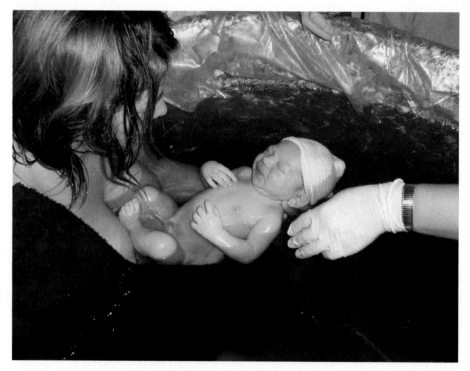

What characterizes the use of waterbirth in delivering a baby?

for delivery. The rationale for waterbirth is that the baby has been in an amniotic sac for many months and that delivery in a similar environment is likely to be less stressful for the baby and the mother. Researchers have found mixed results for the use of waterbirth (Field, 2007; Thoni & Moroder, 2004).

- Massage is increasingly used as a procedure prior to and during delivery (Field, 2007). Researchers have found that massage can reduce pain and anxiety during labor (Chang, Chen, & Huang, 2006; Eogan, Daly, & O'Herlihy, 2006). A recent research review concluded that massage reduces the incidence of perineal trauma (damage to genitalia) following birth (Beckmann & Garrett, 2006).

- *Acupuncture*, the insertion of very fine needles into specific locations in the body, is used as a standard procedure to reduce the pain of childbirth in China, although it only recently has begun to be used in the United States for this purpose. A recent study revealed that acupuncture resulted in less time spent in labor and a reduction in the need for oxytocin to augment labor (Gaudernack, Forbord, & Hole, 2006). Further research is needed to determine the effectiveness of acupuncture as childbirth procedure (Lee & Chan, 2006).

Cesarean Delivery Normally, the baby's head comes through the vagina first. But if the baby is in a *breech position*, the baby's buttocks are the first part to emerge from the vagina. In 1 of every 25 deliveries, the baby's head is still in the uterus when the rest of the body is out. Breech position can prevent the baby from breathing normally. As a result, if the baby is in a breech position, what is called a cesarean section, or a cesarean delivery, is usually preformed. In a *cesarean delivery*, the baby is removed from the mother's uterus through an incision made in her abdomen.

Cesarean deliveries also are performed if the baby is lying crosswise in the uterus, if the baby's head is too large to pass through the mother's pelvis, if the baby develops complications, or if the mother is bleeding vaginally. Cesarean deliveries can be life-saving, but like any major surgery they do bring risks. Compared with vaginal deliveries, they involve a higher infection rate, longer hospital stays, and the greater expense and stress that generally accompany surgery.

The benefits and risks of cesarean sections continue to be debated (Bailit, Love, & Dawson, 2006; London & others, 2007). Some critics believe that too many babies are delivered by cesarean section in the United States. More cesarean sections are performed in the United States than in any other country in the world. The cesarean delivery rate jumped 7.5 percent from 2002 to 2004 in the United States to 29.1 percent of all births, the highest level since these data began to be reported on birth certificates in 1989 (Hoyert & others, 2006). Higher cesarean delivery rates may be due to a better ability to identify infants in distress during birth and the increase in overweight and obese pregnant women (Coleman & others, 2005). Also, some doctors may be overly cautious and recommend a cesarean delivery to defend against a potential lawsuit.

How Would You...? As a health-care professional, how would you advise a woman in her first trimester about the options available for her baby's birth and for her own comfort during the delivery process?

The Transition from Fetus to Newborn

Much of our discussion of birth so far has focused on the mother. Being born also involves considerable stress for the baby. If the delivery takes too long, the baby can develop *anoxia*, a condition in which the fetus or newborn has an insufficient supply of oxygen. Anoxia can cause brain damage (Aylott, 2006).

The baby has considerable capacity to withstand the stress of birth. Large quantities of adrenaline and noradrenaline, hormones that protect the fetus in the event of oxygen deficiency, are secreted in the newborn's body during the birth process (Van Beveren, 2007).

Immediately after birth, the umbilical cord is cut and the baby is on its own. Before birth, oxygen came from the mother via the umbilical cord, but now the baby is self-sufficient and can breathe independently.

Almost immediately after birth, a newborn is taken to be weighed, cleaned up, and tested for signs of developmental problems that might require urgent attention. The **Apgar Scale** is widely used to assess the health of newborns at one and five minutes after birth. The Apgar Scale evaluates infants' heart rate, respiratory effort, muscle tone, body color, and reflex irritability. An obstetrician or a nurse does the evaluation and gives the newborn a score, or reading, of 0, 1, or 2 on each of these five health signs. A total score of 7 to 10 indicates that the newborn's condition is good. A score of 5 indicates there may be developmental difficulties. A score of 3 or below signals an emergency and warns that the baby might not survive. The Apgar Scale is especially good at assessing the newborn's ability to respond to the stress of the delivery and its new environment (Fallis & others, 2006). It also identifies high-risk infants who need resuscitation.

Nurses often play important roles in the birth of a baby. To read about the work of a nurse who specializes in the care of women during labor and delivery, see the Careers in Life-Span Development profile.

Low Birth Weight and Preterm Infants

Three related conditions pose threats to many newborns: low birth weight, being preterm, and being small for date. *Low birth weight* infants weigh less than 5½ pounds at birth. *Very low birth weight* newborns weigh under 3 pounds, and *extremely low birth weight* newborns under 2 pounds. Preterm infants are those born three weeks or more before the pregnancy has reached its full term—in other words, 35 or fewer weeks after conception. Small for date infants (also called *small for gestational age infants*) are those whose birth weight is below normal when the length of the pregnancy is considered. They weigh less than 90 percent of all babies of the same gestational age. Small for date infants may be preterm or full term. One recent study found that small for date infants had a 400 percent greater risk of death (Regev & others, 2003).

The preterm birth rate in the United States increased 18 percent from 1990 to 2004 (Hoyert & others, 2006). One of every eight U.S. births is now preterm (Ashton, 2006). The increase in preterm birth is likely due to such factors as the increasing number of births to women 35 years and older, increasing rates of multiple births, increased management of maternal and fetal conditions (for example, inducing labor preterm if medical technology indicates it will increase the likelihood of survival), increased substance abuse (tobacco, alcohol), and increased stress (Goldenberg & Culcane, 2007). Ethnic variations characterize preterm birth. For example, in 2003, the likelihood of being born preterm was 1 in 8 for all U.S. infants, but the rate was 1 in 6 for African American infants (Ashton, 2006).

Incidences and Causes of Low Birth Weight

Most, but not all, preterm babies are also low birth weight babies. The incidence of low birth weight varies considerably from country to country. In some developing countries, such as Bangladesh, where poverty is rampant and the health and nutrition of mothers are poor, the percentage of low birth weight babies reaches as high as 50 percent. In the United States, there has been an increase in low birth weight infants in the last two decades, and the U.S. low birth weight rate of 8.1 percent in 2004 is considerably higher than that of many other developed countries (Cuevas & others, 2005). For example, only 4 percent of the infants born in Sweden, Finland, the Netherlands, and Norway are low birth weight, and only 5 percent of those born in New Zealand, Australia, France, and Japan are low birth weight.

Recently, there has been considerable interest generated in the role that progestin might play in reducing preterm births. In one study, weekly injections of the hormone progesterone, which is naturally produced by the ovaries, lowered the rate of preterm births by one-third (Meis & Peaceman, 2003). Recent studies provide further support for the use of progestin in the second trimester of pregnancy in reducing the risk of preterm delivery (Coommarasamy & others, 2006; Lamont & Jaggat, 2007). A recent survey indicated that the use of progestin to prevent preterm birth by maternal-fetal medicine surveys increased from 38 percent of these specialists to 67 percent in 2005 (Ness & others, 2006).

Consequences of Low Birth Weight

Although most low birth weight infants are normal and healthy, as a group they have more health and developmental problems than normal birth weight infants (Moss, 2006). The number and severity of these problems increase as birth weight decreases.

At school age, children who were born low in birth weight are more likely than their normal birth weight counterparts to have a learning disability, attention deficit hyperactivity disorder, or breathing problems such as asthma (Wocadlo & Rieger, 2006). Approximately 50 percent of all low birth weight children are enrolled in special education programs.

Note that not all of these adverse consequences can be attributed solely to being born low in birth weight. Some of the less severe but more common developmental and physical delays occur because many low birth weight children come from disadvantaged environments (Malamitsi-Puchner & Boutsikou, 2006).

Kangaroo Care and Massage Therapy

Kangaroo care is a way of holding an infant so that there is skin-to-skin contact; it is a common intervention for preterm newborns (Ludington-Hoe & others, 2006). The baby, wearing only a diaper, is held upright against the parent's bare chest, much as a baby kangaroo is carried by its mother. Another component of kangaroo care is breast feeding on demand. Kangaroo care is typically practiced for two to three hours per day over an extended time in early infancy (Johnson, 2007).

A new mother learning how to practice kangaroo care. *What is kangaroo care?*

Why use kangaroo care with preterm infants? Preterm infants often have difficulty coordinating their breathing and heart rate, and the close physical contact with the parent in kangaroo care has been found to help to stabilize the preterm infant's heartbeat, temperature, and breathing (Kennell, 2006). Further, preterm infants who experience kangaroo care have been found to have longer periods of sleep, gain more weight, decrease their crying, have longer periods of alertness, and earlier hospital discharge (Worku & Kassir, 2005). Increasingly kangaroo care is being recommended for full-term infants as well (Johnson, 2005).

Many preterm infants experience less touch than full-term infants because they are isolated in temperature-controlled incubators (Chia, Selleck, & Gans, 2006). The research of Tiffany Field and her colleagues (2004, 2006, 2007) has led to a surge of interest in the role that massage might play in improving the developmental outcomes for preterm infants. In Field's first study in this area, massage therapy consisting of firm stroking with the palms of the hands was given three times per day for 15-minute periods to preterm infants (Field & others, 1986). The massage therapy led to 47 percent greater weight gain than standard medical treatment. The massaged infants also were more active and alert than preterm infants who were not massaged, and they performed better on developmental tests.

In later studies, Field demonstrated the benefits of massage therapy for infants who faced a variety of problems. For example, preterm infants exposed to cocaine in utero who received massage therapy gained weight and improved their scores on developmental tests (Field, 2001). In another investigation, newborns born to HIV-positive mothers were randomly assigned to a massage therapy group or to a control group that did not receive the therapy (Scafidi & Field, 1996). The massaged infants showed superior performance on a wide range of assessments, including daily weight gain. Another study investigated 1- to 3-month-old infants born to depressed adolescent mothers (Field & others, 1996). The infants of depressed mothers who received massage therapy had lower stress—as well as improved emotionality, sociability, and soothability—compared with the nonmassaged infants of depressed mothers.

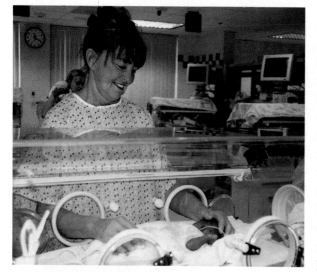

Tiffany Field is shown here massaging a newborn infant. *What types of infants have massage therapy been shown to help?*

In a recent study, Field and her colleagues (2004) taught mothers how to massage their full-term infants. Once a day before bedtime the mothers massaged the babies using either light or moderate pressure. Infants who were massaged with moderate pressure "gained more weight, were greater length, performed better on the orientation scale of the Brazelton, had lower Brazelton excitability and depression scores, and exhibited less agitation during sleep" (p. 435).

In a review of the use of massage therapy with preterm infants, Field and her colleagues (2004) concluded that the most consistent findings involve two positive results: (1) increased weight gain and (2) discharge from the hospital from three to six days earlier.

How Would You...?
As a health-care professional, how would you advise hospital administrators about implementing kangaroo care or massage therapy in the newborn intensive care unit?

Bonding

A special component of the parent-infant relationship is bonding, the formation of a connection, especially a physical bond between parents and the newborn in the period shortly after birth. In the mid-twentieth century, U.S. hospitals seem almost determined to deter bonding. Anesthesia given to the mother during delivery would make the mother drowsy, interfering with her ability to respond to and stimulate the newborn. Mothers and newborns were often separated shortly after delivery, and preterm infants were isolated from their mothers even more than full-term mothers. In recent decades these practices have changed, but to some extent they are still followed in many hospitals.

Do these practices do any harm? Some physicians believe that during the period shortly after birth, the parents and newborn need to form an emotional attachment as a foundation for optimal development in years to come (Kennell, 2006; Kennell & McGrath, 1999). Is there evidence that close contact between mothers in the first several days after birth is critical for optimal development later in life? Although some research supports this bonding hypothesis (Klaus & Kennell, 1976), a body of research challenges the significance of the first few days of life as a critical period (Bakeman & Brown, 1980; Rode & others, 1981). Indeed, the extreme form of the bonding hypothesis—that the newborn *must* have close contact with the mother in the first few days of life to develop optimally—simply is not true.

Nonetheless, the weakness of the bonding hypothesis should not be used as an excuse to keep motivated mothers from interacting with their newborns. Such contact brings pleasure to many mothers and may dispel maternal anxiety about the baby's health and safety. In some mother-infant pairs—including preterm infants, adolescent mothers, and mothers from disadvantaged circumstances—early close contact is key to establishing a climate for improved interaction after the mother and infant leave the hospital.

Many hospitals now offer a *rooming-in* arrangement, in which the baby remains in the mother's room most of the time during its hospital stay. However, if parents choose not to use this rooming-in arrangement, the weight of the research suggests that this decision will not harm the infant emotionally (Lamb, 1994).

postpartum period The period after childbirth when the mother adjusts, both physically and psychologically, to the process of childbirth. This period lasts for about six weeks or until her body has completed its adjustment and returned to a near prepregnant state.

The Postpartum Period

The **postpartum period** is the period after childbirth or delivery that lasts for about six weeks or until the mother's body has completed its adjustment and has returned to a nearly prepregnant state. It is a time when the woman adjusts, both physically and psychologically, to the process of childbearing. Many health professionals believe that the best way to meet these challenges is with a family-centered approach that uses the family's resources to support an early and smooth adjustment to the newborn by all family members. The adjustments needed are physical, emotional, and psychological.

Physical Adjustments

A woman's body makes numerous physical adjustments in the first days and weeks after childbirth. She may have a great deal of energy or feel exhausted and let down. Most new mothers feel tired and need rest. Though these changes are normal, the fatigue can undermine the new mother's sense of well-being and confidence in her ability to cope with a new baby and a new family life (Runquist, 2007).

After delivery, a mother's body undergoes sudden and dramatic changes in hormone production. When the placenta is delivered, estrogen and progesterone levels drop steeply and remain low until the ovaries start producing hormones again. The woman will probably begin menstruating again in four to eight weeks if she is not breast feeding. If she is breast feeding, she might not menstruate for several months to a year or more, though ovulation can occur during this time. The first several menstrual periods following delivery might be heavier than usual, but periods soon return to normal.

Involution is the process by which the uterus returns to its prepregnant size five or six weeks after birth. Immediately following birth, the uterus weighs 2 to 3 pounds. By the end of five or six weeks, the uterus weighs 2 to 3½ ounces. Nursing the baby helps contract the uterus at a rapid rate.

If the woman regularly engaged in conditioning exercises during pregnancy, exercise will help her recover her former body contour and strength. With a caregiver's approval, the new mother can begin some exercises as soon as one hour after delivery. A recent study found that women who maintained or increased their exercise from prepregnancy to postpartum had better maternal well-being than women who engaged in no exercise or decreased their exercise from prepregnancy to postpartum (Blum, Beaudoin, & Caton-Lemos, 2005).

Relaxation techniques are also helpful during the postpartum period. Five minutes of slow breathing on a stressful day in the postpartum period can relax and refresh the new mother, as well as the new baby.

Emotional and Psychological Adjustments

Emotional fluctuations are common for mothers in the postpartum period. For some women, emotional fluctuations decrease within several weeks after the delivery, but other women experience more long-lasting emotional swings.

About 70 percent of new mothers in the United States have what are called "baby blues." About two to three days after birth, they begin to feel depressed, anxious, and upset. These feelings may come and go for several months after the birth, often peaking about three to five days after birth. Even without treatment, these feelings usually go away after one or two weeks.

For other women, emotional fluctuations persist and can produce feelings of anxiety, depression, and difficulty in coping with stress (Morrissey, 2007; Tam & Chung, 2007).

Postpartum depression involves a major depressive episode that typically occurs about four weeks after delivery. In other words, women with postpartum depression have such strong feelings of sadness, anxiety, or despair that for at least a two-week period they have trouble coping with their daily tasks. Without treatment, postpartum depression may become worse and last for many months (Driscoll, 2006). About 10 percent of new mothers experience postpartum depression. Between 25 to 50 percent of these depressed new mothers have episodes that last six months or longer (Beck, 2002). If untreated, approximately 25 of these women are still depressed a year later.

The postpartum period is a time of considerable adjustment and adaptation for both the mother and the father. Fathers can provide an important support system for mothers, especially in helping mothers care for young infants. *What kinds of tasks might the father of a newborn do to support the mother?*

How Would You...? As a human development and family studies professional, how would talk with mothers and fathers about vulnerabilities in mental health and relationships in the postpartum period?

Fathers also undergo considerable adjustment in the postpartum period, even when they work away from home all day (Cox, 2006; Pinheiro & others, 2006). Many fathers feel that the baby comes first and gets all of the mother's attention; some feel that they have been replaced by the baby.

To help the father adjust, parents should set aside some special time to be together with each other. The father's postpartum reaction also likely will be improved if he has taken childbirth classes with the mother and is an active participant in caring for the baby.

Summary

The Evolutionary Perspective

Natural selection is the process by which those individuals of a species that are best adapted survive and reproduce. Darwin proposed that natural selection fuels evolution. In evolutionary theory, adaptive behavior is behavior that promotes the organism's survival in a natural habitat. Evolutionary psychology holds that adaptation, reproduction, and "survival of the fittest" are important in shaping behavior. Ideas proposed by evolutionary developmental psychology include the view that an extended "juvenile" period is needed to develop a large brain and learn the complexity of human social communities. Like other theoretical approaches to development, evolutionary psychology has limitations and has been criticized.

Genetic Foundations of Development

Except in the sperm and egg, the nucleus of each human cell contains 46 chromosomes, which are composed of DNA. Short segments of DNA constitute genes, the units of hereditary information that direct cells to reproduce and manufacture proteins. Genes act collaboratively, not independently. Genes are passed on to new cells when chromosomes are duplicated during the processes of mitosis and meiosis. When an egg and a sperm unite in the fertilization process, the result is a zygote. Genetic principles include those involving dominant-recessive genes, sex-linked genes, and polygenic inheritance. Chromosome abnormalities produce Down syndrome as well a sex-linked chromosomal abnormalities such as Klinefelter syndrome, fragile X syndrome, Turner syndrome, and XYY syndrome. Gene-linked abnormalities involve defective genes. Gene-linked disorders include phenylketonuria (PKU) and sickle-cell anemia.

Heredity and Environment Interaction: The Nature–Nurture Debate

Behavior genetics is the field concerned with the degree and nature of behavior's hereditary basis. Methods used by behavior geneticists include twin studies and adoption studies. In Scarr's heredity-environment correlations view, heredity directs the types of environments that children experience. She describes three genotype-environment correlations: passive, evocative, and active (niche-picking). The epigenetic view emphasizes that development is the result of an ongoing, bidirectional interchange between heredity and environment. The interaction of heredity and environment is extensive.

Prenatal Development

Prenatal development is divided into three periods: germinal, embryonic, and fetal. Amniocentesis, ultrasound sonography, chorionic villus sampling, and maternal blood screening are used to determine whether a fetus is developing normally. Approximately 10 to 15 percent of U.S. couples have infertility problems. A teratogen is any agent that can potentially cause a birth defect or negatively alter cognitive and behavioral outcomes. The dose, time of exposure, and genetic susceptibility influence the severity of the damage to an unborn child and the type of defect that occurs. Some prescription drugs and nonprescription drugs can harm the unborn child. The psychoactive drugs caffeine, alcohol, nicotine, cocaine, metamphetamine, marijuana, and heroin are potentially harmful to offspring. Incompatibility of the mother's and the father's blood types can also harm the fetus. Problems may also result if a pregnant woman has rubella (German measles), syphilis, genital herpes, or AIDS. A developing fetus depends entirely on its mother for nutrition, and it may be harmed if the mother is malnourished, overweight, has a diet deficient in folic acid, or consumes significant amounts of fish polluted by mercury or PCBs. High anxiety and stress in the mother are linked with less than optimal prenatal and birth outcomes. Maternal age can negatively affect the offspring's development if the mother is an adolescent or over 35 and older. Paternal factors also can adversely affect prenatal development. Potential environmental hazards include radiation, environmental pollutants, and toxic wastes. Prenatal care varies extensively, and there are cultural variations in beliefs about pregnancy.

Birth and the Postpartum Period

Childbirth occurs in three stages. The first stage, which lasts about 12 to 24 hours for a woman having her first child, is the longest stage. Childbirth strategies involve the childbirth setting and attendants. In many countries, a doula attends a childbearing woman. Methods of delivery include medicated, natural and prepared, and cesarean. Increasingly, nonmedicated techniques, such as waterbirth, are being used to reduce childbirth pain. Being born involves considerable stress for the baby, but the baby is well prepared and adapted to handle the stress. Low birth weight, preterm, and small for date infants are at risk for developmental problems, although most of these infants are normal and healthy. Kangaroo care and massage therapy have been shown to have benefits for preterm infants. Early bonding has not been found to be critical in the development of a competent infant. The postpartum period is the period after childbirth that lasts for about six weeks or until the body has completed its adjustment; the development of postpartum depression is a concern.

Key Terms

evolutionary psychology 37
chromosomes 39
DNA 39
genes 39
mitosis 40
meiosis 40
genotype 41
phenotype 41

Down syndrome 43
behavior genetics 45
twin study 45
adoption study 46
epigenetic view 47
germinal period 49
embryonic period 49
organogenesis 49

fetal period 50
teratogen 52
fetal alcohol syndrome (FAS) 53
natural childbirth 64
prepared childbirth 64
Apgar Scale 66
postpartum period 69

3

Physical and Cognitive Development in Infancy

Stories of Life-Span Development: Newborn Babies in Ghana and Nigeria

Latonya is a newborn baby in Ghana. During her first days of life she has been kept apart from her mother and bottle-fed. Manufacturers of infant formula provide the hospital where she was born with free or subsidized milk powder. LaTonya's mother has been persuaded to bottle feed rather than breast feed her. When her mother bottle-feeds Latonya, she overdilutes the milk formula with unclean water. Latonya's feeding bottles have not been sterilized. Latonya becomes very sick. She dies before her first birthday.

Ramona was born in Nigeria with a "baby-friendly" program. In this program, babies are not separated from their mothers when they are born, and the mothers are encouraged to breast feed them. The mothers are told of the perils that bottle feeding can bring because of unsafe water and unsterilized bottles. They also are informed about the advantages of breast milk, which include its nutritious and hygienic qualities, its ability to immunize babies against common illnesses, and its role

in reducing the mother's risk of breast and ovarian cancer. Ramona's mother is breast feeding her. At 1 year of age, Ramona is very healthy.

For many years, maternity units in hospitals favored bottle feeding and did not give mothers adequate information about the benefits of breast feeding. In recent years, the World Health Organization and UNICEF have tried to reverse the trend toward bottle feeding of infants in many impoverished countries. They instituted the "baby-friendly" program in

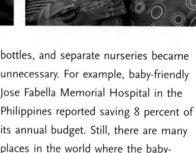

(*Left*) An HIV-infected mother breast feeding her baby in Nairobi, Africa; (*Right*) A Rhwandan mother bottle feeding her baby. *What are some concerns about breast versus bottle feeding in impoverished African countries?*

The advantages of breast feeding in impoverished countries are substantial. However, these advantages must be balanced against the risk of passing HIV to the baby through breast milk if the mothers have the virus; the majority of mothers don't know that they are infected (de Baets & others, 2007; Doherty & others, 2006). In some areas of Africa more than 30 percent of mothers have the HIV virus.

many countries. They also persuaded the International Association of Infant Formula Manufacturers to stop marketing their baby formulas to hospitals in countries where the governments support the baby-friendly initiatives (Grant, 1993). For the hospitals themselves, costs actually were reduced as infant formula, feeding

bottles, and separate nurseries became unnecessary. For example, baby-friendly Jose Fabella Memorial Hospital in the Philippines reported saving 8 percent of its annual budget. Still, there are many places in the world where the baby-friendly initiatives have not been implemented (UNICEF, 2004).

In the first two years of life, an infant's body and brain undergo remarkable growth and development (Field, 2007). In this chapter we explore how this takes place: through physical growth, motor development, sensory and perceptual development, cognitive development, and language development. ∎

Physical Growth and Development in Infancy

At birth, an infant has few of the physical abilities we associate with being human. Its head, which is huge relative to the rest of the body, flops around uncontrollably. Apart from some basic reflexes and the ability to cry, the newborn is unable to perform many actions. Over the next 12 months, however, the infant becomes capable of sitting, standing, stooping, climbing, and usually walking. During the

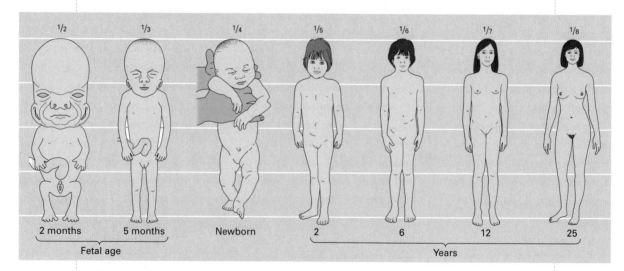

Figure 3.1 Changes in Proportions of the Human Body During Growth
As individuals develop from infancy through adulthood, one of the most noticeable physical changes is that the head becomes smaller in relation to the rest of the body. The fractions listed refer to head size as a proportion of total body length at different ages.

second year, while growth slows, rapid increases in such activities as running and climbing take place. Let's now examine in greater detail the sequence of physical development in infancy.

cephalocaudal pattern The sequence in which the earliest growth always occurs at the top—the head—with physical growth in size, weight, and feature differentiation gradually working from top to bottom.

proximodistal pattern The sequence in which growth starts at the center of the body and moves toward the extremities.

Patterns of Growth

During prenatal development and early infancy, the head occupies an extraordinary proportion of the total body (see Figure 3.1). The **cephalocaudal pattern** is the sequence in which the earliest growth always occurs at the top—the head—with physical growth and differentiation of features gradually working their way down from top to bottom (shoulders, middle trunk, and so on). This same pattern occurs in the head area, as the top parts of the head—the eyes and brain—grow faster than the lower parts, such as the jaw.

Sensory and motor development generally proceed according to the cephalocaudal pattern. For example, infants see objects before they can control their torso, and they can use their hands long before they can crawl or walk. However, development does not follow a rigid blueprint. One recent study found that infants reached for toys with their feet four weeks earlier, on average, than they reached for them with their hands (Galloway & Thelen, 2004).

Growth also follows the **proximodistal pattern**, the sequence in which growth starts at the center of the body and moves toward the extremities. For example, infants control the muscles of their trunk and arms before they control their hands, and they use their whole hands before they can control several fingers.

Height and Weight

The average North American newborn is 20 inches long and weighs $7\frac{1}{2}$ pounds. Ninety-five percent of full-term newborns are 18 to 22 inches long and weigh between $5\frac{1}{2}$ and 10 pounds.

In the first several days of life, most newborns lose 5 to 7 percent of their body weight before they adjust to feeding by sucking, swallowing, and digesting. They then grow rapidly, gaining an average of 5 to 6 ounces per week during the first month. They double their birth weight by the age of 4 months and nearly triple it by their first birthday. Infants grow about 1 inch per month during the first year, reaching approximately $1\frac{1}{2}$ times their birth length by their first birthday.

Growth slows considerably in the second year of life. By 2 years of age, children weigh approximately 26 to 32 pounds, having gained a quarter to half a pound per month during the second year; now they have reached about one-fifth of their adult weight. At 2 years of age, the average child is 32 to 35 inches tall, nearly half of their eventual adult height.

The Brain

How Would You...?

As a health-care professional, how would you talk with parents about shaken baby syndrome?

At birth, the infant that began as a single cell has a brain that contains tens of billions of nerve cells, or neurons. Extensive brain development continues after birth, through infancy, and later (Nelson, 2007; Nelson, Thomas, & de Haan, 2006). Because the brain is still developing so rapidly in infancy, the infant's head should be protected from falls or other injuries and the baby should never be shaken. *Shaken baby syndrome*, which includes brain swelling and hemorrhaging, affects hundreds of babies in the United States each year (Gerber & Coffman, 2007; Walls, 2006).

The Brain's Development

At birth, the newborn's brain is about 25 percent of its adult weight. By the second birthday, the brain is about 75 percent of its adult weight. However, the brain's areas do not mature uniformly.

Mapping the Brain Scientists analyze and categorize areas of the brain in numerous ways. Of greatest interest is the portion farthest from the spinal cord known as the *forebrain,* which includes the cerebral cortex and several structures beneath it. The *cerebral cortex* covers the forebrain like a wrinkled cap. It has two halves, or hemispheres. Based on ridges and valleys in the cortex, scientists distinguish four main areas, called lobes, in each hemisphere: the *frontal lobes,* the *occipital lobes,* the *temporal lobes,* and the *parietal lobes* (see Figure 3.2).

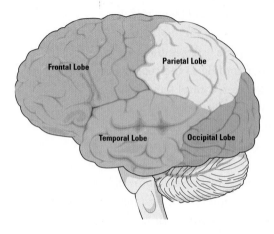

Figure 3.2 The Brain's Four Lobes
Shown here are the locations of the brain's four lobes: frontal, occipital, temporal, and parietal.

Although these areas are found in the cerebral cortex of each hemisphere, the two hemispheres are not identical in anatomy or function. **Lateralization** is the specialization of function in one hemisphere or the other. Researchers continue to explore the degree to which each is involved in various aspects of thinking, feeling, and behavior (Stephan, Fink, & Marshall, 2006). At birth, the hemispheres of the cerebral cortex already have started to specialize: Newborns show greater electrical brain activity in the left hemisphere than the right when they are listening to speech sounds (Hahn, 1987).

The most extensive research on brain lateralization has focused on language (Killgore, Gruber, & Yurgelun-Todd, 2007). Speech and grammar are localized to the left hemisphere in most people, but some aspects of language, such as appropriate language use in different contexts and the use of metaphor and humor, involve the right hemisphere. Thus, language is not controlled exclusively by the brain's left hemisphere (Jabbour & others, 2005). Further, most neuroscientists agree that complex functions—such as reading, performing music, and creating art—are the outcome of communication between both sides of the brain.

How are the areas of the brain different in the newborn and the infant than in an adult, and why do the differences matter? Important differences have been documented at both the cellular and the structural level.

Changes in Neurons Within the brain, neurons send electrical and chemical signals, communicating with each other. A **neuron** is a nerve cell that handles information processing (see Figure 3.3). Extending from the neuron's cell body are two types of fibers known as *axons* and *dendrites.* Generally, the axon carries signals away from the cell body and dendrites carry signals toward it. A *myelin sheath,* which is a layer of fat cells, encases many axons (see Figure 3.3). The myelin sheath provides insulation and helps electrical signals travel faster down the axon. At the end of the axon are terminal buttons, which release chemicals called *neurotransmitters* into *synapses,* which are tiny gaps between neurons' fibers. Chemical interactions in synapses connect axons and dendrites, allowing information to pass from neuron to neuron.

Neurons change in two very significant ways during the first years of life. First, *myelination,* the process of encasing axons with fat cells, begins prenatally and continues throughout childhood, even into adolescence (Dubois & others, 2007). Second, connectivity among neurons increases, creating new neural pathways, as Figure 3.4 illustrates. New dendrites grow, connections among dendrites increase, and synaptic connections between axons and dendrites proliferate. Whereas myelination speeds up neural transmissions, the expansion of dendritic connections facilitates the spreading of neural pathways in infant development.

Researchers have discovered an intriguing aspect of synaptic connections. Nearly twice as many of these connections are made as will ever be used (Huttenlocher & Dabholkar, 1997). The connections that are used become strengthened and survive, while the unused ones are replaced by other pathways or disappear. In the language of neuroscience, these connections will be "pruned" (Giedd & others, 2006).

Changes in Regions of the Brain Figure 3.5 vividly illustrates the dramatic growth and later pruning of synapses in the visual, auditory, and prefrontal cortex (Huttenlocher & Dabholkar, 1997). Notice that "blooming and pruning" vary considerably by brain region. For example, the peak of synaptic overproduction in the visual cortex occurs at about the fourth postnatal month, followed by a gradual retraction until the middle to end of the preschool years (Huttenlocher & Dabholkar, 1997). In areas of the brain involved in hearing and language, a similar, though somewhat later, course is detected. However, in the *prefrontal cortex,* the area of the brain where higher-level thinking and self-regulation occur, the peak of overproduction takes

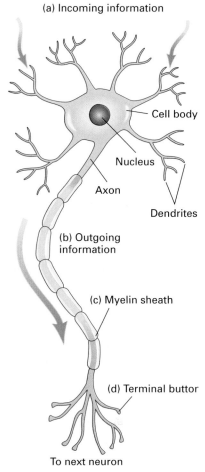

(a) Incoming information

Cell body

Nucleus

Axon

Dendrites

(b) Outgoing information

(c) Myelin sheath

(d) Terminal buttor

To next neuron

Figure 3.3 The Neuron
(*a*) The dendrites of the cell body receive information from other neurons, muscles, or glands through the axon. (*b*) Axons transmit information away from the cell body. (*c*) A myelin sheath covers most axons and speeds information transmission. (*d*) As the axon ends, it branches out into terminal buttons.

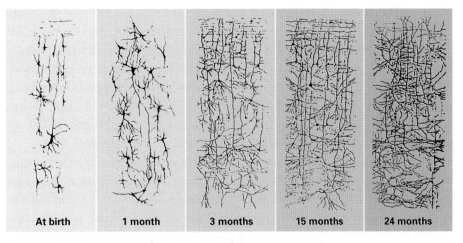

At birth   1 month   3 months   15 months   24 months

Figure 3.4 The Development of Dendritic Spreading
Note the increase in connectedness between neurons over the course of the first two years of life. Reprinted by permission of the publisher from *The Postnatal Development of the Human Cerebral Cortex, Vols. I-VIII* by Jesse LeRoy Conel, Cambridge, Mass.: Harvard University Press, Copyright © 1939, 1975 by the President and Fellows of Harvard College.

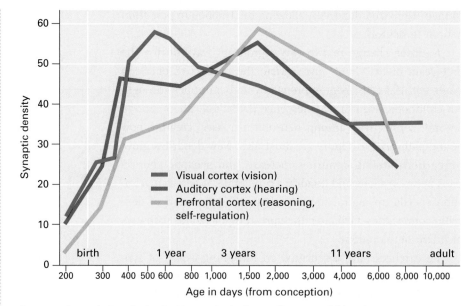

Figure 3.5 Synaptic Density in the Human Brain from Infancy to Adulthoods
The graph shows the dramatic increase and then pruning in synaptic density for three regions of the brain: visual corex, auditory cortex, and prefrontal cortex. Synaptic density is believed to be an important indication of the extent of connectivity between neurons.

place at about 1 year of age; it is not until middle to late adolescence that the adult density of synapses is achieved. Both heredity and environment are thought to influence the timing and course of synaptic overproduction and subsequent retraction.

Meanwhile, the pace of myelination also varies in different areas of the brain. Myelination for visual pathways occurs rapidly after birth and is completed in the first six months. Auditory myelination is not completed until 4 or 5 years of age.

Early Experience and the Brain

What determines how these changes in the brain occur? The infant's brain is literally waiting for experiences to determine how connections are made (Johnson 2005). Before birth, it appears that genes mainly directed how the brain establishes basic wiring patterns; after birth, environmental experiences guide the brain's development. The inflowing stream of sights, sounds, smells, touches, language, and eye contact help shape the brain's neural connections (Johnson, 2007). It may not surprise us, then, that depressed brain activity has been found in children who grow up in a deprived environment (Nelson, Jeanah, & Fox, 2007). Infants whose caregivers expose them to a variety of stimulation—talking, touching, playing—are most likely to develop to their full potential.

The profusion of neural connections described earlier provides the growing brain with flexibility and resilience. As an extreme example, consider 16-year-old Michael Rehbein. When Michael was 4$\frac{1}{2}$, he began to experience uncontrollable seizures—as many as 400 a day. Doctors said that the only solution was to remove the left hemisphere of his brain, where the seizures were occurring. Michael had his first major surgery at age 7 and another at age 10. Although recovery was slow, his right hemisphere began to reorganize and eventually took over functions, such as speech, that normally occur in the brain's left hemisphere (see Figure 3.6).

Patients like Michael are living proof of the growing brain's remarkable ability to adapt and recover from a loss of brain tissue.

Sleep

The typical newborn sleeps 16 to 17 hours a day, but there is considerable individual variation in how much infants sleep. The range is from about 10 hours to about 21 hours.

Infants also vary in their preferred times for sleeping and their patterns of sleep. Although the total amount of time spent sleeping remains somewhat consistent, a given infant may change from sleeping 7 or 8 hours two or three times a day to sleeping for only a few hours three or four times a day. By about 1 month of age, many American infants have begun to sleep longer at night. By about 4 months of age, they usually have moved closer to adultlike sleep patterns, spending the most time sleeping at night and the most time awake during the day (Daws, 2000). A good book to read on strategies for improving infants' sleep habits is *Healthy Sleep Habits, Happy Child* (Weissbluth, 2003).

REM Sleep

A much greater amount of time is taken up by *REM (rapid eye movement)* sleep in infancy than at any other point in the life span. Unlike adults, who spend about one-fifth of their night in REM sleep, infants spend about half of their sleep time in REM sleep, and they often begin their sleep cycle with REM sleep rather than non-REM sleep. By the time infants reach 3 months of age, the percentage of time they spend in REM sleep decreases to about 40 percent, and REM sleep no longer begins their sleep cycle.

Why do infants spend so much time in REM sleep? Researchers are not certain. The large amount of REM sleep may provide infants with added self-stimulation, since they spend less time awake than do older children. REM sleep also might promote the brain's development in infancy (Graven, 2006).

(a)

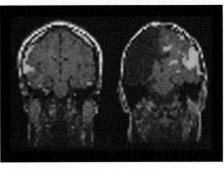

(b)

Figure 3.6 Plasticity in the Brain's Hemispheres
(a) Michael Rehbein at 14 years of age.
(b) Michael's right hemisphere (*right*) has reorganized to take over the language functions normally carried out by corresponding areas in the left hemisphere of an intact brain (*left*). However, the right hemisphere is not as efficient as the left, and more areas of the brain are recruited to process speech.

SIDS

Sudden infant death syndrome (SIDS) is a condition that occurs when an infant stops breathing, usually during the night, and dies suddenly without an apparent cause. SIDS remains the highest cause of infant death in the United States with nearly 3,000 infant deaths annually attributed to SIDS. Risk of SIDS is highest at 1 to 3 months of age (Centers in Disease Control and Prevention, 2007).

Since 1992, The American Academy of Pediatrics (AAP) has recommended that infants be placed to sleep on their backs to

sudden infant death syndrome (SIDS) A condition that occurs when an infant stops breathing, usually during the night, and suddenly dies without an apparent cause.

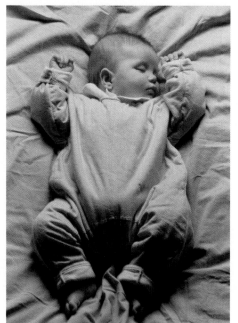

Is this a good sleep position for infants? Why or why not?

reduce the risk of SIDS, and the frequency of U.S. infants sleeping on their stomachs has dropped dramatically (AAP, 2000). Researchers have found that SIDS does indeed decrease when infants sleep on their backs rather than on their stomachs or sides (Alm, Lagercrantz, & Wennergren, 2006). Among the reasons given for prone sleeping (lying face downward) being a high risk factor for SIDS are that it impairs the infant's arousal from sleep and restricts the infant's ability to swallow effectively (Ariagno, van Liempt, & Mirmiran, 2006). SIDS is also more common in low birth weight infants, infants who are passively exposed to cigarette smoke, and infants who sleep in soft bedding (Mcgarvey & others, 2006; Sharma, 2007). And SIDS is less likely to occur in infants who use a pacifier when they go to sleep (Li & others, 2006).

How Would You...?
As a health-care professional how would you advise parents about preventing SIDS?

Nutrition

From birth to 1 year of age, human infants nearly triple their weight and increase their length by 50 percent. What do they need to sustain this growth?

Breast Versus Bottle Feeding

For the first four to six months of life, human milk or an alternative formula is the baby's source of nutrients and energy. For years, debate has focused on whether breast feeding is better for the infant than bottle feeding. The growing consensus is that breast feeding is better for the baby's health (Narra More, 2007; Wardlaw & Hampel, 2007). Since the 1970s, breast feeding by U.S. mothers has soared (see Figure 3.7). In 2004 more than two-thirds of U.S. mothers breast fed their newborns, and more than a third breast fed their 6-month-olds. The American Academy of Pediatrics (AAP) and the American Dietetic Association strongly endorse breast feeding throughout the infant's first year (James & Dobson, 2005).

What are some of the benefits of breast feeding? During the first two years of life and beyond, these benefits include appropriate weight gain and lowered risk of childhood obesity (Miralles & others, 2006); fewer allergies (Host & Halken, 2005); prevention or reduction of diarrhea, respiratory infections (such as pneumonia and bronchitis), bacterial and urinary tract infections, and otitis media (a middle ear infection) (Jackson & Nazar, 2006). Other benefits include denser bones in childhood and adulthood (Gibson & others, 2000); reduced childhood cancer and reduced incidence of breast cancer in mothers and their female offspring (Kwan & others 2004); lower incidence of SIDS

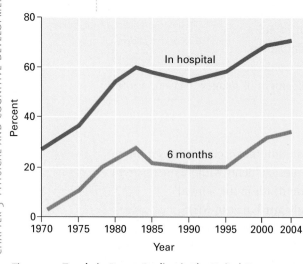

Figure 3.7 Trends in Breast Feeding in the United States: 1970–2004

(Fredrickson, 1993); more advanced neurological and cognitive development (Eidelman & Feldman, 2004); more advanced language and motor development (Dee & others, 2007) and better visual acuity (Makrides & others, 1995).

Are there circumstances when mothers should not breast feed? Yes: A mother should not breast feed if she (1) is infected with AIDS or any other infectious disease that can be transmitted through her milk, (2) has active tuberculosis, or (3) is taking any drug that may not be safe for the infant (Doherty & others, 2006).

Some women cannot breast feed their infants because of physical difficulties; others feel guilty if they terminate breast feeding early (Walshaw & Owens, 2006). Mothers also may worry that they are depriving their infants of important emotional and psychological benefits if they bottle feed rather than breast feed. Some researchers have found, however, that there are no psychological differences between breast fed and bottle fed infants (Ferguson, Harwood, & Shannon, 1987; Young, 1990).

Nutritional Needs

Individual differences among infants in terms of their nutrient reserves, body composition, growth rates, and activity patterns make defining actual nutrient needs difficult (James & Ashwill, 2007; Krebs, 2007). However, because parents need guidelines, nutritionists recommend that infants consume approximately 50 calories per day for each pound they weigh—more than twice an adult's requirement per pound.

A recent national study of more than 3,000 randomly selected 4- to 24-month-olds documented that many U.S. parents are feeding their babies too few fruits and vegetables, and too much junk food (Fox & others, 2004). Up to one-third of the babies ate no vegetables and fruit; almost half of the 7- to 8-month-old babies were fed desserts, sweets, or sweetened drinks. By 15 months, French fries were the most common vegetables the babies ate.

In sum, adequate early nutrition is an important aspect of healthy development. To be healthy, children need a nurturant, supportive environment (Boyle & Long, 2007; Wardlaw & Hampl, 2007). One individual who has stood out as an advocate of caring for children is T. Berry Brazelton, who is featured in the Careers in Life-Span Development profile.

A Healthy Start

So far we have seen that it is important for infants to get off to a healthy start in their journey through life. Unfortunately, this doesn't happen for some children, whose circumstances place them at risk for developmental problems. One program that has been successful in helping high-risk infants and their families is the Family Support/Healthy Start Program that began in 1985 (Allen, Brown, & Finlay, 1992). It was designed by the Hawaii Family Stress Center in Honolulu, which already had been making home visits to improve family functioning and reduce child abuse for more than a decade. Participation is voluntary. Families of newborns are screened for family risk factors, including unstable housing, histories of substance abuse, depression, parents' abuse as a child, late or no prenatal care, fewer than 12 years of schooling, poverty, and unemployment. Healthy Start workers screen and interview new mothers in the hospital. They also screen families referred by physicians, nurses,

CAREERS IN LIFE-SPAN DEVELOPMENT

T. Berry Brazelton, Pediatrician

T. Berry Brazelton is America's best-known pediatrician as a result of his numerous books, television appearances, and newspaper and magazine articles about parenting and children's health. He takes a family-centered approach to child development issues and communicates with parents in easy to understand ways.

Dr. Brazelton founded the Child Development Unit at Boston Children's Hospital and created the Brazelton Neonatal Behavioral Assessment Scale, a widely used measure of the newborn's health and well-being. He also has conducted a number of research studies on infants and children and has been president of the Society for Research in Child Development, a leading research organization.

Pediatricians, such as T. Berry Brazelton, monitor infants' and children's health, work to prevent disease or injury, help children attain optimal health, and treat children with health problems. Pediatricians have earned a medical degree and completed a three- to five-year residency in pediatrics. Pediatricians may work in private practice, a medical clinic, a hospital, or a medical school. Many pediatricians who are on the faculty of medical schools also teach and conduct research on children's health and diseases.

T. Berry Brazelton with a young child.

The Hawaii Family Support/ Healthy Start Program provides many home-visitor services for overburdened families of new-borns and young children. This program has been very successful in reducing abuse and neglect in families. *What are some examples of the home-visitor services in this program?*

and others. Because the demand for services outstrips available resources, only families with a substantial number of risk factors can participate.

Each new participating family receives a weekly visit from a family support worker. Each of the program's eight home visitors works with approximately 25 families at a time. The worker helps the family cope with any immediate crisis, such as unemployment or substance abuse. The family also is linked directly with a pediatrician to ensure that the children receive regular health care. Infants are screened for developmental delays and are immunized on schedule. Pediatricians are notified when a child is enrolled in Healthy Start and when a family at risk stops participating.

The Family Support/Healthy Start Program recently hired a child development specialist to work with families of children with special needs. In some instances, the program's male family support worker visits a father to talk about his role in the family. The support workers encourage parents to participate in group activities held each week at the program center located in a neighborhood shopping center.

Over time, parents are encouraged to assume more responsibility for their family's health and well-being. Families can participate in Healthy Start until the child is 5 and enters public school. One recent study found that the Hawaiian Healthy Start program produced a lower incidence of maternal alcohol abuse and partner violence but did not reduce child abuse (Duggan & others, 2004).

dynamic systems theory
The perspective on motor development that seeks to explain how motor behaviors are assembled for perceiving and acting.

Motor Development

How do infants develop their motor skills, and which skills do they develop when?

The Dynamic Systems View

According to **dynamic systems theory**, infants assemble motor skills for perceiving and acting; perception and action are coupled together (Smith & Brea Zeal, 2007; Thelen & Smith, 2006). In order to develop motor skills, infants must perceive something in the environment that motivates them to act, then use their perceptions to fine-tune their movements. Motor skills represent solutions to the infant's goals.

How is a motor skill developed according to this theory? When infants are motivated to do something, they might create a new motor behavior. The new behavior is the result of many converging factors: the development of the nervous system, the body's physical properties and its possibilities for movement, the goal the child is motivated to reach, and the environmental support for the skill. For example, babies learn to walk only when maturation of the nervous system allows them to control certain leg muscles, when their legs have grown enough to support their weight, and when they want to move.

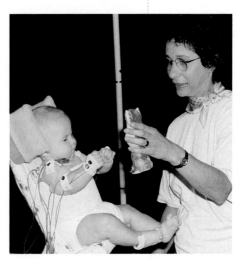

Mastering a motor skill requires the infant's active efforts to coordinate several components of the skill (Adolph & Joh, 2007, 2008). Infants explore and select possible solutions to the demands of a new task; they assemble adaptive patterns by modifying their current movement patterns. The first step occurs when the infant is motivated by a new challenge—such as the desire to cross a room—and initiates this task by taking a few stumbling steps. The infant then "tunes" these movements to make them smoother and more effective. The tuning is achieved through repeated cycles of action and perception of the consequences of that action. According to the dynamic systems view, even universal milestones, such as crawling, reaching, and walking, are learned through this process of adaptation: infants modulate their movement patterns to fit a new task by exploring and selecting possible configurations (Thelen & Smith, 2006).

Thus, according to dynamic systems theory, motor development is not a passive process in which genes dictate the unfolding of a sequence of skills. Rather, the infant actively puts together a skill in order to achieve a goal within the constraints set by the infant's body and environment. Nature and nurture, the infant and the environment, are all working together as part of an ever-changing system (Adolph & Joh, 2007, 2008).

Esther Thelen is shown conducting an experiment to discover how infants learn to control their arms to reach and grasp for objects. A computer device is used to monitor the infant's arm movements and to track muscle patterns. Thelen's research is conducted from a dynamic systems perspective. *What is the nature of this perspective?*

As we examine the course of motor development, we will describe how dynamic systems theory applies to some specific skills. First, though, let's examine how the story of motor development begins with reflexes.

Reflexes

The newborn is not completely helpless. Among other things, the newborn has some basic reflexes. *Reflexes* are built-in reactions to stimuli, and they govern the newborn's movements. Reflexes are genetically carried survival mechanisms which are automatic and involuntary. They allow infants to respond adaptively to their environment before they have had the opportunity to learn. For example, if immersed in water, the newborn automatically holds its breath and contracts its throat to keep water out.

Other important examples are the rooting and sucking reflexes. Both have survival value for newborn mammals, who must find a mother's breast to obtain nourishment. The *rooting reflex* occurs when the infant's cheek is stroked or the side of the mouth is touched. In response, the infant turns its head toward the side that was touched in an apparent effort to find something to suck. The *sucking reflex* occurs when newborns automatically suck an object placed in their mouth. This reflex enables newborns to get nourishment before they have associated a nipple with food.

Another example is the *Moro reflex*, which occurs in response to a sudden, intense noise or movement. When startled, the newborn arches its back, throws back its head, and flings out its arms and legs. Then the newborn rapidly closes its arms and legs. The Moro reflex is believed to be a way of grabbing for support while falling; it would have had survival value for our primate ancestors. An overview of the reflexes we have discussed, along with others, is presented in Figure 3.8.

Reflex	Stimulation	Infant's Response	Developmental Pattern
Blinking	Flash of light, puff of air	Closes both eyes	Permanent
Babinski	Sole of foot stroked	Fans out toes, twists foot in	Disappears after 9 months to 1 year
Grasping	Palms touched	Grasps tightly	Weakens after 3 months, disappears after 1 year
Moro (startle)	Sudden stimulation, such as hearing loud noise or being dropped	Startles, arches back, throws head back, flings out arms and legs and then rapidly closes them to center of body	Disappears after 3 to 4 months
Rooting	Cheek stroked or side of mouth touched	Turns head, opens mouth, begins sucking	Disappears after 3 to 4 months
Stepping	Infant held above surface and feet lowered to touch surface	Moves feet as if to walk	Disappears after 3 to 4 months
Sucking	Object touching mouth	Sucks automatically	Disappears after 3 to 4 months
Swimming	Infant put face down in water	Makes coordinated swimming movements	Disappears after 6 to 7 months
Tonic neck	Infant placed on back	Forms fists with both hands and usually turns head to the right (sometimes called the "fencer's pose" because the infant looks like it is assuming a fencer's position)	Disappears after 2 months

Figure 3.8 Infant Reflexes
This chart describes some of the infant's reflexes

Some reflexes—coughing, sneezing, blinking, shivering, and yawning, for example—persist throughout life. They are as important for the adult as they are for the infant. Other reflexes, though, disappear several months after birth, as the infant's brain matures, and voluntary control over many behaviors develops. The rooting, sucking, and Moro reflexes, for example, all tend to disappear when the infant is 3 to 4 months old.

The movements of some reflexes eventually become incorporated into more complex, voluntary actions. One important example is the *grasping reflex,* which occurs when something touches the infant's palm. The infant responds by grasping tightly. By the end of the third month, the grasping reflex diminishes, and the infant shows a more voluntary grasp. For example, when an infant sees a mobile turning slowly above a crib, it may reach out and try to grasp it. As its motor development becomes smoother, the infant will grasp objects, carefully manipulate them, and explore their qualities.

gross motor skills Motor skills that involve large-muscle activities, such as walking.

Newly crawling infant

Gross Motor Skills

Gross motor skills are skills that involve large-muscle activities, such as moving one's arms and walking. Newborn infants cannot voluntarily control their posture. Within a few weeks, though, they can hold their heads erect, and soon they can lift their heads while prone. By 2 months of age, babies can sit while supported on a lap or an infant seat, but they cannot sit independently until they are 6 or 7 months of age. Standing also develops gradually during the first year of life. By about 8 months of age, infants usually learn to pull themselves up and hold on to a chair, and by about 10 to 12 months of age they can often stand alone.

Locomotion and postural control are closely linked, especially in walking upright (Adolph & Joh, 2007, 2008). To walk upright, the baby must be able both to balance on one leg as the other is swung forward and to shift the weight from one leg to the other (Thelen & Smith, 2006).

Infants must also learn what kinds of places and surfaces are safe for crawling or walking (Adolph & Berger, 2006). Karen Adolph (1997) investigated how experienced and inexperienced crawling infants and walking infants go down steep slopes (see Figure 3.9). Newly crawling infants, who averaged about $8^{1}/_{2}$ months in age, rather indiscriminately went down the steep slopes, often falling in the process (with their mothers next to the slope to catch them). After weeks of practice, the crawling babies became more adept at judging which slopes were too steep to crawl down and which ones they could navigate safely.

You might expect that babies who learned that a slope was too steep for crawling would know when they began

Experienced walker

Figure 3.9 The Role of Experience in Crawling and Walking Infants' Judgments of Whether to Go Down a Slope Karen Adolph (1997) found that locomotor experience rather than age was the primary predictor of adaptive responding on slopes of varying steepness. Newly crawling and walking infants could not judge the safety of the various slopes. With experience, they learned to avoid slopes where they would fall. When expert crawlers began to walk, they again made mistakes and fell, even though they had judged the same slope accurately when crawling. Adolph referred to this as the *specificity of learning* because it does not transfer across crawling and walking.

walking whether a slope was safe. But Adolph's research indicated that newly walking infants could not judge the safety of the slopes. Only when infants became experienced walkers were they able to accurately match their skills with the steepness of the slopes. They rarely fell downhill, either refusing to go down the steep slopes or going down backward in a cautious manner. Experienced walkers perceptually assessed the situation—looking, swaying, touching, and thinking before they moved down the slope. With experience, both the crawlers and the walkers learned to avoid the risky slopes where they would fall, integrating perceptual information with the development of a new motor behavior. In this research, we again see the importance of perceptual-motor coupling in the development of motor skills.

The First Year: Milestones and Variations

Figure 3.10 summarizes important accomplishments in gross motor skills during the first year, culminating in the ability to walk easily. The timing of these milestones, especially the later ones, may vary by as much as two to four months, and experiences can modify the onset of these accomplishments. For example, since 1992, when pediatricians began recommending that parents put their infants to sleep on their backs, fewer babies crawl and the age of onset of crawling is later (Davis & others, 1998). Moreover, some infants do not follow

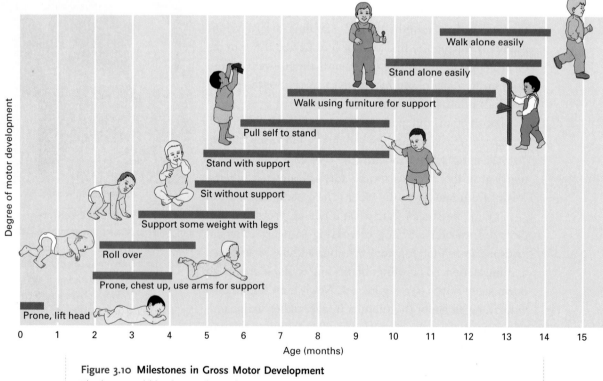

Figure 3.10 Milestones in Gross Motor Development
The horizontal blue bars indicate the range in which most infants reach various milestones in gross motor development.

the standard sequence of motor accomplishments. For example, many American infants never crawl on their belly or on their hands and knees. They may discover an idiosyncratic form of locomotion before walking such as rolling, or they might never locomote until they get upright (Adolph, 2002). In the African Mali tribe, most infants do not crawl (Bril, 1999).

fine motor skills Motor skills that involve more finely tuned movements, such as finger dexterity.

According to Karen Adolph and Sarah Berger (2005), "The old-fashioned view that growth and motor development reflect merely the age-related output of maturation is, at best, incomplete. Rather, infants acquire new skills with the help of their caregivers in a real-world environment of objects, surfaces, and planes" (p. 273).

Development in the Second Year

The motor accomplishments of the first year bring increasing independence, allowing infants to explore their environment more extensively and to initiate interaction with others more readily. In the second year of life, toddlers become more mobile as their motor skills are honed. Child development experts believe that motor activity during the second year is vital to the child's competent development and that few restrictions, except for safety, should be placed on their adventures (Fraiberg, 1959).

By 13 to 18 months, toddlers can pull a toy attached to a string and use their hands and legs to climb up a number of steps. By 18 to 24 months, toddlers can walk quickly or run stiffly for a short distance, balance on their feet in a squatting position while playing with objects on the floor, walk backward without losing their balance, stand and kick a ball without falling, stand and throw a ball, and jump in place.

Fine Motor Skills

Whereas gross motor skills involve large muscle activity, **fine motor skills** involve finely tuned movements. Grasping a toy, using a spoon, buttoning a shirt, or anything that requires finger dexterity demonstrates fine motor skills. At birth, infants have very little control over fine motor skills, but they do have many components of what will become finely coordinated arm, hand, and finger movements.

The onset of reaching and grasping marks a significant achievement in infants' ability to interact with their surroundings (Rocha, Silva, & Tudella, 2006). During the first two years of life, infants refine how they reach and grasp. Initially, infants reach by moving their shoulders and elbows crudely, swinging toward an object. Later, when infants reach for an object they move their wrists, rotate their hands, and coordinate their thumb and forefinger. Infants do not have to see their own hands in order to reach for an object (Clifton & others, 1993); rather, their reaching is guided by cues from muscles, tendons, and joints.

Perceptual-motor coupling is necessary for the infant to coordinate grasping (Keen, 2005). Which perceptual system the infant is most likely to use in coordinating grasping varies with age. Whereas 4-month-old infants rely greatly on touch

How Would You...?
As a human development and family studies professional, how would you advise parents who are concerned that their infant is one or two months behind the average gross motor milestones?

MOTOR DEVELOPMENT

sensation The product of the interaction between information and the sensory receptors—the eyes, ears, tongue, nostrils, and skin.

to determine how they will grip an object, whereas 8-month-olds are more likely to use vision as a guide (Newell & others, 1989). This developmental change is efficient because vision lets infants preshape their hands as they reach for an object.

Experience plays a role in reaching and grasping (Needham, 2008). In one recent study, 3-month-old infants participated in play sessions wearing "sticky mittens"—"mittens with palms that stuck to the edges of toys and allowed the infants to pick up the toys" (Needham, Barrett, & Peterman, 2002, p. 279) (see Figure 3.11). Infants who participated in sessions with the mittens grasped and manipulated objects earlier in their development than a control group of infants who did not receive the "mitten" experience. The experienced infants looked at the objects longer, swatted at them more during visual contact, and were more likely to mouth the objects.

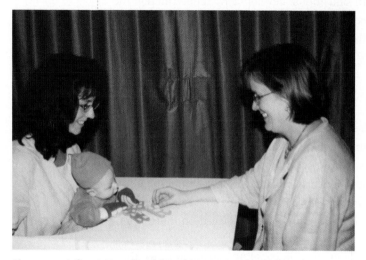

Figure 3.11 Infants' Use of "Sticky Mittens" to Explore Objects
Amy Needham and her colleagues (2002) found that "sticky mittens" enhanced young infants' object exploration skills.

Just as infants need to exercise their gross motor skills, they also need to exercise their fine motor skills (Barrett, Davis, & Needham, 2007; Needham, 2008). Especially when they can manage a pincer grip, infants delight in picking up small objects. Many develop the pincer grip and begin to crawl at about the same time, and infants at this time pick up virtually everything in sight, especially on the floor, and put the objects in their mouth. Thus, parents need to be vigilant in regularly monitoring what objects are within the infant's reach.

Sensory and Perceptual Development

Can a newborn see? If so, what can it perceive? How do sensations and perceptions develop? Can an infant put together information from two modalities, such as sight and sound? These are among the intriguing questions that we explore in this section.

Exploring Sensory and Perceptual Development

How does a newborn know that her mother's skin is soft rather than rough? How does a 5-year-old know what color his hair is? Infants and children "know" these things as a result of information that comes through the senses.

Sensation occurs when information interacts with sensory *receptors*—the eyes, ears, tongue, nostrils, and skin. The sensation of hearing occurs when waves of pulsating air are collected by the outer ear and transmitted through the bones of the inner ear to the auditory nerve. The sensation of vision occurs as rays of light contact the eyes, become focused on the retina, and are transmitted by the optic nerve to the visual centers of the brain.

Perception is the interpretation of what is sensed. The air waves that contact the ears might be interpreted as noise or as musical sounds, for example. The physical energy transmitted to the retina of the eye might be interpreted as a particular color, pattern, or shape, depending on how it is perceived.

The Ecological View

For the past several decades, much of the research on perceptual development in infancy has been guided by the ecological view of Eleanor and James J. Gibson (E. Gibson, 1969, 1989, 2001; J. Gibson, 1966, 1979). They argue that we do not have to take bits and pieces of data from sensations and build up representations of the world in our minds. Instead, our perceptual system can select from the rich information that the environment itself provides.

According to the Gibsons' **ecological view**, we directly perceive information that exists in the world around us. Perception brings us into contact with the environment in order to interact with and adapt to it. Perception is designed for action. Perception gives people such information as when to duck, when to turn their bodies through a narrow passageway, and when to put their hands up to catch something.

Studying the Infant's Perception

Studying the infant's perception is not an easy task. Unlike most research participants, infants cannot write, type on a computer keyboard, or speak well enough to explain to an experimenter what their responses are to a given stimulus or condition. Yet scientists have developed several ingenious research methods to examine infants' sensory and perceptual development (Bendersky & Sullivan, 2007; Slater & Lewis, 2007).

Visual Preference Method Robert Fantz (1963), a pioneer in this effort, made an important discovery: Infants look at different things for different lengths of time. Fantz placed infants in a "looking chamber," which had two visual displays on the ceiling above the infant's head. An experimenter viewed the infant's eyes by looking through a peephole. If the infant was gazing at one of the displays, the experimenter could see the display's reflection in the infant's eyes. This allowed the experimenter to determine how long the infant looked at each display. Fantz (1963) found that infants only 2 days old would gaze longer at patterned stimuli (such as faces or concentric circles) than at red, white, or yellow discs. Similar results were found with infants 2 to 3 weeks old (see Figure 3.12). Fantz's research method—studying whether infants can distinguish one stimulus from another by measuring the length of time they attend to different stimuli—is referred to as the **visual preference method.**

Habituation and Dishabituation Another way that researchers have studied infant perception is to present a stimulus (such as a sight or a sound) a number of times. If the infant decreases its response to the stimulus after several presentations, it indicates that the infant is no longer interested in the stimulus. If the researcher now presents a new stimulus, the infant's response will recover—indicating the infant could discriminate between the old and new stimulus.

perception The interpretation of what is sensed.

ecological view The view that perception functions to bring us into contact with the environment and to increase adaptation.

visual preference method A method used to determine whether infants can distinguish one stimulus from another by measuring the length of time they attend to different stimuli. A-not-B error (AB error) occurs when infants make the mistake of selecting the familiar hiding place (A) rather than the new hiding place (not B) as they progress into substage 4 in Piaget's sensorimotor stage.

habituation Decreased responsiveness to a stimulus after repeated presentations of the stimulus.

dishabituation Recovery of a habituated response after a change in stimulation.

Habituation is the name given to decreased responsiveness to a stimulus after repeated presentations of the stimulus. **Dishabituation** is the recovery of a habituated response after a change in stimulation. Newborn infants can habituate to repeated sights, sounds, smells, or touches (Rovee-Collier, 2002). Among the measures researchers use in habituation studies are sucking behavior (sucking behavior stops when the young infant attends to a novel object), heart and respiration rates, and the length of time the infant looks at an object.

Other Methods To assess an infant's attention to sound, researchers often use a method called *high-amplitude sucking*. In this method, infants are given a nonnutritive nipple to suck and the nipple is connected to

> a sound generating system. Each suck causes a noise to be generated and the infant learns quickly that sucking brings about this noise. At first, babies suck frequently, so the noise occurs often. Then, gradually, they lose interest in hearing repetitions of the same noise and begin to suck less frequently. At this point, the experimenter changes the sound that is being generated. If the babies renew vigorous sucking, we infer that they have discriminated the sound change and are sucking more because they want to hear the interesting new sound. (Menn & Stoel-Gammon, 2005, p. 71)

To determine if an infant can see or hear a stimulus, researchers might look for the *orienting response,* which involves turning one's head toward a sight or sound (Keen, 2005). Another technique to determine what an infant can see is to monitor the infant's *tracking,* which consists of eye movements that follow (*track*) a moving object.

Technology can facilitate the use of most methods for investigating the infant's perceptual abilities. Videotape equipment allows researchers to investigate elusive

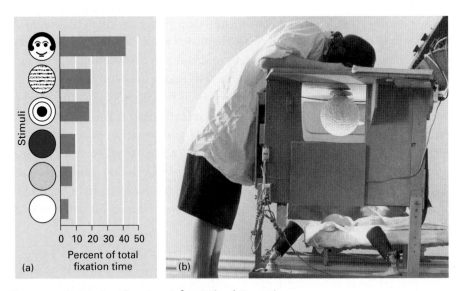

Figure 3.12 Fantz's Experiment on Infants' Visual Perception
(*a*) Infants 2 to 3 weeks old preferred to look at some stimuli more than others. In Fantz's experiment, infants preferred to look at patterns rather than at color or brightness. For example, they looked longer at a face, a piece of printed matter, or a bull's-eye than at red, yellow, or white discs. (*b*) Fantz used a "looking chamber" to study infants' perception of stimuli.

behaviors. High-speed computers make it possible to perform complex data analysis in minutes. Other equipment records respiration, heart rate, body movement, visual fixation, and sucking behavior, which provide clues to what the infant is perceiving. For example, some researchers use equipment that detects if a change in infants' respiration follows a change in the pitch of a sound. If so, it suggests that the infants heard the pitch change. Thus, scientists have become ingenious at assessing the development of infants, discovering ways to "interview" them even though they cannot yet talk.

Visual Perception

Psychologist William James (1890/1950) called the newborn's perceptual world a "blooming, buzzing confusion." A century later, we can safely say that he was wrong (Slater, Field, & Hernandez-Reif, 2007). Even the newborn perceives a world with some order.

Visual Acuity and Color

Just how well can infants see? The newborn's vision is estimated to be 20/600 on the well-known Snellen eye examination chart (Banks & Salapatek, 1983). This means that an object 20 feet away is only as clear to the newborn's eyes as it would be if it were viewed from a distance of 600 feet by an adult with normal vision (20/20). By 6 months of age, though, vision is 20/100 or better, and, by about the first birthday, the infant's vision approximates that of an adult (Banks & Salapatek, 1983). Figure 3.13 shows a computer estimation of what a picture of a face looks like to an infant at different ages from a distance of about 6 inches.

1 month

The infant's color vision also improves. At birth, babies can distinguish between green and red (Adams, 1989). All of the eye's color-sensitive receptors (*cones*) function by 2 months of age.

3 months

Perceiving Patterns

Do infants recognize patterns? As we discussed earlier, Fantz (1963) found that even 2- to 3-week-old infants prefer to look at patterned displays rather than non-patterned displays. For example, they prefer to look at a normal human face rather than one with scrambled features, and prefer to look at a bull's-eye target or black and white stripes rather than a plain circle.

1 year

Even very young infants soon change the way they gather information from the visual world. Researchers observed this by using a special mirror arrangement that photographed infants' eye movements while they viewed a projected image of human faces (Maurer & Salapatek, 1976). The 2-month-old infant scanned much more of the face than the 1-month-old, and the 2-month-old spent more time examining the internal details of the face. Thus, the 2-month-old gained more information about the world than the 1-month-old.

Figure 3.13 Visual Acuity During the First Months of Life The three photographs represent a computer estimation of what a picture of a face looks like to a 1-month-old, a 3-month-old, and 1-year-old (which approximates that of an adult).

Depth Perception

To investigate whether infants have depth perception, Eleanor Gibson and Richard Walk (1960) constructed a miniature cliff with a drop-off covered by glass. They placed 6- to 12-month-old infants on the edge of this visual cliff and had their

Figure 3.14 Examining Infants' Depth Perception on the Visual Cliff Eleanor Gibson and Richard Walk (1960) found that most infants would not crawl out on the glass, which indicated that they had depth perception.

mothers coax them to crawl onto the glass (see Figure 3.14). Most infants would not crawl out on the glass, choosing instead to remain on the shallow side, an indication that they could perceive depth. Although researchers do not know exactly how early in life infants can perceive depth, they have found that infants develop the ability to use binocular (two-eyed) cues to depth by about 3 to 4 months of age.

Other Senses

Other sensory systems besides vision also develop during infancy. We explore development in hearing, touch and pain, smell, and taste.

Hearing

During the last two months of pregnancy, as the fetus nestles in its mother's womb, it can hear sounds such as the mother's voice, music, and so on (Kisilevsky & others, 2005; Smith, Muir, & Kisilevsky, 2001). In one study, researchers had sixteen women read *The Cat in the Hat* aloud to their fetuses during the last months of pregnancy (DeCasper & Spence, 1986). Then, shortly after their babies were born, the mothers read aloud either *The Cat in the Hat* or a story with a different rhyme and pace, *The King, the Mice and the Cheese* (which had not been read during prenatal development). The infants sucked on a nipple in a different way when the mothers read the two stories, suggesting that the infants recognized the pattern and tone of *The Cat in the Hat* (see Figure 3.15).

Newborns are especially sensitive to human speech sounds (Saffran, Werker, & Warner, 2006). Just a few days after birth, newborns will turn to the sound of a familiar caregiver's voice.

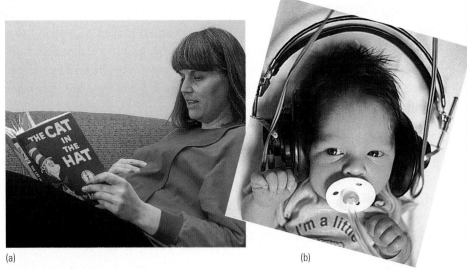

(a) (b)

Figure 3.15 Hearing in the Womb
(a) Pregnant mothers read *The Cat in the Hat* to their fetuses during the last few months of pregnancy. (b) When they were born, the babies preferred listening to a recording of their mothers reading *The Cat in the Hat*, as evidenced by their sucking on a nipple that produced this recording, rather than another story, *The King, the Mice and the Cheese*.

What changes in hearing take place during infancy? They involve perception of a sound's loudness, pitch, and localization: (1) Immediately after birth, infants cannot hear soft sounds quite as well as adults can; a stimulus must be louder for the newborn to hear it (Trehub & others, 1991). (2) Infants are also less sensitive to the pitch of a sound than adults are. *Pitch* is the frequency of a sound; a soprano voice sounds high pitched, a bass voice low pitched. Infants are less sensitive to low-pitched sounds and are more likely to hear high-pitched sounds (Aslin, Jusczyk, & Pisoni, 1998). By 2 years of age, infants have considerably improved their ability to distinguish sounds with different pitches. (3) Even newborns can determine the general location from where a sound is coming, but by 6 months of age, they are more proficient at *localizing* sounds, detecting their origins. The ability to localize sounds continues to improve in the second year (Saffran, Werker, & Warner, 2006).

Touch and Pain

Newborns respond to touch. A touch to the cheek produces a turning of the head; a touch to the lips produces sucking movements. Newborns can also feel pain (Gunnar & Quevado, 2007). The issue of an infant's pain perception often becomes important to parents who give birth to a son and need to consider whether he should be circumcised (Gunnar & Quevedo, 2007). An investigation by Megan Gunnar and her colleagues (1987) found that although newborn infant males cry intensely during circumcision, they also display amazing resiliency. Within several minutes after the surgery (which is performed without anesthesia), they can nurse and interact in a normal manner with their mothers.

Smell

Newborns can differentiate odors (Delaunay-El Allam, Marlier, & Schaal, 2006). The expressions on their faces indicate that they like the scents of vanilla and strawberry but do not like the scent of rotten eggs or fish (Steiner, 1979). In one investigation, 6-day-old infants who were breast fed showed a clear preference for smelling their mother's breast pad rather than a clean breast pad (MacFarlane, 1975) (see Figure 3.16). However, when they were 2 days old, they did not show this preference, indicating that they require several days of experience to recognize this scent.

Taste

Sensitivity to taste might be present even before birth. In one very early experiment, when saccharin was added to the amniotic fluid of a near-term fetus, swallowing increased (Windle, 1940). In another study, even at only 2 hours of age, babies made different facial expressions when they tasted sweet, sour, and bitter solutions (Rosenstein & Oster, 1988) (see Figure 3.17). At about 4 months of age, infants begin to prefer salty tastes, which as newborns they had found to be aversive (Harris, Thomas, & Booth, 1990).

Figure 3.16 Newborns' Preference for the Smell of Their Mother's Breast Pad In the experiment by MacFarlane (1975), 6-day-old infants preferred to smell their mother's breast pad rather than a clean one that had never been used, but 2-day-old infants did not show the preference, indicating that this odor preference requires several days of experience to develop.

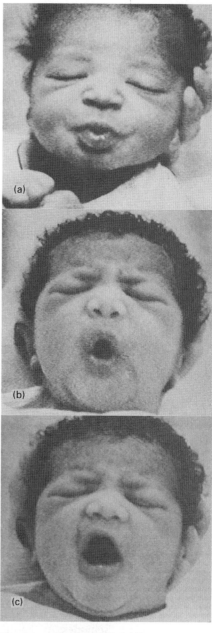

(a)

(b)

(c)

Figure 3.17 Newborns' Facial Responses to Basic Tastes Facial expressions elicited by (a) a sweet solution, (b) a sour solution, and (c) a bitter solution.

intermodal perception The ability to relate and integrate information from two or more sensory modalities, such as vision and hearing.

schemes In Piaget's theory, actions or mental representations that organize knowledge.

Intermodal Perception

Imagine yourself playing basketball or tennis. You are experiencing many visual inputs: the ball coming and going, other players moving around, and so on. However, you are experiencing many auditory inputs as well: the sound of the ball bouncing or being hit, the grunts and groans, and so on. There is good correspondence between much of the visual and auditory information: When you see the ball bounce, you hear a bouncing sound; when a player stretches to hit a ball, you hear a groan. When you look at and listen to what is going on, you do not experience just the sounds or just the sights; you put all these things together. You experience a unitary episode. This is **intermodal perception**, which involves integrating information from two or more sensory modalities, such as vision and hearing.

A basic form of intermodal perception exists even in newborns (Chen, Striano, & Rakozczy, 2004). For example, newborns turn their eyes and their head toward the sound of a voice or rattle when the sound is maintained for several seconds (Clifton & others, 1993). Intermodal perception becomes sharpened with experience in the first year of life (Bahrick & Hollich, 2008). In the first six months, infants have difficulty connecting sensory input from different modes (such as vision and sound), but in the second half of the first year they show an increased ability to make this connection mentally.

Cognitive Development

The competent infant not only develops motor and perceptual skills, but also develops cognitive skills. Our coverage of cognitive development in infancy focuses on Piaget's theory and sensorimotor stage as well as how infants learn, remember, and conceptualize.

Piaget's Theory

Piaget's theory is a general, unifying story of how biology and experience sculpt cognitive development. Piaget thought that, just as our physical bodies have structures that enable us to adapt to the world, we build mental structures that help us to adapt to the world. *Adaptation* involves adjusting to new environmental demands. Piaget stressed that children actively construct their own cognitive worlds; information is not just poured into their minds from the environment. He sought to discover how children at different points in their development think about the world and how systematic changes in their thinking occur.

Processes of Development

What processes do children use as they construct their knowledge of the world? Piaget developed several concepts to answer this question.

Schemes As the infant or child seeks to construct an understanding of the world, said Piaget (1954), the developing brain creates **schemes**. These are actions or mental representations that organize knowledge. In Piaget's theory, infants create behavioral schemes (physical activities) whereas toddlers and older children create mental schemes (cognitive activities) (Lamb, Bornstein, & Teti, 2002). A baby's schemes are structured by simple actions that can be performed on objects such as sucking, looking, and grasping. Older children's schemes include strategies and plans for solving problems.

Assimilation and Accommodation To explain how children use and adapt their schemes, Piaget offered two concepts: assimilation and accommodation. **Assimilation** occurs when children use their existing schemes to deal with new information or experiences. **Accommodation** occurs when children adjust their schemes to take new information and experiences into account.

Think about a toddler who has learned the word *car* to identify the family's car. The toddler might call all moving vehicles on roads "cars," including motorcycles and trucks; the child has assimilated these objects to his or her existing scheme. But the child soon learns that motorcycles and trucks are not cars and fine-tunes the category to exclude motorcycles and trucks. The child has then accommodated the scheme.

Organization To make sense out of their world, said Piaget, children cognitively organize their experiences. **Organization** in Piaget's theory is the grouping of isolated behaviors and thoughts into a higher-order system. Continual refinement of this organization is an inherent part of development. A child who has only a vague idea about how to use a hammer may also have a vague idea about how to use other tools. After learning how to use each one, she relates these uses, organizing her knowledge.

Equilibration and Stages of Development Assimilation and accommodation always take the child to a higher ground, according to Piaget. In trying to understand the world, the child inevitably experiences cognitive conflict, or *disequilibrium*. That is, the child is constantly faced with inconsistencies and counterexamples to his or her existing schemes. For example, if a child believes that pouring water from a short and wide container into a tall and narrow container changes the amount of water, then the child might be puzzled by where the "extra" water came from and whether there is actually more water to drink. The puzzle creates disequilibrium; for Piaget, an internal search for equilibrium creates motivation for change. The child assimilates and accommodates, adjusting old schemes, developing new schemes, and organizing and reorganizing the old and new schemes. Eventually, the organization is fundamentally different from the old organization; it becomes a new way of thinking. **Equilibration** is the name Piaget gave to this mechanism by which children shift from one stage of thought to the next. Equilibration does not, however, happen all at once. There is considerable movement between states of cognitive equilibrium and disequilibrium as assimilation and accommodation work in concert to produce cognitive change.

A result of these processes, according to Piaget, is that individuals go through four stages of development. A different way of understanding the world makes one stage more advanced than another. Cognition is *qualitatively* different in one stage compared with another. In other words, the way children reason at one stage is different from the way they reason at another stage. Here our focus is on Piaget's stage of infant cognitive development. In Chapters 5, 7, and 9, we explore the last three Piagetian stages.

assimilation Piagetian concept of the incorporation of new information into existing schemes

accommodation Piagetian concept of adjusting schemes to fit new information and experiences.

organization Piaget's concept of grouping isolated behaviors into a higher-order, more smoothly functioning cognitive system.

equilibration A mechanism that Piaget proposed to explain how children shift from one stage of thought to the next.

Sensorimotor Stage

The **sensorimotor stage** lasts from birth to about age 2. In this stage, infants construct an understanding of the world by coordinating sensory experiences (such as seeing and hearing) with physical, motoric actions—hence the term "sensorimotor." At the beginning of this stage, newborns have little more than reflexes with which to work. At the end of the sensorimotor stage, 2-year-olds can produce complex sensorimotor patterns and use primitive symbols. We first summarize Piaget's descriptions of how infants develop. Later we consider criticisms of his view.

Substages Piaget divided the sensorimotor stage into six substages: (1) simple reflexes; (2) first habits and primary circular reactions; (3) secondary circular reactions; (4) coordination of secondary circular reactions; (5) tertiary circular reactions, novelty, and curiosity; and (6) internalization of schemes.

The first sensorimotor substage, *simple reflexes*, corresponds to the reflexes we discussed earlier that are present in newborns. In this substage, sensation and action are coordinated primarily through reflexive behaviors, such as rooting and sucking. Soon the infant produces behaviors that resemble reflexes in the absence of the usual stimulus for the reflex. For example, a newborn will reflexively suck a nipple only when it is placed directly in the baby's mouth or touched to the lips. But soon the infant might also make sucking motions with the mouth at the sight of a bottle or nipple nearby.

First habits and primary circular reactions is the second sensorimotor substage, which develops between 1 and 4 months of age. In this substage, the infant coordinates sensation and two types of schemes: habits and primary circular reactions. A *habit* is a scheme based on a reflex that has become completely separated from its eliciting stimulus. For example, infants in substage 1 suck when bottles are put to their lips or when they see a bottle. Infants in substage 2 might suck even when no bottle is present. A *circular reaction* is a repetitive action.

A *primary circular reaction* is a scheme based on the attempt to reproduce an event that initially occurred by chance. For example, suppose an infant accidentally sucks his fingers when they are placed near his mouth. Later, he searches for his fingers to suck them again, but the fingers do not cooperate because the infant cannot coordinate visual and manual actions.

Habits and circular reactions are stereotyped—that is, the infant repeats them the same way each time. During this substage, the infant's own body remains the infant's center of attention. There is no outward pull by environmental events.

Secondary circular reactions is the third sensorimotor substage, which develops between 4 and 8 months of age. In this substage, the infant becomes more object-oriented, moving beyond preoccupation with the self. The infant's schemes are not intentional or goal-directed, but they are repeated because of their consequences. By chance, an infant might shake a rattle and produce a sound. The infant repeats this action for the sake of its fascination with the sound. This is a *secondary circular reaction:* an action repeated because of its consequences. The infant also imitates some simple actions, such as the baby talk or burbling of adults, and some physical gestures. However, the baby imitates only actions that he or she is already able to produce.

Coordination of secondary circular reactions is Piaget's fourth sensorimotor substage, which develops between 8 and 12 months of age. To progress into this substage the infant must coordinate vision and touch, eye and hand. Actions become more outwardly directed. Significant changes during this sub-stage involve the coordination of schemes and intentionality. Infants readily combine and recombine previously learned schemes in a coordinated way. They might look at an object and grasp it simultaneously, or they might visually inspect a toy, such as a rattle, and finger it simultaneously, exploring it tactilely. Actions are even more outwardly directed than before. Related to this coordination is the second achievement—the presence of intentionality. For example, infants might manipulate a stick in order to bring a desired toy within reach or they might knock over one block in order to reach and play with another one.

Tertiary circular reactions, novelty, and curiosity is Piaget's fifth sensorimotor substage, which develops between 12 and 18 months of age. In this substage, infants become intrigued by the many properties of objects and by the many things that they can make happen to objects. A block can be made to fall, spin, hit another object, and slide across the ground. *Tertiary circular reactions* are schemes in which the infant purposely explores new possibilities with objects, continually doing new things to them and exploring the results. Piaget says that this stage marks the starting point for human curiosity and interest in novelty.

Internalization of schemes is Piaget's sixth and final sensorimotor substage, which develops between 18 and 24 months of age. In this substage, the infant develops the ability to use primitive symbols. For Piaget, a *symbol* is an internalized sensory image or word that represents an event. Primitive symbols permit the infant to think about concrete events without directly acting them out or perceiving them. Moreover, symbols allow the infant to manipulate and transform the represented events in simple ways. In a favorite Piagetian example, Piaget's young daughter saw a matchbox being opened and closed. Later, she mimicked the matchbox by opening and closing her mouth, indicating that she had internalized the event. This was an obvious expression of her image of the event.

Object Permanence Object permanence is the understanding that objects continue to exist even when they cannot be seen, heard, or touched. Acquiring the sense of object permanence is one of the infant's most important accomplishments, according to Piaget.

How could anyone know whether or not an infant had a sense of object permanence? The principal way that object permanence is studied is by watching an infant's reaction when an interesting object disappears (see Figure 3.18). If infants search for the object, it is inferred that they know it continues to exist.

Evaluating Piaget's Sensorimotor Stage Piaget opened up a new way of looking at infants with his view that their main task is to coordinate their sensory impressions with their motor activity. However, the infant's cognitive world is not as neatly packaged as Piaget portrayed it, and some of Piaget's explanations for the cause of change are debated. In the past several decades, there have been many research studies on infant development using sophisticated experimental techniques. Much of the new research suggests that Piaget's view of sensorimotor development needs to be modified.

One modification concerns Piaget's claim that certain processes are crucial in stage transitions. The data do not always support his explanations. For example, in Piaget's theory, an important feature in the progression into substage 4 is an infant's inclination to search for a hidden object in a familiar location rather than

Figure 3.18 Object Permanence
Piaget argued that object permanence is one of infancy's landmark cognitive accomplishments. For this 5-month-old boy, "out of sight" is literally out of mind. The infant looks at the toy monkey *(top)*, but, when his view of the toy is blocked *(bottom)*, he does not search for it. Several months later, he will search for the hidden toy monkey, reflecting the presence of object permanence.

to look for the object in a new location. For example, if a toy is hidden twice, initially at location A and subsequently at location B, 8- to 12-month-old infants search correctly at location A initially. But when the toy is subsequently hidden at location B, they make the mistake of continuing to search for it at location A. **A-not-B error** (also called A$\overline{B}$ error) is the term used to describe this common mistake. Older infants are less likely to make the A-not-B error because their concept of object permanence is more complete.

Researchers have found, however, that the A-not-B error does not show up consistently (Sophian, 1985). The evidence indicates that A-not-B errors are sensitive to the delay between hiding the object at B and the infant's attempt to find it (Diamond, 1985). Thus, the A-not-B error might be due to a failure in memory. Another explanation is that infants tend to repeat a previous motor behavior (Clearfield & others, 2006).

A number of theorists, such as Eleanor Gibson (1989) and Elizabeth Spelke (1991; Spelke & Newport, 1998), conclude that infants' perceptual abilities are highly developed very early in development. For example, intermodal perception—the ability to coordinate information from two more sensory modalities, such as vision and hearing—develops much earlier than Piaget would have predicted (Spelke & Owsley, 1979).

Object permanence also develops earlier than Piaget thought. In his view, object permanence does not develop until approximately 8 to 9 months of age. However, research by Renée Baillargeon and her colleagues (1995, 2004; Aguiar & Baillargeon, 2002) document that infants as young as 3 to 4 months expect objects to be *substantial* (in the sense that other objects cannot move through them) and *permanent* (in the sense that they continue to exist when they are hidden).

Today's researchers believe that infants see objects as bounded, unitary, solid, and separate from their background, possibly at birth or shortly thereafter, but definitely by 3 to 4 months of age, much earlier than Piaget envisioned. Young infants still have much to learn about objects, but the world appears both stable and orderly to them.

Many researchers conclude that Piaget wasn't specific enough about how infants learn about their world and that infants are more competent than Piaget thought (Cohen & Cashon, 2006; Mandler, 2004). As they have examined the specific ways that infants learn, the field of infant cognition has become very specialized. If there is a unifying theme, it is that investigators in infant development seek to understand more precisely how developmental changes in cognition take place.

Learning, Remembering, and Conceptualizing

In Chapter 1, we described the behavioral and social cognitive theories, as well as information-processing theory. These theories emphasize that cognitive development does not unfold in a stagelike process as Piaget proposed, but rather advances more gradually. In this section we explore what researchers using these approaches can tell us about how infants learn, remember, and conceptualize.

Conditioning

In Chapter 1, we discussed Skinner's operant conditioning, in which the consequences of a behavior produce changes in the probability of the behavior's occurrence. Infants can learn through operant conditioning: If an infant's behavior is followed by a rewarding stimulus, the behavior is likely to recur.

Operant conditioning has been especially helpful to researchers in their efforts to determine what infants perceive (Kraebel, Fable, & Gerhardstein, 2004). For example, infants will suck faster on a nipple when the sucking behavior is followed by a visual display, music, or a human voice (Rovee-Collier & Barr, 2004).

Carolyn Rovee-Collier (1987) has also demonstrated how infants can retain information from the experience of being conditioned. In a characteristic experiment, Rovee-Collier places a 2¹⁄₂-month-old baby in a crib under an elaborate mobile (see Figure 3.19). She then ties one end of a ribbon to the baby's ankle and the other end to the mobile. Subsequently, she observes that the baby kicks and makes the mobile move. The movement of the mobile is the reinforcing stimulus (which increases the baby's kicking behavior) in this experiment. Weeks later, the baby is returned to the crib, but its foot is not tied to the mobile. The baby kicks, which suggests it has retained the information that if it kicks a leg, the mobile will move.

Attention

Attention, the focusing of mental resources on select information, improves cognitive processing on many tasks. Even newborns can detect a contour and fix their attention on it. Older infants scan patterns more thoroughly (Colombo, 2007). By 4 months of age, infants can selectively attend to an object.

Closely linked with attention are the processes of habituation and dishabituation, which we discussed earlier in this chapter. Infants' attention is strongly governed by novelty and habituation. When an object becomes familiar, attention becomes shorter, making infants more vulnerable to distraction (Oakes, Kannass, & Shaddy, 2002). One recent study found that 10-month-olds were more easily distracted than 26-month-olds (Ruff & Capozzoli, 2003).

Another aspect of attention that is an important aspect of infant development is **joint attention**, in which individuals focus on the same object or event. Joint attention requires (1) an ability to track another's behavior, such as following the gaze of someone; (2) one person directing another's attention, and (3) reciprocal interaction (Butterworth, 2004). Early in infancy, joint attention usually involves a caregiver pointing or using words to direct an infant's attention (LizKowski, 2007). Emerging forms of joint attention occur at about 7 to 8 months, but it is not until 10 to 11 months that joint attention skills are frequently observed (Heimann & others, 2006; Meltzoff & Brooks, 2006). By their first birthday, infants have begun to direct adults' to objects that capture their interest (Heimann & others, 2006).

Joint attention plays important roles in many aspects of infant development and considerably increases infants' ability to learn from other people (Striano, Reid, & Hochl, 2006). Nowhere is this more apparent than in observations of interchanges between caregivers and infants as infants are learning language

attention The focusing of mental resources.

joint attention Occurs when individuals focus on the same object and an ability to track another's behavior is present, one individual directs another's attention, and reciprocal interaction is present.

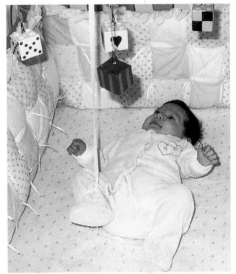

Figure 3.19 The Technique Used in Rovee-Collier's Investigation of Infant Memory
In Rovee-Collier's experiment, operant conditioning was used to demonstrate that infants as young as 2¹⁄₂ months of age can retain information from the experience of being conditioned. *What did infants recall in Rovee-Collier's experiment?*

A mother and her infant daughter engaging in joint attention. *What about this photograph tells you that joint attention is occurring? Why is joint attention an important aspect of infant development?*

How Would You...?
As a human development and family studies professional, what strategies would likely help parents improve an infant's development of attention?

COGNITIVE DEVELOPMENT

99

deferred imitation Imitation that occurs after a delay of hours or days.

memory A central feature of cognitive development, pertaining to all situations in which an individual retains information over time.

implicit memory Memory without conscious recollection; involves skills and routine procedures that are automatically performed.

explicit memory Conscious memory of facts and experiences.

(Poulin-Dubois & Graham, 2007; Tomasello, Carpenter, & LiszKowski, 2007). When caregivers and infants frequently engage in joint attention, infants say their first word earlier and develop a larger vocabulary (Carpenter, Nagell, & Tomasello, 1998; Flom & Pick, 2003).

Imitation

Can infants imitate someone else's emotional expressions? If an adult smiles, will the baby respond with a smile? If an adult protrudes her lower lip, wrinkles her forehead, and frowns, will the baby show a sad face?

Infant development researcher Andrew Meltzoff (2005) has conducted numerous studies of infants' imitative abilities. He sees infants' imitative abilities as biologically based, because infants can imitate a facial expression within the first few days after birth. He also emphasizes that the infant's imitative abilities do not resemble a hardwired response but rather involve flexibility and adaptability. In Meltzoff's observations of infants across the first 72 hours of life, the infants gradually displayed more complete imitation of an adult's facial expression, such as protruding the tongue or opening the mouth wide (see Figure 3.20).

Not all experts on infant development accept Meltzoff's conclusions that newborns are capable of imitation. Some say that these babies were engaging in little more than automatic responses to a stimulus.

Meltzoff (2005) also has studied **deferred imitation**, which occurs after a time delay of hours or days. Piaget held that deferred imitation doesn't occur until about 18 months of age, but Meltzoff's research suggests that it occurs much earlier. In one study, Meltzoff (1988) demonstrated that 9-month-old infants could imitate actions— such as pushing a recessed button in a box, which produced a beeping sound—that they had seen performed 24 hours earlier. Imitative behavior picks up in the second year of life (Fenstermacher & Saudino, 2006). One- to two-year-olds have been observed to acquire as many as one to two new behaviors a day through imitation (Barr & Hayne, 2003).

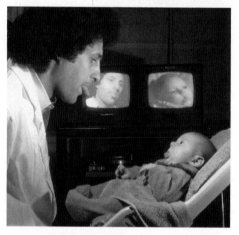

Figure 3.20 Infant Imitation
Infant development researcher Andrew Meltzoff protrudes his tongue in an attempt to get the infant to imitate his behavior. *How do Meltzoff's findings about imitation compare with Piaget's descriptions of infants' abilities?*

Memory

Meltzoff's studies of deferred imitation suggest that infants have another important cognitive ability: **memory**, which involves the retention of information over time. Sometimes information is retained only for a few seconds, and at other times it is retained for a lifetime. What can infants remember, when?

Some researchers such as Rovee-Collier have concluded that infants as young as 2 to 6 months of age can remember some experiences through 1½ to 2 years of age (Rovee-Collier & Barr, 2004, 2007). However, critics such as Jean Mandler (2000), a leading expert on infant cognition, argue that the infants in Rovee-Collier's experiments are displaying only implicit memory. **Implicit memory** refers to memory without conscious recollection—memories of skills and routine procedures that are performed automatically. In contrast, **explicit memory** refers to the conscious memory of facts and experiences.

When people think about memory, they are usually referring to explicit memory. Most researchers find that babies do not show explicit memory until the second half of the first year (Bauer, 2006, 2007). Then, explicit memory improves substantially during the second year of life (Bauer, 2006, 2007). In one longitudinal study, infants were assessed several times during their second year (Bauer & others, 2000). The older infants showed more accurate memory and required fewer prompts to demonstrate their memory than younger infants.

Let's examine another aspect of memory. Do you remember your third birthday party? Probably not. Most adults can remember little if anything from the first 3 years of their life. This is called *infantile* or *childhood amnesia*. The few memories that adults are able to report of their lives at age 2 or 3 are at best very sketchy (Neisser, 2004). Moreover, even by elementary school age, children have lost most memory of their early child years (Lie & Newcombe, 1999; Newcombe, 2007).

What is the cause of infantile amnesia? One reason older children and adults have difficulty recalling events from their infant and early child years is that during these early years the prefrontal lobes of the brain are immature; this area of the brain is believed to play an important role in storing memories for events (Boyer & Diamond, 1992).

In sum, most of young infants' conscious memories appear to be rather fragile and short-lived, although their implicit memory of perceptual-motor actions can be substantial (Bauer, 2006, 2007).

Concept Formation and Categorization

Along with memory, *concepts* are indispensable to competent cognitive development. To understand what concepts are, we first have to define *categories:* they group objects, events, and characteristics on the basis of common properties. Concepts are ideas about what categories represent, or said another way, the sort of thing we think category members are. Concepts and categories help us to simplify and summarize information. Without concepts, you would see each object and event as unique; you would not be able to make any generalizations.

Do infants have concepts? Yes, they do, although we do not know just how early concept formation begins (Mandler, 2004; Quinn, 2007). By about 7 to 9 months of age, infants are able to form *conceptual categories* that are characterized by perceptual variability. For example, in one study of 7- to 11-month-olds, infants correctly classified birds as animals and airplanes as vehicles, even though the objects were perceptually similar—airplanes and birds with their wings spread (Mandler & McDonough, 1993).

Further advances in categorization occur in the second year of life. Many infants' "first concepts are broad and global in nature, such as 'animal' or 'indoor thing.' Gradually, over the first two years these broad concepts become more differentiated into concepts such as 'land animal,' then 'dog,' or to 'furniture,' then 'chair'" (Mandler, 2006, p. 1).

How Would You...?
As an educator, how would you talk with parents about the importance of their infant developing concepts?

language A form of communication, whether spoken, written, or signed, that is based on a system of symbols.

infinite generativity The ability to produce an endless number of meaningful sentences using a finite set of words and rules.

In sum, the infant's advances in processing information—through attention, memory, imitation, and concept formation—is much richer, more gradual and less stagelike, and occurs earlier than was envisioned by earlier theorists, such as Piaget. As leading infant researcher Jean Mandler (2004) concluded, "The human infant shows a remarkable degree of learning power and complexity in what is being learned and in the way it is represented" (p. 304).

Language Development

In 1799, villagers in the French town of Aveyron observed a nude boy running through the woods. The boy was captured and judged to be about 11 years old. Known as the Wild Boy of Aveyron, he was believed to have lived in the woods alone for six years (Lane, 1976). When found, he made no effort to communicate. He never learned to communicate effectively. Sadly, a modern-day wild child named Genie was discovered in Los Angeles in 1970. Despite intensive intervention, Genie has never acquired more than a primitive form of language. Both cases—the Wild Boy of Aveyron and Genie—raise questions about the biological and environmental determinants of language, topics that we also examine later in the chapter. First, though, we need to define language.

Defining Language

Language is a form of communication—whether spoken, written, or signed—that is based on a system of symbols. Language consists of the words used by a community and the rules for varying and combining them. All human languages have some common characteristics such as organizational rules and infinite generativity (Hoff & Shatz, 2007). Rules describe the way the language works; **infinite generativity** is the ability to produce an endless number of meaningful sentences using a finite set of words and rules (Berko Gleason, 2004).

How Language Develops

Whatever language they learn, infants all over the world follow a similar path in language development. What are some key milestones in this development?

Babbling and Gestures

Babies actively produce sounds from birth onward. The effect of these early communications is to attract attention (Lock, 2004). Babies' sounds and gestures go through this sequence during the first year:

1. *Crying.* Babies cry even at birth. Crying can signal distress, but as we will discuss in chapter 4, there are different types of cries that signal different things.

2. *Cooing.* Babies first coo at about 1 to 2 months. These are gurgling sounds that are made in the back of the throat and usually express pleasure during interaction with the caregiver.

3. *Babbling.* In the middle of the first year babies babble—that is, they produce strings of consonant-vowel combinations, such as "ba, ba, ba, ba."

4. *Gestures.* Infants start using gestures, such as showing and pointing, at about 8 to 12 months of age. They may wave bye-bye, nod to mean "yes," and show an empty cup to want more milk.

Recognizing Language Sounds

Long before they begin to learn words, infants can make fine distinctions among the sounds of the language (Menn & Stoel-Gammon, 2005; Stoel-Gammon & Sosa, 2007). In Patricia Kuhl's (1993, 2000; Kuhl & others, 2006) research, *phonemes* (the basic sound units of a language) from languages all over the world are piped through a speaker for infants to hear (see Figure 3.21). A box with a toy bear in it is placed where the infant can see it. A string of identical syllables is played; then the syllables are changed (for example, *ba ba ba ba,* and then *pa pa pa pa*). If the infant turns its head when the syllables change, the box lights up and the bear dances and drums, rewarding the infant for noticing the change.

Kuhl's research has demonstrated that from birth up to about 6 months of age, infants are "citizens of the world": They recognize when sounds change most of the time no matter what language the syllables come from. But over the next six months, infants get even better at perceiving the changes in sounds from their "own" language, the one their parents speak, and gradually lose the ability to recognize differences that are not important in their own language (Kuhl, 2007).

Figure 3.21 From Universal Linguist to Language-Specific Listener

In Patricia Kuhl's research laboratory babies listen to tape-recorded voices that repeat syllables. When the sounds of the syllables change, the babies quickly learn to look at the bear. Using this technique, Kuhl has demonstrated that babies are universal linguists until about 6 months of age, but in the next six months become language-specific listeners. *Does Kuhl's research give support to the view that either "nature" or "nurture" is the source of language acquisition?*

First Words

Between about 8 and 12 months of age, infants often indicate their first understanding of words. The infant's first spoken word is a milestone eagerly anticipated by every parent. This event usually occurs between 10 to 15 months of age and at an average of about 13 months. However, long before babies say their first words, they have been communicating with their parents, often by gesturing and using their own special sounds. The appearance of first words is a continuation of this communication process (Berko Gleason, 2005).

A child's first words include those that name important people (*dada*), familiar animals (*kitty*), vehicles (*car*), toys (*ball*), food (*milk*), body parts (*eye*), clothes (*hat*), household items (*clock*), and greeting terms (*bye*). These were the first words of babies 50 years ago. They are the first words of babies today. Children often express various intentions with their single words, so that "cookie" might mean, "That's a cookie" or "I want a cookie."

On the average, infants understand about 50 words at about 13 months, but they can't say this many words until about 18 months (Menyuk, Liebergott, & Schultz, 1995). Thus, in infancy *receptive vocabulary* (words the child understands) considerably exceeds *spoken vocabulary* (words the child uses).

The infant's spoken vocabulary rapidly increases once the first word is spoken (Houston-Price, Plunkett, & Harris, 2005; Waxman, 2004; Waxman & Lidz, 2006).

Whereas the average 18-month-old can speak about 50 words, a 2-year-old can speak about 200 words. This rapid increase in vocabulary that begins at approximately 18 months is called the *vocabulary spurt* (Bloom, Lifter, & Broughton, 1985).

Like the timing of a child's first word, the timing of the vocabulary spurt varies (Dale & Goodman, 2004). Figure 3.22 shows the range for these two language milestones in 14 children. On average, these children said their first word at 13 months and had a vocabulary spurt at 19 months. However, the ages for the first word of individual children varied from 10 to 17 months and for their vocabulary spurt from 13 to 25 months.

Children sometimes overextend or underextend the meanings of the words they use (Woodward & Markman, 1998). *Overextension* is the tendency to apply a word to objects that are inappropriate for the word's meaning. For example, children at first may say *"dada"* not only for "father" but also for other men, strangers, or boys. With time, overextensions decrease and eventually disappear. *Underextension* is the tendency to apply a word too narrowly; it occurs when children fail to use a word to name a relevant event or object. For example, a child might use the word *boy* to describe a 5-year-old neighbor but not apply the word to a male infant or to a 9-year-old male.

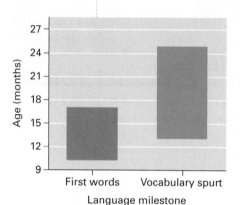

Figure 3.22 Variation in Language Milestones
What are some possible explanations for variations in the timing of these milestones?

Two-Word Utterances

By the time children are 18 to 24 months of age, they usually utter two-word utterances. To convey meaning with just two words, the child relies heavily on gesture, tone, and context. The wealth of meaning children can communicate with a two-word utterance includes the following (Slobin, 1972)—identification— "See doggie"; location—"Book there"; repetition—"More milk"; negation— "Not wolf"; possession—"My candy"; attribution—"Big car"; agent-action— "Mama walk"; action-direct object— "Hit you"; action-indirect object—"Give Papa"; and question—"Where ball?" These examples are from children whose first language is English, German, Russian, Finnish, Turkish, or Samoan.

Notice that the two-word utterances omit many parts of speech and are remarkably succinct. In fact, in every language, a child's first combinations of words have this economical quality; they are telegraphic. **Telegraphic speech** is the use of short and precise words without grammatical markers such as articles, auxiliary verbs, and other connectives. Telegraphic speech is not

Around the world, young children learn to speak in two-word utterances, in most cases, at about 18 to 24 months of age. *What are some examples of these two-word utterances?*

limited to two words; "Mommy give ice cream" and "Mommy give Tommy ice cream" also are examples of telegraphic speech.

Biological and Environmental Influences

We have discussed a number of language milestones in infancy; Figure 3.23 summarizes the time at which infants typically reach these milestones. But what makes this amazing development possible? Everyone who uses language in some way "knows" its rules and has the ability to create an infinite number of words and sentences. Where does this knowledge come from? Is it the product of biology? Is language learned and influenced by experiences?

Typical Age	Language Milestones
Birth	Crying
1 to 2 months	Cooing begins
6 months	Babbling begins
7 to 11 months	Change from universal linguist to language-specific listener
8 to 12 months	Use gestures, such as showing and pointing Comprehension of words appears
13 months	First word spoken
18 months	Vocabulary spurt starts
18 to 24 months	Uses two-word utterances Rapid expansion of understanding of words

Biological Influences

The ability to speak and understand language requires a certain vocal apparatus as well as a nervous system with certain capabilities. The nervous system and vocal apparatus of humanity's predecessors changed over hundreds of thousands, or millions, of years (Fisher & Marcus, 2006). With advances in the nervous system

Figure 3.23 Some Language Milestones in Infancy Despite great variations in the language input received by infants, around the world they follow a similar path in learning to speak.

and vocal structures, *Homo sapiens* went beyond the grunting and shrieking of other animals to develop speech. Although estimates vary, many experts believe that humans acquired language about 100,000 years ago, which in evolutionary time represents a very recent acquisition. It gave humans an enormous edge over other animals and increased the chances of human survival (Lachlan & Feldman, 2003).

Some language scholars view the remarkable similarities in how children acquire language all over the world as strong evidence that language has a biological basis. There is evidence that particular regions of the brain are predisposed to be used for language (Shafer & Garrido-Nag, 2007). Two regions involved in language were first discovered in studies of brain-damaged individuals: *Broca's area,* an area in the left frontal lobe of the brain involved in producing words; and *Wernicke's area,* a region of the brain's left hemisphere involved in language comprehension (see Figure 3.24). Damage to either of these areas produces types of *aphasia,* which is a loss or impairment of language processing. Individuals with damage to Broca's area have difficulty producing speech but can comprehend what others say; individuals with damage to Wernicke's area have poor comprehension and often produce fluent but non-sensical speech.

Linguist Noam Chomsky (1957) proposed that humans are biologically prewired to learn language at a certain time and in a certain way. He said that children are born into the world

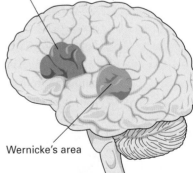

Broca's area

Wernicke's area

Figure 3.24 Broca's Area and Wernicke's Area Broca's area is located in the frontal lobe of the brain's left hemisphere, and it is involved in the control of speech. Wernicke's area is a portion of the left hemisphere's temporal lobe that is involved in understanding language.

with a **language acquisition device (LAD)**, a biological endowment that enables the child to detect the various features and rules of language. Children are prepared by nature with the ability to detect the sounds of language, for example, and follow rules such as how to form plurals and ask questions.

Chomsky's LAD is a theoretical construct, not a physical part of the brain. Is there evidence for the existence of a LAD? Supporters of the LAD concept cite the uniformity of language milestones across languages and cultures, evidence that children create language even in the absence of well-formed input, and biological substrates of language But as we will see, critics argue that even if infants have something like a LAD, it cannot explain the whole story of language acquisition.

Environmental Influences

Decades ago, behaviorists opposed Chomsky's hypothesis and argued that language represents nothing more than chains of responses acquired through reinforcement (Skinner, 1957). A baby happens to babble "Ma-ma"; Mama rewards the baby with hugs and smiles; the baby says "Mama" more and more. Bit by bit, said the behaviorists, the baby's language is built up. According to behaviorists, language is a complex learned skill, much like playing the piano or dancing.

The behaviorist view of language learning has several problems. First, it does not explain how people create novel sentences—sentences that people have never heard or spoken before. Second, children learn the syntax of their native language even if they are not reinforced for doing so. Social psychologist Roger Brown (1973) spent long hours observing parents and their young children. He found that parents did not directly or explicitly reward or correct the syntax of most children's utterances. That is, parents did not say "good," "correct," "right," "wrong," and so on. Parents also did not offer direct corrections such as "You should say two shoes, not two shoe." However, as we will see shortly, many parents do expand on their young children's grammatically incorrect utterances and recast many of those that have grammatical errors (Bonvillian, 2005).

The behavioral view is no longer considered a viable explanation of how children acquire language (Gathercole & Hoff, 2007). But a great deal of research describes ways in which children's environmental experiences influence their language skills. Many language experts argue that a child's experiences, the particular language to be learned, and the context in which learning takes place can strongly influence language acquisition (Snow & Yang, 2006; Tomasello, Carpenter, & LiszKowski, 2007).

Language is not learned in a social vacuum. Most children are bathed in language from a very early age (Tomasello, 2006), whereas the Wild Boy of Aveyron, who never learned to communicate effectively, had lived in social isolation for years. The support and involvement of caregivers and teachers greatly facilitate a child's language learning (Snow & Yang, 2006). For example, one study found that when mothers immediately smiled and touched their 8-month-old infants after they babbled, the infants subsequently made more complex speechlike sounds than when mothers responded to their infants in a random manner (Goldstein, King, & West, 2003) (see Figure 3.25).

Michael Tomasello (2003, 2006) stresses that young children are intensely interested in their social world and that early in their development they can understand the intentions of other people. His *interaction view* of language emphasizes that children learn language in specific contexts. For example, when a toddler and

How Would You...? As a social worker, how would you intervene in a family in which a child like Genie (described on page 30) has lived in social isolation for years?

Figure 3.25 Social Interaction and Babbling
One study focused on two groups of mothers and their eight-month-old infants (Goldstein, King & West, 2003). One group of mothers was instructed to smile and touch their infants immediately after the babies cooed and babbled; the other group was also told to smile and touch their infants but in a random manner, unconnected to sounds the infants made. The infants whose mothers immediately responded in positive ways to their babbling subsequently made more complex, speechlike sounds, such as "da" and "gu." The research setting for this study, which underscores how important caregivers are in the early development of language, is shown here.

a father are jointly focused on a book, the father might say, "See the birdie." In this case, even a toddler understands that the father intends to name something and knows to look in the direction of the pointing. Through this kind of joint attention, early in their development children are able to use their social skills to acquire language (Jaswal & Fernald, 2007).

In particular, researchers have found that the child's vocabulary development is linked to the family's socioeconomic status and the type of talk that parents direct to their children. What characteristics of a family make a difference to a child's language development? Socioeconomic status has been linked with how much parents talk to their children and with young children's vocabulary. Betty Hart and Todd Risley (1995) observed the language environments of children whose parents were professionals and children whose parents were on welfare. Compared with the professional parents, the parents on welfare talked much less to their young children, talked less about past events, and provided less elaboration. As indicated in Figure 3.26, the children of the professional parents had a much larger vocabulary at 36 months of age than the children of the welfare parents. Keep in mind, though, that individual variations characterize language development and that some welfare parents do spend considerable time talking to their children.

child-directed speech Language
spoken in a higher pitch than
normal with simple words and
sentences.

One intriguing component of the young child's linguistic environment is **child-directed speech**, language spoken in a higher pitch than normal with simple words and sentences (Zangl & Mills, 2007). It is hard for most adults to use child-directed speech when not in the presence of a baby. As soon as adults start talking to a baby, though, they often shift into child-directed speech. Much of this is automatic and something most parents are not aware they are doing. Even 4-year-olds speak in simpler ways to 2-year-olds than to their 4-year-old friends. Child-directed speech serves the important function of capturing the infant's attention and maintaining communication.

Adults often use strategies other than child-directed speech to enhance the child's acquisition of language, including recasting, expanding, and labeling. *Recasting* is rephrasing something the child has said, perhaps turning it into a question or restating the child's immature utterance in the form of a fully grammatical sentence. For example, if the child says, "The dog was barking," the adult can respond by asking, "When was the dog barking?" Effective recasting lets the child indicate an interest and then elaborates on that interest. *Expanding* is restating, in a linguistically sophisticated form, what a child has said. For example, a child says, "Doggie eat," and the parent replies, "Yes, the doggie is eating." *Labeling* is identifying the names of objects. Young children are forever being asked to identify the names of objects. Roger Brown (1958) called this "the original word game" and claimed that much of a child's early vocabulary is motivated by this adult pressure to identify the words associated with objects.

Parents use these strategies naturally and in meaningful conversations. Parents do not (and should not) use any deliberate method to teach their children to talk, even for children who are slow in learning language. Children usually benefit when parents guide their discovery of language rather than overloading them; "following in order to lead" helps a child learn language. If children are not ready to take in some information, they are likely to indicate this, perhaps by turning away. Thus, giving the child more information is not always better.

Researchers find that the encouragement of language development, not drill and practice, is the key. Language

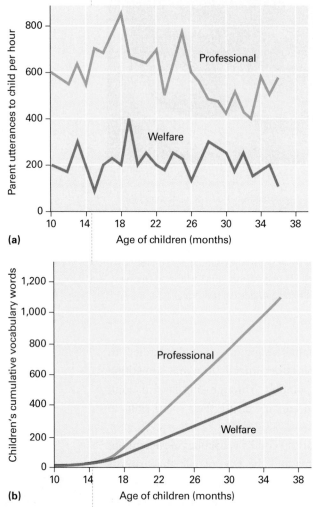

(a)

(b)

Figure 3.26 Language Input in Professional and Welfare Families and Young Children's Vocabulary Development (a) In this study (Hart & Risley, 1995) parents from professional families talked with their young children more than parents from welfare families. (b) All of the children learned to talk, but children from professional families developed vocabularies that were twice as large as those from welfare families. Thus, by the time children go to preschool, they already have experienced considerable differences in language input in their families and developed different levels of vocabulary that are linked to their socioeconomic context. *Does this study indicate that poverty caused deficiencies in vocabulary development?*

It is a good idea for parents to begin talking to their babies at the start. The best language teaching occurs when the talking is begun before the infant becomes capable of intelligible speech. *What are some other guidelines for parents to follow in helping their infants and toddlers develop their language?*

development is not a simple matter of imitation and reinforcement. What are some effective ways that that parents can facilitate children's language development?

In *Growing Up with Language,* linguist Naomi Baron (1992) provided ideas to help parents facilitate their child's language development. A summary of her ideas follows:

Infants *Be an active conversational partner.* Initiate conversation with the infant. If the infant is in a day-long child-care program, ensure that the baby receives adequate language stimulation from adults.

Talk as if the infant understands what you are saying. Parents can generate self-fulfilling prophecies by addressing their young children as if they understand what is being said. The process may take four to five years, but children gradually rise to match the language model presented to them.

Use a language style with which you feel comfortable. Don't worry about how you sound to other adults when you talk with your child. Your affect, not your content, is more important when talking with an infant. Use whatever type of baby talk with which you feel comfortable.

Toddlers *Continue to be an active conversational partner.* Engaging toddlers in conversation, even one-sided conversation, is the most important thing a parent can do to nourish a child linguistically.

Remember to listen. Since toddlers' speech is often slow and laborious, parents are often tempted to supply words and thoughts for them. Be patient and let toddlers express themselves, no matter how painstaking the process is or how great a hurry you are in.

How Would You...?
As a human development and family studies professional, how would you encourage parents to talk with their infants and toddlers?

Use a language style with which you are comfortable, but consider ways of expanding your child's language abilities and horizons. For example, using long sentences need not be problematic. Use rhymes. Ask questions that encourage answers other than "yes" and "no." Actively repeat, expand, and recast the child's utterances. Introduce new topics. And use humor in your conversation.

Adjust to your child's idiosyncrasies instead of working against them. Many toddlers have difficulty pronouncing words and making themselves understood. Whenever possible, make toddlers feel that they are being understood.

An Interactionist View

If language acquisition depended only on biology, then Genie and the Wild Boy of Aveyron (discussed earlier in the chapter) should have talked without difficulty. A child's experiences, then, do influence language acquisition (Jaswal & Fernald, 2007; Snow, 2007). But we have seen that language also has strong biological foundations. No matter how much you converse with a dog, it won't learn to talk. In contrast, children are biologically prepared to learn language. Children all over the world acquire language milestones at about the same time and in about the same order. An interactionist view emphasizes that both biology and experience contribute to language development (Tomasello & Slobin, 2004).

This interaction of biology and experience can be seen in the variations in the acquisition of language. Children vary in their ability to acquire language, and this variation cannot be readily explained by differences in environmental input alone. For children who are slow in developing language skills, however, opportunities to talk and be talked with are important. Children whose parents provide them with a rich verbal environment show many positive benefits. Parents who pay attention to what their children are trying to say, expand their children's utterances, read to them, and label things in the environment, are providing valuable, if unintentional, benefits (Berko Gleason, 2005).

Summary

Physical Growth and Development in Infancy

Most development follows cephalocaudal and proximodistal patterns. The cephalocaudal pattern is the sequence in which growth occurs at the top (the head) and works its way from top to bottom. The proximodistal pattern is the sequence in which growth starts at the center of the body and moves toward the extremities. Physical growth is rapid in the first year but rate of growth slows in the second year. Dramatic changes characterize the brain's development in the first two years. Newborns usually sleep 16 to 17 hours a day, but by 4 months of age, many

American infants approach adultlike sleeping patterns. Sudden infant death syndrome (SIDS) is a condition that occurs when a sleeping infant suddenly stops breathing and dies without an apparent cause. Infants need to consume about 50 calories per day for each pound they weigh. The growing consensus is that breast feeding is superior to bottle feeding.

Motor Development

Dynamic systems theory seeks to explain how motor behaviors are assembled for perceiving and acting. Perception and action are coupled. Reflexes—automatic movements—govern the newborn's behavior. Gross motor skills involve large-muscle activities. Key gross motor skills developed during infancy include control of posture and walking. Fine motor skills involve finely tuned movements. The onset of reaching and grasping marks a significant accomplishment, and this becomes more refined during the first two years of life.

Sensory and Perceptual Development

Sensation occurs when information interacts with sensory receptors. Perception is the interpretation of sensation. Created by the Gibsons, the ecological view states that perception brings people in contact with the environment to interact with and adapt to it. Researchers have developed a number of methods to assess the infant's perception. The infant's visual acuity increases dramatically in the first year of life, and all of the eye's color-sensitive receptors function in adultlike ways by 2 months of age. By 3 months of age, infants show size and shape constancy. In Gibson and Walk's classic study, infants as young as 6 months of age had depth perception. The fetus can hear several weeks prior to birth. Immediately after birth, newborns can hear, but their sensory threshold is higher than that of adults. Newborns can respond to touch and feel pain. Newborns can differentiate odors, and sensitivity to taste may be present before birth. A basic form of intermodal perception is present in newborns and becomes sharpened over the first year of life.

Cognitive Development

In Piaget's theory, children construct their own cognitive worlds, building mental structures to adapt to their world. Schemes, assimilation and accommodation, organization, and equilibration are key processes in Piaget's theory. According to Piaget, there are four qualitatively different stages of thought. In sensorimotor thought, the first of Piaget's four stages, the infant organizes and coordinates sensations with physical movements. The stage lasts from birth to about 2 years of age and has six substages. One key accomplishment of this stage is object permanence. Piaget opened up a whole new way of looking at infant development in terms of coordinating sensory input with motoric actions. In the past decades, revisions of Piaget's view have been proposed based on research. A different approach than Piaget's focuses on infants' operant conditioning, attention, imitation, memory, and concept formation. Operant conditioning occurs in infants. In infancy, attention is closely linked with habituation. Joint attention is an important aspect of infant attention. Meltzoff has shown that newborns can match their behaviors (such as protruding their tongue) to a model. His research also shows that deferred imitation occurs as early as 9 months of age. Infants as young as 2 months of age can retain information about perceptual-motor actions. However, many experts argue that what we commonly think of as memory (consciously remembering the past) does not occur until the second half of the first year of life. Mandler argues that it is not until about 7 to 9 months of age that infants form conceptual categories. Infants' first concepts are broad. Over the first two years of life, these broad concepts gradually become more differentiated.

Language Development

Language is characterized by infinite generativity. Infants reach a number of milestones in development. Chomsky argues that children are born with the ability to detect basic features and rules of language. The behavioral view has not been supported. Adults help children acquire language through child-directed speech, recasting, expanding, and labeling. Parents should talk extensively with an infant, especially about what the baby is attending to. How much of the language is biologically determined, and how much depends on interaction with others, is a subject of debate among linguists and psychologists. However, all agree that both biological capacity and relevant experience are necessary.

Key Terms

cephalocaudal pattern 75
proximodistal pattern 75
lateralization 76
neuron 76
sudden infant death
  syndrome (SIDS) 79
dynamic systems theory 83
gross motor skills 85
fine motor skills 87
sensation 88
perception 89
ecological view 89
visual preference
  method 89

habituation 90
dishabituation 90
intermodal perception 94
schemes 94
assimilation 95
accommodation 95
organization 95
equilibration 95
sensorimotor stage 96
object permanence 97
A-not-B Error (A$\overline{\text{B}}$
  Error) 98

attention 99
joint attention 99
deferred imitation 100
memory 100
implicit memory 100
explicit memory 100
language 102
infinite generativity 102
telegraphic speech 104
language acquisition
  device (LAD) 106
child-directed speech 108

4

Socioemotional Development in Infancy

Stories of Life–Span Development: Tom and His Father

Seventeen-month-old Tom is getting excited. His father just asked him if he wants to go outside and play. Tom toddles down the hall as fast as he can to get his shoes, coat, and hat, which he knows he wears when he goes outside. He grabs his hat and says, "Play, play," which at this point in his development is what he labels going outside and exploring the yard and its flowers, bugs, and bees. On the weekend, his parents take him to the zoo, where they point out and name various animals—like lions, tigers, elephants—as Tom looks wide-eyed at the creatures. When they get home, Tom's parents ask him about some of the sounds and movements the zoo animals make. Tom correctly roars at the mention of *lion* and imitates the movements of monkeys.

On weekdays, Tom's father, a writer, cares for him during the day while his mother works full-time away from home. Tom's father is doing a great job of caring for him. Tom's father keeps Tom nearby while he is writing and spends lots of time talking to him and playing with him. From their interactions, it is clear that they genuinely enjoy each other.

Last month, Tom began spending one day a week at a child-care center. His parents carefully selected the center after observing a number of centers and interviewing teachers and center directors. His parents placed him in the center one day a week because they wanted

Tom to get some experience with peers and to give his father some time out from his caregiving.

Tom's father looks to the future and imagines the Little League games Tom will play in and the many other activities he can enjoy with Tom. Remembering how little time his own father spent with him, he is dedicated to making sure that Tom has an involved, nurturing experience with his father. Of course, not all fathers today are as emotionally involved with their infants as Tom's father is.

When Tom's mother comes home in the evening, she spends considerable time with him. Tom shows a positive attachment to both his mother and his father. By cooperating, his parents have successfully juggled their careers and work schedules to provide Tom with excellent child care.

In Chapter 3, you read about how infants perceive, learn, and remember. Infants also are socioemotional beings, capable of displaying emotions and initiating social interaction with people close to them. The main topics that we explore in this chapter are emotional and personality development, attachment, and the social contexts of the family and child care. ∎

Emotional and Personality Development

Anyone who has been around infants for even a brief time detects that they are emotional beings. Not only do infants express emotions, but they also vary in their temperament. Some are shy and others are outgoing. Some are active and others much less so. Let's explore these and other aspects of emotional and personality development in infants.

Emotional Development

Imagine your life without emotion. Emotion is the color and music of life, as well as the tie that binds people together. How do psychologists define and classify emotions, and why are they important to development? How do emotions develop during the first two years of life?

What Are Emotions?

We will define **emotion** as feeling, or affect, that occurs when a person is in a state or an interaction that is important to them, especially to their well-being (Campos, 2004). Emotion is characterized by behavior that reflects or expresses the pleasantness or unpleasantness of the individual's state or transactions.

Psychologists classify the broad range of emotions in many ways, but almost all classifications designate an emotion as either positive (pleasant) or negative (unpleasant). Positive emotions include pleasant states such as happiness, joy, love, and enthusiasm. Negative emotions include anxiety, anger, guilt, and sadness.

Biological and Environmental Influences

Emotions are influenced both by biological foundations and by a person's experience (Keller, 2007). Facial expressions of emotions have a strong biological foundation (Leppanen & others, 2007). For example, children who are blind from birth and have never observed the smile or frown on another person's face smile and frown in the same way that children

How do East Asian mothers handle their infants' and children's emotional development differently than non-Latino White mothers?

with normal vision do. Moreover, facial expressions of basic emotions such as happiness, surprise, anger, and fear are the same across cultures.

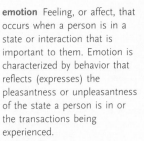

These biological factors, however, are only part of the story of emotion. Display rules—when, where, and how emotions should be expressed—are not culturally universal (Shiraev & Levy, 2007). For example, researchers have found that East Asian infants display less frequent and less intense positive and negative emotions than non-Latino White infants (Camras & others, 1998; Cole & Tan, 2007). Throughout childhood, East Asian parents encourage their children to show emotional reserve rather than be emotionally expressive (Chen & others, 1998).

Emotions serve important functions in our relationships (Field, 2007). As we discuss later in this section, emotions are the first language with which parents and infants communicate (Maccoby, 1992). Emotion-linked interchanges provide the foundation for the infant's developing attachment to the parent.

Early Emotions

Emotions that infants express in the first six months of life include surprise, interest, joy, anger, sadness, fear, and disgust (see Figure 4.1). Other emotions that appear in infancy include jealousy, empathy, embarrassment, pride, shame, and guilt, most of these occurring for the first time at some point in the second half of the first year through the second year. These later developing emotions have been called self-conscious emotions, or other-conscious emotions, because they involve the emotional reactions of others when they are generated (Lewis, 2007; Saarni & others, 2006).

Joy   Sadness

Emotional Expression and Social Relationships

Emotional expressions are involved in infants' first relationships. The ability of infants to communicate emotions permits coordinated interactions with their caregivers and the beginning of an emotional bond between them. Not only do parents change their emotional expressions in response to infants' emotional expressions (and each other), but infants also modify

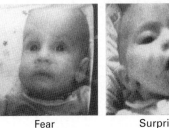

Fear   Surprise

Figure 4.1 Expression of Different Emotions in Infants

their emotional expressions in response to their parents' emotional expressions. In other words, these interactions are mutually regulated. Because of this coordination, the interactions are described as *reciprocal,* or *synchronous,* when all is going well. Sensitive, responsive parents help their infants grow emotionally, whether the infants respond in distressed or happy ways (Laible & Thompson, 2007; Thompson, 2006).

Crying Cries and smiles are two emotional expressions that infants display when interacting with parents. These are babies' first forms of emotional communication. Crying is the most important mechanism newborns have for

basic cry A rhythmic pattern usually consisting of a cry, a briefer silence, a shorter inspiratory whistle that is higher pitched than the main cry, and then a brief rest before the next cry.

anger cry A cry similar to the basic cry, with more excess air forced through the vocal cords.

pain cry A sudden appearance of loud crying without preliminary moaning, followed by breath holding.

reflexive smile A smile that does not occur in response to external stimuli. It appears during the first month after birth, usually during sleep.

social smile A smile in response to an external stimulus, which, early in development, typically is a face.

communicating with their world (Jaswal & Fernald, 2007). The first cry verifies that the baby's lungs have filled with air. Cries also may provide information about the health of the newborn's central nervous system. Newborns even tend to respond with cries and negative facial expressions when they hear other newborns cry (Dondi, Simion, & Caltran, 1999).

Babies have at least three types of cries:

- **Basic cry:** A rhythmic pattern that usually consists of a cry, followed by a briefer silence, then a shorter whistle that is somewhat higher in pitch than the main cry, then another brief rest before the next cry. Some infancy experts believe that hunger is one of the conditions that incites the basic cry.

- **Anger cry:** A variation of the basic cry, with more excess air forced through the vocal cords.

- **Pain cry:** A sudden long, initial loud cry followed by breath holding; no preliminary moaning is present. The pain cry may be stimulated by physical pain or by any high-intensity stimulus.

What are some different types of cries?

Most adults can determine whether an infant's cries signify anger or pain (Zeskind, Klein, & Marshall, 1992). Parents can distinguish the cries of their own baby better than those of another baby.

Should parents respond to an infant's cries? Many developmentalists recommend that parents soothe a crying infant, especially in the first year. This reaction should help infants develop a sense of trust and secure attachment to the caregiver. One recent study examined how mothers responded when their 2- to 6-month-old infants were inoculated (Jahromi, Putnam, & Stifter, 2004). A combination of holding and gently rocking the baby resulted in reduced intensity and duration of infant crying. A good book to read about how to calm a crying baby is *The Happiest Baby on the Block* (Karp, 2002).

How Would You...?
As a health-care professional, how would you explain to a worried parent that a sudden loud cry does not necessarily signify physical pain?

Smiling Parents and caregivers are often delighted when they observe a baby smiling. Infant smiles, however, are different from adult smiles (Messinger, 2007). Two types of smiling can be distinguished in infants:

- **Reflexive smile:** A smile that does not occur in response to external stimuli and appears during the first month after birth, usually during sleep.

- **Social smile:** A smile that occurs in response to an external stimulus, typically a face in the case of the young infant. Social smiling occurs as early as 4 weeks of age in response to a caregiver's voice (Campos, 2005).

By 6 months of age, infants smile more at familiar than unfamiliar people, and by the time they are 1 year old they display several types of smiles (Dickson, Fogel, & Messinger, 1998). For example, when they are with their parents, their smiles are often strong with their cheeks fully raised, but if they smile when they meet an unfamiliar stranger, the smile is usually more reserved. A recent study found that 8-month-olds rarely smiled when they were playing alone with toys, but most often smiled when their mothers were attentive and responsive to them (Jones & Hong, 2005).

Fear One of a baby's earliest emotions is fear, which typically first appears at about 6 months of age and peaks at about 18 months. However, abused and neglected infants can show fear as early as 3 months (Campos, 2005). The most frequent expression of an infant's fear involves **stranger anxiety**, in which an infant shows a fear and wariness of strangers.

Stranger anxiety usually emerges gradually. It first appears at about 6 months of age in the form of wary reactions. By age 9 months, the fear of strangers is often more intense, and it continues to escalate through the infant's first birthday (Emde, Gaensbauer, & Harmon, 1976).

Not all infants show distress when they encounter a stranger. Besides individual variations, whether an infant shows stranger anxiety also depends on the social context and the characteristics of the stranger.

Infants show less stranger anxiety when they are in familiar settings. For example, in one study, 10-month-olds showed little stranger anxiety when they met a stranger in their own home but much greater fear when they encountered a stranger in a research laboratory (Sroufe, Waters, & Matas, 1974). Also, infants show less stranger anxiety when they are sitting on their mothers' laps than when placed in an infant seat several feet away from their mothers (Bohlin & Hagekull, 1993). Thus, it appears that, when infants feel secure, they are less likely to show stranger anxiety.

Who the stranger is and how the stranger behaves also influence stranger anxiety in infants. Infants are less fearful of child strangers than adult strangers. They also are less fearful of friendly, outgoing, smiling strangers than of passive, unsmiling strangers (Bretherton, Stolberg, & Kreye, 1981).

In addition to stranger anxiety, infants experience fear of being separated from their caregivers. The result is **separation protest**—crying when the caregiver leaves. Separation protest tends to peak at about 15 months among U.S. infants. A study of four different cultures found, similarly, that separation protest peaked at about 13 to 15 months (Kagan, Kearsley, & Zelazo, 1978). As indicated in Figure 4.2, the percentage

How Would You...? As a human development and family studies professional, how would you respond to the parents of a 13-month-old baby who are concerned because their son has suddenly started crying every morning when they drop him off at child care despite the fact that he has been going to the same child care for over six months?

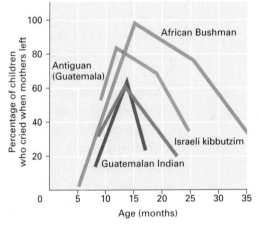

Figure 4.2 Separation Protest in Four Cultures
Note that separation protest peaked at about the same time in all four cultures in this study (13 to 15 months of age) (Kagan, Kearsley, & Zelazo, 1978). However, a higher percentage (100 percent) of infants in an African Bushman culture engaged in separation protest compared to only about 60 percent of infants in Guatemalan Indian and Israeli Kibbutzim cultures. *What might explain the fact that separation protest peaks at about the same time in these cultures?* Reprinted by permission of the publisher from *Infancy: Its Place in Human Development* by Jerome Kagan, Richard B. Kearsley, and Philip R. Zelazo, p. 107, Cambridge, Mass.: Harvard University Press, Copyright © 1978 by the President and Fellows of Harvard College.

social referencing "Reading" emotional cues in others to help determine how to act in a particular situation.

of infants who engaged in separation protest varied across cultures, but the infants reached a peak of protest at about the same age—just before the middle of the second year of life.

Social Referencing

Infants not only express emotions like fear but "read" the emotions of other people. **Social referencing** involves "reading" emotional cues in others to help determine how to act in a particular situation. The development of social referencing helps infants to interpret ambiguous situations more accurately, as when they encounter a stranger and need to know whether to fear the person (Mumme, Fernald, & Herrera, 1996; Thompson, 2006). By the end of the first year, a parent's facial expression—either smiling or fearful—influences whether an infant will explore an unfamiliar environment.

Infants become better at social referencing in the second year of life. At this age, they tend to "check" with their mother before they act; they look at her to see if she is happy, angry, or fearful. For example, in one study, 14- to 22-month-old infants were more likely to look at their mother's face as a source of information for how to act in a situation than were 6- to 9-month-old infants (Walden, 1991).

Emotional Regulation and Coping

During the first year of life, the infant gradually develops an ability to inhibit, or minimize, the intensity and duration of emotional reactions (Eisenberg, Spinrad, & Smith, 2004). From early in infancy, babies put their thumbs in their mouths to soothe themselves. In their second year, they may say things to help soothe themselves. When placed in his bed for the night, after a little crying and whimpering, a 20-month-old was overhead saying, "Go sleep, Alex. Okay." But at first, infants mainly depend on caregivers to help them soothe their emotions, as when a caregiver rocks an infant to sleep, sings lullabyes to the infant, gently strokes the infant, and so on.

The caregivers' actions influence the infant's neurobiological regulation of emotions (Laible & Thompson, 2007; Saarni & others, 2006). By soothing the infant, caregivers help infants to modulate their emotion and reduce the level of stress hormones (Gunnar & Quevado, 2007). Many developmentalists believe it is a good strategy for a caregiver to soothe an infant before the infant gets into an intense, agitated, uncontrolled state (Thompson, 2006).

Later in infancy, when they become aroused, infants sometimes redirect their attention or distract themselves in order to reduce their arousal (Grolnick, Bridges, & Connell, 1996). By 2 years of age, children can use language to define their feeling states and the context that is upsetting them (Kopp & Neufeld, 2002). A 2-year-old might say, "Feel bad. Dog scare." This type of communication may help caregivers to help the child in regulating emotion.

Contexts can influence emotional regulation (Denham, Bassett, & Wyatt, 2007; Saarni & others, 2006). Infants are often affected by fatigue, hunger, time of day, which people are around them, and where they are. Infants must learn to adapt to different contexts that require emotional regulation. Further, new demands appear as the infant becomes older and parents modify their expectations. For example, a

How Would You...?
As a social worker, how would you advise a parent who is frustrated with her 18-month-old child because she tends to whine and cry excessively compared to her 3-year-old sibling?

parent may take it in stride if a 6-month-old infant screams in a restaurant but may react very differently if a 1½-year-old starts screaming. Earlier, we described some strategies for calming a crying infant.

Temperament

Do you get upset easily? Does it take much to get you angry, or to make you laugh? Even at birth, babies seem to have different emotional styles. One infant is cheerful and happy much of the time; another baby seems to cry constantly. These tendencies reflect **temperament**, which is an individual's behavioral style and characteristic way of responding.

Describing and Classifying Temperament

How would you describe your temperament or the temperament of a friend? Researchers have described and classified the temperament of individuals in different ways. Here we examine three of those ways.

Chess and Thomas' Classification Psychiatrists Alexander Chess and Stella Thomas (Chess & Thomas, 1977; Thomas & Chess, 1991) identified three basic types, or clusters, of temperament:

- **Easy child:** This child is generally in a positive mood, quickly establishes regular routines in infancy, and adapts easily to new experiences.

- **Difficult child:** This child reacts negatively and cries frequently, engages in irregular daily routines, and is slow to accept change.

- **Slow-to-warm-up child:** This child has a low activity level, is somewhat negative, and displays a low intensity of mood.

In their longitudinal investigation, Chess and Thomas found that 40 percent of the children they studied could be classified as easy, 10 percent as difficult, and 15 percent as slow to warm up. Notice that 35 percent did not fit any of the three patterns. Researchers have found that these three basic clusters of temperament are moderately stable across the childhood years.

"Oh, he's cute, all right, but he's got the temperament of a car alarm." Copyright © The New Yorker Collection 1999 Barbara Smaller from cartoonbank.com. All Rights Reserved.

Kagan's Behavioral Inhibition Another way of classifying temperament focuses on the differences between a shy, subdued, timid child and a sociable, extraverted, bold child. Jerome Kagan (2002; Kagan & Fox, 2006; Kagan & Snidman, 1991) regards shyness with strangers (peers or adults) as one feature of a broad temperament category called *inhibition to the unfamiliar*. Inhibited children react to many aspects of unfamiliarity with initial avoidance, distress, or subdued affect, beginning around 7 to 9 months of age.

Effortful Control (Self-Regulation) Mary Rothbart and John Bates (2006) stress that effortful control (self-regulation) is an important dimension of temperament. Infants who are high on effortful control show an ability to keep their arousal from getting too high and have strategies for soothing themselves. By contrast, children low on effortful control are often unable to control their arousal; they are easily agitated and become intensely emotional.

Biological Foundations and Experience

How does a child acquire a certain temperament? Kagan (2002) argues that children inherit a physiology that biases them to have a particular type of temperament. However, through experience they may learn to modify their temperament to some degree. For example, children may inherit a physiology that biases them to be fearful and inhibited but then learn to reduce their fear and inhibition to some degree.

How might caregivers help a child become less fearful and inhibited? An important first step is to find out what frightens the child. Comforting and assuring the child, and addressing their specific fears also are good strategies.

Biological Influences Physiological characteristics have been linked with different temperaments (Rothbart & Bates, 2006). In particular, an inhibited temperament is associated with a unique physiological pattern that includes a high and stable heart rate, high level of the hormone cortisol, and high activity in the right frontal lobe of the brain (Kagan & Fox, 2006). This pattern may be tied to the excitability of the amygdala, a structure in the brain that plays an important role in fear and inhibition (LeDoux, 1998).

What is heredity's role in the biological foundations of temperament? Twin and adoption studies suggest that heredity has a moderate influence on differences in temperament within a group of people (Plomin & others, 1994).

Gender, Culture, and Temperament Gender may be an important factor shaping the context that influences temperament. Parents might react differently to an infant's temperament depending on whether the baby is a boy or a girl (Kerr, 2001). For example, in one study, mothers were more responsive to the crying of irritable girls than to the crying of irritable boys (Crockenberg, 1986).

Similarly, the reaction to an infant's temperament may depend in part on culture. For example, an active temperament might be valued in some cultures (such as the United States) but not in other cultures (such as China) (Cole & Tan, 2007). Indeed, children's temperament can vary across cultures (Putnam, Sanson, & Rothbart, 2002). For example, behavioral inhibition is more highly valued in China than in North America (Cole & Tan, 2007).

In short, many aspects of a child's environment can encourage or discourage the persistence of temperament characteristics (Shiner, 2006). One useful way of thinking about these relationships applies the concept of goodness of fit, which we examine next.

Goodness of Fit and Parenting

Goodness of fit refers to the match between a child's temperament and the environmental demands the child must cope with. Suppose Jason is an active toddler who is made to sit still for long periods of time and Jack is a slow-to-warm-up toddler who is abruptly pushed into new situations on a regular basis. Both Jason and Jack face a lack of fit between their temperament and environmental demands. Lack of fit can produce adjustment problems (Rothbart & Bates, 2006; Schoppe-Sullivan & others, 2007).

Many parents don't become believers in temperament's importance until the birth of their second child. They viewed their first child's behavior as a result of how they treated the child. But then they find that some strategies that worked with their first child are not as effective with the second child. Some problems experienced with the first child (such as those involved in feeding, sleeping, and coping with strangers) may not exist with the second child, but new problems arise. Such experiences strongly suggest that children differ from each other very early in life, and that these differences have important implications for parent-child interaction (Rothbart & Putnam, 2002).

What are the implications of temperamental variations for parenting? Although research does not yet allow for many highly specific conclusions, temperament experts Ann Sanson and Mary Rothbart (1995) recommend the following strategies for temperament-sensitive parenting:

- *Attention to and respect for individuality.* One implication is that it is difficult to generate general prescriptions for "good parenting." A goal might be accomplished in one way with one child and in another way with another child, depending on the child's temperament. Parents need to be sensitive and flexible to the infant's signals and needs.

- *Structuring the child's environment.* Crowded, noisy environments can pose greater problems for some children (such as a "difficult child") than others (such as an "easy child"). We might also expect that a fearful, withdrawing child would benefit from slower entry into new contexts.

- *Avoid applying negative labels to the child.* Acknowledging that some children are harder than others to parent is often helpful, and advice on how to handle particular difficult circumstances can be helpful. However, labeling a child "difficult" runs the risk of becoming a self-fulfilling prophecy. That is, if a child is identified as "difficult," people may treat the child in a way that elicits "difficult" behavior.

How Would You...?
As a social worker, how would you apply information about an infant's temperament to maximize the goodness of fit in a clinical setting?

Personality Development

Emotions and temperament form key aspects of *personality*, the enduring personal characteristics of individuals. Let's now examine characteristics that often are thought of as central to personality development during infancy: trust and the development of self and independence.

Trust

According to Erik Erikson (1968), the first year of life is characterized by the trust-versus-mistrust stage of development. Following a life of regularity, warmth, and protection in the mother's womb, the infant faces a world that is less secure. Erikson proposed that infants learn trust when they are cared for in a consistently nurturant manner. If the infant is not well fed and kept warm on a consistent basis, a sense of mistrust is likely to develop.

In Erikson's view, trust versus mistrust is not resolved once and for all in the first year of life. It arises again at each successive stage of development, which can have positive or negative outcomes. For example, children who leave infancy with a sense of trust can still have their sense of mistrust activated at a later stage, perhaps if their parents are separated or divorced under conflicting circumstances.

The Developing Sense of Self

Individuals carry with them a sense of who they are and what makes them different from everyone else. They cling to this identity and begin to feel secure in the knowledge that their identity is becoming more stable. Real or imagined, the sense of self is a strong motivating force in life. When does the individual begin to sense a separate existence from others?

Studying the self in infancy—like studying most other aspects of infants' socioemotional development—is difficult mainly because infants cannot tell us how they experience themselves. Infants cannot verbally express their views of the self. They also cannot understand complex instructions from researchers.

A rudimentary form of self-recognition—being attentive and positive toward one's image in a mirror—appears as early as 3 months of age (Mitchell, 1993; Pipp, Fischer, & Jennings, 1987). However, a central, more complete index of self-recognition—the ability to recognize one's physical features—does not emerge until the second year (Thompson, 2006).

One ingenious strategy to test infants' visual self-recognition is the use of a mirror technique, in which an infant's mother first puts a dot of rouge (or lipstick) on the infant's nose. An observer then watches to see how often the infant touches its nose. Next, the infant is placed in front of a mirror, and observers detect whether nose touching increases. Why does this matter? The idea is that increased nose touching indicates that the infant recognizes the self in the mirror and is trying to touch or rub off the rouge because the rouge violates the infant's view of the self. Increased touching indicates that the infant realizes that it is the self in the mirror—but that something is not right, since the real self does not have a dot of rouge on it.

Figure 4.3 displays the results of two investigations that used the mirror technique. The researchers found that before they were 1 year old, infants did not recognize themselves in the mirror (Amsterdam, 1968; Lewis & Brooks-Gunn, 1979). Signs of self-recognition began to appear among some infants when they were 15 to 18 months old. By the time they were 2 years old, most children recognized themselves in the mirror. In sum, infants begin to develop a self-understanding called self-recognition at approximately 18 months of age (Hart & Karmel, 1996).

In one recent study, researchers conducted biweekly assessments of children from 15 to 23 months of age (Courage, Edison, & Howe, 2004). Self-recognition gradually emerged over this time, first appearing in the form of mirror recognition, followed by use of the personal pronoun and then by the children recognizing a photo of themselves. These aspects of self-recognition are often referred to as the first indications of children's understanding of the mental state of me, "that they are objects in their own mental representation of the world" (Lewis, 2005, p. 363).

Late in the second year and early in the third year, toddlers show other emerging forms of self-awareness that reflect a sense of "me" (Thompson, 2006). For

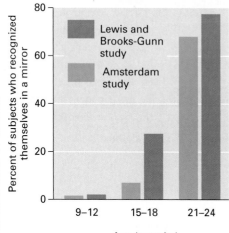

Figure 4.3 The Development of Self-Recognition in Infancy The graph shows the findings of two studies in which infants less than 1 year of age did not recognize themselves in the mirror. A slight increase in the percentage of infant self-recognition occurred around 15 to 18 months of age. By 2 years of age, a majority of children recognized themselves. *Why do researchers study whether infants recognize themselves in a mirror?*

example, they refer to themselves such as by saying, "Me big"; they label their internal experiences such as emotions ("I silly"; "I mad"); they monitor themselves as when a toddler says, "Do it myself"; and claim things as being "mine" (Fasig, 2000).

Independence

How Would You...?
As a human development and family studies professional, how would you work with a parent who shows signs of being overly protective or critical to the point of impairing their toddler's autonomy?

Not only does the infant develop a sense of self in the second year of life, but independence also becomes a more central theme in the infant's life. Erikson (1968) stressed that independence is an important issue in the second year of life. Erikson's second stage of development is identified as autonomy versus shame and doubt. Autonomy builds as the infant's mental and motor abilities develop. At this point, not only can infants walk, but they can also climb, open and close, drop, push and pull, and hold and let go. Infants feel pride in these new accomplishments and want to do everything themselves, whether the activity is flushing a toilet, pulling the wrapping off a package, or deciding what to eat. It is important for parents to recognize the motivation of toddlers to do what they are capable of doing at their own pace. Then they can learn to control their muscles and their impulses themselves. Conversely, when caregivers are impatient and do for toddlers what they are capable of doing themselves, shame and doubt develop. To be sure, every parent has rushed a child from time to time, and one instance of rushing is unlikely to result in impaired development. It is only when parents consistently overprotect toddlers or criticize accidents (wetting, soiling, spilling, or breaking, for example) that children are likely to develop an excessive sense of shame and doubt about their ability to control themselves and their world.

Erikson believed that autonomy versus shame and doubt is the key developmental theme of the toddler years. *What are some good strategies for parents to use with their toddlers?*

Erikson also argued that the stage of autonomy versus shame and doubt has important implications for the development of independence and identity during adolescence. The development of autonomy during the toddler years gives adolescents the courage to be independent individuals who can choose and guide their own future.

Attachment

Earlier in this chapter, we examined how important emotions are in developing a temperament style and saw how emotions set the tone for our early experiences in life. But emotions also write the lyrics because they are at the core of our relationships with others. Foremost among these relationships is attachment.

What Is Attachment?

Attachment is a close emotional bond between two people. There is no shortage of theories about infant attachment. Three theorists discussed in Chapter 1— Freud, Erikson, and Bowlby—proposed influential views.

Freud theorized that infants become attached to the person or object that provides oral satisfaction. For most infants, this is the mother, since she is most likely to feed the infant. Is feeding as important as Freud thought? A classic study by Harry Harlow (1958) indicates that the answer is no (see Figure 4.4).

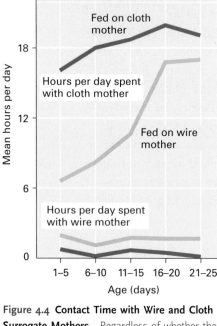

Figure 4.4 Contact Time with Wire and Cloth Surrogate Mothers Regardless of whether the infant monkeys were fed by a wire or a cloth mother, they overwhelmingly preferred to spend contact time with the cloth mother. *How do these results compare with what Freud's theory and Erikson's theory would predict about human infants?*

Harlow removed infant monkeys from their mothers at birth; for six months they were reared by surrogate (substitute) "mothers." One surrogate mother was made of wire, the other of cloth. Half of the infant monkeys were fed by the wire mother, half by the cloth mother. Periodically, the amount of time the infant monkeys spent with either the wire or the cloth mother was computed. Regardless of which mother fed them, the infant monkeys spent far more time with the cloth mother. Even if the wire mother but not the cloth mother provided nourishment, the infant monkeys spent more time with the cloth mother. And when Harlow frightened the monkeys, those "raised" by the cloth mother ran to the mother and clung to it; those raised by the wire mother did not. Whether the mother provided comfort seemed to determine whether the monkeys associated the mother with security. This study clearly demonstrated that feeding is not the crucial element in the attachment process, and that contact comfort is important.

Physical comfort also plays a role in Erik Erikson's (1968) view of the infant's development. Recall Erikson's proposal that in the first year of life, infants are in the stage of trust versus mistrust. Physical comfort and sensitive care, according to Erikson (1968), are key to establishing a basic trust in infants. The infant's sense of trust, in turn, is the foundation for attachment and sets the stage for a lifelong expectation that the world will be a good and pleasant place to be.

The ethological perspective of British psychiatrist John Bowlby (1969, 1989) also stresses the importance of attachment in the first year of life and the responsiveness of the caregiver. Bowlby believes both infants and its primary caregivers are biologically predisposed to form attachments. He argues that the newborn is biologically equipped to elicit attachment behavior. The baby cries, clings, coos, and smiles. Later, the infant crawls, walks, and follows the mother. The immediate result is to keep the primary caregiver nearby; the long-term effect is to increase the infant's chances of survival (Thompson, 2006).

Attachment does not emerge suddenly but rather develops in a series of phases, moving from a baby's general preference for humans to a partnership with primary caregivers. Following are four such phases based on Bowlby's conceptualization of attachment (Schaffer, 1996):

- *Phase 1: From birth to 2 months.* Infants instinctively direct their attachment to human figures. Strangers, siblings, and parents are equally likely to elicit smiling or crying from the infant.

- *Phase 2: From 2 to 7 months.* Attachment becomes focused on one figure, usually the primary caregiver, as the baby gradually learns to distinguish familiar from unfamiliar people.

- *Phase 3: From 7 to 24 months.* Specific attachments develop. With increased locomotor skills, babies actively seek contact with regular caregivers, such as the mother or father.

- *Phase 4: From 24 months on.* Children become aware of others' feelings, goals, and plans and begin to take these into account in forming their own actions.

Bowlby argued that infants develop an *internal working model* of attachment, a simple mental model of the caregiver, their relationship, and the self as deserving of nurturant care. The infant's internal working model of attachment with the caregiver influences the infant's, and later the child's, subsequent responses to other people (Goldsmith, 2007; Koren-Karie, Oppenheim, & Goldsmith, 2007). The internal model of attachment also has played a pivotal role in the discovery of links between attachment and subsequent emotion, understanding, conscious development, and self-concept (Thompson, 2006).

Attachment, then, emerges from the social cognitive advances that allow infants to develop expectations for the caregiver's behavior and to determine the affective quality of their relationship (Laible & Thompson, 2007). These social cognitive advances include recognizing the caregiver's face, voice, and other features, as well as expecting that the caregiver provides pleasure in social interaction and relief from distress.

Individual Differences in Attachment

Although attachment to a caregiver intensifies midway through the first year, isn't it likely that that quality of babies' attachment experiences varies? Mary Ainsworth (1979) thought so. Ainsworth created the **Strange Situation**, an observational measure of infant attachment in which the infant experiences a series of introductions, separations, and reunions with the caregiver and an adult stranger in a prescribed order. In using the Strange Situation, researchers hope that their observations will provide information about the infant's motivation to be near the caregiver and the degree to which the caregiver's presence provides the infant with security and confidence.

Based on how babies respond in the Strange Situation, they are described as being securely attached or insecurely attached (in one of three ways) to the caregiver:

- **Securely attached babies** use the caregiver as a secure base from which to explore the environment. When in the presence of their caregiver, securely attached infants explore the room and examine toys that have been placed in it. When the caregiver departs, securely attached infants might mildly protest; when the caregiver returns, these infants reestablish positive interaction with her, perhaps by smiling or climbing on her lap. Subsequently, they often resume playing with the toys in the room.

- **Insecure avoidant babies** show insecurity by avoiding the caregiver. In the Strange Situation, these babies engage in little interaction with the caregiver, are not distressed when she leaves the room, usually do not reestablish contact with her on her return, and may even turn their back on her. If contact is established, the infant usually leans away or looks away.

- **Insecure resistant babies** often cling to the caregiver and then resist her by fighting against the closeness, perhaps by kicking or pushing away. In the

Strange Situation An observational measure of infant attachment that requires the infant to move through a series of introductions, separations, and reunions with the caregiver and an adult stranger in a prescribed order.

securely attached babies Babies that use the caregiver as a secure base from which to explore the environment.

insecure avoidant babies Babies that show insecurity by avoiding the caregiver.

insecure resistant babies Babies that often cling to the caregiver, then resist him/her by fighting against the closeness, perhaps by kicking or pushing away.

insecure disorganized
babies Babies that show
insecurity by being disorganized
and disoriented.

Strange Situation, these babies often cling anxiously to the caregiver and don't explore the playroom. When the caregiver leaves, they often cry loudly and push away if she tries to comfort them on her return.

- **Insecure disorganized babies** are disorganized and disoriented.

In the Strange Situation, these babies might appear dazed, confused, and fearful. To be classified as disorganized, babies must show strong patterns of avoidance and resistance or display certain specified behaviors, such as extreme fearfulness around the caregiver.

Interpreting Differences in Attachment

What is the nature of secure and insecure attachment?

Do individual differences in attachment matter? Ainsworth proposed that secure attachment in the first year of life provides an important foundation for psychological development later in life. The securely attached infant moves freely away from the caregiver but keeps track of where she is through periodic glances. The securely attached infant responds positively to being picked up by others and, when put back down, freely moves away to play. An insecurely attached infant, by contrast, avoids the caregiver or is ambivalent toward her, fears strangers, and is upset by minor, everyday separations.

If early attachment to a caregiver is important, it should relate to a child's social behavior later in development. For some children, early attachments seem to foreshadow later functioning (Berlin & others, 2007). In an extensive longitudinal study conducted by Alan Sroufe and his colleagues (2005a, b), early secure attachment (assessed by the Strange Situation at 12 and 18 months) was linked with positive emotional health, high self-esteem, self-confidence, and socially competent interaction with peers, teachers, camp counselors, and romantic partners through adolescence. Another recent study found that infants who were securely attached at 15 months of age were more cognitively and socioemotionally competent at age 4 than their counterparts who were insecurely attached at 15 months of age (Fish, 2004).

How Would You...?
As a psychologist, how would you identify an insecurely attached toddler? How would you encourage a parent to strengthen the attachment bond?

For some children, though, there is little continuity (Thompson & Goodvin, 2005). Not all research reveals the power of infant attachment to predict subsequent development. In one longitudinal study, attachment classification (secure and insecure attachment) in infancy did not predict attachment classification at 18 years of age (Lewis, 1997). In this study, the infants whose attachment was insecure did not necessarily have an insecure attachment classification at age 18. Instead, the best predictor of an insecure attachment classification at 18 was the occurrence of parental divorce in the intervening years. Other research suggests that consistently positive caregiving over a number of years is an important factor in connecting early attachment and the child's functioning later in development.

Some developmentalists believe that too much emphasis has been placed on the attachment bond in infancy. Jerome Kagan (1987, 2002), for example, sees infants as highly resilient and adaptive; he argues that they are evolutionarily equipped to stay on a positive developmental course, even in the face of wide variations in parenting. Kagan and others stress that genetic characteristics and temperament play more important roles in a child's social competence than the attachment theorists, such as Bowlby and Ainsworth, are willing to acknowledge (Chaudhuri & Williams, 1999). For example, if some infants inherit a low tolerance for stress, this, rather than an insecure attachment bond, may be responsible for an inability to get along with peers.

Another criticism of attachment theory is that it ignores the diversity of socializing agents and contexts that exists in an infant's world. A culture's value system can influence the nature of attachment (Cole & Tan, 2007; Kagitcibasi, 2007). Expectations for an infant's independence in northern Germany may be responsible for German infants showing little distress upon a brief maternal separation, whereas the Japanese mother's motivation for extreme close proximity to her infant may explain why Japanese infants become upset when they are separated from the mother. Also, in some cultures, infants show attachments to many people. Among the Hausa (who live in Nigeria), both grandmothers and siblings provide a significant amount of care for infants (Harkness & Super, 1995). Infants in agricultural societies tend to form attachments to older siblings, who are assigned a major responsibility for younger siblings' care. Researchers recognize the importance of competent, nurturant caregivers in an infant's development (Bornstein, 2006; Parke & Buriel, 2006). At issue, though, is whether or not secure attachment, especially to a single caregiver, is critical (Lamb, 2005; Thompson, 2006).

In the Hausa culture, siblings and grandmothers provide a significant amount of care for infants. *How might these variations in care affect attachment?*

Despite such criticisms, there is ample evidence that security of attachment is important to development (Juffer, Bakersman-Kranenburg, & van IJzendoorn, 2007; Laible & Thompson, 2007). Secure attachment in infancy is important because it reflects a positive parent-infant relationship and provides the foundation that supports healthy socioemotional development in the years that follow.

Caregiving Styles and Attachment

Is the style of caregiving linked with the quality of the infant's attachment? Securely attached babies have caregivers who are sensitive to their signals and are consistently available to respond to their infants' needs (Main, 2000). These caregivers often let their babies have an active part in determining the onset and pacing of interaction in the first year of life.

How do the caregivers of insecurely attached babies interact with them? Caregivers of avoidant babies tend to be unavailable or rejecting (Berlin & Cassidy, 2000). They often don't respond to their babies' signals and have little physical contact with them. When they do interact with their babies, they may behave in an angry and irritable way. Caregivers of resistant babies tend to be inconsistent; sometimes they respond to their babies' needs, and sometimes they don't. In general, they tend not to be very affectionate with their babies and show little synchrony when interacting with them. Caregivers of disorganized babies often neglect or physically abuse them (Steele & others, 2007).

How Would You...?
As a health-care professional, how would you use an infant's attachment style and/or a parent's caregiving style to determine if an infant may be at risk for neglect or abuse?

Social Contexts

Now that we have explored the infant's emotional and personality development and attachment, let's examine the social contexts in which these occur. We begin by studying a number of aspects of the family and then turn to a social context in which infants increasingly spend time—child care.

The Family

The family can be thought of as a constellation of subsystems—a complex whole made up of interrelated, interacting parts—defined in terms of generation, gender, and role (Minuchin, 2001). Each family member participates in several subsystems. The father and child represent one subsystem; the mother and father another; the mother-father-child represent yet another; and so on.

These subsystems have reciprocal influences on each other, as Figure 4.5 highlights (Belsky, 1981). For example, Jay Belsky (1981) stresses that marital relations, parenting, and infant behavior and development can have both direct and indirect effects on each other. An example of a direct effect is the influence of the parents' behavior on the child. An indirect effect is how the relationship between the spouses mediates the way a parent acts toward the child (Crockenberg, Leerkes, & Lekka, 2007). For example, marital conflict might reduce the efficiency of parenting, in which case marital conflict would indirectly affect the child's behavior. The simple fact that two people are becoming parents may have profound effects on their relationship.

Figure 4.5 Interaction Between Children and Their Parents: Direct and Indirect Effects
Children socialize parents just as parents socialize children.

Marital
relationship

Child
behavior and
development

Parenting

The Transition to Parenthood

Whether people become parents through pregnancy, adoption, or stepparenting, they face disequilibrium and must adapt (Vondra, Sysko, & Belsky, 2005). Parents want to develop a strong attachment with their infant, but they still want to maintain strong attachments to their spouse and friends, and possibly continue their careers. Parents ask themselves how this new being will change their lives. A baby places new restrictions on partners; no longer will they be able to rush out to a movie on a moment's notice, and money may not be readily available for vacations and other luxuries. Dual-career parents ask, "Will it harm the baby to place her in child care? Will we be able to find responsible baby-sitters?"

In a longitudinal investigation of couples from late pregnancy until 3 ¹/₂-years after the baby was born, couples enjoyed more positive marital relations before the baby was born than after (Cowan & Cowan, 2000; Cowan & others, 2005). Still, almost one-third of the couples showed an increase in marital satisfaction. Some couples said that the baby had both brought them closer together and moved them farther apart; being parents enhanced their sense of themselves and gave them a new, more stable identity as a couple. Babies opened men up to a concern with intimate relationships, and the demands of juggling work and family roles stimulated women to manage family tasks more efficiently and pay attention to their own personal growth.

The Bringing Home Baby project is a workshop for new parents that emphasizes strengthening the couples' relationship, understanding and becoming acquainted with the baby, resolving conflict, and developing parenting skills. Evaluations of the project revealed that parents who participated improved in

CHAPTER 4 SOCIOEMOTIONAL DEVELOPMENT IN INFANCY

their ability to work together as parents, fathers were more involved with their baby and sensitive to the baby's behavior, mothers had a lower incidence of postpartum depression symptoms, and their baby showed better overall development than participants in a control group (Gottman & others, 2004; Shapiro & Gottman, 2005).

reciprocal socialization
Socialization that is bidirectional; children socialize parents, just as parents socialize children.

scaffolding Parents time interactions so that infants experience turn-taking with the parents.

Reciprocal Socialization

For many years, socialization between parents and children was viewed as a one-way process: Children were considered to be the products of their parents' socialization techniques. According to more recent research, however, parent-child interaction is reciprocal (Parke & Buriel, 2006). **Reciprocal socialization** is socialization that is bidirectional. That is, children socialize parents just as parents socialize children. For example, the interaction of mothers and their infants is like a dance or a dialogue in which successive actions of the partners are closely coordinated. This coordinated dance or dialogue can assume the form of mutual synchrony in which each person's behavior depends on the partner's previous behavior (Moreno, Posado, & Goldyn, 2006). Or it can be reciprocal in the sense that actions of the partners are matched, as when one partner imitates the other or when there is mutual smiling.

An important form of reciprocal socialization is **scaffolding**, in which parents time interactions in such a way that the infant experiences turn-taking with the parents. Scaffolding involves parental behavior that supports children's efforts, allowing them to be more skillful than they would be if they were to rely only on their own abilities. In using scaffolding, caregivers provide a positive, reciprocal framework in which they and their children interact. For example, in the game peek-a-boo, the mother initially covers the baby. Then she removes the cover and registers "surprise" at the infant's reappearance. As infants become more skilled at peek-a-boo, pat-a-cake, and so on, there are other caregiver games that exemplify scaffolding and turn-taking sequences. In one study, infants who had more extensive scaffolding experiences with their parents (especially in the form of turn-taking) were more likely to engage in turn-taking when they interacted with their peers (Vandell & Wilson, 1988). Engaging in turn-taking and games like peek-a-boo reflect the development of joint attention by the caregiver and infant, which we discussed in Chapter 3 (Tomasello & Carpenter, 2007).

How Would You...?
As an educator, how would you explain the value of games and the role of scaffolding in the development of infants and toddlers?

Maternal and Paternal Caregiving

In stressful circumstances, do infants prefer their mother or father? In one study, 20 12-month-olds were observed interacting with their parents (Lamb, 1977). With both parents present, the infants preferred neither their mother nor their father. The same was true when the infants were alone with the mother or the father. However, the entrance of a stranger, combined with boredom and fatigue, produced a shift in the infants' social behavior toward the mother. In stressful circumstances, then, infants show a stronger attachment to the mother.

Can fathers take care of infants as competently as mothers can? Male primates are notoriously low in their interest in offspring, but when forced to live with infants whose female caregivers are absent, the adult male competently rears the infants. Observations of human fathers and their infants suggest that fathers have the ability to act sensitively and responsively with their infants (Parke & Buriel, 2006).

The typical father behaves differently toward an infant than the typical mother. Maternal interactions usually center on child-care activities—feeding, changing diapers, bathing. Paternal interactions are more likely to include play. Fathers engage in more rough-and-tumble play. They bounce infants, throw them up in the air, tickle them, and so on (Lamb, 1986, 2000). Mothers do play with infants, but their play is less physical and arousing than that of fathers.

Child Care

Many U.S. children today experience multiple caregivers. Most do not have a parent staying home to care for them; instead, the children have some type of care provided by others—"child care." Many parents worry that child care will have adverse effects, such as reducing their infants' emotional attachment to them, retarding the infants' cognitive development, failing to teach them how to control anger, or allowing them to be unduly influenced by their peers. Are the worries of these parents justified?

Parental Leave

Today far more young children are in child care than at any other time in history. About 2 million children in the United States currently receive formal, licensed child care, and uncounted millions of children are cared for by unlicensed baby-sitters. In part, these numbers reflect the fact that U.S. adults cannot receive paid leave from their jobs to care for their young children.

Unlike the United States, many countries provide extensive parental leave policies. Sheila Kammerman (1989, 2000a, b) has conducted extensive examinations of parental leave policies around the world. Policies vary in eligibility criteria, leave duration, benefit level, and the extent to which parents take advantage of these policies. Europe led the way in creating new standards of parental leave: The European Union (EU) mandated a paid 14-week maternity leave in 1992. Among advanced industrialized countries, the United States grants the shortest period of parental leave and is among the few countries that offers only unpaid leave. (Australia and New Zealand are the others.)

Kammerman puts parental leave from employment into five categories:

- *Maternity leave.* In some countries a period of pre-birth leave is compulsory, as is a 6- to 10-week leave following birth.

- *Paternity leave.* This time off work for new fathers is usually much briefer than maternity leave. It may be especially important when a second child is born and the first child requires care.

- *Parental leave.* This gender-neutral leave usually follows a maternity leave and allows either women or men to share the leave policy or choose which of them will use it. In 1998, the European Union mandated a three-month parental leave.

- *Child-rearing leave.* In some countries, this is a supplement to a maternity leave or a variation on a parental leave. A child-rearing leave is usually longer than a maternity leave and is typically paid at a much lower level.

- *Family leave.* This covers reasons other than the birth of a new baby and can allow time off from employment to care for an ill child or other family members, time to accompany a child to school for the first time, or time to visit a child's school.

How are child-care policies in many European countries, such as Sweden, different than those in the United States?

How Would You...?

As a social worker, how would you use your knowledge of parental leave policies in various countries to advise an immigrant family about parental leave and child-care options in the United States?

Sweden has one of the most extensive leave policies. Paid for by the government at 80 percent of wages, one year of parental leave is allowed (including maternity leave). Maternity leave may begin 60 days prior to the expected birth and ends six weeks after birth. Another six months of parental leave can be used until the child's eighth birthday (Kammerman, 2000a). Virtually all eligible mothers take advantage of the leave policy, and approximately 75 percent of eligible fathers take at least some part of the leave they are allowed. In addition, employed grandparents now have the right to take time off to care for an ill grandchild.

Variations in Child Care

Because the United States does not have a policy of paid leave to care for a child, child care in the United States has become a major national concern (Lamb & Ahnert, 2006). Many factors influence the effects of child care, including the age of the child, the type of child care, and the quality of the program.

The type of child care varies extensively (Lamb & Ahnert, 2006). Child care is provided in large centers with elaborate facilities and in private homes. Some child-care centers are commercial operations; others are nonprofit centers run by churches, civic groups, and employers. Some child-care providers are professionals; others are mothers who want to earn extra money while staying home with their own children.

The type of child care makes a difference. Researchers have found that children show more stress when they spend long hours in center-based care than in other types of care (Sagi & others, 2002). Further, children who have a fearful or easily frustrated temperament style are often the most negatively influenced by spending long hours in center-based care (Burrous, Crockenberg, & Leekes, 2005).

Quality also makes a difference. What constitutes a high-quality child-care program for infants? The demonstration program developed by Jerome Kagan and his colleagues (Kagan, Kearsley, & Zelazo, 1978) at Harvard University is exemplary. The child-care center included a pediatrician, a nonteaching director, an infant–teacher ratio of 3 to 1, and additional teachers' aides. The teachers and aides were trained to smile frequently, to talk with the infants, and to provide them with a safe environment, which included many stimulating toys. No adverse effects of child care were observed in this project.

Children are more likely to experience poor-quality child care if they come from families with few resources (psychological, social, and economic) (Lamb, 1994). Many researchers have examined the role of poverty in quality of child care (Burchinal, 2006; Phillips, 2006). A recent study found that extensive child care was harmful to low-income children only when the care was of low quality (Votruba-Drzal & others, 2004). Even if the child was in child care more than 45 hours a week, high-quality care was linked with fewer internalizing problems (anxiety, for example) and externalizing problems (aggressive and destructive behaviors, for example).

To read about one individual who provides quality child care to individuals from impoverished backgrounds, see the Careers in Life-Span Development profile.

How Would You...?
As an educator, how would you design the ideal child-care program to promote optimal infant development?

CAREERS IN LIFE-SPAN DEVELOPMENT
Rashmi Nakhre, Child-Care Director

Rashmi Nakhre has two master's degrees—one in psychology, the other in child development—and is director of a child-care center in Wilson, North Carolina. Rashmi received the Distinguished Woman of North Carolina Award for 1999–2000.

Rashmi Nakhre, child-care director, working with some of the children at her center.

Rashmi first worked at the child-care center soon after she arrived in the United States 25 years ago. She says that she took the job initially because she needed the money but "ended up falling in love with my job." Rashmi has turned the Wilson, North Carolina, child-care center into a model for other centers. The center almost closed several years after she began working there because of financial difficulties. Rashmi played a major role in raising funds not only to keep it open but to improve it. The center provides quality child-care for the children of many Latino migrant workers.

Child care workers like Rashmi Nakhre nurture and teach children who are not yet in formal schooling. In some cases, they also care for older children in before- and after-school settings. Educational requirements for child care workers range from a high school diploma to a college degree. Approximately one-third of child care workers are self-employed.

National Longitudinal Study of Child Care

In 1991, the National Institute of Child Health and Human Development (NICHD) began a comprehensive, longitudinal study of child-care experiences. Data were collected on a diverse sample of almost 1,400 children and their families at

10 locations across the United States over a period of seven years. Researchers used multiple methods (trained observers, interviews, questionnaires, and testing), and they measured many facets of children's development, including physical health, cognitive development, and socioemotional development. Following are some of the results (NICHD Early Child Care Research Network, 2001, 2002, 2003, 2004, 2005, 2006):

- *Patterns of use.* Many families placed their infants in child care very soon after the child's birth, and there was considerable instability in the child-care arrangements. By 4 months of age, nearly three-fourths of the infants had entered some form of nonmaternal child care. Almost half of the infants were cared for by a relative when they first entered care; only 12 percent were enrolled in child-care centers. Socioeconomic factors were linked to the amount and type of care. For example, mothers with higher incomes and families that were more dependent on the mother's income placed their infants in child care at an earlier age. Mothers who believed that maternal employment has positive effects on children were more likely than other mothers to place their infant in nonmaternal care for more hours. Low-income families were more likely than more affluent families to use child care, but infants from low-income families who were in child care averaged as many hours as other income groups. In the preschool years, mothers who were single, those with more education, and families with higher incomes used more hours of center care than other families. Minority families and mothers with less education used more hours of care by relatives.

- *Quality of care.* Evaluations of quality of care were based on such characteristics as group size, child–adult ratio, physical environment, caregiver characteristics (such as formal education, specialized training, and child-care experience), and caregiver behavior (such as sensitivity to children). An alarming conclusion is that a majority of the child care in the first three years of life was of unacceptable low quality. Positive caregiving by nonparents in child-care settings was infrequent—only 12 percent of the children studied experienced positive nonparental child care (such as positive talk, lack of detachment and flat affect, and language stimulation)! Further, infants from low-income families experienced lower-quality child care than infants from higher-income families. When quality of caregivers' care was high, children performed better on cognitive and language tasks, were more cooperative with their mothers during play, showed more positive and skilled interaction with peers, and had fewer behavior problems. Caregiver training and good child–staff ratios were linked with higher cognitive and social competence when children were 54 months of age. A recent analysis of the NICHD data revealed that higher-quality early child care was linked to higher vocabulary scores in the fifth grade (Belsky & others, 2007).

  Higher-quality child care was also related to higher-quality mother-child interaction among the families that used nonmaternal care. Further, poor-quality care was related to an increase of insecure attachment to the mother among infants who were 15 months of age, but only when the mother was low in sensitivity and responsiveness. However, child-care quality was not linked to attachment security at 36 months of age.

How Would You...?

As a psychologist, what factors would you encourage parents to consider in deciding whether to place their infant in child care so that both parents can return to work?

- *Amount of child care.* The quantity of child care predicted some child outcomes. When children spent extensive amounts of time in child care beginning in infancy, they experienced less sensitive interactions with their mother, showed more behavior problems, and had higher rates of illness (Vandell, 2004). Many of these comparisons involved children in child care for less than 30 hours a week versus those in child care for more than 45 hours a week. In general, though, when children spent 30 hours or more per week in child care, their development was less than optimal (Ramey, 2005).

- *Family and parenting influences.* The influence of families and parenting was not weakened by extensive child care. Parents played a significant role in helping children to regulate their emotions. Especially important parenting influences were being sensitive to children's needs, being involved with children, and cognitively stimulating them.

What are some strategies parents can follow in regard to child care? Child-care expert Kathleen McCartney (2003, p. 4) offered this advice:

- *Recognize that the quality of your parenting is a key factor in your child's development.*

- *Make decisions that will improve the likelihood you will be good parents.* "For some this will mean working full-time"—for personal fulfillment, income, or both. "For others, this will mean working part-time or not working outside the home."

- *Monitor your child's development.* "Parents should observe for themselves whether their children seem to be having behavior problems." They should also talk with child-care providers and pediatrician about their child's behavior.

- *Take some time to find the best child care.* Observe different child-care facilities and be certain that you like what you see. "Quality child care costs money, and not all parents can afford the child care they want."

Summary

Emotional and Personality Development

Emotion is feeling, or affect, that occurs when a person is in a state or an interaction that is important to them. Emotional development is influenced by biological factors and experiences. Infants display a number of emotions early in their development. Crying is the most important mechanism newborns have for communicating with their world. Babies have at least three types of cries—basic, anger, and pain cries. Social smiling in response to a caregiver's voice occurs as early as 4 weeks of age. Two fears that infants develop are stranger anxiety and separation from a caregiver (which is reflected in separation protest). Social referencing increases in the second year of life. As infants develop, it is important for them to engage in emotional regulation. Temperament is an individual's behavioral style and characteristic way of emotional responding.

Chess and Thomas classified infants as (1) easy, (2) difficult, or (3) slow to warm up. Kagan proposed that inhibition to the unfamiliar is an important temperament category. Rothbart and Bates' emphasize that effortful control (self-regulation) is an important temperament dimension. Goodness of fit refers to the match between a child's temperament and the environmental demands the child must cope with. Goodness of fit can be an important aspect of a child's adjustment. Erikson argued that an infant's first year is characterized by the stage of trust versus mistrust. A rudimentary form of self-recognition occurs as early as 3 months of age, but the infant develops a more complete, central form of self-recognition at about 18 months of age. Independence becomes a central theme in the second year of life. Erikson stressed that the second year of life is characterized by the stage of autonomy versus shame and doubt.

Attachment

Attachment is a close emotional bond between two people. In infancy, contact comfort and trust are important in the development of attachment. Bowlby's ethological theory stresses that the caregiver and the infant are biologically predisposed to form an attachment. Attachment develops in four phases during infancy. Securely attached babies use the caregiver, usually the mother, as a secure base from which to explore the environment. Three types of insecure attachment are avoidant, resistant, and disorganized. Ainsworth created the Strange Situation, an observational measure of attachment. Ainsworth argues that secure attachment in the first year of life provides an important foundation for psychological development later in life. The strength of the link between early attachment and later development has varied somewhat across studies. Some critics argue that attachment theorists have not given adequate attention to genetics and temperament. Other critics stress that they have not adequately taken into account the diversity of social agents and contexts. Caregivers of secure babies are sensitive to the babies' signals and are consistently available to meet their needs. Caregivers of avoidant babies tend to be unavailable or rejecting. Caregivers of resistant babies tend to be inconsistently available to their babies and usually are not very affectionate. Caregivers of disorganized babies often neglect or physically abuse their babies.

Social Contexts

The transition to parenthood requires considerable adaptation and adjustment on the part of parents. Children socialize parents just as parents socialize children. Belsky's model describes direct and indirect effects. Mutual regulation and scaffolding are important aspects of reciprocal socialization. The mother's primary role when interacting with the infant is caregiving; the father's is playful interaction. More U.S. children are in child care now than at any earlier point in history. The quality of child care is uneven, and child care remains a controversial topic. Quality child care can be achieved and seems to have few adverse effects on children. In the NICHD child-care study, infants from low-income families were more likely to receive the lowest quality of care. Also, higher quality of child care was linked with fewer child problems.

Key Terms

5

Physical and Cognitive Development in Early Childhood

Stories of Life-Span Development: Reggio Emilia's Children

The Reggio Emilia approach is an educational program for young children that was developed in the northern Italian city of Reggio Emilia. Children of single parents and children with disabilities have priority in admission; other children are admitted according to a scale of needs. Parents pay on a sliding scale based on income.

The children are encouraged to learn by investigating and exploring topics that interest them. A wide range of stimulating media and materials is available for children to use as they learn music,

movement, drawing, painting, sculpting, collages, puppets and disguises, and photography, for example (Follari, 2007; Strong-Wilson & Ellis, 2007).

In this program, children often explore topics in a group, which fosters a sense of community, respect for diversity, and a collaborative approach to problem solving (Hyson, Copple, & Jones, 2006). Two co-teachers are present to serve as guides for children The Reggio Emilia teachers consider a project as an adventure, which can start from an adult's suggestion, from a child's idea, or from an

event, such as a snowfall or something else unexpected. Every project is based on what the children say and do. The teachers allow children enough time to think and craft a project.

At the core of the Reggio Emilia approach is the image of children who are competent and have rights, especially the right to outstanding care and education. Parent participation is considered essential, and cooperation is a major theme in the schools. Many early childhood education experts believe the Reggio Emilia approach

137

provides a supportive, stimulating context in which children are motivated to explore their world in a competent and confident manner (New, 2005, 2007).

Parents and educators who clearly understand how young children develop can play an active role in creating programs that foster their natural interest in learning, rather than stifling it. In this chapter, the first of two chapters on early childhood (approximately 3 to 5 years of age), we explore the physical, cognitive, and language changes that typically occur as the toddler develops into the preschooler and then examine different approaches to early childhood education. ▌

A Reggio Emilia classroom in which young children explore topics that interest them.

Physical Changes

Remember from Chapter 3 that a child's growth in infancy is rapid and follows cephalocaudal and proximodistal patterns. The growth rate slows in early childhood. Otherwise, we would be a species of giants.

Body Growth and Change

Despite the slowing of growth in height and weight that characterizes early childhood, this growth is still the most obvious physical change in this period of development. Yet unseen changes in the brain and nervous system are no less significant in preparing children for advances in cognition and language.

Height and Weight

The average child grows 2^1/$_2$ inches in height and gains between 5 and 7 pounds a year during early childhood. As the preschool child grows older, the percentage of increase in height and weight decreases with each additional year. Girls are only slightly smaller and lighter than boys during these years, a difference that continues until puberty. During the preschool years, both boys and girls slim down as the trunks of their bodies lengthen. Although their heads are still somewhat large for their bodies, by the end of the preschool years most children have lost the top-heavy look they had as toddlers. Body fat also shows a slow, steady decline during the preschool years. The chubby baby often looks much leaner by the end of early childhood. Girls have more fatty tissue than boys; boys have more muscle tissue.

Growth patterns vary individually. Think back to your preschool years. This was probably the first time you noticed that some children were taller than you, some shorter; some were fatter, some thinner;

The bodies of 5-year-olds and 2-year-olds are different. Notice that the 5-year-old not only is taller and weighs more, but also has a longer trunk and legs than the 2-year-old. *Can you think of some other physical differences between 2- and 5-year-olds?*

some were stronger, some weaker. Much of the variation was due to heredity, but environmental experiences were also involved. A review of the height and weight of children around the world concluded that the two most important contributors to height differences are ethnic origin and nutrition (Meredith, 1978). The urban, middle-socioeconomic-status, and firstborn children were taller than rural, lower-socioeconomic-status, and later-born children. In the United States, African American children are taller than White children.

myelination The process by which the axons are covered and insulated with a layer of fat cells, which increases the speed at which information travels through the nervous system.

The Brain

One of the most important physical developments during early childhood is the continuing development of the brain and other parts of the nervous system (Nelson, Thomas, & de Haan, 2006). The increasing maturation of the brain, combined with opportunities to experience a widening world, contribute to children's emerging cognitive abilities (Cornish, 2004). In particular, changes in the brain during early childhood enable children to plan their actions, attend to stimuli more effectively, and make considerable strides in language development.

Although the brain does not grow as rapidly during early childhood as in infancy, it does undergo dramatic anatomical changes (Toga, Thompson, & Sowell, 2006). By repeatedly obtaining brain scans of the same children for up to four years, researchers have found that children's brains experience rapid, distinct spurts of growth. The overall size of the brain does not increase dramatically from ages 3 to 15; what does dramatically change are local patterns within the brain. The amount of brain material in some areas can nearly double in as little as a year, followed by a drastic loss of tissue as unneeded cells are purged and the brain continues to reorganize itself.

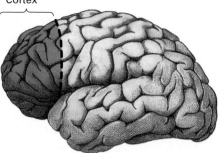

Prefrontal Cortex

Figure 5.1 The Prefrontal Cortex
This evolutionarily advanced portion (shaded in purple) of the brain shows extensive development from 3 to 6 years of age and is believed to play important roles in attention and working memory.

From 3 to 6 years of age the most rapid growth in the brain takes place in part of the frontal lobe involved in planning and organizing new actions and in maintaining attention to tasks (Blumenthal & others, 1999). This part of the frontal lobe is known as the *prefrontal cortex* (see Figure 5.1).

The continuation of two changes discussed in Chapter 3 contributes to the increase in the brain's size during early childhood. First, the number and size of dendrites increase and second, myelination continues. Recall from Chapter 3 that **myelination** is the process in which axons (nerve fibers that carry signals away from the cell body) are covered with a layer of fat cells, which increases the speed and efficiency of information traveling through the nervous system (see Figure 5.2). Myelination is important in the development of a number of children's abilities (Nelson, Thomas, & de Haan, 2006). For example, myelination in the areas of the brain related to hand-eye coordination is not complete until about 4 years of age. One recent fMRI study of children (mean age: 4 years) found that children with developmental delay of motor and cognitive milestones had significantly reduced levels of myelination (Pujol & others, 2004). Myelination in the areas of the brain related to focusing attention is not complete until the end of middle or late childhood.

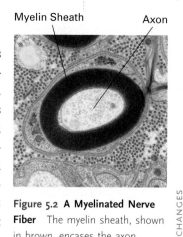

Myelin Sheath   Axon

Figure 5.2 A Myelinated Nerve Fiber The myelin sheath, shown in brown, encases the axon (white). This image was produced by an electron microscope that magnified the nerve fiber 12,000 times. *What role does myelination play in the brain's development?*

PHYSICAL CHANGES

139

Motor Development

Running as fast as you can, falling down, getting right back up and running just as fast as you can . . . building towers with blocks . . . scribbling, scribbling, and scribbling some more . . . cutting paper with scissors . . . During your preschool years, you probably developed the ability to perform all of these activities.

Gross Motor Skills

The preschool child no longer has to make an effort simply to stay upright and to move around. As children move their legs with more confidence and carry themselves more purposefully, moving around in the environment becomes more automatic (Edwards & Sarwark, 2005).

At 3 years of age, children enjoy simple movements, such as hopping, jumping, and running back and forth, just for the sheer delight of performing these activities. They take considerable pride in showing how they can run across a room and jump all of 6 inches. The run-and-jump will win no Olympic gold medals, but for the 3-year-old the activity is a source of considerable pride and accomplishment.

How Would You...?
As a health-care professional, how would you advise parents who want to get their talented 4-year-old child in a soccer league for preschool children?

At 4 years of age, children are still enjoying the same kind of activities, but they have become more adventurous. They scramble over low jungle gyms as they display their athletic prowess. Although they have been able to climb stairs with one foot on each step for some time, they are just beginning to be able to come down the same way.

By age 5, children are even more adventuresome than when they were 4. It is not unusual for self-assured 5-year-olds to perform hair-raising stunts on practically any climbing object. Five-year-olds run hard and enjoy races with each other and their parents.

Fine Motor Skills

By the time they turn 3, children have had the ability to pick up the tiniest objects between their thumb and forefinger for some time, but they are still somewhat clumsy at it. Three-year-olds can build surprisingly high block towers, each block placed with intense concentration but often not in a completely straight line. When 3-year-olds play with a simple jigsaw puzzle, they are rather rough in placing the pieces. Even when they recognize the hole a piece fits into, they are not very precise in positioning the piece. They often try to force the piece into the hole or pat it vigorously.

By age 4, children's fine motor coordination has improved substantially and becomes much more precise. Sometimes 4-year-olds have trouble building high towers with blocks because, in their desire to place each of the blocks perfectly, they may upset those already stacked. Fine motor coordination continues to improve so that by age 5, hand, arm, and body all move together under better command of the eye. Mere towers no longer interest the 5-year-old, who now wants to build a house or a church, complete with steeple, though adults might still need to be told what each finished project is meant to be.

Handedness

As children become able to throw balls and draw pictures, adults are likely to become aware of whether the child is right- or left-handed. For centuries, left-handers suffered unfair discrimination in a world designed for right-handers. In past generations, teachers forced all children to write with their right hand, even if they had a left-hand tendency. Fortunately, today most teachers let children write with the hand they favor (Wenze & Wenze, 2004). However, a recent study found that in the Republic of Malawi in Southern Africa, adults still encourage children to use their right hand rather than their left hand (Zverev, 2006).

What is the origin of hand preference? Genetic inheritance seems to be a strong influence. In one study, the handedness of adopted children was not related to the handedness of their adopted parents, but it was related to the handedness of their biological parents (Carter-Saltzman, 1980). Right-handedness is dominant in all cultures (it appears in a ratio of about 9 right-handers to 1 left-hander) and it appears before the impact of culture.

Are there differences in the abilities of left- and right-handers? Left-handers are more likely to have reading problems (Natsopoulos & others, 1998). Left-handers also tend to have unusually good visual-spatial skills and the ability to imagine spatial layouts (Holtzen, 2000). Left-handedness is more common than expected among mathematicians, musicians, architects, and artists (Michelangelo, Leonardo da Vinci, and Picasso were all left-handed) (Schacter & Ransil, 1996). Also, in one study of more than 100,000 students taking the SAT, 20 percent of the top-scoring group was left-handed, twice the rate of left-handedness found in the general population (10 percent) (Bower, 1985).

Nutrition

Eating habits are important aspects of development during early childhood. What children eat affects their skeletal growth, body shape, and susceptibility to disease.

An average preschool child requires 1,700 calories per day, but energy needs of individual children of the same age, sex, and size vary. Their requirements depend on factors such as their physical activity and the efficiency with which they use energy (Sutte, 2006).

Overweight Young Children

Being overweight has become a serious health problem in early childhood (Li & others, 2007; Torjesen, 2007). The Centers for Disease Control and Prevention (2007) has a category of obesity for adults but does not have an obesity category for children and adolescents because of the stigma the label may bring. Rather they have categories for being overweight or at risk for being overweight in childhood and adolescence. These categories are determined by body mass index (BMI), which is computed by a formula that takes into account height and weight. Only children and adolescents at or above the 95th percentile of BMI are included in the overweight category, and those at or above the 85th percentile are included in the at risk for being overweight category.

What are some trends in the eating habits and weight of young children?

How Would You...?
As a human development and family studies professional, how would you communicate with parents who are not aware that their 5-year-old child is overweight?

The percentages of young children who are overweight or at risk for being overweight in the United States has increased dramatically in recent decades, and the percentages are likely to grow unless changes occur in children's lifestyles (Franks & others, 2007). In one recent study, the body mass index of more than 1,000 children was obtained from their health records at seven different times from 2 to 12 years of age (Nader & others, 2006). Eighty percent of the children who were at risk for being overweight at 3 years of age were also at risk for being overweight or were overweight at 12 years of age. Forty-percent of the children who were in the 50th BMI percentile or above at 3 years of age were at risk for being overweight or were overweight at 12 years of age.

Being overweight can be a serious problem in early childhood (Wardlaw & Hampl, 2007). For example, physicians are now seeing type 2 (adult-onset) diabetes, a condition directly linked with obesity and a low level of fitness, in children as young as 5 years of age (Tresaco & others, 2004). Moreover, as early as 5 years of age, being overweight is associated with lower self-esteem (Davison & Birth, 2001).

The Hip-Hop to Health Jr. is a family-oriented program for African American and Latino children attending Head Start programs in Chicago that is designed to help overweight children lose weight (Fitzgibbon & others, 2002, 2005; Stolley & others 2003). The program targets African American and Latino children because they have higher rates of being overweight than non-Latino White children. The Hip-Hop to Health Jr. program consists of a 45-minute class three times a week for 14 weeks that focuses on hands-on, fun activities that promote healthy eating as well as a 20-minute aerobic activity each class. The parent component of the program consists of a weekly newsletter, homework assignments, and participation in an aerobics class twice a week. In a recent two-year follow-up of the Hip-Hop to Health Jr. program, children who were randomly assigned to the program had a smaller increase in body mass index compared to children who did not participate in the program (Fitzgibbon & others, 2005).

How Would You...?

As a health-care professional, how would you work with parents to increase the nutritional value of meals and snacks they provide to their young children?

In sum, to prevent children from becoming overweight, parents and children should learn to view food as a way to satisfy hunger and nutritional needs, not as proof of love or as a reward for good behavior (Golan & Crow, 2004). Snack foods should be low in fat, simple sugars, and salt, as well as high in fiber. Routine physical activity should be a daily occurrence (Robbins, Powers, & Burgess, 2008). The child's life should be centered around activities, not meals. We have much more to say about overweight children in Chapter 7, "Physical and Cognitive Development in Middle and Late Childhood."

Malnutrition

Poor nutrition affects many young children from low-income families (Greco & others, 2006). Many of these children do not get essential amounts of iron, vitamins, or protein. In the United States, the Special Supplemental Nutrition Program for Women, Infants, and Children (WIC), which serves approximately 7,500,000 participants, has positive influences on young children's nutrition and health (Herman, Harrison, & Jenks, 2006). For example, one study found that participating in the WIC program was linked with a lower risk of being overweight in young Mexican American children (Melgar-Quinonez & Kaiser, 2004). In another study, participation in the WIC program was related to improved nutrition in preschool children, including higher intake of fruit and lower intake of sugar from snacks (Siega-Riz & others, 2004).

Some researchers argue that malnutrition is directly linked to cognitive deficits because of negative effects on brain development

(Liu & others, 2003). However, an increasing number of researchers argue that the links between child undernutrition, physical growth, and cognitive development are more complex (Marcon, 2003). The context in which undernutrition occurs must be considered. Children who vary considerably from the norm in physical growth also differ on other biological and socioemotional factors that might influence cognitive development. For example, children who are underfed are also often less supervised, less stimulated, and less educated than children who are well nourished (Wachs, 1995). Poverty interacts with children's nutritional status to affect physical and cognitive development (Marcon, 2003).

Malnutrition may be linked to other aspects of development in addition to cognitive deficits. One longitudinal study found that U.S. children who were malnourished at 3 years of age showed more aggressive and hyperactive behavior at age 8, more externalizing problems at age 11, and more excessive motor behavior at age 17 (Liu & others, 2004).

Illness and Death

What are the leading causes of death in young children in the United States? What are the greatest risks to their health? How pervasive is death among young children around the world?

The United States

In the United States, accidents are the leading cause of death in young children, followed by cancer and cardiovascular disease (National Vital Statistics Report, 2004). In addition to motor vehicle accidents, other accidental deaths in children involve drowning, falls, and poisoning (Bessey & others, 2006).

Children's safety is influenced not only by their own skills and safety behaviors but also by characteristics of their family and home, school and peers, and the community's actions (Degutis & Greve, 2006). Figure 5.3 describes steps that can be taken in each of these contexts to enhance children's safety and prevent injury (Sleet & Mercy, 2003).

How Would You...?

As a health-care professional, how would you talk with parents about the impact of secondhand smoke on children's health to encourage parents to stop smoking?

One characteristic of the home that may threaten children's health is parental smoking. Approximately 22 percent of children in the United States are exposed to tobacco smoke in the home. An increasing number of studies conclude that children are at risk for health problems when they live in homes in which a parent smokes (Polanska & others, 2006). For example, children exposed to tobacco smoke in the home are more likely to develop wheezing symptoms and asthma than children in nonsmoking homes (Arshad, 2005). They may also have significantly lower levels of vitamin C in their blood than their counterparts in nonsmoking homes (Preston & others, 2003).

Individual

Development of social skills and ability to regulate emotions

Impulse control (such as not darting out into a street to retrieve a ball)

Frequent use of personal protection (such as bike helmets and safety seats)

Family/Home

High awareness and knowledge of child management and parenting skills

Frequent parent protective behaviors (such as use of child safety seats)

Presence of home safety equipment (such as smoke alarms and cabinet locks)

School/Peers

Promotion of home/school partnerships

Absence of playground hazards

Injury prevention and safety promotion policies and programs

Community

Availability of positive activities for children and their parents

Active surveillance of environmental hazards

Effective prevention policies in place (such as pool fencing)

Figure 5.3 Characteristics That Enhance Young Children's Safety In each context of a child's life, steps can be taken to create conditions that enhance the child's safety and reduce the likelihood of injury. *How are the contexts listed in the figure related to Bronfenbrenner's theory (described in Chapter 1)?*

Another concern is the poor health status of many young children from low-income families in the United States (Howell, Pettit, & Kingsley, 2005; Ramey, Ramey, & Lanzi, 2006). The families of many of these children do not have adequate medical insurance, and thus the children receive less adequate medical care compared with children living in higher socioeconomic conditions (Olson, Tang, & Newacheck, 2005). At the same time, children living in poverty face increased risks to their health, such as malnutrition. Approximately 11 million preschool children in the United States are malnourished, and many have lowered resistance to diseases, including minor ones, such as colds, and major ones, such as influenza.

The State of Illness and Health of the World's Children

Each year UNICEF produces a report entitled *The State of the World's Children.* In a recent report, UNICEF (2006) emphasized the importance of information about a nation's under-5 mortality rate. UNICEF concluded that the under-5 mortality rate is the result of a wide range of factors, including the nutritional health and health knowledge of mothers, access to immunizations, and the availability of maternal and child health services, clean water and safe sanitation, family income and food, and the overall safety of the child's environment.

Many children in impoverished countries die before reaching the age of 5 from dehydration and malnutrition brought about by diarrhea. *What are some of the other main causes of death in young children around the world?*

Many of the deaths of young children around the world could be prevented by a reduction in poverty and improvements in nutrition, sanitation, education, and health services (Bhutta & others, 2005). High poverty rates have devastating effects on the health of a country's young children, as they often experience lives of hunger, malnutrition, illness, inadequate access to health care, unsafe water, and a lack of protection from harm (UNICEF, 2006, 2007).

In the last decade, there has been a dramatic increase in the number of young children who have died because of HIV/AIDS transmitted to them by their parents (Kalichman & others, 2005). Deaths of young children due to HIV/AIDS especially occur in countries with high rates of poverty and low levels of education (UNICEF, 2006, 2007).

Cognitive Changes

The cognitive world of the preschool child is creative, free, and fanciful. Preschool children's imaginations work overtime, and their mental grasp of the world improves. Our coverage of cognitive development in early childhood focuses on three theories: Piaget's, Vygotsky's, and information processing.

Piaget's Preoperational Stage

Remember from Chapter 3 that during Piaget's first stage of development, the sensorimotor stage, the infant progresses in the ability to organize and coordinate sensations and perceptions with physical movements and actions. The **preoperational stage**, which lasts from approximately 2 to 7 years of age, is the second Piagetian stage. In this stage, children begin to represent the world with words, images, and drawings. They form stable concepts and begin to reason. At the same time, the young child's cognitive world is dominated by egocentrism and magical beliefs.

Because Piaget called this stage "preoperational," it might sound like an unimportant waiting period. Not so. However, the label *preoperational* emphasizes that the child does not yet perform **operations**, which are reversible mental actions; they allow children to do mentally what before they could do only physically. Mentally adding and subtracting numbers are examples of operations. *Preoperational thought* is the beginning of the ability to reconstruct in thought what has been established in behavior. It can be divided into two substages: the symbolic function substage and the intuitive thought substage.

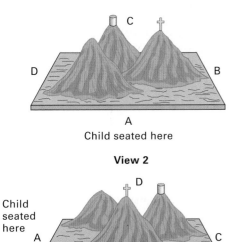

View 1

C

D B

A
Child seated here

View 2

D

Child
seated
here
A C

B

Figure 5.4 The Three Mountains Task
View 1 shows the child's perspective from where he or she is sitting. View 2 is an example of one of the photographs the child would be shown, along with other photographs taken from different perspectives. It shows what the mountains look like to a person sitting at spot B. When asked what a view of the mountains looks like from position B, the preoperational child selects a photograph taken from location A, the child's view at the time. A child who thinks in a preoperational way cannot take the perspective of a person sitting at another spot.

preoperational stage Piaget's second stage, lasting from about 2 to 7 years of age, during which children begin to represent the world with words, images, and drawings, and symbolic thought goes beyond simple connections of sensory information and physical action; stable concepts are formed, mental reasoning emerges, egocentrism is present, and magical beliefs are constructed.

operations In Piaget's theory, internalized reversible sets of actions that allow children to do mentally what they formerly did physically.

symbolic function substage Piaget's first substage of preoperational thought, in which the child gains the ability to mentally represent an object that is not present (between about 2 and 4 years of age).

egocentrism The inability to distinguish between one's own perspective and someone else's (salient feature of the first substage of preoperational thought).

The Symbolic Function Substage

The **symbolic function substage** is the first substage of preoperational thought, occurring roughly between the ages of 2 and 4. In this substage, the young child gains the ability to mentally represent an object that is not present. This ability vastly expands the child's mental world (DeLoache, 2004). In this substage, children use scribble designs to represent people, houses, cars, clouds, and so on; they begin to use language more effectively and engage in pretend play. However, although young children make distinct progress during this substage, their thought still has important limitations, two of which are egocentrism and animism.

Egocentrism is the inability to distinguish between one's own perspective and someone else's perspective. The following telephone conversation between 4-year-old Marie, who is at home, and her father, who is at work, typifies Marie's egocentric thought: Father: Marie, is Mommy there?; Marie: (silently nods); Father: Marie, may I speak to Mommy?; Marie: (nods again silently). Marie's response is egocentric in that she fails to consider her father's perspective before replying. A nonegocentric thinker would have responded verbally.

Piaget and Barbel Inhelder (1969) initially studied young children's egocentrism by devising the three mountains task (see Figure 5.4). The child walks around the model of the mountains and becomes familiar with what

animism The belief that inanimate objects have lifelike qualities and are capable of action.

intuitive thought substage Piaget's second substage of preoperational thought, in which children begin to use primitive reasoning and want to know the answers to all sorts of questions (between about 4 and 7 years of age).

the mountains look like from different perspectives, and she can see that there are different objects on the mountains. The child is then seated on one side of the table on which the mountains are placed. The experimenter moves a doll to different locations around the table, at each location asking the child to select from a series of photos the one photo that most accurately reflects the view that the doll is seeing. Children in the preoperational stage often pick their own view rather than the doll's view. Preschool children frequently show the ability to take another's perspective on some tasks but not others.

Animism, another limitation of preoperational thought, is the belief that inanimate objects have lifelike qualities and are capable of action (Gelman & Opfer, 2004). A young child might show animism by saying, "That tree pushed the leaf off, and it fell down," or "The sidewalk made me mad; it made me fall down." A young child who uses animism fails to distinguish the appropriate occasions for using human and nonhuman perspectives.

The Intuitive Thought Substage

The **intuitive thought substage** is the second substage of preoperational thought, occurring between approximately 4 and 7 years of age. In this substage, children begin to use primitive reasoning and want to know the answers to all sorts of questions. Consider 4-year-old Terrell, who is at the beginning of the intuitive thought substage. Although he is starting to develop his own ideas about the world he lives in, his ideas are still simple, and he is not very good at thinking things out. He has difficulty understanding events that he knows are taking place but which he cannot see. His fantasized thoughts bear little resemblance to reality. He cannot yet answer the question "What if?" in any reliable way. For example, he has only a vague idea of why he needs to avoid getting hit by a car. He also has difficulty negotiating traffic because he cannot do the mental calculations necessary to estimate whether an approaching car will hit him when he crosses the road.

By the age of 5 children have just about exhausted the adults around them with "why" questions. The child's questions signal the emergence of interest in reasoning and in figuring out why things are the way they are. Following are some samples of the questions children ask during the questioning period of 4 to 6 years of age (Elkind, 1976): "What makes you grow up?" "Why does a woman have to be married to have a baby?" "Who was the mother when everybody was a baby?" "Why do leaves fall?" "Why does the sun shine?"

Piaget called this substage *intuitive* because young children seem so sure about their knowledge and understanding yet are unaware of how they know what they know. That is, they know something but know it without the use of rational thinking and are sometimes wrong as a result.

"I still don't have all the answers, but I'm beginning to ask the right questions."

Centration and the Limits of Preoperational Thought

Another limitation of preoperational thought is **centration**, a centering of attention on one characteristic to the exclusion of all others. Centration is most clearly evidenced in young children's lack of **conservation**, the awareness that altering an object's or a substance's appearance does not change its basic properties. For example, to adults, it is obvious that a certain amount of liquid stays the same when poured from one container to another, regardless of a container's shapes. But this is not at all obvious to young children.

The situation that Piaget devised to study conservation is his most famous task. In the conservation task, children are presented with two identical beakers, each filled to the same level with liquid (see Figure 5.5). They are asked if these beakers have the same amount of liquid, and they usually say yes. Then the liquid from one beaker is poured into a third beaker, which is taller and thinner than the first two. The children are then asked if the amount of liquid in the tall, thin beaker is equal to that which remains in one of the original beakers. Children who are less than 7 or 8 years old usually say no and justify their answers in terms of the differing height or width of the beakers. They are typically struck by the height of the liquid in a tall, narrow container, and focus on that characteristic to the exclusion of others. Older children usually answer yes and justify their answers appropriately ("If you poured the water back, the amount would still be the same").

In Piaget's theory, failing the conservation of liquid task is a sign that children are at the preoperational stage of cognitive development. The failure demonstrates not only centration but also an inability to mentally reverse actions. For example,

centration The focusing of attention on one characteristic to the exclusion of all others.

conservation In Piaget's theory, awareness that altering an object's or a substance's appearance does not change its basic properties.

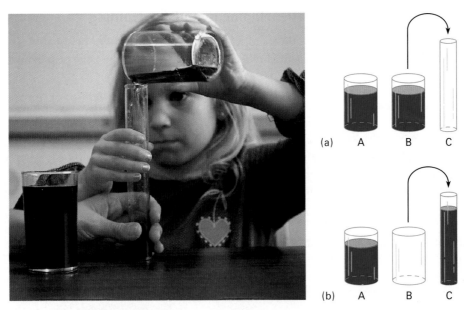

Figure 5.5 Piaget's Conservation Task
The beaker test is a well-known Piagetian test to determine whether a child can think operationally—that is, can mentally reverse actions and show conservation of the substance. (a) Two identical beakers are presented to the child. Then, the experimenter pours the liquid from B into C, which is taller and thinner than A or B, (b) The child is asked if these beakers (A and C) have the same amount of liquid. The preoperational child says "no." When asked to point to the beaker that has more liquid, the preoperational child points to the tall, thin beaker.

COGNITIVE CHANGES

147

social constructivist approach An approach that emphasizes the social contexts of learning and that knowledge is mutually built and constructed. Vygotsky's theory reflects this approach.

in the conservation of matter example shown in Figure 5.6, preoperational children say that the longer shape has more clay because they assume that "longer is more." Preoperational children cannot mentally reverse the clay-rolling process to see that the amount of clay is the same in both the shorter ball shape and the longer stick shape.

In addition to failing to conserve volume, preoperational children also fail to conserve number, matter, length, and area. However, children often vary in their performance on different conservation tasks. Thus, a child might be able to conserve volume but not number.

Some developmentalists do not believe Piaget was entirely correct in his estimate of when children's conservation skills emerge. For example, Rochel Gelman (1969) showed that when the child's attention to relevant aspects of the conservation task is improved, the child is more likely to conserve. Gelman has also demonstrated that attentional training on one dimension, such as number, improves the preschool child's performance on another dimension, such as mass. Thus, Gelman believes that conservation appears earlier than Piaget thought and that attention is especially important in explaining conservation.

Vygotsky's Theory

Like Piaget, Vygotsky was a constructivist, but Vygotsky's theory is a **social constructivist approach**, which emphasizes the social contexts of learning and the construction of knowledge through social interaction (Daniels, Wertsch, & Cole, 2007). In Chapter 1, we described some basic ideas about Vygotsky's theory. Here we expand on his theory, exploring his ideas about the zone of proximal development, scaffolding, and the young child's use of language.

The Zone of Proximal Development and Scaffolding

Vygotsky's belief in the importance of social influences, especially instruction, on children's cognitive development is reflected in his concept of the zone of proximal

How Would You...?
As a human development and family studies professional, how would you explain the child's response in the following scenario: A parent gives a 3-year-old a cookie. The child says, "I want two cookies." The parent breaks the cookie in half and hands the two pieces to the child, who happily accepts them.

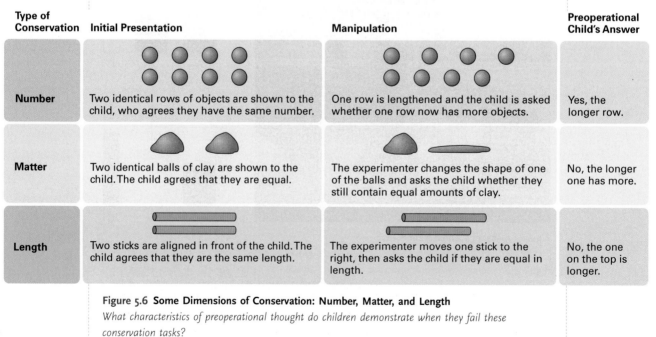

Type of Conservation	Initial Presentation	Manipulation	Preoperational Child's Answer
Number	Two identical rows of objects are shown to the child, who agrees they have the same number.	One row is lengthened and the child is asked whether one row now has more objects.	Yes, the longer row.
Matter	Two identical balls of clay are shown to the child. The child agrees that they are equal.	The experimenter changes the shape of one of the balls and asks the child whether they still contain equal amounts of clay.	No, the longer one has more.
Length	Two sticks are aligned in front of the child. The child agrees that they are the same length.	The experimenter moves one stick to the right, then asks the child if they are equal in length.	No, the one on the top is longer.

Figure 5.6 Some Dimensions of Conservation: Number, Matter, and Length
What characteristics of preoperational thought do children demonstrate when they fail these conservation tasks?

development (Bodrova & Leong, 2007). **Zone of proximal development (ZPD)** is Vygotsky's term for the range of tasks that are too difficult for the child to master alone but that can be learned with guidance and assistance of adults or more-skilled children. Thus, the lower limit of the ZPD is the level of skill reached by the child working independently. The upper limit is the level of additional responsibility the child can accept with the assistance of an able instructor (see Figure 5.7). The ZPD captures the child's cognitive skills that are in the process of maturing and can be accomplished only with the assistance of a more-skilled person (Alvarez & del Rio, 2007). Vygotsky (1962) called these the "buds" or "flowers" of development, to distinguish them from the "fruits" of development, which the child already can accomplish independently.

zone of proximal development (ZPD) Vygotsky's term for tasks too difficult for children to master alone but that can be mastered with assistance.

How Would You...? As an educator, how would you apply Vygotsky's ZPD theory and the concept of scaffolding to help a young child complete a puzzle?

Closely linked to the idea of the ZPD is the concept of scaffolding, which was introduced in the context of parent-infant interaction in Chapter 4. *Scaffolding* means changing the level of support. Over the course of a teaching session, a more-skilled person (a teacher or advanced peer) adjusts the amount of guidance to fit the child's current performance (Daniels, 2007). When the student is learning a new task, the skilled person may use direct instruction. As the student's competence increases, less guidance is given.

Language and Thought

According to Vygotsky, children use speech not only for social communication, but also to help them solve tasks. Vygotsky (1962) further believed that young children use language to plan, guide, and monitor their behavior. This use of language for self-regulation is called *private speech*. For Piaget private speech is egocentric and immature, but for Vygotsky it is an important tool of thought during the early childhood years (John-Steiner, 2007; Wertsch, 2007).

Vygotsky said that language and thought initially develop independently of each other and then merge. He emphasized that all mental functions have external, or social, origins. Children must use language to communicate with others before they can focus inward on their own thoughts. Children also must communicate externally and use language for a long period of time before they can make the transition from external to internal speech. This transition period occurs between 3 and 7 years of age and involves talking to oneself. After a while, the self-talk becomes second nature to children, and they can act without verbalizing. When this occurs, children have internalized their egocentric speech in the form of *inner speech*, which becomes their thoughts.

Vygotsky saw children who use a lot of private speech as more socially competent than those who don't. He argued that private speech represents an early transition in becoming more socially communicative. For Vygotsky, when young

Upper limit
Level of additional responsibility child can accept with assistance of an able instructor

Zone of proximal development (ZPD)

Lower limit
Level of problem solving reached on these tasks by child working alone

Figure 5.7 Vygotsky's Zone of Proximal Development Vygotsky's zone of proximal development has a lower limit and an upper limit. Tasks in the ZPD are too difficult for the child to perform alone. They require assistance from an adult or a more-skilled child. As children experience the verbal instruction or demonstration, they organize the information in their existing mental structures, so they can eventually perform the skill or task alone.

COGNITIVE CHANGES

149

children talk to themselves, they are using language to govern their behavior and guide themselves. For example, a child working on a puzzle might say to herself, "Which pieces should I put together first? I'll try those green ones first. Now I need some blue ones. No, that blue one doesn't fit there. I'll try it over here."

Researchers have found support for Vygotsky's view that private speech plays a positive role in children's development (Winsler, Carlton, & Barry, 2000). Children use private speech more when tasks are difficult, when they have made errors, and when they are not sure how to proceed (Berk, 1994). Researchers have also found that children who use private speech are more attentive and improve their performance more than children who do not use private speech (Berk & Spuhl, 1995).

Teaching Strategies Based on Vygotsky's Theory

Vygotsky's theory has been embraced by many teachers and has been successfully applied to education (Bodrova & Leong, 2007; Daniels, 2007). Here are some ways Vygotsky's theory can be used by educators:

1. *Assess the child's ZPD.* Like Piaget, Vygotsky did not believe that formal, standardized tests are the best way to assess children's learning. Rather, Vygotsky argued that assessment should focus on determining the child's zone of proximal development. The skilled helper presents the child with tasks of varying difficulty to determine the best level at which to begin instruction.

2. *Use the child's zone of proximal development in teaching.* Teaching should begin toward the zone's upper limit, so that the child can reach the goal with help and move to a higher level of skill and knowledge. Offer just enough assistance. You might ask, "What can I do to help you?" Or simply observe the child's intentions and attempts, providing support only when needed.

3. *Use more-skilled peers as teachers.* Remember that it is not just adults that are important in helping children learn. Children also benefit from the support and guidance of more-skilled children.

4. *Monitor and encourage children's use of private speech.* Be aware of the developmental change from externally talking to oneself when solving a problem during the preschool years to privately talking to oneself in the early elementary school years. In the elementary school years, encourage children to internalize and self-regulate their talk to themselves.

5. *Place instruction in a meaningful context.* Educators today are moving away from abstract presentations of material, instead providing students with opportunities to experience learning in real-world settings. For example, instead of just memorizing math formulas, students work on math problems with real-world implications.

Tools of the Mind is an early childhood education curriculum that emphasizes children's development of self-regulation and the cognitive foundations of literacy (Hyson, Copple, & Jones, 2006). The curriculum was created by Elena Bodrova and Deborah Leong (2001, 2007) and has been implemented in more than 200 classrooms. Most of the children in the Tools of the Mind programs are at-risk because of their living circumstances, which in many instances involve poverty and other difficult conditions such as being homeless and having parents with drug problems.

With these applications of Vygotsky's theory in mind, let's examine an early childhood program that reflects these applications. Tools of the Mind is grounded in Vygotsky's (1962) theory with special attention given to cultural tools and developing self-regulation, the zone of proximal development, scaffolding, private speech, shared activity, and play as important activity. In a Tools of the Mind classroom, dramatic play has a central role. Teachers guide children in creating themes that are based on the children's interests, such as treasure hunt, store, hospital, and restaurant. Teachers also incorporate field trips, visitor presentations, videos, and books in the development of children's play. They also help children develop a play plan, which increased the maturity of their play. Play plans describe what the children expect to do in the play period, including the imaginary context, roles, and props to be used. The play plans increase the quality of their play and self-regulation.

Scaffolding writing is another important theme in the Tools of the Mind classroom. Teachers guide children in planning their own message by drawing a line to stand for each word the child says. Children then repeat the message, pointing to each line as they say the word. Then the child writes on the lines, trying to represent each word with some letters or symbols.

Research assessments of children's writing in Tools of the Mind classrooms revealed that they have more advanced writing skills than children in other early childhood programs (Bodrova & Leong, 2001, 2007). For example, they write more complex messages, use more words, spell more accurately, show better letter recognition, and have a better understanding of the concept of a sentence.

Evaluating Vygotsky's Theory

How does Vygotsky's theory compare with Piaget's? We already have mentioned several comparisons, such as Vygotsky's emphasis on the importance of inner speech in development and Piaget's view that such speech is immature. Figure 5.8 compares the theories. The implication of Piaget's theory for teaching is that

	Vygotsky	Piaget
Sociocultural Context	Strong emphasis	Little emphasis
Constructivism	Social constructivist	Cognitive constructivist
Stages	No general stages of development proposed	Strong emphasis on stages (sensorimotor, pre-operational, concrete operational, and formal operational)
Key Processes	Zone of proximal development, language, dialogue, tools of the culture	Assimilation, accommodation, operations, conservation, classification, hypothetical-deductive reasoning
Role of Language	A major role; language plays a powerful role in shaping thought	Language has a minimal role; cognition primarily directs language
View on Education	Education plays a central role, helping children learn the tools of the culture	Education merely refines the child's cognitive skills that have already emerged
Teaching Implications	Teacher is a facilitator and guide, not a director; establish many opportunities for children to learn with the teacher and more-skilled peers	Also views teacher as a facilitator and guide, not a director; provide support for children to explore their world and discover knowledge

Figure 5.8 Comparison of Vygotsky's and Piaget's Theories

COGNITIVE CHANGES

children need support to explore their world and discover knowledge. The main implication of Vygotsky's theory for teaching is that students need many opportunities to learn with a teacher and more-skilled peers. In both Piaget's and Vygotsky's theories, teachers serve as facilitators and guides, rather than as directors and molders.

Even though their theories were proposed at about the same time, most of the world learned about Vygotsky's theory later than they learned about Piaget's theory, so Vygotsky's theory has not yet been evaluated as thoroughly. Vygotsky's view of the importance of sociocultural influences on children's development fits with the current belief that it is important to evaluate the contextual factors in learning (Cole & Gajdamaschko, 2007; Karpov, 2006).

Some critics say Vygotsky overemphasized the role of language in thinking. His emphasis on collaboration and guidance, too, has potential pitfalls. Might facilitators be too helpful in some cases, as when a parent becomes too overbearing and controlling? Further, some children might become lazy and expect help when they might have done something on their own.

Information Processing

Piaget's and Vygotsky's theories provided important ideas about how young children think and how their thinking changes. More recently, the information-processing approach has generated research that illuminates how children process information during the preschool years. What are the limitations and advances in the young child's ability to pay attention to the environment, to remember, to develop strategies and solve problems, and to understand their own mental processes and those of others?

Attention

Recall that in Chapter 3 we defined *attention* as the focusing of cognitive resources. The child's ability to pay attention improves significantly during the preschool years. In at least two ways, however, the preschool child's control of attention is still developing:

- *Salient versus relevant dimensions.* Preschool children are likely to pay attention to stimuli that stand out, or are *salient,* even when those stimuli are not relevant to solving a problem or performing a task. For example, if a flashy, attractive clown presents the directions for solving a problem, preschool children are likely to pay more attention to the clown than to the directions. After the age of 6 or 7, children attend more efficiently to the dimensions of the task that are relevant, such as the directions for solving a problem. This change reflects a shift to cognitive control of attention, so that children act less impulsively and reflect more.

- *Planfulness.* When experimenters ask children to judge whether two complex pictures are the same, preschool children tend to use a haphazard comparison strategy, not examining all of the details before making a judgment. By comparison, elementary-school-age children are more likely to systematically compare the details across the pictures, one detail at a time.

Preschool children's ability to control and sustain their attention is related to both their achievement-related skills and their social skills (NICHD Early Child

Care Research Network, 2005). For example, one recent study of more than 1,000 children found that their ability to sustain their attention at age 4¹/₂ was linked to their school readiness (which included achievement and language skills) (NICHD Early Child Care Research Network, 2005). Another study found that young children who have difficulty regulating their attention are more likely than other children to experience peer rejection and to engage in aggressive behavior (Eisenberg, Spinrad, & Smith, 2004).

short-term memory The memory component in which individuals retain information for up to 30 seconds, assuming there is no rehearsal of the information.

Memory

Memory—the retention of information over time—is a central process in children's cognitive development. In Chapter 3, we saw that most of an infant's memories are fragile and, for the most part, short-lived—except for the memory of perceptual-motor actions, which can be substantial (Mandler, 2004). Thus, we saw that to understand the infant's capacity to remember we need to distinguish *implicit memory* from *explicit memory*. Explicit memory itself comes in many forms. One distinction occurs between relatively permanent or *long-term memory* and short-term memory.

Short-Term Memory In **short-term memory**, individuals retain information for only about 30 seconds without rehearsal of the information. But by using rehearsal (repeating information after it has been presented), we can keep information in short-term memory for a much longer period. One method of assessing short-term memory is the memory-span task. The participant hears a short list of stimuli—usually digits—presented at a rapid pace (one per second, for example) and is then asked to repeat the digits.

Research with the memory-span task suggests that short-term memory increases during early childhood. For example, in one investigation, memory span increased from about 2 digits in 2- to 3-year-old children to about 5 digits in 7-year-old children, yet between 7 and 13 years of age memory span increased only by 1¹/₂ digits (Dempster, 1981) (see Figure 5.9). Keep in mind, though, that memory span varies from one individual to another.

Why does memory span change with age? Rehearsal of information is one reason; older children are better able to rehearse the digits than younger children. Speed and efficiency of processing information are important, too, especially the speed with which memory items can be identified (Schneider, 2004).

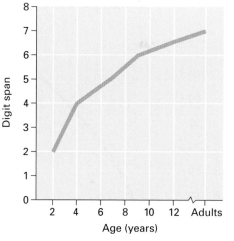

Figure 5.9 Developmental Changes in Memory Span In one study, from 2 years of age to 7 years of age, children's memory span increased about 3 digits to 5 digits (Dempster, (1981). By 12 years of age, memory span had increased on average only another 1½ digits, to 7 digits. *What factors might contribute to the increase in memory span during childhood?*

How Accurate Are Young Children's Long-Term Memories?

Not only does short-term memory span increase during the early childhood years, young children's memory also becomes more accurate. Young children can remember a great deal of information if they are given appropriate cues and prompts. Increasingly, young children are even being allowed to testify in court, especially if they are the only witnesses to abuse, a crime, and so forth (Pipe, 2007).

Several factors can influence the accuracy of a young child's memory (Bruck & Ceci, 1999). Preschool children are more susceptible to misleading or incorrect postevent information than elementary-school-age children (Ghetti & Alexander, 2004). Despite these age differences, there is still concern about older children when they are subjected to suggestive interviews (Poole & Lindsay, 1996). There are also individual differences; some preschoolers are highly resistant to interviewers' suggestions, whereas others immediately succumb to the slightest suggestion (Crossman, Scullin, & Melnyk, 2004; Gilstrap & Ceci, 2005). A recent research review found that suggestibility is linked to low self-concept, low support from parents, and mothers' insecure attachment in romantic relationships (Bruck & Melnyk, 2004). Further, interviewing techniques can produce substantial distortions in children's reports about highly salient events. Children are suggestible not just about peripheral details but also about the central aspects of an event (Bruck, Ceci, & Hembrooke, 1998).

The Young Child's Theory of Mind

Even young children are curious about the nature of the human mind. They have a **theory of mind**, which refers to awareness of one's own mental processes and the mental processes of others. Studies of theory of mind view the child as "a thinker who is trying to explain, predict, and understand people's thoughts, feelings, and utterances" (Harris, 2006). Children's theory of mind changes as they develop through childhood (Flavell, Miller, & Miller, 2002). The main changes occur at 2 to 3 years of age, 4 to 5 years of age, and beyond 5 years.

2 to 3 Years of Age In this time frame, children begin to understand the following three mental states. (1) *Perceptions*—the child realizes that another person sees what is in front of her eyes and not necessarily what is in front of the child's eyes. (2) *Emotions*—the child can distinguish between positive (for example, happy) and negative (sad, for example) emotions. A child might say, "Vic feels bad." (3) *Desires*—the child understands that if someone wants something, he or she will try to get it. A child might say, "I want my mommy."

Children refer to desires earlier and more frequently than they refer to cognitive states such as thinking and knowing (Harris, 2006). Two- to 3-year-olds understand the way that desires are related to actions and to simple emotions (Harris, 2006). For example, they understand that people will search for what they want and that if they obtain it, they are likely to feel happy, but if they don't they will keep searching for it and are likely to feel sad or angry (Hadwin & Perner, 2001; Wellman & Woolley, 1990).

4 to 5 Years of Age Children come to understand that the mind can represent objects and events accurately or inaccurately. The realization that people can have *false beliefs*—beliefs that are not true—develops in a majority of children by the time they are 5 years old (Wellman, Cross, & Watson, 2001) (see Figure 5.10). In one study of false beliefs, young children were shown a Band-Aids box and asked what was inside (Jenkins & Astington, 1996).

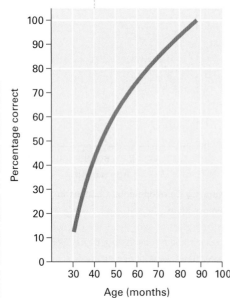

Figure 5.10 Development Changes in False-Belief Performance False-belief performance—the child's understanding that a person has a false belief that contradicts reality—dramatically increases from 2½ years of age through the middle of the elementary school years. In a summary of the results of many studies, 2½-year-olds gave correct responses about 20 percent of the time (Wellman, Cross, & Watson, 2001). At 3 years, 8 months, they were correct about 50 percent of the time, and after that, gave increasingly correct responses.

To the children's surprise, the box actually contained pencils. When asked what a child who had never seen the box would think was inside, 3-year-olds typically responded "pencils." However, the 4- and 5-year-olds, grinning at the anticipation of the false beliefs of other children who had not seen what was inside the box, were more likely to say "Band-Aids."

Children's understanding of thinking has some limitations in early childhood (Doherty, 2007; Harris, 2006). They often underestimate when mental activity is likely occurring. For example, they fail to attribute mental activity to someone who is sitting quietly, reading, or talking (Flavell, Green & Flavell, 1995). Their understanding of their own thinking is also limited.

Beyond Age 5 It is only beyond the preschool years that children have a deepening appreciation of the mind itself rather than just an understanding of mental states (Wellman, 2004). Not until middle and late childhood do children see the mind as an active constructor of knowledge or processing center (Flavell, Green, & Flavell, 2000). It is only then that they move from understanding that beliefs can be false to realizing that the same event can be open to multiple interpretations (Carpendale & Chandler, 1996).

Language Development

Young children move rather quickly from producing two-word utterances to creating three-, four-, and five-word combinations. Between 2 and 3 years of age they begin the transition from saying simple sentences that express a single proposition to saying complex sentences (Bloom, 1998).

As young children learn the special features of their own language, there are extensive regularities in how they acquire that particular language (Berko Gleason, 2005). For example, children learn the prepositions *on* and *in* before other prepositions. Children learning other languages, such as Russian or Chinese, also acquire the particular features of those languages in a consistent order.

Understanding Phonology and Morphology

In Chapter 3, we defined *phonology* as the sound system of a language, including the sounds that are used and how they may be combined. During the preschool years, most children gradually become more sensitive to the sounds of spoken words and become increasingly capable of producing all the sounds of their language (National Research Council, 1999). They notice rhymes, enjoy poems, make up silly names for things by substituting one sound for another (such as *bubblegum, bubblebum, bubbleyum*), and clap along with each syllable in a phrase.

By the time children move beyond two-word utterances, they demonstrate a knowledge of morphology rules (Carlisle, 2004). **Morphology** refers to the units of meaning involved in word formation. Preschool children begin using the plural and possessive forms of nouns (such as *dogs* and *dog's*). They put appropriate endings on verbs (such as *-s* when the subject is third-person singular and *-ed* for the past tense). They use prepositions (such as *in* and *on*), articles (such as *a* and *the*), and various forms of the verb *to be* (such as "I *was* going to the store"). Some of the best evidence for changes in children's use of morphological rules occurs in

morphology Units of meaning involved in word formation.

syntax The ways words are combined to form acceptable phrases and sentences.

semantics The meaning of words and sentences.

their overgeneralization of the rules, as when a preschooler say "foots" instead of "feet," or "goed" instead of "went."

Children's understanding of morphological rules was the subject of a classic experiment by children's language researcher Jean Berko (1958). Berko presented preschool and first-grade children with cards such as the one shown in Figure 5.11. Children were asked to look at the card while the experimenter read the words on it aloud. Then the children were asked to supply the missing word. This might sound easy, but Berko was interested not just in the children's ability to recall the right word but also in their ability to say it "correctly" with the ending that was dictated by morphological rules. *Wugs* is the correct response for the card in Figure 5.11. Although the children were not perfectly accurate, they were much better than chance would dictate. Moreover, they demonstrated their knowledge of morphological rules not only with the plural forms of nouns ("There are two wugs") but also with the possessive forms of nouns and with the third-person singular and past-tense forms of verbs.

Berko's study demonstrated not only that the children relied on rules, but also that they had *abstracted* the rules from what they had heard and could apply them to novel situations. What makes Berko's study impressive is that all of the words were *fictional;* they were created especially for the experiment. Thus, the children could not base their responses on remembering past instances of hearing the words. Instead, they were forced to rely on *rules*. Their performance suggested that they did so successfully.

This is a wug.

Now there is another one.
There are two of them.
There are two _____.

Figure 5.11 Stimuli in Berko's Study of Young Children's Understanding of Morphological Rules In Jean Berko's (1958) study, young children were presented cards, such as this one with a "wug" on it. Then the children were asked to supply the missing word; in supplying the missing word, they had to say it correctly too. "Wugs" is the correct response here.

Changes in Syntax and Semantics

Preschool children also learn and apply rules of **syntax**, which involves the way words are combined to form acceptable phrases and sentences. They show a growing mastery of complex rules for how words should be ordered (Marchman & Thal, 2005).

Consider *wh-* questions, such as "Where is Daddy going?" or "What is that boy doing?" To ask these questions properly, the child must know two important differences between *wh-* questions and affirmative statements (for instance, "Daddy is going to work" and "That boy is waiting on the school bus"). First, a *wh-* word must be added at the beginning of the sentence. Second, the auxiliary verb must be inverted—that is, exchanged with the subject of the sentence. Young children learn quite early where to put the *wh-* word, but they take much longer to learn the auxiliary-inversion rule. Thus, preschool children might ask, "Where Daddy is going?" and "What that boy is doing?"

Gains in **semantics**, the aspect of language that involves the meaning of words and sentences, also characterize early childhood. Vocabulary development is dramatic. Some experts have concluded that between 18 months and 6 years of age, young children learn about one new word every waking hour

(Carey, 1978; Gelman & Kalish, 2006). By the time they enter first grade, it is estimated that children know about 14,000 words (Clark, 1993).

Advances in Pragmatics

Changes in **pragmatics**, the appropriate use of language in different contexts, also characterize young children's language development (Bryant, 2005). A 6-year-old is simply a much better conversationalist than a 2-year-old is. What are some of the improvements in pragmatics during the preschool years?

As children get older they become increasingly able to talk about things that are not here (grandma's house, for example) and not now (what happened to them yesterday or might happen tomorrow, for example). A preschool child can tell you what she wants for lunch tomorrow, something that would not have been possible at the two-word stage of language development.

Around 4 to 5 years of age, children learn to change their speech style to suit the situation. For example, even 4-year-old children speak differently to a 2-year-old than to a same-aged peer; they use shorter sentences with the 2-year-old. They also speak differently to an adult than to a same-aged peer, using more polite and formal language with the adult (Shatz & Gelman, 1973).

How Would You…? As an educator, how would you design playtime activities to promote language development in young children?

Young Children's Literacy

What should a literacy program for preschool children be like? Instruction should be built on what children already know about oral language, reading, and writing (McGee & Richgels, 2008). Further, early precursors of literacy and academic success include language skills, phonological and syntactic knowledge, letter identification, and knowledge about print and its functions (Jalongo, 2007; Vukelich, Christie, & Enz, 2008). A longitudinal study found that knowledge of letter names, letter and word naming speed, and phonological awareness in kindergarten were linked to reading success in the first and second grade (Schattschneider & others, 2004). In another longitudinal study, the number of letters children knew in kindergarten was strongly linked with their reading achievement in high school (Stevenson & Newman, 1986).

All young children should experience feelings of success and pride in their early reading and writing exercises (Fields, Groth, & Spangler, 2008; Graves, Juel, &

Anna Mudd began writing stories when she was 4 years old. Above is her story, "The devl and the babe goste," which she wrote as a 6-year-old. The story includes poetic images, sophisticated syntax, and vocabulary that reflects advances in language development. *What are some guidelines parents and teachers can follow in helping young children develop literacy skills?*

child-centered kindergarten
Education that involves the whole child by considering both the child's physical, cognitive, and socioemotional development and the child's needs, interests, and learning styles.

Montessori approach An educational philosophy in which children are given considerable freedom and spontaneity in choosing activities and are allowed to move from one activity to another as they desire.

Graves, 2007). Children's early writing attempts should be encouraged without concern for the proper formation of letters or correct conventional spelling. Children should be encouraged to take risks in reading and writing, and errors should be viewed as a natural part of the child's growth (Soderman & Farrell, 2008). Teachers and parents should take time to regularly read to children from a wide variety of poetry, fiction, and nonfiction (Otto, 2008).

The advances in language that take place in early childhood lay the foundation for later development in the elementary school years, which we discuss in Chapter 7.

Early Childhood Education

To the teachers at a Reggio Emilia program (described in the chapter opening), preschool children are active learners, exploring the world with their peers, constructing their knowledge of the world in collaboration with their community, aided but not directed by the teachers. In many ways, the Reggio Emilia approach applies ideas consistent with the views of Piaget and Vygotsky discussed in this chapter. Does it matter to the children? How do other early education programs treat children, and how do the children fare? Our exploration of early childhood education focuses on variations in programs, education for children who are disadvantaged, and some controversies in early childhood education.

Variations in Early Childhood Education

There are many variations in the way young children are educated (Brewer, 2007; Driscoll & Nagel, 2008). The foundation of early childhood education has been the child-centered kindergarten.

The Child–Centered Kindergarten

Nurturing is a key aspect of the **child-centered kindergarten**, which emphasizes the education of whole child and concern for his or her physical, cognitive, and socioemotional development (Morrison, 2008). Instruction is organized around the child's needs, interests, and learning styles. Emphasis is on the process of learning, rather than what is learned (Feeney, Christensen, & Moravicik, 2006). The child-centered kindergarten honors three principles: Each child follows a unique developmental pattern; young children learn best through firsthand experiences with people and materials; and play is extremely important in the child's total development.

The Montessori Approach

Montessori schools are patterned after the educational philosophy of Maria Montessori (1870–1952), an Italian physician-turned-educator, who crafted a revolutionary approach to young children's education at the beginning of the twentieth century. The **Montessori approach** is a philosophy of education in which children are given considerable freedom and spontaneity in choosing activities. They are allowed to move from one activity to another as they desire. The teacher acts as a facilitator rather than a director. The teacher shows the child how to perform intellectual activities, demonstrates interesting ways to explore curriculum materials, and offers help when the child requests it. "By encouraging children to make decisions from an early age, Montessori programs seek to develop self-regulated problem solvers who can make choices and manage their time effectively" (Hyson, Copple, & Jones, 2006, p. 14). The number of Montessori schools in the United States has expanded dramatically in recent years, from one school in 1959 to 355 schools in 1970 to approximately 4,000 in 2005 (Whitescarver, 2006).

developmentally appropriate practice Education that focuses on the typical developmental patterns of children (age appropriateness) and the uniqueness of each child (individual appropriateness).

Some developmentalists favor the Montessori approach, but others believe that it neglects children's socioemotional development (Chattin-McNichols, 1992). For example, while Montessori fosters independence and the development of cognitive skills, it deemphasizes verbal interaction between the teacher and child and peer interaction. Montessori's critics also argue that it restricts imaginative play and that its heavy reliance on self-corrective materials may not adequately allow for creativity and for a variety of learning styles (Goffin & Wilson, 2001).

Larry Page and Sergey Brin, founders of the highly successful Internet search engine, Google, recently said that their early years at Montessori schools were a major factor in their success (International Montessori Council, 2006). During an interview with Barbara Walters, they said they learned how to be self-directed and self-starters at Montessori (ABC News, 2005). They commented that Montessori experiences encouraged them to think for themselves and allowed them the freedom to develop their own interests.

Developmentally Appropriate and Inappropriate Education

A growing number of educators and psychologists believe that preschool and young elementary school children learn best through active, hands-on teaching methods such as games and dramatic play. They know that children develop at varying rates and that schools need to allow for these individual differences (Brewer, 2007). They also believe that schools should focus on improving children's socioemotional development, as well as their cognitive development (Hyson, 2007; Hyson, Copple, & Jones, 2006). Educators refer to this type of schooling as **developmentally appropriate practice**, which is based on knowledge of the typical development of children within an age span (age appropriateness) as well as the uniqueness of the child (individual appropriateness) (Bredekamp, 1997; NAEYC, 1986). In contrast, developmentally inappropriate practice for a young child relies on abstract paper-and-pencil activities presented to large groups (Kostelnik, Soderman, & Whiren, 2007).

One study compared 182 children from five developmentally appropriate kindergarten classrooms (with hands-on activities and integrated curriculum tailored to meet age group, cultural, and individual learning styles) and five developmentally inappropriate kindergarten classrooms (which had an academic, direct instruction emphasis with extensive use of workbooks/worksheets, seatwork, and rote drill/practice activities) in a Louisiana school system (Hart & others, 2003). Children from the two types of classrooms did not differ in pre-kindergarten readiness, and the classrooms were balanced in terms of sex and socioeconomic status.

Teacher ratings of child behavior and scores on the California Achievement Test were obtained through the third grade. Children taught in developmentally inappropriate classrooms had slower growth in vocabulary, math application, and math computation.

However, not all studies show significant positive benefits for developmentally appropriate education (Hyson, 2007; Hyson, Copple, & Jones, 2006). Among the reasons it is difficult to generalize about research on developmentally appropriate education is that individual programs often vary, and developmentally appropriate education is an evolving concept. Recent changes in the concept have given more attention to sociocultural factors, the teacher's active involvement and implementation of systematic intentions, as well as how strong academic skills should be emphasized and how they should be taught.

How Would You...? As an educator, how would you design a developmentally appropriate lesson to teach kindergartners the concept of gravity?

Education for Young Children Who Are Disadvantaged

For many years, U.S. children from low-income families did not receive any education before they entered the first grade. As a result, they began first grade already several steps behind their classmates who had attended kindergarten and possibly preschool. In the summer of 1965, the federal government began an effort to break the cycle of poverty and poor education for young children in the United States through **Project Head Start.** It is a compensatory program designed to provide children from low-income families the opportunity to acquire the skills and experiences important for success in school.

The goals and methods of Head Start programs vary greatly around the country. The U.S. Congress is considering whether to infuse Head Start programs with a stronger academic focus. Some worry that the emphasis on academic skills will come at the expense of reduced health services and decreased emphasis on socioemotional skills (Stipek, 2004).

How Would You...? As a health-care professional, how would you explain the importance of health services being a component of an effective Head Start program?

Head Start programs are not all created equal. One estimate is that 40 percent of the 1,400 Head Start programs are of questionable quality (Zigler & Styfco, 1994). More attention needs to be given to developing consistently high-quality Head Start programs. One individual who is strongly motivated to make Head Start a valuable learning experience for young children from disadvantaged backgrounds is Yolanda Garcia. To read about her work, see the Careers in Life-Span Development profile.

Evaluations support the positive influence of quality early childhood programs on both the cognitive and social worlds of disadvantaged young children (Chambers, Chung, & Slavin, 2006; Ryan, Fauth, & Brooks-Gunn, 2006). One high-quality early childhood education program (although not a Head Start program) is the Perry Preschool program in Ypsilanti, Michigan, a two-year preschool program that includes weekly home visits from program personnel. In analyses of the long-term effects of the program, adults who had been in the Perry Preschool program were compared with a control group of adults from the same background who did not receive the enriched early childhood education (Schweinhart & others, 2005; Weikart, 1993). Those who had been in the Perry Preschool program had fewer teen pregnancies and higher high school graduation rates and at age 40 more were in the workforce, owned their own homes, had a savings account, and had fewer arrests.

Controversies in Early Childhood Education

Currently there is controversy about what the curriculum of U.S. early childhood education should be (Hyson, 2007; Hyson, Copple, & Jones, 2006). On one side are those who advocate a child-centered, constructivist approach much like that emphasized by the National Association for the Education of Young Children (NAEYC) along the lines of developmentally appropriate practice. On the other side are those who advocate an academic, direct instruction approach.

How Would You...?
As a psychologist, how would you advise preschool teachers to balance the development of young children's skills for academic achievement with opportunities for healthy social interaction?

In reality, many high-quality early childhood education programs include both academic and constructivist approaches. Many education experts like Lilian Katz (1999), though, worry about academic approaches that place too much pressure on young children to achieve and don't provide any opportunities to actively construct knowledge. Competent early childhood programs also should focus on cognitive development *and* socioemotional development, not exclusively on cognitive development (Kagan & Scott-Little, 2004).

Early childhood education should encourage adequate preparation for learning, varied learning activities, trusting relationships between adults and children, and increased parental involvement (Brewer, 2007). Too many young children go to substandard early childhood programs (Driscoll & Naqel, 2008). According to a report by the Carnegie Corporation (1996), four out of five early childhood programs did not meet quality standards.

Especially because so many young children do not experience an environment that approximates a good early childhood program, there are increasing calls for instituting preschool education for all U.S. 4-year-old children (Zigler, Gilliam, & Jones, 2006). Attending preschool is rapidly becoming the norm for U.S. children. In 2002, 43 states funded pre-kindergarten programs, and 55 percent of U.S. 3- and 4-year-old children attended center-based programs (NAEYC, 2005). Many other 3- and 4-year-old children attend private preschool programs.

Edward Zigler and his colleagues (2006) recently argued that the United States should have universal preschool education. They emphasize that quality preschools prepare children for school readiness and academic success. Zigler and his colleagues (2006) cite research that shows quality preschool programs increase the likelihood that once children go to elementary and secondary school they will be less likely to be retained in a grade or drop out of school. They also point to analyses indicating that universal preschool would bring considerable cost savings on the order of billions of dollars because of a diminished need for remedial and justice services (Karoly & Bigelow, 2005). A number of early childhood education experts agree with Zigler and his colleagues that U.S. 4-year-olds would benefit from universal preschool education (Finn-Stevenson, 2006).

Critics of universal preschool education argue that the gains attributed to preschool and kindergarten education are often overstated. They especially stress that research has not proven that nondisadvantaged children improve as a result of attending a preschool. Thus, the critics say it is more important to improve preschool education for young children who are disadvantaged rather than funding preschool education for all 4-year-old children. Some critics, especially home-schooling advocates, emphasize that young children should be educated by their parents, not by schools. Thus, controversy continues to characterize whether universal preschool education should be implemented.

Cross-Cultural Variations

What characterizes early childhood education in Japan?

A kindergarten class in Kingston, Jamaica. *What characterizes kindergarten in many developing countries like Jamaica?*

In Japan and many developing countries, the goals of early childhood education are quite different from those of American programs, although there is diversity in early childhood education in all countries. Some Japanese kindergartens have specific aims, such as early musical training or the practice of Montessori strategies. In large cities, some kindergartens are attached to universities that have elementary and secondary schools. In most Japanese preschools, however, less emphasis is placed on academic instruction than in U.S. preschools. The vast majority of young Japanese children are taught to read at home by their parents. In many Japanese kindergartens, children wear the same uniforms, including caps, which are of different colors to indicate the classrooms to which they belong. They have identical sets of equipment, kept in identical drawers and shelves. This is not intended to turn the young children into robots, as some Americans have observed, but to impress on them that other people, just like themselves, have needs and desires that are equally important (Hendry, 1995).

Japan is a highly advanced industrialized country. What about developing countries—how do they compare to the United States in educating young children? The wide range of programs and emphasis on the education of the whole child—physically, cognitively, and socio-emotionally—that characterizes U.S. early childhood does not exist in many developing countries (Rooparnine & Metingdogan, 2006). Economic pressures and parents' belief that education should be academically rigorous have produced teacher-centered rather child-centered early childhood education programs in most developing countries. Among the countries in which this type of early childhood education has been observed are Jamaica, China, Thailand, Kenya, and Turkey. In these countries, young children are usually given few choices and are educated in highly structured settings. Emphasis is on learning academic skills through rote memory and recitation (Lin, Johnson, & Johnson, 2003). Programs in Mexico, Singapore, Korea, and Hong Kong have been observed to be closer to those in the United States in their emphasis on curriculum flexibility and play-based methods (Cisneros-Cohernour, Moreno, & Cisneros, 2000).

Summary

Physical Changes

The average child grows $2^{1}/_{2}$ inches in height and gains between 5 and 7 pounds a year during early childhood. Growth patterns vary individually, though. Some of the brain's increase in size in early childhood is due to increases in the number and size of dendrites, some to myelination. From 3 to 6 years of age, the most rapid growth in the brain occurs in the frontal lobes. Gross motor skills increase dramatically during early childhood. Fine motor skills also improve substantially during early childhood. Left-handed children are as competent in motor skills and intellect as right-handed children, although left-handers have more reading problems. Both genetic and environmental explanations of handedness have been given. Energy requirements vary according to rate of growth, level of activity, and energy used. Too many young children in the United States are being raised on diets that are too high in fat. Increasingly, young children are overweight. The child's life should be centered on activities, not meals. Other nutritional concerns include malnutrition and the inadequate diets of many children living in poverty. A special concern is the poor health status of many young children in low-income families. There has been a dramatic increase in HIV/AIDS in young children in developing countries in the last decade.

Cognitive Changes

According to Piaget, in the preoperational stage children cannot yet perform operations, but they begin to present the world with symbols, to form stable concepts, and to reason. During the symbolic function substage, which occurs between approximately 2 and 4 years of age, children begin to create symbols, but their thought is limited by egocentrism and animism. During the intuitive thought substage, which stretches from about 4 to 7 years of age, children begin to reason and to bombard adults with questions. Thought at this substage is called intuitive because children seem so sure about their knowledge yet are unaware of how they know what they know. Centration and a lack of conservation also characterize the preoperational stage. Vygotsky's theory represents a social constructivist approach to development. According to Vygotsky, adults should assess and use the child's zone of proximal development (ZPD) and scaffold children's learning. He also emphasized that private speech is an important aspect of the young child's thought. The child's ability to attend to stimuli dramatically improves during early childhood, but the child attends to the salient rather than the relevant features of a task. Significant improvement in short-term memory occurs during early childhood. With good prompts, young children's long-term memories can be accurate, although young children can be led into developing false memories. Theory of mind is the awareness of one's own mental processes and the mental processes of others. Children begin to understand mental states involving perceptions, desires, and emotions at 2 to 3 years of age and at 4 to 5 years of age realize that people can have false beliefs. It is only beyond the early childhood years that children have a deepening appreciation of the mind itself rather than just understanding mental states.

Language Development

Young children increase their grasp of language's rule systems. In terms of phonology, most young children become more sensitive to the sounds of spoken language. Berko's classic experiment demonstrated that young children understand morphological rules. Preschool children learn and apply rules of syntax and how words should be ordered. In terms of semantics, vocabulary development increases dramatically during early childhood. Young children's conversational skills improve, and they learn to change their speech style to suit the situation. Instruction should be built on what young children already know about language. Early precursors of literacy and academic success include language skills such as phonological and syntactic knowledge, letter identification, and knowledge about print.

Early Childhood Education

The child-centered kindergarten emphasizes the education of the whole child, with particular attention to individual variation, the process of learning, and the importance of play in development. The Montessori approach is an increasingly popular early childhood education choice. Developmentally appropriate practice focuses on the typical patterns of children (age appropriateness) and the uniqueness of each child (individual appropriateness). The U.S. government has tried to break the poverty cycle with programs such as Head Start. Model programs have been shown to have positive effects on children who live in poverty. Controversy characterizes early childhood education curricula. On the one side are the child-centered, constructivist advocates; on the other are those who advocate an instructivist, academic approach. Another controversy focuses on whether universal preschool education should be implemented.

Key Terms

myelination 139
preoperational stage 145
operations 145
symbolic function
  substage 145
egocentrism 145
animism 146
intuitive thought
  substage 146

centration 147
conservation 147
social constructivist
  approach 148
zone of proximal
  development (ZPD) 149
short-term memory 153
theory of mind 154
morphology 155

syntax 156
semantics 156
pragmatics 157
child-centered
  kindergarten 158
Montessori approach 158
developmentally
  appropriate practice 159
Project Head Start 160

6

Socioemotional Development in Early Childhood

Stories of Life–Span Development: Craig Lesley's Complicated Early Emotional and Social Life

In his memoir, *Burning Fence: A Western Memoir of Fatherhood,* award-winning novelist Craig Lesley describes one memory from his early childhood:

Lifting me high above his head, my father placed me in the crotch of the Bing cherry tree growing beside my mother's parents' house in The Dalles. A little frightened at the dizzying height, I pressed my palms into the tree's rough, peeling bark. My father stood close, reassuring. I could see his olive skin, dazzling smile, and sharp-creased army uniform.

"Rudell, don't let him fall." My mother watched, her arms held out halfway, as if to catch me....

The cherries were ripe and robins flittered through the green leaves, pecking at the Bings. Tipping my head back I could see blue sky beyond the extended branches.

"That's enough. Bring him down now." My mother's arms reached out farther.

Laughing, my father grabbed me under the arms, twirled me around, and plunked me into the grass. I wobbled a little. Imprinted on my palms was the pattern of the

tree bark, and I brushed off the little bark pieces on my dungarees.

In a moment, my grandmother gave me a small glass of lemonade...

This first childhood memory of my father remains etched in my mind....

When I grew older, I realized that my father had never lifted me into the cherry tree. After Rudell left, I never saw him until I was fifteen. My grandfather had put me in the tree. Still, the memory of my father lifting me into the tree persists. Even today, I remain half-convinced by the details, the press of bark against my palms, the taste of lemonade, the texture of my father's serge uniform. Apparently, my mind has cross-wired the photographs of my handsome father in his army uniform with the logical reality that my grandfather set me in the crotch of the tree.

Why can I remember the event so vividly? I guess because I wanted so much for my father to be there. I have no easy answers. (Lesley, 2005, pp. 8–10)

Like millions of children, Lesley experienced a family torn by divorce; he would also experience abuse by a stepfather. When his father left, Lesley was an infant, but even as a preschooler, he felt his father's absence. Once he planned to win a gift for his father so that his grandmother "could take it to him and then he'd come to see me" (Lesley, 2005, p. 16). In just a few years, the infant had become a child with a complicated emotional and social life.

In early childhood, children's emotional lives and personalities develop in significant ways, and their small worlds widen. In addition to the continuing influence of family relationships, peers assume a more significant role in children's development, play fills the days of many young children's lives—and, for many children, more time is spent watching television. ∎

Emotional and Personality Development

Many changes characterize young children's socioemotional development in early childhood. Their developing minds and social experiences produce remarkable advances in the development of their self, emotional maturity, moral understanding, and gender awareness.

The Self

We learned in Chapter 4 that during the second year of life children make considerable progress in self-recognition. In the early childhood years, young children develop in many ways that enable them to enhance their self-understanding.

Initiative Versus Guilt

In Chapter 1, you read about Erik Erikson's (1968) eight developmental stages that are encountered during certain time periods in the human life span. As you learned in Chapter 4, Erikson's first stage, trust versus mistrust, describes what he considers to be the main developmental task of infancy. Erikson's psychosocial stage associated with early childhood is *initiative versus guilt*. By now, children have become convinced that they are persons of their own; during early childhood, they begin to discover what kind of person they will become. They identify intensely with their parents, who most of the time appear to them to be powerful and beautiful, although often unreasonable, disagreeable, and sometimes even dangerous. During early childhood, children use their perceptual, motor, cognitive, and language skills to make things happen. They have a surplus of energy that permits them to forget failures quickly and to approach new areas that seem desirable— even if dangerous—with undiminished zest and some increased sense of direction. On their own initiative, then, children at this stage exuberantly move out into a wider social world.

The great governor of initiative is *conscience*. Their initiative and enthusiasm may bring them not only rewards but also guilt, which lowers self-esteem.

Self-Understanding and Understanding Others

Recent research studies have revealed that young children are more pychologically aware—of themselves and others—than used to be thought (Harris, 2006;

Thompson, 2006). This increased psychological awareness reflects young children's expanding psychological sophistication.

In Erikson's portrait of early childhood, the young child clearly has begun to develop **self-understanding**, which is the representation of self, the substance and content of self-conceptions (Harter, 2006). Though not the whole of personal identity, self-understanding provides its rational underpinnings (Damon & Hart, 1992). Mainly through interviews, researchers have probed children's conceptions of many aspects of self-understanding (Harter, 2006).

As we saw in Chapter 4, "Socioemotional Development in Infancy," early self-understanding involves self-recognition. In early childhood, young children think that the self can be described by many material characteristics, such as size, shape, and color. They distinguish themselves from others through many physical and material attributes. Says 4-year-old Sandra, "I'm different from Jennifer because I have brown hair and she has blond hair." Says 4-year-old Ralph, "I am different from Hank because I am taller, and I am different from my sister because I have a bicycle." Physical activities are also a central component of the self in early childhood (Keller, Ford, & Meacham, 1978). For example, preschool children often describe themselves in terms of activities such as play. In sum, in early childhood, children often provide self-descriptions that involve body attributes, material possessions, and physical activities.

Although young children mainly describe themselves in terms of concrete, observable features and action tendencies, at about 4 to 5 years of age, as they hear others use psychological trait and emotion terms, they begin to include these in their own self-descriptions (Marsh, Ellis, & Craven, 2002; Thompson, 2006). Thus, in a self-description, 4-year-old Kadir might say, "I'm not scared. I'm always happy."

Young children's self-descriptions are typically unrealistically positive, as reflected in the comment of 4-year-old Kadier, who says he is always happy, which he is not (Harter, 2006). This occurs because they don't yet distinguish between their desired competence and their actual competence.

Children also make advances in their understanding of others in early childhood (Gelman, Heyman, Legare, 2007). As we saw in Chapter 5, "Physical and Cognitive Development in Early Childhood," young children's theory of mind includes understanding that other people have emotions and desires. And at about 4 to 5 years of age, children not only start describing themselves in terms of psychological traits, but they also begin to perceive others in terms of psychological traits. Thus, a 4-year-old might say, "My teacher is nice."

Individual differences characterize young children's social understanding (Laible & Thompson, 2007). Some young children are better than others at understanding what people are feeling and what they desire, for example. To some degree, these individual differences are linked to conversations care-

Young children are more psychologically aware of themselves and others than once thought. Some children are better than others at understanding people's feelings and desires, and to some degree, these individual differences are influenced by conversations caregivers have with young children about feelings and desires.

self-understanding The child's cognitive representation of self, the substance and content of the child's self-conceptions.

givers have with young children about other people's feelings and desires, and children's opportunities to observe others talking about people's feelings and desires. For example, a mother might say to her 3-year-old, "You should think about Raphael's feelings next time before you hit him."

Emotional Development

The young child's growing awareness of self is linked to the ability to feel an expanding range of emotions. Young children, like adults, experience many emotions during the course of a day. Their emotional development in early childhood allows them to try to make sense of other people's emotional reactions and to begin to control their own emotions.

Self-Conscious Emotions

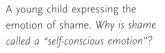

Recall from Chapter 4 that even young infants experience emotions such as joy and fear, but to experience *self-conscious emotions*, children must be able to refer to themselves and be aware of themselves as distinct from others (Lewis, 2007). Pride, shame, embarrassment, and guilt are examples of self-conscious emotions. Self-conscious emotions do not appear to develop until self-awareness appears around 18 months of age.

During the early childhood years, emotions such as pride and guilt become more common. They are especially influenced by parents' responses to children's behavior. For example, a young child may experience shame when a parent says, "You should feel bad about biting your sister."

A young child expressing the emotion of shame. *Why is shame called a "self-conscious emotion"?*

Young Children's Emotion Language and Understanding of Emotion

Among the most important changes in emotional development in early childhood are an increased understanding of emotion and an increased ability to talk about one's own and others' emotions (Kuebli, 1994). Between 2 and 4 years of age, children considerably increase the number of terms they use to describe emotions (Ridgeway, Waters, & Kuczaj, 1985). During this time, they are also learning about the causes and consequences of feelings (Denham, Bassett, & Wyatt, 2007).

When they are 4 to 5 years of age, children show an increased ability to reflect on emotions (Denham, 2006). They also begin to understand that the same event can elicit different feelings in different people. Moreover, they show a growing awareness that they need to manage their emotions to meet social standards (Bruce, Olen, & Jensen, 1999).

Emotion-Coaching and Emotion-Dismissing Parents

Parents can play an important role in helping young children regulate their emotions (Laible & Thompson, 2007; Thompson, 2006). Depending on how they talk with their children about emotion, parents can be described as taking an *emotion-coaching* or an *emotion-dismissing* approach (Katz, 1999). The distinction between these approaches is most evident in the way the parent deals with the child's negative emotions (anger, frustration, sadness, and so on). *Emotion-coaching parents* monitor their children's emotions, view their children's negative emotions as opportunities for teaching, assist them in labeling emotions, and coach them in how to deal effectively with emotions. In contrast, *emotion-dismissing parents* view their role as to deny, ignore, or change negative emotions. Researchers have observed that emotion-coaching parents interact with their children in a less rejecting manner, use more scaffolding and praise, and are more nurturant than are emotion-dismissing parents (Gottman & DeClaire, 1997). Moreover, the children of emotion-coaching parents were better at soothing themselves when they got upset, more effective in regulating their negative affect, focused their attention better, and had fewer behavior problems than the children of emotion-dismissing parents.

Regulation of Emotion and Peer Relations

Emotions play a strong role in determining the success of a child's peer relationships (Saarni & others, 2006). Specifically, the ability to modulate one's emotions is an important skill that benefits children in their relationships with peers. Moody and emotionally negative children are more likely to experience rejection by their peers, whereas emotionally positive children are more popular (Stocker & Dunn, 1990).

Moral Development

Unlike a crying infant, a screaming 5-year-old is likely to be thought responsible for making a fuss. The parents may worry about whether the 5-year-old is a "bad" child. Although there are some who view children as innately good, many developmentalists believe that just as parents help their children become good readers, musicians, or athletes, parents must nurture goodness and help their children develop morally. **Moral development** involves the development of thoughts, feelings, and behaviors regarding rules and conventions about what people should do in their interactions with other people. Major developmental theories have focused on different aspects of moral development.

Moral Feelings

Feelings of anxiety and guilt are central to the account of moral development provided by Freud's psychoanalytic theory (introduced in Chapter 1). According to Freud, to reduce anxiety, avoid punishment, and maintain parental affection, children identify with parents, internalizing their standards of right and wrong, and thus form the *superego*, the moral element of personality.

Freud's ideas are not backed by research, but guilt certainly can motivate moral behavior. Other emotions, however, also contribute to the child's moral development, including positive feelings. One important example is *empathy*, which is responding to another person's feelings with an emotion that echoes the other's feelings (Eisenberg, Fabes, & Spinrad, 2006).

Infants have the capacity for some purely empathic responses, but empathy often requires the ability to discern another's inner psychological states, or what is called *perspective taking*. Learning how to identify a wide range of emotional states in others, and to anticipate what kinds of action will improve another person's emotional state, help to advance children's moral development (Johansson, 2006).

moral development
Development that involves thoughts, feelings, and actions regarding rules and conventions about what people should do in their interactions with other people.

heteronomous morality The first stage of moral development in Piaget's theory, occurring from approximately 4 to 7 years of age. Justice and rules are conceived of as unchangeable properties of the world, removed from the control of people.

autonomous morality The second stage of moral development in Piaget's theory, displayed by older children (about 10 years of age and older). The child becomes aware that rules and laws are created by people and, in judging an action, one should consider the actor's intentions as well as the consequences.

immanent justice The concept that, if a rule is broken, punishment will be meted out immediately.

Piaget extensively observed and interviewed 4- to 12-year-old children as they played games to learn how they used and thought about the games' rules.

Moral Reasoning

Interest in how children think about moral issues was stimulated by Piaget (1932), who extensively observed and interviewed children from the ages of 4 through 12. Piaget watched children play marbles to learn how they used and thought about the game's rules. He also asked children about ethical issues—theft, lies, punishment, and justice, for example. Piaget concluded that children go through two distinct stages in how they think about morality.

- From about 4 to 7 years of age, children display **heteronomous morality,** the first stage of moral development in Piaget's theory. Children think of justice and rules as unchangeable properties of the world, removed from the control of people.

- From 7 to 10 years of age, children are in a transition, showing some features of the first stage of moral reasoning and some stages of the second stage, autonomous morality.

- From about 10 years of age and older, children show **autonomous morality.** They become aware that rules and laws are created by people, and in judging an action, they consider the actor's intentions as well as the consequences.

Because young children are heteronomous moralists, they judge the rightness or goodness of behavior by considering its consequences, not the intentions of the actor. For example, to the heteronomous moralist, breaking twelve cups accidentally is worse than breaking one cup intentionally. As children develop into moral autonomists, intentions become more important than consequences.

The heteronomous thinker also believes that rules are unchangeable and are handed down by all-powerful authorities. When Piaget suggested to young children that they use new rules in a game of marbles, they resisted. By contrast, older children—moral autonomists—accept change and recognize that rules are merely convenient to conventions, subject to change.

The heteronomous thinker also believes in **immanent justice,** the concept that if a rule is broken, punishment will be meted out immediately. The young child believes that a violation is connected automatically to its punishment. Thus, young children often look around worriedly after doing something wrong, expecting inevitable punishment. Immanent justice also implies that if something unfortunate happens to someone, the person must have transgressed earlier. Older children, who are moral autonomists, recognize that punishment occurs only if someone witnesses the wrongdoing and that, even then, punishment is not inevitable.

How do these changes in moral reasoning occur? Piaget argued that, as children develop, they become more sophisticated in thinking about social matters, especially about the possibilities and conditions of cooperation. Piaget stressed that this social understanding comes about through the mutual give-and-take of peer relations. In the peer group, where others have power and status similar to the child's, plans are negotiated and coordinated, and disagreements are reasoned about and eventually settled. Parent-child relations, in which parents have the

How Would You...? As a health-care professional, how would you expect a child in the heteronomous stage of moral development to judge the behaviors of a doctor who unintentionally caused the child pain during a medical procedure?

power and children do not, are less likely to advance moral reasoning, because rules are often handed down in an authoritarian way.

Building on Piaget's ideas, Lawrence Kohlberg developed a theory of moral development that also emphasized moral reasoning and the influence of the give-and-take of peer relations. Like Piaget, Kohlberg concluded from his research that children begin as heteronomous moralists and decide whether an act is right and wrong by whether it is rewarded or punished. Later, in Chapter 8, we examine Kohlberg's theory and his stages of moral development, the evidence his theory is based on, and its critics.

Moral Behavior

The behavioral and social cognitive approach, initially described in Chapter 1, focuses on moral behavior rather than moral reasoning (Bugental & Grusec, 2006; Grusec, 2006). It holds that the processes of reinforcement, punishment, and imitation explain the development of moral behavior. When children are rewarded for behavior that is consistent with laws and social conventions, they are likely to repeat that behavior. When models who behave morally are provided, children are likely to adopt their actions. And, when children are punished for immoral behavior, those behaviors are likely to be reduced or eliminated. However, because punishment may have adverse side effects, as discussed later in this chapter, it needs to be used judiciously and cautiously.

If a 4-year-old boy has been rewarded by his mother for telling the truth when he breaks a glass at home, does that mean that he is likely to tell the truth to his preschool teacher when he knocks over a vase and breaks it? Not necessarily; the situation influences behavior. More than half a century ago, a comprehensive study of thousands of children in many situations—at home, at school, and at church, for example—found that the totally honest child was virtually nonexistent; so was the child who cheated in all situations (Hartshorne & May, 1928–1930). Behavioral and social cognitive researchers emphasize that what children do in one situation is often only weakly related to what they do in other situations. A child might cheat in class but not in a game; a child might steal a piece of candy when alone but not steal it when others are present.

Social cognitive theorists also believe that the ability to resist temptation is closely tied to the development of self-control (Mischel, 2004). To achieve this self-control, children must learn to delay gratification. According to social cognitive theorists, cognitive factors are important in the child's development of self-control (Bandura, 2002).

Gender

Recall from Chapter 1 that *gender* refers to the social and psychological dimensions of being male or female, and even preschool children display many of these dimensions. **Gender identity** is the sense of being male or female, which most children acquire by the time they are 3 years old. **Gender roles** are sets of expectations that prescribe how females or males should think, act, and feel. During the preschool years, most children increasingly act in ways that match their culture's gender roles.

gender identity The sense of being male or female, which most children acquire by the time they are 3 years old.

gender roles Sets of expectations that prescribe how females or males should think, act, and feel.

First imagine that this is a photograph of a baby girl. *What expectations would you have for her?* Then imagine that this is a photograph of a baby boy. *What expectations would you have for him?*

EMOTIONAL AND PERSONALITY DEVELOPMENT

171

social role theory A theory that gender differences result from the contrasting roles of men and women.

psychoanalytic theory of gender A theory deriving from Freud's view that the preschool child develops a sexual attraction to the opposite-sex parent, by approximately 5 or 6 years of age renounces this attraction because of anxious feelings, and subsequently identifies with the same-sex parent, unconsciously adopting the same-sex parent's characteristics.

social cognitive theory of gender A theory that emphasizes that children's gender development occurs through the observation and imitation of gender behavior and through the rewards and punishments children experience for gender-appropriate and gender-inappropriate behavior.

How do these and other gender differences come about? Biology clearly plays a role, as we saw in Chapter 2. Among the possible biological influences are chromosomes, hormones, and evolution. However, our focus here—in this chapter on socioemotional development in early childhood—is on the social aspects of gender.

Social Influences

Many social scientists do not locate the cause of psychological gender differences in biological dispositions. Rather, they argue that these differences are due to social experiences (Denmark, Rabinowitz, & Sechzer, 2005). Explanations for how gender differences come about through experience include both social and cognitive theories.

Social Theories of Gender Three main social theories of gender have been proposed—social role theory, psychoanalytic theory, and social cognitive theory. Alice Eagly (2001) proposed **social role theory**, which states that gender differences result from the contrasting roles of women and men. In most cultures around the world, women have less power and status than men, and they control fewer resources (UNICEF, 2007). Compared with men, women perform more domestic work, spend fewer hours in paid employment, receive lower pay, and are more thinly represented in the highest levels of organizations. In Eagly's view, as women adapted to roles with less power and less status in society, they showed more cooperative, less dominant profiles than men. Thus, the social hierarchy and division of labor are important causes of gender differences in power, assertiveness, and nurture (Wood & Eagly, 2007).

The **psychoanalytic theory of gender** stems from Freud's view that the preschool child develops a sexual attraction to the opposite-sex parent. This is the process known as the Oedipus (for boys) or Electra (for girls) complex. At 5 or 6 years of age, the child renounces this attraction because of anxious feelings. Subsequently, the child identifies with the same-sex parent, unconsciously adopting the same-sex parent's characteristics. However, developmentalists have observed that gender development does not proceed as Freud proposed (Callan, 2001). Children become gender-typed much earlier than 5 or 6 years of age, and they become masculine or feminine even when the same-sex parent is not present in the family.

The social cognitive approach discussed in Chapter 2 provides an alternative explanation of how children develop gender-typed behavior. According to the **social cognitive theory of gender**, children's gender development occurs through observing and imitating what other people say and do, and through being rewarded and punished for gender-appropriate and gender-inappropriate behavior (Bussey & Bandura, 1999). From birth onward, males and females are treated differently. When infants and toddlers show gender differences, adults tend to reward them. Parents often use rewards and punishments to teach their daughters to be feminine ("Karen, you are being a good girl when you play gently with your doll") and their sons to be masculine ("Keith, a boy as big as you is not supposed to cry"). Parents, however, are only one of many sources through which children learn gender roles (Ruble, Martin, & Bernenbaum, 2006). Culture, schools, peers, the media, and other family members also provide gender role models (Matlin, 2008).

For example, children also learn about gender from observing other adults in the neighborhood and on television (Bugental & Grusec, 2006). As children get older, peers become increasingly important. Let's take a closer look at the influence of parents and peers.

Parental Influences Parents, by action and by example, influence their children's gender development (Leaper & Friedman, 2007). Both mothers and fathers are psychologically important to their children's gender development (Grusec & Davidov, 2007). Cultures around the world, however, tend to give mothers and fathers different roles (Kagitcibasi, 2007). A recent research review provided these conclusions (Bronstein (2006):

- *Mothers' socialization strategies.* In many cultures mothers socialize their daughters to be more obedient and responsible than their sons. They also place more restrictions on daughters' autonomy.

- *Fathers' socialization strategies.* Fathers show more attention to sons than daughters, engage in more activities with sons, and put forth more effort to promote sons' intellectual development.

How Would You...?
As a human development and family studies professional, how would you describe the ways in which parents influence their children's notions of gender roles?

Thus, according to Bronstein (2006, pp. 269–270), "Despite an increased awareness in the United States and other Western cultures of the detrimental effects of gender stereotyping, many parents continue to foster behaviors and perceptions that are consonant with traditional gender role norms."

Peer Influences Parents provide the earliest discrimination of gender roles, but before long, peers join the process of responding to and modeling masculine and feminine behavior. In fact, peers become so important to gender development that the playground has been called "gender school" (Luria & Herzog, 1985).

Peers extensively reward and punish gender behavior (Leaper & Friedman, 2007). For example, when children play in ways that the culture says are sex-appropriate, their peers tend to reward them. But peers often reject children who act in a manner that is considered more characteristic of the other gender (Matlin, 2004). A little girl who brings a doll to the park may find herself surrounded by new friends; a little boy might be jeered. However, there is greater pressure for boys to conform to a traditional male role than for girls to conform to a traditional female role (Fagot, Rogers, & Leinbach, 2000). For example, a preschool girl who wants to wear boys' clothing receives considerably more approval than a boy who wants to wear a dress. The very term "tomboy" implies broad social acceptance of girls' adopting traditional male behaviors.

Gender molds important aspects of peer relations. It influences the composition of children's groups, the size of groups, and interactions within a group (Maccoby, 1998, 2002):

- *Gender composition of children's groups.* Around the age of 3, children already show a preference to spend time with same-sex playmates. From 4 to 12 years of age, this preference for playing in same-sex groups increases, and during the elementary school years children spend a large majority of their free time with children of their own sex (see Figure 6.1).

- *Group size.* From about 5 years of age onward, boys are more likely to associate together in larger clusters than girls are. Boys are also more likely to participate in organized group games than girls are. In one study, same-sex groups of six children were permitted to use play materials in any way they wished (Benenson, Apostolaris, & Parnass, 1997). Girls were more likely than boys to play in dyads or triads, while boys were more likely to interact in larger groups and seek to attain a group goal.

- *Interaction in same-sex groups.* Boys are more likely than girls to engage in rough-and-tumble play, competition, conflict, ego displays, risk taking, and seeking dominance. By contrast, girls are more likely to engage in "collaborative discourse," in which they talk and act in a more reciprocal manner.

Cognitive Influences

Observation, imitation, rewards and punishment—these are the mechanisms by which gender develops according to social cognitive theory. Interactions between the child and the social environment are the main keys to gender development in this view. Some critics who adopt a cognitive approach argue that this explanation pays too little attention to the child's own mind and understanding, and portrays the child as passively acquiring gender roles (Martin & Ruble, 2004).

One influential cognitive theory is **gender schema theory**, which states that gender typing emerges as children gradually develop gender schemas of what is gender-appropriate and gender-inappropriate in their culture (Ruble, Martin, & Berenbaum, 2006). A *schema* is a cognitive structure, a network of associations that guide an individual's perceptions. A *gender schema* organizes the world in terms of female and male. Children are internally motivated to perceive the world and to act in accordance with their developing schemas. Bit by bit, children pick up what is gender-appropriate and gender-inappropriate in their culture, and develop gender schemas that shape how they perceive the world and what they remember. Children are motivated to act in ways that conform with these gender schemas. Thus, gender schemas fuel gender typing.

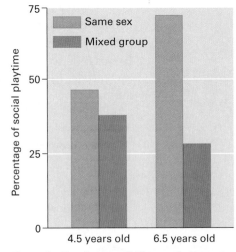

Figure 6.1 Developmental Changes in Percentage of Time Spent in Same-Sex and Mixed-Group Settings Observations of children show that they are more likely to play in same-sex than mixed-sex groups. This tendency increases between 4 to 6 years of age.

How Would You...? As an educator, how would you create a classroom climate that promotes healthy gender development for both boys and girls?

Families

Attachment to a caregiver is a key social relationship during infancy, but we saw in Chapter 4 that some experts maintain that secure attachment and the infant years have been overdramatized as determinants of life-span development. Social and emotional development is also shaped by other relationships and by temperament, contexts, and social experiences in the early childhood years and later. Consider Craig Lesley, whose story opened this chapter. As an infant he was securely attached to his mother, but his abandonment by his father also mattered. For years he missed him; he missed his love; he felt "the terrible pull of my father's blood...he drew me like a lodestone" (Lesley, 2005, p. 141). In this section, we discuss social relationships of early childhood beyond attachment. We explore the different types of parenting, sibling relationships, and variations in family structures.

Parenting

To understand variations in parenting, let's consider the styles parents use when they interact with their children, how they discipline their children, and the cooperative practice of coparenting.

Baumrind's Parenting Styles

Diana Baumrind (1971) stresses that parents should be neither punitive nor aloof. Rather, they should develop rules for their children and be affectionate with them. She has described four types of parenting styles:

- **Authoritarian parenting** is a restrictive, punitive style in which parents exhort the child to follow their directions and respect their work and effort. The authoritarian parent places firm limits and controls on the child and allows little verbal exchange. For example, an authoritarian parent might say, "You do it my way or else." Authoritarian parents also might spank the child frequently, enforce rules rigidly but not explain them, and show anger toward the child. Children of authoritarian parents are often unhappy, fearful, and anxious about comparing themselves with others; they also fail to initiate activity, and have weak communication skills.

- **Authoritative parenting** encourages children to be independent but still places limits and controls on their actions. Extensive verbal give-and-take is allowed, and parents are warm and nurturant toward the child. An authoritative parent might put his arm around the child in a comforting way and say, "You know you should not have done that. Let's talk about how you can handle the situation better next time." Authoritative parents show pleasure and support in response to children's constructive behavior. They also expect independent, age-appropriate behavior by children. Children whose parents are authoritative are often cheerful, self-controlled and self-reliant, and achievement-oriented; they tend to maintain friendly relations with peers, cooperate with adults, and cope well with stress.

- **Neglectful parenting** is a style in which the parent is very uninvolved in the child's life. Children whose parents are neglectful develop the sense that other aspects of the parents' lives are more important than they are. These children tend to be socially incompetent. Many have poor self-control and don't handle independence well. They frequently have low self-esteem, are immature, and may be alienated from the family. In adolescence, they may show patterns of truancy and delinquency.

- **Indulgent parenting** is a style in which parents are highly involved with their children but place few demands or controls on them. Such parents let their children do what they want. Some parents deliberately rear their children in this way because they believe the combination of warm involvement and few restraints will produce a creative, confident child. However, children whose parents are

authoritarian parenting A restrictive punitive style in which parents exhort the child to follow their directions and to respect work and effort. The authoritarian parent places firm limits and controls on the child and allows little verbal exchange. Authoritarian parenting is associated with children's social incompetence.

authoritative parenting A parenting style in which parents encourage their children to be independent but still place limits and controls on their actions. Extensive verbal give-and-take is allowed, and parents are warm and nurturant toward the child. Authoritative parenting is associated with children's social competence.

neglectful parenting A style of parenting in which the parent is very uninvolved in the child's life; it is associated with children's social incompetence, especially a lack of self-control.

indulgent parenting A style of parenting in which parents are highly involved with their children but place few demands or controls on them. Indulgent parenting is associated with children's social incompetence, especially a lack of self-control.

How Would You...?
As a human development and family studies professional, how would you characterize the parenting style that prevails within your own family?

FAMILIES

175

indulgent rarely learn respect for others and have difficulty controlling their behavior. They might be domineering, egocentric, noncompliant, and have difficulties in peer relations.

These four classifications of parenting involve combinations of acceptance and responsiveness on the one hand and demand and control on the other (Maccoby & Martin, 1983). How these dimensions combine to produce authoritarian, authoritative, neglectful, and indulgent parenting is shown in Figure 6.2.

	Accepting, responsive	Rejecting, unresponsive
Demanding, controlling	Authoritative	Authoritarian
Undemanding, uncontrolling	Indulgent	Neglectful

Figure 6.2 Classification of Parenting Styles The four types of parenting styles (authoritative, authoritarian, indulgent, and neglectful) involve the dimensions of acceptance and responsiveness, on the one hand, and demand and control on the other. For example, authoritative parenting involves being both accepting/responsive and demanding/controlling.

Parenting Styles in Context

Among Baumrind's four parenting styles, authoritative parenting clearly conveys the most benefits to the child and to the family as a whole. Do the benefits of authoritative parenting transcend the boundaries of ethnicity, socioeconomic status, and household composition? Although some exceptions have been found, evidence linking authoritative parenting with competence on the part of the child occurs in research across a wide range of ethnic groups, social strata, cultures, and family structures (Steinberg & Silk, 2002).

Nonetheless, researchers have found that in some ethnic groups, aspects of the authoritarian style may be associated with more positive child outcomes than Baumrind predicts (Parke & Buriel, 2006). In the Arab world, many families today are very authoritarian, dominated by the father's rule, and children are taught strict codes of conduct and family loyalty (Booth, 2002). As another example, Asian American parents often continue aspects of traditional Asian child-rearing practices that have sometimes been described as authoritarian. The parents exert considerable control over their children's lives. However, Ruth Chao (2001, 2005, 2007; Chao & Tseng, 2002) argues that the style of parenting used by many Asian American parents is distinct from the domineering control of the authoritarian style. Instead, Chao argues that the control reflects concern and involvement in children's lives and is best conceptualized as a type of training. The high academic achievement of Asian American children may be a consequence of their parents' "training" (Stevenson & Zusho, 2002).

Punishment

For centuries, corporal (physical) punishment, such as spanking, has been considered a necessary and even desirable method of disciplining children. Use of corporal punishment is legal in every state in America. A recent national survey

How Would You...?
As a psychologist, how would you use the research on parenting styles to design a parent education class that teaches effective skills for interacting with young children?

of U.S. parents with 3- and 4-year-old children found that 26 percent of parents reported spanking their children frequently, and 67 percent of the parents reported yelling at their children frequently (Regaldo & others, 2004). A cross-cultural comparison found that individuals in the United States and Canada were among those with the most favorable attitudes toward corporal punishment and were the most likely to remember it being used by their parents (Curran & others, 2001).

A research review concluded that corporal punishment by parents is associated with higher levels of immediate compliance, but also with increased aggression by the children (Gershoff, 2002). The review also found that children subjected to corporal punishment have lower levels of moral internalization and mental health. A longitudinal study found that spanking before age 2 was related to behavioral problems in middle and late childhood (Slade & Wissow, 2004). And in a recent study, children whose parents who had hit or slapped them in the prior two weeks showed more emotional and adjustment problems than children who had not been hit or slapped by parents in the same time frame (Aucoin, Frick, & Bodin, 2006).

Despite the widespread use of corporal punishment, there have been surprisingly few research studies on physical punishment, and those that have been conducted are correlational. And some critics argue that the research evidence is not yet sound enough to warrant a blanket injunction against corporal punishment, especially mild corporal punishment (Baumrind, Larzelere, & Cowan, 2002; Kazdin & Benjet, 2003).

Among the reasons that many developmentalists recommend not spanking children or using other intense punishments are: (1) when parents spank or yell at children, they present children with an out-of-control model which the children may then imitate (Sim & Ong, 2005); (2) punishment can instill fear, rage, or avoidance in children; (3) punishment tells the child what *not* to do rather than what *to* do; and (4) punishment can be abusive. Parents might unintentionally become so aroused when they are punishing a child that they lose control and abuse the child (Ateah, 2005).

Most child psychologists recommend handling misbehavior by reasoning with the child, especially explaining the consequences of the child's actions for others. *Time out*, in which the child is briefly removed from a setting that offers positive reinforcement, can also be effective. For example, when the child has misbehaved, a parent might take away TV viewing for an age-appropriate specified time.

Coparenting

Coparenting refers to the support that parents provide one another in jointly raising a child. Poor coordination between parents, undermining of the other parent, lack of cooperation and warmth, and disconnection by one parent are conditions that place children at risk for problems (McHale, 2007; McHale & Sullivan, 2007). For example, in one study, 4-year-old children from families characterized by low levels of mutuality and support in coparenting were more likely than their classmates to show difficulties in social adjustment on the playground (McHale, Johnson, & Sinclair, 1999). By contrast, parental cooperation and warmth are linked with children's prosocial behavior and competence in peer relations.

Parents who have difficulty learning to coparent, or who have other problems in child rearing, can benefit from counseling and therapy. The work of marriage and family counselor Darla Botkin is described in the Careers in Life-Span Development profile.

CAREERS IN LIFE-SPAN DEVELOPMENT

Darla Botkin, Marriage and Family Therapist

Darla Botkin is a marriage and family therapist who teaches, conducts research, and engages in marriage and family therapy. She is on the faculty of the University of Kentucky. Darla obtained a bachelor's degree in elementary education with a concentration in special education and then went on to receive a master's degree in early childhood education. She spent the next six years working with children and their families in a variety of settings, including child care, elementary school, and Head Start. These experiences led Darla to recognize the interdependence of the developmental settings that children and their parents experience (such as home, school, and work). She returned to graduate school and obtained a Ph.D. in family studies from the University of Tennessee. Darla then became a faculty member in the Family Studies program at the University of Kentucky. Completing further coursework and clinical training in marriage and family therapy, she became certified as a marriage and family therapist.

Darla's current interests include working with young children in family therapy, gender and ethnic issues in family therapy, and the role of spirituality in family wellness.

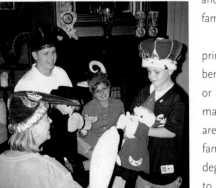

Darla Botkin (*left*), conducting a family therapy session.

Marriage and family therapists, like Darla Botkin, work on the principle that many individuals who have psychological problems benefit when psychotherapy is provided in the context of a marital or family relationship. Marriage and family therapists may provide marital therapy, couple therapy to individuals in a relationship who are not married, and family therapy to two or more members of a family. Marriage and family therapists have a master's or a doctoral degree. They complete a training program in graduate school similar to a clinical psychologist's but with the focus on marital and family relationships. In most states, it is necessary to go through a licensing procedure to practice marital and family therapy.

Child Maltreatment

Unfortunately, punishment sometimes leads to the abuse of infants and children. In 2002, approximately 906,000 U.S. children were found to be victims of child abuse (U.S. Department of Health and Human Services, 2005). Eighty-four percent of these children were abused by a parent or parents. Laws in many states now require physicians and teachers to report suspected cases of child abuse, yet many cases go unreported, especially those of battered infants (Miller-Perrin & Perrin, 2007).

Whereas the public and many professionals use the term *child abuse* to refer to both abuse and neglect, developmentalists increasingly use the term *child maltreatment* (Cicchetti & Toth, 2005, 2006). This term does not have quite the emotional impact of the term *abuse* and acknowledges that maltreatment includes diverse conditions.

Types of Child Maltreatment

The four main types of child maltreatment are physical abuse, child neglect, sexual abuse, and emotional abuse (Child Welfare Information Gateway, 2007):

- *Physical abuse* is characterized by the infliction of physical injury as result of punching, beating, kicking, biting, burning, shaking, or otherwise harming a child. The parent or other person may not have intended to hurt the child; the injury may have resulted from excessive physical punishment (Hornor, 2005).

- *Child neglect* is characterized by failure to provide for the child's basic needs (Sedlak & others, 2006). Neglect can be physical (abandonment, for example), educational (allowing chronic truancy, for example), or emotional (marked inattention to the child's needs, for example).

- *Sexual abuse* includes fondling a child's genitals, intercourse, incest, rape, sodomy, exhibitionism, and commercial exploitation through prostitution or the production of pornographic materials (Edinburgh & others, 2006).

How Would You...?
As a health-care professional, how would you work with parents during infant and toddler checkups to prevent child maltreatment?

- *Emotional abuse (psychological/verbal abuse/mental injury)* includes acts or omissions by parents or other caregivers that have caused, or could cause, serious behavioral, cognitive, or emotional problems (Gelles & Cavanaugh, 2005).

Although any of these forms of child maltreatment may be found separately, they often occur in combination. Emotional abuse is almost always present when other forms are identified.

The Context of Abuse

No single factor causes child maltreatment (Cicchetti & Toth, 2005, 2006). A combination of factors, including the culture, family, and developmental characteristics of the child, likely contribute to child maltreatment.

The extensive violence that takes place in American culture is reflected in the occurrence of violence in the family (Freisthler, Merritt, & Lascala, 2006). A regular diet of violence appears on television screens, and parents often resort to power assertion as a disciplinary technique. In China, where physical punishment is rarely used to discipline children, the incidence of child abuse is reported to be very low.

The family itself is obviously a key part of the context of abuse (Miller-Perrin & Perrin, 2007). The interactions of all family members need to be considered, regardless of who performs the violent acts against the child (Kim & Cicchetti, 2004). For example, even though the father may be the one who physically abuses the child, the behavior of the mother, the child, and siblings also should be evaluated. A mother who conveniently goes shopping whenever the father is angry with the child, or siblings who tease the child for "deserving" a beating, may contribute to the abuse.

Were parents who abuse children abused by their own parents? About one-third of parents who were abused themselves when they were young go on to abuse their own children (Cicchetti & Toth, 2005, 2006). Thus, some, but not a majority, of parents are involved in an intergenerational transmission of abuse (Dixon, Browne, & Hamilton-Giachritsis, 2005). Mothers who break out of the intergenerational transmission of abuse often report having had at least one warm, caring adult in their background; have a close, positive marital relationship; and have received therapy (Egeland, Jacobvitz, & Sroufe, 1988).

This print ad was created by Prevent Child Abuse America to make people aware of its national blue wristband campaign. The campaign's goal is to educate people about child abuse prevention and encourage them to support the organization. *Source: Prevent Child Abuse America*

FAMILIES

Developmental Consequences of Abuse

Among the consequences of child maltreatment in childhood and adolescence are poor emotion regulation, attachment problems, problems in peer relations, difficulty in adapting to school, and other psychological problems such as depression and delinquency (Cicchetti & Toth, 2005, 2006). Later, during the adult years, those who were maltreated as children often have difficulty in establishing and maintaining healthy intimate relationships (Minzenberg, Poole, & Vinogradov, 2006). As adults, maltreated children are also at higher risk for violent behavior toward other adults—especially dating partners and marital partners—as well as for substance abuse, anxiety, and depression (Shea & others, 2005).

How Would You...?

As an educator, how would you explain the potential impact of maltreatment in the home on a child's schooling?

What can be done to prevent or reduce the incidence of child maltreatment? In one recent study of maltreating mothers and their 1-year-olds, two treatments were effective in reducing child maltreatment: (1) home visitation that emphasized improved parenting, coping with stress, and increasing support for the mother; and (2) parent-infant psychotherapy that focused on improving maternal-infant attachment (Cicchetti, Toth, and Rogosch, 2005).

Sibling Relationships and Birth Order

The middle and late childhood years are a time when many children spend a great deal of time interacting with their siblings. How do developmentalists characterize sibling relationships? How extensively does birth order influence behavior?

Approximately 80 percent of American children have one or more siblings— that is, sisters and brothers (Dunn, 2007). Any of you who have grown up with siblings probably have a rich memory of aggressive, hostile interchanges. Siblings in the presence of each other when they are 2 to 4 years of age, on average, have a conflict once every 10 minutes and then the conflicts go down somewhat from 5 to 7 years of age (Kramer, 2006). What do parents do when they encounter siblings having a verbal or physical confrontation? One study revealed that they do one of three things: (1) intervene and try to help them resolve the conflict, (2) admonish or threaten them, or (3) do nothing at all (Kramer & Perozynski, 1999). Of interest is that in families with two siblings 2 to 5 years of age, the most frequent parental reaction is do nothing at all.

Laurie Kramer (2006), who had conducted a number of research studies on siblings, says that not intervening and letting sibling conflict escalate is not a good strategy. She developed a program titled "More Fun with Sisters and Brothers," which teaches 4- to 8-year-old siblings social skills for developing positive interactions (Kramer & Radey, 1997). Among the social skills taught in the program are how to appropriately initiate play, how to accept and refuse invitations to play, perspective taking, how to deal with angry feelings, and how to manage conflict.

However, conflict is only one of the many dimensions of sibling relations. Sibling relations include helping, sharing, teaching, fighting, and playing, and siblings can act as emotional supports, rivals, and communication partners (Pomery & others, 2006).

Judy Dunn (2007), a leading expert on sibling relationships, recently described three important characteristics of sibling relationships:

- *Emotional quality of the relationship.* Both intensive positive and negative emotions are often expressed by siblings toward each other. Many children and adolescents have mixed feelings toward their siblings.

- *Familiarity and intimacy of the relationship.* Siblings typically know each other very well, and this intimacy suggests that they can either provide support or tease and undermine each other, depending on the situation.

- *Variation in sibling relationships.* Some siblings describe their relationships more positively than others. Thus, there is considerable variation in sibling relationships. We just indicated that many siblings have mixed feelings about each other, but some children and adolescents mainly describe their sibling in warm, affectionate ways, while others primarily talk about how irritating and mean a sibling is.

Birth Order

Whether a child has older or younger siblings has been linked to development of certain personality characteristics. For example, compared with later-born children, firstborn children are more adult-oriented, helpful, conforming, and self-controlled. Firstborns excel in academic and professional endeavors, and they have more guilt, anxiety, and difficulty in coping with stressful situations, as well as higher admission to child guidance clinics.

The one-child family is becoming much more common in China because of the strong motivation to limit the country's population growth. The policy is still relatively new, and its effects on children have not been fully examined. *In general, though, what have researchers found the only child to be like?*

What accounts for such differences related to birth order? Proposed explanations usually point to variations in interactions with parents and siblings associated with being in a particular position in the family. This is especially true in the case of the firstborn child (Teti, 2002). The oldest child is the only one who does not have to share parental love and affection with other siblings—until another sibling comes along. An infant requires more attention than an older child; this means that the firstborn sibling receives less attention after the newborn arrives. Does this result in conflict between parents and the firstborn? In one research study, mothers became more negative, coercive, and restraining and played less with the firstborn following the birth of a second child (Dunn & Kendrick, 1982).

What is the only child like? The popular conception is that the only child is a "spoiled brat," with such undesirable characteristics as dependency, lack of self-control, and self-centered behavior. But researchers present a more positive portrayal of the only child. Only children often are achievement-oriented and display a desirable personality, especially in comparison with later-borns and children from large families (Falbo & Poston, 1993; Jiao, Ji, & Jing, 1996).

So far, our discussion suggests that birth order might be a strong predictor of behavior. However, an increasing number of family researchers believe that when all of the factors that influence behavior are considered, birth order itself shows limited ability to predict behavior. Think about some of the other important factors in children's lives that influence their behavior beyond birth order. They include heredity, models of competency or incompetency that parents present to children on a daily basis, peer influences, school influences, socioeconomic factors, sociohistorical factors, and cultural variations. When someone says firstborns are always like this but last-borns are always like that, the person is making overly

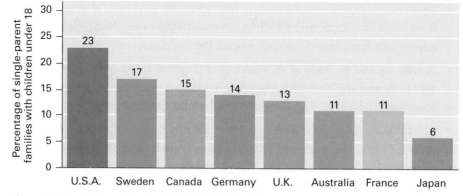

Figure 6.3 Single-Parent Families in Different Countries

simplistic statements that do not adequately take into account the complexity of influences on a child's development.

The Changing Family in a Changing Society

Beyond variations in the number of siblings, the families that children experience differ in many important ways. The number of children growing up in single-parent families is staggering (Martin, Emery, & Peris, 2004). As shown in Figure 6.3, the United States has one of the highest percentage of single-parent families in the world. Among two-parent families, there are those in which both parents work, or have divorced parents who have remarried, or gay or lesbian parents. Differences in culture and socioeconomic status (SES) also influence families. How do these variations in families affect children?

Working Parents

More than one of every two U.S. mothers with a child under the age of 5 is in the labor force; more than two of every three mothers with a child from 6 to 17 years of age is. Maternal employment is a part of modern life, but its effects are still debated. According to Lois Hoffman (1989), because household operations have become more efficient and family size has decreased, it is not certain that American children today receive less attention when both parents work outside the home than children in the past whose mothers were not employed. Parents might spend less time than in the past keeping the house clean or pursuing hobbies. Time once split among several children might now be focused on just one or two.

It also cannot be assumed that all children would benefit from receiving extra time and attention from stay-at-home parents. Parenting does not always have a positive effect on the child. Parents may overinvest in their children, worrying excessively and discouraging the child's independence. The needs of the growing child require parents to give increasing independence to the child, which may be easier for parents whose jobs provide an additional source of identity and self-esteem.

Work can produce positive and negative effects on parenting (Crouter & McHale, 2005; Heidi, 2006). Recent research indicates that what matters for children's development is the nature of parents' work rather than whether one parent works outside the home (Clarke-Stewart, 2006). Ann Crouter (2006) recently described how parents bring their experiences at work into their homes. She concluded that parents who have poor working conditions, such as long hours, overtime work, stressful work, and lack of autonomy at work, are likely to be more irritable at home and engage in less effective parenting than their counterparts who have better work conditions in their jobs.

Children in Divorced Families

Divorce rates changed rather dramatically in the United States and many countries around the world in the late twentieth century (Amato & Irving, 2006). The U.S. divorce rate increased dramatically in the 1960s and 1970s but has declined since the 1980s. However, the divorce rate in the United States is still much higher than in most other countries.

It is estimated that 40 percent of children born to married parents in the United States will experience their parents' divorce (Hetherington & Stanley-Hagan, 2002). Let's examine some important questions about children in divorced families:

Are children better adjusted in intact, never-divorced families than in divorced families? Most researchers agree that children from divorced families show poorer adjustment than their counterparts in nondivorced families (Hetherington, 2005, 2006; Huurre, Junkkari, & Aro, 2006 (see Figure 6.4). Those who have experienced multiple divorces are at greater risk. Children in divorced families are more likely than children in nondivorced families to have academic problems, to show externalized problems (such as acting out and delinquency) and internalized problems (such as anxiety and depression), to be less socially responsible, to have less competent intimate relationships, to drop out of school, to become sexually active at an early age, to take drugs, to associate with antisocial peers, to have low self-esteem, and to be less securely attached as young adults (Conger & Chao, 1996). For example, one recent study found that experiencing a divorce in childhood was associated with insecure attachment in early adulthood (Brockmeyer, Treboux, & Crowell, 2005). Another recent study revealed that when individuals experienced the divorce of their parents in childhood and adolescence, it was linked to having unstable romantic or marital relationships and low levels of education in adulthood (Amato, 2006). Nonetheless, keep in mind that a majority of children in divorced families do not have significant adjustment problems (Ahrons, 2007; Barber & Demo, 2006). One recent study found that 20 years after their parents had divorced when they were children, approximately 80 percent of adults concluded that their parents' decision to divorce was a wise one (Ahrons, 2004).

Should parents stay together for the sake of the children? Whether parents should stay in an unhappy or conflicted marriage for the sake of their children is one of the most commonly asked questions about divorce (Hetherington, 2005, 2006). If the stresses and disruptions in family relationships associated with an unhappy, conflictual marriage that erode the well-being of children are reduced by the move to a divorced, single-parent family, divorce can be advantageous. However, if the diminished resources and increased risks associated with divorce also are accompanied by inept parenting and sustained or increased conflict, not only between the divorced couple but also among the parents, children, and siblings, the best choice for the

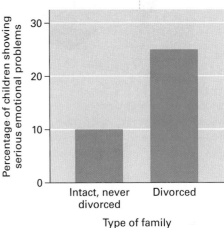

Figure 6.4 Divorce and Children's Emotional Problems In Hetherington's research, 25 percent of children from divorced families showed serious emotional problems compared with only 10 percent of children from intact, never-divorced families. However, keep in mind that a substantial majority (75 percent) of the children from divorced families did not show serious emotional problems.

What concerns are involved in whether parents should stay together for the sake of the children or become divorced?

children would be for an unhappy marriage to be retained (Hetherington & Stanley-Hagan, 2002). It is difficult to determine how these "ifs" will play out when parents either remain together in an acrimonious marriage or become divorced.

Note that marital conflict may have negative consequences for children in the context of marriage or divorce (McDonald & Grych, 2006). A longitudinal study revealed that conflict in nondivorced families was associated with emotional problems in children (Amato, 2006)

How much do family processes matter in divorced families? Family processes matter a great deal (Clarke-Stewart & Brentano, 2006; Kelly, 2007). When divorced parents' relationship with each other is harmonious, and when they use authoritative parenting, the adjustment of children improves (Hetherington, 2005, 2006). A number of researchers have shown that a disequilibrium, which includes diminished parenting skills, occurs in the year following the divorce but that, by two years after the divorce, restabilization has occurred and parenting skills have improved (Hetherington, 1989).

What factors influence an individual child's vulnerability to suffering negative consequences as a result of living in a divorced family? Among the factors involved in the child's risk and vulnerability are the child's adjustment prior to the divorce, as well as the child's personality and temperament, gender, and custody situation (Hetherington, 2005, 2006). Children whose parents later divorce show poorer adjustment before the breakup (Amato & Booth, 1996). Children who are socially mature and responsible, who show few behavioral problems, and who have an easy temperament are better able to cope with their parents' divorce. Children with a difficult temperament often have problems in coping with their parents' divorce (Hetherington, 2005).

Earlier studies reported gender differences in response to divorce, with divorce being more negative for girls than boys in mother-custody families. However, more recent studies have shown that gender differences are less pronounced and consistent than was previously believed. Some of the inconsistency may be due to the increase in father custody, joint custody, and increased involvement of noncustodial fathers, especially in their sons' lives (Palmer, 2004). An analysis of studies found that children in joint-custody families were better adjusted than children in sole-custody families (Bauserman, 2002). Some studies have shown that boys adjust better in father-custody families, girls in mother-custody families, whereas other studies have not (Maccoby & Mnookin, 1992; Santrock & Warshak, 1979).

What role does socioeconomic status play in the lives of children in divorced families? Custodial mothers experience the loss of about one-fourth to one-half of their predivorce income, in comparison with a loss of only one-tenth by custodial fathers (Emery, 1994). This income loss for divorced mothers is accompanied by increased workloads, high rates of job instability, and residential moves to less desirable neighborhoods with inferior schools (Sayer, 2006).

In sum, many factors are involved in determining how divorce influences a child's development (Hetherington, 2005, 2006). In the case of Craig Lesley, whose story opened this chapter, his parents' divorce certainly marked his life, but perhaps not quite in ways we would predict. According to Lesley, his father's "neglect motivated me to raise an alcohol-damaged Indian boy just to show the old man I could succeed as a father where he had fallen down. To be truthful, it was harder than I thought" (Lesley, 2005, p. 7).

From this discussion, we can see that many factors are involved in determining how divorce influences a child's development (Clarke-Stewart & Brentano, 2006; Hetherington, 2006). The following guidelines for communicating with chidren about divorce were developed by Ellen Galinsky and Judy David (1988):

- *Explain the separation.* As soon as daily activities in the home make it obvious that one parent is leaving, tell the children. If possible, both parents should be present when children are told about the separation to come. The reasons for the separation are very difficult for young children to understand. No matter what parents tell children, children can find reasons to argue against the separation. It is extremely important for parents to tell the children who will take care of them and to describe the specific arrangements for seeing the other parent.

- *Explain that the separation is not the child's fault.* Young children often believe their parents' separation or divorce is their own fault. Therefore, it is important to tell children that they are not the cause of the separation. Parents need to repeat this a number of times.

- *Explain that it may take time to feel better.* Tell young children that it's normal to not feel good about what is happening and that many other children feel this way when their parents become separated. It is also okay for divorced parents to share some of their emotions with children, by saying something like, "I'm having a hard time since the separation just like you, but I know it's going to get better after a while." Such statements are best kept brief and should not criticize the other parent.

How Would You...?
As a human development and family studies professional, how would you apply the guidelines on communicating about divorce to help parents discuss the death of a family member with their children?

- *Keep the door open for further discussion.* Tell your children to come to you anytime they want to talk about the separation. It is healthy for children to express their pent-up emotions in discussions with their parents and to learn that the parents are willing to listen to their feelings and fears.

- *Provide as much continuity as possible.* The less children's worlds are disrupted by the separation, the easier their transition to a single-parent family will be. This means maintaining the rules already in place as much as possible. Children need parents who care enough not only to give them warmth and nurturance but also to set reasonable limits.

Gay Male and Lesbian Parents

Increasingly, gay male and lesbian couples are creating families that include children. Approximately 20 percent of lesbians and 10 percent of gay men are parents (Patterson, 2004). There may be more than one million gay and lesbian parents in the United States today.

Like heterosexual couples, gay male and lesbian parents vary greatly. They may be single, or they may have same-gender partners. Many lesbian mothers and gay fathers are noncustodial parents because they lost custody of their children to heterosexual spouses after a divorce.

Most children of gay and lesbian parents were born in a heterosexual relationship that ended in a divorce: in most cases, it was probably a relationship in which one or both parents only later identified themselves as gay male or lesbian. In other cases, lesbians and gay men became parents as a result of donor insemination and surrogates, or through adoption.

What are the research findings regarding the development and psychological well-being of children raised by gay male and lesbian couples?

Parenthood among lesbians and gay men is controversial. Opponents claim that being raised by male or lesbian parents harms the child's development. But researchers have found few differences between children growing up with lesbian mothers or gay fathers on the one hand, and children growing up with heterosexual parents on the other (Patterson, 2004; Patterson & Hastings, 2007). For example, children growing up in gay or lesbian families are just as popular with their peers, and no differences are found in the adjustment and mental health of children living in these families when they are compared with children in heterosexual families (Hyde, 2007). Contrary to the once-popular expectation that being raised by a gay or lesbian parent would result in the child growing up to be gay or lesbian, in fact the overwhelming majority of children from gay or lesbian families have a heterosexual orientation (Tasker & Golombok, 1997).

Cultural, Ethnic, and Socioeconomic Variations

Parenting can be influenced by culture, ethnicity, and socioeconomic status. Recall from Bronfenbrenner's ecological theory (Chapter 1) that a number of social contexts influence the child's development. In Bronfenbrenner's theory, culture, ethnicity, and socioeconomic status are classified as part of the macrosystem because they represent broader, societal contexts.

Cross-Cultural Studies Different cultures often give different answers to such basic questions as what the father's role in the family should be, what support systems are available to families, and how children should be disciplined (Harkness & Super, 2002; Shiraev & Levy, 2007). There are important cross-cultural variations in parenting (Kagitcibasi, 2007). In some cultures (such as Arab countries, mentioned earlier in this chapter), authoritarian parenting is widespread.

Cultural change, brought about by such factors as increasingly frequent international travel, the Internet and electronic communications, and economic globalization, is coming to families in many countries around the world. There are trends toward greater family mobility, migration to urban areas, separation as some family members work in cities or countries far from their homes, smaller families, fewer extended-family households, and increases in maternal employment (Brown & Larson, 2002). These trends can change the resources that are available to children. For example, when several generations no longer live close by, children may lose support and guidance from grandparents, aunts, and uncles. On the positive side, smaller families may produce more openness and communication between parents and children.

Ethnicity Families within different ethnic groups in the United States differ in their typical size, structure, composition, reliance on kinships networks, and levels of income and education (Hernandez, 2007; Hernandez, Denton, & Macartney, 2007). Large and extended families are more common among minority groups than among the White majority. For example, 19 percent of Latino families have three or more children, compared with 14 percent of African American and 10 percent of White families. African American and Latino children interact more with grandparents, aunts, uncles, cousins, and more-distant relatives than do White children.

Single-parent families are more common among African Americans and Latinos than among White Americans (Harris & Graham, 2007; McAdoo, 2006). In comparison with two-parent households, single parents often have more limited resources of time, money, and energy (Ryan, Fauth, & Brooks-Gunn, 2006). Ethnic minority parents also are less educated and more likely to live in low-income circumstances than their White counterparts (Fuligni & Fuligni, 2007). Still, many impoverished ethnic minority families manage to find ways to raise competent children (Huston & Ripke, 2006).

Of course, individual families vary, and how ethnic minority families deal with stress depends on many factors. Whether the parents are native-born or immigrants, how long the family has been in this country, their socioeconomic status, and their national origin all make a difference (Berry, 2007).

The opportunities for cultural adaptation that young children experience depend mainly on their parents and extended family (Garcia Coll & Pachter, 2002). When children spend time in a child-care center, school, church, or other community setting, they are likely to learn the values and behaviors of the dominant culture, and they may be expected to adapt to that culture's norms. When they are at home, these norms may not be reinforced. Thus, children raised in a traditional Latino family where the family's good is valued more highly than the individual's interests may attend a preschool in which children are rewarded for asserting themselves. Chinese American children whose traditional parents value behavioral inhibition may be rewarded outside the home for being active and emotionally expressive. Over time, the differences in the level of acculturation experienced by children and by their parents and extended family may grow.

What are some characteristics of families within different ethnic groups?

Socioeconomic Status In America and most Western cultures, differences have been found in child rearing among different SES groups (Hoff, Laursen, & Tardif, 2002, p. 246):

- "Lower-SES parents (1) are more concerned that their children conform to society's expectations, (2) create a home atmosphere in which it is clear that parents have authority over children," (3) use physical punishment more in disciplining their children, and (4) are more directive and less conversational with their children.

- "Higher-SES parents (1) are more concerned with developing children's initiative" and delay of gratification, "(2) create a home atmosphere in which children are more nearly equal participants and in which rules are discussed as opposed to being laid down" in an authoritarian manner, (3) are less likely to use physical punishment, and (4) "are less directive and more conversational" with their children.

Parents in different socioeconomic groups also tend to think differently about education (Huston & Ripke, 2006; Magnuson & Duncan, 2002). Middle- and upper-income parents more often think of education as something that should be mutually encouraged by parents and teachers. By contrast, low-income parents are more likely to view education as the teacher's job. Thus, increased school-family linkages especially can benefit students from low-income families.

How Would You...?
As an educator, how would you work with low socioeconomic-status families to increase parental involvement in their children's educational activities?

Peer Relations, Play, and Television

The family is an important social context for children's development. However, children's development also is strongly influenced by what goes on in other social contexts, such as in peer groups and when children are playing or watching television.

Peer Relations

As children grow older, they spend an increasing amount of time with their *peers*—children of about the same age or maturity level.

What are the functions of a child's peer group? One of its most important functions is to provide a source of information and comparison about the world outside the family. Children receive feedback about their abilities from their peer group. Children evaluate what they do in terms of whether it is better than, as good as, or worse than what other children do. It is hard to make these judgments at home because siblings are usually older or younger.

Good peer relations can be necessary for normal socioemotional development (Ladd, Herald, & Andrews, 2006). Special concerns focus on children who are withdrawn and aggressive (Bukowski, Brendgen, & Vitaro, 2007). Withdrawn children who are rejected by peers or are victimized and feel lonely are at risk for depression. Children who are aggressive with their peers are at risk for developing a number of problems, including delinquency and dropping out of school (Dodge, Coie, & Lynam, 2006).

Recall from our discussion of gender that by about the age of 3, children already prefer to spend time with same-sex rather than opposite-sex playmates, and this preference increases in early childhood. During these same years, the frequency of peer interaction, both positive and negative, picks up considerably (Hartup, 1983). Although aggressive interaction and rough-and-tumble play increase, the proportion of aggressive exchanges, compared to friendly exchanges, decreases. Many preschool children spend considerable time in peer interaction just conversing with playmates about such matters as "negotiating roles and rules in play, arguing, and agreeing" (Rubin, Bukowski, & Parker, 2006). We have much more to say about peer relations in Chapter 8, "Socioemotional Development in Middle and Late Childhood."

Play

An extensive amount of peer interaction during childhood involves play, but social play is only one type of play. *Play* is a pleasurable activity that is engaged in for its own sake, and its functions and forms vary.

Play's Functions

Play is essential to the young child's health (Frost & others, 2008, Sutterby & Frost, 2006). Theorists have focused on different aspects of play and highlighted a long list of functions.

According to Freud and Erikson, play helps the child master anxieties and conflicts. Because tensions are relieved in play, the child can cope with life's problems. Play permits the child to work off excess physical energy and to release pent-up tensions. Therapists use *play therapy* both to allow the child to work off frustrations and to analyze the child's conflicts and ways of coping with them (Frost & others, 2008).

Children may feel less threatened and be more likely to express their true feelings in the context of play.

Piaget (1962) maintained that play advances children's cognitive development. At the same time, he said that children's cognitive development *constrains* the way they play. Play permits children to practice their competencies and acquired skills in a relaxed, pleasurable way. Piaget thought that cognitive structures need to be exercised, and play provides the perfect setting for this exercise. For example, children who have just learned to add or multiply begin to play with numbers in different ways as they perfect these operations, laughing as they do so.

Vygotsky (1962) also considered play to be an excellent setting for cognitive development. He was especially interested in the symbolic and make-believe aspects of play, as when a child substitutes a stick for a horse and rides the stick as if it were a horse. For young children, the imaginary situation is real. Parents should encourage such imaginary play, because it advances the child's cognitive development, especially creative thought.

Daniel Berlyne (1960) described play as exciting and pleasurable in itself because it satisfies our exploratory drive. This drive involves curiosity and a desire for information about something new or unusual. Play is a means whereby children can safely explore and seek out new information. Play encourages exploratory behavior by offering children the possibilities of novelty, complexity, uncertainty, surprise, and incongruity.

Types of Play

The contemporary perspective on play emphasizes both the cognitive and the social aspects of play (Roskos & Christie, 2007). Among the most widely studied types of children's play today are sensorimotor and practice play, pretense/symbolic play, social play, constructive play, and games (Bergen, 1988).

Sensorimotor and Practice Play **Sensorimotor play** is behavior by infants to derive pleasure from exercising their sensorimotor schemes. The development of sensorimotor play follows Piaget's description of sensorimotor thought, which we discussed in Chapter 7. Infants initially engage in exploratory and playful visual and motor transactions in the second quarter of the first year of life. For example, at 9 months of age, infants begin to select novel objects for exploration and play, especially responsive objects, such as toys that make noise or bounce. At 12 months of age, infants enjoy making things work and exploring cause and effect.

Practice play involves the repetition of behavior when new skills are being learned or when physical or mental mastery and coordination of skills are required for games or sports. Sensorimotor play, which often involves practice play, is primarily confined to infancy, while practice play can be engaged in throughout life. During the preschool years, children often engage in practice play. Although practice play declines in the elementary school years, practice play activities such as running, jumping, sliding, twirling, and throwing balls or other objects are frequently observed on the playgrounds at elementary schools.

sensorimotor play Behavior engaged in by infants to derive pleasure from exercising their existing sensorimotor schemes.

practice play Play that involves repetition of behavior when new skills are being learned or when physical or mental mastery and coordination of skills are required for games or sports.

pretense/symbolic play Play in which the child transforms the physical environment into a symbol.

What types of play are these young children engaging in?

social play Play that involves social interactions with peers.

constructive play Play that combines sensorimotor and repetitive activity with symbolic representation of ideas. Constructive play occurs when children engage in self-regulated creation or construction of a product or a problem solution.

games Activities engaged in for pleasure that include rules and often competition with one or more individuals.

Pretense/Symbolic Play **Pretense/symbolic play** occurs when the child transforms the physical environment into a symbol. Between 9 and 30 months of age, children increase their use of objects in symbolic play. They learn to transform objects—substituting them for other objects and acting toward them as if they were these other objects (Kavanaugh, 2006). For example, a preschool child treats a table as if it were a car and says, "I'm fixing the car," as he grabs a leg of the table.

Many experts on play consider the preschool years the "golden age" of symbolic/pretense play that is dramatic or sociodramatic in nature (Fein, 1986). This type of make-believe play often appears at about 18 months of age and reaches a peak at 4 to 5 years of age, then gradually declines.

Social Play **Social play** is play that involves interaction with peers, and it is the focus of Parten's classification. Social play increases dramatically during the preschool years.

Constructive Play **Constructive play** combines sensorimotor/practice play with symbolic representation. Constructive play occurs when children engage in the self-regulated creation of a product or a solution. Constructive play increases in the preschool years as symbolic play increases and sensorimotor play decreases. Constructive play is also a frequent form of play in the elementary school years, both in and out of the classroom (Van Hoorn & others, 2007).

How Would You...? As an educator, how would you integrate play in the learning process?

Games

Games are activities that are engaged in for pleasure and have rules. Often they involve competition. Preschool children may begin to participate in social games that involve simple rules of reciprocity and turn-taking. However, games take on a much stronger role in the lives of elementary school children. In one study, the highest incidence of game playing occurred between 10 and 12 years of age (Eiferman, 1971). After age 12, games decline in popularity (Bergen, 1988).

Television

Few developments in society in the second half of the twentieth century had a greater impact on children than television (Pecora, Murray, & Wartella, 2007). Although it is only one of the many types of mass media that affect children's behavior, television is the most influential. The persuasive capabilities of television are staggering (Comstock & Scharrer, 2006).

Many children spend more time in front of the television set than they do with their parents. Just how much television do young children watch? Surveys vary, with the figures ranging from an average of two to four hours a day (Kaiser Family Foundation, 2006). Compared with their counterparts in other developed countries, children in the United States watch television for considerably longer periods.

"Mrs. Horton, could you stop by school today?"
Copyright © Martha Campbell.

Television can have a negative influence on children by making them passive learners, distracting them from doing homework, teaching them stereotypes, providing them with violent models of aggression, and presenting them with unrealistic views of the world (Dubow, Huesmann, & Greenwood, 2007). However, television can have a positive influence on children's development by presenting motivating educational programs, increasing their information about the world beyond their immediate environment, and providing models of prosocial behavior (Bryant, 2007).

Effects of Television on Children's Aggression

The extent to which children are exposed to violence and aggression on television raises special concern (Dubow, Huessman, & Greenwood, 2007; Murray, 2007). For example, Saturday morning cartoons show average more than 25 violent acts per hour. In one experiment, preschool children were randomly assigned to one of two groups: One group watched television shows taken directly from violent Saturday morning cartoons on 11 days; the second group watched television cartoon shows with all of the violence removed (Steur, Applefield, & Smith, 1971). The children were then observed during play at their preschool. The preschool children who had seen the TV cartoon shows with violence kicked, choked, and pushed their playmates more than did the preschool children who watched nonviolent TV cartoon shows. Because the children were randomly assigned to the two conditions (TV cartoons with violence versus nonviolent TV cartoons), we can conclude that exposure to TV violence *caused* the increased aggression in the children in this investigation.

Other research has found links between watching television violence as a child and acting aggressively years later. For example, in one study, exposure to media violence at 6 to 10 years of age was linked with young adult aggressive behavior (Huesmann & others, 2003). In another study, long-term exposure to television violence was significantly related to the likelihood of aggression in 1,565 12- to 17-year-old boys (Belson, 1978). Boys who watched the most aggression on television were the most likely to commit a violent crime, swear, be aggressive in sports, threaten violence toward another boy, write slogans on walls, or break windows. These studies are *correlational*, so we can conclude from them that television violence is *associated with* aggressive behavior.

How is television violence linked to children's aggression?

In addition to television violence, there is increased concern about children who play violent video games, especially those that are highly realistic (Anderson, 2007; Anderson, Gentile, & Buckle, 2007). Children can become so deeply immersed in some electronic games that they experience an altered state of consciousness in which rational thought is suspended and arousing aggressive scripts are learned (Roberts, Henrikson, & Foehr, 2004). The direct rewards that players receive ("winning points") for their actions may also enhance the influence of video games.

Correlational studies indicate that children who extensively play violent electronic games are more aggressive than their counterparts who spend less time playing the games or do not play them at all (Cohen, 1995). Experiments have not yet been conducted to demonstrate increased aggression subsequent to playing violent video games, although an analysis of research studies concluded that playing violent video games is linked to aggression in both males and females (Anderson & Bushman, 2001).

Effects of Television on Children's Prosocial Behavior

How Would You...?
As a human development and family studies professional, how would you talk with parents about strategies for improving television viewing by their children?

Television also can teach children that it is better to behave in positive, prosocial ways than in negative, antisocial ways (Bryant, 2007), as Aimee Leifer (1973) demonstrated. She selected episodes from the television show *Sesame Street* that reflected positive social interchanges that taught children how to use their social skills. For example, in one interchange, two men were fighting over the amount of space available to them; they gradually began to cooperate and to share the space. Children who watched these episodes copied these behaviors, and in later social situations they applied the prosocial lessons they had learned.

Summary

Emotional and Personality Development

In Erikson's theory, early childhood is a period when development involves resolving the conflict of initiative versus guilt. The toddler's rudimentary self-understanding develops into the preschooler's representation of the self in terms of body parts, material possessions, and physical activities. At about 4 to 5 years of age, children also begin to use traitlike self-descriptions. Young children display more sophisticated self-understanding and understanding of others than previously thought. Young children's range of emotions expands during early childhood as they increasingly experience self-conscious emotions such as pride, shame, and guilt. Emotion-coaching parents have children who engage in more effective self-regulation of their emotions than do emotion-dismissing parents. Moral development involves thoughts, feelings, and actions regarding rules and regulations about what people should do in their interactions with others. Freud's psychoanalytic theory emphasizes the importance of feelings in the development of the superego. Positive emotions, such as empathy, also contribute to the child's moral development. Piaget analyzed moral reasoning and concluded that children from about 4 to 7 years of age display heteronomous morality, judging behavior by its consequences. According to behavioral and social cognitive theorists, moral behavior develops as a result of reinforcement, punishment and imitation, and there is considerable situational variability in moral behavior. Gender refers to the social and psychological dimensions of being male or female. Both psychoanalytic theory and social cognitive theory emphasize the adoption of parents' gender characteristics. Peers are especially adept at rewarding gender-appropriate behavior. Gender schema theory emphasizes the role of cognition in gender development.

Families

Authoritarian, authoritative, neglectful, and indulgent are four main parenting styles. Authoritative parenting is the most widely used style around the world and is the style most often associated with children's social competence. However, ethnic variations in parenting styles suggest that in Asian American families some aspects of control may benefit children. Physical punishment is widely used by U.S. parents, but there are a number of reasons why it is not a good choice. Coparenting has positive effects on children's development. Child maltreatment may take the form of physical abuse, child neglect, sexual

abuse, and emotional abuse. Siblings interact with each other in positive and negative ways. Birth order is related in certain ways to child characteristics, but by itself it is not a good predictor of behavior. In general, having both parents employed full-time outside the home has not been shown to have negative effects on children. However, the nature of parents' work can affect their parenting quality. Divorce can have negative effects on children's adjustment, but so can an acrimonious relationship between parents who stay together for their children's sake. If divorced parents develop a harmonious relationship and practice authoritative parenting, children's adjustment improves. Researchers have found few differences between children growing up in gay or lesbian families and children growing up in heterosexual families. Cultures vary on a number of issues regarding families. African American and Latino children are more likely than White American children to live in single-parent families and larger families and to have extended family connections. Lower-SES parents create a home atmosphere that involves more authority and physical punishment with children than higher-SES parents. Higher-SES parents are more concerned about developing children's initiative and delay of gratification.

Peer Relations, Play, and Television

Peers are powerful socialization agents. Peers provide a source of information and comparison about the world outside the family. Play's functions include affiliation with peers, tension release, advances in cognitive development, exploration, and provision of a safe haven.. The contemporary perspective on play emphasizes both the cognitive and the social aspects of play. Among the most widely studied types of children's play are sensorimotor play, practice play, pretense/symbolic play, social play, constructive play, and games. Television can have both negative influences (such as turning children into passive learners and presenting them with aggressive models) and positive influences (such as providing models of prosocial behavior) on children's development. TV violence is not the only cause of children's aggression, but it can induce aggression. Prosocial behavior on TV can teach children positive behavior.

Key Terms

self-understanding 167
moral development 169
heteronomous
 morality 170
autonomous morality 170
immanent justice 170
gender identity 171
gender roles 171
social role theory 172

psychoanalytic theory of
 gender 172
social cognitive theory of
 gender 172
gender schema theory 174
authoritarian
 parenting 175
authoritative parenting 175
neglectful parenting 175

indulgent parenting 175
sensorimotor play 189
practice play 189
pretense/symbolic
 play 189
social play 190
constructive play 190
games 190

7

Physical and Cognitive Development in Middle and Late Childhood

Stories of Life-Span Development: Angie and Her Weight

The following comments are by Angie, an elementary-school-age girl:

When I was eight years old, I weighed 125 pounds. My clothes were the size that large teenage girls wear. I hated my body, and my classmates teased me all the time. I was so overweight and out of shape that when I took a P.E. class my face would get red and I had trouble breathing. I was jealous of the kids who played sports and weren't overweight like I was.

I'm nine years old now and I've lost 30 pounds. I'm much happier and proud of myself. How did I lose the weight? My mom said she had finally decided enough was enough. She took me to a pediatrician who specializes in helping children lose weight and keep it off. The pediatrician counseled my mom about my eating and exercise habits, then had us join a group that he had created for overweight children and their parents. My mom and I go to the group once a week, and we've now been participating in the program for six months. I no longer eat fast-food meals, and my mom is cooking more healthy meals. Now that I've lost weight, exercise is not as hard for me, and I don't get teased by the kids at school. My mom's pretty happy, too, because she's lost 15 pounds herself since we've been in the counseling program.

Not all overweight children are as successful as Angie at reducing their weight. Indeed, being overweight in childhood has become a major national concern in the United States. Later in the chapter, we further explore being overweight in childhood.

During the middle and late childhood years, which last from approximately

6 years of age to 10 or 11 years of age, children grow taller, heavier, and stronger, and become more adept at using their physical skills. During these years, disabilities may emerge that call for special attention and intervention. It is also in this age period that children's cognitive abilities increase dramatically. Their command of grammar becomes proficient, they learn to read, and they may acquire a second language. ■

Physical Changes and Health

Continued growth and change in proportions characterize children's bodies during middle and late childhood. During this time period, some important changes in the brain take place and motor skills also improve. Developing a healthy lifestyle that involves regular exercise and good nutrition is a key aspect of making these years a time of healthy growth and development.

Body Growth and Change

The period of middle and late childhood involves slow, consistent growth. This is a period of calm before the rapid growth spurt of adolescence. During the elementary school years, children grow an average of 2 to 3 inches a year until, at the age of 11, the average girl is 4 feet, $10^1/_4$ inches tall, and the average boy is 4 feet, 9 inches tall. During the middle and late childhood years, children gain about 5 to 7 pounds a year. The weight increase is due mainly to increases in the size of the skeletal and muscular systems, as well as the size of some body organs.

Proportional changes are among the most pronounced physical changes in middle and late childhood. Head and waist circumference decrease in relation to body height. A less noticeable physical change is that bones continue to ossify during middle and late childhood, though they still yield to pressure and pull more than do mature bones.

Muscle mass and strength gradually increase during these years as "baby fat" decreases. The loose movements and knock-knees of early childhood give way to improved muscle tone. Thanks to both heredity and to exercise, children double their strength capabilities during these years. Because of their greater number of muscle cells, boys are usually stronger than girls.

The Brain

The development of brain-imaging techniques, such as MRI, has led to an increase in research on changes in the brain during middle and late childhood, and how these brain changes are linked to improvements in cognitive development (Toga, Thompson, & Sowell, 2006). Total brain volume stabilizes by the end of middle and late childhood, but significant changes in various structures and regions of the brain continue to occur. In particular, the brain pathways and circuitry involving the prefrontal cortex, the highest level in the brain, continue to increase in middle and late childhood (Durston & Casey, 2006). These advances in the prefrontal cortex are linked to children's improved attention, reasoning, and cognitive control. See Figure 5.1 in Chapter 5 for the location of the prefrontal cortex in the brain.

Changes also occur in the thickness of the cerebral cortex (cortical thickness) in middle and late childhood (Toga, Thompson, & Sowell, 2006). One study used brain scans to assess cortical thickness in 5- to 11-year-old children (Sowell &

others, 2004). Cortical thickening across a two-year time period was observed in the temporal and frontal lobe areas that function in language, which may reflect improvements in language abilities such as reading.

As children develop, activation of some brain areas increases while others decrease (Dowker, 2006). One shift in activation that occurs as children develop is from diffuse, larger areas to more focal, smaller areas (Turkeltaub & others, 2003). This shift is characterized by synaptic pruning, in which areas of the brain not being used lose synaptic connections, and those being used show an increase in connections. In a recent study, researchers found less diffusion and more focal activation in the prefrontal cortex from 7 to 30 years of age (Durston & others, 2007). The activation change was accompanied by increased efficiency in cognitive performance, especially in *cognitive control*, which involves flexible and effective control in a number of areas. These areas include controlling attention, reducing interfering thoughts, inhibiting motor actions, and being cognitive flexible in switching between competing choices (Munkata, 2006).

Motor Development

During middle and late childhood, children's motor skills become much smoother and more coordinated than they were in early childhood. Running, climbing, skipping rope, swimming, and bicycle riding are just a few of the many physical skills elementary school children can master. In such gross motor skills, boys usually outperform same-age girls.

Increased myelination of the central nervous system is reflected in the improvement of fine motor skills during middle and late childhood. Children can more adroitly use their hands as tools. Six-year-olds can hammer, paste, tie shoes, and fasten clothes. By 7 years of age, children's hands have become steadier. At this age, children prefer a pencil to a crayon for printing, and printing becomes smaller. At 8 to 10 years of age, the hands can be used independently with more ease and precision. Fine motor coordination develops to the point at which children can write rather than print words. Cursive letter size then becomes progressively smaller and more even. At 10 to 12 years of age, children begin to show manipulative skills similar to the abilities of adults. They can master the complex, intricate, and rapid movements needed to produce fine-quality crafts or to play a difficult piece on a musical instrument. Girls usually outperform same-age boys in their use of fine motor skills.

Exercise

Elementary school children need to be active as they mature physically. They are more fatigued by long periods of sitting than by running, jumping, or bicycling. Physical action, such as batting a ball, skipping rope, or balancing on a beam, is essential for these children to refine their developing skills. Research is making it increasingly clear that exercise plays an important role in children's growth and development (Corbin & others, 2008). As we will see later in this section, exercise is also related to maintaining a healthy body weight.

Are U.S. children getting enough exercise? A recent study found that 61 percent of 9- to 13-year-old U.S. children do not participate in any organized physical activity during their nonschool hours, and 23 percent do not engage in any free-time

How Would You...?
As an educator, how would you structure the curriculum to ensure that elementary school students are getting adequate physical activity throughout the day?

physical activity at all (Centers for Disease Control and Prevention, 2003). One historical comparison found that the percentage of children involved in daily P.E. programs in schools decreased from 80 percent in 1969 to 20 percent in 1999 (Health Management Resources, 2001) (see Figure 7.1).

Here are some practical ways to get children to exercise more:

- Improve physical fitness activities in schools.

- Offer more physical activity programs run by volunteers at school facilities.

- Have children plan community and school activities that really interest them.

- Encourage families to focus more on physical activity and encourage parents to exercise more. Caregivers who model an active lifestyle and provide children with opportunities to be active influence children's activity level.

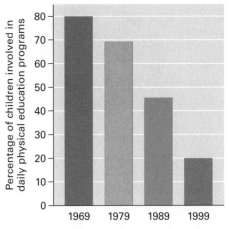

Figure 7.1 Percentage of Children Involved in Daily Physical Education Programs in the United States from 1969 to 1999 There has been a dramatic drop in the percentage of children participating in daily physical education programs in the United States, from 80 percent in 1969 to only 20 percent in 1999.

Health, Illness, and Disease

For the most part, middle and late childhood is a time of excellent health. Disease and death are less prevalent at this time than during other periods in childhood and in adolescence.

Accidents and Injuries

Injuries are the leading cause of death during middle and late childhood, and the most common cause of severe injury and death in this period is motor vehicle accidents, either as a pedestrian or as a passenger (James, 2007). The use of safety-belt restraints greatly reduces the severity of motor vehicle injuries. Other serious injuries involve bicycles, skateboards, roller skates, and other sports equipment.

Most accidents occur in or near the child's home or school. The most effective prevention strategy is to educate the child about proper use of equipment and the hazards of risk taking (Leiffer, 2007). Safety helmets, protective eye and mouth shields, and protective padding are recommended for children who engage in active sports (Briem & others, 2004).

How Would You...? As a health-care professional, how would you work with school-age children to reduce their chances of injury due to accidents?

Cancer

Cancer is the second leading cause of death in U.S. children 5 to 14 years of age. One in every 330 children in the United States develops cancer before the age of 19. Moreover, the incidence of cancer in children is increasing (Maule & others, 2007).

Child cancers mainly attack the white blood cells (leukemia), brain, bone, lymph system, muscles, kidneys, and nervous system. All are characterized by an uncontrolled proliferation of abnormal cells (McHugh, 2007). As indicated in Figure 7.2, the most common cancer in children is leukemia, a cancer in which bone marrow manufactures an abundance of abnormal white blood cells, which

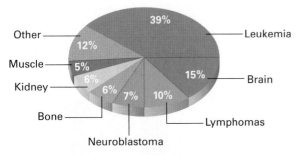

Figure 7.2 Types of Cancer in Children
Cancers in children have a different profile from adult cancers, which attack mainly the lungs colon, breast, prostate, and pancreas.

crowd out normal cells, making the child susceptible to bruising and infection (Hijiya & others, 2007).

Child life specialists are among the health professionals who work to make the lives of children with diseases such as cancer less stressful. Read about the work of child life specialist Sharon McCleod in the Careers in Life-Span Development profile.

CAREERS IN LIFE-SPAN DEVELOPMENT

Sharon McLeod, Child Life Specialist

Sharon McLeod is a child life specialist who is Clinical Director of the Child Life and Recreational Therapy Department at the Children's Hospital Medical Center in Cincinnati.

Under Sharon's direction, the goals of the Child Life Department are to promote children's optimal growth and development, reduce the stress of health-care experiences, and provide support to child patients and their families. These goals are accomplished through therapeutic play and developmentally appropriate activities, educating and psychologically preparing children for medical procedures, and serving as a resource for parents and other professionals regarding children's development and health-care issues.

Sharon says that human growth and development provides the foundation for her profession of child life specialist. She also describes her best times as a student when she conducted fieldwork, had an internship, and experienced hands-on theories and concepts she learned in her courses.

Sharon McLeod, child life specialist, working with a child at Children's Hospital Medical Center in Cincinnati.

Child life specialists like Sharon McLeod work with children and their families when the child needs to be hospitalized. They monitor the child's activities, seek to reduce the child's stress, and help the child to cope and to enjoy the hospital experience as much as possible. Child life specialists may provide parent education and develop individualized treatment plans based on an assessment of the child's devel opment, temperament, medical plan, and available social supports. Child life specialists have an undergraduate degree. They have taken courses in child development and education and usually completed additional courses in a child life program.

Cardiovascular Disease

Cardiovascular disease is uncommon in children. Nonetheless, environmental experiences and behavior in the childhood years can sow the seeds for cardiovascular disease in adulthood. Many elementary-school-age children already possess one or more of the risk factors for cardiovascular disease, such as hypertension and obesity (Yang & others, 2007). A study of more than 5,000 U.S. children revealed that high blood pressure was most likely to be present in Latino children (25 percent) and least characteristic of Asian American children (14 percent) (Sorof & others, 2004).

Overweight Children

Being overweight is an increasing health problem (Insel & Roth, 2008). Recall from Chapter 5, "Physical and Cognitive Development in Early Childhood," that being overweight is defined in terms of body mass index (BMI), which is computed by a formula that takes into account height and weight—children at or above the 95th percentile of BMI are included in the overweight category, and children at or above the 85th percentile are described as at risk for being overweight (Centers for Disease Control and Prevention, 2007). Over the last three decades, the percentage of U.S. children who are at risk for being overweight has doubled from 15 percent in the 1970s to almost 30 percent today, and the percentage of children who are overweight has tripled during this time frame (Paxson & others, 2006). In Chapter 5, we described research that found being overweight at 3 years of age was a risk factor for being overweight at 12 years of age (Nader & others, 2006). In that study, it also was revealed that the more times that children were overweight at 7, 9, or 11 years of age, the more likely they would also be overweight at 12 years of age. Eighty percent of the children who were overweight at any time during the elementary school years remained overweight at 12 years of age. Researchers have found that being overweight as a child is a risk factor for being obese as an adult. For example, a longitudinal study revealed that girls who were overweight in childhood were 11 to 30 times more likely to be obese in adulthood (Thompson & others, 2007).

Girls are more likely than boys to be overweight (Flegal, Ogden, & Carroll, 2004). Being overweight is less common in African American than in non-Latino White children during childhood, but during adolescence this reverses.

The increase in overweight children in recent decades is cause for great concern because being overweight raises the risk for many medical and psychological problems (Freedman & others, 2007). Overweight children can develop lung problems and hip problems (Daniels, 2006). Obese children are also prone to have high blood pressure, elevated blood cholesterol levels, and type 2 diabetes (Jolliffe & Janssen, 2007). The problems faced by Angie, whose comments opened this chapter, illustrate some of the psychological difficulties encountered by many overweight children. Low self-esteem and depression are common outgrowths of being overweight. Furthermore, overweight children often have problems in peer relations and may be shunned by their peers (Janssen & others, 2004).

What are the causes for the increase in overweight children? Changes in diet are one suspect (Franks & others, 2007). From the late 1970s through the late 1990s, key dietary shifts took place among U.S. children as young as 2 years of age through the adult years: greater away-from-home consumption; large increases in total calories from salty snacks, soft drinks, and pizza; and large decreases in calories from low- and medium-fat milk and medium- and high-fat beef and pork (Nielsen, Siega-Riz, & Popkin, 2002). Children's total caloric intake has also increased.

Other characteristics of how today's children live may also be culprits in the increase in children who are overweight (Lindsay & others, 2006). One study found that time spent watching TV and the number of soft drinks consumed were both related to children being overweight (Giammattei & others, 2003). And a recent U.S. study revealed that children who watched more television and ate fewer family meals when they were kindergarten age were more likely to be consistently overweight across four years of assessment than their counterparts who

learning disability Includes three components: (1) a minimum IQ level; (2) a significant difficulty in a school-related area (especially reading and/or mathematics); and (3) exclusion of severe emotional disorders, second-language background, sensory disabilities, and/or specific neurological deficits.

watched less television and ate more meals with their family (Gable, Chang, & Krull, 2007).

Inadequate levels of exercise, which we discussed earlier in this section, are also related to being overweight (Roemmick & others, 2007). One study found that one additional hour of physical education per week in the first grade was linked to girls being less likely to be overweight (Datar & Sturm, 2004). In Chapter 11, we focus on the importance of exercise in the treatment of obesity in young adults.

Parents play an important role in preventing children from becoming overweight and helping them lose weight if they become overweight (Boyle & Long, 2007). They can encourage healthy eating habits in children by eating more family meals together, making healthy foods available, and not keeping sugar-sweetened beverages and other unhealthy foods in the home (Fulkerson & others, 2007). They also can help reduce the likelihood their children will become overweight by reducing children's TV time, getting children involved in sports and other physical activities, and being healthy, physically active models themselves (Salmon, Campbell, & Crawford, 2006). A recent study revealed that Latino parents who monitored what their children ate had children who ate healthier foods and exercised more than their counterparts whose eating habits were not monitored (Arrendono & others, 2006). As we learned in Angie's story, a combination of behavioral modification, parental involvement, and a structured program can effectively help overweight children.

What can parents do to prevent their children from being overweight or obese?

How Would You...?
As a social worker, how would you use your knowledge of overweight risk factors to design a workshop for parents and children about healthy lifestyle choices?

Children with Disabilities

The elementary school years are a time when children with disabilities become more sensitive about their differentness and how it is perceived by others. Approximately 10 percent of children in the United States receive special education or related services. Among children with disabilities who receive such services, more than 40 percent have a learning disability or attention deficit hyperactivity disorder (National Center for Education Statistics, 2003). Substantial percentages of children have speech or language impairments (17 percent), mental retardation (9 percent) or an emotional disturbance (7 percent).

Learning Disabilities

After examining the research on learning disabilities, leading expert Linda Siegel (2003) concluded that a definition of **learning disabilities** should include these components: (1) a minimum IQ level; (2) a significant difficulty in a school-related area, especially reading and/or mathematics; and (3) exclusion of severe emotional disorders, second-language background, sensory disabilities, and/or specific neurological deficits.

A recent national survey revealed that 8 percent of U.S. children have a learning disability (Bloom & Dey, 2006). About three times as many boys as girls are classified as having a learning disability (U.S. Department of Education, 1996).

Among the explanations for this gender difference are a greater biological vulnerability among boys and *referral bias*. That is, boys are more likely to be referred by teachers for treatment because of troublesome behavior (Liederman, Kantrowitz, & Flannery, 2005).

The most common problem that characterizes children with a learning disability involves reading (Bursuck & Damer, 2007; Johnston & Morrison, 2007). Children with learning disabilities often have difficulties in handwriting, spelling, or composition. Their writing may be extremely slow, it may be virtually illegible, and they may make numerous spelling errors because of their inability to match up sounds and letters. **Dyslexia** is a category reserved for individuals who have a severe impairment in their ability to read and spell.

dyslexia A category of learning disabilities involving a severe impairment in the ability to read and spell.

attention deficit hyperactivity disorder (ADHD) A disability in which children consistently show one or more of the following characteristics: (1) inattention, (2) hyperactivity, and (3) impulsivity.

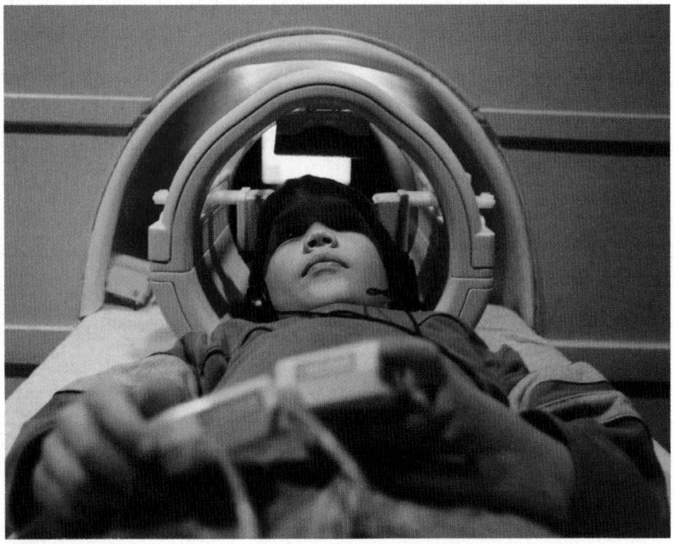

Figure 7.3 Brain Scans and Learning Disabilities
An increasing number of studies are using MRI brain scans to examine the brain pathways involved in learning disabilities. Shown here is 9-year-old Patrick Price, who has dyslexia, going through an MRI scanner disguised by drapes to look like a child-friendly castle. Inside the scanner, children must lay virtually motionless as words and symbols flash on a screen. They are asked to identify them by clicking different buttons.

The precise causes of learning disabilities have not yet been determined. However, some possible causes have been proposed (Bender, 2008; Fletcher & others, 2007). Learning disabilities tends to run in families with one parent having a disability such as dyslexia, although the specific genetic transmission of learning disabilities has not been discovered (Shastry, 2007). Some leading researchers argue that some reading disabilities are likely due to genetics but that the majority are the result of environmental influences (Shaywitz, Lyon, & Shaywitz, 2006).

How Would You...?
As an educator, how would you explain the nature of learning disabilities to a parent whose child has recently been diagnosed with a learning disability?

Researchers also use brain-imaging techniques, such as magnetic resonance imaging, to reveal any regions of the brain that might be involved in learning disabilities (Berninger, 2006; Shaywitz, Lyon, & Shaywitz, 2006) (see Figure 7.3). This research indicates that it is unlikely learning disabilities reside in a single, specific brain location. More likely learning disabilities are due to problems in integrating information from multiple brain regions or subtle difficulties in brain structures and functions.

Attention Deficit Hyperactivity Disorder (ADHD)

Attention deficit hyperactivity disorder (ADHD) is a disability in which children consistently show one or more of these characteristics over a period of time: (1) inattention, (2) hyperactivity, and (3) impulsivity. Children who are inattentive have such difficulty focusing on any one thing that they may get bored with a task after only a few minutes—or even seconds. Children who are hyperactive show high levels of physical activity, seeming to be almost constantly in motion. Children who are impulsive have difficulty curbing their reactions; they do not do a good job of thinking before they act. Depending on the characteristics that children with ADHD display, they can be diagnosed as (1) ADHD with predominantly inattention, (2) ADHD with predominantly hyperactivity/impulsivity, or (3) ADHD with both inattention and hyperactivity/impulsivity.

The number of children diagnosed and treated for ADHD has increased substantially in recent decades, by some estimates doubling in the 1990s. The disorder occurs as much as four to nine times more in boys than in girls. There is controversy, however, about the increased diagnosis of ADHD (Zentall, 2006). Some experts attribute the increase mainly to heightened awareness of the disorder. Others are concerned that many children are being incorrectly diagnosed.

How Would You...? As a health-care professional, how would you respond to these statements by a parent? "I do not believe that ADHD is a real disorder. Children are supposed to be active."

Definitive causes of ADHD have not been found. However, a number of causes have been proposed, such as low levels of certain neurotransmitters (chemical messengers in the brain), prenatal and postnatal abnormalities, and heredity (Stein & others, 2007; Waldman & Gizer, 2006). Thirty to 50 percent of children with ADHD have a sibling or parent who has the disorder (Heiser & others, 2004).

Many children with ADHD show impulsive behavior, such as this child who is jumping out of his seat and throwing a paper airplane at other children. *How would you handle this situation if you were a teacher and this were to happen in your classroom?*

It used to be assumed that ADHD decreased in adolescence, but now many experts believe this often is not the case. Estimates suggest that ADHD decreases in only about one-third of adolescents. Increasingly, it is being recognized that these problems may continue into adulthood (Waldman & Gizer, 2006).

Stimulant medication such as Ritalin or Adderall (which has fewer side effects than Ritalin), is effective in improving the attention of many children with ADHD, but it usually does not improve their attention to the same level as children who do not have ADHD (Barbaresi & others, 2006; Pliszka, 2007). Researchers have found that a combination of medication (such as Ritalin) and behavior management improves the behavior of children with ADHD better than medication alone or behavior management alone (Daly & others, 2007; Greydanus, Pratt, & Patel, 2007).

How Would You...? As a human development and family studies professional, how would you advise parents who are hesitant about medicating their child who was recently diagnosed with a mild form of ADHD?

Critics argue that many physicians are too quick to prescribe stimulants for children with milder forms of ADHD (Marcovitch, 2004). Also, in 2006, the U.S. government issued a warning about the cardiovascular risks of stimulant medication to treat ADHD.

Recent studies are focusing on the possibility that exercise might reduce ADHD (Azrin, Ehle, & Beaumont, 2006; Tantillo & others, 2002). Some mental health experts now recommend that children with ADHD exercise several times a day and speculate that the increase in rates of ADHD have coincided with the decline in U.S. children's exercise (Ratey, 2006).

Educational Issues

Until the 1970s most U.S. public schools either refused enrollment to children with disabilities or inadequately served them. This changed in 1975, when *Public Law 94-142*, the Education for All Handicapped Children Act, required that all students with disabilities be given a free, appropriate public education. In 1990, Public Law 94-142 was recast as the *Individuals with Disabilities Education Act (IDEA)*. IDEA was amended in 1997 and then reauthorized in 2004 and renamed the Individuals with Disabilities Education Improvement Act (Mastropieri & Scruggs, 2007).

Elaboration is an important strategy that involves more extensive processing of the information one wants to remember, such as thinking of examples or relating the information to one's own life. Elaboration makes the information more meaningful. When individuals engage in elaboration, their memory benefits (Terry, 2006).

The use of elaboration changes developmentally (Pressley & Harris, 2006). Adolescents are more likely to use elaboration spontaneously than are children. Elementary school children can be taught to use elaboration strategies on a learning task, but they will be less likely than adolescents to use the strategies on other learning tasks in the future. Nonetheless, verbal elaboration can be an effective strategy for processing information even for young elementary school children.

Fuzzy Trace Theory Might something other than knowledge and strategies be responsible for the improvement in memory during the elementary school years? Charles Brainerd and Valerie Reyna (1993; Reyna, 2004) argue that *fuzzy traces*—imprecise memory representations that are relatively easy to access—account for much of this improvement. Their **fuzzy trace theory** states that memory is best understood by considering two types of memory representations: (1) verbatim memory trace, and (2) gist. The *verbatim memory trace* consists of the precise details of the information, whereas *gist* refers to the central idea of the information. When gist is used, fuzzy traces are built up. Although individuals of all ages use gist, young children tend to store and retrieve verbatim traces. At some point during the early elementary school years, children begin to use gist more and, according to the theory, this contributes to the improved memory and reasoning of older children because fuzzy traces are more enduring and less likely to be forgotten than verbatim traces.

Thinking

Thinking involves manipulating and transforming information in memory. Two ways that children engage in thinking is to think critically or creatively.

Critical Thinking **Critical thinking** involves thinking reflectively and productively, as well as evaluating the evidence. In this book, the "How Would You…?" questions in the margins of each chapter challenge you to think critically about a topic or an issue related to the discussion. There is considerable interest in improving children's critical thinking (Halpern, 2007).

Jacqueline and Martin Brooks (2001) lament that few schools really teach students to think critically and develop a deep understanding of concepts. Deep understanding occurs when students are stimulated to rethink previously held ideas. In Brooks and Brooks' view, schools spend too much time getting students to give a single correct answer in an imitative way, rather than encouraging them to expand their thinking by coming up with new ideas and rethinking earlier conclusions. They observe that too often teachers ask students to recite, define, describe, state, and list, rather than to analyze, infer, connect, synthesize, criticize, create, evaluate, think, and rethink. Many successful students complete their assignments, do well on tests and get good grades, yet they don't ever learn to think critically and deeply. They think superficially, staying on the surface of problems rather than stretching their minds and becoming deeply engaged in meaningful thinking.

elaboration An important strategy that involves engaging in more extensive processing of information.

fuzzy trace theory States that memory is best understood by considering two types of memory representations: (1) verbatim memory trace and (2) gist. In this theory, older children's better memory is attributed to the fuzzy traces created by extracting the gist of information.

thinking Manipulating and transforming information in memory

critical thinking Thinking reflectively and productively, as well as evaluating the evidence.

COGNITIVE CHANGES

creative thinking The ability to think in novel and unusual ways and to come up with unique solutions to problems.

convergent thinking Thinking that produces one correct answer and is characteristic of the kind of thinking tested by standardized intelligence tests.

divergent thinking Thinking that produces many answers to the same question and is characteristic of creativity.

brainstorming A technique in which individuals are encouraged to come up with creative ideas in a group, play off each other's ideas, and say practically whatever comes to mind.

Creative Thinking Cognitively competent children not only think critically, but also creatively (Runco, 2006). **Creative thinking** is the ability to think in novel and unusual ways and to come up with unique solutions to problems. Thus, intelligence and creativity are not the same thing. This difference was recognized by J. P. Guilford (1967), who distinguished between **convergent thinking**, which produces one correct answer and characterizes the kind of thinking required on conventional tests of intelligence, and **divergent thinking**, which produces many different answers to the same question and characterizes creativity. For example, a typical item on a conventional intelligence test is "How many quarters will you get in return for 60 dimes?" In contrast, the following question has many possible answers: "What image comes to mind when you hear the phrase 'sitting alone in a dark room' or 'some unique uses for a paper clip'?"

It is important to recognize that children will show more creativity in some domains than others (Kaufmann, 2006). A child who shows creative thinking skills in mathematics may not exhibit these skills in art, for example.

What are some strategies for increasing children's creative thinking?

- *Provide children with environments that stimulate creativity.* Some settings nourish creativity; others depress it (Csikszentmihalyi & Nakamura, 2006). People who encourage children's creativity often rely on children's natural curiosity. They provide exercises and activities that stimulate children to find insightful solutions to problems, rather than asking a lot of questions that require rote answers. Adults also encourage creativity by taking children to locations where creativity is valued. Science, discovery, and children's museums may offer rich opportunities to stimulate children's creativity (Gardner, 1993).

What do you mean, "What is it?" It's the spontaneous, unfettered expression of a young mind not yet bound by the restraints of narrative or pictorial representation. ScienceCartoonsPlus.Com. Used with permission.

- *Don't overcontrol.* Formal evaluations and asking children questions that have just one right answer can inhibit creativity. Adults are more likely to nurture children's natural curiosity if they allow children to select their own interests and support their inclinations rather than dictating activities and judging performance.

- *Encourage internal motivation.* The excessive use of prizes, such as gold stars, money, or toys, can stifle creativity by undermining the intrinsic pleasure children derive from creative activities. Creative children's motivation is the satisfaction generated by the work itself. Competition for prizes often undermines intrinsic motivation and creativity (Amabile & Hennesey, 1992).

- *Introduce children to creative people.* Who are the most creative people in your community? Teachers can invite these people to their classrooms and ask them to describe what helps them become creative or to demonstrate their creative skills. Writers, poets, musicians, scientists, and many others can bring their props and productions to the class, turning it into a theater for stimulating students' creativity.

- *Have children engage in brainstorming.* **Brainstorming** is a problem-solving technique in which children are encouraged to come up with creative ideas in a group, play off each other's ideas, and say practically anything that comes

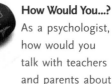

How Would You...?
As a psychologist, how would you talk with teachers and parents about ways to improve children's creative thinking?

to mind. The more ideas children produce, the better their chance of creating something unique. Creative children are not afraid of failing or getting something wrong. They may go down twenty dead-end streets before they come up with an innovative idea.

Metacognition

One expert in children's thinking, Deanna Kuhn (1999), believes that to help students become better thinkers, schools should pay more attention to helping students develop awareness of what they (and others) know. In other words, schools should do more to develop **metacognition**, which is cognition about cognition, or knowing about knowing (Flavell, 2004).

The majority of developmental studies of metacognition have focused on *metamemory,* or knowledge about memory. This includes general knowledge about memory, such as knowing that recognition tests are easier than recall tests. It also encompasses knowledge about one's own memory, such as a student's ability to monitor whether she has studied enough for a test that is coming up next week.

Young children do have some general knowledge about memory. By 5 or 6 years of age, children usually already know that familiar items are easier to learn than unfamiliar ones, that short lists are easier than long ones, that recognition is easier than recall, and that forgetting is more likely to occur over time (Lyon & Flavell, 1993). However, in other ways young children's metamemory is limited. They don't understand that related items are easier to remember than unrelated ones, or that remembering the gist of a story is easier than remembering information verbatim (Kreutzer, Leonard, & Flavell, 1975). By the fifth grade, students understand that gist recall is easier than verbatim recall.

Young children also have only limited knowledge about their own memory. They have an inflated opinion of their memory abilities. For example, in one study a majority of young children predicted that they would be able to recall all 10 items on a list of 10 items. When tested for this, none of the young children managed this feat (Flavell, Friedrichs, & Hoyt, 1970). As they move through the elementary school years, children give more realistic evaluations of their memory skills (McCormick, 2003).

In addition to metamemory, metacognition includes knowledge about strategies. In the view of Michael Pressley (2000, 2007; Pressley & others, 2007), the key to education is helping students learn a rich repertoire of problem-solving strategies. Good thinkers routinely use strategies and effective planning to solve problems. Good thinkers also know when and where to use strategies. Understanding when and where to use strategies often results from monitoring the learning situation (McCormick, 2003).

Pressley and his colleagues (Pressley & Harris, 2006; Pressley & Hilden, 2006; Pressley & others, 2004) have spent considerable time in recent years observing teachers' strategy instruction and students' use of strategies in elementary and secondary school classrooms. They conclude that strategy instruction is far less complete and intense than what students need in order to learn how to use strategies effectively. They argue that education needs to be restructured so that students receive more opportunities to become competent strategic learners.

How Would You...? As an educator, how would advise teachers and parents about ways to improve their child's metacognitive skills?

intelligence Problem-solving skills and the ability to learn from, and adapt to, the experiences of everyday life.

individual differences The stable, consistent ways in which people are different from each other.

mental age (MA) Binet's measure of an individual's level of mental development, compared with that of others.

intelligence quotient (IQ) A person's mental age divided by chronological age, multiplied by 100.

normal distribution A symmetrical distribution with most scores falling in the middle of the possible range of scores and few scores appearing toward the extremes of the range.

Intelligence

Just what is meant by the concept of "intelligence"? Some experts describe intelligence as problem-solving skills. Others describe it as the ability to adapt to and learn from life's everyday experiences. Combining these ideas, we can arrive at a definition of **intelligence** as problem-solving skills and the ability to learn from, and adapt to, life's everyday experiences.

Interest in intelligence has often focused on individual differences and assessment. **Individual differences** are the stable, consistent ways in which people are different from each other. We can talk about individual differences in personality or any other domain, but it is in the domain of intelligence that the most attention has been directed at individual differences. For example, an intelligence test purports to inform us about whether a student can reason better than others who have taken the test. Let's go back in history and see what the first intelligence test was like.

The Binet Tests

In 1904, the French Ministry of Education asked psychologist Alfred Binet to devise a method of identifying children who were unable to learn in school. School officials wanted to reduce crowding by placing students who did not benefit from regular classroom teaching in special schools. Binet and his student Theophile Simon developed an intelligence test to meet this request. The test is called the 1905 Scale. It consisted of 30 questions on topics ranging from the ability to touch one's ear to the ability to draw designs from memory and define abstract concepts.

Binet developed the concept of **mental age (MA)**, an individual's level of mental development relative to others. Not much later, in 1912, William Stern created the concept of **intelligence quotient (IQ)**, a person's mental age divided by chronological age (CA), multiplied by 100. That is: $IQ = MA/CA \times 100$. If mental age is the same as chronological age, then the person's IQ is 100. If mental age is above chronological age, then IQ is more than 100. If mental age is below chronological age, then IQ is less than 100.

The Binet test has been revised many times to incorporate advances in the understanding of intelligence and intelligence tests. These revisions are called the *Stanford-Binet tests* (Stanford University is where the revisions have been done). By administering the test to large numbers of people of different ages (from preschool through late adulthood) from different backgrounds, researchers have found that scores on the Stanford-Binet approximate a normal distribution (see Figure 7.6). A **normal distribution** is symmetrical, with a majority of the scores falling in the middle of the possible range of scores and few scores appearing toward the extremes of the range.

The Wechsler Scales

Another set of widely used tests is called the *Wechsler scales,* developed by David Wechsler. They include the Wechsler Preschool and Primary Scale of Intelligence–III (WPPSI-III) to test children 4 to 6½ years of age; the Wechsler Intelligence Scale for Children–IV Integrated (WISC-IV Integrated) for children and adolescents 6 to 16 years of age; and the Wechsler Adult Intelligence Scale–III (WAIS-III).

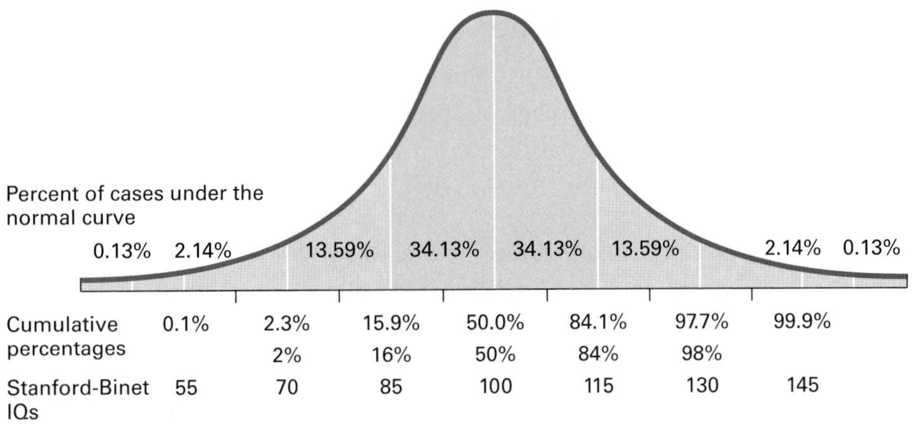

Figure 7.6 The Normal Curve and Stanford Binet IQ Scores

The distribution of IQ scores approximates a normal curve. Most of the population falls in the middle range of scores. Notice that extremely high and extremely low scores are very rare. Slightly more than two-thirds of the scores fall between 85 and 115. Only about 1 in 50 individuals has an IQ of more than 130, and only about 1 in 50 individuals has an IQ of less than 70.

Not only do the Wechsler scales provide an overall IQ, but they also yield verbal and performance IQs. Verbal IQ is based on six verbal subscales, performance IQ on five performance subscales. This allows the examiner to quickly see patterns of strengths and weaknesses in different areas of the student's intelligence. Three of the Wechsler subscales are shown in Figure 7.7.

Verbal Subscales

Similarities

A child must think logically and abstractly to answer a number of questions about how things might be similar.

Example: "In what way are a lion and a tiger alike?"

Comprehension

This subscale is designed to measure an individual's judgment and common sense.

Example: "What is the advantage of keeping money in a bank?"

Nonverbal Subscales

Block Design

A child must assemble a set of multicolored blocks to match designs that the examiner shows. Visual-motor coordination, perceptual organization, and the ability to visualize spatially are assessed.

Example: "Use the four blocks on the left to make the pattern on the right."

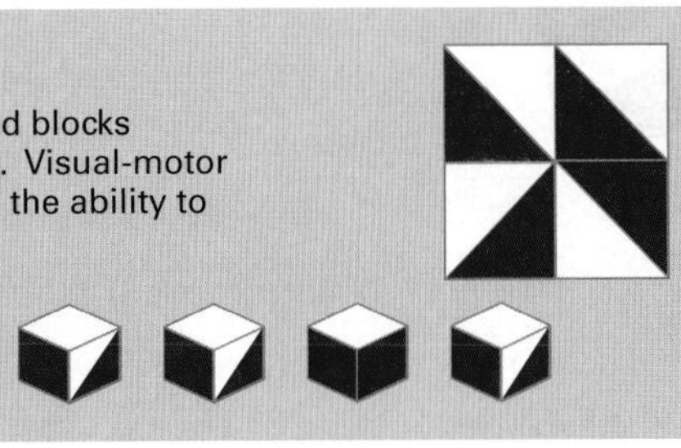

The Wechsler includes 11 subscales, 6 verbal and 5 nonverbal.
Three of the subscales are shown here.

Figure 7.7 Sample Subscales of the Wechsler Intelligence Scale for Children (WISC-IV Integrated)

The Wechsler includes 11 subscales, 6 verbal and 5 nonverbal. Three of the subscales are shown here. Simulated items similar to those found in the *Wechsler Intelligence Scale for Children– Fourth Edition* Copyright © 2003 by Harcourt Assessment, Inc. Reproduced by permission. All rights reserved.

triarchic theory of intelligence
Sternberg's theory that
intelligence consists of
analytical intelligence, creative
intelligence, and practical
intelligence.

Types of Intelligence

Is it more appropriate to think of a child's intelligence as a general ability or as a number of specific abilities? Robert Sternberg and Howard Gardner have proposed influential theories oriented to this second viewpoint.

Sternberg's Triarchic Theory Robert J. Sternberg (1986, 2004, 2006, 2008) developed the **triarchic theory of intelligence**, which states that intelligence comes in three forms: (1) *analytical intelligence*—this refers to the ability to analyze, judge, evaluate, compare, and contrast; (2) *creative intelligence*—this consists of the ability to create, design, invent, originate, and imagine; and (3) *practical intelligence*—this involves the ability to use, apply, implement, and put ideas into practice.

Sternberg (2002) says that children with different triarchic patterns "look different" in school. Students with high analytic ability tend to be favored in conventional schooling. They often do well under direct instruction, in which the teacher lectures and gives students objective tests. They often are considered to be "smart" students who get good grades, show up in high-level tracks, do well on traditional tests of intelligence and the SAT, and later get admitted to competitive colleges.

In contrast, children who are high in creative intelligence often are not on the top rung of their class. Many teachers have specific expectations about how assignments should be done, and creatively intelligent students may not conform to those expectations. Instead of giving conformist answers, they give unique answers, for which they might get reprimanded or marked down. No teacher wants to discourage creativity, but Sternberg believes that too often a teacher's desire to improve students' knowledge supresses creative thinking.

Like children high in creative intelligence, children who are practically intelligent often do not relate well to the demands of school. However, many of these children do well outside of the classroom's walls. They may have excellent social skills and good common sense. As adults, some become successful managers, entrepreneurs, or politicians in spite of having undistinguished school records.

Children in the Key School form "pods," in which they pursue activities of special interest to them. Every day, each child can choose from activities that draw on Gardner's eight frames of mind. The school has pods that range from gardening to architecture to gliding to dancing. *What are some of the main ideas of Gardner's theory and its application to education?*

Gardner's Eight Frames of Mind Howard Gardner (1983, 1993, 2002) suggests there are eight types of intelligence, or "frames of mind." These are described here, with examples of the types of vocations in which they are reflected as strengths (Campbell, Campbell, & Dickinson, 2004):

- *Verbal:* The ability to think in words and use language to express meaning.

   Occupations: Authors, journalists, speakers.
- *Mathematical:* The ability to carry out mathematical operations.

   Occupations: Scientists, engineers, accountants.
- *Spatial:* The ability to think three-dimensionally.

   Occupations: Architects, artists, sailors.
- *Bodily-Kinesthetic:* The ability to manipulate objects and be physically adept.

   Occupations: Surgeons, craftspeople, dancers, athletes.

- *Musical:* A sensitivity to pitch, melody, rhythm, and tone.

  Occupations: Composers, musicians, and sensitive listeners.

- *Interpersonal:* The ability to understand and interact effectively with others.

  Occupations: Successful teachers, mental health professionals.

- *Intrapersonal:* The ability to understand oneself.

  Occupations: Theologians, psychologists.

- *Naturalist:* The ability to observe patterns in nature and understand natural and human-made systems.

  Occupations: Farmers, botanists, ecologists, landscapers.

According to Gardner, everyone has all of these intelligences to varying degrees. As a result, we prefer to learn and process information in different ways. People learn best when they can do so in a way that uses their stronger intelligences.

How Would You...?
As a psychologist, how would you use Gardner's theory of multiple intelligences to respond to children who are distressed by their below-average score on a traditional intelligence test?

Evaluating the Multiple–Intelligence Approaches Sternberg's and Gardner's approaches have much to offer. They have stimulated teachers to think more broadly about what makes up children's competencies. And they have motivated educators to develop programs that instruct students in multiple domains. These approaches have also contributed to interest in assessing intelligence and classroom learning in innovative ways, such as by evaluating student portfolios (Moran & Gardner, 2006).

Still, doubts about multiple-intelligences approaches persist. A number of psychologists think that the multiple-intelligence views have taken the concept of specific intelligences too far (Johnson & others, 2004). Some argue that a research base to support the three intelligences of Sternberg or the eight intelligences of Gardner has not yet emerged. One expert on intelligence, Nathan Brody (2006), observes that people who excel at one type of intellectual task are likely to excel in others. Thus, individuals who do well at memorizing lists of digits are also likely to be good at solving verbal problems and spatial layout problems. If musical skill reflects a distinct type of intelligence, ask other critics, why not label the skills of outstanding chess players, prizefighters, painters, and poets as types of intelligence? The argument between those who support the concept of general intelligence and those who advocate the multiple-intelligences view is ongoing (Sternberg, 2007).

Culture and Intelligence Differences in conceptions of intelligence occur not only among psychologists but also among cultures. What is viewed as intelligent in one culture may not be thought of as intelligent in another (Cole, 2006; Zang & Sternberg, 2008). For example, people in Western cultures tend to view intelligence in terms of reasoning and thinking skills, whereas people in Eastern cultures see intelligence as a way for members of a community to engage successfully in social roles (Nisbett, 2003). One study found that Taiwanese Chinese conceptions of intelligence emphasize understanding and relating to others, including when to show and when not to show one's intelligence (Yang & Sternberg, 1997).

Interpreting Differences in IQ Scores

The IQ scores that result from tests such as the Stanford-Binet and Wechsler scales provide information about children's mental abilities. However, interpreting what performance on an intelligence test means is debated.

The Influence of Genetics

How strong is the effect of genetics on intelligence? The concept of heritability attempts to tease apart the effects of heredity and environment in a population. **Heritability** is the fraction of the variance in a population that is attributed to genetics. The heritability index is computed using correlational techniques, which we first discussed in Chapter 1. Thus, 1.00 is the highest degree of heritability that is hypothetically possible, and correlations of .70 and above suggest a strong genetic influence. A committee of respected researchers convened by the American Psychological Association concluded that by late adolescence, the heritability of intelligence is about .75, which reflects a strong genetic influence (Neisser & others, 1996).

Most research on heredity and environment does not include environments that differ radically. Thus, it is not surprising that many genetic studies show environment to be a fairly weak influence on intelligence (Fraser, 1995).

The heritability index has several flaws. It is only as good as the data entered into its analysis and the interpretations made from it (Sternberg, Grigorenko, & Kidd, 2005, 2006). The data are virtually all from traditional IQ tests, which some experts think are not always the best indicator of intelligence (Gardner, 2002; Sternberg, 2006). Also, the heritability index assumes that we can treat genetic and environmental influences as factors that can be separated, with each part contributing a distinct amount of influence. As we discussed in Chapter 2, genes and the environment interact: Genes always exist in an environment and the environment shapes their activity.

One strategy for examining the role of heredity in intelligence is to compare the IQs of identical and fraternal twins, which we initially discussed in Chapter 2. Recall that identical twins have exactly the same genetic makeup, but fraternal twins do not. If intelligence is genetically determined, say some investigators, identical twins' IQs should be more similar than the intelligence of fraternal twins. A research review of many studies found that the difference in the average correlation of intelligence between identical and fraternal twins was .15, a relatively low correlation (Grigorenko, 2000).

Today, most researchers agree that genetics and environment interact to influence intelligence (Gottlieb, Wahlsten, & Lickliter, 2006; Sternberg, 2006). For most people, this means that modifications in environment can change their IQ scores considerably. Although genetic endowment may always influence a person's intellectual ability, the environmental influences and opportunities we provide children and adults do make a difference (Ramey, Ramey, & Lanzi, 2006; Sternberg, 2006).

Environmental Influences

In Chapter 3, we described one study that demonstrated the influence of parents on cognitive abilities. Researchers went into homes and observed how extensively parents from welfare and middle-income professional families talked and communicated with their young children (Hart & Risley, 1995). They found that the middle-income professional parents were much more likely to communicate with their young children than the welfare parents were. How much the parents communicated with their children in the first three years of their lives was correlated with the children's Stanford-Binet IQ scores at age 3. The more parents communicated with their children, the higher the children's IQs were.

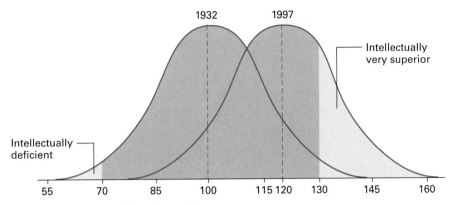

Figure 7.8 The Increase in IQ Scores from 1932 to 1997
As measured by the Stanford-Binet intelligence test, American children seem to be getting smarter. Scores of a group tested in 1932 fell along a bell-shaped curve with half below 100 and half above. Studies show that if children took that same test today, half would score above 120 on the 1932 scale. Very few of them would score in the "intellectually deficient" end, on the left side, and about one-fourth would rank in the "very superior" range.

Schooling also influences intelligence (Ceci & Gilstrap, 2000). The biggest effects have been found when large groups of children have been deprived of formal education for an extended period, resulting in lower intelligence. Another possible effect of education can be seen in rapidly increasing IQ test scores around the world (Flynn, 1999, 2006). IQ scores have been increasing so fast that a high percentage of people regarded as having average intelligence at the turn of the century would be considered below average in intelligence today (see Figure 7.8). If a representative sample of people today took the Stanford-Binet test version used in 1932, about 25 percent would be defined as having very superior intelligence, a label usually accorded to fewer than 3 percent of the population (Horton, 2001). Because the increase has taken place in a relatively short time, it can't be due to heredity, but rather may be due to increasing levels of education attained by a much greater percentage of the world's population, or to other environmental factors such as the explosion of information to which people are exposed. The worldwide increase in intelligence test scores that has occurred over a short time frame has been called the *Flynn effect* after the researcher who discovered it, James Flynn.

Researchers are increasingly concerned about improving the early environment of children who are at risk for impoverished intelligence (McLoyd, Aikens, & Burton, 2006; Ramey, Ramey, & Lanzi, 2006). For various reasons, many low-income parents have difficulty providing an intellectually stimulating environment for their children. Programs that educate parents to be more sensitive caregivers and better teachers, as well as support services such as quality child-care programs, can make a difference in a child's intellectual development. Thus the efforts to counteract a deprived early environment's effect on intelligence emphasize prevention rather than remediation.

A review of the research on early interventions concluded that (1) high-quality child-care center-based interventions are associated with increases in children's intelligence and school achievement; (2) the interventions are most successful with poor children and children whose parents have little education; (3) the positive benefits continue through adolescence, but are not as strong as in early childhood or the beginning of elementary school; and (4) the programs that continue into middle and late childhood have the best long-term results (Brooks-Gunn, 2003).

culture-fair tests Tests of intelligence that are designed to be free of cultural bias.

Group Differences

On the average, African American schoolchildren in the United States score 10 to 15 points lower on standardized intelligence tests than White American schoolchildren do (Brody, 2000; Lynn, 1996). Children from Latino families also score lower than White children. These are *average scores,* however; there is significant overlap in the distribution of scores. About 15 to 25 percent of African American schoolchildren score higher than half of White schoolchildren do, and many White schoolchildren score lower than most African American schoolchildren.

As African Americans have gained social, economic, and educational opportunities, the gap between African Americans and Whites on standardized intelligence tests has begun to narrow (Ogbu & Stern, 2001; Onwuegbuzi & Daley, 2001). This gap especially narrows in college, where African American and White students often experience more similar environments than in the elementary and high school years (Myerson & others, 1998). Also, when children from disadvantaged African American families are adopted into more-advantaged middle-socioeconomic-status families, their scores on intelligence tests more closely resemble national averages for middle-socioeconomic-status children than for lower-socioeconomic-status children (Scarr & Weinberg, 1983).

Group differences in average IQ scores may be due in part to biased test items. Many of the early tests of intelligence favored urban children over rural children, children from middle-SES families over children from low-income families, and White children over minority children (Miller-Jones, 1989). The standards for the early tests were almost exclusively based on White middle-SES children. And some of the test items were culturally biased. For example, one item on an early test asked what you should do if you find a 3-year-old in the street. The correct answer was "Call the police." However, children from impoverished inner-city families might not choose this answer if they have had bad experiences with the police. Children living in rural areas might not have police nearby. More recent versions of intelligence tests are designed to reduce such cultural bias.

Even if the content of test items is appropriate, however, another problem can characterize intelligence tests. Since many items are verbal, minority individuals may encounter problems in understanding the language of the items.

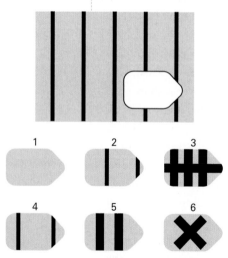

Figure 7.9 Sample Item from the Raven's Progressive Matrices Test Individuals are presented with a matrix arrangement of symbols, such as the one at the top of this figure, and must then complete the matrix by selecting the appropriate missing symbol from a group of symbols, such as the ones at the bottom. Simulated item similar to those found in the *Raven's Progressive Matrices.* Copyright © 1998 by Harcourt Assessment, Inc. Reproduced with permission. All rights reserved.

Creating Culture-Fair Tests

Culture-fair tests are tests of intelligence that are intended to be free of cultural bias. Two types of culture-fair tests have been devised. The first includes items that are familiar to children from all socioeconomic and ethnic backgrounds, or items that at least are familiar to the children taking the test. For example, a child might be asked how a bird and a dog are different, on the assumption that all children have been exposed to birds and dogs. The second type of culture-fair test has no verbal questions. Figure 7.9 shows a sample item from the Raven Progressive Matrices Test. Even though tests such as the Raven Progressive

Matrices are designed to be culture-fair, people with more education still score higher on them than do those with less education.

Why is it so hard to create culture-fair tests? Most tests tend to reflect what the dominant culture thinks is important (Greenberg & others, 2006). If tests have time limits, that will bias the test against groups not concerned with time. If languages differ, the same words might have different meanings for different language groups. Even pictures can produce bias because some cultures have less experience with drawings and photographs (Anastasi & Urbina, 1996). Within the same culture, different subgroups could have different attitudes, values, and motivation, and this could affect their performance on intelligence tests. Items that ask why buildings should be made of brick are biased against children who have little or no experience with brick houses. Questions about railroads, furnaces, snow, distances between cities, and so on can be biased against groups who have less experience than others with these contexts. Recall, too, that cultures define what is intelligent differently.

These attempts to produce culture-fair tests remind us that conventional intelligence tests probably are culturally biased, yet the effort to create a truly culture-fair test has not yielded a successful alternative.

Using Intelligence Tests

Psychological tests are tools. Like all tools, their effectiveness depends on the knowledge, skill, and integrity of the user. A hammer can be used to build a beautiful kitchen cabinet, or it can be used as a weapon of assault. Like a hammer, psychological tests can be used for positive purposes, or they can be badly abused. Here are some cautions about IQ that can help you avoid the pitfalls of using information about a child's intelligence in negative ways:

- *Avoid stereotyping and expectations.* A special concern is that the scores on an IQ test easily can lead to stereotypes and expectations about students. Sweeping generalizations are too often made on the basis of an IQ score. An IQ test should always be considered a measure of current performance. It is not a measure of fixed potential. Maturational changes and enriched environmental experiences can advance a student's intelligence.

- *now that IQ is not a sole indicator of competence.* Another concern about IQ tests occurs when they are used as the main or sole assessment of competence. A high IQ is not the ultimate human value. As we have seen in this chapter, it is important to consider not only students' intellectual competence in such areas as verbal skills but also their creative and practical skills.

- *Use caution in interpreting an overall IQ score.* In evaluating a child's intelligence, it is wiser to think of intelligence as consisting of a number of domains. Keep in mind the different types of intelligence described by Sternberg and Gardner. Remember that, by considering the different domains of intelligence, you can find that every child has at least one or more strengths.

How Would You...?
As a social worker, how would you explain the role and purpose of intelligence test scores to a parent whose child is preparing to take a standardized intelligence test?

Extremes of Intelligence

Intelligence tests have been used to discover indications of mental retardation or intellectual giftedness, the extremes of intelligence. At times, intelligence tests have been misused for this purpose. Keeping in mind the theme that an intelligence test should not be used as the sole indicator of mental retardation or giftedness, we will explore the nature of these intellectual extremes.

COGNITIVE CHANGES

mental retardation A
condition of limited mental
ability in which an individual
has a low IQ, usually below
70 on a traditional test of
intelligence, and has difficulty
adapting to everyday life.

organic retardation Mental
retardation that involves
some physical damage and is
caused by a genetic disorder
or brain damage.

cultural-familial retardation
Retardation characterized by
no evidence of organic brain
damage, but the individual's
IQ generally is between 50
and 70.

gifted Having above-average
intelligence (an IQ of 130 or
higher) and/or superior
talent for something.

A child with Down syndrome.
*What causes a child to develop
Down syndrome? In which major
classification of mental retardation
does the condition fall?*

Mental Retardation

Mental retardation is a condition of limited mental ability in which an individual has a low IQ, usually below 70 on a traditional intelligence test, and has difficulty adapting to everyday life. About 5 million Americans fit this definition of mental retardation.

There are several classifications of mental retardation (Hodapp & Dykens, 2006). About 89 percent of individuals with mental retardation fall into the mild category, with IQs of 55 to 70; most of them are able to live independently as adults and work at a variety of jobs. About 6 percent fall into the moderate category, with IQs of 40 to 54; these people can attain a second-grade level of skills and may be able to support themselves as adults through some types of labor. About 3.5 percent of individuals with mental retardation fall into the severe category, with IQs of 25 to 39; these individuals learn to talk and accomplish very simple tasks but require extensive supervision. Less than 1 percent have IQs below 25; they fall into the profound classification and require constant supervision.

Mental retardation can have an organic cause, or it can be social and cultural in origin:

- **Organic retardation** is mental retardation that is caused by a genetic disorder or by brain damage; the word *organic* refers to the tissues or organs of the body, indicating physical damage. Most people who suffer from organic retardation have IQs that range between 0 and 50. However, children with Down syndrome have an average IQ of approximately 50. As discussed in Chapter 2, Down syndrome is caused by an extra copy of chromosome 21.

- **Cultural-familial retardation** is a mental deficit in which no evidence of organic brain damage can be found; individuals' IQs generally range from 50 to 70. Psychologists suspect that such mental deficits result from the normal variation that distributes people along the range of intelligence scores combined with growing up in a below-average intellectual environment.

Giftedness

There have always been people whose abilities and accomplishments outshine others'—the whiz kid in class, the star athlete, the natural musician. People who are **gifted** have above-average intelligence (an IQ of 130 or higher) and/or superior talent for something. When it comes to programs for the gifted, most school systems select children who have intellectual superiority and academic aptitude, whereas children who are talented in the visual and performing arts (arts, drama, dance), athletics, or other special aptitudes tend to be overlooked (Tassell-Baska & Stambaugh, 2006; Winner, 2006).

What are the characteristics of children who are gifted? Despite speculation that giftedness is linked with having a mental disorder, no relation between giftedness and mental disorder has been found. Similarly, the idea that gifted children are maladjusted is a myth, as Lewis Terman (1925) found when he conducted an extensive study of 1,500 children whose Stanford-Binet IQs averaged 150. The children in Terman's study were socially well adjusted, and many went on to become successful doctors, lawyers, professors, and scientists. Recent studies support the conclusion that gifted people tend to be more mature than others, have fewer emotional problems than others, and grow up in a positive family climate (Davidson, 2000; Feldman, 2001).

Ellen Winner (1996) described three criteria that characterize gifted children, whether in art, music, or academic domains:

1. *Precocity.* Gifted children are precocious. They begin to master an area earlier than their peers. Learning in their domain is more effortless for them than for ordinary children. In most instances, these gifted children are precocious because they have an inborn high ability in a particular domain or domains.

2. *Marching to their own drummer.* Gifted children learn in a qualitatively different way than ordinary children. One way that they march to a different drummer is that they need minimal help, or scaffolding, from adults to learn. In many instances, they resist any kind of explicit instruction. They often make discoveries on their own and solve problems in unique ways.

3. *A passion to master.* Gifted children are driven to understand the domain in which they have high ability. They display an intense, obsessive interest and an ability to focus. They motivate themselves, says Winner, and do not need to be "pushed" by their parents.

Is giftedness a product of heredity or environment? Likely both. Individuals who are gifted recall that they had signs of high ability in a particular area at a very young age, prior to or at the beginning of formal training (Howe & others, 1995). This suggests the importance of innate ability in giftedness. However, researchers have also found that individuals with world-class status in the arts, mathematics, science, and sports all report strong family support and years of training and practice (Bloom, 1985). Deliberate practice is an important characteristic of individuals who become experts in a particular domain. For example, in one study, the best musicians engaged in twice as much deliberate practice over their lives as did the least successful ones (Ericsson, Krampe, & Tesch, 1993).

At 2 years of age, art prodigy Alexandra Nechita colored in coloring books for hours and also took up pen and ink. She had no interest in dolls or friends. By age 5 she was using watercolors. Once she started school, she would start painting as soon as she got home. At the age of 8, in 1994, she saw the first public exhibit of her work. In succeeding years, working quickly and impulsively on canvases as large as 5 feet by 9 feet, she has completed hundreds of paintings, some of which sell for close to $100,000 apiece. As a teenager, she continues to paint—relentlessly and passionately. It is, she says, what she loves to do. *What are some characteristics of children who are gifted?*

How Would You...?
As an educator, how would you structure educational programs for children who are gifted that would challenge and expand their unique cognitive abilities?

Language Development

Children gain new skills as they enter school that make it possible to learn to read and write: These include increased use of language to talk about things that are not physically present, learning what a word is, and learning how to recognize and talk about sounds (Berko Gleason, 2003). They also learn the *alphabetic principle*, that the letters of the alphabet represent sounds of the language.

Vocabulary, Grammar, and Metalinguistic Awareness

During middle and late childhood, changes occur in the way children's mental vocabulary is organized. When asked to say the first word that comes to mind when they hear a word, preschool children typically provide a word that often

metalinguistic awareness
Refers to knowledge about language, such as knowing what a preposition is or the ability to discuss the sounds of a language.

whole-language approach
An approach to reading instruction based on the idea that instruction should parallel children's natural language learning. Reading materials should be whole and meaningful.

follows the word in a sentence. For example, when asked to respond to "dog" the young child may say "barks," or to the word "eat" respond with "lunch." At about 7 years of age, children begin to respond with a word that is the same part of speech as the stimulus word. For example, a child may now respond to the word "dog" with "cat" or "horse." To "eat," they now might say "drink." This is evidence that children now have begun to categorize their vocabulary by parts of speech (Berko Gleason, 2003).

The process of categorizing becomes easier as children increase their vocabulary. Children's vocabulary increases from an average of about 14,000 words at age 6 to an average of about 40,000 words by age 11.

Children make similar advances in grammar (Lust, 2007). During the elementary school years, children's improvement in logical reasoning and analytical skills helps them understand such constructions as the appropriate use of comparatives (*shorter, deeper*) and subjectives ("If you were president..."). During the elementary school years, children become increasingly able to understand and use complex grammar, such as the following sentence: *The boy who kissed his mother wore a hat.* They also learn to use language in a more connected way, producing connected discourse. They become able to relate sentences to one another to produce descriptions, definitions, and narratives that make sense. Children must be able to do these things orally before they can be expected to deal with them in written assignments.

These advances in vocabulary and grammar during the elementary school years are accompanied by the development of **metalinguistic awareness**, which is knowledge about language, such as knowing what a preposition is or the ability to discuss the sounds of a language. Metalinguistic awareness allows children "to think about their language, understand what words are, and even define them" (Berko Gleason, 2005, p. 4). It improves considerably during the elementary school years. Defining words becomes a regular part of classroom discourse, and children increase their knowledge of syntax as they study and talk about the components of sentences such as subjects and verbs (Ely, 2005).

Children also make progress in understanding how to use language in culturally appropriate ways—pragmatics. By the time they enter adolescence, most children know the rules for the use of language in everyday contexts; that is, what is appropriate and inappropriate to say.

Reading

Before learning to read, children learn to use language to talk about things that are not present; they learn what a word is; and they learn how to recognize sounds and talk about them (Berko Gleason, 2003). Children who begin elementary school with a robust vocabulary have an advantage when it comes to learning to read (Paris & Paris, 2006). For example, a recent study revealed that a good vocabulary was linked with high reading comprehension in second-grade students (Berninger & Abbott, 2005). A fluent vocabulary helps readers access word meaning effortlessly.

How should children be taught to read? Currently, debate focuses on the whole-language approach versus the phonics approach (Reutzel & Cooter, 2008).

The **whole-language approach** stresses that reading instruction should parallel children's natural language learning. In some whole-language classes, beginning readers are taught to recognize whole words or even entire sentences, and to use the context of what they are reading to guess at the meaning of words. Reading materials that support the whole-language approach are whole and meaningful—that is, children are given material in its complete form, such as stories and poems, so that they learn to understand language's communicative function. Reading is connected with listening and writing skills. Although there are variations in whole-language programs, most share the premise that reading should be integrated with other skills and subjects, such as science and social studies, and that it should focus on real-world material. Thus, a class might read newspapers, magazines, or books, and then write about and discuss them.

In contrast, the **phonics approach** emphasizes that reading instruction should teach basic rules for translating written symbols into sounds. Early phonics-centered reading instruction should involve simplified materials. Only after children have learned correspondence rules that relate spoken phonemes to the alphabet letters that are used to represent them should they be given complex reading materials, such as books and poems.

What are the main approaches to teaching children how to read?

Which approach is better? Research suggests that children can benefit from both approaches, but instruction in phonics needs to be emphasized (Rasinski & Padak, 2008). An increasing number of experts in the field of reading now conclude that direct instruction in phonics is a key aspect of learning to read (Mraz, Padak, & Rasinski, 2008).

Bilingualism and Second Language Learning

Learning a second language is more readily accomplished by children than adolescents or adults. Adults make faster initial progress, but their eventual success in the second language is not as great as children's. For example, in one study, Chinese and Korean adults who had immigrated to the United States at different ages were given a test of grammatical knowledge (Johnston & Newport, 1991). Those who began learning English when they were 3 to 7 years old scored as well as native speakers on the test, but those who arrived in the United States and started learning English in later childhood or adolescence had lower test scores. Children's ability to pronounce words with a nativelike accent in a second language typically decreases with age, with an especially sharp drop occurring after the age of about 10 to 12 (Asher & Garcia, 1969). In sum, researchers have found that early exposure to a second language is optimal (Lessow-Hurley, 2005; Petitto, Kovelman, & Harasymowycz, 2003).

Students in the United States are far behind their counterparts in many developed countries in learning a second language. For example, in Russia, schools have 10 grades, called *forms*, which roughly correspond to the 12 grades in American schools. Russian children begin school at age 7 and begin learning English in the third form. Because of this emphasis on teaching English, most Russian citizens under the age of 40 today are able to speak at least some English. The United States is the only technologically advanced Western nation that does not have a national foreign language requirement at the high school level, even for students in rigorous academic programs.

U.S. students who do not learn a second language may be missing more than the chance to acquire a skill. *Bilingualism*—the ability to speak two languages—has a positive effect on children's cognitive development (Gibbons & Ng, 2004). Children who are fluent in two languages perform better than their single-language counterparts on tests of control of attention, concept formation, analytical reasoning, cognitive flexibility, and cognitive complexity (Bialystok, 1999, 2001). They also are more conscious of the structure of spoken and written language and better at noticing errors of grammar and meaning, skills that benefit their reading ability (Bialystok, 1993, 1997).

How Would You...?
As a human development and family studies professional, how would you describe the advantages of promoting bilingualism in the home for school-age children who come from families whose first language is not English?

In the United States, many immigrant children go from being monolingual in their home language to bilingual in that language and in English, only to end up monolingual speakers of English. This is called *subtractive bilingualism,* and it can have negative effects on children, who often become ashamed of their home language.

An ongoing controversy related to bilingualism involves bilingual education (Echevarria, Voqt, & Short, 2008). What is the best way for U.S. schools to provide education to the millions of U.S. children who come from homes in which English is not the primary language?

For the last two decades, the preferred strategy has been *bilingual education,* which teaches academic subjects to immigrant children in their native language while gradually teaching English (Diaz-Rico, 2008). Advocates of bilingual education programs argue that if children who do not know English are taught only in English, they will fall behind in academic subjects. How, they ask, can 7-year-olds learn arithmetic or history taught only in English when they do not speak the language?

Critics of bilingual programs point out that it generally takes immigrant children approximately three to five years to develop speaking proficiency and seven years to develop reading proficiency in English. However, many schools provide only one year of bilingual instruction (Hakuta, Butler, & Witt, 2000). Then, too, immigrant children vary in their ability to learn English (Horwitz, 2008). Children who come from lower socioeconomic backgrounds tend to have more difficulty than those from higher socioeconomic backgrounds (Hakuta, 2005). Thus, especially for immigrant children from low socioeconomic backgrounds, more years of bilingual education may be needed than they currently are receiving.

On the other side of the debate are critics who oppose bilingual education; they argue that as a result of these programs, the children of immigrants are not learning English, which puts them at a permanent disadvantage in U.S. society. California, Arizona, and Massachusetts have significantly reduced their bilingual education programs. Some states continue to endorse bilingual education, but they mandate that test scores be reported separately for English-language learners (students whose main language is not English) in the No Child Left Behind state assessments has shifted attention to literacy in English (Snow & Yang, 2006).

A first- and second-grade bilingual English-Cantonese teacher instructing students in Chinese in Oakland, California. *What have researchers found about the effectiveness of bilingual education?*

What have researchers found regarding outcomes of bilingual education programs? Drawing conclusions about the effectiveness of bilingual education programs is difficult because of variations across programs in the number of years they are in effect, type of instruction, qualities of schooling other than bilingual education, teachers, children, and other factors. Further, to date no experiments have been conducted that compare bilingual education with English-only education in the United States (Snow & Yang, 2006). Some experts have concluded that the quality of instruction is more important in determining outcomes than the language in which it is delivered (Lesaux & Siegel, 2003).

Research supports bilingual education in that (1) children have difficulty learning a subject when it is taught in a language they do not understand, and 2) when both languages are integrated in the classroom, children learn the second language more readily and participate more actively (Gonzales, Yawkey, & Minaya-Rowe, 2006; Hakuta, 2005). However, many of the research results report only modest rather than strong support for bilingual education, and some supporters of bilingual education now acknowledge that English-only instruction can produce positive outcomes for English-language learners (Lesaux & Siegel, 2003; Snow & Yang, 2006).

Summary

Physical Changes and Health

The period of middle and late childhood involves slow, consistent growth. During this period, children grow an average of 2 to 3 inches a year. Muscle mass and strength gradually increase. Among the most pronounced changes in body growth and proportion are decreases in head circumference and waist circumference in relation to body height. Changes in the brain in middle and late childhood included advances in functioning in the prefrontal cortex, which are reflected in improved attention, reasoning, and cognitive control. During middle and late childhood, less diffusion and more focal activation occurs in the prefrontal cortex, a change that is associated with an increase in cognitive control. During the middle and late childhood years, motor development becomes much smoother and more coordinated. Increased myelination of the central nervous system is reflected in improved motor skills. Improved fine motor skills appear in the form of handwriting development. Boys are usually better at gross motor skills, girls at fine motor skills. Most American children do not get nearly enough exercise. U.S. children are getting less exercise today and spend less time in physical education classes than in past decades. For the most part, middle and late childhood is a time of excellent health. The most common cause of severe injury and death in childhood is motor vehicle accidents, with most occurring at or near the child's home or school. Cancer is the second leading cause of death in children (after accidents). Leukemia is the most common childhood cancer. Cardiovascular disease is uncommon in children, but the precursors to adult cardiovascular disease are often already apparent in children. Being overweight in childhood poses serious health risks. The increase in the prevalence of being overweight is linked to poor diet, inadequate exercise, and poor eating habits.

Children with Disabilities

Slightly more than 40 percent of students with disabilities are classified as having a learning disability or attention deficit hyperactivity disorder. Children with learning disabilities (1) have a minimum IQ level; (2) have a significant difficulty in a school-related area; and (3) do not have severe emotional disorders, second-language background, sensory disabilities, or specific neurological deficits. Dyslexia is a category of learning disabilities that involves a severe impairment in the ability to read and spell. Attention deficit hyperactivity disorder (ADHD) is a disability in which individuals consistently show problems in one or more of these areas: (1) inattention, (2) hyperactivity, and (3) impulsivity. ADHD has been increasingly diagnosed. In 1975, Public Law 94-142, the Education for All Handicapped Children Act, required that all children with disabilities be given a free, appropriate public education. This law was renamed the Individuals with Disabilities Education Act (IDEA) in 1990 and updated in 2004. IDEA includes requirements that children with disabilities receive an individual education plan (IEP), which is a written plan that spells out a program tailored to the child, and that they be educated in the least restrictive environment (LRE), which is a setting that is as similar as possible to the one in which children without disabilities are educated. The term inclusion means educating children with disabilities full-time in the regular classroom.

Cognitive Changes

Piaget said that the stage of concrete operational thought characterizes children from about 7 to 11 years of age. During this stage children are capable of concrete operations, conservation, classification, seriation, and transitivity. Critics argue that some components of a stage do not appear at the same time, and that culture has more influence on development than Piaget predicted. Neo-Piagetians place more emphasis on how children process information, strategies, speed of information processing, and the division of cognitive problems into more precise steps. Long-term memory increases in middle and late childhood. Knowledge and expertise influence memory. Children can improve their memories by the use of strategies such as imagery and elaboration. Critical thinking involves thinking reflectively and productively, as well as evaluating the evidence. Creative thinking is the ability to think in novel and unusual ways and to come up with unique solutions to problems. A number of strategies can be used to encourage children's creative thinking, including brainstorming. Metacognition is knowing about knowing. Pressley views the key to education as helping students learn a rich repertoire of strategies. Intelligence consists of problem-solving skills and the ability to adapt to, and learn from, life's everyday experiences. Interest in intelligence often focuses on individual differences and assessment. Widely used intelligence tests today include the Stanford-Binet tests and Wechsler scales. Sternberg proposed that intelligence comes in three main forms, whereas Gardner said there are eight types of intelligence. Cultures vary in the way they define intelligence. IQ scores are influenced by both genetics and characteristics of the environment. Mental retardation is low IQ combined with problems in adapting to everyday life. A child who is gifted has above-average intelligence and/or superior talent for something.

Language Development

In the elementary school years, children become more analytical and logical in their approach to words and grammar. They begin to understand comparatives and subjectives. They become increasingly able to use complex grammar and produce narratives that make sense. Improvements in metalinguistic awareness—knowledge about language—are evident during the elementary school years as children increasingly define words, increase their knowledge of syntax, and understand better how to use language in culturally appropriate ways. A current debate in reading focuses on the phonics approach versus the whole-language approach. The phonics approach advocates instruction in the sounds letters make and employs simplified materials. The whole-language approach stresses that reading instruction should parallel children's natural language learning and uses complex, whole-language materials, such as books and poems. Children can benefit when both approaches are used, but experts increasingly view phonics instruction as critical in learning to read. Bilingual education aims to teach academics to immigrant children in their native languages while gradually adding English instruction. Researchers have found that bilingualism does not interfere with performance in either language. Success in learning a second language is greater in childhood than in adolescence.

Key Terms

learning disability 200
dyslexia 201
attention deficit
  hyperactivity disorder
  (ADHD) 201
individualized education
  plan (IEP) 203
least restrictive
  environment (LRE) 203
inclusion 203
seriation 204
transitivity 204
neo-Piagetians 205
long-term memory 206

strategies 206
elaboration 207
fuzzy trace theory 207
thinking 207
critical thinking 207
creative thinking 208
convergent thinking 208
divergent thinking 208
brainstorming 208
metacognition 209
intelligence 210
individual differences 210
mental age (MA) 210
intelligence quotient (IQ) 210

normal distribution 210
triarchic theory of
  intelligence 212
heritability 214
culture-fair tests 216
mental retardation 218
organic retardation 218
cultural-familial retardation
  gifted 218
metalinguistic
  awareness 220
whole-language
  approach 220
phonics approach 221

Socioemotional Development in Middle and Late Childhood

Stories of Life-Span Development: Learning in Troubled Schools

In *The Shame of the Nation,* Jonathan Kozol (2005) described his visits to 60 U.S. schools in urban low-income areas in 11 states. He saw many schools in which the minority population was 80 to 90 percent. Kozol observed numerous inequities—unkempt classrooms, hallways, and restrooms; inadequate textbooks and supplies; and lack of resources. He also saw teachers mainly instructing students to memorize material by rote, especially as preparation for mandated tests, rather than stimulating them to engage in higher-level thinking. Kozol also frequently observed teachers using threatening disciplinary tactics to control the classroom.

However, some teachers Kozol observed were effective in educating children in these undesirable conditions. At P.S. 30 in the South Bronx, Mr. Bedrock teaches fifth grade. One student in his class, Serafina, recently lost her mother to AIDS. When author Jonathan Kozol visited the class, he was told that two other children had taken the role of "allies in the child's struggle for emotional survival" (Kozol, 2005, p. 291). Textbooks are in short supply for the class, and the social studies text is so out of date it claims that Ronald Reagan is the country's president. But Mr. Bedrock told Kozol that it's a "wonderful" class this year. About their teacher, 56-year-old Mr. Bedrock, one student said, "He's getting old... but we love him anyway" (p. 292). Kozol found the students orderly, interested, and engaged.

The years of middle and late childhood bring many changes to children's social and emotional lives. The development of their self-conceptions, moral reasoning, and gendered behavior is significant. Transformations in their relationships with parents and peers occur, and schooling takes on a more academic flavor. ∎

Emotional and Personality Development

In this section, we explore how the self continues to develop during middle and late childhood and the emotional changes that take place during these years. We also discuss children's moral development and many aspects of the role that gender plays in their development in middle and late childhood.

The Self

What is the nature of the child's self-understanding and self-esteem during the elementary school years? What role do self-efficacy and self-regulation play in children's achievement?

The Development of Self–Understanding

In middle and late childhood, especially from 8 to 11 years of age, children increasingly describe themselves with psychological characteristics and traits in contrast to the more concrete self-descriptions of younger children. Older chidren are more likely to describe themselves as *"popular, nice, helpful, mean, smart,* and *dumb"* (Harter, 2006, p. 526).

In addition, during the elementary school years, children become more likely to recognize social aspects of the self (Harter, 2006). They include references to social groups in their self-descriptions, such as referring to themselves as Girl Scouts, as Catholics, or as someone who has two close friends (Livesly & Bromley, 1973).

Children's self-understanding in the elementary school years also includes increasing reference to social comparison (Harter, 2006). At this point in development, children are more likely to distinguish themselves from others in comparative rather than in absolute terms. That is, elementary-school-age children are no longer as likely to think about what they do or do not do, but are more likely to think about what they can do in comparison with others.

Consider a series of studies in which Diane Ruble (1983) investigated children's use of social comparison in their self-evaluations. Children were given a difficult task and then offered feedback on their performance, as well as information about the performances of other children their age. The children were then asked for self-evaluations. Children younger than 7 made virtually no reference to the information about other children's performances. However, many children older than 7 included socially comparative information in their self-descriptions.

In sum, in middle and late childhood, self-description increasingly involves psychological and social characteristics, including social comparison.

How Would You...?

As a psychologist, how would you explain the role of social comparison for the development of a child's sense of self?

self-esteem The global
evaluative dimension of the self.
Self-esteem is also referred to
as self-worth or self-image.

self-concept Domain-specific
evaluations of the self.

Self-Esteem and Self-Concept

High self-esteem and a positive self-concept are important character-istics of children's well-being (Harter, 2006). Investigators sometimes use the terms *self-esteem* and *self-concept* interchangeably or do not precisely define them, but there is a meaningful difference between them. **Self-esteem** refers to global evaluations of the self; it is also called *self-worth* or *self-image*. For example, a child may perceive that she is not merely a person but a *good* person. **Self-concept** refers to domain-specific evalua-tions of the self. Children can make self-evaluations in many domains of their lives—academic, athletic, appearance, and so on. In sum, *self-esteem* refers to global self-evaluations, *self-concept* to domain-specific evaluations.

Self-esteem reflects perceptions that do not always match reality (Baumeister & others, 2003). A child's self-esteem might reflect a belief about whether he or she is intelligent and attractive, for example, but that belief is not neces-sarily accurate. Thus, high self-esteem may refer to accurate, justified perceptions of one's worth as a person and one's successes and accom-plishments, but it can also refer to an arrogant, grandiose, unwarranted sense of superiority over others. In the same manner, low self-esteem may reflect either an accurate perception of one's shortcomings or a distorted, even patho-logical, sense of insecurity and inferiority.

How Would You...?
As an educator,
how would you
work with a child
to develop a
healthy self-
concept
concerning their
academic ability?

Variations in self-esteem have been linked with many aspects of children's development. However, much of the research is *correlational* rather than *experi-mental*. Recall from Chapter 1 that correlation does not equal causation. Thus, if a correlational study finds an association between children's low self-esteem and low academic achievement, low academic achievement could cause the low self-esteem as much as low self-esteem causes low academic achievement—or neither factor may cause the other (Bowles, 1999).

In fact, correlations between school performance and self-esteem are only moder-ate, and these correlations do not suggest that high self-esteem produces better school performance (Baumeister & others, 2003). Efforts to increase students' self-esteem have not always led to improved school performance (Davies & Brember, 1999).

Children with high self-esteem have greater initiative, but this can produce positive or negative outcomes (Baumeister & others, 2003). High-self-esteem chil-dren are prone to both prosocial and antisocial actions.

A current concern is that too many of today's children grow up receiving praise for mediocre or even poor performance and as a consequence have inflated self-esteem (Graham, 2005; Stipek, 2005). They may have difficulty handling competition and criticism. This theme is vividly captured by the title of a book, *Dumbing Down Our Kids: Why American Children Feel Good About Themselves But Can't Read, Write, or Add* (Sykes, 1995).

Increasing Children's Self-Esteem

Teachers, social workers, health-care professionals and others are often concerned about low self-esteem in the children they serve. Researchers have suggested sev-eral strategies to improve self-esteem in at-risk children (Bednar, Wells, & Peterson, 1995; Harter, 2006).

- *Identify the causes of low self-esteem.* Intervention should target the causes of low self-esteem. Children have the highest self-esteem when they perform

How can parents help children develop higher self-esteem?

competently in domains that are important to them. Therefore, it is helpful to encourage children to identify and value their areas of competence. These may include areas such as academic skills, athletic skills, physical attractiveness, and social acceptance.

- *Provide emotional support and social approval.* Some children with low self-esteem come from conflicted families or conditions of abuse or neglect—situations in which emotional support is unavailable. In some cases, alternative sources of support can be arranged either informally through the encouragement of a teacher, a coach, or another significant adult, or more formally, through programs such as Big Brothers and Big Sisters.

- *Help children achieve.* Achievement also can improve children's self-esteem. For example, the straightforward teaching of real skills to children often results in increased achievement and, thus, in enhanced self-esteem. Children develop higher self-esteem when they know which tasks will achieve their goals, and they have successfully performed them or similar tasks.

- *Help children cope.* Self-esteem can be built when a child faces a problem and tries to cope with it, rather than avoiding it. If coping rather than avoidance prevails, children often face problems realistically, honestly, and nondefensively. This produces favorable self-evaluative thoughts, which lead to the self-generated approval that raises self-esteem.

Self–Efficacy

Self-efficacy is the belief that one can master a situation and produce favorable outcomes. Albert Bandura (2001, 2006, 2007a, b), whose social cognitive theory we described in Chapter 1, states that self-efficacy is a critical factor in whether or not students achieve. Self-efficacy is the belief that "I can"; helplessness is the belief that "I cannot." Students with high self-efficacy endorse such statements as "I know that I will be able to learn the material in this class" and "I expect to be able to do well at this activity."

Dale Schunk (2008; Schunk & Zimmerman, 2006) has applied the concept of self-efficacy to many aspects of students' achievement. In his view, self-efficacy influences a student's choice of activities. Students with low self-efficacy for learning may avoid many learning tasks, especially those that are challenging. By contrast, high-self-efficacy counterparts eagerly work at learning tasks (Schunk & Zimmerman, 2006). Students with high self-efficacy are more likely to expend effort and persist longer at a learning task than students with low self-efficacy.

How Would You...?
As an educator, how would you encourage enhanced self-efficacy in a student who says, "I can't do this work!"?

Self–Regulation

One of the most important aspects of the self in middle and late childhood is the increased capacity for self-regulation. This increased capacity is characterized by deliberate efforts to manage one's behavior, emotions, and thoughts that lead to increased social competence and achievement (Gross & Thompson, 2007; Laible & Thompson, 2007).

The increased capacity in self-regulation is linked to developmental advances in the brain's prefrontal cortex, which was discussed in Chapter 7, "Physical and

Cognitive Development in Middle and Late Childhood" (Davidson, Fox, & Kalin, 2007). Recall our discussion there of the increased focal activation in the prefrontal cortex that is linked to improved cognitive control, which includes self-regulation (Durston & others, 2007)

Industry Versus Inferiority

In Chapter 1, we described Erik Erikson's (1968) eight stages of human development. His fourth stage, industry versus inferiority, appears during middle and late childhood. The term *industry* expresses a dominant theme of this period: Children become interested in how things are made and how they work. When children are encouraged in their efforts to make, build, and work—whether building a model airplane, constructing a tree house, fixing a bicycle, solving an addition problem, or cooking—their sense of industry increases. Conversely, parents who see their children's efforts at making things as "mischief" or "making a mess" will tend to foster a sense of inferiority in their children.

Emotional Development

In Chapter 6, we saw that preschoolers become more adept at talking about their own and others' emotions. They also show a growing awareness of the need to control and manage their emotions to meet social standards. In middle and late childhood, children further develop their understanding and self-regulation of emotion (Saarni & others, 2006).

Developmental Changes

Developmental changes in emotions during the middle and late childhood years include the following (Denham, Bassett, & Wyatt, 2007; Kuebli, 1994; Thompson & Goodvin, 2005):

- *Improved emotional understanding.* Children in elementary school, for example, develop an increased ability to understand such complex emotions as pride and shame. These emotions become less tied to the reactions of other people; they become more self-generated and integrated with a sense of personal responsibility.

- *Increased understanding that more than one emotion can be experienced in a particular situation.* A third-grader, for example, may realize that achieving something might involve both anxiety and joy.

- *Increased tendency to be aware of the events leading to emotional reactions.* A fourth-grader may become aware that her sadness today is influenced by her friend moving to another town last week.

- *Ability to suppress or conceal negative emotional reactions.* A fifth-grader has learned to tone down his anger better than he used to when one of his classmates irritates him.

- *The use of self-initiated strategies for redirecting feelings.* In the elementary school years, children become more reflective about their emotional lives and increasingly use strategies to control their emotions. They become more effective at cognitively managing their emotions, such as soothing oneself after an upset.

- *A capacity for genuine empathy.* A fourth-grader, for example, feels sympathy for a distressed person and experiences vicariously the sadness the distressed person is feeling.

Coping with Stress

An important aspect of children's emotional lives is learning how to cope with stress (Taylor & Stanton, 2007). As children get older, they more accurately appraise a stressful situation and determine how much control they have over it. Older children generate more coping alternatives to stressful conditions and use more cognitive coping strategies (Saarni & others, 2006). They are better than younger children at intentionally shifting their thoughts to something that is less stressful; and at reframing, or changing one's perception of a stressful situation. For example, a younger child may be very disappointed that a teacher did not say hello when the child arrived in the classroom. An older child may reframe the situation and think, "My teacher may have been busy with other things and just forgot to say hello."

What are some effective strategies to help children cope with traumatic events, such as the terrorist attacks on the United States on 9/11/2001 and Hurricane Katrina in September, 2005?

By 10 years of age, most children are able to use these cognitive strategies to cope with stress (Saarni, 1999). However, in families that have not been supportive and are characterized by turmoil or trauma, children may be so overwhelmed by stress that they do not use such strategies (Klingman, 2006).

The terrorist attacks on the World Trade Center in New York City and the Pentagon in Washington, D.C., on September 11, 2001, and hurricanes Katrina and Rita in September 2005, raised special concerns about how to help children cope with such stressful events (Osofsky, 2007). Researchers have offered some recommendations for parents, teachers, and other adults caring for children (Gurwitch & others, 2001, pp. 4–11):

- Reassure children (numerous times, if necessary) of their safety and security.

- Allow children to retell events and be patient in listening to them.

- Encourage children to talk about any disturbing or confusing feelings, reassuring them that such feelings are normal after a stressful event.

- Protect children from reexposure to frightening situations and reminders of the trauma—for example, by limiting discussion of the event in front of the children.

- Help children make sense of what happened, keeping in mind that children may misunderstand what took place. For example, young children "may blame themselves, believe things happened that did not happen, believe that terrorists are in the school, etc. Gently help children develop a realistic understanding of the event" (p. 10).

How Would You...?

As a social worker, how would you counsel a child who has been exposed to a traumatic event?

Traumatic events may cause individuals to think about the moral aspects of life. Hopelessness and despair may short-circuit moral development when a child is confronted by the violence of war zones and impoverished inner cities (Nadar, 2001). Let's further explore children's moral development.

preconventional reasoning The lowest level in Kohlberg's theory of moral development. The individual's moral reasoning is controlled primarily by external rewards and punishment.

heteronomous morality Kohlberg's first stage in preconventional reasoning in which moral thinking is tied to punishment.

Moral Development

Remember from Chapter 6 our description of Piaget's view of moral development. Piaget proposed that younger children are characterized by heteronomous morality, but that by 10 years of age, they have moved into a higher stage called autonomous morality. According to Piaget, older children consider the intentions of the individual, believe that rules are subject to change, and are aware that punishment does not always follow wrongdoing.

A second major perspective on moral development was proposed by Lawrence Kohlberg (1958, 1986). Piaget's cognitive stages of development serve as the underpinnings for Kohlberg's theory, but Kohlberg proposed six stages of moral development, which he believed are universal. Development from one stage to another, said Kohlberg, is fostered by opportunities to take the perspective of others and to experience conflict between one's current stage of moral thinking and the reasoning of someone at a higher stage.

The Kohlberg Stages

Kohlberg's stages fall into three levels of moral thinking, each of which is characterized by two stages (see Figure 8.1).

Preconventional reasoning is Kohlberg's lowest level of moral reasoning. At this level, children interpret good and bad in terms of external rewards and punishments.

- *Stage 1.* **Heteronomous morality** is the first stage in preconventional reasoning. At this stage, moral thinking is tied to punishment. For example, children think that they must obey because they fear punishment for disobedience.

LEVEL 1 Preconventional Level No Internalization	LEVEL 2 Conventional Level Intermediate Internalization	LEVEL 3 Postconventional Level Full Internalization
Stage 1 Heteronomous Morality *Children obey because adults tell them to obey. People base their moral decisions on fear of punishment.*	**Stage 3** Mutual Interpersonal Expectations, Relationships, and Interpersonal Conformity *Individuals value trust, caring, and loyalty to others as a basis for moral judgments.*	**Stage 5** Social Contract or Utility and Individual Rights *Individuals reason that values, rights, and principles undergird or transcend the law.*
Stage 2 Individualism, Purpose, and Exchange *Individuals pursue their own interests but let others do the same. What is right involves equal exchange.*	**Stage 4** Social System Morality *Moral judgments are based on understanding of the social order, law, justice, and duty.*	**Stage 6** Universal Ethical Principles *The person has developed moral judgments that are based on universal human rights. When faced with a dilemma between law and conscience, a personal, individualized conscience is followed.*

Figure 8.1 Kohlberg's Three Levels and Six Stages of Moral Development
Kohlberg argued that people everywhere develop their moral reasoning by passing through these age-based *stages. Where does Kohlberg's theory stand on the nature-nurture and continuity-discontinuity issues discussed in Chapter 1?*

- *Stage 2.* **Individualism, instrumental purpose, and exchange** is the second stage of preconventional reasoning. At this stage, children reason that pursuing their own interests is the right thing to do, but they let others do the same. Thus, they think that what is right involves an equal exchange. They reason that if they are nice to others, others will be nice to them in return.

Conventional reasoning is the second, or intermediate, level in Kohlberg's theory of moral development. At this level, individuals apply certain standards, but they are the standards set by others, such as parents or the government.

- *Stage 3.* **Mutual interpersonal expectations, relationships, and interpersonal conformity** is Kohlberg's third stage of moral development. At this stage, individuals value trust, caring, and loyalty to others as a basis of moral judgments. Children and adolescents often adopt their parents' moral standards at this stage, seeking parental approval as a "good girl" or a "good boy."

- *Stage 4.* **Social systems morality** is the fourth stage in Kohlberg's theory of moral development. At this stage, moral judgments are based on understanding the social order, law, justice, and duty. For example, adolescents may reason that in order for a community to work effectively, it needs to be protected by laws that community members obey.

Postconventional reasoning is the highest level in Kohlberg's theory of moral development. At this level, the individual recognizes alternative moral courses, explores the options, and then decides on a personal moral code.

- *Stage 5.* **Social contract or utility and individual rights** is the fifth Kohlberg stage. At this stage, individuals reason that values, rights, and principles undergird or transcend the law. A person evaluates the validity of actual laws, and social systems can be examined in terms of the degree to which they preserve and protect fundamental human rights and values.

- *Stage 6.* **Universal ethical principles** is the sixth and highest stage in Kohlberg's theory of moral development. At this stage, the person has developed a moral standard based on universal human rights. When faced with a conflict between law and conscience, the person reasons that conscience should be followed, even though the decision might bring risk.

Kohlberg believed that these levels and stages occur in a sequence and are age related: Before age 9, most children use level 1, preconventional reasoning based on external rewards and punishments. By early adolescence, moral reasoning is increasingly based on level 2, the application of standards set by others. Most adolescents reason at the higher part of level 2 (stage 3), with some signs of stages 2 and 4. Not everyone progresses beyond level 2, even in adulthood, but by early adulthood a small number of individuals reason in postconventional ways (level 3).

individualism, instrumental purpose, and exchange The second Kohlberg stage of moral development. At this stage, individuals pursue their own interests but also let others do the same.

conventional reasoning The second, or intermediate, level in Kohlberg's theory of moral development. At this level, individuals abide by certain standards, but they are the standards of others such as parents or the laws of society.

mutual interpersonal expectations, relationships, and interpersonal conformity Kohlberg's third stage of moral development. At this stage, individuals value trust, caring, and loyalty to others as a basis of moral judgments.

social systems morality The fourth stage in Kohlberg's theory of moral development. Moral judgments are based on understanding the social order, law, justice, and duty.

postconventional reasoning The highest level in Kohlberg's theory of moral development. At this level, the individual recognizes alternative moral courses, explores the options, and then decides on a personal moral code.

social contract or utility and individual rights The fifth Kohlberg stage. At this stage, individuals reason that values, rights, and principles undergird or transcend the law.

universal ethical principles The sixth and highest stage in Kohlberg's theory of moral development. Individuals develop a moral standard based on universal human rights.

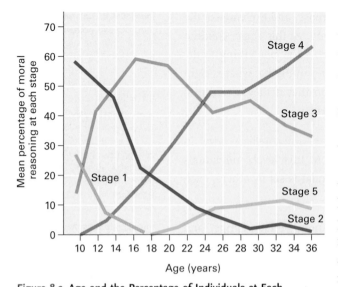

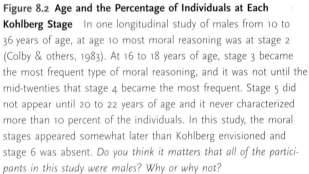

Figure 8.2 Age and the Percentage of Individuals at Each Kohlberg Stage In one longitudinal study of males from 10 to 36 years of age, at age 10 most moral reasoning was at stage 2 (Colby & others, 1983). At 16 to 18 years of age, stage 3 became the most frequent type of moral reasoning, and it was not until the mid-twenties that stage 4 became the most frequent. Stage 5 did not appear until 20 to 22 years of age and it never characterized more than 10 percent of the individuals. In this study, the moral stages appeared somewhat later than Kohlberg envisioned and stage 6 was absent. *Do you think it matters that all of the participants in this study were males? Why or why not?*

What evidence supports this description of development? A 20-year longitudinal investigation found that use of stages 1 and 2 decreased with age (Colby & others, 1983) (see Figure 8.2). Stage 4, which did not appear at all in the moral reasoning of 10-year-olds, was reflected in the moral thinking of 62 percent of the 36-year-olds. Stage 5 did not appear in any individuals until age 20 to 22, and even later in adulthood it never characterized more than 10 percent of the individuals. Thus, this research found that the moral stages appeared somewhat later than Kohlberg initially envisioned, and reasoning at the higher stages, especially stage 6, was rare.

Influences on the Kohlberg Stages

What factors influence movement through Kohlberg' stages? Although moral reasoning at each stage presupposes a certain level of cognitive development, Kohlberg argued that advances in children's cognitive development did not ensure development of moral reasoning. Instead, moral reasoning also reflects children's experiences in dealing with moral questions and moral conflict.

Several investigators have tried to advance individuals' levels of moral development by having a model present arguments that reflect moral thinking one stage above the individuals' established levels. This approach applies the Vygotsky principle of scaffolding; it also applies the concepts of equilibrium and conflict that Piaget used to explain cognitive development. By presenting arguments slightly beyond the children' level of moral reasoning, the researchers created a disequilibrium that motivated the children to restructure their moral thought. The upshot of studies using this approach is that virtually any plus-stage discussion, for any length of time, seems to promote more advanced moral reasoning (Walker, 1982).

Kohlberg believed that peer interaction is a critical part of the social stimulation that challenges children to change their moral reasoning. Whereas adults characteristically impose rules and regulations on children, the give-and-take among peers gives children an opportunity to take the perspective of another person and to generate rules democratically. Kohlberg stressed that encounters with any peers can produce perspective-taking opportunities that may advance a child's moral reasoning.

How Would You...? As a human development and family studies professional, how would you explain the progression of moral reasoning skills that develop during the elementary school years?

Kohlberg's Critics

Kohlberg's theory provoked much debate, research, and criticism (Lapsley & Narvaez, 2006; Turiel, 2006; Walker, 2006). Key criticisms involve the link between moral thought and moral behavior, the roles of culture and the family in moral development, and the significance of concern for others.

Moral Thought and Moral Behavior Does Kohlberg's theory place too much emphasis on moral thought and not enough emphasis on moral behavior? Critics argue that moral reasons can sometimes be a shelter for immoral behavior. We have only to read the news to observe that politicians and corporate executives may endorse the loftiest of moral virtues in public but engage in serious breaches of ethics. There seems to be no shortage of cheaters and thieves who can reason at the postconventional level; the cheaters and thieves may know what is right yet still do what is wrong.

Culture and Moral Reasoning Kohlberg viewed his stages of moral reasoning as universal, but some critics find his theory to be culturally biased (Miller, 2006, 2007; Wainryb, 2006). Both Kohlberg and his critics may be partially correct.

One review of 45 studies in 27 mostly non-European cultures around the world provided support for the universality of Kohlberg's first four stages (Snarey, 1987). Individuals in diverse cultures developed through these four stages in sequence as Kohlberg predicted. Stages 5 and 6, however, were not found in all cultures.

Furthermore, this review found that Kohlberg's system failed to recognize the higher-level moral reasoning of certain cultures and thus that moral reasoning is more culture-specific than Kohlberg envisioned (Snarey, 1987). For example, researchers encountered moral judgments based on principles of communal equity and collective happiness in Israel, the unity and sacredness of all life-forms in India, and collective moral responsibility in New Guinea (Snarey, 1987). These examples of moral reasoning would not be scored at the highest level in Kohlberg's system because they are not based on principles of justice. Similar results occurred in a study that assessed the moral development of 20 adolescent male Buddhist monks in Nepal (Huebner & Garrod, 1993). Justice, a basic theme in Kohlberg's theory, was not of paramount importance in the monks' moral views, and their concerns about the prevention of suffering and the role of compassion are not captured by Kohlberg's theory.

This 14-year-old boy in Nepal is thought to be the sixth holiest Buddhist in the world. *How might the moral reasoning of this boy be different than Kohlberg's theory predicts?*

In sum, although Kohlberg's approach does represent much of the moral reasoning voiced in various cultures around the world, it misses or miscontrues some important moral concepts in particular cultures (Miller, 2007; Wainryb, 2006).

Families and Moral Development Kohlberg did not view family processes as especially important in children's moral development. As noted earlier, he argued that parent-child relationships usually provide children with little opportunity for give-and-take or perspective taking. Rather, Kohlberg said that such opportunities are more likely to be provided by children's peer relations (Brabeck, 2000).

Did Kohlberg underestimate the contribution of family relationships to moral development? A number of developmentalists emphasize that *inductive discipline,* which uses reasoning and focuses children's attention on how their actions affect others, positively influences moral development (Hoffman, 1970). They also stress that parents' moral values influence children's developing moral thoughts, and parents influence children's moral development by being proactive to avert potential misbehavior by children (Thompson, McGlinly, & Meyer, 2006). Nonetheless, most developmentalists agree with Kohlberg, and Piaget, that peers play an important role in the development of moral reasoning.

justice perspective A moral perspective that focuses on the rights of the individual; individuals independently make moral decisions.

care perspective The moral perspective of Carol Gilligan, which views people in terms of their connectedness with others and emphasizes interpersonal communication, relationships with others, and concern for others.

Gender and the Care Perspective Perhaps the most publicized criticism of Kohlberg's theory has come from Carol Gilligan (1982, 1992, 1996), who argues that Kohlberg's theory reflects a gender bias. According to Gilligan, Kohlberg's theory is based on a male norm that puts abstract principles above relationships and concern for others and sees the individual as standing alone and independently making moral decisions. It puts justice at the heart of morality. In contrast to Kohlberg's **justice perspective**, Gilligan argues for a **care perspective**, which is a moral perspective that views people in terms of their connectedness with others and emphasizes interpersonal communication, relationships with others, and concern for others.

According to Gilligan, Kohlberg greatly underplayed the care perspective, perhaps because he was a male, because most of his research was with males rather than females, and because he used male responses as a model for his theory.

In extensive interviews with girls from 6 to 18 years of age, Gilligan and her colleagues found that girls consistently interpret moral dilemmas in terms of human relationships and base these interpretations on listening and watching other people (Gilligan, 1992, 1996; Gilligan & others, 2003). However, a meta-analysis (a statistical analysis that combines the results of many different studies) cast doubt on Gilligan's claim of substantial gender differences in moral judgment (Jaffee & Hyde, 2000). Overall, this analysis found only a small gender difference in care-based reasoning, and the difference was greater in adolescence than childhood. When differences in moral reasoning occurred, they were better explained by the nature of the dilemma than by gender. For example, both males and females tended to use care reasoning to deal with interpersonal dilemmas and justice reasoning to handle societal dilemmas. In sum, experts have now concluded that there is no evidence to support Gilligan's claim that Kohlberg downplayed females' moral thinking (Hyde, 2005, 2007; Walker, 2006).

Carol Gilligan is shown with some of the students she has interviewed about the importance of relationships in a female's development. *What is Gilligan's view of moral development?*

However, other research does find differences in how boys and girls tend to interpret some aspects of moral situations (Eisenberg, Fabes, & Spinrad, 2006; Eisenberg & Morris, 2004). In support of this idea, one study found that females rated prosocial dilemmas (those emphasizing altruism and helping) as more significant than males did (Wark & Krebs, 2000). Another study revealed that young adolescent girls used more care-based reasoning about dating dilemmas than did boys (Weisz & Black, 2002).

Prosocial Behavior

Whereas Kohlberg's and Gilligan's theories have focused primarily on the development of moral reasoning, the study of prosocial moral behavior has placed more emphasis on the behavioral aspects of moral development (Hastings, Utendale, & Sullivan, 2007). Children engage in both immoral antisocial acts, such as lying and cheating, and prosocial moral behavior, such as showing empathy or helping others altruistically (Carlo, 2006). Even during the preschool years, children may care for others or comfort someone in distress, but prosocial behavior is more prevalent in adolescence than in childhood (Eisenberg & Morris, 2004).

How does children's sharing change from the preschool to the elementary school years?

Sharing is one aspect of prosocial behavior that researchers have studied. Children's sharing comes to reflect a more complex sense of what is just and right during middle and late childhood. By the start of the elementary school years, children begin to express objective ideas about fairness (Eisenberg, Fabes, & Spinrad, 2006). It is common to hear 6-year-old children use the word *fair* as synonymous with *equal* or *same*. By the mid- to late elementary school years, children come to believe that equity can also mean that people with special merit or special needs deserve special treatment.

gender stereotypes Broad categories that reflect our impressions and beliefs about females and males.

Gender

Gilligan's claim that Kohlberg's theory of moral development reflects gender bias reminds us of the pervasive influence of gender on development. Long before elementary school, boys and girls show preferences for different toys and activities. As we discussed in Chapter 6, preschool children display a gender identity and gender-typed behavior that reflects biological, cognitive, and social influences. Here we examine gender stereotypes, gender similarities and differences, and gender-role classification.

Gender Stereotypes

In the nineteenth and early twentieth centuries, a well-adjusted boy was supposed to be independent, aggressive, and powerful. A well-adjusted girl was supposed to be dependent, nurturant, and uninterested in power. These notions are **gender stereotypes**, broad categories that reflect general impressions and beliefs about females and males.

Recent research has found that gender stereotypes are, to a great extent, still present in today's world, both in the lives of children and adults (Bigler, Averhart, & Liben, 2003; Hyde, 2005, 2007). A recent study revealed that children's gender stereotyping increased from preschool through the fifth grade (Miller & others, 2007). In this study, preschoolers stereotyped dolls and appearance as characteristic of girls' interests and toys and behaviors (such as action heroes and hitting) as the province of boys. During middle and late childhood, children expanded the range and extent of their gender stereotyping in such areas as occupations, sports, and school tasks. Researchers also have found that boys' gender stereotypes are more rigid than girls' (Ruble, Martin, & Berenbaum, 2006).

Gender Similarities and Differences

What is the reality behind gender stereotypes? Let's examine some of the similarities and differences between boys and girls, keeping in mind that (1) the differences are averages—not all boys versus all girls; (2) even when differences are reported, there is considerable gender overlap; and (3) the differences may be due primarily to biological factors, sociocultural factors, or both. First, we examine physical similarities and differences, and then we turn to cognitive and socioemotional similarities and differences.

Physical Development On the average, males grow to be 10 percent taller than females. Other physical differences are less obvious. From conception on, females have a longer life expectancy than males, and females are less likely than males to develop physical or mental disorders. Males have twice the risk of coronary disease as females.

Differences in hormones contribute to many of these physical differences between the sexes. Androgens such as testosterone are male sex hormones and estrogens are female sex hormones, although both males and females produce androgens and estrogens. Male hormones promote the growth of long bones; female hormones stop such growth at puberty. Estrogen strengthens the immune system, making females more resistant to infection, for example.

Does gender matter when it comes to brain structure and function? Human brains are much alike, whether the brain belongs to a male or a female (Halpern, 2001). However, researchers have found some differences in the brains of males and females (Goldstein & others, 2001; Kimura, 2000). The following are among the differences that have been discovered:

- Although female brains are smaller than male brains, they have more folds; the larger folds (called convolutions) allow more surface brain tissue within the skulls of females than males (Luders & others, 2004).

- One part of the hypothalamus responsible for sexual behavior is larger in men than in women (Swaab & others, 2001).

- Portions of the corpus callosum—the band of tissues through which the brain's two hemispheres communicate—are larger in females than in males (Le Vay, 1994).

- An area of the parietal lobe that functions in visuospatial skills is larger in males than in females (Frederikse & others, 2000).

- The areas of the brain involved in emotional expression show more metabolic activity in females than in males (Gur & others, 1995).

Cognitive Development In a classic review of gender differences, Eleanor Maccoby and Carol Jacklin (1974) concluded that males have better math and visuospatial skills (the kinds of skills an architect needs to design a building's angles and dimensions), whereas females have better verbal abilities. However, Maccoby subsequently (1987) revised her conclusion about several gender dimensions. She found that the accumulation of research evidence suggested that verbal differences between females and males had virtually disappeared, but that math and visuospatial differences still existed. For example, despite equal participation in the National Geography Bee, in most years all 10 finalists were boys (Liben, 1995).

"So according to the stereotype, you can put two and two together, but I can read the handwriting on the wall." Copyright © 1994 Joel Pett. All Rights Reserved.

Some experts, such as Janet Shibley Hyde (2005, 2007), suggest that the cognitive differences between females and males have been exaggerated. For example, Hyde has found considerable overlap in the distributions of female and male scores on math and visuospatial tasks. In a national study, boys did slightly better than girls did at math and science (National Assessment of Educational Progress, 2005). Overall, though, girls were far superior students, and they were significantly better than boys in reading. In another national study, females had better writing skills than males in grades 4, 8, and 12, with the gap widening as students progressed through school (Coley, 2001).

Socioemotional Development Three areas of socioemotional development in which gender similarities and differences have been studied extensively are aggression, emotion, and prosocial behavior.

One of the most consistent gender differences is that boys are more physically aggressive than girls. The difference occurs in all cultures and appears very early in children's development (White, 2001). The difference in physical aggression is especially pronounced when children are provoked. Although boys are consistently more physically aggressive than girls, might girls be just as aggressive or even more aggressive than boys in other ways? When verbal aggression, such as yelling, is examined, females are often as aggressive, or even more aggressive, than males (Eagly & Steffen, 1986). However, research on gender differences in *relational aggression,* which involves such behaviors as spreading malicious rumors in order to get others to dislike a child or ignoring someone when angry at him or her, are mixed (Crick, Ostrov, & Werner, 2006; Underwood, 2004). Some studies show girls engaging in more relational aggression, others indicate no differences.

Are there gender differences in emotion? Beginning in the elementary school years, boys are more likely to hide their negative emotions, such as sadness, and girls are less likely to express disappointment that might hurt others' feelings (Eisenberg, Martin, & Fabes, 1996). Beginning in early adolescence, girls say they experience more sadness, shame, and guilt, and report more intense emotions, whereas boys are more likely to deny that they experience these emotions (Ruble, Martin, & Berenbaum, 2006). Males usually show less self-regulation of emotion than females, and this low self-control can translate into behavioral problems (Eisenberg & others, 2002). In one study, children's low self-regulation was linked with greater aggression, teasing of others, overreaction to frustration, low cooperation, and inability to delay gratification (Block & Block, 1980).

Are there gender differences in prosocial behavior? Females view themselves as more prosocial and empathic (Eisenberg & Morris, 2004). Across childhood and adolescence, females engage in more prosocial behavior (Eisenberg, Fabes, & Spinrad, 2006). The biggest gender difference occurs for kind and considerate behavior with a smaller difference in sharing.

Earlier in the chapter, we discussed Carol Gilligan's theory that many females are more sensitive about relationships and have better relationship skills than males do. In Chapter 12, "Socioemotional Development in Early Adulthood," we further explore this area of gender.

How Would You...?
As a psychologist, how would you discuss gender similarities and differences with a parent or teacher who is concerned about a child's academic progress and social skills?

Gender-Role Classification

Not very long ago, it was accepted that boys should grow up to be masculine and girls to be feminine. In the 1970s, however, as both females and males became dissatisfied with the burdens imposed by their stereotypic roles, alternatives to femininity and masculinity were proposed. Instead of describing masculinity and femininity as a continuum in which more of one means less of the other, it was proposed that individuals could have both masculine and feminine traits.

androgyny The presence of positive masculine and feminine characteristics in the same individual.

This thinking led to the development of the concept of **androgyny**, the presence of positive masculine and feminine characteristics in the same person (Bem, 1977; Spence & Helmreich, 1978). The androgynous boy might be assertive (masculine) and nurturant (feminine). The androgynous girl might be powerful (masculine) and sensitive to others' feelings (feminine). Recent studies confirmed that societal changes are leading females to be more assertive (Spence & Buckner, 2000) and that sons were more androgynous than their fathers (Guastello & Guastello, 2003).

Gender experts such as Sandra Bem argue that androgynous individuals are more flexible, competent, and mentally healthy than their masculine or feminine counterparts. To some degree, though, which gender-role classification is best depends on context. For example, in close relationships, feminine and androgynous orientations might be more desirable. One recent study found that children high in femininity showed a stronger interest in caring than did children high in masculinity (Karniol, Groz, & Schorr, 2003). However, masculine and androgynous orientations might be more desirable in traditional academic and work settings because of the achievement demands in these contexts.

Despite talk about the "sensitive male," William Pollack (1999) argues that little has been done to change traditional ways of raising boys. He says that the "boy code" tells boys that they should show little if any emotion and should act tough. Boys learn the boy code in many contexts, especially peer contexts—sandboxes, playgrounds, schoolrooms, camps, hangouts. The result, according to Pollack, is a "national crisis of boyhood." Pollack and others suggest that boys would benefit from being socialized to express their anxieties and concerns and to better regulate their aggression.

Gender in Context

The concept of androgyny and gender stereotypes both talk about people in terms of personality traits such as "aggressive" or "caring." However, which traits people display may vary with the situation (Galambos, 2004). Thus, the nature and extent of gender differences may depend on the context (Leaper & Friedman, 2007; Matlin, 2008).

Consider helping behavior. The stereotype is that females are better than males at helping. But it depends on the situation. Females are more likely than males to volunteer their time to help children with personal problems and to engage in caregiving behavior. However, in situations in which males feel a sense of competence and that involve danger, males are more likely than females to help (Eagly & Crowley, 1986). For example, a male is more likely than a female to stop and help a person stranded by the roadside with a flat tire. Indeed, one recent study documented that males are more likely to help when the context is masculine in nature (MacGeorge, 2003).

In China, females and males are usually socialized to behave, feel, and think differently. The old patriarchal traditions of male supremacy have not been completely uprooted. Chinese women still make considerably less money than Chinese men do, and, in rural China (such as here in the Lixian Village of Sichuan) male supremacy still governs many women's lives.

The importance of considering gender in context is nowhere more apparent than when examining what is culturally prescribed behavior for females and males in different countries around the world (Denmark, Rabinowitz, & Sechzer, 2005). Although there has been greater acceptance of androgyny and similarities in male and female behavior in the United States, in many countries gender roles have remained gender-specific.

For example, in many Middle Eastern countries, the division of labor between males and females is dramatic. Males are socialized and schooled to work in the public sphere, females in the private world of home and child rearing. For example, in Iran, the dominant view is that the man's duty is to provide for his family and the woman's is to care for her family and household. China is another example of a male-dominant culture. Although women have made some strides in China, especially in urban areas, the male role is still dominant. Most males in China do not accept androgynous behavior and gender equity.

Families

Our further discussion of parenting and families in this section focuses on how parent-child interactions typically change in middle and late childhood, parents as managers, and how children are affected by living with stepparents and by being left on their own after school.

Developmental Changes in Parent-Child Relationships

As children move into the middle and late childhood years, parents spend considerably less time with them. In one study, parents spent less than half as much time with their children aged 5 to 12 in caregiving, instruction, reading, talking, and playing as when the children were younger (Hill & Stafford, 1980). Although parents spend less time with their children in middle and late childhood than in early childhood, parents continue to be extremely important in their children's lives. In a recent analysis of the contributions of parents in middle and late childhood, the following conclusion was reached: "Parents serve as gatekeepers and provide scaffolding as children assume more responsibility for themselves and . . . regulate their own lives" (Huston & Ripke, 2006, p. 422).

Parents especially play an important role in supporting and stimulating children's academic achievement in middle and late childhood (Huston & Ripke, 2006). The value parents place on education can mean the difference in whether children do well in school. Parents not only influence children's in-school achievement, but they also make decision about children's out-of-school activities. Whether children participate in such activities as sports, music, and other activities is heavily influenced by the extent to which parents sign up children for such activities and encourage their participation (Simpkins & others, 2006).

Elementary school children tend to receive less physical discipline than they did as preschoolers. Instead of spanking or coercive holding, their parents are more likely to use deprivation of privileges, appeals to the child's self-esteem, comments designed to increase the child's sense of guilt, and statements that the child is responsible for his or her actions.

During middle and late childhood, some control is transferred from parent to child. The process is gradual, and it produces *coregulation* rather than control by either the child or the parent alone (Maccoby,

What are some changes in the focus of parent-child relationships in middle and late childhood?

1984). Parents continue to exercise general supervision and control, while children are allowed to engage in moment-to-moment self-regulation. The major shift to autonomy does not occur until about the age of 12 or later. A key developmental task as children move toward autonomy is learning to relate to adults outside the family on a regular basis—adults who interact with the child much differently than parents, such as teachers.

Parents as Managers

Parents can play important roles as managers of children's opportunities, as monitors of their behavior, and as social initiators and arrangers (Parke & Buriel, 2006). Mothers are more likely than fathers to engage in a managerial role in parenting.

Researchers have found that family management practices are positively related to students' grades and self-responsibility, and negatively to school-related problems (Eccles, 2007; Taylor & Lopez, 2005). Among the most important family management practices in this regard are maintaining a structured and organized family environment, such as establishing routines for homework, chores, bedtime, and so on, and effectively monitoring the child's behavior. A recent research review of family functioning in African American students' academic achievement found that when African American parents monitored their son's academic achievement by ensuring that homework was completed, restricted time spent on nonproductive distractions (such as videogames and TV), and participated in a consistent, positive dialogue with teachers and school officials, their son's academic achievement benefited (Mandara, 2006).

Stepfamilies

Not only has divorce become commonplace in the United States, so has getting remarried (Hetherington, 2006). It takes time for parents to marry, have children, get divorced, and then remarry. Consequently, there are far more elementary and secondary school children than infants or preschool children living in stepfamilies.

The number of remarriages involving children has grown steadily in recent years. Also, divorces occur at a 10 percent higher rate in remarriages than in first marriages (Cherlin & Furstenberg, 1994). About half of all children whose parents divorce will have a stepparent within four years of the separation.

Remarried parents face some unique tasks. The couple must define and strengthen their marriage and at the same time renegotiate the biological parent-child relationships and establish stepparent-stepchild and stepsibling relationships (Ganong, Coleman, & Hans, 2006). The complex histories and multiple relationships make adjustment difficult in a stepfamily (Goldscheider & Saggler, 2006). Only one-third of stepfamily couples stay remarried.

In some cases, the stepfamily may have been preceded by the death of a spouse. However, by far the largest number of stepfamilies are preceded by divorce rather than death (Pasley & Moorefield, 2004). Three common types of stepfamily structure are (1) stepfather, (2) stepmother, and (3) blended or complex. In stepfather families,

How does living in a stepfamily influence a child's development?

the mother typically had custody of the children and remarried, introducing a stepfather into her children's lives. In stepmother families, the father usually had custody and remarried, introducing a stepmother into his children's lives. In a blended or complex stepfamily, both parents bring children from previous marriages to live in the newly formed stepfamily.

In Hetherington's (2006) most recent longitudinal analyses, children and adolescents who had been in a simple stepfamily (stepfather or stepmother) for a number of years were adjusting better than in the early years of the remarried family and were functioning well in comparison to children and adolescents in conflicted nondivorced families and children and adolescents in complex (blended) stepfamilies. More than 75 percent of the adolescents in long-established simple stepfamilies described their relationships with their stepparents as "close" or "very close." Hetherington (2006) concluded that in long-established simple stepfamilies adolescents seem to eventually benefit from the presence of a stepparent and the resources provided by the stepparent.

Children often have better relationships with their custodial parents (mothers in stepfather families, fathers in stepmother families) than with stepparents (Santrock, Sitterle, & Warshak, 1988). Also, children in simple families (stepmother, stepfather) often show better adjustment than their counterparts in complex (blended) families (Hetherington, 2006).

How Would You...?
As a human development and family studies professional, how would you advise divorced parents on strategies to ease their children's adjustment to remarriage?

As in divorced families, children in stepfamilies show more adjustment problems than children in nondivorced families (Hetherington, 2006). The adjustment problems are similar to those found among children of divorced parents—academic problems and lower self-esteem, for example (Anderson & others, 1999). However, it is important to recognize that a majority of children in stepfamilies do not have problems. In one analysis, 25 percent of children from stepfamilies showed adjustment problems compared with 10 percent in intact, never-divorced families (Hetherington & Kelly, 2002). Adolescence is an especially difficult time for the formation of a stepfamily (Anderson & others, 1999). This may occur because becoming part of a stepfamily exacerbates normal adolescent concerns about identity, sexuality, and autonomy.

Latchkey Children

We concluded in Chapter 6 that both parents' working outside the home does not necessarily have negative outcomes for their children. However, the subset of children sometimes called "latchkey children" deserves further scrutiny. The term comes from the fact that these children use the key to their home to let themselves in after school while their parents are still at work. Latchkey children are largely unsupervised for two to four hours a day during each school week. During the summer months, they might be unsupervised for entire days, five days a week.

Although latchkey children may be vulnerable to problems, the experiences of latchkey children vary enormously, as do the experiences of all children with working parents. Parents need to give special attention to the ways in which their latchkey children's lives can be effectively monitored. Variations in latchkey experiences suggest that parental monitoring and authoritative parenting help the child cope more effectively with latchkey experiences, especially in resisting peer pressure (Galambos & Maggs, 1989; Steinberg, 1986).

For parents who work, are there good alternatives to allowing their school-children to be home by themselves after school? One recent study of 819 10- to 14-year-olds found that out-of-home care, whether supervised or unsupervised, was linked to delinquency, drug and alcohol use, and school problems (Coley, Morri, & Hernandez, 2004). Other research, however, found more positive outcomes for children in some after-school programs. In one study, attending a formal after-school program that included academic, recreational, and remedial activities was associated with better academic achievement and social adjustment, in comparison with self-care and with other types of after-school care such as informal adult supervision (Posner & Vandell, 1994).

How Would You...?
As a health-care professional, how would you design a school-based program to increase the health, safety, and well-being of latchkey children?

Practitioners and policy makers recommend that after-school programs have warm and supportive staff, a flexible and relaxed schedule, multiple activities, and opportunities for positive interactions with staff and peers (Pierce, Hamm, & Vandell, 1997). Such programs, however, are not widely available and tend to be expensive when they do exist. A recent study found, perhaps not surprisingly, that low-income parents were especially dissatisfied with the quality of options available in after-school programs (Wallace Foundation, 2004).

Peers

Positive relationships with peers are especially important in middle and late childhood. Engaging in positive interactions with peers, resolving conflicts with peers in nonaggressive ways, and having quality friendships in middle and late adulthood not only have positive outcomes at this time in children's lives, but also are linked to more positive relationship outcomes in adolescence and adulthood (Huston & Ripke, 2006). For example, in one longitudinal study, being popular with peers and engaging in low levels of aggression at 8 years of age were related to higher levels of occupational status at 48 years of age (Huesmann & others, 2006). Another study found that peer competence (a composite measure that included social contact with peers, popularity with peers, friendship, and social skills) in middle and late childhood was linked to having better relationships with coworkers in early adulthood (Collins & van Dulmen, 2006).

Developmental Changes

As children enter the elementary school years, reciprocity becomes especially important in peer interchanges. Researchers estimate that the percentage of time spent in social interaction with peers increases from approximately 10 percent at 2 years of age to more than 30 percent in middle and late childhood (Rubin, Bukowski, & Parker, 2006). In one early study, a typical day in elementary school included approximately 300 episodes with peers (Barker & Wright, 1951). As children move through middle and late childhood, the size of their peer group increases, and peer interaction is less closely supervised by adults (Rubin, Bukowski, & Parker, 2006). Until about 12 years of age, children's preference for same-sex peer groups increases.

Peer Status

Which children are likely to be popular with their peers and which ones are disliked? Developmentalists address this and similar questions by examining *sociometric status*, a term that describes the extent to which children are liked or disliked by their peer group (Ladd, Herald, & Andrews, 2006). Sociometric status is typically assessed by asking children to rate how much they like or dislike each of their classmates. Or it may be assessed by asking children to nominate the children they like the most and those they like the least.

What are some statuses that children have with their peers?

Developmentalists have distinguished five peer statuses (Wentzel & Asher, 1995):

- **Popular children** are frequently nominated as a best friend and are rarely disliked by their peers.

- **Average children** receive an average number of both positive and negative nominations from their peers.

- **Neglected children** are infrequently nominated as a best friend but are not disliked by their peers.

- **Rejected children** are infrequently nominated as someone's best friend and are actively disliked by their peers.

- **Controversial children** are frequently nominated both as someone's best friend and as being disliked.

Popular children have a number of social skills that contribute to their being well liked. They give out reinforcements, listen carefully, maintain open lines of communication with peers, are happy, control their negative emotions, act like themselves, show enthusiasm and concern for others, and are self-confident without being conceited (Hartup, 1983; Rubin, Bukowski, & Parker, 1998).

Neglected children engage in low rates of interaction with their peers and are often described as shy by peers. The goal of many training programs for neglected children is to help them attract attention from their peers in positive ways and to hold that attention by asking questions, by listening in a warm and friendly way, and by saying things about themselves that relate to the peers' interests.

Rejected children often have more serious adjustment problems than those who are neglected (Bukowski, Brendgen, & Vitaro, 2007). One study found that in kindergarten, children who were rejected by their peers were less likely to engage in classroom participation, more likely to express a desire to avoid school, and more likely to report being lonely than children who were accepted by their peers (Buhs & Ladd, 2001). The combination of being rejected by peers and being aggressive forecasts problems. One study evaluated 112 fifth-grade boys over a period of seven years until the end of high school (Kupersmidt & Coie, 1990). The best predictor of whether rejected children would engage in delinquent behavior or drop out of school later during adolescence was aggression toward peers in elementary school.

John Coie (2004, pp. 252–253) provided three reasons why aggressive peer-rejected boys have problems in social relationships:

> First, the rejected, aggressive boys are more impulsive and have problems sustaining attention. As a result, they are more likely to be disruptive of ongoing activities in the

How Would You...?

As a social worker, how would you help a neglected child become more involved in peer activities?

classroom and in focused group play. Second, rejected, aggressive boys are more emotionally reactive. They are aroused to anger more easily and probably have more difficulty calming down once aroused. Because of this they are more prone to become angry at peers and attack them verbally and physically. . . . Third, rejected children have fewer social skills in making friends and maintaining positive relationships with peers.

Not all rejected children are aggressive (Ladd, Herald, & Andres, 2006). Although aggression and its related characteristics of impulsiveness and disruptiveness underlie rejection about half the time, approximately 10 to 20 percent of rejected children are shy.

How can rejected children be trained to interact more effectively with their peers? They may be asked to engage in role playing or to discuss hypothetical situations involving negative encounters with peers, such as when a peer cuts into a line ahead of them. This can help them to more accurately assess whether or not the intentions of their peers are negative (Bierman, 2004). In some programs, children are shown videotapes of appropriate peer interaction and asked to draw lessons from what they have seen (Ladd, 2005).

Social Cognition

A boy accidentally trips and knocks another boy's drink out of his hand. That boy misinterprets the encounter as hostile, which leads him to retaliate aggressively against the boy who tripped. Through repeated encounters of this kind, the aggressive boy's classmates come to perceive him as habitually acting in inappropriate ways.

This encounter demonstrates the importance of *social cognition*—thinking about social matters, such as the aggressive boy's interpretation of an encounter as hostile and his classmates' perception of his behavior as inappropriate (Gauvain & Perez, 2007). Children's social cognition about their peers becomes increasingly important for understanding peer relationships in middle and late childhood. Of special interest are the ways in which children process information about peer relations and their social knowledge (Dodge, Coie, & Lynam, 2006).

How Would You...?
As a psychologist, how would you characterize differences in the social cognition of aggressive children compared to children who behave in less hostile ways?

Kenneth Dodge (1983) argues that children go through five steps in processing information about their social world. They decode social cues, interpret, search for a response, select an optimal response, and enact. Dodge has found that aggressive boys are more likely to perceive another child's actions as hostile when the child's intention is ambiguous. Further, when aggressive boys search for cues to determine a peer's intention, they respond more rapidly, less efficiently, and less reflectively than do nonaggressive children. These are among the social cognitive factors believed to be involved in children's conflicts.

Social knowledge also is involved in children's ability to get along with peers. They need to know what goals to pursue in poorly defined or ambiguous situations, how to initiate and maintain a social bond, and what scripts to follow to get other children to be their friends. For example, as part of the script for getting friends, it helps to know that saying nice things, regardless of what the peer does or says, will increase the peer's liking for the child.

Bullying

Significant numbers of students are victimized by bullies (DeRosier & Marcus, 2005; Evertson & Weinstein, 2006). In one national survey of more than 15,000 sixth- through tenth-grade students, nearly one of every three students said that they had experienced occasional or frequent involvement as a victim or perpetrator in bullying (Nansel & others, 2001). In this study, bullying was defined as verbal or physical behavior intended to disturb someone less powerful. As shown in Figure 8.3, being belittled about looks or speech was the most frequent type of bullying.

Who is likely to be bullied? In the study just described, boys and younger middle school students were most likely to be affected (Nansel & others, 2001). Children who said they were bullied reported more loneliness and difficulty in making friends, whereas those who did the bullying were more likely to have a poor academic record and to smoke and drink alcohol. Researchers have found that anxious, socially withdrawn, and aggressive children are often the victims of bullying (Hanish & Guerra, 2004). Anxious and socially withdrawn children may be victimized because they are nonthreatening and unlikely to retaliate if bullied, whereas aggressive children may be the targets of bullying because their behavior is irritating to bullies (Rubin, Bukowski, & Parker, 2006).

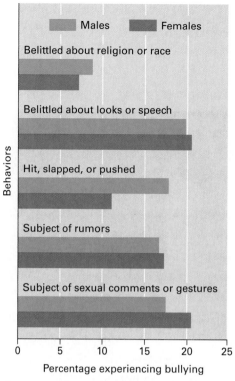

Figure 8.3 Bullying Behaviors Among U.S. Youth This graph shows the type of bullying most often experienced by U.S. youth. The percentages reflect the extent to which bullied students said that they had experienced a particular type of bullying. In terms of gender, note that when they were bullied, boys were more likely to be hit, slapped, or pushed than girls were.

How Would You...?
As a health-care professional, how would you characterize the health risks that bullying poses to the victims of bullying?

What are the outcomes of bullying? A recent study of 9- to 12-year-old children in the Netherlands found that the victims of bullies had a much higher incidence of headaches, sleeping problems, abdominal pain, feeling tired, and depression than children not involved in bullying behavior (Fekkes, Pijpers, & Verloove-Vanhorick, 2004).

To reduce bullying, teachers and schools can employ several strategies (Hyman & others, 2006; Limber, 1997, 2004; Milsom & Gallo, 2006):

- Get older peers to serve as monitors for bullying and intervene when they see it taking place.

- Develop school-wide rules and sanctions against bullying and post them throughout the school.

- Incorporate the message of the antibullying program into places of worship, school, and other community activities where children and youth are involved.

- Identify bullies and victims early, and use social skills training to improve their behavior. Teaching empathy, especially perspective taking; promoting self-control; and training social skills have been found to reduce the negative behavior of bullies.

How Would You...?
As an educator, how would you design and implement a bullying reduction program at your school?

Friends

Like adult friendships, children's friendships are typically characterized by similarity. Throughout childhood, friends are more similar than dissimilar in terms of age, sex, race, and many other factors. Friends often have similar attitudes toward school, similar educational aspirations, and closely aligned achievement orientations.

Why are children's friendships important? Children's friendships can serve six functions (Gottman & Parker, 1987):

- *Companionship.* Friendship provides children with a familiar partner and playmate, someone who is willing to spend time with them and join in collaborative activities.

- *Stimulation.* Friendship provides children with interesting information, excitement, and amusement.

- *Physical support.* Friendship provides time, resources, and assistance.

- *Ego support.* Friendship provides the expectation of support, encouragement, and feedback, which helps children maintain an impression of themselves as competent, attractive, and worthwhile individuals.

- *Social comparison.* Friendship provides information about where the child stands vis-à-vis others and whether the child is doing okay.

- *Affection and intimacy.* Friendship provides children with a warm, close, trusting relationship with another individual. **Intimacy in friendships** is characterized by self-disclosure and the sharing of private thoughts. Research suggests that intimate friendships may not appear until early adolescence (Berndt & Perry, 1990).

What are some characteristics of children's friendships?

Although having friends can be a developmental advantage, not all friendships are alike. People differ in the company they keep—that is, who their friends are. Developmental advantages occur when children have friends who are socially skilled and supportive. However, it is not developmentally advantageous to have coercive and conflict-ridden friendships (Berndt, 2002; Rubin, Bukowski, & Parker, 2006).

The importance of friendship was recently underscored in a two-year longitudinal study (Wentzel, Barry, & Caldwell, 2004). Sixth-grade students who did not have a friend engaged in less prosocial behavior (cooperation, sharing, helping others), had lower grades, and were more emotionally distressed (depression, low well-being) than their counterparts who had one or more friends. Two years later, in the eighth grade, the students who had been friendless in the sixth grade were still more emotionally distressed.

Schools

What does the transition to attending school signify for a child's development? Does the process of educating children involve controversy and opposing ideals? What effect do socioeconomic status and ethnicity have on schooling? Is school achievement a universal phenomenon, or does it have cross-cultural differences?

Contemporary Approaches to Student Learning

For most children, entering the first grade signals a change from being a "homechild" to being a "schoolchild." They take up a new role (being a student) and experience new obligations. They develop new relationships and develop new standards by which to judge themselves. School provides children with a rich source of new ideas to shape their sense of self. The children will spend many years in schools as members of small societies in which there are tasks to be accomplished, people to be socialized and socialized by, and rules that define and limit behavior, feelings, and attitudes. By the time students graduate from high school, they have spent 12,000 hours in the classroom. In short, it is justifiable to be concerned about the impact of schools on children.

Controversy swirls about the best way to teach children and how to hold schools and teachers accountable for whether children are learning.

Constructivist and Direct Instruction Approaches

The **constructivist approach** is a learner-centered approach that emphasizes the importance of individuals actively constructing their knowledge and understanding with guidance from the teacher. In the constructivist view, teachers should not attempt to simply pour information into children's minds. Rather, children should be encouraged to explore their world, discover knowledge, reflect, and think critically with careful monitoring and meaningful guidance from the teacher (Stiggins, 2008). The constructivist belief is that for too long in American education children have been

Is this classroom more likely constructivist or direct instruction? Explain.

required to sit still, be passive learners, and rotely memorize irrelevant as well as relevant information (Silberman, 2006).

Today, constructivism may include an emphasis on collaboration—children working with each other in their efforts to know and understand (Bodrova & Leong, 2007). A teacher with a constructivist instructional philosophy would not have children memorize information rotely but would give them opportunities to meaningfully construct the knowledge and understand the material while guiding their learning (Kafai, 2006).

By contrast, the **direct instruction approach** is a structured, teacher-centered approach that is characterized by teacher direction and control, high teacher expectations for students' progress, maximum time spent by students on academic tasks, and efforts by the teacher to keep negative affect to a minimum. An important goal in the direct-instruction approach is maximizing student learning time.

Advocates of the constructivist approach argue that the direct instruction approach turns children into passive learners and does not adequately challenge them to think in critical and creative ways (Oakes & Lipton, 2007). Direct instruction enthusiasts, on the other hand, say that the constructivist approach does not give enough attention to the content of a discipline, such as history or science. They view the constructivist approach as too relativistic and vague.

Some experts in educational psychology believe that many effective teachers use both a constructivist *and* a direct instruction approach rather than exclusively using one or the other (Bransford & others, 2006; Darling-Hammond & Bransford, 2005). Further, some circumstances may call more for a constructivist approach, others for a direction instruction approach. For example, experts increasingly recommend an explicit, intellectually engaging direct instruction approach when teaching students with a reading or a writing disability (Berninger, 2006). As another example, subject matter where creativity is important, such as art, might be more effectively taught with a constructivist approach.

Accountability

Since the 1990s, the U.S. public and governments at every level have demanded increased accountability from schools. One result was the spread of state-mandated tests to measure just what students had or had not learned (Johnson & others, 2008; McNergney & McNergney, 2007). Many states identified objectives for students in their state and created tests to measure whether students were meeting those objectives. This approach became national policy in 2002 when the No Child Left Behind (NCLB) legislation was signed into law.

Advocates argue that state-wide standardized testing will have a number of positive effects. These include improved student performance; more time teaching the subjects that are tested; high expectations for all students; identification of poorly performing schools, teachers, and administrators; and improved confidence in schools as test scores rise.

Most educators support high expectations and high standards for students (Revelle, 2004). At issue, however, is whether the tests and procedures mandated by NCLB are the best ones for achieving high standards (McMillan, 2007).

Critics are concerned that the NCLB legislation will do more harm than good (Connors, 2007). One criticism stresses that using a single test as the sole indicator of students' progress and competence presents a very narrow view of students' skills (Lewis, 2007). This criticism is similar to the one leveled at IQ tests, which we described in Chapter 7. To assess student progress and achievement, many psychologists and educators emphasize that an array of measures should be used, including tests, quizzes, projects, portfolios, classroom observations, and so on. Another criticism is that the tests used as part of NCLB don't measure creativity, motivation, persistence, flexible thinking, or social skills (Ercikan, 2006). There is concern that teachers may end up "teaching to the test"—drilling students and having them memorize isolated facts—at the expense of building thinking skills, which students need for success in life. Despite such criticisms, most U.S. schools are making accommodations to meet the requirements of NCLB.

Socioeconomic Status and Ethnicity

Children from low-income, ethnic minority backgrounds have more difficulties in school than do their middle-socioeconomic-status, White counterparts. Why? Critics argue that schools have not done a good job of educating low-income, ethnic minority students to overcome the barriers to their achievement (Banks, 2008; Spring, 2007). Let's further explore the roles of socioeconomic status and ethnicity in schools.

Educating Students from Low-Income Backgrounds

How Would You...?
As a health-care professional, how would you advise school administrators about health and nutrition challenges faced by low-income students that may impact their performance on achievement tests?

Many children in poverty face problems that present barriers to their learning (Diaz, Pelletier, & Provenzo, 2006; Ryan, Fauth, & Brooks-Gunn, 2006). They might have parents who don't set high educational standards for them, who are incapable of reading to them, and who don't have enough money to pay for educational materials and experiences, such as books and trips to zoos and museums. They might live in a crowded, noisy apartment where it is difficult to find a quiet place to do homework or even to sleep. They might be malnourished; they might live in a dangerous neighborhood where crime, violence, and fear are a way of life.

Compared with schools in higher income areas, schools in low-income areas are more likely to have more students with low achievement test scores, low graduation rates, and small percentages of students going to college; they are more likely to have young teachers with less experience; and they are more likely to encourage rote learning (McLaren, 2007). Too few schools in low-income neighborhoods provide students with environments that are conducive to learning (Aber, Jones, & Raver, 2006). Many of the schools' buildings and classrooms are old and crumbling. These are the types of undesirable conditions Jonathan Kozol (2005) observed in many inner-city schools, including the South Bronx in New York City, as described at the beginning of the chapter.

Ethnicity in Schools

More than one-third of all African American and almost one-third of all Latino students attend schools in the 47 largest city school districts in the United States, compared with only 5 percent of all White and 22 percent of all Asian American students. Many of these inner-city schools are grossly underfunded, do not provide adequate opportunities for children to learn effectively, and are still segregated

What are some strategies that effective teachers use regarding diversity issues?

despite integration measures that have been in place for decades (Koppelman & Goodheart, 2008). Even outside of inner-city schools, school segregation remains a factor in U.S. education (Nieto & Bode, 2008). Almost one-third of all African American and Latino students attend schools in which 90 percent or more of the students are from minority groups (Banks, 2008). Thus, the effects of SES and the effects of ethnicity are often intertwined.

The school experiences of students from different ethnic groups vary considerably (Banks, 2008; Bennett, 2007). African American students are twice as likely as Latinos, Native Americans, or Whites to be suspended from school. African American and Latino students are much more likely than non-Latino White or Asian American students to be enrolled in remedial and special education programs, and much less likely to be enrolled in college preparatory programs. Asian

American students are far more likely than other ethnic minority groups to take advanced math and science courses in high school.

Some experts charge that a form of institutional racism, by which teachers accept a low level of performance from children of color, permeates many American schools (Ogbu & Stern, 2001; Spencer, 1999). American anthropologist John Ogbu (1989) proposed that ethnic minority students are placed in a position of subordination and exploitation in the American educational system. He believes that students of color, especially African Americans and Latinos, have inferior educational opportunities, are exposed to teachers and school administrators who have low academic expectations for them, and encounter negative stereotypes (Ogbu & Stern, 2001). In one study of middle schools in predominantly Latino areas of Miami, Latino and White teachers rated African American students as having more behavioral problems than African American teachers rated the same students as having (Zimmerman & others, 1995).

Following are some strategies for improving relationships among ethnically diverse students:

How Would You...? As an educator, how would you structure a lesson plan using the jigsaw strategy?

- *Turn the class into a jigsaw classroom.* When Eliot Aronson was a professor at the University of Texas at Austin, the school system contacted him for ideas on how to reduce the increasing racial tension in classrooms. Aronson (1986) developed the concept of "jigsaw classroom," in which students from different cultural backgrounds are placed in a cooperative group in which they have to construct different parts of a project to reach a common goal. Aronson used the term *jigsaw* because he saw the technique as much like a group of students cooperating to put different pieces together to complete a jigsaw puzzle. How might this work? Team sports, drama productions, and music performances are examples of contexts in which students participate cooperatively to reach a common goal; however, the jigsaw technique also lends itself to group science projects, history reports, and other learning experiences with a variety of subject matter.

- *Encourage students to have positive personal contact with diverse other students.* Mere contact does not do the job of improving relationships with diverse others. For example, busing ethnic minority students to predominantly White schools, or vice versa, has not reduced prejudice or improved interethnic relations (Minuchin & Shapiro, 1983). What matters is what happens after children get to school. Especially beneficial in improving interethnic relations is sharing one's worries, successes, failures, coping strategies, interests, and other personal information with people of other ethnicities. When this happens, people tend to look at others as individuals rather than as members of a homogeneous group.

- *Reduce bias.* Teachers can reduce bias by displaying images of children from diverse ethnic and cultural groups, selecting play materials and classroom activities that encourage cultural understanding, helping students resist stereotyping, and working with parents to reduce children's exposure to bias and prejudice at home.

- *View the school and community as a team.* James Comer (1988, 2004, 2006) advocates a community, team approach as the best way to educate children. Three important aspects of the Comer Project for Change are (1) a governance and management team that develops a comprehensive school plan, assessment strategy, and staff development plan; (2) a mental health or school support team; and (3) a parent's program. Comer believes that the entire school community should have a cooperative rather than an adversarial attitude. The Comer program is currently operating in more than 600 schools in 26 states. Read further about James Comer's work in the Careers in Life-Span Development profile.

- *Be a competent cultural mediator.* Teachers can play a powerful role as cultural mediators by being sensitive to biased content in materials and classroom interactions, learning more about different ethnic groups, being sensitive to children's ethnic attitudes, viewing students of color positively, and thinking of positive ways to get parents of color more involved as partners with teachers in educating children.

CAREERS IN LIFE SPAN DEVELOPMENT
James Comer, Child Psychiatrist

James Comer grew up in a low-income neighborhood in East Chicago, Indiana, and credits his parents with leaving no doubt about the importance of education. He obtained a BA degree from Indiana University. He went on to obtain a medical degree from Howard University College of Medicine, a Master of Public Health degree from the University of Michigan School of Public Health, and psychiatry training at the Yale University School of Medicine's Child Study Center. He currently is the Maurice Falk Professor of Child Psychiatry at the Yale University Child Study Center and an associate dean at the Yale University Medical School. During his years at Yale, James has concentrated his career on promoting a focus on child development as a way of improving schools. His efforts in support of healthy development of young people are known internationally.

James is perhaps best known for the founding of the School Development program in 1968, which promotes the collaboration of parents, educators, and community to improve social, emotional, and academic outcomes for children.

Psychiatrists like James Comer obtain a medical degree and then do a residency in psychiatry. Medical school takes approximately four years, and the psychiatry residency another three to four years. Unlike most psychologists (who do not go to medical school), psychiatrists can administer drugs to clients. (Recently, several states gave clinical psychologists the right to prescribe drugs.) Like clinical psychologists, psychiatrists might specialize in working with children (child psychiatry) or with older adults (geriatric psychiatry). Psychiatrists might work in medical schools in teaching and research roles, in a medical clinic or hospital, or in private practice. In addition to administering drugs to help improve the lives of people with psychological problems, psychiatrists also may conduct psychotherapy.

James Comer *(left)* is shown with some of the inner-city African American children who attend a school that became a better learning environment because of Comer's intervention.

Cross–Cultural Comparisons of Achievement

American children are more achievement-oriented than their counterparts in many countries. However, the relatively poor performance of American children in math and science in comparison with their counterparts in some other countries, especially Asian countries, has been highly publicized in recent decades. In the most recent international comparisons, in 2003, fourth-grade students in five countries (Singapore, Chinese Taipei, Japan, Hong Kong, and England) had higher math scores than U.S. students, who had higher math scores than students in 19 countries (Gonzales & others, 2004). In science comparisons, fourth-graders in 11 countries (highest scores were for Singapore, Hong Kong, Japan, and Chinese Taipei) had higher scores than their U.S. counterparts, who had higher scores than fourth-graders in 13 countries.

Harold Stevenson and his colleagues (Stevenson, 1995, 2000; Stevenson & Hofer, 1999; Stevenson & others, 1990; Stevenson & Zusko, 2002) have completed five cross-cultural comparisons of students in the United States, China, Taiwan, and Japan. In these studies, Asian students consistently outperform American students in mathematics. And, the longer the students are in school, the wider the gap becomes between Asian and American students—the lowest difference is in the first grade, the highest in the eleventh grade (the highest grade studied).

To learn more about the reasons for these large cross-cultural differences, Stevenson and his colleagues spent thousands of hours observing in classrooms, as well as interviewing and surveying teachers, students, and parents. They found that the Asian teachers spent more of their time teaching math than did the American teachers. For example, more than one-fourth of total classroom time in the first grade was spent on math instruction in Japan, compared with only one-tenth of the time in the U.S. first-grade classrooms. Moreover, the Asian students were in school an average of 240 days a year, compared with 178 days in the United States.

Differences were also found between the Asian and American parents. American parents were more likely to believe that their children's math achievement was due to innate ability, whereas the Asian parents were more likely to say that their children's math achievement was the consequence of effort and training (see Figure 8.4).

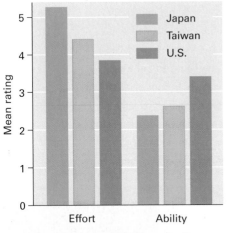

Figure 8.4 Mothers' Beliefs About the Factors Responsible for Children's Math Achievement in Three Countries In one study, mothers in Japan and Taiwan were more likely to believe that their children's math achievement was due to effort rather than innate ability, while U.S. mothers were more likely to believe their children's math achievement was due to innate ability (Stevenson, Lee, & Stigler, 1986). If parents believe that their children's math achievement is due to innate ability and their children are not doing well in math, the implication is that they are less likely to think their children will benefit from putting forth more effort.

Related to the differences in Asian and U.S. parents involving explanations of effort and ability, Carol Dweck (2006) described the importance of children's **mindset**, which she defines as the cognitive view individuals develop for themselves. She concludes that individuals have one of two mindsets: (1) *a fixed mindset,* in which they believe that their qualities are carved in stone and cannot change; or (2) *a growth mindset,* in which they believe their qualities can change and improve through their effort.

Dweck (2006) argued that individuals' mindsets influence whether they will be optimistic or pessimistic, what their goals will be and how hard they will strive to reach those goals, and their achievement. Dweck says that mindsets begin to be shaped in childhood as children interact with parents, teachers, and coaches, who themselves have either a fixed mindset or a growth mindset. She described the growth mindset of Chicago second-grade teacher Marva Collins, a masterful teacher. Collins' goal is to change apathetic, fixed-mindset children into growth-mindset children. On the first day of school, she tells her students, many of whom are repeating the second grade:

> I know most of you can't spell your name. You don't know the alphabet, you don't know how to read, you don't know homonyms or how to syllabicate. I promise you that you will. None of you has ever failed. School may have failed you. Well, goodbye to failure, children. Welcome to success. You will read hard books in here

and understand what you read. You will write every day. . . . But you must help me to help you. If you don't give anything, don't expect anything. Success is not coming to you, you must come to it. (Dweck, 2006, pp. 188–189)

Marva Collins' second-grade students usually have to start off with the lowest level of reader available, but by the end of the school year, most of the students are reading at the fifth-grade level.

Returning to Stevenson's research, the American parents also had much lower expectations for their children's education and achievement than did the Asian parents. In Stevenson's view, the change that is needed most in U.S. education is higher expectations for achievement. Other experts, such as Phylis Blumenfeld, Jacquelynne Eccles, and Joyce Epstein (Blumenfeld, Kempler, & Krajcik, 2006; Eccles, 2007; Epstein & Sheldon, 2006) conclude that high achievement standards, as well as teacher concern for individual children, engaging children in meaningful and interesting learning tasks, and positive connections between schools and families, are key aspects of improving U.S. children's academic achievement.

Summary

Emotional and Personality Development

Self-descriptions increasingly involve psychological and social characteristics, including social comparison, in middle and late childhood. Self-concept refers to domain-specific evaluations of the self. Self-esteem refers to global evaluations of the self and is also referred to as self-worth or self-image. Self-efficacy and self-regulation are linked to children's competence and achievement. Erikson's fourth stage of development, industry versus inferiority, characterizes the middle and late childhood years. Developmental changes in emotion occur in middle and late childhood. As children get older, they use a greater variety of coping strategies and more cognitive strategies. Kohlberg argued that moral development consists of three levels—preconventional, conventional, and postconventional—and six stages (two at each level). Kohlberg believed that these stages were age related. Criticisms of Kohlberg's theory have been made, especially by Gilligan, who advocates a stronger care perspective. Prosocial behavior involves positive moral behaviors such as sharing. Gender stereotyping is present in children's lives, and recent research indicates it increases during middle and late childhood. Boys have more rigid stereotypes than girls. A number of physical differences exist between males and females. Some experts argue that cognitive differences between males and females have been exaggerated. In terms of socioemotional differences, males are more physically aggressive than females, whereas females regulate their emotions better and engage in more prosocial behavior than males. Gender-role classification focuses on how masculine, feminine, or androgynous individuals are. Androgyny means having both positive feminine and masculine characteristics. It is important to think about gender in terms of context.

Families

Parents spend less time with children during middle and late childhood than in early childhood. New parent-child issues emerge and discipline changes. Control is more coregulatory. Parents can play important roles as managers of children's opportunities. Children living in stepparent families have more adjustment problems than their counterparts in nondivorced families. Children who are not monitored by adults in the after-school hours may find their way into trouble more easily than other children, although contextual variations characterize latchkey children's experiences.

Peers

Among the developmental changes in peer relations in middle and late childhood are increased preference for same-sex groups, an increase in time spent in peer interaction and the size of the peer group, and less supervision of the peer group by adults. Peer statuses—popular children, neglected children, rejected children, controversial children, and average children are important in middle and late childhood. Social information-processing skills and social knowledge are two important dimensions of social cognition in peer relations. Significant numbers of children are bullied, and this can result in short-term and long-term negative effects for both the victims and bullies. Like adult friends, children who are friends tend to be similar to each other. Children's friendships serve six functions: companionship, stimulation, physical support, ego support, social comparison, and intimacy/affection.

Schools

Contemporary approaches to student learning include constructivist (a learner-centered approach) and direct instruction (a teacher-centered approach). In the United States, standardized testing of elementary school students has been mandated by both many state governments and by the No Child Left Behind federal legislation. Children in poverty face many barriers to learning at school as well as at home. The effects of SES and ethnicity on schools are intertwined, as many U.S. schools are segregated. Low expectations for ethnic minority children represent one of the barriers to their learning. American children are more achievement-oriented than children in many countries, but perform more poorly in math and science than many children in Asian countries, such as China, Taiwan, and Japan. Mindset is the cognitive view, either fixed or growth, that individuals develop for themselves. Dweck argues that a key aspect of children's development is to guide them in developing a growth mindset. A number of experts conclude that the United States has expectations for children's achievement that are too low.

Key Terms

self-esteem 228
self-concept 228
self-efficacy 229
preconventional
  reasoning 232
heteronomous morality 232
individualism,
  instrumental purpose,
  and exchange 233
conventional
  reasoning 233
mutual interpersonal
  expectations,
  relationships, and
  interpersonal
  conformity 233

social systems
  morality 233
postconventional
  reasoning 233
social contract or utility
  and individual rights 233
universal ethical
  principles 233
justice perspective 236
care perspective 236
gender stereotypes 237
androgyny 240
popular children 245
average children 245
neglected children 245
rejected children 245

controversial children 245
intimacy in
  friendships 248
constructivist
  approach 249
direct instruction
  approach 249
mindset 254

Physical and Cognitive Development in Adolescence

Stories of Life-Span Development: Annie, Arnie, and Katie

Fifteen-year-old Annie developed a drinking problem, and recently she was kicked off the cheerleading squad at her school for missing practice so often—but that didn't stop her drinking. She and her friends began skipping school regularly so they could drink.

Fourteen-year-old Arnie is a juvenile delinquent. Last week he stole a TV set, struck his mother and bloodied her face, broke some streetlights in the neighborhood, and threatened a boy with a wrench and hammer.

Twelve-year old Katie, more than just about anything else, wanted a playground in her town. She knew that other kids also wanted one so she put together a group, which generated funding ideas for the playground. They presented their ideas to the town council. Her group got more youth involved, and they raised money by selling candy and sandwiches door-to-door. The playground became a reality, a place where, as Katie says, "People can have picnics and make friends."

Katie's advice: "You won't get anywhere if you don't try."

Adolescents like Annie and Arnie are the ones we hear about the most. But there are many adolescents like Katie, who contribute in positive ways to their community, and competently make the transition through adolescence. Indeed, for most adolescents, adolescence is not a time of rebellion, crisis, pathology, and deviance. A far more accurate vision of adolescence is of a time of evaluation, of decision making, of commitment, of carving out a place in the world. Most of the problems of today's youth are not with the youth themselves. What adolescents need is access to a range of legitimate opportunities and to long-term support from adults who care deeply about them (Benson, 2006).

Adolescence is a transitional period in the human life span, entered at approximately 10 to 12 years of age and exited at about 18 to 22 years of age. We begin this chapter by examining some general characteristics of adolescence followed by coverage of major

physical changes and health issues of adolescence. Then we describe the significant cognitive changes that characterize adolescence and various aspects of schools for adolescents. ∎

The Nature of Adolescence

As in development during childhood, genetic, biological, environmental, and social factors interact in adolescent development. During their childhood years of development, adolescents experienced thousands of hours of interactions with parents, peers, and teachers, but now they face dramatic biological changes, new experiences, and new developmental tasks. Relationships with parents take a different form, moments with peers become more intimate, and dating occurs for the first time, as do sexual exploration and possibly intercourse. The adolescent's thoughts are more abstract and idealistic. Biological changes trigger a heightened interest in body image. Adolescence has both continuity and discontinuity with childhood.

There is a long history of worrying about how adolescents will "turn out." In 1904, G. Stanley Hall proposed the "storm-and-stress" view that adolescence is a turbulent time charged with conflict and mood swings. However, when Daniel Offer and his colleagues (1988) studied the self-images of adolescents in the United States, Australia, Bangladesh, Hungary, Israel, Italy, Japan, Taiwan, Turkey, and West Germany, at least 73 percent of the adolescents displayed a healthy self-

Growing up has never been easy. However, adolescence is not best viewed as a time of rebellion, crisis, pathology, and deviance. A far more accurate vision of adolescence as a time of evaluation, of decision making, of commitment, and of carving out a place in the world. Most of the problems of today's youth are not with the youth themselves. What adolescents need is access to a range of legitimate opportunities and to long-term support from adults who deeply care about them. *What might be some examples of such support and caring?*

image. Although there were differences among them, the adolescents were happy most of the time, they enjoyed life, they perceived themselves as able to exercise self-control, they valued work and school, they felt confident about their sexual selves, they expressed positive feelings toward their families, and they felt they had the capability to cope with life's stresses: not exactly a storm-and-stress portrayal of adolescence.

puberty A period of rapid physical and sexual maturation that occurs mainly during early adolescence.

Public attitudes about adolescence emerge from a combination of personal experience and media portrayals, neither of which produce an objective picture of how normal adolescents develop (Feldman & Elliott, 1990). Some of the readiness to assume the worst about adolescents likely involves the short memories of adults. Many adults measure their current perceptions of adolescents by their memories of their own adolescence. Adults may portray today's adolescents as more troubled, less respectful, more self-centered, more assertive, and more adventurous than they were.

However, in matters of taste and manners, the young people of every generation have seemed unnervingly radical and different from adults—different in how they look, in how they behave, in the music they enjoy, in their hairstyles, and in the clothing they choose. It is an enormous error, though, to confuse adolescents' enthusiasm for trying on new identities and enjoying moderate amounts of outrageous behavior with hostility toward parental and societal standards. Acting out and boundary testing are time-honored ways in which adolescents move toward accepting, rather than rejecting, parental values.

Most adolescents negotiate the lengthy path to adult maturity successfully, but too large a group does not (Dryfoos & Barkin, 2006). Ethnic, cultural, gender, socioeconomic, age, and lifestyle differences influence the actual life trajectory of every adolescent (Patterson & Hastings, 2007). Different portrayals of adolescence emerge, depending on the particular group of adolescents being described (Benson & others, 2006). Today's adolescents are exposed to a complex menu of lifestyle options through the media, and many face the temptations of drug use and sexual activity at increasingly young ages. Too many adolescents are not provided with adequate opportunities and support to become competent adults (Conger & Dogan, 2007).

Physical Changes

One father remarked that the problem with his teenage son was not that he grew, but that he did not know when to stop growing. As we will see, there is considerable variation in the timing of the adolescent growth spurt. In addition to pubertal changes, other physical changes we will explore involve sexuality and the brain.

Puberty

Puberty is not the same as adolescence. For most of us, puberty ends long before adolescence does, although puberty is the most important marker of the beginning of adolescence. **Puberty** is a period of rapid physical maturation involving hormonal and bodily changes that occur primarily during early adolescence. Puberty is not a single, sudden event. We know whether a young boy or girl is going through puberty, but pinpointing puberty's beginning and end is difficult. Among the most noticeable changes are signs of sexual maturation and increases in height and weight.

Sexual Maturation, Height, and Weight

Think back to the onset of your puberty. Of the striking changes that were taking place in your body, what was the first to occur? Researchers have found that male pubertal characteristics typically develop in this order: increase in penis and testicle size, appearance of straight pubic hair, minor voice change, first ejaculation (which usually occurs through masturbation or a wet dream), appearance of kinky pubic hair, onset of maximum growth in height and weight, growth of hair in armpits, more detectable voice changes, and, finally, growth of facial hair.

ZITS By Jerry Scott and Jim Borgman

© ZITS Partnership. Reprinted with permission of King Features Syndicate.

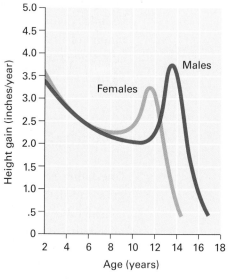

What is the order of appearance of physical changes in females? First, either the breasts enlarge or pubic hair appears. Later, hair appears in the armpits. As these changes occur, the female grows in height and her hips become wider than her shoulders. **Menarche**—a girl's first menstruation—comes rather late in the pubertal cycle. Initially, her menstrual cycles may be highly irregular. For the first several years, she may not ovulate every menstrual cycle; some girls do not ovulate at all until a year or two after menstruation begins. No voice changes comparable to those in pubertal males occur in pubertal females. By the end of puberty, the female's breasts have become more fully rounded.

Marked weight gains coincide with the onset of puberty. During early adolescence, girls tend to outweigh boys, but by about age 14 boys begin to surpass girls. Similarly, at the beginning of the adolescent period, girls tend to be as tall as or taller than boys of their age, but by the end of the middle school years most boys have caught up, or, in many cases, surpassed girls in height.

Figure 9.1 Pubertal Growth Spurt

On the average, the peak of the growth spurt during puberty occurs 2 years earlier for girls (11¹/₂) than for boys (13¹/₂). *How are hormones related to the growth spurt and to the difference between the average height of adolescent boys and girls?* From J. M. Tanner et al., in *Archives of Diseases in Childhood* 41, 1966. Reproduced with permission from the BMJ Publishing Group.

As indicated in Figure 9.1, the growth spurt occurs approximately two years earlier for girls than for boys. The mean age at the beginning of the growth spurt in girls is 9; for boys, it is 11. The peak rate of pubertal change occurs at 11¹/₂ years for girls and 13¹/₂ years for boys. During their growth spurt, girls increase in height about 3¹/₂ inches per year, boys about 4 inches. Boys and girls who are shorter or taller than their peers before adolescence are likely to remain so during adolescence; however, as much as 30 percent of an individual's height in late adolescence is unexplained by his or her height in the elementary school years.

hormones Powerful chemical substances secreted by the endocrine glands and carried through the body by the bloodstream.

hypothalamus A structure in the higher portion of the brain that monitors eating and sex.

pituitary gland An important endocrine gland that controls growth and regulates other glands, including the gonads.

gonads The sex glands—the testes in males and the ovaries in females.

Hormonal Changes

Behind the first whisker in boys and the widening of hips in girls is a flood of **hormones**, powerful chemical substances secreted by the endocrine glands and carried through the body by the bloodstream. The endocrine system's role in puberty involves the interaction of the hypothalamus, the pituitary gland, and the gonads. The **hypothalamus** is a structure in the brain that monitors eating and sex. The **pituitary gland** is an important endocrine gland that controls growth and regulates other glands; among these, the **gonads**—the testes in males, the ovaries in females—are particularly important in giving rise to pubertal changes in the body.

The concentrations of certain hormones increase dramatically during adolescence (Dorn & others, 2006). *Testosterone* is a hormone associated in boys with the development of genitals, an increase in height, and a change in voice. *Estradiol* is a type of estrogen; in girls it is associated with breast, uterine, and skeletal development. In one study, testosterone levels increased eighteenfold in boys but only twofold in girls during puberty; estradiol increased eightfold in girls but only twofold in boys (Nottelmann & others, 1987). Thus, both testosterone and estradiol are present in the hormonal makeup of both boys and girls, but testosterone dominates in male pubertal development, estradiol in female pubertal development.

What are some of the differences in the ways girls and boys experience pubertal growth?

The same influx of hormones that grows hair on a male's chest and increases the fatty tissue in a female's breasts may also contribute to psychological development in adolescence (Dorn & others, 2006). In one study of boys and girls ranging in age from 9 to 14, a higher concentration of testosterone was present in boys who rated themselves as more socially competent (Nottelmann & others, 1987). In another study of 60 normal boys and girls in the same age range, the girls with higher estradiol levels expressed more anger and aggression than their lower-estradiol peers (Inoff-Germain & others, 1988). However, hormonal effects by themselves do not account for adolescent development (Graber & Brooks-Gunn, & Warren, 2006). For example, in one study, social factors accounted for two to four times as much variance as did hormonal factors in young adolescent girls' depression and anger (Brooks-Gunn & Warren, 1989). Behavior and moods also can affect hormones. Stress, eating patterns, exercise, sexual activity, tension, and depression can activate or suppress various aspects of the hormonal system. In sum, the hormone-behavior link is complex (Dorn & others, 2006).

How Would You...?

As a psychologist, how would you explain the role of biological and physical changes on adolescent mood swings?

Timing and Variations in Puberty

Imagine a toddler displaying all the features of puberty—a 3-year-old girl with fully developed breasts or a preschool boy with a deep voice. That is what we would see by the year 2250 if the age at which puberty arrives were to keep getting younger at its present pace. In Norway today, menarche occurs at just over 13 years of age, compared with 17 years of age in the 1840s. In the United States—where children mature up to a year earlier than children in European countries—the average age of menarche has declined significantly since the mid-nineteenth century (McDowell, Brody, & Hughes, 2007) (see Figure 9.2). Fortunately, however, we are unlikely to see pubescent tod-

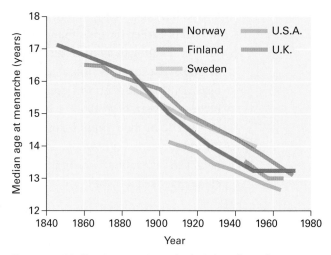

Figure 9.2 Median Ages at Menarche in Selected Northern European Countries and the United States from 1845 to 1969 Notice the steep decline in the age at which girls experienced menarche in four northern European countries and the United States from 1845 to 1969. Recently the age at which girls experience menarche has been leveling off.

dlers, since what has happened in the past century is likely the result of improved nutrition and health (Hermann-Giddens, 2006, 2007). The available historical information suggests that menarche began to occur earlier at about the time of the Industrial Revolution, which brought improved standards of living and advances in medical science (Petersen, 1979).

Why do the changes of puberty occur when they do, and how can variations in their timing be explained? The basic genetic program for puberty is wired into the species, but nutrition, health, and other environmental factors also affect puberty's timing and makeup (Hirschhorn, 2005).

For most boys, the pubertal sequence may begin as early as age 10 or as late as 13½, and may end as early as age 13 or as late as 17. Thus the normal range is wide enough that, given two boys of the same chronological age, one might complete the pubertal sequence before the other one has begun it. For girls, menarche is considered within the normal range if it appears between the ages of 9 and 15.

How Would You...?
As a health-care professional, how would you use your knowledge of puberty to reassure adolescents who are concerned that they are maturing slower than their friends?

Body Image

One psychological aspect of physical change in puberty is certain: Adolescents are preoccupied with their bodies and develop images of what their bodies are like (Ayala & others, 2007; Nollen & others, 2006). Preoccupation with body image is strong throughout adolescence, but it is especially acute during puberty, a time when adolescents are more dissatisfied with their bodies than in late adolescence (Graber & Brooks-Gunn, 2001).

Gender differences characterize adolescents' perceptions of their bodies. In general, girls are less happy with their bodies and have more negative body images than boys throughout puberty (Bearman & others, 2006). As pubertal change proceeds, girls often become more dissatisfied with their bodies, probably because their body fat increases. In contrast, boys become more satisfied as they move through puberty, probably because their muscle mass increases (Bearman & others, 2006).

How Would You...?
As a human development and family studies professional, how would you counsel parents about communicating with their adolescent daughter about changes in her behavior that likely reflect a downward turn in her body image?

Early and Late Maturation

Some of you entered puberty early, others late, and still others right on time. Adolescents who mature earlier or later than their peers perceive themselves differently. In the Berkeley Longitudinal Study some years ago, early-maturing boys perceived themselves more positively and had more successful peer relations than did their late-maturing counterparts (Jones, 1965). When the late-maturing boys were in their thirties, however, they had developed a stronger sense of identity than the early-maturing boys had (Peskin, 1967). This may have occurred because the late-maturing boys had more time to explore life's options, or because the early-maturing boys continued to focus on their advantageous physical status instead of on career development and achievement. More recent research confirms, though, that at least during adolescence it is advantageous to be an early-maturing rather than a late-maturing boy (Graber, Brooks-Gunn, & Warren, 2006).

An increasing number of researchers have found that early maturation increases girls' vulnerability to a number of problems (Graber, 2007; Graber, Brooks-Gunn, & Warren, 2006; Lynne & others, 2007). Early-maturing girls are more likely to smoke, drink, be depressed, have an eating disorder, struggle for earlier independence from their parents, and have older friends; and their bodies are likely to elicit responses from males that lead to earlier dating and earlier sexual experiences (Wiesner & Ittel, 2002).

How Would You...?

As a social worker, how would you design a community program to identify and assist early-maturing adolescent girls who are at risk for delinquency and early sexual behaviors?

corpus callosum The location where fibers connect the brain's left and right hemispheres

amygdala The region of the brain that is the seat of emotions.

The Brain

Along with the rest of the body, the brain is changing during adolescence, but the study of adolescent brain development is in its infancy. As advances in technology take place, significant strides will also likely be made in charting developmental changes in the adolescent brain (Kuhn & Franklin, 2006; Nelson, Thomas, & de Haan, 2006). What do we know now?

Using fMRI brain scans, scientists have recently discovered that adolescents' brains undergo significant structural changes (Eshel & others, 2006; Steinberg, 2007; Toga, Thompson, & Sowell, 2006). The **corpus callosum**, where fibers connect the brain's left and right hemispheres, thickens in adolescence, and this improves adolescents' ability to process information (Giedd & others, 2006). We described advances in the development of the *prefrontal cortex*—the highest level of the frontal lobes involved in reasoning, decision making, and self-control—in Chapters 5 and 7. However, the prefrontal cortex doesn't finish maturing until the emerging adult years, approximately 18 to 25 years of age, or later, but the **amygdala**—the seat of emotions such as anger—matures earlier than the prefrontal cortex. Figure 9.3 shows the locations of the corpus callosum, prefrontal cortex, and amygdala.

Leading researcher Charles Nelson (2003; Nelson, Thomas, & de Haan, 2006) points out that—although adolescents are capable of very strong emotions—their prefrontal cortex hasn't adequately developed to the point at which they can control these passions. It is as if their brain doesn't have the brakes to slow down their emotions. Or consider this interpretation of the development of emotion and cognition in adolescents: "early activation of strong 'turbo-charged' feelings with a relatively un-skilled set of 'driving skills' or cognitive abilities to modulate strong emotions and motivations" (Dahl, 2004, p. 18).

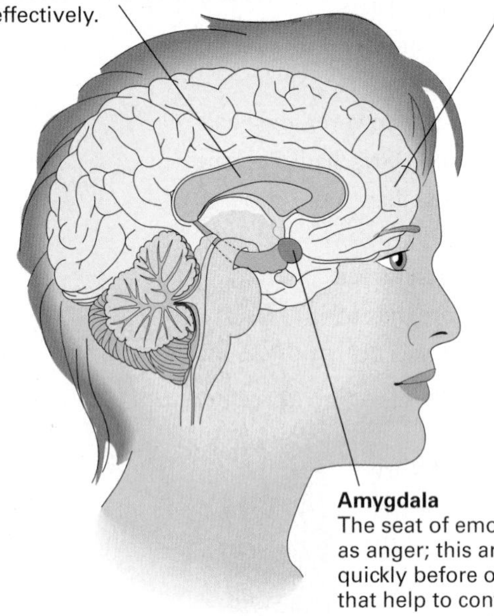

Corpus callosum
These nerve fibers connect the brain's two hemispheres; they thicken in adolescence to process information more effectively.

Prefrontal cortex
This "judgment" region reins in intense emotions but doesn't finish developing until at least age 20.

Amygdala
The seat of emotions such as anger; this area develops quickly before other regions that help to control it.

Figure 9.3 **Changes in the Adolescent Brain**

Adolescent Sexuality

Not only are adolescents characterized by substantial changes in physical growth and the development of the brain, but adolescence also is a bridge between the asexual child and the sexual adult (Feldman, 1999). Adolescence is a time of sexual exploration and experimentation, of sexual fantasies and realities, of incorporating sexuality into one's identity.

Developing a Sexual Identity

Mastering emerging sexual feelings and forming a sense of sexual identity is a multifaceted and lengthy process. It involves learning to manage sexual feelings (such as sexual arousal and attraction), developing new forms of intimacy, and learning the skills to regulate sexual behavior to avoid undesirable consequences. The sexual identity must also be related to other developing identities, which are discussed in Chapter 10.

An adolescent's sexual identity involves activities, interests, styles of behavior, and an indication of sexual orientation (whether an individual has same-sex or other-sex attractions) (Buzwell & Rosenthal, 1996). For example, some adolescents have a high anxiety level about sex, others a low level. Some adolescents are strongly aroused sexually, others less so. Some adolescents are very active sexually, others not at all. Some adolescents are sexually inactive in response to their strong religious upbringing; others go to church regularly, yet their religious training does not inhibit their sexual activity (Thorton & Camburn, 1989).

It is commonly believed that most gay and lesbian individuals quietly struggle with same-sex attractions in childhood, do not engage in heterosexual dating, and gradually recognize that they are gay or lesbian in mid- to late adolescence (Diamond, 2003). Many youth do follow this developmental pathway, but others do not (Diamond & Lucas, 2004). For example, many youth have no recollection of early same-sex attractions and experience a more abrupt sense of their same-sex attraction in late adolescence (Savin-Williams, 2006). Researchers also have found that the majority of adolescents with same-sex attractions also experience some degree of other-sex attractions (Garofalo & others, 1999). Even though some adolescents who are attracted to individuals of their same sex fall in love with these individuals, others claim that their same-sex attractions are purely physical (Savin-Williams, 2006).

In sum, gay and lesbian youth have diverse patterns of initial attraction, often have bisexual attractions, and may have physical or emotional attraction to same-sex individuals but do not always fall in love with them (Savin-Williams & Diamond, 2004). In Chapter 11, "Physical and Cognitive Development in Early Adulthood," we further explore same-sex and heterosexual attraction.

The Timing of Adolescent Sexual Behaviors

How Would You...?

As a psychologist, how would you describe the cultural and ethnic differences in the timing of an adolescent's first sexual experience?

The timing of sexual initiation varies by country as well as by gender and other socioeconomic characteristics. In one cross-cultural study, among females, the proportion having first intercourse by age 17 ranged from 72 percent in Mali to 47 percent in the United States and 45 percent in Tanzania (Singh & others, 2000). The percentage of males who had their first intercourse by age 17 ranged from 76 percent in Jamaica to 64 percent in the United States and 63 percent in Brazil. Within the United States, male, African American, and inner-city adolescents report being the most sexually active, whereas Asian American adolescents have the most restrictive sexual timetable (Feldman, Turner, & Araujo, 1999).

A national survey of U.S. adolescents further revealed the timing of their sexual activities (Alan Guttmacher Institute, 1998). Most young adolescents had not had sexual intercourse: 8 in 10 girls and 7 in 10 boys were virgins at age 15. The probability that adolescents had engaged in sexual intercourse increased steadily with age, but 1 in 5 individuals have not yet had sexual intercourse by age 19. Most teenagers initially had sexual intercourse in the mid- to late adolescent years. More recent data collected in 2005 in a national U.S. survey found similar developmental trends, with 63 percent of twelfth-graders reporting that they had experienced sexual intercourse compared with 34 percent of ninth-graders (MMWR, 2006).

What is the progression of sexual behaviors in adolescence?

Many adolescents are not emotionally prepared to handle sexual experiences, especially in early adolescence. Early sexual activity is linked with risky behaviors such as drug use, delinquency, and school-related problems (Dryfoos & Barkin, 2006). In a longitudinal study from 10 to 12 years of age to 25 years of age, early sexual intercourse and affiliation with deviant peers were linked to substance use disorders in emerging adulthood (Cornelius & others, 2006). Another recent study indicated that low parental monitoring was linked with early initiation of sexual activity by adolescents, more sexual partners, and less likelihood of condom use (Wight, Williamson, & Henderson, 2006). And a recent research review revealed that the amount of time adolescents reported being home alone with the opposite sex (or being home without a parent) and perceiving that peers have had sex were related to early initiation of sexual intercourse (Buhi & Goodson, 2007).

Contraceptive Use

Sexual activity carries with it considerable risks if appropriate safeguards are not taken (Strong & others, 2008). Youth encounter two kinds of risks: unintended unwanted pregnancy and sexually transmitted infections. Both of these risks can be reduced significantly if contraception is used.

The good news is that adolescents are increasing their use of contraceptives (Santelli & others, 2007). For example, a recent study examined trends in U.S. ninth- to twelfth-graders' contraceptive use from 1991 to 2003 (Anderson, Santelli, & Morrow, 2006). Approximately one-third of the adolescents reported being sexually active in the previous three months. The use of condoms by males increased from 46 percent in 1991 to 63 percent in 2003. The percentage of adolescents who used either withdrawal or no method steadily declined from 33 percent in 1991 to 19 percent in 2003.

Although adolescent contraceptive use is increasing, many sexually active adolescents still do not use contraceptives, or they use them inconsistently (Ball, 2007; Davies & others, 2006). A national survey of U.S. 15- to 19-year-olds who have had sexual intercourse found that 47 percent of the boys said they always use a condom but only 28 percent of the girls said they always use one (National Center for Health Statistics, 2004). Eleven percent of the boys and 18 percent of the girls said they never use a condom.

Sexually active younger adolescents are less likely than older adolescents to take contraceptive precautions. Those who do are more likely to use a condom or withdrawal, whereas older adolescents are more likely to use the pill or a diaphragm.

How Would You...? As a social worker, how would you design an educational campaign to increase adolescents' effective use of contraception?

Sexually Transmitted Infections

Some forms of contraception, such as birth control pills or implants, do not protect against sexually transmitted infections, or STIs. **Sexually transmitted infections (STIs)** are contracted primarily through sexual contact, including oral-genital and anal-genital contact. Every year more than 3 million American adolescents (about one-fourth of those who are sexually experienced) acquire an STI (Centers for Disease Control and Prevention, 2006). In a single act of unprotected sex with an infected partner, a teenage girl has a 1 percent risk of getting HIV, a 30 percent risk of acquiring genital herpes, and a 50 percent chance of contracting gonorrhea (Glei, 1999). Yet another very widespread STI is chlamydia. In Chapter 11, we describe these and other sexually transmitted infections.

Psychologists are exploring ways to encourage adolescents to make less risky sexual decisions. Here an adolescent participates in an interactive video session developed by Julie Downs and her colleagues at the Department of Social and Decision Making Sciences at Carnegie Mellon University. The videos help adolescents evaluate their responses and decisions in high-risk sexual contexts.

Adolescent Pregnancy

In cross-cultural comparisons, the United States continues to have one of the highest adolescent pregnancy and childbearing rates in the industrialized world, despite a considerable decline in the 1990s (Centers for Disease Control and Prevention, 2002). As Figure 9.4 shows, the U.S. adolescent pregnancy rate is eight times as high as in the Netherlands. This dramatic difference exists in spite of the fact that U.S. adolescents are no more sexually active than their counterparts in the Netherlands.

Despite the negative comparisons of the United States with many other developed countries, there are encouraging trends in U.S. adolescent pregnancy rates. In 2004, births to adolescent girls fell to a record low (Child Trends, 2006). The rate of births to adolescent girls has dropped 30 percent since 1991. Reasons for these declines include increased contraceptive use and fear of sexually transmitted infections such as AIDS (Santelli & others, 2007).

Outcomes Adolescent pregnancy creates risks for both the mother and the baby. Adolescent mothers often drop out of school. Although many adolescent mothers resume their education later in life, they generally never catch up economically with women who postpone childbearing until their twenties. A recent study revealed that adolescent mothers also are at risk for a rapid subsequent pregnancy (Raneri & Constance, 2007). Infants born to adolescent mothers are more likely to have low birth weights—a prominent factor in infant mortality—as well as neurological problems and childhood illness (Malamitsi-Puchner & Boutsikou, 2006).

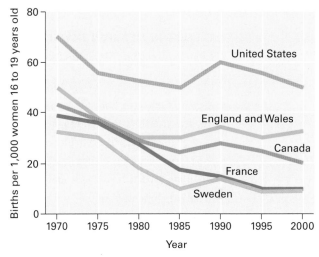

Figure 9.4 Cross-Cultural Comparisons of Adolescent Pregnancy Rates Pregnancy rates among U.S. adolescents are among the highest in the industrialized world (Centers for Disease Control and Prevention, 2002).

Though the consequences of America's high adolescent pregnancy rate are cause for great concern, it often is not pregnancy alone that leads to negative consequences for an adolescent mother and her offspring (Oxford & others, 2006). Adolescent mothers are more likely to come from low-SES backgrounds (Crosby & Holtgrave, 2006). Many adolescent mothers also were not good students before they became pregnant (Malamitsi-Puchner & Boutsikou, 2006). However, not every adolescent female who bears a child lives a life of poverty and low achievement. Thus, although adolescent pregnancy is a high-risk circumstance and adolescents who do not become pregnant generally fare better than those who do, some adolescent mothers do well in school and have positive outcomes (Leadbeater & Way, 2000).

Serious, extensive efforts are needed to help pregnant adolescents and young mothers enhance their educational and occupational opportunities. Adolescent mothers also need help in obtaining competent child care and in planning for the future.

All adolescents can benefit from age-appropriate family life education (Dryfoos & Barkin, 2006). Family and consumer science educators teach life skills, such as effective decision making, to adolescents. The Careers in Life-Span Development profile describes the work of one family and consumer science educator.

How Would You...?
As an educator, how would you incorporate sex education throughout the curriculum to encourage adolescents' healthy, responsible sexual development?

Reducing Adolescent Pregnancy Girls, Inc., has four programs that are intended to increase adolescent girls' motivation to avoid pregnancy until they are mature enough to make responsible decisions about motherhood (Roth & others, 1998). Growing Together, a series of five two-hour workshops for adolescent girls and their mothers and Will Power/Won't Power, a series of six two-hour sessions that focus on assertiveness training, are designed for 12- to 14-year-old girls. For older adolescent girls, Taking Care of Business provides nine sessions that emphasize career planning as well as information about sexuality, reproduction, and contraception. Health Bridge coordinates health and education services—girls can participate in this program as one of their club activities. Girls who participated in these programs were less likely to get pregnant than girls who did not participate (Girls, Inc., 1991).

CAREERS IN LIFE-SPAN DEVELOPMENT

Lynn Blankenship, Family and Consumer Science Educator

Lynn Blankenship is a family and consumer science educator. She has an undergraduate degree in this area from the University of Arizona. She has taught for more than 20 years, the last 14 at Tucson High Magnet School.

Lynn was awarded the Tucson Federation of Teachers Educator of the Year Award for 1999–2000 and the Arizona Teacher of the Year in 1999.

Lynn especially enjoys teaching life skills to adolescents. One of her favorite activities is having students care for an automated baby that imitates the needs of real babies. She says that this program has a profound impact on students because the baby must be cared for around the clock for the duration of the assignment. Lynn also coordinates real-world work experiences and training for students in several child-care facilities in the Tucson area.

Family and consumer science educators like Lynn Blankenship may specialize in early childhood education or instruct middle and high school students about such matters as nutrition, interpersonal relationships, human sexuality, parenting, and human development. Hundreds of colleges and universities throughout the United States offer two- and four-year degree programs in family and consumer science. These programs usually require an internship. Additional education courses may be needed to obtain a teaching certificate. Some family and consumer educators go on to graduate school for further training, which provides a background for possible jobs in college teaching or research.

Lynn Blankenship (*center*) teaching life skills to students.

There has recently been a major controversy over whether schools should provide sex education in the form of an abstinence-only program or a program that emphasizes contraceptive knowledge (Santelli & others, 2006). A recent review of research found that some abstinence-only programs and some contraceptive-knowledge programs were effective in changing adolescents' sexual behavior (Bennett & Assefi, 2005). However, the positive outcomes were modest and most lasted only for a short time. Although critics of contraceptive-knowledge programs charge that such programs increase adolescent sexual activity, the research review found that they do not. An important point to note about comparing sex education programs is that the variation in samples, interventions, and outcome measures makes it difficult to draw meaningful conclusions about which programs are most effective.

Issues in Adolescent Health

Adolescence is a critical juncture in the adoption of behaviors that are relevant to health (McCracken, Jiles, & Blanck, 2007; Sanchez & others, 2007). Many of the behaviors that are linked to poor health habits and early death in adults begin during adolescence. Conversely, the early formation of healthy behavior patterns, such as regular exercise and a preference for foods low in fat and cholesterol, not only has immediate health benefits but helps in adulthood to delay or prevent disability and mortality from heart disease, stroke, diabetes, and cancer (Anderson & others, 2006; te Velde & others, 2007).

Nutrition and Exercise

Concerns are growing about adolescents' nutrition and exercise (Nelson & Gordon-Larsen, 2006). The percentage of overweight U.S. 12- to 19-year-olds increased from 11 to 17 percent from the early 1990s through 2004 (Eaton & others, 2006). Other research also indicates increases in being overweight during adolescence in European countries (Irwin, 2004). In a comparison of adolescents in 28 countries, U.S. adolescents ate more junk food than adolescents in most other countries (World Health Organization, 2000). U.S. adolescents were more likely to eat fried foods and less likely to eat fruits and vegetables than adolescents in most other countries studied. The National Youth Risk Survey found that U.S. high school students decreased their intake of fruits and vegetables from 1999 through 2005 (MMWR, 2006) (see Figure 9.5).

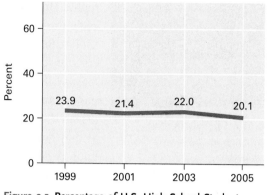

Figure 9.5 Percentage of U.S. High School Students Who Ate Fruits and Vegetables at Least Five Times a Day, 1999 to 2005. This figure shows the percentage of high school students over time who had eaten fruits and vegetables—100% fruit juice, fruit, green salad, potatoes (excluding French fries, fried potatoes, or potato chips), carrots, or other vegetables—at least five times/day during the seven days preceding the National Youth Risk Survey (MHWR, 2005).

How Would You...?
As a health-care professional, how would you explain the benefits of physical fitness in adolescence to adolescents, parents, and teachers?

In a cross-cultural study, just two-thirds of U.S. adolescents exercised at least twice a week, compared with 80 percent or more of adolescents in Ireland, Austria, Germany, and the Slovak Republic (World Health Organization, 2000). U.S. boys and girls become less active as they reach and progress through adolescence (Merrick & others, 2005). A recent study of more than 3,000 U.S. adolescents found that 34 percent were in the lowest fitness category (Carnethon, Gulati, & Greenland, 2005).

Sleep Patterns

Like nutrition and exercise, sleep is an important influence on well-being. Might changing sleep patterns in adolescence contribute to adolescents' health-compromising behaviors? Recently there has been a surge of interest in adolescent sleep patterns (Carskadon, 2005, 2006; Chen, Wang, & Yeng, 2006; Dahl, 2006).

The National Sleep Foundation (2006) conducted a U.S. survey of 1,602 caregivers and their 11- to 17-year-olds. Forty-five percent of the adolescents got inadequate sleep on school nights (less than eight hours). Older adolescents (ninth- to twelfth-graders) got markedly less sleep on school nights than younger adolescents (sixth- to eighth-graders)—62 percent of the older adolescents got inadequate sleep compared with 21 percent of the younger adolescents. Adolescents who got inadequate sleep (eight hours or less) on school nights were more likely to feel more tired or sleepy, more cranky and irritable, fall asleep in school, be in a depressed mood, and drink caffeinated beverages than their counterparts who got optimal sleep (nine or more hours).

Mary Carskadon and her colleagues (2005, 2006; Carskadon, Acebo, & Jenni, 2004; Carskadon, Mindell, & Drake, 2006) have conducted a number of research studies on adolescent sleep patterns. They found that when given the opportunity adolescents will sleep an average of 9 hours and 25 minutes a

In Mary Carskadon's sleep laboratory at Brown University, an adolescent girl's brain activity is being monitored. Carskadon (2005) says that in the morning, sleep-deprived adolescents' "brains are telling them it's nighttime… and the rest of the world is saying it's time to go to school" (p. 19)

night. Most get considerably less than nine hours of sleep, especially during the week. This shortfall creates a sleep deficit, which adolescents often attempt to make up on the weekend. The researchers also found that older adolescents tend to be more sleepy during the day than younger adolescents. They theorized that this sleepiness was not due to academic work or social pressures. Rather, their research suggests that adolescents' biological clocks undergo a shift as they get older, delaying their period of wakefulness by about one hour. A delay in the nightly release of the sleep-inducing hormone melatonin, which is produced in the brain's pineal gland, seems to underlie this shift. Melatonin is secreted at about 9:30 P.M. in younger adolescents and approximately an hour later in older adolescents.

Carskadon has suggested that early school starting times may cause grogginess, inattention in class, and poor performance on tests. Based on her research, school officials in Edina, Minnesota, decided to start classes at 8:30 A.M. rather than the usual 7:25 A.M. Since then there have been fewer referrals for discipline problems, and the number of students who report being ill or depressed has decreased. The school system reports that test scores have improved for high school students, but not for middle school students. This finding supports Carskadon's suspicion that early start times are likely to be more stressful for older than for younger adolescents.

How Would You...?
As an educator, how would you use developmental research to convince your school board to change the starting time of high school?

Leading Causes of Death in Adolescence

The three leading causes of death in adolescence are accidents, homicide, and suicide. More than half of all deaths in adolescents ages 10 to 19 are due to accidents, and most of those, especially among older adolescents, involve motor vehicles. Risky driving habits, such as speeding, tailgating, and driving under the influence of alcohol or other drugs, may be more important causes of these accidents than is lack of driving experience. In about 50 percent of the motor vehicle fatalities involving an adolescent, the driver has a blood alcohol level of 0.10 percent, twice the level needed to be "under the influence" in some states. A high rate of intoxication is also often present in adolescents who die as pedestrians or while using recreational vehicles.

Homicide is the second leading cause of death in adolescence, especially among African American male adolescents (National Center for Health Statistics, 2006). The adolescent suicide rate has tripled since the 1950s. Suicide accounts for 6 percent of the deaths in the 10-to-14 age group and 12 percent of deaths in the 15-to-19 age group. We discuss suicide further in Chapter 10.

How Would You...?
As a health-care professional, how would you use research on the rates and risks of adolescents' substance abuse to advocate for government funding of drug and alcohol education programs?

Substance Use and Abuse

Each year since 1975, Lloyd Johnston and his colleagues at the Institute of Social Research at the University of Michigan have monitored the drug use of America's high school seniors in a wide range of public and private high schools. Since 1991, they also have surveyed drug use by eighth- and tenth-graders. In 2006, the

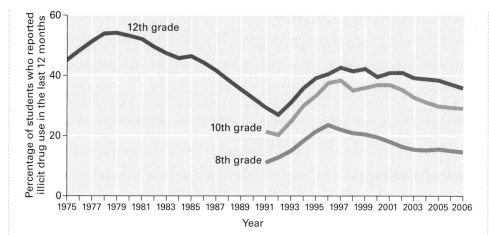

Figure 9.6 **Trends in Drug Use by U.S. Eighth-, Tenth-, and Twelfth-Grade Students**
This graph shows the percentage of U.S. eighth-, tenth-, and twelfth-grade students who reported having taken an illicit drug in the last 12 months from 1991 to 2006 for eighth- and tenth-graders, and from 1975 to 2006 for twelfth-graders (Johnston & others, 2007).

University of Michigan study, called the Monitoring the Future Study, surveyed 50,000 students in nearly 400 secondary schools.

According to this study, the proportions of eighth-, tenth-, and twelfth-grade U.S. students who used any illicit drug declined in the late 1990s and first years of the twenty-first century (Johnston & others, 2007) (see Figure 9.6). Nonetheless, even with the recent decline in use, the United States still has one of the highest rates of adolescent drug use of any industrialized nation. For example, one study revealed that a higher percentage of U.S. adolescents have used an illicit drug than adolescents in most European countries (Hibell & others, 2004).

The Roles of Development, Parents, Peers, and Schools

A special concern involves adolescents who begin to use drugs early in adolescence or even in childhood (Dawson, Grant, & Li, 2007; King & Chassin, 2007). A recent study revealed that individuals who began drinking alcohol before 14 years of age were more likely to become alcohol dependent than their counterparts who began drinking alcohol at 21 years of age or older (Hingson, Heeren, & Winter, 2006). A longitudinal study of individuals from 8 to 42 years of age also found that early onset of drinking was linked to increased risk of heavy drinking in middle age (Pitkanen, Lyra, & Pulkkinen, 2005)

Parents, peers, and schools can play important roles in preventing adolescent drug abuse (Eitle, 205; Engels & others, 2005). Positive relationships with parents and others can reduce adolescents' drug use. In one study, parental control and monitoring were linked with a lower incidence of problem behavior by adolescents, including substance abuse (Fletcher, Steinberg, & Williams-Wheeler, 2004). A recent study of more than 5,000 middle school students revealed that having friends in their school's social network, and having fewer friends who use substances, were related to a lower level of substance use (Ennett & others, 2006). Another recent study found that having good school connectedness at 13 to 14 years of age was linked with lower substance abuse at 16 years of age (Bond & others, 2007).

What roles do parents play in adolescents' drug use?

How Would You...?
As a human development and family studies professional, how would you explain to parents the importance of parental monitoring in preventing adolescent substance abuse?

ISSUES IN ADOLESCENT HEALTH

anorexia nervosa An eating
disorder that involves the
relentless pursuit of thinness
through starvation.

bulimia nervosa An eating
disorder in which the individual
consistently follows a binge-and-
purge pattern.

Eating Disorders

Eating disorders have become increasingly common among adolescents (Kirsh & others, 2007; Stice & others, 2007). Earlier in the
chapter under the topic of health, we described the increase in being
overweight in adolescence. Let's now examine two other eating problems that often appear for the first time in adolescence: anorexia
nervosa and bulimia nervosa.

Anorexia Nervosa

Although most U.S. girls have been on a diet at some point, slightly less than 1
percent ever develop anorexia nervosa (Walters & Kendler, 1994). **Anorexia nervosa**
is an eating disorder that involves the relentless pursuit of thinness through starvation. It is a serious disorder that can lead to death (Agras & others, 2004). Three
main characteristics of anorexia nervosa are (1) weighing less than 85 percent of what
is considered normal for a person's age and height, (2) having an intense fear of
gaining weight (the fear does not decrease with weight loss), and (3) having a distorted body image (Rigaud & others, 2007). Even when they are extremely thin, they
see themselves as too fat. They never think they are thin enough, especially in the
abdomen, buttocks, and thighs. They usually weigh themselves frequently, often take their body measurements, and gaze critically at themselves in mirrors (Seidenfeld, Sosin, & Rickert, 2004).

Anorexia nervosa typically begins in the early to middle teenage
years, often following an episode of dieting and some type of life
stress (Lee & others, 2005). It is about 10 times more likely to occur
in females than males.

Most anorexics are White adolescent or young adult females from
well-educated, middle- and upper-income families and are competitive
and high-achieving (Schmidt, 2003). They set high standards, become
stressed about not being able to reach the standards, and are intensely
concerned about how others perceive them (Striegel-Moore, Silberstein, & Rodin, 1993). Unable to meet these high expectations, they
turn to something they can control: their weight. Problems in family
functioning are increasingly being found to be linked to the appearance of anorexia nervosa in adolescent girls (Benninghoven & others,
2007), and a recent research review indicated that family therapy is
often the most effective treatment of adolescent girls with anorexia
nervosa (Bulik & others, 2007).

Anorexia nervosa has become an
increasing problem for adolescent
girls and young adult women.
*What are some possible causes of
anorexia nervosa?*

The fashion image in U.S. culture contributes to the incidence of anorexia
nervosa. The media portray thin as beautiful in their choice of fashion models,
who many adolescent girls strive to emulate (Wiseman, Sunday, & Becker, 2005).
And many adolescent girls who strive to be thin hang out together. A recent study
of adolescent girls revealed that friends often share similar body image and eating problems (Hutchinson & Rapee, 2007). In this study, an individual girl's
dieting and extreme weight loss behavior could be predicted from her friends'
dieting and extreme weight loss behavior.

Bulimia Nervosa

Whereas anorexics control their eating by restricting it, most bulimics cannot.
Bulimia nervosa is an eating disorder in which the individual consistently follows

a binge-and-purge pattern. The bulimic goes on an eating binge and then purges by self-inducing vomiting or using a laxative. Although many people binge and purge occasionally, and some experiment with it, a person is considered to have a serious bulimic disorder only if the episodes occur at least twice a week for three months.

As with anorexics, most bulimics are preoccupied with food, have a strong fear of becoming overweight, and are depressed or anxious (Speranza & others, 2005). A recent study revealed that bulimics overvalued their body weight and shape, and this overvaluation was linked to higher depression and lower self-esteem (Hrabosky & others, 2007). Unlike anorexics, people who binge and purge typically fall within a normal weight range, which makes bulimia more difficult to detect.

Approximately 1 to 2 percent of U.S. women are estimated to develop bulimia nervosa, and about 90 percent of bulimics are women (Gotesdam & Agras, 1995). Bulimia nervosa typically begins in late adolescence or early adulthood. Many women who develop bulimia nervosa were somewhat overweight before the onset of the disorder, and the binge eating often began during an episode of dieting. As with anorexia nervosa, about 70 percent of individuals who develop bulimia nervosa eventually recover from the disorder (Agras & others, 2004).

How Would You...?
As a health-care professional, how would you educate parents to identify the signs and symptoms that may signal an eating disorder?

Adolescent Cognition

Adolescents' developing power of thought opens up new cognitive and social horizons. Let's examine what their developing power of thought is like, beginning with Piaget's theory (1952).

Piaget's Theory

As we discussed in Chapter 7, Piaget proposed that around 7 years of age children enter the *concrete operational stage* of cognitive development. They can reason logically about concrete events and objects, and they make gains in the ability to classify objects and to reason about the relationships between classes of objects. Around age 11, according to Piaget, the fourth and final stage of cognitive development, the formal operational stage, begins.

The Formal Operational Stage

What are the characteristics of the formal operational stage? Formal operational thought is more abstract than concrete operational thought. Adolescents are no longer limited to actual, concrete experiences as anchors for thought. They can conjure up make-believe situations, abstract propositions, and events that are purely hypothetical, and can try to reason logically about them.

The abstract quality of thinking during the formal operational stage is evident in the adolescent's verbal problem-solving ability. The concrete operational thinker needs to see the concrete elements A, B, and C to be able to make the logical inference that if A = B and B = C, then A = C, whereas the formal operational thinker can solve this problem merely through verbal presentation.

Another indication of the abstract quality of adolescents' thought is their increased tendency to think about thought itself. One adolescent commented,

hypothetical-deductive reasoning Piaget's formal operational concept that adolescents have the cognitive ability to develop hypotheses, or best guesses, about ways to solve problems, such as an algebraic equation.

"I began thinking about why I was thinking what I was. Then I began thinking about why I was thinking about what I was thinking about what I was." If this sounds abstract, it is, and it characterizes the adolescent's enhanced focus on thought and its abstract qualities.

Accompanying the abstract nature of formal operational thought is thought full of idealism and possibilities, especially during the beginning of the formal operational stage, when assimilation dominates. Adolescents engage in extended speculation about ideal characteristics—qualities they desire in themselves and in others. Such thoughts often lead adolescents to compare themselves with others in regard to such ideal standards. And their thoughts are often fantasy flights into future possibilities.

At the same time that adolescents think more abstractly and idealistically, they also think more logically. Children are likely to solve problems through trial and error; adolescents begin to think more as a scientist thinks, devising plans to solve problems and systematically testing solutions. This type of problem solving requires **hypothetical-deductive reasoning**, which involves creating a hypothesis and deducing its implications, which provides ways to test the hypothesis. Thus, formal operational thinkers develop hypotheses about ways to solve problems and then systematically deduce the best path to follow to solve the problem.

Might adolescents' ability to reason hypothetically and to evaluate what is ideal versus what is real lead them to engage in demonstrations, such as this protest related to better ethnic relations? What other causes might be attractive to adolescents' newfound cognitive abilities of hypothetical-deductive reasoning and idealistic thinking?

Evaluating Piaget's Theory

Researchers have challenged some of Piaget's ideas on the formal operational stage (Kuhn & Franklin, 2006). Among their findings is that there is much more individual variation than Piaget envisioned: Only about one in three young adolescents is a formal operational thinker, and many American adults never become formal operational thinkers; neither do many adults in other cultures.

Furthermore, education in the logic of science and mathematics promotes the development of formal operational thinking. This point recalls a criticism of Piaget's theory that we discussed in Chapter 7: Culture and education exert stronger influences on cognitive development than Piaget argued (Cole, 2006; Rogoff & others, 2007).

Piaget's theory of cognitive development has been challenged on other points as well (Bauer, 2006, 2007). As we noted in Chapter 7, Piaget conceived of stages as unitary structures of thought, with various aspects of a stage emerging at the same time. However, most contemporary developmentalists agree that cognitive development is not as stagelike as Piaget thought (Kellman &

Arterberry, 2006). Furthermore, children can be trained to reason at a higher cognitive stage, and some cognitive abilities emerge earlier than Piaget thought (Cohen & Cashon, 2006). For example, even 2-year-olds are nonegocentric in some contexts. When they realize that another person will not see an object, they investigate whether the person is blindfolded or looking in a different direction. Some understanding of the conservation of number has been demonstrated as early as age 3, although Piaget did not think it emerged until 7. Other cognitive abilities can emerge later than Piaget thought (Kuhn & Franklin, 2006). As we just noted, many adolescents still think in concrete operational ways or are just beginning to master formal operations, and even many adults are not formal operational thinkers.

Despite these challenges to Piaget's ideas, we owe him a tremendous debt. Piaget was the founder of the present field of cognitive development, and he developed a long list of masterful concepts of enduring power and fascination: assimilation, accommodation, object permanence, egocentrism, conservation, and others. Psychologists also owe him the current vision of children as active, constructive thinkers. And they have a debt to him for creating a theory that generated a huge volume of research on children's cognitive development.

Piaget also was a genius when it came to observing children. His careful observations demonstrated inventive ways to discover how children act on, and adapt to, their world. He also showed us how children need to make their experiences fit their schemes yet simultaneously adapt their schemes to experience. Piaget also revealed how cognitive change is likely to occur if the context is structured to allow gradual movement to the next higher level. Concepts do not emerge suddenly, full-blown, but instead develop through a series of partial accomplishments that lead to increasingly comprehensive understanding (Gelman & Kalish, 2006).

Adolescent Egocentrism

Adolescent egocentrism is the heightened self-consciousness of adolescents. David Elkind (1976) maintains that adolescent egocentrism has two key components—the imaginary audience and personal fable. The **imaginary audience** is adolescents' belief that others are as interested in them as they themselves are, as well as attention-getting behavior—attempts to be noticed, visible, and "on stage." For example, an eighth-grade boy might walk into the classroom and thinks that all eyes are riveted on his spotty complexion. Adolescents sense that they are "on stage" in early adolescence, believing they are the main actors and all others are the audience.

According to Elkind, the **personal fable** is the part of adolescent egocentrism involving a sense of uniqueness and invincibility (or invulnerability). For example, 13-year-old Adrienne says this about herself: "No one understands me, particularly my parents. They have no idea of what I am feeling." Adolescents' sense of personal uniqueness makes them feel that no one can understand how they really feel. As part of their effort to retain a sense of personal uniqueness, adolescents

Many adolescent girls spend long hours in front of the mirror, depleting cans of hairspray, tubes of lipstick, and jars of cosmetics. *How might this behavior be related to changes in adolescent cognitive and physical development?*

might craft a story about the self that is filled with fantasy, immersing themselves in a world that is far removed from reality. Personal fables frequently show up in adolescent diaries.

Adolescents also often show a sense of invincibility or invulnerability. For example, during a conversation with a girl her same age, 14-year-old Margaret says, "Are you kidding? I won't get pregnant." This sense of invincibility may also lead them to believe that they themselves are invulnerable to dangers and catastrophes (such as deadly car wrecks) that happen to other people. As a result, some adolescents engage in risky behaviors such as drag racing, drug use, suicide, and having sexual intercourse without using contraceptives or barriers against STIs.

A recent study of sixth- through twelfth-graders examined whether aspects of the personal fable were linked to various aspects of adolescent adjustment (Aalsma, Lapsley, & Flannery, 2006). A sense of invincibility or invulnerability was linked to engaging in risky behaviors, such as smoking cigarettes, drinking alcohol, and delinquency, while a sense of personal uniqueness was related to depression and suicidal thoughts.

Information Processing

According to Deanna Kuhn (Kuhn & Franklin, 2006), the most important cognitive change in adolescence is improvement in *executive functioning*, which involves higher-order cognitive activities such as reasoning, making decisions, monitoring thinking critically, and monitoring one's cognitive progress. Improvements in executive functioning permit more effective learning and an improved ability to determine how attention will be allocated, to make decisions, and to engage in critical thinking.

Decision Making

Adolescence is a time of increased decision making—which friends to choose, which person to date, whether to have sex, buy a car, go to college, and so on (Wigfield, Byrnes, & Eccles, 2006). How competent are adolescents at making decisions? Older adolescents are described as more competent than younger adolescents, who in turn are more competent than children (Keating, 1990).

Compared with children, young adolescents are more likely to generate different options, examine a situation from a variety of perspectives, anticipate the consequences of decisions, and consider the credibility of sources.

However, older adolescents' decision-making skills are far from perfect, as are adults' (Klaczynski, 2005). Indeed, some researchers have found that adolescents and adults do not differ in their decision-making skills (Quadrel, Fischoff, & Davis, 1993). Furthermore, some personality traits may influence

What are some of the decisions adolescents have to make? What characterizes their decision making?

decision making. Adolescents who are impulsive and seek sensation are often not very effective decision makers, for example (Byrnes, 2005).

Being able to make competent decisions does not guarantee that one will make them in everyday life, where breadth of experience often comes into play (Keating, 1990). As an example, driver-training courses improve adolescents' cognitive and motor skills to levels equal, or sometimes superior, to those of adults. However, driver training has not been effective in reducing adolescents' high rate of traffic accidents (Potvin, Champagne, & Laberge-Nadeau, 1988).

How Would You...?
As an educator, how would you incorporate decision-making exercises into the school curriculum for adolescents?

Adolescents need more opportunities to practice and discuss realistic decision making. Many real-world decisions on matters such as sex, drugs, and daredevil driving occur in an atmosphere of stress that includes time constraints and emotional involvement. One strategy for improving adolescent decision making is to provide more opportunities for them to engage in role playing and peer group problem solving.

Critical Thinking

Adolescence is an important transitional period in the development of critical thinking (Keating, 1990). In one study of fifth-, eighth-, and eleventh-graders, critical thinking increased with age but still occurred in only 43 percent of even the eleventh-graders, and many adolescents showed self-serving biases in their reasoning (Klaczynski & Narasimham, 1998).

If fundamental skills (such as literacy and math skills) are not developed during childhood, critical-thinking skills are unlikely to mature in adolescence. For the subset of adolescents who lack such fundamental skills, potential gains in adolescent thinking are unlikely. For other adolescents, however, cognitive changes that allow improved critical thinking in adolescence include (1) increased speed, automaticity, and capacity of information processing, which free cognitive resources for other purposes; (2) more breadth of content knowledge in a variety of domains; (3) increased ability to construct new combinations of knowledge; and (4) a greater range and more spontaneous use of strategies or procedures for applying or obtaining knowledge, such as planning, considering alternatives, and cognitive monitoring.

Schools

What is the transition from elementary to middle or junior high school like? What are the characteristics of effective schools for adolescents? How can adolescents benefit from service learning?

The Transition to Middle or Junior High School

The first year of middle school or junior high school can be difficult for many students (Wigfield, Brynes, & Eccles, 2006). For example, in one study of the transition from sixth grade in an elementary school to the seventh grade in a junior high school, adolescents' perceptions of the quality of their school life plunged in the seventh grade (Hirsch & Rapkin, 1987). Compared with their earlier feelings as sixth-graders, the seventh-graders were less satisfied with school, were less committed to school, and liked their teachers less. The drop in school satisfaction occurred regardless of how academically successful the students were.

The transition to middle or junior high school takes place at a time when many changes—in the individual, in the family, and in school—are occurring simultaneously. These changes include puberty and related concerns about body image; the emergence of at least some aspects of formal operational thought, including accompanying changes in social cognition; increased responsibility and decreased dependency on parents; change to a larger, more impersonal school structure; change from one teacher to many teachers and from a small, homogeneous set of peers to a larger, more heterogeneous set of peers; and an increased focus on achievement and performance. Moreover, when students make the transition to middle or junior high school, they experience the **top-dog phenomenon**, moving from being the oldest, biggest, and most powerful students in the elementary school to being the youngest, smallest, and least powerful students in the middle or junior high school.

The transition from elementary to middle or junior high school occurs at the same time as a number of other developmental changes. *What are some of these other developmental changes?*

There can also be positive aspects to the transition to middle or junior high school. Students are more likely to feel grown up, have more subjects from which to select, have more opportunities to spend time with peers and locate compatible friends, and enjoy increased independence from direct parental monitoring. They also may be more challenged intellectually by academic work.

Effective Schools for Young Adolescents

Educators and psychologists worry that junior high and middle schools have become watered-down versions of high schools, mimicking their curricular and extracurricular schedules. Critics argue that these schools should offer activities that reflect a wide range of individual differences in biological and psychological development among young adolescents. The Carnegie Corporation (1989) issued an extremely negative evaluation of our nation's middle schools. It concluded that most young adolescents attended massive, impersonal schools; were taught from irrelevant curricula; trusted few adults in school; and lacked access to health care and counseling. It recommended that the nation should develop smaller "communities" or "houses" to lessen the impersonal nature of large middle schools, have lower student-to-counselor ratios (10 to 1 instead of several hundred to 1), involve parents and community leaders in schools, develop new curricula, have teachers team teach in more flexibly designed curriculum blocks that integrate several disciplines, boost students' health and fitness with more in-school programs, and help students who need public health care to get it. Twenty-five years later, experts are still finding that middle schools throughout the nation need a major redesign if they are to be effective in educating adolescents (Eccles, 2007).

How Would You...? As an educator, how would you design school programs to enhance students' smooth transition into middle school?

High School

Just as there are concerns about U.S. middle school education, so are there concerns about U.S. high school education. Critics stress that many high schools foster passivity and that schools should create a variety of pathways for students to achieve an identity. Many students graduate from high school with inadequate reading, writing, and mathematical skills—including many who go on to college and have to enroll in remediation classes there. Other students drop out of high school and do not have skills that will allow them to obtain decent jobs, much less to be informed citizens.

In the last half of the twentieth century and the first several years of the twenty-first century, U.S. high school dropout rates declined (National Center for Education Statistics, 2005) (see Figure 9.7). In the 1940s, more than half of U.S. 16- to 24-year-olds had dropped out of school; by 2003, this figure had decreased to only 9.9 percent. The dropout rate of Latino adolescents remains high, although it is decreasing in the twenty-first century. The highest dropout rate in the United States, though, likely occurs for Native American youth—less than 50 percent finish their high school education.

Students drop out of schools for many reasons (Christensen & Thurlow, 2004). In one study, almost 50 percent of the dropouts cited school-related reasons for leaving school, such as not liking school or being expelled or suspended (Rumberger, 1995). Twenty percent of the dropouts (but 40 percent of the Latino students) cited economic reasons for leaving school. One-third of the female students dropped out for personal reasons such as pregnancy or marriage.

According to a recent review, the most effective programs to discourage dropping out of high school provide early reading programs, tutoring, counseling, and mentoring (Lehr & others, 2003). They also emphasize the creation of caring environments and relationships, use block scheduling, and offer community-service opportunities.

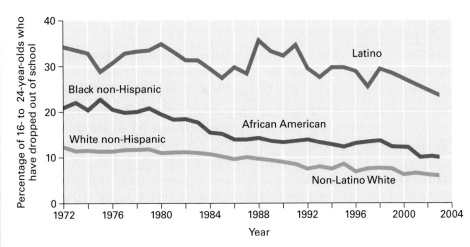

Figure 9.7 Trends in High School Dropout Rates
From 1972 through 2003, the school dropout rate for Latinos remained very high (23.5 percent of 16- to 24-year-olds in 2003). The African American dropout rate was still higher (10.9 percent) than the White non-Latino rate (6.3 percent) in 2000. The overall dropout rate declined considerably from the 1940s through the 1960s but has declined only slightly since 1972. (Source: National Center for Education Statistics, 2005).

service learning A form of
education that promotes social
responsibility and service to the
community.

Service Learning

Service learning is a form of education that promotes social responsibility and service to the community. In service learning, adolescents engage in activities such as tutoring, helping older adults, working in a hospital, assisting at a child-care center, or cleaning up a vacant lot to make a play area. An important goal of service learning is for adolescents to become less self-centered and more strongly motivated to help others (Benson & others, 2006). Service learning is often more effective when two conditions are met (Nucci, 2006): (1) giving students some degree of choice in the service activities in which they participate, and (2) providing students opportunities to reflect about their participation.

Researchers have found that service learning benefits adolescents in a number of ways (Reinders & Youniss, 2006). These improvements in adolescent development related to service learning include higher grades in school, increased goal setting, higher self-esteem, an improved sense of being able to make a difference for others, and an increased likelihood that they will serve as volunteers in the future (Benson & others, 2006; Hart, Atkins, & Donnelly, 2006).

What are some outcomes of service learning?

How Would You...? As an educator, how would you devise a program to increase adolescents' motivation to participate in service learning?

Summary

The Nature of Adolescence

Many stereotypes of adolescents are too negative. Most adolescents today successfully negotiate the path from childhood to adulthood. However, too many of today's adolescents are not provided with adequate opportunities and support to become competent adults. It is important to view adolescents as a heterogeneous group because different portraits of adolescents emerge, depending on the particular set of adolescents being described.

Physical Changes

Puberty is a period of rapid physical maturation involving hormonal and bodily changes that occur primarily during early adolescence. Puberty's determinants include nutrition, health, and heredity. The endocrine system's influence on puberty involves an interaction of the hypothalamus, the pituitary gland, and the gonads (sex glands). The initial onset of the pubertal growth spurt occurs on the average at 9 years for girls and 11 for boys, reaching a peak change for girls at $11^1/_2$ and for boys at $13^1/_2$. Individual variation in pubertal changes is substantial. Adolescents show considerable interest in their body image, with girls having more negative body images than boys do. For boys, early maturation brings benefits, at least during early adolescence. Early-maturing girls are vulnerable to a number of risks. Changes in the brain during adolescence involve the thickening of the corpus callosum and gap in maturation between the amygdala and the prefrontal cortex, which functions in reasoning and self-regulation. Adolescence is a time of sexual exploration and sexual experimentation. Having sexual intercourse in early adolescence is associated with negative developmental outcomes. Contraceptive use by adolescents is increasing. About one in four sexually experienced adolescents acquire a sexually transmitted infection (STI). America's adolescent pregnancy rate is high but has been decreasing in recent years.

Issues in Adolescent Health

Adolescence is a critical juncture in health because many of the factors related to poor health habits and early death in the adult years begin during adolescence. Poor nutrition, lack of exercise, and inadequate sleep are concerns. The three leading causes of death in adolescence are accidents, homicide, and suicide. Despite recent declines in use, the United States has the highest rate of adolescent illicit drug use of any industrialized nation. Parents and peers play important roles in whether adolescents take drugs. Eating disorders have increased in adolescence, with a substantial increase in the percentage of adolescents who are overweight. Two eating disorders that may emerge in adolescence are anorexia nervosa and bulimia nervosa.

Adolescent Cognition

During the formal operational stage, Piaget's fourth stage of cognitive development, thought is more abstract, idealistic, and logical than during the concrete operational stage. However, many adolescents are not formal operational thinkers but are consolidating their concrete operational thought. Elkind describes adolescent egocentrism as the heightened self-consciousness of adolescents that consists of two parts: imaginary audience and personal fable. Changes in information processing in adolescence are mainly reflected in improved executive functioning, which includes advances in decision making and critical thinking.

Schools

The transition to middle or junior high school coincides with many social, familial, and individual changes in the adolescent's life, and this transition is often stressful. One source of stress is the move from the top-dog to the lowest position in school. Some critics argue that a major redesign of U.S. middle schools is needed. Critics say that U.S. high schools foster passivity and do not develop student's academic skills adequately. The overall high school dropout rate declined considerably in the last half of the twentieth century, but the dropout rates of Latino and Native American youth remain very high. Service learning, a form of education that promotes social responsibility and service to the community, is related to a number of positive benefits for adolescents.

Key Terms

Socioemotional Development in Adolescence

Stories of Life-Span Development: Jewel Cash, Teen Dynamo

The mayor of the city says she is "everywhere." She recently persuaded the city's school committee to consider ending the practice of locking tardy students out of their classrooms. She also swayed a neighborhood group to support her proposal for a winter jobs program. According to one city councilman, "People are just impressed with the power of her arguments and the sophistication of the argument" (Silva, 2005, pp. B1, B4). She is Jewel E. Cash, and she is only 16 years old.

A junior at Boston Latin Academy, Jewel was raised in one of Boston's housing projects by her mother, a single parent. Today she is a member of the Boston Student Advisory Council, mentors children, volunteers at a women's shelter, manages and dances in two troupes, and is a member of a neighborhood watch group—among other activities. Jewel is far from typical, but her

Jewel Cash, seated next to her mother, participating in a crime watch meeting at a community center.

activities illustrate that cognitive and socioemotional development allows even adolescents to be capable, effective individuals.

Significant changes characterize socioemotional development in adolescence. These changes include searching for identity. Changes also occur in the social contexts of adolescents' lives, with transformations occurring in relationships with families and peers in cultural contexts. Adolescents also may develop socioemotional problems, such as delinquency and depression. ▌

Identity

Jewel Cash told an interviewer from the *Boston Globe,* "I see a problem and I say, 'How can I make a difference?'... I can't take on the world, even though I can try.... I'm moving forward but I want to make sure I'm bringing people with me" (Silva, 2005, pp. B1, B4). Jewel's confidence and positive identity sound at least as impressive as her activities. This section examines how adolescents develop characteristics like these. How much did you understand yourself during adolescence, and how did you acquire the stamp of your identity? Is your identity still developing?

What Is Identity?

Identity is a self-portrait composed of many pieces, including these:

- The career and work path the person wants to follow (vocational/career identity)

- Whether the person is conservative, liberal, or middle-of-the-road (political identity)

- The person's spiritual beliefs (religious identity)

- Whether the person is single, married, divorced, and so on (relationship identity)

- The extent to which the person is motivated to achieve and is intellectual (achievement, intellectual identity)

- Whether the person is heterosexual, homosexual, or bisexual (sexual identity)

- Which part of the world or country a person is from and how intensely the person identifies with his or her cultural heritage (cultural/ethnic identity)

- The kind of things a person likes to do, which can include sports, music, hobbies, and so on (interest)

What are some important dimensions of identity?

- The individual's personality characteristics (such as being introverted or extra-verted, anxious or calm, friendly or hostile, and so on) (personality)

- The individual's body image (physical identity)

Synthesizing the identity components can be a long and drawn-out process, with many negations and affirmations of various roles and faces. Identity development gets done in bits and pieces. Decisions are not made once and for all, but have to be made again and again. Identity development does not happen neatly, and it does not happen cataclysmically (Cote, 2006; Kroger, 2007).

Erikson's View

Questions about identity surface as common, virtually universal, concerns during adolescence. Some decisions made during adolescence might seem trivial: whom to date, whether or not to break up, which major to study, whether to study or play, whether or not to be politically active, and so on. Over the years of adolescence, however, such decisions begin to form the core of what the individual is all about as a human being—what is called his or her identity.

It was Erik Erikson (1950, 1968) who first understood how central questions about identity are to understanding adolescent development. That identity is now believed to be a key aspect of adolescent development is a result of Erikson's masterful thinking and analysis.

Erikson's theory was introduced in Chapter 1. Recall that his fifth developmental stage, which individuals experience during adolescence, is **identity versus identity confusion.** During this time, said Erikson, adolescents are faced with deciding who they are, what they are all about, and where they are going in life.

The search for an identity during adolescence is aided by a *psychosocial moratorium,* which is Erikson's term for the gap between childhood security and adult autonomy. During this period, society leaves adolescents relatively free of responsibilities and free to try out different identities. Adolescents in effect search their culture's identity files, experimenting with different roles and personalities. They may want to pursue one career one month (lawyer, for example) and another career the next month (doctor, actor, teacher, social worker, or astronaut, for example). They may dress neatly one day, sloppily the next. This experimentation is a deliberate effort on the part of adolescents to find out where they fit in the world. Most adolescents eventually discard undesirable roles.

Developmental Changes

Although questions about identity may be especially important during adolescence, identity formation neither begins nor ends during these years. It begins with the appearance of attachment, the development of the sense of self, and the emergence of independence in infancy; the process reaches its final phase with a life review and integration in old age. What is important about identity development in adolescence,

crisis Marcia's term for a period of identity development during which the adolescent is exploring alternatives.

commitment Marcia's term for the part of identity development in which adolescents show a personal investment in forming an identity.

identity diffusion Marcia's term for adolescents who have not yet experienced a crisis (explored meaningful alternatives) or made any commitments.

identity foreclosure Marcia's term for adolescents who have made a commitment but have not experienced a crisis.

identity moratorium Marcia's term for adolescents who are in the midst of a crisis, but their commitments are either absent or vaguely defined.

identity achievement Marcia's term for adolescents who have undergone a crisis and have made a commitment.

especially late adolescence, is that for the first time, physical development, cognitive development, and socioemotional development advance to the point at which the individual can begin to sort through and synthesize childhood identities and identifications to construct a viable path toward adult maturity.

How do individual adolescents go about the process of forming an identity? Eriksonian researcher James Marcia (1980, 1994) believes that Erikson's theory of identity development contains four *statuses* of identity, or ways of resolving the identity crisis: identity diffusion, identity foreclosure, identity moratorium, and identity achievement. What determines an individual's identity status? Marcia classifies individuals based on the existence or extent of their crisis or commitment (see Figure 10.1). **Crisis** is defined as a period of identity development during which the individual is exploring alternatives. Most researchers use the term *exploration* rather than crisis. **Commitment** is personal investment in identity.

The four statuses of identity are:

- **Identity diffusion**, the status of individuals who have not yet experienced a crisis or made any commitments. Not only are they undecided about occupational and ideological choices, they are also likely to show little interest in such matters.

- **Identity foreclosure** is the status of individuals who have made a commitment but not experienced a crisis. This occurs most often when parents hand down commitments to their adolescents, usually in an authoritarian way, before adolescents have had a chance to explore different approaches, ideologies, and vocations on their own.

- **Identity moratorium** is the status of individuals who are in the midst of a crisis but whose commitments are either absent or are only vaguely defined.

- **Identity achievement** is the status of individuals who have undergone a crisis and made a commitment.

How Would You...?
As a psychologist, how would you apply Marcia's theory of identity formation to describe your current identity status or adolescents you know?

Beyond Erikson

A consensus is developing that the key changes in identity are more likely to take place in emerging adulthood, the period from about 18 to 25 years of age (Kroger,

Position on Occupation and Ideology	Identity Status			
	Identity diffusion	Identity foreclosure	Identity moratorium	Identity achievement
Crisis	Absent	Absent	Present	Present
Commitment	Absent	Present	Absent	Present

Figure 10.1 Marcia's Four Statuses of Identity

According to Marcia, an individual's status in developing an identity can be described as identity diffusion, identity foreclosure, identity moratorium, or identity achievement. The status depends on the presence or absence of (1) a crisis or exploration of alternatives and (2) a commitment to an identity. *What is the identity status of most young adolescents?*

2007; Pals, 2006). For example, Alan Waterman (1985, 1992) has found that from the years preceding high school through the last few years of college, the number of individuals who are identity achieved increases, whereas the number of individuals who are identity diffused decreases. Many young adolescents are identity diffused. College upperclassmen are more likely than high school students or college freshmen to be identity achieved.

Resolution of the identity issue during adolescence does not mean that identity will be stable through the remainder of life. Many individuals who develop positive identities follow what are called "MAMA" cycles; that is, their identity status changes from *moratorium* to *achievement* to *moratorium* to *achievement* (Marcia, 1994). These cycles may be repeated throughout life. Marcia (2002) believes that the first identity is just that—it is not, and should not be expected to be, the final product.

In short, questions about identity come up throughout life. An individual who develops a healthy identity is flexible and adaptive, open to changes in society, in relationships, and in careers. This openness assures numerous reorganizations of identity throughout the individual's life.

Family Influences

Parents are important figures in the adolescent's development of identity (Luyckx & others, 2006). Researchers have found that a family atmosphere that promotes both individuality and connectedness is important in the adolescent's identity development (Cooper & Grotevant, 1989):

- **Individuality** consists of two dimensions: self-assertion (the ability to have and communicate a point of view) and separateness (the use of communication patterns to express how one is different from others).

- **Connectedness** also consists of two dimensions: mutuality, which involves sensitivity to, and respect for, others' views, and permeability, which involves openness to others' views.

In general, Cooper's research indicates that identity formation is enhanced by family relationships that are both individuated, which encourages adolescents to develop their own point of view, and connected, which provides a secure base from which adolescents can explore their widening social worlds. When connectedness is strong and individuation weak, adolescents often have an identity foreclosure status. When connectedness is weak, adolescents often reveal identity confusion.

Ethnic Identity

Throughout the world, ethnic minority groups have struggled to maintain their ethnic identities while blending in with the dominant culture (Erikson, 1968). **Ethnic identity** is an enduring aspect of the self that includes a sense of membership in an ethnic group, along with the attitudes and feelings related to

individuality Individuality consists of two dimensions: self-assertion (the ability to have and communicate a point of view) and separateness (the use of communication patterns to express how one is different from others).

connectedness Connectedness consists of two dimensions: mutuality (sensitivity to, and respect for, others' views) and permeability (openness to others' views).

ethnic identity An enduring, basic aspect of the self that includes a sense of membership in an ethnic group and the attitudes and feelings related to that membership.

Michelle Chin, age 16: "Parents do not understand that teenagers need to find out who they are, which means a lot of experimenting, a lot of mood swings, a lot of emotions and awkwardness. Like any teenager, I am facing an identity crisis. I am still trying to figure out whether I am a Chinese American or an American with Asian eyes."

that membership. Thus, for adolescents from ethnic minority groups, the process of identity formation has an added dimension: the choice between two or more sources of identification—their own ethnic group and the mainstream, or dominant culture (Phinney & others, 2006). Many adolescents resolve this choice by developing a *bicultural identity*. That is, they identify in some ways with their ethnic group and in other ways with the majority culture (Phinney, 2006). One recent study of Mexican American and Asian American college students found that they identified both with the American mainstream culture and their culture of origin (Devos, 2006).

For ethnic minority individuals, adolescence is often a special juncture in their development (Umana-Taylor, Bhanot, & Shin, 2006). Although children are aware of some ethnic and cultural differences, individuals consciously confront their ethnicity for the first time in adolescence. Unlike children, adolescents have the ability to interpret ethnic and cultural information, to reflect on the past, and to speculate about the future.

How Would You...?
As a human development and family studies professional, how would you design a community program that assists ethnic minority adolescents to develop a healthy bicultural identity?

The indicators of identity change often differ for each succeeding generation (Berry, 2007; Phinney, 2006). First-generation immigrants are likely to be secure in their identities and unlikely to change much; they may or may not develop a new identity. The degree to which they begin to feel "American" appears to be related to whether or not they learn English, develop social networks beyond their ethnic group, and become culturally competent in their new country. Second-generation immigrants are more likely to think of themselves as "American," possibly because citizenship is granted at birth. Their ethnic identity is likely to be linked to retention of their ethnic language and social networks. In the third and later generations, the issues become more complex. Historical, contextual, and political factors that are unrelated to acculturation may affect the extent to which members of this generation retain their ethnic identities. For non-European ethnic groups, racism and discrimination influence whether ethnic identity is retained.

Families

Adolescence typically alters the relationship between parents and their children. Among the most important aspects of family relationships in adolescence are those that involve autonomy, attachment, and parent-adolescent conflict.

Autonomy and Attachment

With most adolescents, parents are likely to find themselves engaged in a delicate balancing act, weighing competing needs for autonomy and control, for independence and connection.

The Push for Autonomy

The typical adolescent's push for autonomy and responsibility puzzles and angers many parents. As parents see their teenager slipping from their grasp, they may have an urge to take stronger control. Heated emotional exchanges may ensue, with either side calling names, making threats, and doing whatever seems necessary to gain control. Parents may seem frustrated because they *expect* their teenager to heed their advice, to want to spend time with the family, and to grow up to do what is right. Most parents anticipate that their teenager will have some difficulty adjusting to the changes that adolescence brings, but few parents imagine and predict just how strong an adolescent's desires will be to spend time with peers or how intensely adolescents will want to show that it is they—not their parents—who are responsible for their successes and failures.

Adolescents' ability to attain autonomy and gain control over their behavior is acquired through appropriate adult reactions to their desire for control (Collins & Steinberg, 2006). At the onset of adolescence, the average individual does not have the knowledge to make appropriate or mature decisions in all areas of life. As the adolescent pushes for autonomy, the wise adult relinquishes control in those areas where the adolescent can make reasonable decisions, but continues to guide the adolescent to make reasonable decisions in areas in which the adolescent's knowledge is more limited. Gradually, adolescents acquire the ability to make mature decisions on their own.

Gender differences characterize autonomy-granting in adolescence. Boys are given more independence than girls. In one study, this was especially true in U.S. families with a traditional gender-role orientation (Bumpus, Crouter, & McHale, 2001).

What are strategies parents can use to guide adolescents in effectively handling their increased motivation for autonomy?

The Role of Attachment

Recall from Chapter 4 that one of the most widely discussed aspects of socioemotional development in infancy is secure attachment to caregivers. In the past decade, researchers have explored whether secure attachment also might be an important concept in adolescents' relationships with their parents (Collins & Steinberg, 2006). For example, Joseph Allen and his colleagues (Allen, 2007; Allen & others, 2002, 2005) found that securely attached adolescents were less likely than those who were insecurely attached to engage in problem behaviors such as juvenile delinquency and drug abuse.

Other research has examined possible links between secure attachment to parents and good relations with peers. Researchers have found that securely attached adolescents have better peer relations than their insecurely attached counterparts (Laible, Carlo, & Raffaeli; 2000; Zimmerman, 2007). However, the correlations between adolescent-parent attachments and adolescent outcomes are moderate, indicating that the success or failure of parent-adolescent attachments does not necessarily guarantee success or failure in peer relationships.

Parent–Adolescent Conflict

Although parent-adolescent conflict increases in early adolescence, it does not reach the tumultuous proportions G. Stanley Hall envisioned at the beginning of the twentieth century (Collins & Steinberg, 2006; Smetana, Campione-Barr, & Metzger, 2006). Rather, much of the conflict involves the everyday events of family

Old Model

Autonomy, detachment from parents; parent and peer worlds are isolated

Intense, stressful conflict throughout adolescence; parent-adolescent relationships are filled with storm and stress on virtually a daily basis

New Model

Attachment and autonomy; parents are important support systems and attachment figures; adolescent-parent and adolescent-peer worlds have some important connections

Moderate parent-adolescent conflict is common and can serve a positive developmental function; conflict greater in early adolescence

Figure 10.2 **Old and New Models of Parent-Adolescent Relationships**

life, such as keeping a bedroom clean, dressing neatly, getting home by a certain time, and not talking forever on the phone. The conflicts rarely involve major dilemmas such as drugs or delinquency.

Conflict with parents often escalates during early adolescence, remains somewhat stable during the high school years, and then lessens as the adolescent reaches 17 to 20 years of age. Parent-adolescent relationships become more positive if adolescents go away to college than if they attend college while living at home (Sullivan & Sullivan, 1980).

The everyday conflicts that characterize parent-adolescent relationships may actually serve a positive developmental function. These minor disputes and negotiations facilitate the adolescent's transition from being dependent on parents to becoming an autonomous individual. For example, in one study, adolescents who expressed disagreement with their parents explored identity development more actively than did adolescents who did not express disagreement with their parents (Cooper & others, 1982). Recognizing that conflict and negotiation can serve a positive developmental function can tone down parental hostility.

The old model of parent-adolescent relationships suggested that as adolescents mature they detach themselves from parents and move into a world of autonomy apart from parents. The old model also suggested that parent-adolescent conflict is intense and stressful throughout adolescence. The new model emphasizes that parents serve as important attachment figures and support systems while adolescents explore a wider, more complex social world (Allen, 2007; Furman, 2007). The new model also emphasizes that, in most families, parent-adolescent conflict is moderate rather than severe, and that the everyday negotiations and minor disputes not only are normal but also can serve the positive developmental function of helping the adolescent make the transition from childhood dependency to adult independence (see Figure 10.2).

Still, a high degree of conflict characterizes some parent-adolescent relationships (Ouerbeek & others, 2007). One estimate of the proportion of parents and adolescents who engage in prolonged, intense, repeated, unhealthy conflict is about one in five families (Montemayor, 1982). While this figure represents a minority of adolescents, it indicates that 4 to 5 million American families encounter serious, highly stressful parent-adolescent conflict. And this prolonged, intense conflict is associated with various adolescent problems: movement out of the home, juvenile delinquency, school dropout, pregnancy and early marriage, membership in religious cults, and drug abuse (Brook & others, 1990).

How Would You...?

As a social worker, how would you counsel a mother who is experiencing stress about anticipated family conflicts as her child enters adolescence?

Competent adolescent development is most likely when adolescents have parents who:

1. Show them warmth and respect, and avoid the tendency to be too controlling or too permissive.

2. Demonstrate sustained interest in their lives—for example, by spending time with them and by monitoring their activities.

3. Understand and adapt to their cognitive and socioemotional development.

4. Communicate expectations for high standards of conduct and achievement.

5. Recognize that moderate conflict is a normal part of the adolescent's desire for independence and search for an identity.

6. Display constructive ways of dealing with problems and conflict.

7. Understand that adolescence is a long journey; adolescents don't become adults overnight.

Peers

Peers play powerful roles in the lives of adolescents. When you think back to your own adolescent years, you probably recall many of your most enjoyable moments as experiences shared with peers. Peer relations undergo important changes in adolescence, including changes in friendships and in peer groups and the beginning of romantic relationships. In middle and late childhood, as we discussed in Chapter 8, the focus of peer relations is on being liked by classmates and being included in games or lunchroom conversations. Being overlooked or, worse yet, being rejected can have damaging effects on children's development that sometimes are carried forward to adolescence (Bukowski, Brendgen, & Vitaro, 2007; Rubin, Bukowski, & Parker, 2006).

Friendships

For most children, being popular with their peers is a strong motivator. Beginning in early adolescence, however, teenagers typically prefer to have a smaller number of friendships that are more intense and intimate than those of young children.

Harry Stack Sullivan (1953) was the most influential theorist to discuss the importance of adolescent friendships. In contrast to other psychoanalytic theorists who focused almost exclusively on parent-child relationships, Sullivan argued that friends are also important in shaping the development of children and adolescents. Everyone, said Sullivan, has basic social needs, such as the need for tenderness (secure attachment), playful companionship, social acceptance, intimacy, and sexual relations. Whether or not

What changes take place in friendship during the adolescent years?

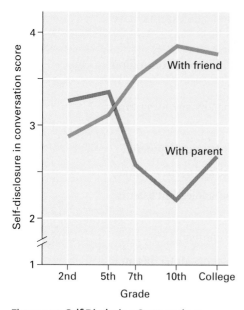

Figure 10.3 Self-Disclosing Conversations
In this study children and youth completed a 5-point rating scale, with a higher score representing greater self-disclosure (Buhrmester, 1998). The data shown here represent the means for each age group. Self-disclosing conversations with friends increased dramatically in adolescence while declining in an equally dramatic fashion with parents. However, self-disclosing conversations with parents began to pick up somewhat during the college years.

these needs are fulfilled largely determines our emotional well-being. For example, if the need for playful companionship goes unmet, then we become bored and depressed; if the need for social acceptance is not met, we suffer a lowered sense of self-worth.

During adolescence, said Sullivan, friends become increasingly important in meeting social needs. In particular, Sullivan argued that the need for intimacy intensifies during early adolescence, motivating teenagers to seek out close friends. If adolescents fail to forge such close friendships, they experience loneliness and a reduced sense of self-worth. The nature of relationships with friends during adolescence can foreshadow the quality of romantic relationships in emerging adulthood. For example, a longitudinal study revealed that having more secure relationships with close friends at 16 years of age was linked with more positive romantic relationships at 20 to 23 years of age (Simpson & others 2007).

Many of Sullivan's ideas have withstood the test of time (Buhrmester, 2005). For example, adolescents report disclosing intimate and personal information to their friends more often than do younger children (Buhrmester, 1998) (see Figure 10.3). Adolescents also say they depend more on friends than on parents to satisfy their needs for companionship, reassurance of worth, and intimacy. The ups and downs of experiences with friends shape adolescents' well-being (Berndt, 2002).

Although most adolescents develop friendships with individuals who are close to their own age, some adolescents become best friends with younger or older individuals. Do older friends encourage adolescents to engage in delinquent behavior or early sexual behavior? Adolescents who interact with older youth do engage in these behaviors more frequently, but it is not known whether the older youth guide younger adolescents toward deviant behavior or whether the younger adolescents were already prone to deviant behavior before they developed the friendship with the older youth (Billy, Rodgers, & Udry, 1984).

Peer Groups

How extensive is peer pressure in adolescence? What roles do cliques and crowds play in adolescents' lives? As we see next, researchers have found that the standards of peer groups and the influence of crowds and cliques become increasingly important during adolescence.

Peer Pressure

Young adolescents conform more to peer standards than children do. Around the eighth and ninth grades, conformity to peers—especially to their antisocial standards—peaks (Leventhal, 1994). At this point, adolescents are most likely to go along with a peer to steal hubcaps off a car, draw graffiti on a wall, or steal cosmetics from a store counter. One study found that U.S. adolescents are more likely than Japanese adolescents to put pressure on their peers to resist parental influence (Rothbaum & others, 2000).

Cliques and Crowds

Cliques and crowds assume more important roles in the lives of adolescents than children (Brown, 2004). **Cliques** are small groups that range from 2 to about 12 individuals and average about 5 to 6 individuals. The clique members are usually of the same sex and about the same age.

Cliques can form because adolescents engage in similar activities, such as being in a club or on a sports team. Some cliques also form because of friendship. Several adolescents may form a clique because they have spent time with each other, share mutual interests, and enjoy each other's company. Not necessarily friends, they often develop a friendship if they stay in the clique. What do adolescents do in cliques? They share ideas and hang out together. Often they develop an in-group identity in which they believe that their clique is better than other cliques.

Crowds are larger than cliques and less personal. Adolescents are usually members of a crowd based on reputation, and they may or may not spend much time together. Many crowds are defined by the activities adolescents engage in (such as "jocks" who are good at sports or "druggies" who take drugs) (Brown, 2004; Verkooijen, de Vries, & Nielsen, 2007). Reputation-based crowds often appear for the first time in early adolescence and usually become less prominent in late adolescence (Collins & Steinberg, 2006).

In one study, crowd membership was associated with adolescent self-esteem (Brown & Lohr, 1987). The crowds included jocks (athletically oriented), populars (well-known students who led social activities), normals (middle-of-the-road students who made up the masses), druggies or toughs (known for illicit drug use or other delinquent activities), and nobodies (low in social skills or intellectual abilities). The self-esteem of the jocks and the populars was highest, whereas that of the nobodies was lowest. One group of adolescents not in a crowd had self-esteem equivalent to that of the jocks and the populars; this group was the independents, who indicated that crowd membership was not important to them. Keep in mind that these data are correlational; self-esteem could increase an adolescent's probability of becoming a crowd member, just as crowd membership could increase the adolescent's self-esteem.

Dating and Romantic Relationships

Adolescents spend considerable time either dating or thinking about dating. Dating can be a form of recreation, a source of status, a setting for learning about close relationships, as well as a way of finding a mate.

Developmental Changes in Dating

Can you remember confiding to a friend in middle school or junior high that you "liked" someone? Or what is was like when you first had an exclusive relationship with someone, "going out" with that person and only that person? One study found that 40 percent of the sixth-graders studied had announced that "I like" someone (Buhrmester, 2001). But it wasn't until the tenth grade that half of the adolescents had had a romantic relationship that lasted two months or longer. By the twelfth grade, a quarter of the adolescents still had not had a

clique A small group that ranges from 2 to about 12 individuals, averaging about 5 to 6 individuals, and can form because adolescents engage in similar activities.

crowd A larger group structure than a clique, a crowd is usually formed based on reputation, and members may or may not spend much time together.

What are dating relationships like in adolescence?

romantic relationship that lasted two months or longer. Another study found that 35 percent of 15- to 16-year-olds and almost 60 percent of 17- and 18-year-olds had had dating relationships that endured for 11 months or longer (Carver, Joyner, & Udry, 2003).

In their early exploration of romantic relationships, today's adolescents often find comfort in numbers and begin hanging out together in mixed-sex groups. Sometimes they just hang out at someone's house or get organized enough to get someone to drive them to a mall or a movie (Peterson, 1997). Or they may try *cyberdating*— "dating" over the Internet—as another alternative to traditional dating (Thomas, 1998). Cyberdating is popular especially among middle school students. Of course, cyberdating is hazardous since one does not know who is really at the other end of the computer link. By the time they reach high school and are able to drive, most adolescents are more interested in real-life dating.

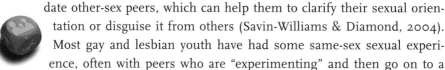

How Would You...?
As a psychologist, how would you explain the risks of cyberdating during middle school based on the cognitive development of adolescents?

Dating in Gay and Lesbian Youth

Recently, researchers have begun to study romantic relationships in gay, lesbian, and bisexual youth (Savin-Williams, 2006). Many sexual minority youth date other-sex peers, which can help them to clarify their sexual orientation or disguise it from others (Savin-Williams & Diamond, 2004). Most gay and lesbian youth have had some same-sex sexual experience, often with peers who are "experimenting" and then go on to a primarily heterosexual orientation. However, relatively few have same-sex romantic relationships because of limited opportunities and social disapproval of same-sex relationships (Diamond, 2003). In one study, gay and lesbian youth rated the breakup of a current romance as their second most stressful problem, second only to disclosure of their sexual orientation to their parents (D'Augelli, 1991).

How Would You...?
As a human development and family studies professional, how would you explain to parents the developmental challenges faced by a gay or lesbian adolescent?

Sociocultural Contexts and Dating

The sociocultural context exerts a powerful influence on adolescents' dating patterns. This influence may be seen in differences in dating patterns among ethnic groups within the United States. For example, one recent study found that Asian American adolescents were less likely to have been involved in a romantic relationship in the past 18 months than African American or Latino adolescents (Carver, Joyner, & Udry, 2003).

Values, religious beliefs, and traditions often dictate the age at which dating begins, how much freedom in dating is allowed, whether dates must be chaperoned by adults or parents, and the roles of males and females in dating. For example, Latino and Asian American cultures have more conservative standards regarding adolescent dating than does the Anglo-American culture. Dating may become a source of conflict within a family if the parents have immigrated from cultures in which dating begins at a late age, little freedom in dating is allowed, dates are chaperoned, and adolescent girl dating is especially restricted. When immigrant adolescents choose to adopt the ways of the dominant U.S. culture (such as unchaperoned dating), they often clash with parents and extended-family members who have more traditional values.

In recent research, Latina young adults in the midwestern United States reflected on their experiences in dating during adolescence (Raffaeli & Ontai, 2004). They said that their parents placed strict boundaries on their romantic involvement. As a result, the young women said that their adolescent dating experiences were filled with tension and conflict. Over half of the Latinas engaged in "sneak dating" without their parents' knowledge.

What are some ethnic variations in dating during adolescence?

Culture and Adolescent Development

We live in an increasingly diverse world, one in which there is increasing contact between adolescents from different cultures and ethnic groups. In this section, we explore these differences as they relate to adolescents. We explore how adolescents in various cultures spend their time, and some of the rites of passage they undergo. We also examine how ethnicity affects U.S. adolescents and their development.

Cross-Cultural Comparisons

What traditions remain for adolescents around the globe? What circumstances are changing adolescents' lives?

Traditions and Changes in Adolescence around the Globe

Consider some of the variations of adolescence around the world (Brown & Larson, 2002):

- Two-thirds of Asian Indian adolescents accept their parents' choice of a marital partner for them.

- In the Philippines, many female adolescents sacrifice their own futures by migrating to the city to earn money that they can send home to their families.

- In the Middle East, many adolescents are not allowed to interact with the other sex, even in school.

- Street youth in Kenya and other parts of the world learn to survive under highly stressful circumstances (Nsamenang, 2002). In some cases abandoned by their parents, they may engage in delinquency or prostitution to provide for their economic needs.

- Whereas individuals in the United States are marrying later than in past generations, youth in Russia are marrying earlier to legitimize sexual activity (Stetsenko, 2002).

Asian Indian adolescents in a marriage ceremony

Thus, depending on the culture being observed, adolescence may involve many different experiences (Larson & Wilson, 2004).

Some cultures have retained their traditions regarding adolescence, but rapid global change is altering the experience of adolescence in many places, presenting new opportunities and challenges to young people's health and well-being. Around the world, adolescents' experiences may differ.

Muslim school in Middle East with boys only

Health Adolescent health and well-being have improved in some respects but not in others. Overall, fewer adolescents around the world die from infectious diseases and malnutrition now than in the past (UNICEF, 2007). However, a number of adolescent health-compromising behaviors (especially illicit drug use and unprotected sex) are increasing in frequency (Blum & Nelson-Mmari, 2004). Extensive increases in the rates of HIV in adolescents have occurred in many sub-Saharan countries (UNICEF, 2007).

How Would You...? As a health-care professional, how would you explain to policy makers and insurance providers the importance of cultural context when creating guidelines for adolescent health coverage?

Gender Around the world, the experiences of male and female adolescents continue to be quite different (Brown & Larson, 2002). Except in a few regions, such as Japan, the Philippines, and Western countries, males have far greater access to educational opportunities than females (UNICEF, 2007). In many countries, adolescent females have less freedom than males to pursue a variety of careers and engage in various leisure activities. Gender differences in sexual expression are widespread, especially in India, Southeast Asia, Latin America, and Arab countries where there are far more restrictions on the sexual activity of adolescent females than on males. These gender differences do appear to be narrowing over time, however. In some countries, educational and career opportunities for women are expanding, and control over adolescent girls' romantic and sexual relationships is weakening.

Street youth in Rio de Janeiro

Family In some countries, adolescents grow up in closely knit families with extensive extended-kin networks that retain a traditional way of life. For example, in Arab countries, "adolescents are taught strict codes of conduct and loyalty" (Brown & Larson, 2002, p. 6). However, in Western countries such as the United States, parenting is less authoritarian than in the past, and much larger numbers of adolescents are growing up in divorced families and stepfamilies.

In many countries around the world, current trends "include greater family mobility, migration to urban areas, family members working in distant cities or countries, smaller families, fewer extended-family households, and increases in mothers' employment" (Brown & Larson, 2002, p. 7). Unfortunately, many of these changes may reduce the ability of families to spend time with their adolescents.

Peers Some cultures give peers a stronger role in adolescence than others (Brown & Larson, 2002). In most Western nations, peers figure prominently in adolescents' lives, in some cases taking on roles that are otherwise assumed by parents. Among street youth in South America, the peer network serves as a surrogate family that supports survival in dangerous and stressful settings. In other regions of the world, such as in Arab countries, peer relations are restricted, especially for girls (Booth, 2002).

Adolescents' lives, then, are characterized by a combination of change and tradition. Researchers have found both similarities and differences in the experiences of adolescents in different countries (Larson & Wilson, 2004).

rite of passage A ceremony or ritual that marks an individual's transition from one status to another. Most rites of passage focus on the transition to adult status.

Rites of Passage

Another variation in the experiences of adolescents in different cultures is whether the adolescents go through a rite of passage. Some societies have elaborate ceremonies that signal the adolescent's move to maturity and achievement of adult status (Kottak, 2004). A **rite of passage** is a ceremony or ritual that marks an individual's transition from one status to another. Most rites of passage focus on the transition to adult status. In many primitive cultures, rites of passage are the avenue through which adolescents gain access to sacred adult practices, to knowledge, and to sexuality. These rites often involve dramatic practices intended to facilitate the adolescent's separation from the immediate family, especially the mother. The transformation is usually characterized by some form of ritual death and rebirth, or by means of contact with the spiritual world. Bonds are forged between the adolescent and the adult instructors through shared rituals, hazards, and secrets

These Congolese Kota boys painted their faces as part of a rite of passage to adulthood. *What rites of passage do American adolescents have?*

to allow the adolescent to enter the adult world. This kind of ritual provides a forceful and discontinuous entry into the adult world at a time when the adolescent is perceived to be ready for the change.

An especially rich tradition of rites of passage for adolescents has prevailed in African cultures, especially sub-Saharan Africa. Under the influence of Western industrialized culture, many of these rites are disappearing today, although they are still prevalent in locations where formal education is not readily available.

Do we have such rites of passage for American adolescents? We certainly do not have universal formal ceremonies that mark the passage from adolescence to adulthood. Certain religious and social groups do, however, have initiation ceremonies that indicate that an advance in maturity has been reached: the Jewish bar and bat mitzvah, the Catholic confirmation, and social debuts, for example. School graduation ceremonies come the closest to being culture-wide rites of passage in the United States. The high school graduation ceremony has become nearly universal for middle-class adolescents and increasing numbers of adolescents from low-income backgrounds.

How Would You...?
As an educator, how would you modify high school graduation to be a more meaningful rite of passage for adolescents in the United States?

Ethnicity

Earlier in this chapter we explored the identity development of ethnic minority adolescents. Here, we further examine immigration and the relationship between ethnicity and socioeconomic status.

assimilation The absorption of
ethnic minority groups into the
dominant group, which often
involves the loss of some or
virtually all of the behavior and
values of the ethnic minority
group.

pluralism The coexistence of
distinct ethnic and cultural
groups in the same society.
Individuals with a pluralistic
stance usually advocate that
cultural differences be
maintained and appreciated.

Immigration

Relatively high rates of immigration are contributing to the growth of
ethnic minorities in the United States (Berry, 2007). Immigrants
often experience stressors uncommon to, or less prominent among,
longtime residents such as language barriers, dislocations and separations from support networks, changes in SES status, and the dual
struggle to preserve identity and to acculturate.

The adjustment of immigrants to their new country may be complicated by the fact that both native-born Americans and immigrants
may be torn between two values related to ethnic issues: assimilation
and pluralism.

- **Assimilation** is the absorption of ethnic minority groups into the dominant
  group, which often means the loss of some or virtually all of the behavior and
  values of the ethnic minority group. Individuals who endorse assimilation
  usually advocate that ethnic minority groups become more American.

- **Pluralism** is the coexistence of distinct ethnic and cultural groups in the same
  society, each of which maintains its cultural differences.

Many of the families that have immigrated in recent decades to the United
States, such as Mexican Americans and Asian Americans, come from collectivist cultures in which family obligation is strong (Fuligni & Hardway, 2004). For
adolescents, this family obligation may take the form of assisting parents in
their occupations and contributing to the family's welfare (Parke & Buriel,
2006). This often means helping out in jobs in construction, gardening,
cleaning, or restaurants. In some cases, the long hours immigrant youth work
in such jobs can be detrimental to their academic achievement.

Ethnicity and Socioeconomic Status

Much of the research on ethnic minority adolescents has
failed to tease apart the influences of ethnicity and socioeconomic status. Ethnicity and socioeconomic status can
interact in ways that exaggerate the influence of ethnicity
because ethnic minority individuals are overrepresented
in the lower socioeconomic levels of American society.
Consequently, researchers too often have given ethnic
explanations for aspects of adolescent development that
were largely due instead to socioeconomic status.

Not all ethnic minority families are poor. However,
poverty contributes to the stressful life experiences of
many ethnic minority adolescents (McLoyd, Aikens, &
Burton, 2006). Thus, many ethnic minority adolescents
experience a double disadvantage: (1) prejudice, discrimination, and bias because of their ethnic minority
status; and (2) the stressful effects of poverty.

Although some ethnic minority youth have middle-
income backgrounds, economic advantage does not
entirely enable them to escape the prejudice, discrimination, and bias associated with being a member of an
ethnic minority group (Banks, 2008). Even Japanese

Jason Leonard age 15: "I want America to know
that most of us Black teens are not troubled
people from broken homes and headed to jail. . . .
In my relationships with my parents, we show
respect for each other and we have values in our
house. We have traditions we celebrate together,
including Christmas and Kwanzaa."

Americans, who are often characterized as a "model minority" because of their strong achievement orientation and family cohesiveness, still experience stress associated with ethnic minority status.

Adolescent Problems

In Chapter 9, we described several adolescent problems: substance abuse, sexually transmitted infections, and eating disorders. In this chapter, we examine the problems of juvenile delinquency, depression, and suicide. We also explore interrelationships among adolescent problems and how such problems can be prevented or remedied.

Juvenile Delinquency

The label **juvenile delinquent** is applied to an adolescent who breaks the law or engages in behavior that is considered illegal. Like other categories of disorders, juvenile delinquency is a broad concept; legal infractions range from littering to murder. Because the adolescent technically becomes a juvenile delinquent only after being judged guilty of a crime by a court of law, official records do not accurately reflect the number of illegal acts juvenile delinquents commit. Estimates of the number of juvenile delinquents in the United States are sketchy, but FBI statistics indicate that at least 2 percent of all youth are involved in juvenile court cases.

U.S. government statistics reveal that juvenile court caseloads for males were three times higher than for females in 2002 (National Center for Juvenile Justice, 2006). In the last two decades, however, there has been a greater increase in female delinquency than in male delinquency (National Center for Juvenile Justice, 2006). For both male and female delinquents, rates for property offenses are higher than for other rates of offenses (such as offenses against persons, drug offenses, and public order offenses). Arrests of adolescent males for delinquency still are much higher than for adolescent females.

Delinquency rates among minority groups and lower-socioeconomic-status youth are especially high in proportion to the overall population of these groups. However, such groups have less influence over the judicial decision-making process in the United States and, therefore, may be judged delinquent more readily than their White, middle-socioeconomic-status counterparts.

Causes of Delinquency

What causes delinquency? Many causes have been proposed, including heredity, identity problems, community influences, and family experiences. Erik Erikson (1968), for example, argues that adolescents whose development has restricted them from acceptable social roles, or made them feel that they cannot measure up to the demands placed on them, may choose a negative identity. Adolescents with a negative identity may find support for their delinquent image among peers, reinforcing the negative identity. For Erikson, delinquency is an attempt to establish an identity, although a negative one.

Although delinquency is less exclusively a phenomenon of lower socioeconomic status than it was in the past, some characteristics of lower-class culture might promote delinquency. The norms of many lower-SES peer groups and gangs are antisocial, or counterproductive, to the goals and norms of society at large. Getting into and staying out of trouble are prominent features of life for some adolescents in low-income neighborhoods (Flannery & others, 2003). Being "tough" and "masculine" are high-status traits for lower-SES boys, and these traits are often measured by the adolescent's success in performing and getting away with delinquent acts. Furthermore, adolescents in communities with high crime rates observe many models who engage in criminal activities. These communities may be characterized by poverty, unemployment, and feelings of alienation toward the middle class. Quality schooling, educational funding, and organized neighborhood activities may be lacking in these communities (Sabol, Coulton, & Korbin, 2004).

How Would You...?

As a social worker, how would you apply your knowledge of juvenile delinquency and adolescent development to improve the juvenile justice system?

Certain characteristics of family support systems are also associated with delinquency (Dodge, Coie, & Lynam, 2006; Feinberg & others, 2007). Parents of delinquents are less skilled in discouraging antisocial behavior and in encouraging skilled behavior than are parents of nondelinquents. Parental monitoring of adolescents is especially important in determining whether an adolescent becomes a delinquent (Coley, Morris, & Hernandez, 2004). Family discord and inconsistent and inappropriate discipline are also associated with delinquency (Bor, McGee, & Fagan, 2004). And an increasing number of studies have found that siblings can have a strong influence on delinquency (Bank, Burraston, & Snyder, 2004). In one study, high levels of hostile sibling relationships and older sibling delinquency were linked with younger sibling delinquency in both brother and sister pairs (Slomkowski & others, 2001). Finally, having delinquent peers greatly increases the risk of becoming delinquent (Dodge & Dishion, 2006).

One individual whose goal is to help at-risk adolescents, such as juvenile delinquents, cope more effectively with their lives is Rodney Hammond. Read about his work in the Careers in Life-Span Development profile.

Depression and Suicide

What is the nature of depression in adolescence? What causes an adolescent to commit suicide?

Depression

Depression is more likely to occur in adolescence than in childhood and more likely to occur in adulthood than adolescence. Further, adolescent girls consistently have higher rates of depression than adolescent boys (Nolen-Hoeksema, 2007). Among the reasons for this gender difference are that females tend to ruminate in their depressed mood and amplify it; females' self-images, especially their body images, are more negative than males'; females face more discrimination than males do; and puberty occurs earlier for girls than for boys. As a result girls experience a piling up of changes and life experiences in the middle school years that can increase depression.

Certain family factors place adolescents at risk for developing depression (Eley & others, 2004). These include having a depressed parent, emotionally unavailable parents, parents who have high marital conflict, and parents with financial problems (Sheeber & others, 2007).

CAREERS IN LIFE-SPAN DEVELOPMENT

Rodney Hammond, Health Psychologist

Rodney Hammond described his college experiences:

> When I started as an undergraduate at the University of Illinois, Champaign-Urbana, I hadn't decided on my major. But to help finance my education, I took a part-time job in a child development research program sponsored by the psychology department. There, I observed inner-city children in settings designed to enhance their learning. I saw firsthand the contribution psychology can make, and I knew I wanted to be a psychologist. (American Psychological Association, 2003, p. 26)

Rodney Hammond went on to obtain a doctorate in school and community psychology with a focus on children's development. For a number of years, he trained clinical psychologists at Wright State University in Ohio and directed a program to reduce violence in ethnic minority youth. There, he and his associates taught at-risk youth how to use social skills to effectively manage conflict and to recognize situations that could lead to violence. Today, Rodney is Director of Violence Prevention at the Centers for Disease Control and Prevention in Atlanta. Rodney says that if you are interested in people and problem solving, psychology is a wonderful way to put these together.

Rodney Hammond, counseling an adolescent girl about the risks of adolescence and how to effectively cope with them.

School psychology was one of Rodney's Hammond's doctoral concentrations. School psychologists focus on improving the psychological and intellectual well-being of elementary, middle/junior, and high school students. They give psychological tests, interview students and their parents, consult with teachers, and may provide counseling to students and their families. They may work in a centralized office in a school district or in one or more schools. School psychologists usually have a master's or doctoral degree in school psychology. In graduate school, they take courses in counseling, assessment, learning, and other areas of education and psychology.

Poor peer relationships also are associated with adolescent depression (Kistner & others, 2006). Not having a close relationship with a best friend, having less contact with friends, and experiencing peer rejection all increase depressive tendencies in adolescents. Problems in adolescent romantic relationships can also trigger depression, especially for girls (Davila & Steinberg, 2006).

Suicide

Suicide behavior is rare in childhood but escalates in adolescence and then increases further in emerging adulthood (Park & others, 2006). Suicide is the third-leading cause of death in 10- to 19-year-olds today in the United States (National Center for Health Statistics, 2005). After increasing to high levels in the 1990s, suicide rates in adolescents have declined in recent years. In 2004, 4,214 U.S. individuals from 15 to 24 years of age committed suicide (Minino, Heron, & Smith, 2006).

Although a suicide threat should always be taken seriously, far more adolescents contemplate or attempt it unsuccessfully than actually commit it. In a national study, in 2005, 17 percent of U.S. high school students said that they had seriously considered or attempted suicide in the last 12 months (Eaton & others, 2006). As

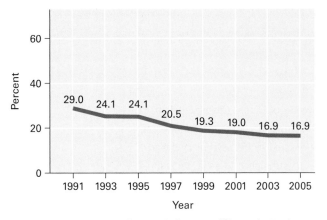

Figure 10.4 **Percentage of U.S. Ninth- to Twelfth-Grade Students Who Seriously Considered Attempting Suicide in the Previous 12 Months from 1991–2005**

What are some characteristics of adolescents who become depressed? What are some factors that are linked with suicide attempts by adolescents?

shown in Figure 10.4, this percentage has declined since 1991. In the national survey, in 2005, 2.3 percent reported a suicide attempt that resulted in an injury, poisoning, or drug overdose that had been treated by a doctor. Females were more likely to attempt suicide than males, but males were more likely to succeed in committing suicide (Whetstone, Morrissey, & Cummings, 2007). Males use more lethal means, such as guns, in their suicide attempts, whereas adolescent females are more likely to cut their wrists or take an overdose of sleeping pills—methods less likely to result in death. A recent study of adolescents indicated that suicide ideation peaked at age 15 (Rueter & Kwon, 2005).

Both early and later experiences may be involved in suicide attempts (Favaro, Ferrara, & Santonastaso, 2007). The adolescent might have a long-standing history of family instability and unhappiness. Lack of affection and emotional support, high control, and pressure for achievement by parents during childhood are likely to show up as factors in suicide attempts. One recent review of research found a link that adolescents who had been physically or sexually abused were more likely to have suicidal thoughts than adolescents who had not experienced such abuse (Evans, Hawton, & Rodham, 2005). The adolescent might also lack supportive friendships. Recent and current stressful circumstances, such as getting poor grades in school and experiencing the breakup of a romantic relationship, may trigger suicide attempts (Antai-Oton, 2003).

How Would You...?
As a psychologist, how would you talk with an adolescent who has just threatened suicide?

The Interrelation of Problems and Successful Prevention/Intervention Programs

We have described some of the major adolescent problems in this chapter and in Chapter 9: substance abuse; juvenile delinquency; school-related problems, such as dropping out of school; adolescent pregnancy and sexually transmitted infections; eating disorders; depression; and suicide.

The four problems that affect the most adolescents are (1) drug abuse, (2) juvenile delinquency, (3) sexual problems, and (4) school-related problems (Dryfoos, 1990; Dryfoos & Barkin, 2006). The adolescents most at risk have more than one of these problems. Researchers are increasingly finding that problem behaviors in adolescence are interrelated (Nation & Heflinger, 2006; Thompson, Ho, & Kingree, 2007). For example, heavy substance abuse is related to early sexual activity, lower grades, dropping out of school, and delinquency (Mason, Hitchings, & Spoth, 2007). Early initiation of sexual activity is associated with the use of cigarettes and alcohol, the use of marijuana and other illicit drugs, lower grades, dropping out of school, and delinquency. Delinquency is related to early sexual activity, early pregnancy, substance abuse, and dropping out of school. As many as 10 percent of adolescents in the United States have been estimated to engage in all four of these problem behaviors (for example, adolescents who have dropped out of school, are behind in their grade level, are users of heavy drugs, regularly use cigarettes and marijuana, and are sexually active but do not use contraception). In 1990, it was estimated that another 15 percent of high-risk youth engage in two or three of the four main problem behaviors (Dryfoos, 1990). Recently, this figure was increased to 20 percent of all U.S. adolescents (Dryfoos & Barkin, 2006).

A review of the programs that have been successful in preventing or reducing adolescent problems found these common components (Dryfoos, 1990; Dryfoos & Barkin, 2006):

1. *Intensive individualized attention.* In successful programs, high-risk adolescents are attached to a responsible adult, who gives the adolescent attention and deals with the adolescent's specific needs. This theme occurs in a number of programs. In a successful substance-abuse program, a student assistance counselor is available full-time for individual counseling and referral for treatment.

2. *Community-wide multiagency collaborative approaches.* The basic philosophy of community-wide programs is that a number of different programs and services have to be in place. In one successful substance-abuse program, a community-wide health promotion campaign has been implemented that uses local media and community education, in concert with a substance-abuse curriculum in the schools.

3. *Early identification and intervention.* Reaching younger children and their families before children develop problems, or at the beginning of their problems, is a successful strategy (Aber & others, 2006). One preschool program serves as an excellent model for the prevention of delinquency, pregnancy, substance abuse, and dropping out of school. Operated by the High/Scope Foundation in Ypsilanti, Michigan, the Perry Preschool has had a long-term positive impact on its students. This enrichment program, directed by David Weikart, serves disadvantaged African American children. They attend a high-quality two-year preschool program and receive weekly home visits from program personnel. Based on official police records, by age 19, individuals who had attended the Perry Preschool program were less likely to have been arrested and reported fewer adult offenses than a control group did. The Perry Preschool students also were less likely to drop out of school, and teachers rated their social behavior as more competent than that of a control group who had not received the enriched preschool experience (High/Scope Resource, 2005).

Summary

Identity

Identity development is complex and is done in bits and pieces. Erikson argues that identity versus identity confusion is the fifth stage of the human life span, which individuals experience during adolescence. A psychosocial moratorium during adolescence allows the personality and role experimentation that are important aspects of identity development. James Marcia proposed four identity statuses—identity diffusion, foreclosure, moratorium, and achievement—that are based on crisis (exploration) and commitment. Increasingly, experts argue the main changes in identity occur in emerging adulthood rather than adolescence. Individuals often follow *moratorium-achievement-moratorium-achievement* (MAMA) cycles in their lives. Identity development is facilitated by family relations that promote both individuality and connectedness. Throughout the world, ethnic minority groups have struggled to maintain their identities while blending into the majority culture.

Families

Many parents have a difficult time handling the adolescent's push for autonomy, even though the push is one of the hallmarks of adolescence. Adolescents do not simply move into a world isolated from parents; attachment to parents increases the probability that an adolescent will be socially competent. Parent-adolescent conflict increases in adolescence. The conflict is usually moderate rather than severe, and the increased conflict may serve the positive developmental function of promoting autonomy and identity. A subset of adolescents experiences high parent-adolescent conflict, which is linked with negative outcomes.

Peers

Harry Stack Sullivan argued that there is a dramatic increase in the psychological importance and intimacy of close friends in early adolescence. The pressure to conform to peers is strong during adolescence, especially during the eighth and ninth grades. Cliques and crowds assume more importance in the lives of adolescents than in the lives of children. Membership in certain crowds is associated with increased self-esteem. Dating can have many functions. Younger adolescents often begin to hang out together in mixed-sex groups. Many gay male and lesbian youth date other-sex peers, which can help them to clarify their sexual orientation or disguise it from others. Culture can exert a powerful influence on adolescent dating.

Culture and Adolescent Development

In some countries, traditions are being continued in the socialization of adolescents, whereas in others, substantial changes in the experiences of adolescents are taking place. Ceremonies mark an individual's transition from one status to another, especially into adulthood. In primitive cultures, rites of passage are often well defined. In contemporary America, rites of passage to adulthood are ill-defined. Many of the families that have immigrated in recent decades to the United States come from collectivist cultures in which there is a strong sense of family obligation. Much of the research on ethnic minority adolescents has not teased apart the influences of ethnicity and socioeconomic status. Because of this failure, too often researchers have given ethnic explanations for characteristics that were largely due to socioeconomic factors. Although not all ethnic minority families are poor, poverty contributes to the stress of many ethnic minority adolescents.

Adolescent Problems

A juvenile delinquent is an adolescent who breaks the law or engages in conduct that is considered illegal. Heredity, identity problems, community influences, and family experiences have been proposed as causes of juvenile delinquency. Adolescents have a higher rate of depression than children. Female adolescents are more likely to have mood and depressive disorders than male adolescents are. Adolescent suicide is the third leading cause of death in U.S. adolescents. Both early and later experiences may be involved in suicide's causes. Researchers are increasingly finding that problem behaviors in adolescence are interrelated. Dryfoos found a number of common components in successful programs designed to prevent or reduce adolescent problems: They provide individual attention to high-risk adolescents, they develop community-wide intervention, and they include early identification and intervention.

Key Terms

crisis 286
commitment 286
identity diffusion 286
identity foreclosure 286
identity moratorium 286

identity achievement 286
individuality 287
connectedness 287
ethnic identity 287
clique 293

crowd 293
rite of passage 297
assimilation 298
pluralism 298
juvenile delinquent 299

11

Physical and Cognitive Development in Early Adulthood

Stories of Life-Span Development: Dave Eggers, Pursuing a Career in the Face of Stress

Dave was a senior in college when both of his parents died of cancer within five weeks of each other. What would he do? He and his 8-year-old brother left Chicago to live in California, where his older sister was entering law school. Dave would take care of his younger brother, but he needed a job. That first summer, he took a class in furniture-painting; then he worked for a geological surveying company, re-creating maps on a computer. Soon, though, he did something very different—with friends from high school,

Dave Eggers started *Might*, a satirical magazine for twentysomethings. It was an edgy, highly acclaimed publication, but not a moneymaker. After a few years, Eggers had to shut down the magazine, and he abandoned California for New York.

This does not sound like a promising start for a career. But within a decade after his parents' death, Eggers had not only raised his young brother but also had founded a quarterly journal and Web site, *McSweeney's*, and had written a best

seller, *A Heartbreaking Work of Staggering Genius,* which received the National Book Critics Circle Award and was nominated for a Pulitzer Prize. It is a slightly fictionalized account of Eggers' life as he helped care for his dying mother, raised his brother, and searched for his own place in the world. Despite the pain of his loss and the responsibility for his brother, Eggers quickly built a record of achievement as a young adult.

Recall from Chapter 1 that *early adulthood* is the developmental period that begins in the late teens or early twenties and lasts through the thirties. In this chapter, we explore many aspects of physical and cognitive development in early adulthood. These include some of the areas that were so important in David Eggers' life, such as maximizing his creative talents and pursuing a career. We also explore changes in physical development, sexuality, and cognitive development. However, we begin where we left off in Chapter 10 and address the transition from adolescence to adulthood, a time during which Dave Eggers displayed resilience in face of intense stress. ▮

Dave Eggers, talented and insightful author.

The Transition from Adolescence to Adulthood

When does an adolescent become an adult? In Chapter 9, we saw that it is not easy to tell when a girl or a boy enters adolescence. The task of determining when an individual becomes an adult is more difficult.

Becoming an Adult

For most individuals, becoming an adult involves a lengthy transition period. Recently, the transition from adolescence to adulthood has been referred to as **emerging adulthood**, which occurs from approximately 18 to 25 years of age (Arnett, 2006, 2007). Experimentation and exploration characterize the emerging adult. At this point in their development, many individuals are still exploring which career path they want to follow, what they want their identity to be, and which lifestyle they want to adopt (for example, single, cohabiting, or married).

Key Features

Jeffrey Arnett (2006) recently concluded that five key features characterize emerging adulthood:

- *Identity exploration, especially in love and work.* Emerging adulthood is the time during which key changes in identity take place for many individuals.

- *Instability.* Residential changes peak during early adulthood, a time during which there also is often instability in love, work, and education.

- *Self-focused.* According to Arnett (2006, p. 10), emerging adults "are self-focused in the sense that they have little in the way of social obligations, little in the way of duties and commitments to others, which leaves with a great deal of autonomy in running their own lives."

- *Feeling in-between.* Many emerging adults don't consider themselves adolescents or full-fledged adults.

- *The age of possibilities, a time when individuals have an opportunity to transform their lives.* Arnett (2006) describes two ways in which emerging adulthood is the age of possibilities: (1) many emerging adults are optimistic about their future; and (2) for emerging adults who have experienced difficult times while growing up, emerging adulthood presents an opportunity to direct their lives in a more positive direction (Schulenberg & Zarrett, 2006).

Consider the changing life of Michael Maddaus (Broderick, 2003; Masten, Obradovic, & Burt, 2006). Growing up as a child and adolescent in Minneapolis, his mother drank heavily and his stepfather abused him. He coped by spending increasing time on the streets, being arrested more than 20 times for his delinquency, frequently being placed in

detention centers, and rarely going to school. At 17, he joined the Navy and the experience helped him to gain self-discipline and hope. After his brief stint in the Navy, he completed a GED and began taking community college classes. However, he continued to have some setbacks with drugs and alcohol. A defining moment as an emerging adult came when he delivered furniture to a surgeon's home. The surgeon became interested in helping Michael, and his mentorship led to Michael volunteering at a rehabilitation center, then to a job with a neurosurgeon. Eventually, he obtained his undergraduate degree, went to medical school, got married, and started

Dr. Michael Maddaus talking with a troubled youth.

a family. Today, Michael Maddaus is a successful surgeon. One of his most gratifying volunteer activities is telling his story to troubled youth.

In a longitudinal study, Ann Masten and her colleagues (2006) found that emerging adults who became competent after experiencing difficulties while growing up were more intelligent, experienced higher parenting quality, and were less likely to grow up in poverty or low-income circumstances than their counterparts who did not become competent as emerging adults. A further analysis focused on individuals who were still showing maladaptive patterns in emerging adulthood but had gotten their lives together by the time they were in the late twenties and early thirties. The three characteristics shared by these "late-bloomers" were support by adults, being planful, and showing positive aspects of autonomy. In some cases, "...military service, marriage and romantic relationships, higher education, religion affiliations, and work opportunities may provide turning-point opportunities for changing the life course during emerging adulthood" (Masten, Obradovic, & Burt, 2006, p. 179).

How Would You...?
As a social worker, how would you apply your knowledge of contemporary society to counsel a client making the transition into adulthood?

Markers of Becoming an Adult

In the United States, the most widely recognized marker of entry into adulthood is holding a more or less permanent full-time job, which usually happens when an individual finishes school—high school for some, college for others, graduate or professional school for still others. However, other criteria are far from clear. Economic independence is one marker of adult status, but achieving it is often a long process. College graduates are increasingly returning to live with their parents as they attempt to establish themselves economically. A longitudinal study found that at age 25 only slightly more than half of the participants were fully financially independent of their family of origin (Cohen & others, 2003). The most dramatic findings in this study, though, involved the extensive variability in the individual trajectories of adult roles across ten years from 17 to 27 years of age; many of the participants moved back and forth between increasing and decreasing economic dependency.

Other studies show us that taking responsibility for oneself is likely an important marker of adult status for many individuals. For example, in one study more than 70 percent of college students said that being an adult means accepting responsibility for the consequences of one's actions, deciding on one's own beliefs and values, and establishing a relationship with parents as an equal adult (Arnett, 1995).

What we have said about the markers of adult status mainly characterize individuals in industrialized societies, especially Americans. Are the criteria for adulthood the same in developing countries as they are in the United States? In developing countries, marriage is more often a significant marker for entry into adulthood, and this usually occurs much earlier than the adulthood markers in the United States (Arnett, 2004).

The Transition from High School to College

For many individuals in developed countries, going from high school to college is an important aspect of the transition to adulthood. Just as the transition from elementary school to middle or junior high school involves change and possible stress, so does the transition from high school to college. The two transitions have many parallels. Going from being a senior in high school to being a freshman in college replays the top-dog phenomenon of transferring from the oldest and most powerful group of students to the youngest and least powerful group of students that occurred earlier as adolescence began. For many students, the transition from high school to college involves movement to a larger, more impersonal school structure; interaction with peers from more diverse geographical and sometimes more diverse ethnic backgrounds; and increased focus on achievement and its assessment. And like the transition from elementary to middle or junior high school, the transition from high school to college can involve positive features. Students are more likely to feel grown up, have more subjects from which to select, have more time to spend with peers, have more opportunities to explore different lifestyles and values, enjoy greater independence from parental monitoring, and be challenged intellectually by academic work (Santrock & Halonen, 2008).

Most college campuses have a counseling center with access to mental health professionals who can help you to learn effective ways to cope with stress. Counselors can provide good information about coping with stress and academic matters. To read about the work of college counselor Grace Leaf, see the Careers in Life-Span Development profile.

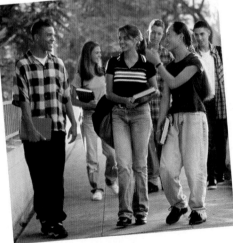

The transition from high school to college often involves positive as well as negative features. In college, students are likely to feel grown up, be able to spend more time with peers, have more opportunities to explore different lifestyles and values, and enjoy greater freedom from parental monitoring. However, college involves a larger, more impersonal school structure and an increased focus on achievement and its assessment. *What was your transition to college like?*

Grace Leaf, College/Career Counselor

Grace Leaf is a counselor at Spokane Community College in Washington. She has a master's degree in educational leadership and is working toward a doctoral degree in educational leadership at Gonzaga University in Washington. Her job involves teaching orientation for international students, conducting individual and group advising, and doing individual and group career planning. Grace tries to connect students with goals and values and help them design an educational program that fits their needs and visions.

College counselors help students to cope with adjustment problems, identify their abilities and interests, develop academic plans, and explore career options. Some have an undergraduate degree, others a master's degree like Grace Leaf. Some college counselors have a graduate degree in counseling; others may have an undergraduate degree in psychology or another discipline.

Grace Leaf, counseling college students at Spokane Community College about careers.

Physical Development

As emerging and young adults learn more about healthy lifestyles and how they contribute to a longer life span, they are increasingly interested in learning about their physical performance, health, nutrition, exercise, and addiction.

Physical Performance and Development

Most of us reach our peak physical performance before the age of 30, often between the ages of 19 and 26. This peak of physical performance occurs not only for the average young adult, but for outstanding athletes as well. Even though athletes as a group keep getting better than their predecessors—running faster, jumping higher, and lifting more weight—the age at which they reach their peak performance has remained virtually the same.

Different types of athletes, however, reach their peak performances at different ages. Most swimmers and gymnasts peak in their late teens. Golfers and marathon runners tend to peak in their late twenties. In other areas of athletics, peak performance is often in the early to mid-twenties.

Not only do we reach our peak in physical performance during early adulthood, it is also during this age period that we begin to decline in physical performance. Muscle tone and strength usually begin to show signs of decline around the age of 30. Sagging chins and protruding abdomens also may begin to appear for the first time. The lessening of physical abilities is a common complaint among the just-turned thirties. Sensory systems show little change in early adulthood, but the lens of the eye loses some of its elasticity and becomes less able to change shape and focus on near objects. Hearing peaks in adolescence, remains constant in the first part of early adulthood, and then begins to decline in the last part of early adulthood. And in the mid- to late twenties, the body's fatty tissue increases.

Health

Emerging adults have more than twice the mortality rate of adolescents (Park & others, 2006) (see Figure 11.1). As indicated in Figure 11.1, males are mainly responsible for the higher mortality rate of emerging adults.

Although emerging adults have a higher death rate than adolescents, emerging adults have few chronic health problems, and they have fewer colds and respiratory problems than when they were children (Rimsza & Kirk, 2005). Although most college students know what it takes to prevent illness and promote health, they don't fare very well when it comes to applying this information to themselves (Murphy-Hoefer, Alder, & Higbee, 2004).

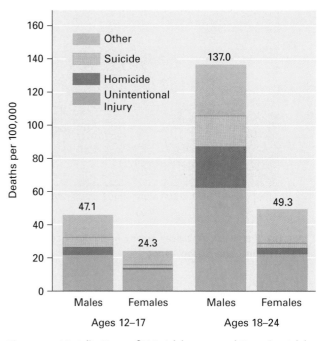

Figure 11.1 Mortality Rates of U.S. Adolescents and Emerging Adults

A longitudinal study revealed that most bad health habits engaged in during adolescence increased in emerging adulthood (Harris & others, 2006). Inactivity, diet, obesity, substance use, reproductive health care, and health-care access worsened in emerging adulthood. For example, when they were 12 to 18 years of age, only 5 percent reported no weekly exercise but when they became 19 to 26 years of age, 46 percent said they did not exercise during a week.

In emerging and early adulthood, few individuals stop to think about how their personal lifestyles will affect their health later in their adult lives. As emerging adults, many of us develop a pattern of not eating breakfast, not eating regular meals, and relying on snacks as our main food source during the day, eating excessively to the point where we exceed the normal weight for our age, smoking moderately or excessively, drinking moderately or excessively, failing to exercise, and getting by with only a few hours of sleep at night (Cousineau, Goldstein, & Franco, 2005). These lifestyles are associated with poor health, which in turn impacts life satisfaction. In the Berkeley Longitudinal Study—in which individuals were evaluated over a period of 40 years—physical health at age 30 predicted life satisfaction at age 70, more so for men than for women (Mussen, Honzik, & Eichorn, 1982).

The health profile of emerging and young adults can be improved by reducing the incidence of certain health-impairing lifestyles, such as overeating, and by engaging in health-improving lifestyles that include good eating habits, exercising regularly, and not abusing drugs (Robbins, Powers, & Burgess, 2008).

Why might it be easy to develop bad health habits in emerging and early adulthood?

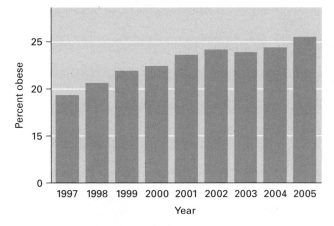

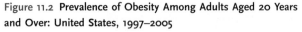

Figure 11.2 **Prevalence of Obesity Among Adults Aged 20 Years and Over: United States, 1997–2005**

Eating and Weight

In Chapters 5 and 7, we discussed aspects of overweight children's lives, and in Chapter 9 we examined the eating disorders of anorexia nervosa and bulimia nervosa in adolescence. Now, we turn our attention to obesity and the extensive preoccupation that many young adults have with dieting.

Obesity

Obesity is a serious and pervasive health problem for many individuals (Centers for Disease Control and Prevention, 2006; Corbin & others, 2008). As shown in Figure 11.2, the prevalence of obesity in U.S. adults 20 years of age and older increased from 19 percent in 1997 to 25 percent in 2005 (Centers for Disease Control and Prevention, 2006). In this survey, obesity was defined as having a body mass index (which takes into account height and weight) of 30 or more. In the survey, 22 percent of U.S. adults 20 to 39 years of age were classified as obese in 2005.

Obesity is linked to increased risk of hypertension, diabetes, and cardiovascular disease (Hahn, Payne, & Lucas, 2008). For individuals who are 30 percent overweight, the probability of dying in middle adulthood increases by about 40 percent.

Dieting

How Would You...?
As a health-care professional, how would you counsel young women of normal weight to accept their body image and set point for weight management?

Ironically, while obesity is on the rise, dieting has become an obsession with many Americans (Malik & Hu, 2007). Although many Americans regularly embark on a diet, few are successful in keeping weight off long term. Some critics argue that all diets fail (Wooley & Garner, 1991).

However, studies show that some individuals do lose weight and maintain the loss (Brownell & Cohen, 1995). How often this occurs, and whether some diet programs work better than others, are still open questions.

What we do know about losing weight is that the most effective programs include exercise (Fahey, Insel, & Roth, 2007). Exercise not only burns up calories, but continues to elevate the person's metabolic rate for several hours *after* exercising (Janssen & others, 2004). A recent study of approximately 2,000 U.S. adults found that exercising 30 minutes a day, planning meals, and weighing themselves daily were the main strategies that successful dieters used compared to unsuccessful dieters (Kruger, Blanck, & Gillepse, 2006) (see Figure 11.3).

Even when diets do produce weight loss, they can place the dieter at risk for other health problems (Cunningham & Hyson, 2006). One main concern focuses on weight cycling—yo-yo dieting—in which the person is in a recurring cycle of weight loss and weight gain (Janacek & others, 2005). Also, liquid diets and other very low calorie strategies are linked with gallbladder damage.

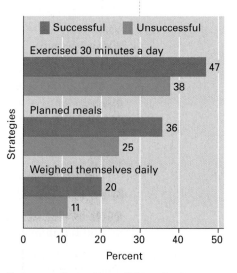

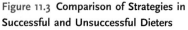

Figure 11.3 **Comparison of Strategies in Successful and Unsuccessful Dieters**

With these problems in mind, when overweight people diet and maintain their weight loss, they do become less depressed and reduce their risk for a number of health-impairing disorders (Daubenmeir & others, 2007; Mensah & Brown, 2007).

Regular Exercise

One of the main reasons that health experts want people to exercise is that it helps to prevent diseases, such as heart disease and diabetes (Hoeger & Hoeger, 2008). Many health experts recommend that young adults engage in 30 minutes or more of aerobic exercise a day, preferably every day. **Aerobic exercise** is sustained exercise—jogging, swimming, or cycling, for example—that stimulates heart and lung activity. Most health experts recommend that you raise your heart rate to at least 60 percent of your maximum heart rate. Only about one-fifth of adults, however, are active at these recommended levels of physical activity.

Researchers have found that exercise benefits not only physical health, but mental health as well. In particular, exercise improves self-concept and reduces anxiety and depression (Brenes & others, 2007). Meta-analyses have shown that exercise can be as effective in reducing depression as psychotherapy (Richardson & others, 2005). One recent study of more than 600 adults found that exercise was associated with positive mental health, and obesity was linked to poor mental health (Rohrer, Pierce, & Blackburn, 2005).

Substance Abuse

In Chapter 9, we explored substance abuse in adolescence. Fortunately, by the time individuals reach their mid-twenties, many have reduced their use of alcohol and drugs. Let's take a closer look at use of alcohol and nicotine by young adults and at the nature of addiction.

Alcohol

Let's examine two problems associated with drinking: binge drinking and alcoholism.

Binge Drinking Heavy binge drinking often increases in college, and it can take its toll on students (Wu & others, 2007). Chronic binge drinking is more common among college men than women and students living away from home, especially in fraternity houses (Schulenberg & others, 2000).

In a national survey of drinking patterns on 140 campuses (Wechsler & others, 1994), almost half of the binge drinkers reported problems that included missing classes, physical injuries, troubles with police, and having unprotected sex. For example, binge-drinking college students were 11 times more likely to fall behind in school, 10 times more likely to drive after drinking, and twice as likely to have unprotected sex than college students who did not binge drink. Also, one study found that after an evening of binge drinking memory retrieval was significantly impaired during the alcohol hangover the next morning (Verster & others, 2002).

A special concern is the increase in binge drinking by females during emerging adulthood. One study found a 125 percent increase in binge drinking at all-women colleges from 1993 through 2001 (Wechsler & others, 2002).

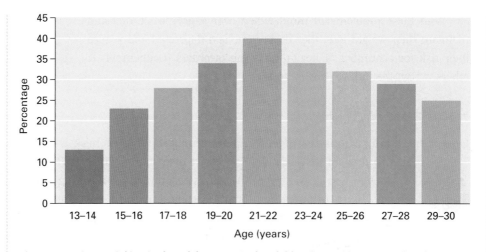

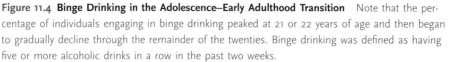

Figure 11.4 **Binge Drinking in the Adolescence–Early Adulthood Transition**   Note that the percentage of individuals engaging in binge drinking peaked at 21 or 22 years of age and then began to gradually decline through the remainder of the twenties. Binge drinking was defined as having five or more alcoholic drinks in a row in the past two weeks.

How Would You…?

As a social worker, how would you apply your understanding of binge drinking to develop a program to encourage responsible alcohol use on college campuses?

When does binge drinking peak during development? A longitudinal study revealed that binge drinking peaks at about 21 to 22 years of age and then declines through the remainder of the twenties (Bachman & others, 2002) (see Figure 11.4).

Alcoholism   *Alcoholism* is a disorder that involves long-term, repeated, uncontrolled, compulsive, and excessive use of alcoholic beverages and that impairs the drinker's health and social relationships. One in nine individuals who drinks continues the path to alcoholism. Those who do are disproportionately related to alcoholics (Redgrave & others, 2007). Family studies consistently reveal a high frequency of alcoholism in the first-degree relatives of alcoholics (Conway, Swendsen, & Merikangas, 2003). Indeed, researchers have found that heredity likely plays a role in alcoholism, although the precise hereditary mechanism has not been found (Miles & Williams, 2007). An estimated 50 to 60 percent of individuals who become alcoholics are believed to have a genetic predisposition for it.

Although studies reveal a genetic influence on alcoholism, they also show that environmental factors play a role (Ksir, Hart, & Ray, 2008). For example, family studies indicate that many individuals who suffer from alcoholism do not have close relatives who are addicted to alcohol (Martin & Sher, 1994). Large cultural variations in alcohol also underscore the environment's role in alcoholism.

Cigarette Smoking and Nicotine

Converging evidence from a number of studies underscores the dangers of smoking or being around those who do (Akhter & others, 2007). For example, smoking is linked to 30 percent of cancer deaths, 21 percent of heart disease deaths, and 82 percent of chronic pulmonary disease deaths. Secondhand smoke is implicated in as many as 9,000 lung cancer deaths a year. Children of smokers are at special risk for respiratory and middle-ear diseases (Wallace-Bell, 2003).

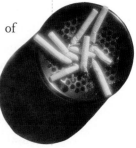

Fewer people smoke today than in the past, and almost half of all living adults who ever smoked have quit. In the United States, the prevalence of smoking in men has dropped from 42 percent in 1965 to 21 percent today (Centers for Disease Control and Prevention, 2006). However, more than 50 million Americans still smoke cigarettes today. And cigar smoking and tobacco chewing, with risks similar to those of cigarette smoking, have increased.

Most adult smokers would like to quit, but their addiction to nicotine often makes quitting a challenge (Pineda & Oberman, 2006). Nicotine, the active drug in cigarettes, is a stimulant that increases the smoker's energy and alertness, a pleasurable and reinforcing experience. Nicotine also stimulates neurotransmitters that have a calming or pain-reducing effect.

Studies indicate that when people do stop smoking, their risk of cancer is reduced (Hughes, 2003). Five years after people stop smoking, their health risk is noticeably lower than people who continue to smoke (U.S. Surgeon General's Report, 1990).

"there's no shooting—we just make you keep smoking."

Sexuality

We do not need sex for everyday survival the way we need food and water, but we do need it for the survival of the species. In Chapter 9, we explored at how adolescents develop a sexual identity and become sexually active. What happens to their sexuality in adulthood? Let's examine the sexual activity of Americans and their sexual orientation, as well as some of the problems that can be associated with sexual activity.

Sexual Activity in Emerging Adulthood

At the beginning of emerging adulthood (age 18), surveys indicate that slightly more than 60 percent of individuals have experienced sexual intercourse, but by the end of emerging adulthood (age 25), most individuals have had sexual intercourse (Lefkowitz & Gillen, 2006). Also, the average age of marriage in the United States is currently 27 for males and 26 for females (Poponoe & Whitehead, 2006). Thus, emerging adulthood is a time frame during which most individuals are "both sexually active and unmarried" (Lefkowitz & Gillen, 2006, p. 235).

Patterns of heterosexual behavior for males and females in emerging adulthood include the following (Lefkowitz & Gillen, 2006): (1) Males have more casual sexual partners, and females report being more selective about their choice of a sexual partner. (2) Casual sex is a more common in emerging adulthood than in young adulthood. One study indicated that 30 percent of emerging adults said they had "hooked up" with someone and had sexual intercourse during college (Paul, McManus, & Hayes, 2000).

Sexual Orientation and Behavior

Obtaining accurate information about such a private activity as sexual behavior is not easy. The best information we currently have comes from what is often referred to as the 1994 Sex in America survey. In this well-designed, comprehensive study

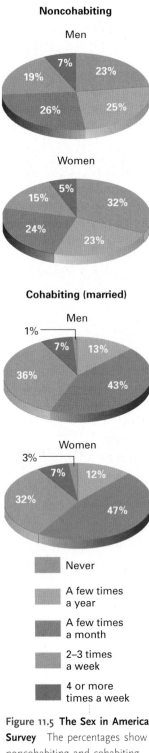

Noncohabiting

Men

Women

Cohabiting (married)

Men

1%

Women

3%

■ Never

■ A few times
a year

■ A few times
a month

■ 2–3 times
a week

■ 4 or more
times a week

Figure 11.5 The Sex in America Survey The percentages show noncohabiting and cohabiting (married) males' and females' responses to the question "How often have you had sex in the past year?" in a 1994 survey (Michael & others, 1994). *What was one feature of the Sex in America survey that made it superior to most surveys of sexual behavior?*

of American adults' sexual patterns, Robert Michael and his colleagues (1994) interviewed more than 3,000 people from 18 to 59 years of age who were randomly selected, a sharp contrast from earlier samples that were based on unrepresentative groups of volunteers.

Heterosexual Attitudes and Behavior

Here are some of the key findings from the 1994 Sex in America survey:

- Americans tend to fall into three categories: One-third have sex twice a week or more, one-third a few times a month, and one-third a few times a year or not at all.
- Married (and cohabiting) couples have sex more often than non-cohabiting couples (see Figure 11.5).
- Most Americans do not engage in kinky sexual acts. When asked about their favorite sexual acts, the vast majority (96 percent) said that vaginal sex was "very" or "somewhat" appealing. Oral sex was in third place, after an activity that many have not labeled a sexual act—watching a partner undress.
- Adultery is clearly the exception rather than the rule. Nearly 75 percent of the married men and 85 percent of the married women indicated that they have never been unfaithful.
- Men think about sex far more than women do—54 percent of the men said they think about it every day or several times a day, whereas 67 percent of the women said they think about it only a few times a week or a few times a month.

In sum, one of the most powerful messages in the 1994 survey was that Americans' sexual lives are more conservative than previously believed. Although 17 percent of the men and 3 percent of the women said they have had sex with at least 21 partners, the overall impression from the survey was that sexual behavior is ruled by marriage and monogamy for most Americans.

Sources of Sexual Orientation

Until the end of the nineteenth century, it was generally believed that people were either heterosexual or homosexual. Today, it is more accepted to view sexual orientation, not as an either/or proposition, but as a continuum from exclusive male-female relations to exclusive same-sex relations (Strong & others, 2008). Some individuals are also *bisexual,* being sexually attracted to people of both sexes.

In the Sex in America survey, 2.7 percent of the men and 1.3 percent of the women reported that they had had same-sex relations in the past year (Michael & others, 1994). Why are some individuals lesbian, gay, or bisexual (LGB) and others heterosexual? Speculation about this question has been extensive (Crooks & Baur, 2008).

All people, regardless of their sexual orientation, have similar physiological responses during sexual arousal and seem to be aroused by the same types of tactile stimulation. Investigators typically find

What likely determines an individual's sexual preference?

no differences between LGBs and heterosexuals in a wide range of attitudes, behaviors, and adjustments (Peplau & Fingerhut, 2007).

Recently, researchers have explored the possible biological basis of same-sex relations. The results of hormone studies have been inconsistent (Gooren, 2006). If gay males are given male sex hormones (androgens), their sexual orientation doesn't change. Their sexual desire merely increases. A very early prenatal critical period might influence sexual orientation (James, 2005). In the second to fifth months after conception, exposure of the fetus to hormone levels characteristic of females might cause the individual (male or female) to become attracted to males (Ellis & Ames, 1987). If this critical-period hypothesis turns out to be correct, it would explain why clinicians have found that sexual orientation is difficult, if not impossible, to modify.

An individual's sexual orientation—same-sex, heterosexual, or bisexual—is most likely determined by a combination of genetic, hormonal, cognitive, and environmental factors (Baldwin & Baldwin, 1998). Most experts on same-sex relations believe that no one factor alone causes sexual orientation, and that the relative weight of each factor can vary from one individual to the next.

Attitudes and Behavior of Lesbians and Gay Males

Many gender differences that appear in heterosexual relationships occur in same-sex relationships (Savin-Williams, 2006). For example, like heterosexual women, lesbians have fewer sexual partners than gay men, and lesbians have less permissive attitudes about casual sex outside a primary relationship than gay men (Peplau & Fingerhut, 2007).

How can lesbians and gay males adapt to a world in which they are a minority? According to psychologist Laura Brown (1989), lesbians and gay males experience life as a minority in a dominant, majority culture. For lesbians and gay men, developing a *bicultural identity* creates new ways of defining themselves. Brown believes that lesbians and gay males adapt best when they don't define themselves in polarities, such as trying to live in an encapsulated lesbian or gay male world completely divorced from the majority culture or completely accepting the dictates and bias of the majority culture.

How Would You...?
As a human development and family studies professional, what information would you include in a program designed to educate young adults about healthy sexuality and sexual relationships?

SEXUALITY

317

Sexually Transmitted Infections

Sexually transmitted infections (STIs) are diseases that are primarily contracted through sex—intercourse as well as oral-genital and anal-genital sex. STIs affect about one of every six U.S. adults (National Center for Health Statistics, 2006). Among the most prevalent STIs are bacterial infections—such as gonorrhea, syphilis, and chlamydia—and STIs caused by viruses—such as AIDS (acquired immune deficiency syndrome), genital herpes, and genital warts. Figure 11.6 describes these sexually transmitted infections.

No single disease has had a greater impact on sexual behavior, or created more public fear in the last several decades, than infection with the human immunodeficiency virus (HIV) (Strong & others, 2008). HIV is a virus that destroys the body's immune system. Once infected with HIV, the virus breaks down and overpowers the immune system, which leads to AIDS. An individual sick with AIDS has such a weakened immune system that a common cold can be life-threatening.

As of January 1, 2005, 310,000 cases of AIDS in 25- to 34-year-olds had been reported in the United States, with about 80 percent of these being males and almost half intravenous (IV) drug users (Centers for Disease Control and Prevention, 2006). Because of education and the development of more effective drug treatments, deaths due to HIV/AIDS have begun to decline in the United States (Centers for Disease Control and Prevention, 2006).

STI	Description/cause	Incidence	Treatment
Gonorrhea	Commonly called the "drip" or "clap." Caused by the bacterium *Neisseria gonorrhoeae*. Spread by contact between infected moist membranes (genital, oral-genital, or anal-genital) of two individuals. Characterized by discharge from penis or vagina and painful urination. Can lead to infertility.	500,000 cases annually in U.S.	Penicillin, other antibiotics
Syphilis	Caused by the bacterium *Treponema pallidum*. Characterized by the appearance of a sore where syphilis entered the body. The sore can be on the external genitals, vagina, or anus. Later, a skin rash breaks out on palms of hands and bottom of feet. If not treated, can eventually lead to paralysis or even death.	100,000 cases annually in U.S.	Penicillin
Chlamydia	A common STI named for the bacterium *Chlamydia trachomatis*, an organism that spreads by sexual contact and infects the genital organs of both sexes. A special concern is that females with chlamydia may become infertile. It is recommended that adolescent and young adult females have an annual screening for this STI.	About 3 million cases annually in U.S.	Antibiotics
Genital herpes	Caused by a family of viruses with different strains. Involves an eruption of sores and blisters. Spread by sexual contact.	One of five U.S. adults	No known cure but antiviral medications can shorten outbreaks
AIDS	Caused by the human immunodeficiency virus (HIV), which destroys the body's immune system. Semen and blood are the main vehicles of transmission. Common symptoms include fevers, night sweats, weight loss, chronic fatigue, and swollen lymph nodes.	More than 300,000 cumulative cases of HIV virus in U.S. 25–34-year-olds; epidemic incidence in sub-Saharan countries	New treatments have slowed the progression from HIV to AIDS; no cure
Genital warts	Caused by the human papillomavirus, which does not always produce symptoms. Usually appear as small, hard painless bumps in the vaginal area, or around the anus. Very contagious. Certain high-risk types of this virus cause cervical cancer and other genital cancers. May recur despite treatment. HPV vaccine approved by the FDA in 2006 offers protection against 4 HPV strains.	About 5.5 million new cases annually; considered the most common STI in the U.S.	A topical drug, freezing, or surgery

Globally, the total number of individuals with the HIV virus reached 39.5 million in 2006 (UNAIDS, 2006). The greatest concern about HIV/AIDS is in sub-Saharan Africa, where it has reached epidemic proportions, with 24.7 million individuals infected with HIV in 2006 (UNAIDS, 2006).

rape Forcible sexual intercourse with a person who does not consent to it.

What are some good strategies for protecting against HIV and other sexually transmitted infections? They include:

- *Knowing your and your partner's risk status.* Anyone who has had previous sexual activity with another person might have contracted an STI without being aware of it. Spend time getting to know a prospective partner before you have sex. Use this time to inform the other person of your STI status and inquire about your partner's. Remember that many people lie about their STI status.

- *Obtaining medical examinations.* Many experts recommend that couples who want to begin a sexual relationship should have a medical checkup to rule out STIs before they engage in sex. If cost is an issue, contact your campus health service or a public health clinic.

- *Having protected, not unprotected, sex.* When correctly used, latex condoms help to prevent many STIs from being transmitted. Condoms are most effective in preventing gonorrhea, syphilis, chlamydia, and HIV. They are less effective against the spread of herpes.

- *Not having sex with multiple partners.* One of the best predictors of getting an STI is having sex with multiple partners. Having more than one sex partner elevates the likelihood that you will encounter an infected partner.

How Would You...?
As a health-care professional, how would you advise a patient who is sexually active, does not use condoms, and does not want to be tested for any sexually transmitted infections?

Forcible Sexual Behavior and Sexual Harassment

Too often, sex involves the exercise of power. Here we briefly look at three of the problems that may result: two types of rape and sexual harassment.

Rape

Rape is forcible sexual intercourse with a person who does not give consent. Legal definitions of rape differ from state to state. For example, in some states, husbands are not prohibited from forcing their wives to have intercourse, although this has been challenged in several of those states.

Because victims may be reluctant to suffer the consequences of reporting rape, the actual incidence is not easily determined (Carroll, 2007). Rape occurs most often in large cities, where it has been reported that 8 of every 10,000 women 12 years and older are raped each year. Nearly 200,000 rapes are reported each year in the United States. Although most victims of rape are women, rape of men does occur (McLean, Balding, & White, 2005). Men in prisons are especially vulnerable to rape, usually by heterosexual males who use rape as a means of establishing their dominance and power.

Why does rape of women occur so often in the United States? Among the causes given are that males are socialized to be sexually aggressive, to regard women as inferior beings, and to view their own pleasure as the most important

date or acquaintance rape Coercive sexual activity directed at someone with whom the perpetrator is at least casually acquainted.

objective in sexual relations (Beech, Ward, & Fisher, 2006). Researchers have found that male rapists share the following characteristics: aggression enhances their sense of power or masculinity; they are angry at women in general; and they want to hurt and humiliate their victims.

Rape is a traumatic experience for the victims and those close to them (Kilmartin & Allison, 2007). As victims strive to get their lives back to normal, they may experience depression, fear, anxiety, and increased substance use for months or years (Herrera & others, 2006). Sexual dysfunctions, such as reduced sexual desire and an inability to reach orgasm, occur in 50 percent of female rape victims (Sprei & Courtois, 1988). Recovery depends on the victim's coping abilities, psychological adjustments prior to the assault, and social support (White & Frabult, 2006). Parents, partner, and others close to the victim can provide important support for recovery, as can mental health professionals.

An increasing concern is **date or acquaintance rape**, which is coercive sexual activity directed at someone with whom the victim is at least casually acquainted (Caron, 2007). By some estimates, one in three adolescent girls will be involved in a controlling, abusive relationship before she graduates from high school, and two-thirds of college freshman women report having been date raped or having experienced an attempted date rape at least once (Watts & Zimmerman, 2002). About two-thirds of college men admit that they fondle women against their will, and half admit to forcing sexual activity.

Sexual Harassment

Sexual harassment is a manifestation of power of one person over another. It takes many forms—from inappropriate sexual remarks and physical contact (patting, brushing against one's body) to blatant propositions and sexual assaults. Millions of women experience sexual harassment each year in work and educational settings. Sexual harassment of men by women also occurs but to a far lesser extent than sexual harassment of women by men.

In a recent survey of 2,000 college women, 62 percent reported that they had experienced sexual harassment while attending college (American Association of University Women, 2006). Most of the college women said that the sexual harassment involved noncontact forms such as crude jokes, remarks, and gestures. However, almost one-third said that the sexual harassment was physical in nature. A recent study of almost 1,500 college women revealed that when they had been sexually harassed they reported an increase in psychological distress, greater physical illness, and an increase in disordered eating (Huerta & others, 2006).

Sexual harassment can result in serious psychological consequences for the victim. Sexual harassment is a manifestation of power of one person over another. The elimination of such exploitation requires the development of work and academic environments that provide equal opportunities to develop a career and obtain education in a climate free of sexual harassment (Hock, 2007).

Cognitive Development

Are there changes in cognitive performance during these years? To explore the nature of cognition in early adulthood, we focus on issues related to cognitive stages and creative thinking.

Cognitive Stages

Are young adults more advanced in their thinking than adolescents are? Let's examine what Piaget and others have said about this intriguing question.

Piaget's View

Piaget concluded that an adolescent and an adult think qualitatively in the same way. That is, Piaget argued that at approximately 11 to 15 years of age, adolescents enter the formal operational stage, which is characterized by more logical, abstract, and idealistic thinking than the concrete operational thinking of 7- to 11-year-olds. Piaget did believe that young adults are more *quantitatively* advanced in their thinking in the sense that they have more knowledge than adolescents. He also believed, as do information-processing psychologists, that adults especially increase their knowledge in a specific area, such as a physicist's understanding of physics or a financial analyst's knowledge about finance. According to Piaget, however, formal operational thought is the final stage in cognitive development, and it characterizes adults as well as adolescents.

Some developmentalists theorize it is not until adulthood that many individuals consolidate their formal operational thinking. That is, they may begin to plan and hypothesize about intellectual problems in adolescence, but they become more systematic and sophisticated at this as young adults. Nonetheless, even many adults do not think in formal operational ways at all (Keating, 2004).

Realistic and Pragmatic Thinking

Some developmentalists propose that as young adults move into the world of work, their way of thinking does change. One idea is that as they face the constraints of reality, which work promotes, their idealism decreases (Labouvie-Vief, 1986). A related change in thinking is that in early adulthood individuals often switch from acquiring knowledge to applying knowledge as they pursue success in their work (Schaie & Willis, 2000).

Reflective and Relativistic Thinking

William Perry (1999) also described changes in cognition that take place in early adulthood. He said that adolescents often view the world in terms of polarities—right/wrong, we/they, or good/bad. As youth age into adulthood, they gradually move away from this type of absolutist thinking as they become aware of the diverse opinions and multiple perspectives of others. Thus, in Perry's view, the absolutist, dualistic thinking of adolescence gives way to the reflective, relativistic thinking of adulthood. Other developmentalists also believe that reflective thinking is an important indicator of cognitive change in young adults (Fischer & Bidell, 2006).

What are some ways that young adults might think differently than adolescents?

postformal thought A form of thought that is qualitatively different from Piaget's formal operational thought. It involves understanding that the correct answer to a problem can require reflective thinking, that the correct answer can vary from one situation to another, and that the search for truth is often an ongoing, never-ending process. It also involves the belief that solutions to problems need to be realistic, and that emotion and subjective factors can influence thinking.

Is There a Fifth, Postformal Stage?

Some theorists have pieced together cognitive changes in young adults and proposed a new stage of cognitive development, **postformal thought**, which is qualitatively different from Piaget's formal operational thought (Sinnott, 2003). Postformal thought involves understanding that the correct answer to a problem requires reflective thinking and can vary from one situation to another, and that the search for truth is often an ongoing, never-ending process (Kitchener, King, & DeLuca, 2006). Postformal thought also includes the belief that solutions to problems need to be realistic, and that emotion and subjective factors can influence thinking.

How strong is the evidence for a fifth, postformal stage of cognitive development? Researchers have found that young adults are more likely to engage in this postformal thinking than adolescents are (Commons & Bresette, 2006). But critics argue that research has yet to document that postformal thought is a qualitatively more advanced stage than formal operational thought.

How Would You...? As an educator, how would you characterize the differences in the intellectual development of adolescents and adults? How would this distinction change the way you teach to these different populations?

Creativity

Early adulthood is a time of great creativity for some people. At the age of 30, Thomas Edison invented the phonograph, Hans Christian Andersen wrote his first volume of fairy tales, and Mozart composed The Marriage of Figaro. One early study of creativity found that individuals' most creative products were generated in their thirties, and that 80 percent of the most important creative contributions were completed by age 50 (Lehman, 1960). Even though a decline in creative contributions is often found in the fifties and later, the decline is not as great as commonly thought.

Any consideration of decline in creativity with age requires consideration of the field of creativity involved. In such fields as philosophy and history, older adults often show as much creativity as when they were in their thirties and forties. By contrast, in such fields as lyric poetry, abstract math, and theoretical physics, the peak of creativity is often reached in the twenties or thirties.

Can you make yourself more creative? In Chapter 7, "Physical and Cognitive Development in Middle and Late Childhood," we presented some strategies for stimulating creative thinking in children, and these strategies can also be used by adults. Other strategies for becoming more creative have been suggested by Mihaly Csikszentmihalyi (pronounced ME-high CHICK-sent-me-high-ee).

Csikszentmihalyi (1995) interviewed 90 leading figures in art, business, government, education, and science to learn how creativity works. He discovered that creative people regularly experience a state he calls *flow*, a heightened state of pleasure experienced when we are engaged in mental and physical challenges that absorb us. Csikszentmihalyi (2000) believes everyone is capable of achieving flow. Based on his interviews with some of the most creative people in the world,

Mihaly Csikszentmihalyi, in the setting where he gets his most creative ideas. *When and where do you get your most creative thoughts?*

the first step toward a more creative life is cultivating your curiosity and interest. How can you do this?

- *Try to be surprised by something every day.* Maybe it is something you see, hear, or read about. Become absorbed in a lecture or a book. Be open to what the world is telling you. Life is a stream of experiences. Swim widely and deeply in it, and your life will be richer.

- *Try to surprise at least one person every day.* In a lot of things you do, you have to be predictable and patterned. Do something different for a change. Ask a question you normally would not ask. Invite someone to go to a show or a museum you never have visited.

- Write down each day what surprised you and how you surprised others. Most creative people keep a diary, notes, or lab records to ensure that their experience is not fleeting or forgotten. Start with a specific task. Each evening record the most surprising event that occurred that day and your most surprising action. After a few days, reread your notes and reflect on your past experiences. After a few weeks, you might see a pattern of interest emerging in your notes, one that might suggest an area you can explore in greater depth.

- When something sparks your interest, follow it. Usually when something captures your attention, it is short-lived—an idea, a song, a flower. Too often we are too busy to explore the idea, song, or flower further. Or we think these areas are none of our business because we are not experts about them. Yet the world is our business. We can't know which part of it is best suited to our interests until we make a serious effort to learn as much about as many aspects of it as possible.

- Wake up in the morning with a specific goal to look forward to. Creative people wake up eager to start the day. Why? Not necessarily because they are cheerful, enthusiastic types but because they know that there is something meaningful to accomplish each day, and they can't wait to get started.

- Spend time in settings that stimulate your creativity. In Csikszent- mihalyi's (1995) research, he gave people an electronic pager and beeped them randomly at different times of the day. When he asked them how they felt, they reported the highest levels of creativity when walking, driving, or swimming. I (your author) do my most creative thinking when I'm jogging. These activities are semiautomatic in that they take a certain amount of attention while leaving some time free to make connections among ideas. Another setting in which highly creative people report coming up with novel ideas is the sort of half-asleep, half-awake state we are in when we are deeply relaxed or barely awake.

How Would You...? As an educator, how would you use your understanding of creativity to become a more effective teacher?

Careers and Work

Earning a living, choosing an occupation, establishing a career, and developing in a career—these are important themes of early adulthood. What are some of the factors that go into choosing a job or career, and how does work typically affect the lives of young adults?

Developmental Changes

Many children have idealistic fantasies about what they want to be when they grow up. For example, many young children want to be superheroes, sports stars, or movie stars. In the high school years, they often have begun to think about careers on a somewhat less idealistic basis. In their late teens and early twenties, their career decision making has usually turned more serious as they explore different career possibilities and zero in on the career they want to enter. In college, this often means choosing a major or specialization that is designed to lead to work in a particular field. By their early and mid-twenties, many individuals have completed their education or training and started to enter a full-time occupation. From the mid-twenties through the remainder of early adulthood, individuals often seek to establish their emerging career in a particular field. They may work hard to move up the career ladder and improve their financial standing.

Monitoring the Occupational Outlook

"Uh-huh. Uh-huh. And for precisely how long were you a hunter-gatherer at I.B.M.?"

As you explore the type of work you are likely to enjoy and in which you can succeed, it is important to be knowledgeable about different fields and companies. Occupations may have many job openings one year but few in another year as economic conditions change. Thus, it is critical to keep up with the occupational outlook in various fields. An excellent source for doing this is the U.S. government's *Occupational Outlook Handbook*, which is revised every two years.

According to the 2006–2007 handbook, service industries, especially education and health services, and professional and business services, are projected to account for the most new jobs in the next decade. Projected job growth varies widely by educational requirements. Jobs that require a college degree are expected to grow the fastest. Most of the highest-paying occupations require a college degree (*Occupational Outlook Handbook*, 2006–2007).

The Impact of Work

Work defines people in fundamental ways (Blustein, 2006; Schultz & Adams, 2007). It is an important influence on their financial standing, housing, the way they spend their time, where they live, their friendships, and their health. Some people define their identity through their work. Work also creates a structure and rhythm to life that is often missed when individuals do not work for an extended period. When unable to work, many individuals experience emotional distress and low self-esteem.

Most individuals spend about one-third of their lives at work. In one survey, 35 percent of Americans worked 40 hours a week, but 18 percent worked 51 hours or more per week (Center for Survey Research at the University of Connecticut, 2000). Only 10 percent worked less than 30 hours a week.

Of course, work also creates stress. Four characteristics of work settings are linked with employee stress and health problems (Moos, 1986): (1) high job demands such as having a heavy workload and time pressure, (2) inadequate opportunities to participate in decision making, (3) a high level of supervisor control, and (4) a lack of clarity about the criteria for competent performance.

Work During College

Eighty percent of U.S. undergraduate college students worked during the 1999–2000 academic year (National Center for Education Statistics, 2002). Forty-eight percent of undergraduates identified themselves mainly as students working to meet school expenses and 32 percent as employees who decided to enroll in school. Undergraduate students who identified themselves as working to meet expenses worked an average of 26 hours per week; those who considered themselves to be employees worked an average of 40 hours per week.

Working can pay or help offset some costs of schooling, but working also can restrict students' opportunities to learn. For those who identified themselves primarily as students, one recent national study found that as the number of hours worked per week increased, their grades suffered (National Center for Education Statistics, 2002) (see Figure 11.7). Other research has found that as the number of hours college students work increases, the more likely they are to drop out of college (National Center for Education Statistics, 2002). Thus, college students need to carefully examine whether the number of hours they work is having a negative impact on their college success.

Of course, jobs also can contribute to your education. More than 1,000 colleges in the United States offer *cooperative (co-op) programs*, which are paid apprenticeships in a field that you are interested in pursuing. (You may not be permitted to participate in a co-op program until your junior year.) Other useful opportunities for working while going to college include internships and part-time or summer jobs relevant to your field of study. In a national survey of employers, almost 60 percent said their entry-level college hires had co-op or internship experience (Collins, 1996). Participating in these work experiences can be a key factor in whether you land the job you want when you graduate.

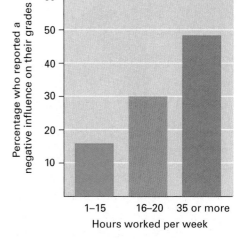

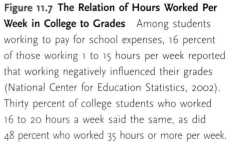

Figure 11.7 The Relation of Hours Worked Per Week in College to Grades Among students working to pay for school expenses, 16 percent of those working 1 to 15 hours per week reported that working negatively influenced their grades (National Center for Education Statistics, 2002). Thirty percent of college students who worked 16 to 20 hours a week said the same, as did 48 percent who worked 35 hours or more per week.

How Would You...?
As an educator, how would you advise a student who works a full-time job while taking college classes?

Dual-Career Couples

Dual-career couples may have particular problems finding a balance between work and the rest of life (Pitt-Catsouphes, Kossek, & Sweet, 2006). If both partners are working, who cleans up the house or calls the repairman or takes care of the other endless details involved in maintaining a home? If the couple has children, who is responsible for being sure that the children get to school or to piano practice, who writes the notes to approve field trips or meets the teacher or makes the dental appointments?

Although single-earner married families still make up a sizeable minority of families, the two-earner couple has increased considerably in the last three decades (Barnett, 2001). As more U.S. women worked outside the home, the division of

How has the diversity of the workplace changed in recent years?

responsibility for work and family changed. Research suggests that (Barnett, 2001; Barnett & others, 2001):

- *U.S. husbands are taking increased responsibility for maintaining the home.* Men in dual-career families do about 45 percent of the housework.

- *U.S. women are taking increased responsibility for breadwinning.* In about one-third of two-earner couples, wives earn as much as or more than their husbands.

- *U.S. men are showing greater interest in their families and parenting.* Young adult men are reporting that family is at least as important to them as work.

Diversity in the Workplace

The workplace is becoming increasingly diverse (*Occupational Outlook Handbook,* 2006–2007). Whereas at one time few women were employed outside the home, in developed countries women have increasingly entered the labor force (UNICEF, 2007). In 2004 in the United States, men made up 53.6 percent of the labor force, women 46.4 percent (*Occupational Outlook Handbook,* 2006–2007). In the United States, more than one-fourth of all lawyers, physicians, computer scientists, and chemists today are females.

Ethnic diversity also is increasing in the workplace in every developed country except France. In the United States, between 1980 and 2004, the percentage of Latinos and Asian Americans more than doubled in the workplace, a trend that is expected to continue (*Occupational Outlook Handbook,* 2006–2007; U.S. Bureau of Labor Statistics, 2005). Latinos are projected to constitute a larger percentage of the labor force than African Americans by 2014, growing from 12 percent to 15 percent (*Occupational Outlook Handbook,* 2006–2007). Asian Americans will continue to be the fastest growing of the labor force groups. The increasing diversity in the workplace requires a sensitivity to cultural differences, and the cultural values that workers bring to a job need to be recognized and appreciated (Powell, 2004).

Despite the increasing diversity in the workplace, women and ethnic minorities experience difficulty in breaking through the *glass ceiling.* This invisible barrier to career advancement prevents women and ethnic minorities from holding managerial or executive jobs regardless of their accomplishments and merits.

Summary

The Transition from Adolescence to Adulthood

Emerging adulthood is the term now given to the transition from adolescence to adulthood. Its age range is about 18 to 25 years of age, and it is characterized by experimentation and exploration. There is both continuity and change in the transition from adolescence to adulthood. Two criteria for adult status are economic independence and independent decision making. The transition from high school to college can involve both positive and negative features. U.S. college students today report experiencing more stress than did college students of the 1980s.

Physical Development

Peak physical performance is often reached between 19 and 26 years of age. Toward the latter part of early adulthood, a detectable slowdown in physical performance is apparent for most individuals. Obesity is a serious problem. Most diets don't work long term. For those that do, exercise is usually an important component. Both moderate and intense exercise produce important physical and psychological gains. By the mid-twenties a reduction in drug use often takes place. Binge drinking among college students is still a major concern. Alcoholism is a disorder that impairs an individual's health and social relationships. A number of strategies, such as nicotine substitutes, have shown some success in getting smokers to quit.

Sexuality

Patterns of sexual activity change during emerging adulthood, a time when casual sex is more common than in early adulthood. In the 1994 Sex in America survey, American adults' sexual lives were portrayed as more conservative than in earlier surveys. An individual's sexual preference likely is the result of a combination of genetic, hormonal, cognitive, and environmental factors. Also called STIs, sexually transmitted infections are contracted primarily through sexual contact. The human immunodeficiency virus (HIV) can lead to AIDS (acquired immune deficiency syndrome). Rape is forcible sexual intercourse with a person who does not give consent. Date or acquaintance rape involves coercive sexual activity directed at someone with whom the victim is at least casually acquainted. Sexual harassment occurs when one person uses his or her power over another individual in a sexual manner and can result in serious psychological consequences for the victim.

Cognitive Development

Formal operational thought, entered at age 11 to 15, is Piaget's final cognitive stage. According to Piaget, although adults are quantitatively more knowledgeable than adolescents, adults do not enter a new, qualitatively different stage. Some experts argue that the idealism of Piaget's formal operational stage declines in young adults, and is replaced by more realistic, pragmatic thinking. Some propose that differences like these constitute a qualitatively different, fifth cognitive stage, called postformal thought. Creativity peaks in adulthood, often in the forties, and then declines. However, there is extensive individual variation in lifetime creative output. Csikszentmihalyi proposed that the first step toward living a creative life is to cultivate curiosity and interest.

Careers and Work

Many young children have idealistic fantasies about a career. In the late teens and early twenties, their career thinking has usually turned more serious. By their early to mid-twenties, many individuals have completed their education or training and started in a career. In the remainder of early adulthood, they seek to establish their emerging career and start moving up the career ladder. Jobs that require a college education will be the fastest growing and highest paying in the United States in the next decade. Work defines people in fundamental ways and is a key aspect of their identity. Most individuals spend about one-third of their adult life at work. Eighty percent of U.S. college students work while going to college. Working during college can have positive or negative outcomes. The increasing number of women who work in careers outside the home has led to new work-related issues. Because of dual-career households, there has been a considerable increase in the time men spend in household work and child care. The U.S. workplace has become increasingly diverse.

Key Terms

emerging adulthood 308
aerobic exercise 313
sexually transmitted infections (STIs) 318

rape 319
date or acquaintance rape 320
postformal thought 322

12

Socioemotional Development in Early Adulthood

Stories of Life-Span Development: Gwenna's Pursuit and Greg's Lack of Commitment

Commitment is an important issue in a romantic relationship for most individuals. Consider Gwenna, who decides that it is time to have a talk with Greg about his commitment to their relationship (Lerner, 1989, pp. 44–45):

> She shared her perspective on both the strengths and weaknesses of their relationship and what her hopes were for the future. She asked Greg to do the same. Unlike earlier conversations, this one was conducted without her pursuing him, pres-

suring him, or diagnosing his problems with women. At the same time, she asked Greg some clear questions, which exposed his vagueness.

"How will you know when you are ready to make a commitment? What specifically would you need to change or be different than it is today?"

"I don't know," was Greg's response. When questioned further, the best he could come up with was that he'd just feel it.

"How much more time do you need to make a decision one way or another?"

"I'm not sure," Greg replied. "Maybe a couple of years, but I really can't answer a question like that. I can't predict my feelings."

And so it went.

Gwenna really loved this man, but two years (and maybe longer) was longer than she could comfortably wait. So, after much thought, she told Greg that she would wait till fall (about ten months), but that she would move on if he couldn't commit himself to marriage by then. She was open about her wish to marry and have a family

329

with him, but she was equally clear that her first priority was a mutually committed relationship. If Greg was not at that point by fall, then she would end the relationship—painful though it would be.

During the waiting period, Gwenna was able to not pursue him and not get distant or otherwise reactive to his expressions of ambivalence and doubt. In this way she gave Greg emotional space to struggle with his dilemma and the relationship had its best chance of succeeding. Her

bottom-line position ("a decision by fall") was not a threat or an attempt to rope Greg in, but rather, a clear statement of what was acceptable to her.

When fall arrived, Greg told Gwenna he needed another six months to make up his mind. Gwenna deliberated a while and decided she could live with that. But when the six months were up, Greg was uncertain and asked for more time. It was then that Gwenna took the painful but ultimately empowering step of ending their relationship.

Love is of central importance in each of our lives, as it is in Gwenna and Greg's lives. Shortly, we discuss the many faces of love, as well as the diversity of adult lifestyles, marriage and the family, and the role of gender in relationships. To begin, though, we will return to an issue we initially raised in Chapter 1: stability and change. ∎

Stability and Change from Childhood to Adulthood

For adults, socioemotional development revolves around adaptively integrating our emotional experiences into enjoyable relationships with others on a daily basis (Thompson & Goodvin, 2005). Young adults like Gwenna and Greg face choices and challenges in adopting lifestyles that will be emotionally satisfying, predictable, and manageable for them. They do not come to these tasks as blank slates, but do their decisions and actions simply reflect the persons they had already become when they were 5 years old or 10 years old or 20 years old?

Current research shows that the first 20 years of life are not meaningless in predicting an adult's socioemotional life (Caspi & Shiner, 2006). And there is also every reason to believe that experiences in the early adult years are important in determining what the individual is like later in adulthood. A common finding is that the smaller the time intervals over which we measure socioemotional characteristics, the more similar an individual will look from one measurement to the next. Thus, if we measure an individual's self-concept at the age of 20, and then again at the age of 30, we will probably find more stability than if we measured the individual's self-concept at the age of 10 and then again at the age of 30.

In trying to understand the young adult's socioemotional development, it would be misleading to look at an adult's life only in the present tense, ignoring the unfolding of social relationships and emotions. So, too, it would be a mistake to search only through a 30-year-old's first five to ten years of life in trying to understand why he or she is having difficulty in a close relationship. To further explore stability and change, let's examine attachment.

Attachment appears during infancy and plays an important part in socioemotional development. We discussed its role in infancy and adolescence (see Chapters 4 and 10). How do these earlier patterns of attachment and adults' attachment styles influence the lives of adults?

Although relationships with romantic partners differ from those with parents, romantic partners fulfill some of the same needs for adults as parents do for their children (Shaver & Mikulincer, 2007). Recall from Chapter 4 that *securely attached* infants are defined as those who use the caregiver as a secure base from which to explore the environment. Similarly, adults may count on their romantic partners to be a secure base to which they can return and obtain comfort and security in stressful times.

Do adult attachment patterns with partners reflect childhood attachment patterns with parents? In a retrospective study, Cindy Hazen & Philip Shaver (1987) revealed that young adults who were securely attached in their romantic relationships were more likely to describe their early relationship with their parents as securely attached. In a longitudinal study, infants who were securely attached at 1 year of age were securely attached twenty years later in their adult romantic relationships (Steele & others, 1998). However, in another longitudinal study, links between early attachment styles and later attachment styles were lessened by stressful and disruptive experiences, such as the death of a parent or instability of caregiving (Lewis, Feiring, & Rosenthal, 2000).

attachment-related anxiety Involves the extent to which individuals feel secure or insecure about whether a partner will be available, responsive, and attentive.

attachment-related avoidance Involves the degree to which individuals feel secure or insecure in relying on others, opening up to them, and being intimate with them.

How do we know whether adults are "securely attached"? Researchers have used varying methods to describe and classify adult attachment (Hazen, Gur-Yaish, & Campa, 2007). Increasingly, they are conceptualizing and measuring adult attachment in terms of two dimensions (Brennan, Clark, & Shaver, 1998):

- **Attachment-related anxiety:** Involves the extent to which individuals feel secure or insecure about whether a partner will be available, responsive, and attentive.

- **Attachment-related avoidance:** Involves the degree to which individuals feel secure or insecure in relying on others, opening up to them, and being intimate with them.

Thus, saying that adults are securely attached indicates that they score low on measures of attachment-related anxiety and attachment-related avoidance.

What are some key dimensions of attachment in adulthood, and how are they related to relationship patterns and well-being?

Researchers also are studying links between adults' current attachment styles and many aspects of adults' lives (Rholes & Simpson, 2007). Securely attached adults are more satisfied with their close relationships than insecurely attached adults, and the relationships of securely attached adults are more likely to be characterized by trust, commitment, and longevity (Feeney & Collins, 2007). Securely attached adults also are more likely than insecurely attached adults to provide support when they are distressed and more likely to give support when their partner is distressed (Simpson, Rholes, & Nelligan, 1992). One recent study found that adults with avoidant and anxious attachment styles were more likely to be depressed than securely attached adults (Hankin, Kassel, & Abela, 2005).

Love and Close Relationships

Love refers to a vast and complex territory of human behavior, spanning a range of relationships that includes friendship, romantic love, affectionate love and consummate love. In most of these types of love, one recurring theme is intimacy.

Intimacy

Self-disclosure and the sharing of private thoughts are hallmarks of intimacy. As we discussed in Chapter 10, adolescents have an increased need for intimacy. At the same time, they are engaged in the essential tasks of developing an identity and

How Would You...?
As a human development and family studies professional, how would you help individuals understand how early relationship experiences might influence their close relationships in adulthood?

establishing their independence from their parents. Juggling the competing demands of intimacy, identity, and independence also becomes a central task of adulthood.

Erikson's Stage: Intimacy Versus Isolation

Recall from our discussion in Chapter 10 that Erik Erikson (1968) argues that identity versus identity confusion—pursuing who we are, what we are all about, and where we are going in life—is the most important issue to be negotiated in adolescence. In early adulthood, according to Erikson, after individuals are well on their way to establishing stable and successful identities, they enter the sixth developmental stage, which is intimacy versus isolation. Erikson describes intimacy as finding oneself while losing oneself in another person, and it requires a commitment to another person. If a person fails to develop an intimate relationship in early adulthood, according to Erikson, isolation results.

An inability to develop meaningful relationships with others can harm an individual's personality. It may lead individuals to repudiate, ignore, or attack those who frustrate them. Such circumstances account for the shallow, almost pathetic attempts of youth to merge themselves with a leader. Many youth want to be apprentices or disciples of leaders and adults who will shelter them from the harm of the "out-group" world. If this fails, and Erikson believes that it must, sooner or later the individuals recoil into a self-search to discover where they went wrong. This introspection sometimes leads to painful depression and isolation. It also may contribute to a mistrust of others.

Intimacy and Independence

Development in early adulthood often involves balancing intimacy and commitment on the one hand, and independence and freedom on the other. At the same time as individuals are trying to establish an identity, they face the challenges of increasing their independence from their parents, developing an intimate relationship with another individual, and continuing their friendship commitments. They also face the task of making decisions for themselves without always relying on what others say or do.

The extent to which young adults develop autonomy has important implications for them. For example, young adults who have not sufficiently moved away from parental ties may have difficulty in both interpersonal relationships and a career.

The balance between intimacy and commitment—and independence and freedom—is delicate. Some individuals are able to experience a healthy independence and freedom along with an intimate relationship. Keep in mind that intimacy and commitment, and independence and freedom, are not just concerns of early adulthood. They are important themes of development that are worked and reworked throughout the adult years.

Friendship

Increasingly researchers are finding that friendship plays an important role in development throughout the human life span (Dow & Wood, 2006; Monsour, 2006). As we saw in Chapter 8, friendship can serve many functions—such as companionship, intimacy/affection, support, and a source of self-esteem. In some cases, friends can provide a better buffer from stress and be a better source of emotional support than family members. This might be because friends choose each other, whereas family ties are obligatory. Individuals often select a friend in terms of such criteria as loyalty, trustworthiness, and support. Thus, it is not surprising that in times of stress individuals turn to their friends for emotional support (Fehr, 2000).

As with children, adult friends usually come from the same age group. For many individuals, friendships formed in the twenties often continue through the twenties and into the thirties, although some new friends may be made in the thirties and some lost because of moving or other circumstances.

As in the childhood years, there are gender differences in adult friendship. Compared with men, women have more close friends and their friendships involve more self-disclosure and exchange of mutual support (Dow & Wood, 2006). Women are more likely to listen at length to what a friend has to say and be sympathetic, and women have been labeled as "talking companions" because talk is so central to their relationship (Gouldner & Strong, 1987). Women's friendships tend to be characterized not only by depth but also by breadth: Women share many aspects of their experiences, thoughts, and feelings (Wood, 2001).

Romantic Love

Some friendships evolve into **romantic love**, which is also called passionate love, or eros. Romantic love has strong components of sexuality and infatuation, and it often predominates in the early part of a love relationship (Aron & others, 2005; Brown, 2005).

A complex intermingling of different emotions goes into romantic love—including such emotions as passion, fear, anger, sexual desire, joy, and jealousy (Harris, 2002). Well-known love researcher Ellen Berscheid (1988) says that sexual desire is the most important ingredient of romantic love. Obviously, some of these emotions are a source of anguish (Daley & Hammen, 2002), which can lead to other issues such as depression. One study found that a relationship between romantic lovers was more likely than a relationship between friends to be a cause of depression (Berscheid & Fei, 1977).

How Would You...?
As a health-care professional, how would you advise individuals who are concerned about their sexual functioning because the romantic relationship in which they are involved in seems to be losing its spark?

Affectionate Love

Love is more than just passion. **Affectionate love**, also called *companionate love*, is the type of love that occurs when someone desires to have the other person near and has a deep, caring affection for the person.

The early stages of love have more romantic love ingredients—but as love matures, passion tends to give way to affection (Harvey & Weber, 2002). Phillip Shaver (1986) proposed a developmental model of love in which the initial phase of romantic love is fueled by a mixture of sexual attraction and gratification, a reduced sense of loneliness, uncertainty about the security of developing another attachment, and excitement from exploring the novelty of another human being. With time, he says, sexual attraction wanes, attachment anxieties either lessen or produce conflict

romantic love Also called passionate love, or eros; romantic love has strong sexual and infatuation components and often predominates in the early period of a love relationship.

affectionate love In this type of love, also called companionate love, an individual desires to have the other person near and has a deep, caring affection for the other person.

and withdrawal, novelty is replaced with familiarity, and lovers either find themselves securely attached in a deeply caring relationship or distressed—feeling bored, disappointed, lonely, or hostile, for example. In the latter case, one or both partners may eventually end the relationship and then move on to another relationship.

Consummate Love

So far we have discussed two forms of love: romantic (or passionate) and affectionate (or companionate). According to Robert J. Sternberg (1988), these are not the only forms of love. Sternberg proposed a triarchic theory of love in which love can be thought of as a triangle with three main dimensions—passion, intimacy, and commitment. Passion involves physical and sexual attraction to another. Intimacy relates to the emotional feelings of warmth, closeness, and sharing in a relationship. Commitment is the cognitive appraisal of the relationship and the intent to maintain the relationship even in the face of problems (Rusbult & others, 2001).

In Sternberg's theory, the strongest, fullest form of love is *consummate love,* which involves all three dimensions (see Figure 12.1). If passion is the only ingredient in a relationship (with intimacy and commitment low or absent), we are merely *infatuated.* An affair or a fling in which there is little intimacy and even less commitment is an example. A relationship marked by intimacy and commitment but low or lacking in passion is called *affectionate love,* a pattern often found among couples who have been married for many years. If passion and commitment are present but intimacy is not, Sternberg calls the relationship *fatuous love,* as when one person worships another from a distance. But if couples share all three dimensions—passion, intimacy, and commitment—they experience consummate love.

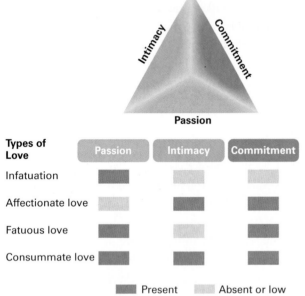

Figure 12.1 Sternberg's Triangle of Love
Sternberg identified three types of love: passion, intimacy, and commitment. Various combinations of these result in infatuation, affectionate love, fatuous love, and consummate love.

Adult Lifestyles

Adults today choose many lifestyles and form many types of families. One of the most striking social changes in recent decades is the decreased stigma attached to people who do not maintain what were long considered conventional families. They may choose to live alone, cohabit, marry, divorce, remarry, or live with someone of the same sex. Let's explore each of these lifestyles and how they affect adults.

Single Adults

There has been a dramatic rise in the percentage of single adults in the United States. As shown in Figure 12.2, the percentage of never-married 30- to 34-year-old single adults more than tripled from 1970 to 2005 (U.S. Census Bureau, 2005).

Even when singles enjoy their lifestyles and are highly competent individuals, they often are stereotyped (DePaulo & Morris, 2005). Stereotypes associated with being single range from the "swinging single" to the "desperately lonely, suicidal" single. Of course, most single adults are somewhere between these extremes. Common problems of single adults may include forming intimate relationships with other adults, confronting loneliness, and finding a niche in a society that is marriage-oriented. Advantages of being single include having time to make decisions about one's life course, time to develop personal resources to meet goals, freedom to make autonomous decisions and pursue one's own schedule and interests, opportunities to explore new places and try out new things, and privacy.

Once adults reach the age of 30, there can be increasing pressure to settle down and get married. This is when many single adults make a conscious decision to marry or to remain single.

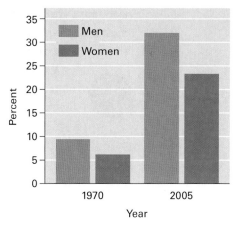

Figure 12.2 Percentage of Never-Married Single Adults 30 to 34 Years of Age in 1970 and 2005 In three decades, the percentage of never-married single adults 30 to 34 years of age in the United States more than tripled.

Cohabiting Adults

Cohabitation refers to living together in a sexual relationship without being married. Cohabitation has undergone considerable changes in recent years. The percentage of U.S. couples who cohabit before marriage has increased from approximately 11 percent in 1970 to more than 50 percent in 2005 (Whitehead & Poponoe, 2006). Cohabiting rates are even higher in some countries—in Sweden, cohabitation before marriage is virtually universal.

A number of couples view their cohabitation not as a precursor to marriage but as an ongoing lifestyle. These couples do not want the official aspects of marriage. In the United States, cohabiting arrangements tend to be short-lived, with one third lasting less than a year (Hyde & DeLamater, 2006). Less than one out of ten lasts five years. Of course, it is easier to dissolve a cohabitation relationship than to divorce.

Do cohabiting relationships differ from marriage in ways other than the legal aspects? Relationships between cohabiting men and women tend to be more equal than those between husbands and wives (Wineberg, 1994).

Although cohabitation offers some advantages, it also can produce some problems (Trask & Koivur, 2007). Researchers have found a higher rate of domestic violence among cohabiting couples than in married couples (Kenney & McLanahan, 2006). Disapproval by parents and other family members can place emotional strain on the cohabiting couple. Some cohabiting couples have difficulty owning property jointly. Legal rights on the dissolution of the relationship are less certain than in a divorce.

If a couple lives together before they marry, does cohabiting help or harm their chances of later having a stable and happy marriage? Researchers increasingly

What are some potential advantages and disadvantages of cohabitation?

have found that couples who marry after cohabiting are more likely to experience marital distress and become divorced than couples who didn't cohabit (Stanley, Rhoades, & Markman, 2006).

How Would You...?

As a psychologist, how would you counsel a couple deciding whether or not to cohabit before marriage?

What might explain the finding that cohabiting is linked with divorce more than not cohabiting? The most frequently given explanation is that the less traditional lifestyle of cohabitation may attract less conventional individuals who are not great believers in marriage in the first place (Whitehead & Popenoe, 2003). An alternative explanation is that the experience of cohabiting changes people's attitudes and habits in ways that increase their likelihood of divorce (Solot & Miller, 2002).

Married Adults

Until about 1930, stable marriage was widely accepted as the endpoint of adult development. In the last 60 years, however, personal fulfillment both inside and outside marriage has emerged as a goal that competes with marital stability. The changing norm of male-female equality in marriage has produced marital relationships that are more fragile and intense than they were earlier in the twentieth century (Trask & Koivur, 2007).

Marital Trends

In recent years, marriage rates in the United States have declined. More adults are remaining single longer today. In 2005, the U.S. average age for a first marriage climbed to just over 27 years for men and 26 years for women, higher than at any point in history (U.S. Census Bureau 2005). In addition, the increase in cohabitation and a slight decline in the percentage of divorced individuals who remarry contributed to the decline in marriage rates in the United States (Whitehead & Poponoe, 2006).

How happy are people who do marry? The average duration of a marriage in the United States is currently just over nine years. As indicated in Figure 12.3, the percentage of married individuals in the United States who said their marriages were "very happy" declined from the 1970s through the early 1990s, but recently has begun to increase (Poponoe & Whitehead, 2005). Notice in Figure 12.3 that men consistently report being happier in their marriage than women.

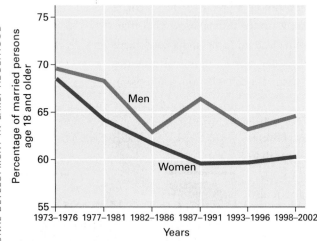

Figure 12.3 **Percentage of Married Persons Age 18 and Older with "Very Happy" Marriages**

The Benefits of a Good Marriage

Are there any benefits to having a good marriage? There are (Coontz, 2007). Individuals who are happily married live longer, healthier lives than either divorced individuals or those who are unhappily married (Cotten, 1999). One study revealed that women in happy marriages had lower levels of biological and cardiovascular risk factors—such as blood pressure, cholesterol levels, and body mass index—and lower levels of depression, anxiety, and anger than women in unhappy marriages (Gallo & others, 2003). Another study revealed that negative spousal behaviors were linked to adults' health problems (Bookwala, 2005). An unhappy marriage increases an individual's risk of getting sick by approximately one third and can even shorten a person's life by an average of four years (Gove, Style, & Hughes, 1990).

What are the reasons for these benefits of a happy marriage? People in happy marriages likely feel less physically and emotionally stressed, which puts less wear and tear on a person's body.

Divorced Adults

Divorce has become epidemic in our culture (Coontz, 2007; Fine & Harvey, 2006). The number of divorced adults rose from 2 percent of the adult population in 1950 to 3 percent in 1970 to 10 percent in 2002. The divorce rate was increasing annually by 10 percent, but has been declining since the 1980s (Amato & Irving, 2006).

Although divorce has increased for all socioeconomic groups, those in some groups have a higher incidence of divorce. Youthful marriage, low educational level, low income, not having a religious affiliation, having parents who are divorced, and having a baby before marriage are groups that are associated with increases in divorce (Rodrigues, Hall, & Fincham, 2006).

If a divorce is going to occur, it usually takes place early in a marriage; most occur in the fifth to tenth year of marriage (National Center for Health Statistics, 2000) (see Figure 12.4). This timing may reflect an effort by partners in troubled marriages to stay in the marriage and try to work things out. If after several years these efforts don't improve the relationship, they may then seek a divorce.

Even those adults who initiated their divorce experience challenges after a marriage dissolves (Ahrons, 2007; Wallerstein & Lewis, 2005). The stress of separation and divorce places both men and women at risk for psychological and physical difficulties (Fine, Ganong, & Demo, 2006). Separated and divorced women and men have higher rates of psychiatric disorders, admission to psychiatric hospitals, clinical depression, alcoholism, and psychosomatic problems, such as sleep disorders, than do married adults.

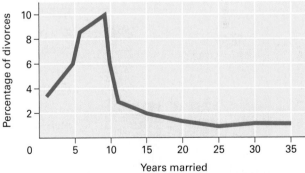

Figure 12.4 The Divorce Rate in Relation to Number of Years Married Shown here is the percentage of divorces as a function of how long couples have been married. Notice that most divorces occur in the early years of marriage, peaking in the fifth to tenth years of marriage.

Remarried Adults

On average, divorced adults remarry within four years after their divorce, with men remarrying sooner than women. Stepfamilies come in many sizes and forms.

The custodial and noncustodial parents and stepparent all might have been married and divorced, in some cases more than once. These parents might have residential children from prior marriages and a large network of grandparents and other relatives. Researchers have found that remarried adults are more likely to have higher levels of depressive symptoms than adults in intact, never-divorced families (Barrett & Turner, 2005).

Why do remarried adults find it so difficult to stay remarried? For one thing, many remarry not for love but for financial reasons, for help in rearing children, and to reduce loneliness. They also might carry into the stepfamily negative patterns that produced failure in an earlier marriage. Remarried couples also experience more stress in rearing children than parents in never-divorced families (Ganong, Coleman, & Hans, 2006).

For remarried couples, strategies for coping with the stress of living in a stepfamily include these (Visher & Visher, 1989):

- *Have realistic expectations.* Allow time for loving relationships to develop, and look at the complexity of the stepfamily as a challenge to overcome.

- *Develop new positive relationships within the family.* Create new traditions and ways of dealing with difficult circumstances. Allocation of time is especially important because so many people are involved. The remarried couple needs to allot time alone for each other.

Gay Male and Lesbian Adults

The legal and social context of marriage creates barriers to breaking up that do not usually exist for same-sex partners. But in other ways, researchers have found that gay and lesbian relationships are similar—in their satisfactions, loves, joys, and conflicts—to heterosexual relationships (Hyde & DeLamater, 2006). For example, like heterosexual couples, gay and lesbian couples need to find the balance of romantic love, affection, autonomy, and equality that is acceptable to both partners (Kurdek, 2006). An increasing number of gay and lesbian couples are creating families that include children (see Figure 12.5).

There are a number of misconceptions about gay male and lesbian couples. Contrary to stereotypes, one partner is masculine and the other feminine in only a small percentage of gay male and lesbian couples. Only a small segment of the gay male population has a large number of sexual partners, and this is uncommon among lesbians. Furthermore, researchers have found that gay male and lesbian couples prefer long-term, committed relationships (Peplau & Fingerhut, 2007). About half of committed gay male couples do have an open relationship that allows the possibility of sex (but not affectionate love) outside of the relationship. Lesbian couples usually do not have this open relationship.

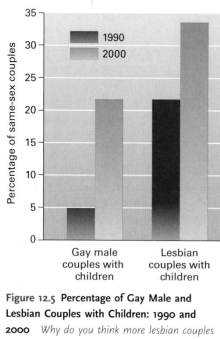

Figure 12.5 Percentage of Gay Male and Lesbian Couples with Children: 1990 and 2000 *Why do you think more lesbian couples have children than gay male couples?*

Challenges in Marriage, Parenting, and Divorce

Whatever lifestyles young adults choose, they will bring certain challenges. Because many choose the lifestyle of marriage, we'll consider some of the challenges in marriage and how to make it work. We also examine some challenges in parenting and trends in childbearing. Given the statistics about divorce rates in previous section, we'll then consider how to deal with divorce.

Making Marriage Work

John Gottman (1994; Gottman & Notarius, 2000; Gottman & Silver, 1999) has been studying married couples' lives since the early 1970s. He uses many methods to analyze what makes marriages work. Gottman interviews couples about the history of their marriage, their philosophy about marriage, and how they view their parents' marriages. He videotapes them talking to each other about how their day went and evaluates what they say about the good and bad times of their marriages. Gottman also uses physiological measures to chart their heart rate, blood flow, blood pressure, and immune functioning moment by moment. He also checks back in with the couples every year to see how their marriage is faring. Gottman's research represents the most extensive assessment of marital relationships available. Currently he and his colleagues are following 700 couples in seven studies.

Among the principles Gottman has found that determine whether a marriage will work are:

- *Establishing love maps.* Individuals in successful marriages have personal insights and detailed maps of each other's life and world. They aren't psychological strangers. In good marriages, partners are willing to share their feelings with each other. They use these "love maps" to express not only their understanding of each other but also their fondness and admiration.

- *Nurturing fondness and admiration.* In successful marriages, partners sing each other's praises. More than 90 percent of the time, when couples put a positive spin on their marriage's history, the marriage is likely to have a positive future.

- *Turning toward each other instead of away.* In good marriages, spouses are adept at turning toward each other regularly. They see each other as friends. This friendship doesn't keep arguments from occurring, but it can prevent differences from overwhelming the relationship. In these good marriages, spouses respect each other and appreciate each other's point of view despite disagreements.

- *Letting your partner influence you.* Bad marriages often involve one spouse who is unwilling to share power with the other. Although power-mongering is more common in husbands, some wives also show this trait. A willingness to share power and to respect the other person's view is a prerequisite to compromising.

- Creating shared meaning. The more partners can speak candidly and respectfully with each other, the more likely it is that they will create shared meaning in their marriage. This also includes sharing goals with one's spouse and working together to achieve each other's goals.

What makes marriages work? What are the benefits of having a good marriage?

In a provocative recent book, *Marriage, History,* Stephanie Coontz (2005) concluded that marriages in America today are fragile not because Americans have become self-centered and career-minded, but because expectations for marriage have become unrealistically high compared with previous generations. However, she states that many marriages today are better than in the past, citing the increase in marriages that are equitable, loving, intimate, and protective of children. To make a marriage work, she emphasizes, like Gottman, that partners need to develop a deep friendship, show respect for each other, and embrace commitment.

Becoming a Parent

For many young adults, parental roles are well planned, coordinated with other roles in life, and developed with the individual's economic situation in mind. For others, the discovery that they are about to become parents is a startling surprise. In either event, the prospective parents may have mixed emotions and romantic illusions about having a child.

Parenting requires a number of interpersonal skills and imposes emotional demands, yet there is little in the way of formal education for this task. Most parents learn parenting practices from their own parents—some they accept, some they discard. Unfortunately, when methods of parents are passed on from one generation to the next, both desirable and undesirable practices are perpetuated. Adding to reality of the task of parenting, husbands and wives may bring different parenting practices to the marriage (Huston & Holmes, 2004). The parents, then, may struggle with each other about which is a better practice to interact with a child.

Parent educators seek to help individuals to become better parents. To read about the work of one parent educator, see the Careers in Life-Span Development profile.

CAREER IN LIFE-SPAN DEVELOPMENT
Janis Keyser, Parent Educator

Janis Keyser is a parent educator and teaches in the Department of Early Childhood Education at Cabrillo College in California. In addition to teaching college classes and conducting parenting workshops, she also has coauthored a book with Laura Davis (1997), *Becoming the Parent You Want to Be: A Source-Book of Strategies for the First Five Years.*

Janis also writes as an expert on the iVillage Web site (www.parentsplace.com). And she also co-authors a nationally syndicated parenting column, "Growing Up, Growing Together." She is the mother of three, stepmother of five, grandmother of twelve, and great-grandmother of six.

Parent educators may have different educational backgrounds and occupational profiles. As just indicated, Janet Keyser has a background in early childhood education and teaches at a college. Many parent educators have majored in areas such as child development as an undergraduate and/or taken a specialization of parenting and family courses in a master's or doctoral degree program in human development and family studies, clinical psychology, counseling psychology, or social work. As part of, or in addition to, their work in colleges and clinical settings, they may conduct parent education groups and workshops.

Janis Keyser *(right), conducting a parenting workshop.*

Trends in Childbearing

As birth control has become common practice, many individuals consciously choose when they will have children and how many children they will rear. The number of one-child families is increasing, for example, and U.S. women overall are having fewer children. These childbearing results are creating several trends:

- By giving birth to fewer children, and reducing the demands of child care, women free up a significant portion of their life spans for other endeavors.

- As working women increase in number, they invest less actual time in the child's development.

- Men are apt to invest a greater amount of time in fathering.

- Parental care is often supplemented by institutional care (child care, for example).

How Would You...?
As a family studies and human development professional, how would you advise a young woman who is inquiring about the best age for her to have children?

As more women show an increased interest in developing a career, they are not only marrying later, but also having fewer children and having them later in life. What are some of the advantages of having children early or late? Some of the advantages of having children early (in the twenties) are that the parents are likely to have more physical energy (for example, they can cope better with such matters as getting up in the middle of the night with infants and waiting up until adolescents come home at night); the mother is likely to have fewer medical problems with pregnancy and childbirth; and the parents may be less likely to build up expectations for their children, as do many couples who have waited many years to have children.

There are also advantages to having children later (in the thirties). The parents will have had more time to consider their goals in life, such as what they want from their family and career roles; the parents will be more mature and will be able to benefit from their life experiences to engage in more competent parenting; and the parents will be better established in their careers and have more income for child-rearing expenses.

Dealing with Divorce

If a marriage doesn't work, what happens after divorce? Psychologically, one of the most common characteristics of divorced adults is difficulty in trusting someone else in a romantic relationship. Following a divorce, though, people's lives can take diverse turns (Ahrons, 2007). For example, in one research study, 20 percent of the divorced group became more competent and better adjusted following their divorce (Hetherington & Kelly, 2002).

Strategies for divorced adults include (Hetherington & Kelly, 2002):

- Thinking of divorce as a chance to grow personally and to develop more positive relationships.

- Making decisions carefully. The consequences of your decision regarding work, lovers, and children may last a lifetime.

- Focusing more on the future than the past. Think about what is most important for you going forward in your life, set some challenging goals, and plan how to reach them.

What are some strategies for divorced adults that improve their adjustment?

rapport talk The language of conversation; it is a way of establishing connections and negotiating relationships.

report talk Talk that is designed to give information and includes public speaking.

- Using your strengths and resources to cope with difficulties.

- Not expecting to be successful and happy in everything you do. The path to a more enjoyable life will likely have a number of twists and turns, and moving forward will require considerable effort and resilience.

Gender, Communication, and Relationships

Stereotypes about differences in men's and women's attitudes toward communication, and about differences in how they communicate with each other, have spawned countless cartoons and jokes. Are the supposed differences real?

When Deborah Tannen (1990) analyzed the talk of women and men, she found that many wives complain about their husbands that "He doesn't listen to me anymore" and "He doesn't talk to me anymore." Lack of communication, though high on women's lists of reasons for divorce, is mentioned much less often by men.

Communication problems between men and women may come in part from differences in their preferred ways of communicating. Tannen distinguishes two ways of communicating: rapport talk and report talk. **Rapport talk** is the language of conversation; it is a way of establishing connections and negotiating relationships. **Report talk** is talk that is designed to give information, which includes public speaking. According to Tannen, women enjoy rapport talk more than report talk, and men's lack of interest in rapport talk bothers many women. In contrast, men prefer to engage in report talk. Men hold center stage through such verbal performances as telling stories and jokes. They learn to use talk as a way of getting and keeping attention.

How Would You...?
As a social worker, how would you educate a marital therapy group about the role of gender in communication and relationships?

How extensive are the gender differences in communication? Research has yielded somewhat mixed results. Recent studies do reveal some gender differences (Anderson, 2006). One study of a sampling of students' e-mails found that people could guess the writer's gender two-thirds of the time (Thompson & Murachver, 2001). Another study revealed that women make 63 percent of phone calls and when talking to another woman stay on the phone longer (7.2 minutes) than men do when talking with other men (4.6 minutes) (Smoreda & Licoppe, 2000). How- ever, recent meta-analyses suggest that overall gender differences in communication are small for both children and adults (Hyde, 2005; Leaper & Smith, 2004).

Summary

Stability and Change from Childhood to Adulthood

The first 20 years are important in predicting an adult's personality, but so, too, are continuing experiences in the adult years. Two main dimensions characterize adult attachment: attachment-related anxiety and attachment-related avoidance. Attachment styles in early adulthood are linked with a number of relationship patterns and developmental outcomes.

Love and Close Relationships

Erikson theorized that intimacy versus isolation is the key developmental issue in early adulthood. Friendship plays an important role in adult development, especially in terms of emotional support. Romantic love, also called passionate love, includes passion, sexuality, and a mixture of emotions, not all of which are positive. Affectionate love, also called companionate love, usually becomes more important as relationships mature. Sternberg proposed a triarchic model of love (passion, intimacy, and commitment).

Adult Lifestyles

Being single has become an increasingly prominent lifestyle. Autonomy is one of its advantages. Intimacy, loneliness, and finding a positive identity in a marriage-oriented society are challenges faced by single adults. Cohabitation is an increasingly popular lifestyle. Cohabitation does not lead to greater marital happiness but rather to no differences or to differences that suggest that cohabitation is not good for a marriage. The age at which individuals marry in U.S. is increasing. Despite a decline in marriage rates, a large percentage of Americans still marry. The benefits of marriage include better physical and mental health and a longer life. The U.S. divorce rate increased dramatically in the twentieth century but began to decline in the 1980s. Divorce is complex and emotional. Stepfamilies are complex and adjustment is difficult. One of the most striking findings about gay male and lesbian couples is how similar their relationships are to heterosexual couples' relationships.

Challenges in Marriage, Parenting, and Divorce

Gottman's research indicates that in marriages that work, couples establish love maps, nurture fondness and admiration, turn toward each other, accept the influence of the partner, and create shared meaning. Families are becoming smaller, and many women are delaying childbirth until they have become well established in a career. There are some advantages to having children earlier in adulthood, and some advantages to having them later. Hetherington identified six pathways taken by people after divorce. About 20 percent became better adjusted and more competent after the divorce.

Gender, Communication, and Relationships

Tannen distinguishes between rapport talk, which many women prefer, and report talk, which many men prefer. A recent meta-analysis found small gender differences in communication.

Key Terms

attachment-related
 anxiety 331
attachment-related
 avoidance 331

romantic love 333
affectionate love 333

rapport talk 342
report talk 342

13

Physical and Cognitive Development in Middle Adulthood

Stories of Life–Span Development: Jim Croce, Time in a Bottle

Our perception of time depends on where we are in the life span. We are more concerned about time at some points in life than others (Carstensen, 2006). Jim Croce's song "Time in a Bottle" reflects a time perspective that develops in the adult years:

If I could save time in a bottle
The first thing that I'd like to do
Is to save every day
Til Eternity passes away
Just to spend them with you . . .

But there never seems to be enough time
To do the things you want to do
Once you find them
I've looked around enough to know
That you're the one I want to go
Through time with

Jim Croce's song connects time with love and the hope of going through time with someone we love. Love and intimacy are important themes of adult development as we saw in Chapter 12. So is time. Middle-aged adults begin to

look back to where they have been, reflecting on what they have done with the time they have had. They look toward to the future more in terms of how much time remains to accomplish what they hope to do with their lives.

When young adults look forward in time to what their lives might be like as middle-aged adults, too often they anticipate that things will go downhill. However, like all periods of the human life span, for most individuals there usually are positive and negative features of middle age. In this first chapter on middle adulthood, we discuss physical changes; cognitive changes; changes in careers, work, and leisure; as well as the importance of religion and meaning in life during middle adulthood. To begin, though, we explore how middle age is changing. ▮

The Nature of Middle Adulthood

Is midlife experienced the same way today as it was 100 years ago? How can middle adulthood be defined, and what are some of its main characteristics?

Changing Midlife

Each year, for $8, about 2.5 to 3 million Americans who have turned 50 become members of the American Association for Retired Persons, now called simply, AARP. There is something incongruous about so many 50-year-olds joining a retirement group when hardly any of them are retired. Indeed, many of today's 50-year-olds are in better shape, more alert, and more productive than their 40-year-old counterparts from a generation or two earlier. As more people lead healthier lifestyles, and medical discoveries help to stave off the aging process, the boundaries of middle age are being pushed upward. It looks like middle age is starting later and lasting longer for increasing numbers of active, healthy, and productive people. One study found that almost half of the individuals 65 to 69 years of age considered themselves middle-aged (National Council on Aging, 2000), and another study found a similar pattern: Half of the 60- to 65-year-olds viewed themselves as in middle age (Lachman, Maier, & Budner, 2000). Also, some individuals consider the upper boundary of midlife as the age at which they make the transition from work to retirement.

When Carl Jung studied midlife transitions early in the twentieth century, he referred to midlife as "the afternoon of life" (Jung, 1933). Midlife serves as an important preparation for late adulthood, "the evening of life" (Lachman, 2004, p. 306). But "midlife" came much earlier in Jung's time. In 1900 the average life expectancy was only 47 years of age; only 3 percent of the population lived past 65. Today, the average life expectancy is 78, and 12 percent of the U.S. population is older than 65. As a much greater percentage of the population lives to an older age, the midpoint of life and what constitutes middle age or middle adulthood are getting harder to pin down. Statistically, the middle of life today is about 39 years of age, but most 39-year-olds don't want to be called "middle-aged." What we think of as middle age comes later—anywhere from 40 or 45 to about 60 or 65 years of age. And as more people live longer, the 60 to 65 years upper boundary will likely be nudged upward.

How is midlife changing?

Compared to previous decades and centuries, an increasing percentage of the population is made up of middle-aged and older adults. In the past, the age structure of the population could be represented by a pyramid, with the largest percentage of the population in the childhood years. Today, the percentages of people at different ages in the life span are more similar, creating what is called the "rectangularization" of the age distribution (a vertical rectangle) (Willis & Martin, 2005).

Although middle adulthood has been a relatively neglected period of the human life span (except for pop psychology portrayals of the midlife crisis), life-span developmentalists are beginning to give more attention to this age period (Brim, Ryff, & Kessler, 2004; Lachman, 2004; Willis & Martin, 2005). One reason for the increased attention is that the largest cohort in U.S. history is currently moving through the middle-age years. From 1990 to 2015, the middle-aged U.S. population is projected to increase from 47 million to 80 million, a 72 percent increase. Because of the size of the baby-boom cohort (recall from Chapter 1 that a *cohort* is a group of people born in a particular year or time period), the median age of the U.S. population will increase from 33 years in 1990 to 42 years in 2050. The baby boomers, born from 1946 to 1964, are of interest to developmentalists not only because of their increased numbers but also because they are the best-educated and most affluent cohort in history to pass through middle age (Willis & Martin 2005).

Defining Middle Adulthood

Though the age boundaries are not set in stone, we will consider **middle adulthood** as the developmental period that begins at approximately 40 years of age and extends to about 60 to 65 years of age. For many people, middle adulthood is a time of declining physical skills and expanding responsibility; a period in which people become more conscious of the young-old polarity and the shrinking amount of time left in life; a point when individuals seek to transmit something meaningful to the next generation; and a time when people reach and maintain satisfaction in their careers. In sum, middle adulthood involves "balancing work and relationship responsibilities in the midst of the physical and psychological changes associated with aging" (Lachman, 2004, p. 305).

In midlife, as in other age periods, individuals make choices, selecting what to do, how to invest time and resources, and evaluating what aspects of their lives they need to change. In midlife, "a serious accident, loss, or illness" may be a "wake-up call" and produce "a major restructuring of time and a reassessment" of life's priorities (Lachman, 2004, p. 310).

As we mentioned earlier, for many increasingly healthy adults, middle age is lasting longer. Indeed, an increasing number of experts on middle adulthood describe the age period of 55 to 65 as *late midlife* (Deeg, 2005). Compared to earlier midlife, late midlife is more likely to be characterized by the death of a parent, the last child leaving the parental home, becoming a grandparent, the preparation for retirement, and in most cases actual retirement. Many people in this age range experience their first confrontation with health problems. Overall, then, although gains and losses may balance each other in early midlife, losses may begin to dominate gains for many individuals in late midlife (Baltes, Lindenberger, & Staudinger, 2006).

Keep in mind, though, that midlife is characterized by individual variations (Perrig-Chiello & Perren, 2005). As life-span expert Gilbert Brim (1992) commented, middle adulthood is full of changes, twists, and turns; the path is not fixed. People move in and out of states of success and failure.

Physical Development

What physical changes accompany the change to middle adulthood? How healthy are middle-aged adults? How sexually active are middle-aged adults?

Physical Changes

Although everyone experiences some physical change due to aging in the middle adulthood years, the rates of this aging vary considerably from one individual to another. Genetic makeup and lifestyle factors play important roles in whether chronic disease will appear and when (Gavrilova & Gavrilova, 2006). Middle age is a window through which we can glimpse later life while there is still time to engage in prevention and to influence some of the course of aging (Lachman, 2004).

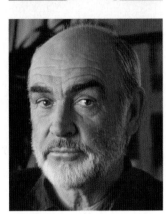

Visible Signs

One of the most visible signs of physical changes in middle adulthood is physical appearance. The first outwardly noticeable signs of aging usually are apparent by the forties or fifties. The skin begins to wrinkle and sag because of a loss of fat and collagen in underlying tissues (Giacomoni & Rein, 2004). Small, localized areas of pigmentation in

How Would You...?
As a human development and family studies professional, how would you characterize the impact of the media in shaping middle-aged adults' expectations about their changing physical appearance?

the skin produce aging spots, especially in areas that are exposed to sunlight, such as the hands and face. For most people, their hair becomes thinner and grayer. Fingernails and toenails develop ridges and become thicker and more brittle.

Since a youthful appearance is stressed in our culture, many individuals whose hair is graying, whose skin is wrinkling, whose bodies are sagging, and whose teeth are yellowing strive to make themselves look younger. Undergoing cosmetic surgery, dyeing hair, wearing wigs, enrolling in weight reduction programs, participating in exercise regimens, and taking heavy doses of vitamins are common in middle age (McCullough & Kelly, 2006). Many baby boomers have shown a strong interest in plastic surgery and Botox, which may reflect their desire to take control of the aging process (Lachman & Firth, 2004).

Famous actor Sean Connery as a young adult in his twenties (*top*) and as a middle-aged adult in his fifties (*bottom*). *What are some of the most outwardly noticeable signs of aging in the middle adulthood years?*

Height and Weight

Individuals lose height in middle age. On average, from 30 to 50 years of age, men lose about $^1/_2$ inch in height, then may lose another $^3/_4$ inch from 50 to 70 years of age (Hoyer & Roodin, 2003). The height loss for women can be as much as 2 inches over a 50-year span from 25 to 75 years of age. Note that there are large variations in the extent to which individuals become shorter with aging. The decrease in height is due to bone loss in the vertebrae.

Although people in middle age may lose height, many gain weight. On average, body fat accounts for about 10 percent of body weight in adolescence; it makes up

How Would You...?
As a social worker, how would you apply the statistics on weight and health to promote healthier lifestyles for middle-aged adults?

20 percent or more in middle age. In a recent national survey, 29 percent of U.S. adults 40 to 59 years of age were classified as obese (Centers for Disease Control and Prevention, 2006). In Chapter 11, we saw that in this survey 22 percent of U.S. adults 20 to 39 years of age were classified as obese. Being overweight is a critical health problem in middle adulthood (Aldwin, Spiro, & Park, 2006). For example, obesity increases the probability that an individual will suffer a number of other ailments, among them hypertension (abnormally high blood pressure) diabetes, and digestive disorders (Hart & others, 2007). A recent large-scale study found that being overweight or obese in middle age increases an individual's risk of dying earlier (Adams & others, 2006).

Strength, Joints, and Bones

As we saw in Chapter 11, maximum physical strength often is attained in the twenties. The term *sarcopenia* is given to age-related loss of muscle mass and strength (Deschennes, 2007). The rate of muscle loss with age occurs at a rate of approximately 1 to 2 percent per year past the age of 50 (Marcell, 2003). A loss of strength especially occurs in the back and legs. Exercise can reduce the decline involved in sarcopenia (Zacker, 2006).

Peak functioning of the body's joints also usually occurs in the twenties. The cartilage that cushions the movement of bones and other connective tissues, such as tendons and ligaments, become less efficient in the middle-adult years, a time when many individuals experience joint stiffness and more difficulty in movement.

Maximum bone density occurs by the mid- to late thirties, from which point there is a progressive loss of bone. The rate of this bone loss begins slowly but accelerates in the fifties (Whitbourne, 2001). Women experience about twice the rate of bone loss as men. By the end of midlife, bones break more easily and heal more slowly (Wehren & others, 2005).

Vision and Hearing

Accommodation of the eye—the ability to focus and maintain an image on the retina—experiences its sharpest decline between 40 and 59 years of age. In particular, middle-aged individuals begin to have difficulty viewing close objects, which means that many individuals have to wear glasses with bifocal lenses, lenses with two sections to see items at different distances (Schieber, 2006). Also, there is some evidence that the retina becomes less sensitive to low levels of illumination.

Hearing also can start to decline by the age of 40 (Roring, Hines, & Charness, 2007). Sensitivity to high pitches usually declines first. The ability to hear low-pitched sounds does not seem to decline much in middle adulthood, though. Men usually lose their sensitivity to high-pitched sounds sooner than women do. However, this gender difference might be due to men's greater exposure to noise in occupations such as mining, automobile work, and so on (Kline & Scialfa, 1996).

Cardiovascular System

Midlife is the time when high blood pressure and high cholesterol take many individuals by surprise (Lachman, 2004). Fatty deposits and scar tissue slowly accumulate in the linings of blood vessels, gradually reducing blood flow to various organs, including the heart and brain (Masoro, 2006).

The level of cholesterol in the blood increases through the adult years and in midlife begins to accumulate on the artery walls, increasing the risk of cardiovascular disease (Kurth & others, 2007). Blood pressure (hypertension), too, usually rises in the forties and fifties (Bloch & Basile, 2007). At menopause, a woman's blood pressure rises sharply and usually remains above that of a man through life's later years (Narkiewicz & others, 2005).

Exercise, weight control, and a diet rich in fruits, vegetables, and whole grains can often help to stave off many cardiovascular problems in middle age (Stanner, 2006). For example, though heredity influences cholesterol levels, LDL (the bad cholesterol) can be reduced and HDL (the good cholesterol) increased by eating food that is very low in saturated fat and cholesterol and by exercising regularly (Ekelund, Griffin, & Wareham, 2007).

Lungs

There is little change in lung capacity through most of middle adulthood. However, at about the age of 55, the proteins in lung tissue become less elastic. This change, combined with a gradual stiffening of connective tissues in the chest wall, decreases the lungs' capacity to shuttle oxygen from the air people breathe to the blood in their veins. As shown in Figure 13.1, the lung capacity of individuals who are smokers drops precipitously in middle age, but if the individuals quit smoking their lung capacity improves, although not to the level of individuals who have never smoked.

Sleep

Some aspects of sleep become more problematic in middle age (Campell & Murphy, 2007). The total number of hours slept usually remains the same as in early adulthood, but beginning in the forties, wakeful periods are more frequent and there is less of the deepest type of sleep (stage 4). The amount of time spent lying awake in bed at night begins to increase in middle age, and this can produce a feeling of being less rested in the morning (Abbott, 2003). Sleep problems in middle-aged adults are more common in individuals who use a higher number of prescription and nonprescription drugs, are obese, have cardiovascular disease, or are depressed (Kaleth & others, 2007).

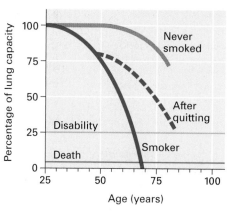

Figure 13.1 The Relation of Lung Capacity to Age and Cigarette Smoking Lung capacity shows little change through middle age for individuals who have not smoked. However, smoking is linked with reduced lung capacity in middle-aged and older adults. When individuals stop smoking their lung capacity becomes greater than those who continue to smoke, but not as great as the lung capacity of individuals who have never smoked.

Health and Disease

In middle adulthood, the frequency of accidents declines, and individuals are less susceptible to colds and allergies than in childhood, adolescence, or early adulthood. Indeed, many individuals live through middle adulthood without having a disease or persistent health problem. For others, however, disease and persistent health problems become more common in middle adulthood than in earlier life stages.

Only 7 percent of individuals in their early forties report having a disability, but that number more than doubles by the early fifties (16 percent), and by the early sixties, 30 percent report having a disability (Lachman, 2004). When individuals in late adulthood were asked to rate their health in early, middle, and late adulthood, they indicated that their health in middle adulthood was not as good as in early adulthood but better than in late adulthood (National Center for Health Statistics, 1999). Men rated their health as somewhat better than women in midlife, but in late adulthood the gender differences virtually disappeared.

Stress is increasingly being found to be a factor in disease (Clays & others, 2007). For example, people who have had major life changes such as loss of a spouse or a job, which might mean an increase in stress overall, have an increased incidence of cardiovascular disease and early death (Taylor, 2006). The cumulative effect of stress often takes a toll on the health of individuals by the time they reach middle age (Aldwin, Spiro, & Park, 2006). Stress is linked to disease through both the immune system and cardiovascular disease (Ah, Kang, & Carpenter, 2007)

climacteric The midlife transition in which fertility declines.

menopause The complete cessation of a woman's menstruation, which usually occurs in the late forties or early fifties.

Cause of Death
1. Heart disease
2. Cancer
3. Cerebrovascular disease
4. Accidents
5. Pulmonary disease

Figure 13.2 **Leading Causes of Death in Middle Adulthood**

Mortality Rates

Infectious disease was the main cause of death until the middle of the twentieth century. As infectious disease rates declined and more individuals lived through middle age, chronic disorders increased. Chronic diseases are now the main causes of death for individuals in middle adulthood (Merrill & Verbrugge, 1999).

In middle age, many deaths are caused by a single, readily identifiable condition, whereas in old age death is more likely to result from the combined effects of several chronic conditions (Gessert, Elliott, & Haller, 2003). Figure 13.2 shows the leading causes of death in middle age. Heart disease is the leading cause, followed by cancer and cerebrovascular disease (National Center for Health Statistics, 2006). In the first half of middle age, cancer claims more lives than heart disease; this is reversed in the second half. Men have higher mortality rates than women for all of the leading causes of death.

Sexuality

What kinds of changes characterize the sexuality of women and men as they go through middle age? **Climacteric** is a term that is used to describe the midlife transition in which fertility declines. Let's explore the substantial differences in the climacteric of women and men during middle adulthood.

Menopause

Most of us know something about menopause. But is what we know accurate? What is menopause, when does it occur, and what are its side effects?

Menopause is the time in middle age, usually in the late forties or early fifties, when a woman's menstrual periods completely cease. The average age at which women have their last period is 51 (Wise, 2006). However, there is large variation in the age at which menopause occurs—from 39 to 59 years of age. A recent study revealed that women who smoke experience menopause earlier while women who exercise reach menopause later (Santoro & others, 2007).

Not only the timing but also the side effects of menopause vary greatly (Dennerstein & others, 2007). In menopause, production of estrogen by the ovaries declines dramatically, and this decline produces uncomfortable symptoms in some women—"hot flashes," nausea, fatigue, and rapid heartbeat, for example. Cross-cultural studies also reveal wide variations in the menopause experience (Anderson & Yoshizawa, 2007; Avis, 1999). For example, hot flashes are uncommon in Mayan women (Beyene, 1986). Asian women report fewer hot flashes than women in Western societies (Payer, 1991). It is difficult to determine the extent to which these cross-cultural variations are due to genetic, dietary, reproductive, or cultural factors.

In the United States, research based on small samples of women who go to physicians or therapists because they are having problems associated with menopause sometimes creates the impression that menopause is necessarily a traumatic event. In fact, in a large-scale study of Americans in midlife, just over 50 percent of middle-aged women reported having no hot flashes at all (Brim, 1999). Almost two-thirds of postmenopausal women said they were relieved that their periods had stopped. Only 1 percent said they felt "only regret" that they no longer had their period. Some menopausal women report depression and irritability, but in some instances these feelings are related to other circumstances such as becoming divorced, losing a job, caring for a sick parent, and so on (Gannon, 1998).

In sum, menopause overall is not the negative experience for most women it was once thought to be (Cheng & others, 2007). However, the loss of fertility is an important marker for women—it means that they have to make final decisions about having children. Women in their thirties who have never had children sometimes speak about being "up against the biological clock" because they cannot postpone choices about having children much longer.

Until recently, hormone replacement therapy was often prescribed as treatment for unpleasant side effects of menopause. *Hormone replacement therapy (HRT)* augments the declining levels of reproductive hormone production by the ovaries (Wathen, 2006). HRT can consist of various forms of estrogen, and usually a progestin.

Researchers have found that almost 50 percent of Canadian and American women have occasional hot flashes, but only 1 in 7 Japanese women do (Lock, 1998). *What factors might account for these variations?*

A study of HRT's effects was halted as evidence emerged that participants who were receiving HRT faced an increased risk of stroke (National Institutes of Health, 2004). Preliminary data also indicated a trend toward increased risk of dementia (deterioration of mental functioning) among those receiving HRT. On the positive side, the study found that estrogen lowered the risk of hip fractures and did not increase the risk of heart attacks or breast cancer.

The National Institutes of Health recommends that women with a uterus who are currently taking hormones should consult with their doctor to determine whether they should continue the treatment. If they are taking HRT for short-term relief of symptoms, the benefits may outweigh the risks. However, the recent evidence of risks associated with HRT suggests that long-term hormone therapy should be seriously reevaluated (Warren, 2007).

How Would You...?
As a human development and family studies professional, how would you counsel middle-aged women who voice the belief that hormone replacement therapy is necessary to "stay young"?

Hormonal Changes in Middle-Aged Men

Do men go through anything like the menopause that women experience? That is, is there a male menopause? During middle adulthood, most men do not lose their capacity to father children, although there usually is a modest decline in their sexual hormone level and activity. Men experience hormonal changes in their fifties and sixties, but nothing like the dramatic drop in estrogen that women experience (Harman, 2006). Testosterone production begins to decline about 1 percent a year during middle adulthood, and sperm count usually shows a slow decline, but men do not lose their fertility in middle age. What has been referred to as "male menopause," then, probably has less to do with hormonal change than with the psychological adjustment men must make when they are faced with declining physical energy and with family and work pressures. Testosterone therapy has not been found to relieve such symptoms, suggesting that they are not induced by hormonal change.

PHYSICAL DEVELOPMENT

351

The gradual decline in men's testosterone levels in middle age can reduce their sexual drive (Gooren, 2003). Their erections are less full and less frequent, and men require more stimulation to achieve them. Researchers once attributed these changes to psychological factors, but increasingly they find that as many as 75 percent of the erectile dysfunctions in middle-aged men stem from physiological problems. Smoking, diabetes, hypertension, and elevated cholesterol levels are at fault in many erectile problems in middle-aged men (Beutel, Weidner, & Brahler, 2006).

Treatment for men with erectile dysfunction has focused recently on the drug Viagra and on similar drugs that appeared after Viagra became popular, such as Levitra and Cialis (Zinner, 2007). Viagra works by allowing increased blood flow into the penis, which produces an erection. Its success rate is nearly 90 percent (Lee & others, 2006).

Sexual Attitudes and Behavior

Although the ability of men and women to function sexually shows little biological decline in middle adulthood, sexual activity usually occurs on a less frequent basis than in early adulthood (Burgess, 2004). Career interests, family matters, energy level, and routine may contribute to this decline (Avis & others, 2005).

In the Sex in America survey (described initially in Chapter 11), the frequency of having sex was greatest for individuals aged 25 to 29 years old (47 percent had sex twice a week or more) and dropped off for individuals in their fifties (23 percent of 50- to 59-year-old males said they had sex twice a week or more, while only 14 percent of the females in this age group reported this frequency) (Michael & others, 1994). Note, though, that the Sex in America survey may underestimate the frequency of sexual activity of middle-aged adults because the data were collected prior to the widespread use of erectile dysfunction drugs such as Viagra.

Living with a spouse or partner makes all the difference in whether people engage in sexual activity, especially for women over 40 years of age. In one study conducted by the MacArthur Foundation, 95 percent of women in their forties with partners said that they have been sexually active in the last six months, compared with only 53 percent of those without partners (Brim, 1999). By their fifties,

How Would You...?

As a psychologist, how would you counsel a couple about the ways that the transition to middle adulthood might affect their sexual relationship?

Age groups	Not at all	A few times per year	A few times per month	2–3 times a week	4 or more times a week
Men					
18–24	15	21	24	28	12
25–29	7	15	31	36	11
30–39	8	15	37	23	6
40–49	9	18	40	27	6
50–59	11	22	43	20	3
Women					
18–24	11	16	2	9	12
25–29	5	10	38	37	10
30–39	9	16	6	33	6
40–49	15	16	44	20	5
50–59	30	22	35	12	2

Percentage engaging in sex

What are some characteristics of middle-aged adults' sexual behavior?

88 percent of women living with a partner have been sexually active in the last six months, but only 37 percent of those who are neither married nor living with someone say they have had sex in the last six months.

crystallized intelligence Accumulated information and verbal skills, which increase in middle age, according to Horn.

fluid intelligence The ability to reason abstractly, which steadily declines from middle adulthood on, according to Horn.

Cognitive Development

We have seen that middle-aged adults may not see as well, run as fast, or be as healthy as they were in their twenties and thirties. We've also seen a decline in their sexual activity. What about their cognitive skills? Do they decline as we enter and move through middle adulthood? To answer this question we explore the possibility of cognitive changes in intelligence and information processing.

Intelligence

Our exploration of possible changes in intelligence in middle adulthood focuses on the concepts of fluid and crystallized intelligence, cohort effects, and the Seattle Longitudinal Study.

Fluid and Crystallized Intelligence

John Horn argues that some abilities begin to decline in middle age, whereas others increase (Horn & Donaldson, 1980). Horn argues that **crystallized intelligence,** an individual's accumulated information and verbal skills, continues to increase in middle adulthood, whereas **fluid intelligence**, one's ability to reason abstractly, begins to decline in the middle adulthood years (see Figure 13.3).

Horn's data were collected in a cross-sectional manner. Remember from Chapter 1, "Introduction," that a cross-sectional study assesses individuals of different ages at the same point in time. For example, a cross-sectional study might assess the intelligence of different groups of 40-, 50-, and 60-year-olds in a single evaluation, such as in 1980. The 40-year-olds in the study would have been born in 1940 and the 60-year-olds in 1920—different eras that offered different economic and educational opportunities. The 60-year-olds likely had fewer educational opportunities as they grew up. Thus, if we find differences between 40- and 60-year-olds on intelligence tests when they are assessed cross-sectionally, these differences might be due to cohort effects related to educational differences rather than to age.

By contrast, remember from Chapter 1 that in a longitudinal study, the same individuals are studied over a period of time. Thus, a longitudinal study of intelligence in middle adulthood might consist of giving the same intelligence test to the same individuals when they are 40, then 50, and then 60 years of age. As we see next, whether data on intelligence are collected cross-sectionally or longitudinally can make a difference in what is found about changes in crystallized and fluid intelligence and about intellectual decline.

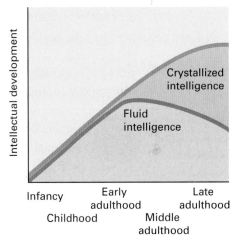

Figure 13.3 Fluid and Crystallized Intellectual Development Across the Life Span According to Horn, crystallized intelligence (based on cumulative learning experiences) increases throughout the life span, but fluid intelligence (the ability to perceive and manipulate information) steadily declines from middle adulthood.

The Seattle Longitudinal Study

K. Warner Schaie (1996; Willis & Schaie, 2005) is conducting an extensive study of intellectual abilities in the adulthood years. Five hundred individuals initially were tested in 1956. New waves of participants are added periodically. The main focus in the Seattle Longitudinal Study has been on individual change and stability in intelligence. The main mental abilities tested are *vocabulary* (ability to understand ideas expressed in words); *verbal memory* (ability to encode and recall meaningful language units, such as a list of words; *number* (ability to perform simple mathematical computations such as addition, subtraction, and multiplication; *spatial orientation* (ability to visualize and mentally rotate stimuli in two- and three-dimensional space); *inductive reasoning* (ability to recognize and understand patterns and relationships in a problem and use this understanding to solve other instances of the problem); and *perceptual speed* (ability to quickly and accurately make simple discriminations in visual stimuli).

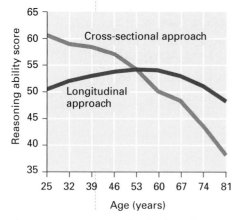

Figure 13.4 Cross-Sectional and Longitudinal Comparisons of Intellectual Change in Middle Adulthood *Why do you think reasoning ability peaks during middle adulthood.*

The highest level of functioning for four of the six intellectual abilities occurred in the middle adulthood years (Willis & Schaie, 2005). For both women and men, peak performance on vocabulary, verbal memory, inductive reasoning, and spatial orientation was attained in middle age. For only two of the six abilities—numerical ability and perceptual speed—were there declines in middle age. Perceptual speed showed the earliest decline, actually beginning in early adulthood. Interestingly, in terms of John Horn's ideas that were discussed earlier, for the participants in the Seattle Longitudinal Study, middle age was a time of peak performance for some aspects of both crystallized intelligence (vocabulary) and fluid intelligence (spatial orientation and inductive reasoning).

How Would You...? As an educator, how might changes in fluid and crystallized intelligence influence the way middle-aged adults learn?

When Schaie (1994, 2007) assessed intellectual abilities both cross-sectionally and longitudinally, he found decline more likely in the cross-sectional than in the longitudinal assessments. For example, as shown in Figure 13.4, when assessed cross-sectionally, inductive reasoning showed a consistent decline in the middle adulthood years. In contrast, when assessed longitudinally, inductive reasoning increased until toward the end of middle adulthood, when it began to show a slight decline. In Schaie's view, it is in middle adulthood, not early adulthood, that people reach a peak in their cognitive functioning for many intellectual skills.

Information Processing

As we saw in our discussion of theories of development (Chapter 1) and of cognitive development from infancy through adolescence (Chapters 3, 5, 7, and 9), the information-processing approach provides another way of examining cognitive abilities. Among the information-processing changes that take place in middle adulthood are those involved in speed of processing information, memory, and expertise.

Speed of Information Processing

As we saw in Schaie's (1996) Seattle Longitudinal Study, perceptual speed begins declining in early adulthood and continues to decline in middle adulthood. A common way to assess speed of information is through a reaction-time task, in which individuals simply press a button as soon as they see a light appear (Hartley, 2006). Middle-aged adults are slower to push the button when the light appears than young adults are. However, keep in mind that the decline is not dramatic—under 1 second in most investigations. Also, for unknown reasons, the decline in reaction time is stronger for women than for men (Salthouse, 1994).

working memory Closely related to short-term memory but places more emphasis on mental work. Working memory is like a mental "workbench" where individuals can manipulate and assemble information when making decisions, solving problems, and comprehending written and spoken language.

Memory

In Schaie's (1994, 1996) Seattle Longitudinal Study, verbal memory peaked in the fifties. However, in some other studies, verbal memory has shown a decline in middle age, especially when assessed in cross-sectional studies. For example, in several studies, when asked to remember lists of words, numbers, or meaningful prose, younger adults outperformed middle-aged adults (Salthouse, 1991; Salthouse & Skovronek, 1992). Although there still is some controversy about whether memory declines in the middle adulthood years, most experts conclude that it does decline, at least in late middle age (Hoyer & Verhaeghen, 2006; Salthouse, 2000).

Aging and cognition expert Denise Park (2001) argues that starting in late middle age, more time is needed to learn new information. The slowdown in learning new information has been linked to changes in **working memory**, the mental "workbench" where individuals manipulate and assemble information when making decisions, solving problems, and comprehending written and spoken language (Baddeley, 2000, 2007). In this view, in late middle age, working memory capacity—the amount of information that can be immediately retrieved and used—becomes more limited (Leonards, Ibanez, & Giannakopoulous, 2002).

Memory decline is more likely to occur when individuals don't use effective memory strategies, such as organization and imagery (Hoyer & Verhaeghen, 2006). By organizing lists of phone numbers into different categories or imagining the phone numbers as representing different objects around the house, many people can improve their memory in middle adulthood.

Expertise

Because it takes so long to attain, expertise often shows up more in the middle adulthood than in the early adulthood years (Kim & Hasher, 2005). Recall from Chapter 7 that *expertise* involves having extensive, highly organized knowledge and understanding of a particular domain. Developing expertise and becoming an "expert" in a field usually is the result of many years of experience, learning, and effort.

Adults in the middle age who have become experts in their fields are likely to do the following: rely on their accumulated experience to solve problems; process information automatically and analyze it more efficiently when solving a problem; devise better strategies and shortcuts to solving problems; and be more creative and flexible in solving problems.

Stephen J. Hawking is a world-renowned expert in physics. Hawking authored the best-selling book, *A Brief History of Time.* Hawking has a neurological disorder that prevents him from walking or talking. He communicates with the aid of a voice-equipped computer. *What distinguishes experts from novices?*

Careers, Work, and Leisure

What are some issues that workers face in midlife? What role does leisure play in the lives of middle-aged adults?

Work in Midlife

The role of work, whether one works in a full-time career, a part-time job, as a volunteer, or a homemaker, is central during the middle years. Middle-aged adults may reach their peak in position and earnings. They may also be saddled with multiple financial burdens from rent or mortgage, child care, medical bills, home repairs, college tuition, loans to family members, or bills from nursing homes.

The progression of career trajectories in middle age is diverse. Some individuals have stable careers, with little mobility, while others move in and out of the labor force, experiencing layoffs and unemployment. Middle-aged adults may experience age discrimination in some job situations, and finding a job in midlife may be difficult because pay demands of older workers are higher than those of younger workers, or technological advances may render the midlife worker's skills outdated or obsolete (Lachman, 2004).

For many people, midlife is a time of evaluation, assessment, and reflection in terms of the work they do and want to do in the future. Among the work issues that some people face in midlife are recognizing limitations in career progress, deciding whether to change jobs or careers, deciding whether to rebalance family and work, and planning for retirement (Sterns & Huyck, 2001).

Career Challenges and Changes

The current middle-aged worker faces several important challenges in the twenty-first century (Moen & Spencer, 2006). These include the globalization of work, rapid developments in information technologies, downsizing of organizations, early retirement, and concerns about pensions and health care (Schulz & Borowksi, 2006).

Globalization has replaced what was once a primarily White male workforce in the United States with employees of different ethnic and national backgrounds who have immigrated from different parts of the world. The proliferation of computer technology compels middle-aged adults to become increasingly computer literate to maintain their work competence (Csaja, 2001). To improve profits, many companies are restructuring, downsizing, and outsourcing jobs. One of the outcomes of this is to offer incentives to middle-aged employees to retire early—in their fifties, or in some cases even forties, rather than their sixties.

The decline in defined-benefit pensions and increased uncertainty about the fate of health insurance are decreasing the sense of personal control for middle-aged workers. As a consequence, many are delaying retirement plans.

Some midlife career changes are self-motivated, others are the consequence of losing one's job (Moen & Spencer, 2006). Some individuals in middle age decide that they don't want to do the same work they have been doing for the rest of

How Would You...?
As a social worker, how would you advise middle-aged adults who are dissatisfied with their careers?

their working lives (Hoyer & Roodin, 2003). One aspect of middle adulthood involves adjusting idealistic hopes to realistic possibilities in light of how much time individuals have before they retire and how fast they are reaching their occupational goals (Levinson, 1978). Individuals could become motivated to change jobs, if they perceive that they are behind schedule, if their goals are unrealistic, if they don't like the work they are doing, or if their job has become too stressful,

leisure The pleasant times after work when individuals are free to pursue activities and interests of their own choosing.

Leisure

As adults, not only must we learn how to work well, but we also need to learn how to relax and enjoy leisure (Stebbins, 2005). **Leisure** refers to the pleasant times after work when individuals are free to pursue activities and interests of their own choosing—hobbies, sports, or reading, for example. In a recent analysis of research on what U.S. adults regret the most, not engaging in more leisure was one of the top six regrets (Roese & Summerville, 2005).

Leisure can be an especially important aspect of middle adulthood (Parkes, 2006). By middle adulthood, more money may be available to many individuals, and there may be more free time and paid vacations. In short, midlife changes may produce expanded opportunities for leisure. For many individuals, middle adulthood is the first time in their lives when they have the opportunity to follow their leisure-time interests.

Sigmund Freud once commented that the two things adults need to do well to adapt to society's demands are to work and to love. To his list we add "to play." In our fast-paced society, it is all too easy to get caught up in the frenzied, hectic pace of our achievement-oriented work world and ignore leisure and play. *Imagine your life as a middle-aged adult. What would be the ideal mix of work and leisure? What leisure activities do you want to enjoy as a middle-aged adult?*

How Would You...?
As a health-care professional, how would you explain the link between work and health to a patient?

Adults at midlife need to begin preparing psychologically for retirement. Developing constructive and fulfilling leisure activities in middle adulthood are an important part of this preparation (Agahi, Ahacic, & Parker, 2006). If an adult develops leisure activities that can be continued into retirement, the transition from work to retirement can be less stressful.

Religion and Meaning in Life

What role does religion play in our development as adults? Is the meaning of life an important theme for many middle-aged adults?

Religion and Adult Lives

Religion is an important aspect of people's lives around the world—98 percent of respondents in India, 88 percent in Italy, 72 percent in France, and 63 percent in Scandinavia say that they believe in God (Gallup, 1987). In the MacArthur Study of Midlife Development, more than 70 percent of U.S. middle-aged adults said they are religious and consider spirituality a major part of their lives (Brim, 1999). However, that does not mean they are committed to a single religion or house of

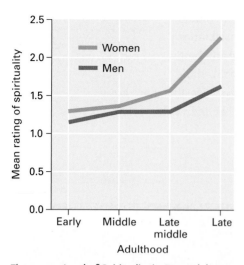

Figure 13.5 **Level of Spirituality in Four Adult Age Periods** In a longitudinal study, the spirituality of individuals in four different adult age periods—early (30s), middle (40s), late middle (mid-50s/early 60s), and late (late 60s/early 70s) adulthood—was assessed (Wink & Dillon, 2002). Based on responses to open-ended questions in interviews, the spirituality of the individuals was coded on a 5-point scale, with 5 being the highest level of spirituality and 1 the lowest.

worship. About half said they attend religious services less than once a month or never. In another study, about three-fourths of U.S. adults said that they pray (*Religion in America,* 1993).

In thinking about religion and adult development, it is important to consider the role of individual differences (McCullough & Laurenceau, 2005). Religion is a powerful influence in some adults' lives, whereas it plays little or no role in others' lives (Myers, 2000). In a longitudinal study of individuals from their early thirties through their late sixties/early seventies, a significant increase in spirituality occurred between late middle (mid-fifties/early sixties) and late adulthood (Wink & Dillon, 2002) (see Figure 13.5).

Females have consistently shown a stronger interest in religion than males have (Bijur & others, 1993). Compared with men, they participate more in both organized and personal forms of religion, are more likely to believe in a higher power or presence, and are more likely to feel that religion is an important dimension of their lives. In the longitudinal study just described, the spirituality of women increased more than men in the second half of life (Wink & Dillon, 2002).

Religion and Health

What might be some of the effects of religion on physical health? Some cults and religious sects encourage behaviors that are damaging to health, such as ignoring sound medical advice. For individuals in the religious mainstream, however, there is generally either no link between religion and physical health or a positive effect (Krause, 2006). Researchers have found that religious attendance is linked to a reduction in hypertension (Gillum & Ingram, 2007). Also, a number of studies have confirmed a positive association between religious participation and longevity (Oman & Thoresen, 2006).

Why might religion promote physical health? There are several possible answers (Hill & Butter, 1995). First, there are *lifestyle issues*—for example, religious individuals have lower drug use than their nonreligious counterparts (Gartner, Larson, & Allen, 1991). Second are *social networks*—the degree to which individuals are connected to others affects their health. Well-connected individuals have fewer health problems (Hill & Pargament, 2003). Religious groups, meetings, and activities provide social connectedness for individuals. A third answer involves *coping with stress*—religion offers a source of comfort and support when individuals are confronted with stressful events.

Religious counselors often advise people about mental health and coping. To read about the work of one religious counselor, see the Careers in Life-Span Development profile.

What roles do religion and spirituality play in the lives of middle-aged adults?

Gabriel Dy-Liacco, Pastoral Counselor

Gabriel Dy-Liacco is a pastoral counselor at the Pastoral Counseling and Consultation Centers of Greater Washington, D.C. He obtained his Ph.D. in pastoral counseling from Loyola College in Maryland and also has experience as a psychotherapist in such mental health settings as a substance abuse program, military family center, psychiatric clinic, and community mental health center. As a pastoral counselor, he works with adolescents and adults in the aspects of their life that they show the most concern about—psychological, spiritual, or the interface of both. Having lived in Peru, Japan, and the Phillipines, he brings considerable multicultural experience to the counseling setting. Dr. Dy-Liacco also is a professor in the Graduate School of Psychology and Counseling at Regent University in the Washington, D.C., area.

Pastoral counselors, like Gabriel Dy-Liacco, are trained in both psychology and theology, which enables them to provide clients with psychological and spiritual guidance. Most pastoral counselors have an undergraduate degree and a master's or doctoral degree in theology and/or pastoral counseling. If they have only an advanced theology degree, they also must take a certain amount of pastoral counseling courses. Pastoral counselors usually work in such care settings as hospitals, nursing homes, rehabilitation facilities, psychiatric facilities, and correctional institutions.

Meaning in Life

Austrian psychiatrist Viktor Frankl's mother, father, brother, and wife died in the concentration camps and gas chambers in Auschwitz, Poland. Frankl survived the concentration camp and went on to write about meaning in life. In his book, *Man's Search for Meaning*, Frankl (1984) emphasized each person's uniqueness and the finiteness of life. He believed that examining the finiteness of our existence and the certainty of death adds meaning to life. If life were not finite, said Frankl, we could spend our life doing just about whatever we please because time would continue forever.

Frankl said that the three most distinct human qualities are spirituality, freedom, and responsibility. Spirituality, in his view, does not have a religious underpinning. Rather, it refers to a human being's uniqueness—to spirit, philosophy, and mind. Frankl proposed that people need to ask themselves such questions as why they exist, what they want from life, and what the meaning of their life is.

It is in middle adulthood that individuals begin to be faced with death more often, especially the deaths of parents and other older relatives. Also faced with less time in their life, many individuals in middle age begin to ask and evaluate the questions that Frankl proposed. And meaning-making coping is especially helpful in times of chronic stress and loss.

Summary

The Nature of Middle Adulthood

As more people live to an older age, what we think of as middle age seems to be occurring later. A major reason developmentalists are beginning to study middle age is because of the dramatic increase in the number of individuals entering this period of the life span. Middle age involves extensive individual variation. With this variation in mind, we will consider middle adulthood to be entered at about 40 and exited at approximately 60 to 65 years of age. For most people, middle adulthood involves declining physical skills, expanding responsibility, being conscious of the young-old polarity, motivation to transmit something meaningful to the next generation, and reaching and maintaining career satisfaction.

Physical Development

The physical changes of midlife are usually gradual. Genetic and lifestyle factors play important roles in whether chronic diseases will appear and when. Among the physical changes of middle adulthood are outwardly noticeable changes in physical appearance (wrinkles, aging spots); height (decrease) and weight (increase); loss of strength and bone density; loss of flexibility in joints; vision and hearing changes; cardiovascular system changes; decreased lung capacity; and sleep changes. In middle age, the leading causes of death, in order, are heart disease, cancer, and cerebrovascular disease. Climacteric is the midlife transition in which fertility declines. The vast majority of women do not have serious physical or psychological problems related to menopause. Recent evidence of risks associated with hormone replacement therapy suggests that its long-term use should be seriously evaluated. Men do not experience an inability to father children in middle age, although their testosterone levels decline. Sexual behavior occurs less frequently in middle adulthood than in early adulthood.

Cognitive Development

Horn argued that crystallized intelligence (accumulated information and verbal skills) continues to increase in middle adulthood, whereas fluid intelligence (ability to reason abstractly) declines. Schaie found that longitudinal assessments of intellectual abilities are less likely than cross-sectional assessments to find declines in middle adulthood and are even more likely to find improvements. The highest level of four intellectual abilities (vocabulary, verbal memory, inductive reasoning, and spatial orientation) occurred in middle age. Speed of information processing, often assessed through reaction time, declines in middle adulthood. Working memory declines in late middle age. Memory is more likely to decline in middle age when individuals don't use effective memory strategies. Expertise often increases in the middle adulthood years.

Careers, Work, and Leisure

For many people midlife is a time of reflection, assessment, and evaluation of their current work and what they plan to do in the future. The progression of career trajectories in midlife is diverse. The current middle-aged worker faces such challenges as the globalization of work, rapid developments in information technologies, downsizing of organizations, early retirement, and concerns about pensions and health care. Midlife job or career changes can be self-motivated or forced on individuals. We not only need to learn to work well, but we also need to learn to enjoy leisure. Midlife may be an especially important time for leisure because of the physical changes that occur and because of preparation for a satisfactory retirement.

Religion and Meaning in Life

Religion is an important dimension of many Americans' lives, as well as the lives of people around the world. Females show a stronger interest in religion than males do. It is important to consider individual differences in religious interest.

In some cases, religion can be negatively linked to physical health, as when cults or religious sects discourage individuals from obtaining medical care. In mainstream religions, religion usually shows either a positive association or no association with physical health. Religion can play an important role in coping for some individuals. Frankl believes that examining the finiteness of our existence leads to exploration of meaning in life. Faced with the death of older relatives and less time to live themselves, many middle-aged individuals increasingly examine life's meaning.

Key Terms

middle adulthood 346
climacteric 350
menopause 350

crystallized
 intelligence 353
fluid intelligence 353

working memory 355
leisure 357

14

Socioemotional Development in Middle Adulthood

Stories of Life-Span Development: Sarah and Wanda, Middle-Age Variations

Forty-five-year-old Sarah feels tired, depressed, and angry when she looks back on the way her life has gone. She became pregnant when she was 17 and married Ben, the baby's father. They stayed together for three years after their son was born, and then Ben left her for another woman. Sarah went to work as a salesclerk to make ends meet. Eight years later, she married Alan, who had two children of his own from a previous marriage. Sarah stopped working for several years to care for the children.

Then, like Ben, Alan started going out on her. She found out about it from a friend. Nevertheless, Sarah stayed with Alan for another year. Finally he was gone so much that she could not take it anymore and decided to divorce him. Sarah went back to work again as a salesclerk; she has been in the same position for 16 years now. During those 16 years, she has dated a number of men, but the relationships never seemed to work out. Her son never finished high school and has drug

problems. Her father just died last year, and Sarah is trying to help her mother financially, although she can barely pay her own bills. Sarah looks in the mirror and does not like what she sees. She sees her past as a shambles, and the future does not look rosy, either.

Forty-five-year-old Wanda feels energetic, happy, and satisfied. As a young woman, she graduated from college and worked for three years as a high school math teacher. She married Andy, who had just finished law school. One year later, they had their first child, Josh. Wanda stayed home with Josh for two years, and then returned to her job as a math teacher. Even during her pregnancy, Wanda stayed active and exercised regularly, playing tennis almost every day. After her pregnancy, she kept up her exercise habits. Wanda and Andy had another child, Wendy. Now, as they move into their middle-age years, their children are both off to college, and Wanda and Andy are enjoying spending more time with each other. Last weekend they visited Josh at his college, and

the weekend before they visited Wendy at her college. Wanda continued working as a high school math teacher until six years ago. She had developed computer skills as part of her job and taken some computer courses at a nearby college, doubling up during the summer months. She resigned her math teaching job and took a job with a computer company, where she has already worked her way into management. Wanda looks in the mirror and likes what she sees. She sees her past as enjoyable, although not without hills and valleys, and she

looks to the future with zest and enthusiasm.

As with Sarah and Wanda, there are individual variations in the way people experience middle age. To begin the chapter, we examine personality theories and development in middle age, including ideas about individual variation. Then we turn our attention to how much individuals change or stay the same as they go through the adult years, and finally we explore a number of aspects of close relationships during the middle adulthood years. ∎

Personality Theories and Development

What is the best way to conceptualize middle age? Is it a stage or a crisis? How extensively is middle age influenced by life events? Do middle-aged adults experience stress differently than young and older adults? Is personality linked with contexts such as the point in history in which individuals go through midlife, their culture, and their gender?

Stages of Adulthood

Adult stage theories have been plentiful, and they have contributed to the view that midlife brings a crisis in development. Two prominent theories that define stages of adult development are Erik Erikson's life-span view and Daniel Levinson's seasons of a man's life.

Erikson's Stage of Generativity Versus Stagnation

Erikson (1968) proposed that middle-aged adults face a significant issue—generativity versus stagnation, which is the name Erikson gave to the seventh stage in his life-span theory. **Generativity** encompasses adults' desire to leave legacies of themselves to the next generation (Petersen, 2002). Through these legacies adults achieve a kind of immortality. By contrast, **stagnation** (sometimes called "self-absorption") develops when individuals sense that they have done little or nothing for the next generation.

Generative adults commit themselves to the continuation and improvement of society as a whole through their connection to the next generation. Generative adults develop a positive legacy of the self and then offer it as a gift to the next generation. Middle-aged adults can develop generativity in a number of ways (Kotre, 1984). Through biological generativity, adults have offspring. Through parental generativity, adults nurture and guide children. Through work generativity, adults develop skills that are passed down to others. And through cultural generativity, adults create, renovate, or conserve some aspect of culture that ultimately survives.

How Would You...?
As an educator, how would you describe ways in which the profession of teaching might establish generativity for someone in middle adulthood?

generativity Adults' desires to leave legacies of themselves to the next generation; the positive side of Erikson's generativity versus stagnation middle adulthood stage.

stagnation Sometimes called "self-absorption"—develops when individuals sense that they have done little or nothing for the next generation; the negative side of Erikson's generativity versus stagnation middle adulthood stage.

Through generativity, adults promote and guide the next generation by parenting, teaching, leading, and doing things that benefit the community (Pratt & others, 2001). One of the participants in a study of aging said: "From twenty to thirty I learned how to get along with my wife. From thirty to forty I learned how to be a success at my job, and at forty to fifty I worried less about myself and more about the children" (Vaillant, 2002, p. 114).

How does research support Erikson's theory that generativity is an important dimension of middle age? In one study, Carol Ryff (1984) examined the views of women and men at different ages and found that middle-aged adults especially were concerned about generativity. In another study, generative women with careers found gratification through work; generative women who had not worked in a career experienced gratification through parenting (Peterson & Stewart, 1996). In a longitudinal study of Smith College women, the desire for generativity increased as the participants aged from their thirties to their fifties (Stewart, Ostrove, & Helson, 2001).

How Would You...?
As a human development and family studies professional, how would you advise a middle-aged woman who never had children and now fears she has little opportunity to leave a legacy to the next generation?

Late adult transition: Age 60 to 65

Era of late adulthood: 60 to ?

Middle adult transition: Age 40 to 45

Culminating life structure for middle adulthood: 55 to 60

Age 50 transition: 50 to 55

Entry life structure for middle adulthood: 45 to 50

Early adult transition: Age 17 to 22

Culminating life structure for early adulthood: 33 to 40

Age 30 transition: 28 to 33

Entry life structure for early adulthood: 22 to 28

Figure 14.1 Levinson's Periods of Adults Development
According to Levinson, adulthood has three main stages, which are surrounded by transition period. Specific tasks and challenges are associated with each stage.

Levinson's Seasons of a Man's Life

In *The Seasons of a Man's Life* (1978), clinical psychologist Daniel Levinson reported the results of extensive interviews with forty middle-aged men. The interviews were conducted with hourly workers, business executives, academic biologists, and novelists. Levinson bolstered his conclusions with information from the biographies of famous men and the development of memorable characters in literature. Although Levinson's major interest focused on midlife change in men, he described a number of stages and transitions during the period from 17 to 65 years of age, as shown in Figure 14.1. Levinson emphasizes that developmental tasks must be mastered at each stage.

At the end of one's teens, according to Levinson, a transition from dependence to independence should occur. This transition is marked by the formation of a dream—an image of the kind of life the youth wants to have, especially in terms of a career and marriage. Levinson sees the twenties as a *novice phase* of adult development. It is a time of reasonably free experimentation and of testing the dream in the real world. In early adulthood, the two major tasks to be mastered are exploring the possibilities for adult living and developing a stable life structure.

From about the ages of 28 to 33, the man goes through a transition period in which he must face the more serious question of determining his goals. During the thirties, he usually focuses on family and career development. In the later years of this period, he enters a phase of *Becoming One's Own Man* (or BOOM, as Levinson calls it). By age 40, he has reached a stable location in his career, has outgrown his earlier, more tenuous attempts at learning to become an adult, and now must look forward to the kind of life he will lead as a middle-aged adult.

According to Levinson, the transition to middle adulthood lasts about five years (ages 40 to 45) and requires the adult male to come to grips with four major conflicts that have existed in his life since adolescence: (1) being young versus being old, (2) being destructive versus being constructive, (3) being masculine versus being feminine, and (4) being attached to others versus being separated from them. Seventy to 80 percent of the men Levinson interviewed found the midlife transition tumultuous and psychologically painful, as many aspects of their lives came into question. According to Levinson, the success of the midlife transition rests on how effectively the individual reduces the polarities and accepts each of them as an integral part of his being.

Because Levinson interviewed middle-aged males, we can consider the data about middle adulthood more valid than the data about early adulthood. When individuals are asked to remember information about earlier parts of their lives, they may distort and forget things. The original Levinson data included no females, although Levinson (1996) reported that his stages, transitions, and the crisis of middle age hold for females as well as males. Levinson's work included no statistical analysis. However, the quality and quantity of the Levinson biographies make them outstanding examples of the clinical tradition.

How Pervasive Are Midlife Crises?

Levinson (1978) views midlife as a crisis, believing that the middle-aged adult is suspended between the past and the future, trying to cope with this gap that threatens life's continuity. George Vaillant (1977) has a different view. Vaillant's study—called the "Grant Study"—involved men who were in their early thirties and in their late forties who initially had been interviewed as undergraduates at Harvard University. He concludes that just as adolescence is a time for detecting parental flaws and discovering the truth about childhood, the forties are a decade of reassessing and recording the truth about the adolescent and adulthood years. However, whereas Levinson sees midlife as a crisis, Vaillant maintains that only a minority of adults experience a midlife crisis.

Today, adult development experts are virtually unanimous in their belief that midlife crises have been exaggerated (Brim, Ryff, & Kessler, 2004;

contemporary life-events approach An approach that emphasizes that how a life event influences the individual's development depends not only on the life event, but also on mediating factors, the individual's adaptation to the life event, the life-stage context, and the sociohistorical context.

Lachman, 2004; Wethington, Kessler, & Pixley, 2004). In sum, the stage theories place too much emphasis on crises in development, especially midlife crises. Also, there often is considerable individual variation in the way people experience the stages, a topic that we turn to next.

The Life-Events Approach

Age-related stages represent one major way to examine adult personality development. A second major way to conceptualize adult personality development is to focus on life events (Schwarzer & Schultz, 2003). In the early version of the life-events approach, life events were viewed as taxing circumstances for individuals, forcing them to change their personality (Holmes & Rahe, 1967). Such events as the death of a spouse, divorce, marriage, and so on were believed to involve varying degrees of stress, and therefore likely to influence the individual's development.

Today's life-events approach is more sophisticated (Cui & Vaillant, 1996; Hultsch & Plemons, 1979). The **contemporary life-events approach** emphasizes that how life events influence the individual's development depends not only on the life event itself but also on mediating factors (physical health, family supports, for example), the individual's adaptation to the life event (appraisal of the threat, coping strategies, for example), the life-stage context, and the sociohistorical context (see Figure 14.2). For example, if individuals are in poor health and have little family support, life events are likely to be more stressful. And a divorce may be more stressful after many years of marriage when adults are in their fifties than when they have only been married several years and are

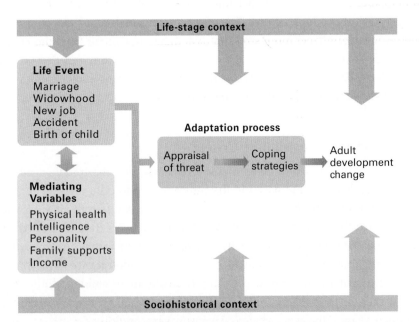

Figure 14.2 A Contemporary Life-Events Framework for Interpreting Adult Development Change
According to the contemporary life-events approach, the influence of a life event depends on the event itself, on mediating variables, on the life-stage and sociohistorical context, and on the individual's appraisal of the event and coping strategies.

in their twenties (Chiriboga, 1982); the life-stage context of an event makes a difference. So does the sociohistorical context. For example, adults may be able to cope more effectively with divorce today than in the 1950s because divorce has become more commonplace and accepted in today's society. Whatever the context or mediating variables, however, one individual may perceive a life event as highly stressful, whereas another individual may perceive the same event as a challenge.

Though the life-events approach is a valuable addition to understanding adult development, like other approaches to adult development, it has its drawbacks (Dohrenwend & Dohrenwend, 1978). One of the most significant drawbacks is that the life-events approach places too much emphasis on change. It does not adequately recognize the stability that, at least to some degree, characterizes adult development. We look more closely at stability in mid adulthood in the next section.

Another drawback of the life-events approach is that it may not be life's major events that are the primary sources of stress, but our daily experiences (Brim, Ryff, & Kessler, 2004; Mak & others, 2005). Enduring a boring but tense job, staying in an unsatisfying marriage, or living in poverty do not show up on scales of major life events. Yet the everyday pounding we take from these living conditions can add up to a highly stressful life and eventually illness. Some psychologists believe we can gain greater insight into the source of life's stresses by focusing less on major events and more on daily hassles and daily uplifts (Lazarus & Folkman, 1984).

Stress and Personal Control in Midlife

As we have seen, there is conclusive evidence that midlife is not a time when a majority of adults experience a tumultuous crisis, and when they do experience a midlife crisis it is often linked to stressful life events. Do middle-aged adults experience stress differently than young adults and older adults? One study using daily diaries over a one-week period found that both young and middle-aged adults had more stressful days than older adults (Almeida & Horn, 2004). In this study, although young adults experienced daily stressors more frequently than middle-aged adults, middle-aged adults experienced more "overload" stressors that involved juggling too many activities at once (Almeida & Horn, 2004).

To what extent do middle-aged adults perceive that they can control what happens to them? Researchers have found that on average a sense of personal control decreases as adults become older (Lachman, 2006). In one study, approximately 80 percent of the young adults (25 to 39 years of age), 71 percent of the middle-aged adults (40 to 59 years of age), and 62 percent of the older adults (60 to 75 years of age) reported that they were often in control of their lives (Lachman & Firth, 2004). However, some aspects of personal control increase with age while others decrease (Lachman, 2006). For example, middle-aged adults feel they have a greater sense of control over their finances, work, and marriage than younger adults but less control over their sex life and their children (Lachman & Firth, 2004; Lachman & Weaver, 1998).

According to the study using adults' daily diaries, the most frequent daily stressor among middle-aged adults is interpersonal tension (Almeida & Horn,

How Would You...?
As a health-care professional, how would you convince a company that it should sponsor a stress-reduction program for its middle-aged employees?

2004). Gender and educational status, however, influence the stress experienced. Midlife women shouldered more "crossover" stressors—simultaneous demands from multiple contexts such as work and family—than their midlife male counterparts, and as a result they reported more distress. Further, midlife adults with lower educational status reported the same number of stressors as midlife adults with higher educational status, but the individuals with lower educational status were more likely to rate the stressors as more severe.

Contexts of Midlife Development

The contemporary life-events approach (like Bronfenbrenner's theory, discussed in Chapter 1) highlights the importance of the complex setting of our lives—of everything from our income and family supports to our sociohistorical circumstances. Let's examine how two aspects of the contexts of life influence development during middle adulthood: historical contexts (cohort effects) and culture.

Historical Contexts (Cohort Effects)

Some developmentalists believe that changing historical times and different social expectations influence how different cohorts—groups of individuals born in the same year or time period—move through the life span (Schaie, 2007). Bernice Neugarten (1964) has been emphasizing the power of age group or cohort since the 1960s. Our values, attitudes, expectations, and behaviors are influenced by the period in which we live. For example, the group of individuals born during the difficult times of the Great Depression may have a different outlook on life than the group born during the optimistic 1950s, says Neugarten.

Neugarten (1986) argues that the social environment of a particular age group can alter its **social clock**—the timetable according to which individuals are expected to accomplish life's tasks, such as getting married, having children, or establishing themselves in a career. Social clocks provide guides for our lives; individuals whose lives are not synchronized with these social clocks find life to be more stressful than those who are on schedule, says Neugarten. She argues that today there is much less agreement than in the past on the right age or sequence for the occurrence of major life events such as having children or retiring.

Trying to tease out universal truths and patterns about adult development from one birth cohort is complicated because the findings may not apply to another birth cohort. Most of the individuals studied by Levinson and Vaillant, for example, were born before and during the Great Depression. What was true for these individuals may not be true for today's 50-year-olds, born in the optimistic aftermath of World War II, or for the post-baby-boom generation as they approach the midlife transition. The midlife men in Levinson's and Vaillant's studies might have been burned out at a premature age rather than being representatives of a normal adult developmental pattern (Rossi, 1989).

Cultural Contexts

In many cultures, especially nonindustrialized cultures, the concept of middle age is not very clear, or in some cases is absent. It is common in nonindustrialized societies to describe individuals as young or old, but not as middle-aged (Grambs,

1989). Some cultures have no words for "adolescent," "young adult," or "middle-aged adult" but they do have other categories they use.

Consider the Gusii culture, located south of the equator in the African country of Kenya. The Gusii divide the life course differently for females and males (LeVine, 1979):

Females	Males
1. Infant	1. Infant
2. Uncircumcised girl	2. Uncircumcised boy
3. Circumcised girl	3. Circumcised boy warrior
4. Married woman	4. Male elder
5. Female elder	

Thus, movement from one status to the next is due primarily to life events, not age, in the Gusii culture.

Although the Gusii do not have a clearly labeled midlife transition, some of the Gusii adults do reassess their lives around the age of 40. At this time, these Gusii adults examine their current status and the limited time they have remaining in their lives. Their physical strength is decreasing, and they know they cannot farm their land forever, so they seek spiritual powers by becoming ritual practitioners or healers. As in the American culture, however, a midlife crisis in the Gusii culture is the exception rather than the rule.

What is middle age like for women in other cultures? It depends on the modernity of the culture and the culture's view of gender roles (Dittmann-Kohli, 2005). Some anthropologists believe that when women become middle-aged in nonindustrialized societies they may experience certain advantages (Brown, 1985). First, they are often freed from cumbersome restrictions that were placed on them when they were younger. For example, in middle age they enjoy greater geographical mobility. Child care has ceased or can be delegated, and domestic chores are reduced. They may venture forth from the village for commercial opportunities, visits to relatives living at a distance, and religious events. Second, with middle age a woman has the right to exercise authority over specified younger kin. Middle-aged women can extract labor from younger family members. The work of middle-aged women tends to be administrative, delegating tasks and making assignments to younger women. Middle-aged women also make important decisions for certain members of the younger generation: what a grandchild is to be named, who is ready to be initiated, and who is eligible to marry whom. A third major change brought on by middle age in nonindustrialized societies is eligibility for special statuses and the possibility that these provide recognition beyond the household. These statuses include the vocations of midwife, curer, holy woman, and matchmaker.

Even among industrialized cultures, the cultural context of middle age development may differ in significant ways. Consider the social clock. In one study, Australian adults were asked the same questions about the best age for experiencing various life circumstances as Neugarten had asked American

Gusii dancers perform on habitat day in Nairobi, Kenya. Movement from one status to another in the Gusii culture is due primarily to life events, not age. The Gusii do not have a clearly labeled midlife transition.

big five factors of personality Openness to experience, conscientiousness, extraversion, agreeableness, and neuroticism (emotional stability).

adults (Peterson, 1996). Compared with the Americans, the Australian adults advocated later ages for marriage and grandparenthood, a younger age for leaving school, and a broader age range for retiring.

Stability and Change

Recall from Chapter 1 that questions about stability and change are an important issue in life-span development. One of the main ways that stability and change are assessed is through longitudinal studies that assess the same individuals at different points in their lives.

Longitudinal Studies

We examine three longitudinal studies to help us understand the extent to which there is stability or change in adult personality development: Costa and McCrae's Baltimore Study, the Berkeley Longitudinal Studies, and Vaillant's studies.

Costa and McCrae's Baltimore Study

A major study of adult personality development continues to be conducted by Paul Costa and Robert McCrae (1998; McCrae & Costa, 2003). They focus on what are called the **big five factors of personality**, which are openness to experience, conscientiousness, extraversion, agreeableness, and neuroticism (emotional stability); they are described in Figure 14.3. (Notice that if you create an acronym from these factor names, you will get the word *OCEAN*.) These traits are sometimes referred to as the Big Five. A number of research studies point toward these factors as important dimensions of personality (McCrae & Costa, 2003).

Using their five-factor personality test, Costa and McCrae (1998, 2000) studied approximately a thousand college-educated men and women ages 20 to 96, assessing the same individuals over many years. Data collection began in the 1950s to the mid-1960s and is ongoing. Costa and McCrae concluded that considerable stability across the adult years occurs for the five personality factors.

Openness	**C**onscientiousness	**E**xtraversion	**A**greeableness	**N**euroticism (emotional stability)
• Imaginative or practical	• Organized or disorganized	• Sociable or retiring	• Softhearted or ruthless	• Calm or anxious
• Interested in variety or routine	• Careful or careless	• Fun-loving or somber	• Trusting or suspicious	• Secure or insecure
• Independent or conforming	• Disciplined or impulsive	• Affectionate or reserved	• Helpful or uncooperative	• Self-satisfied or self-pitying

Figure 14.3 The Big Five Factors of Personality
Each of the broad supertraits encompasses more narrow traits and characteristics. Use the acronym OCEAN to remember the big five personality factors (openness, conscientiousness, extraversion, agreeableness, neuroticism).

A recent meta-analysis of the Big-Five framework revealed more change across the adult years than Costa and McRae found. The meta-analysis of 87 longitudinal studies spanning 10 to 101 years of age indicated that (Roberts, Walton, & Viechtbauer, 2006):

- Results for extraversion were complex until it was subdivided into social dominance (assertiveness, dominance) and social vitality (talkativeness, sociability). Social dominance increased from adolescence through middle adulthood, social vitality increased in adolescence and then decreased in early and late adulthood.
- Agreeableness and conscientiousness increased in early and middle adulthood.
- Neuroticism decreased in early adulthood.
- Openness to experience increased in adolescence and early adulthood and then decreased in late adulthood.

In general, this study revealed that personality traits changed most during early adulthood.

Berkeley Longitudinal Studies

In the Berkeley Longitudinal Studies more than 500 children and their parents were initially studied in the late 1920s and early 1930s. The book *Present and Past in Middle Life* (Eichorn & others, 1981) profiles these individuals as they became middle-aged. The results from early adolescence through a portion of midlife did not support either extreme in the debate over whether personality is characterized by stability or change. Some characteristics were more stable than others, however. The most stable characteristics were the degree to which individuals were intellectually oriented, self-confident, and open to new experiences. The characteristics that changed the most included the extent to which the individuals were nurturant or hostile and whether they had good self-control or not.

George Vaillant's Studies

Longitudinal studies by George Vaillant help us examine a somewhat different question than the studies described so far: Does personality at middle age predict what a person's life will be like in late adulthood? Vaillant (2002) has conducted three longitudinal studies of adult development and aging: (1) a sample of 268 socially advantaged Harvard graduates born about 1920 (called the Grant Study); (2) a sample of 456 socially disadvantaged inner-city men born about 1930; and (3) a sample of 90 middle-SES, intellectually gifted women born about 1910. These individuals have been assessed numerous times (in most cases, every two years),

How Would You...?
As a health care professional, how would you use the results of Vaillant's research to advise a middle-aged adult patient who abuses alcohol and smokes?

beginning in the 1920s to 1940s and continuing today for those still living. The main assessments involve extensive interviews with the participants, their parents, and teachers.

Vaillant categorized 75- to 80-year-olds as "happy-well," "sad-sick," and "dead." He used data collected from these individuals when they were 50 years of age to predict which categories they were likely to end up in at 75 to 80 years of age. Alcohol abuse and smoking at age 50 were the best predictors of which individuals would be dead at 75 to 80 years of age. Other factors at age 50 were linked with being in the "happy-well" category at 75 to 80 years of age: getting regular exercise, avoiding being overweight, being well-educated, having a stable marriage, being

cumulative personality model
States that with time and age, people become more adept at interacting with their environment in ways that promote the stability of personality.

future-oriented, being thankful and forgiving, empathizing with others, being active with other people, and having good coping skills.

Wealth and income at age 50 were not linked with being in the "happy-well" category at 75 to 80 years of age. Generativity in middle age (defined in this study as "taking care of the next generation") was more strongly related than intimacy to whether individuals would have an enduring and happy marriage at 75 to 80 years of age (Vaillant, 2002).

The results for one of Vaillant's studies, the Grant Study of Harvard men, are shown in Figure 14.4. Note that when individuals at 50 years of age were not heavy smokers, did not abuse alcohol, had a stable marriage, exercised, maintained a normal weight, and had good coping skills, they were more likely to be alive and happy at 75 to 80 years of age.

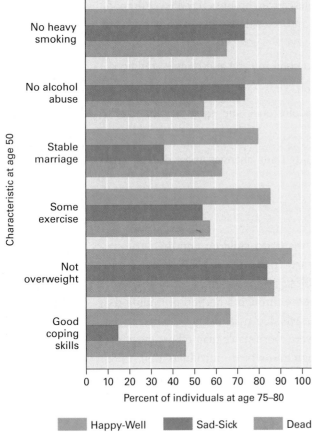

Figure 14.4 Links Between Characteristics at Age 50 and Health and Happiness at Age 75 to 80 In a longitudinal study, the characteristics shown above at age 50 were related to whether individuals were happy-well, sad-sick, or dead at age 75 to 80 (Vaillant, 2002).

Conclusions

What can be concluded about stability and change in personality development during the adult years? Avshalom Caspi and Brent Roberts (2001) concluded that the evidence does not support the view that personality traits become completely fixed at a certain age in adulthood. However, they argue that change is typically limited, and in some cases the changes in personality are small. They also say that age is positively related to stability and that stability peaks in the fifties and sixties. That is, people show greater stability in their personality when they reach midlife than when they were younger adults. These findings support what is called a **cumulative personality model** of development, which states that with time and age, people become more adept at interacting with their environment in ways that promote the stability of personality.

This does not mean that change is absent throughout midlife. Ample evidence shows that social contexts, new experiences, and sociohistorical changes can affect personality development (Mroczek, Spiro, & Griffin, 2006). However, Caspi and Roberts (2001) concluded that as people get older, stability increasingly outweighs change.

Other researchers argue that stability in personality begins to set in at about 30 years of age (Costa & McCrae, 2000). However, some researchers conclude that personality change can be extensive in the adult years (Lewis, 2001). And some people likely change more than others (Mroczek, Spiro, & Griffin, 2006). In sum, there still is disagreement on how much stability and change characterize personality development in adulthood (Caspi & Shiner, 2006; Mrocek, Spiro, & Griffin, 2006; Roberts, 2006).

Close Relationships

There is a consensus among middle-aged Americans that a major component of well-being involves positive relationships with others, especially parents, spouse, and offspring (Lachman, 2004). To begin our examination of midlife relationships, let's explore love and marriage in middle-aged adults.

Love and Marriage at Midlife

Remember from Chapter 12 that two major forms of love are romantic love and affectionate love. The fires of romantic love are strong in early adulthood. Affectionate, or companionate, love increases during middle adulthood. That is, physical attraction, romance, and passion are more important in new relationships, especially those begun in early adulthood. Security, loyalty, and mutual emotional interest become more important as relationships mature, especially in middle adulthood.

What characterizes marriage in middle adulthood?

Even some marriages that were difficult and rocky during early adulthood turn out to be better adjusted during middle adulthood. Although the partners may have lived through a great deal of turmoil, they eventually discover a deep and solid foundation on which to anchor their relationship. In middle adulthood, the partners may have fewer financial worries, less housework and chores, and more time with each other. Middle-aged partners are more likely to view their marriage as positive if they engage in mutual activities.

Most individuals in midlife who are married voice considerable satisfaction with being married. In a large-scale study of individuals in middle adulthood, 72 percent of those who were married said their marriage was either "excellent" or "very good" (Brim, 1999). Possibly by middle age, many of the worst marriages already have dissolved.

Divorce in middle adulthood may be more positive in some ways, more negative in others, than divorce in early adulthood. On the one hand, for mature individuals, the perils of divorce can be fewer and less intense than for younger individuals. They have more resources, and they can use this time as an opportunity to simplify their lives by disposing of possessions, such as a large home, which they no longer need. Their children are adults and may be able to cope with their parents' divorce more effectively. The partners may have gained a better understanding of themselves and may be searching for changes that could include the end to a poor marriage.

How Would You...?

As a social worker, how would you describe the different reasons for divorce between young and middle-aged adults?

On the other hand, the emotional and time commitment to marriage that has existed for so many years may not be lightly given up. Many midlife individuals perceive a divorce as failing in the best years of their lives. The divorcer might see the situation as an escape from an untenable relationship, but the divorced partner usually sees it as betrayal, the ending of a relationship that had been built up over many years and that involved a great deal of commitment and trust.

empty nest syndrome A term
used to indicate a decrease in
marital satisfaction after children
leave home.

A survey by AARP (2004) of 1,148 40- to 79-year-olds who were divorced at least once in their forties, fifties, or sixties found that staying married because of their children was by far the main reason many people took so long to become divorced. Despite the worry and stress involved in going through a divorce, three in four of the divorcees said they had made the right decision to dissolve their marriage and reported a positive outlook on life. Sixty-six percent of the divorced women said they initiated the divorce compared with only 41 percent of the divorced men. The divorced women were much more afraid of having financial problems (44 percent) than the divorced men (11 percent).

Following are the main reasons the middle-aged and older adults cited for their divorce:

Main Causes for Women	Main Causes for Men
1. Verbal, physical, or emotional abuse (23 percent)	1. No obvious problems, just fell out of love (17 percent)
2. Alcohol or drug abuse (18 percent)	2. Cheating (14 percent)
3. Cheating (17 percent)	3. Different values, lifestyles (14 percent)

The Empty Nest and Its Refilling

An important event in a family is the launching of a child into adult life. Parents face new adjustments as a result of the child's absence. Students usually think that their parents suffer from their absence. In fact, parents who live vicariously through their children might experience the **empty nest syndrome**, which includes a decline in marital satisfaction after children leave the home. For most parents, however, marital satisfaction does not decline after children have left home. Rather, for most parents marital satisfaction increases during the years after child rearing (Fingerman & Lang, 2004). With their children gone, marital partners have time to pursue careers, other interests, and more time for each other (Ward & Spitze, 2004).

In today's uncertain economic climate, the refilling of the empty nest is becoming a common occurrence as adult children return to live at home after several years of college, after graduating from college, or to save money after

Doonesbury   BY GARRY TRUDEAU

taking a full-time job (Owen, 2005) Young adults also may move back in with their parents after an unsuccessful career or a divorce. And some individuals don't leave home at all until their middle to late twenties because they cannot financially support themselves. Numerous labels have been applied to these young adults who return to their parents' homes to live, including "boomerang kids," and "B2B" (or Back-to-Bedroom) (Furman, 2005).

What are some strategies that can help parents and their young adult children get along better?

The middle generation has always provided support for the younger generation, even after the nest is bare. Through loans and monetary gifts for education, and through emotional support, the middle generation has helped the younger generation. Adult children appreciate the financial and emotional support their parents provide them at a time when they often feel considerable stress about their career, work, and lifestyle. And parents feel good that they can provide this support.

However, as with most family living arrangements, there are both pluses and minuses when adult children return to live at home. One of the most common complaints voiced by both adult children and their parents is a loss of privacy. The adult children complain that their parents restrict their independence, cramp

How Would You...?
As a psychologist, how would you counsel parents of adult children who return to live at home for a few years following their college?

their sex lives, reduce their rock music listening, and treat them as children rather than adults. Parents often complain that their quiet home has become noisy, that they stay up late worrying when their adult children will come home, that meals are difficult to plan because of conflicting schedules, that their relationship as a married couple has been invaded, and that they have to shoulder too much responsibility for their adult children. In sum, when adult children return home to live, a disequilibrium in family life is created, which requires considerable adaptation on the part of parents and their adult children.

When adult children ask to return home to live, parents and their adult children should agree on the conditions and expectations beforehand. For example, they might discuss and agree on whether young adults will pay rent, wash their own clothes, cook their own meals, do any household chores, pay their phone bills, come and go as they please, be sexually active or drink alcohol at home, and so on. If these conditions aren't negotiated at the beginning, conflict often results because the expectations of parents and young adult children will likely be violated.

Sibling Relationships and Friendships

Sibling relationships persist over the entire life span for most adults (Teti, 2001). Eighty-five percent of today's adults have at least one living sibling. Sibling relationships in adulthood may be extremely close, apathetic, or highly rivalrous. The majority of sibling relationships in adulthood have been found to be close (Cicirelli, 1991). Those siblings who are psychologically close to each other in adulthood tended to be that way in childhood. It is rare for sibling closeness to develop for the first time in adulthood (Dunn, 1984).

Friendships continue to be important in middle adulthood just as they were in early adulthood (Antonucci, 1989). It takes time to develop intimate friendships, so friendships that have endured over the adult years are often deeper than those that have just been formed in middle adulthood.

Grandparenting

What are some grandparents roles?

Many adults become grandparents for the first time during middle age. Researchers have consistently found that grandmothers have more contact with grandchildren than grandfathers (Watson, Randolph, & Lyons, 2005). Perhaps women tend to define their role as grandmothers as part of their responsibility for maintaining ties between family members across generations. Men may have fewer expectations about the grandfather role and see it as more voluntary.

In this section, we consider the following questions: What roles do grandparents assume, and what styles do they use with their grandchildren?

Grandparent Roles

What is the meaning of the grandparent role? Three prominent meanings are attached to being a grandparent (Neugarten & Weinstein, 1964). For some older adults, being a grandparent is a source of biological reward and continuity. For others, being a grandparent is a source of emotional self-fulfillment, generating feelings of companionship and satisfaction that may have been missing in earlier adult-child relationships. And for yet others, being a grandparent is a remote role.

How Would You...?
As a human development and family studies professional, how would you educate parents about the mutual benefits of having grandparents actively involved in their children's lives?

The grandparent role may have different functions in different families, in different ethnic groups and cultures, and in different situations (Watson, Randolph, & Lyons, 2005). For example, in one study of White, African American, and Mexican American grandparents and grandchildren, the Mexican American grandparents saw their grandchildren more frequently, provided more support for the grandchildren and their parents, and had more satisfying relationships with their grandchildren (Bengtson, 1985). And in a study of three generations of families in Chicago, grandmothers had closer relationships with their children and grandchildren and gave more personal advice than grandfathers did (Hagestad, 1985).

The Changing Profile of Grandparents

An increasing number of U.S. grandchildren live with their grandparents (Gerard, Landry-Meyer, & Roe, 2006; Ross & Aday, 2006). In 1980, 2.3 million grandchildren lived with their grandparents, but in 2005 that figure had reached 6.1 million (U.S. Census Bureau, 2006). Divorce, adolescent pregnancies, and drug use by parents are the main reasons that grandparents are thrust back into the "parenting" role they thought they had shed. One study of grandparents raising their grandchildren found that stress was linked with three conditions: being a younger grandparent, having grandchildren with physical and psychological problems, and low family cohesion (Sands & Goldberg-Glen, 2000).

As divorce and remarriage have become more common, a special concern of grandparents is visitation privileges with their grandchildren. In the last 10 to 15 years, more states have passed laws giving grandparents the right to petition a court for visitation privileges with their grandchildren, even if a parent objects. Whether such forced visitation rights for grandparents are in the child's best interest is still being debated.

Intergenerational Relationships

Adults in midlife play important roles in the lives of the young and the old (Wolff & Kasper, 2006). Middle-aged adults share their experience and transmit values to the younger generation (McAdams, 2001). They may be launching children and experiencing the empty nest, adjusting to having grown children return home, or becoming grandparents. They also may be giving or receiving financial assistance, caring for a widowed or sick parent, or adapting to being the oldest generation after both parents have died (Silverstein, Gans, & Yang, 2006).

With each new generation, personality characteristics, attitudes, values, and problems are replicated or changed (Brook & others, 2007; Rhule-Louie & McMahon, 2007). As older family members die, their biological, intellectual, emotional, and personal legacies are carried on in the next generation (De Litvan & Manzano, 2005). Their children become the oldest generation and their grandchildren the second generation. As adult children become middle-aged, they often develop more positive perceptions of their parents (Field, 1999).

For the most part, family members maintain considerable contact across generations (Miller-Day, 2004). As we continue to stay connected with our parents and our children as we age, both similarity and dissimilarity across generations

How Would You...?
As a health-care professional, how would you advise a family contemplating the potential challenges of having a middle-aged child take on primary responsibility for the daily care of a chronically ill parent?

are found. For example, similarity between parents and an adult child is most noticeable in religion and politics, least in gender roles and lifestyle.

What is the nature of intergenerational relationships?

What are the most common conflicts between parents and their adult children? In one study, they included communication and interaction style (such as "He is always yelling" and "She is too critical"), habits and lifestyle choices (such as sexual activity, living arrangements), child-rearing practices and values (such as decisions about having children, being permissive or controlling), politics, religion, and ideology (such as lack of religious involvement) (Clarke & others, 1999). In this study, there were generational differences in perceptions of the main conflicts between parents and adult children. Parents most often listed habits and lifestyle choices; adult children cited communication and interaction style.

Gender differences also characterize intergenerational relationships (Miller-Day, 2004). In one study, mothers and their daughters had much closer relationships during their adult years than mothers and sons, fathers and daughters, and

sandwich generation A term used to describe middle-aged adults because of the responsibilities they have for their adolescent and young children on the one hand and their aging parents on the other.

fathers and sons (Rossi, 1989). Also in this study, married men were more involved with their wives' kin than with their own. And maternal grandmothers and maternal aunts were cited twice as often as their counterparts on the paternal side of the family as the most important or loved relative.

Middle-aged adults have been described as the **sandwich generation** because of the responsibilities they have for their adolescent and young adult children on the one hand and their aging parents on the other (Riley & Bowen, 2005). These simultaneous pressures from adolescents or young adult children and aging parents may contribute to stress in middle adulthood. Many middle-aged adults experience considerable stress when their parents become very ill and die. One survey found that when adults enter midlife 41 percent have both parents alive but that 77 percent leave midlife with no parents alive (Bumpass & Acquilino, 1994).

Summary

Personality Theories and Development

Erikson says that the seventh stage of the human life span, generativity versus stagnation, occurs in middle adulthood. Four types of generativity are biological, parental, work, and cultural. In Levinson's theory, developmental tasks should be mastered at different points in development, and changes in middle age focus on four conflicts: being young versus being old, being destructive versus being constructive, being masculine versus being feminine, and being attached to others versus being separated from them. Levinson proposed that a majority of Americans, especially men, experience a midlife crisis. Research, though, indicates that midlife crises are not pervasive. There is considerable individual variation in development during the middle adulthood years. According to the early version of the life-events approach, life events produce taxing circumstances that create stress in people's lives. In the contemporary version of the life-events approach, how life events influence the individual's development depends not only on the life event but also on mediating factors, adaptation to the event, the life-stage context, and the sociohistorical context. Researchers have found that young and middle-aged adults experience more stressful days than do older adults, and that as adults become older they report less control over their lives. Neugarten argues that the social environment of a particular cohort can alter its social clock—the timetable according to which individuals are expected to accomplish life's tasks. Many cultures do not have a clear concept of middle age. In many nonindustrialized societies, a woman's status improves in middle age.

Stability and Change

In Costa and McCrae's Baltimore Study, the big five personality factors—openness to experience, conscientiousness, extraversion, agreeableness, and neuroticism—showed considerable stability. However, a recent meta-analysis of the big five personality factors found increases and declines of specific factors across the adult years, with the most change occurring in early adulthood. In the Berkeley Longitudinal Studies, the extremes in the stability-change argument were not supported. The most stable characteristics were intellectual orientation, self-confidence, and openness to new experiences. The characteristics that changed the most were nurturance, hostility, and self-control. George Vaillant's research revealed links between a number of characteristics at age 50 and health and well-being at 75 to 80 years of age. The issue of whether personality is stable or changes in adulthood continues to be debated. Some researchers believe that stability peaks in the fifties and sixties, others that it begins to stabilize at about 30, and yet others argue for more change. Some people change more than others.

Close Relationships

Affectionate love increases in midlife, especially in marriages that have endured many years. A majority of middle-aged adults who are married say that their marriage is good or excellent. Researchers recently have found that couples who divorce in midlife are more likely to have a cool, distant, emotionally suppressed relationship, whereas divorcing young adults are more likely to have an emotionally volatile and expressive relationship. Rather than decreasing marital satisfaction as once thought, the empty nest increases it for most parents. An increasing number of young adults are returning home to live with their parents. Sibling relationships continue throughout life. Some are close, others are distant. Friendships continue to be important in middle age. There are different grandparent roles. Grandmothers spend more time with grandchildren than grandfathers, and the grandmother role involves greater expectations for maintaining ties across generations than the grandfather role. The profile of grandparents is changing, due to such factors as divorce and remarriage. An increasing number of U.S. grandchildren live with their grandparents. Family members usually maintain contact across generations. Mothers and daughters have the closest relationships. The middle-aged generation, which has been called the "sandwich generation," plays an important role in linking generations.

Key Terms

generativity 364
stagnation 364
contemporary life-events
 approach 366
social clock 368

big five factors of
 personality 370
cumulative personality
 model 372

empty nest syndrome 374
sandwich generation 378

15

Physical and Cognitive Development in Late Adulthood

Stories of Life-Span Development: Learning to Age Successfully

Jonathan Swift said, "No wise man ever wished to be younger." Without a doubt, a 70-year-old body does not work as well as it once did. It is also true that an individual's fear of aging is often greater than need be. As more individuals live to a ripe and active old age, our image of aging is changing. While on the average a 75-year-old's joints should be stiffening, people can practice not to be average. For example, a 75-year-old man might choose to train for and run a marathon; an 80-year-old woman whose

capacity for work is undiminished might choose to make and sell children's toys.

Consider 85-year-old Sadie Halperin, who has been working out for 11 months at a rehabilitation center for the aged in Boston. She lifts weights and rides a stationary bike. She says that before she started working out, about everything she did—shopping, cooking, walking—was a major struggle. Sadie says she always felt wobbly and held on to a wall when she walked. Now she walks down the cen-

ter of the hallways and reports that she feels wonderful. Initially she could lift only 15 pounds with both legs; now she lifts 30 pounds. At first she could bench-press only 20 pounds; now she bench-presses 50 pounds. Sadie's exercise routine has increased her muscle strength and helps her to battle osteoporosis by slowing the calcium loss from her bones, which can lead to deadly fractures (Ubell, 1992).

The story of Sadie Halperin's physical development and well-being in late

Eighty-five-year-old Sadie Halperin doubled her strength in exercise after just 11 months. Before developing an exercise routine, Sadie felt wobbly and often had to hold on to a wall when she walked. Now she walks down the middle of hallways and says she feels wonderful.

adulthood raises some truly fascinating questions about life-span development, which we explore in this chapter. They include: Why do we age, and what, if anything, can we do to delay the aging process? How long do we live? What chance do you have of living to be 100? How does the body change in old age? What eating and exercise habits help us to live longer? Other questions we will examine are: How well do older adults function cognitively? What roles do work and retirement play in older adults' lives? What can we do to take care of ourselves mentally as we age?

Longevity, Biological Aging, and Physical Development

In his eighties, Linus Pauling argued that vitamin C slows the aging process. Aging researcher Roy Walford fasted two days a week because he believed calorie restriction slows the aging process. What do we really know about longevity? What are the current biological theories about why we age? How does our brain change during this part of our life span? What happens to us physically? Does our sexuality change?

Longevity

We are no longer a youthful society. As more individuals live to older ages, the proportion of individuals at different ages has become increasingly similar. Indeed, the concept of a period called "late adulthood" is a recent one—before the twentieth century most individuals died before they reached 65. In Chapter 1, we indicated that period of late adulthood begins in the sixties or seventies and lasts until death.

Life Span and Life Expectancy

Since the beginning of recorded history, **life span**, the maximum number of years an individual can live, has remained at approximately 120 to 125 years of age. But since 1900 improvements in medicine, nutrition, exercise, and lifestyle have increased our life expectancy an average of 31 additional years.

Recall from Chapter 1 that **life expectancy** is the number of years that the average person born in a particular year will probably live. Sixty-five-year-olds in the United States today can expect to live an average of 18 more years (20 for females, 16 for males) (National Center for Health Statistics, 2006). The average life expectancy of individuals born today in the United States is 77.6 years.

life span The upper boundary of life, the maximum number of years an individual can live. The maximum life span of human beings is about 120 to 125 years of age.

life expectancy The number of years that will probably be lived by the average person born in a particular year.

Differences in Life Expectancy How does the United States fare in life expectancy, compared with other countries around the world? We do considerably better than some, a little worse than some others. Japan has the highest life expectancy at birth today (81 years) (UNICEF, 2004). Differences in life expectancies across countries are due to such factors as health conditions and medical care throughout the life span.

Life expectancy also differs for various ethnic groups within the United States and for men and women (Land & Yang, 2006). For example, life expectancy of African Americans (70 years) in the United States is eight years lower than the low expectancy for non-Latino Whites (78 years) (National Center for Health Statistics, 2006). The life expectancy for females is 80 years of age; for males it is 75. When individuals reach their mid-thirties, females outnumber males; this gap widens during the remainder of the adult years. By the time adults are 75 years of age, more than 61 percent of the population is female; for those 85 and over, the figure is almost 70 percent female.

Why can women expect to live longer than men? Social factors such as health attitudes, habits, lifestyles, and occupation are probably important (Land & Yang, 2006). In the United States, men are more likely than women to die from the leading causes of death associated with lifestyle, such as cancer of the respiratory system, emphysema, motor vehicle accidents, cirrhosis of the liver, and coronary heart disease (Yoshida & others, 2006). For example, the gender difference in deaths due to lung cancer and emphysema occurs because men are heavier smokers than women.

The gender difference in longevity also is influenced by biological factors (van Jaarsveld & others, 2006). In virtually all species, females outlive males. Women have more resistance to infections and degenerative diseases (Candore & others, 2006). For example, the female's estrogen production helps to protect her from arteriosclerosis (hardening of the arteries), which may lead to deadly cardiovascular diseases. And the additional X chromosome that women carry in comparison to men may be associated with the production of more antibodies to fight off disease.

Centenarians

In 1980, there were only 15,000 centenarians (individuals 100 years and older) in the United States. In 2000, there were 77,000, and it is projected that this number will be 834,000 in 2050. Many people expect that "the older you get, the sicker you get." However, researchers are finding that is not true for some centenarians (Perls, 2006). One study of 400 centenarians found that 32 percent of the males and 15 percent of the females had never been diagnosed with common age- and lifestyle-associated diseases such as heart disease, cancer, and stroke (Evert & others, 2003). Another recent study of 93 centenarians revealed that despite some physical limitations, they had a low rate of age-associated diseases and most had good mental health (Selim & others, 2005).

What chance do you have of living to be 100? Genes play an important role in surviving to an extreme old age (Ford & Tower, 2006; Kim, 2007). But there are also other factors at work such as family history, health (weight, diet, smoking, and exercise), education, personality, and lifestyle. It may also make a difference in where you live geographically live and in what food is available in that region.

Biological Theories of Aging

Even if we stay remarkably healthy, we begin to age at some point. In fact, some life-span experts argue that biological aging begins at birth (Schaie, 2000). Three biological explanations provide intriguing explanations of why we age: cellular clock theory, free-radical theory, and hormonal stress theory.

Cellular Clock Theory

Cellular clock theory is Leonard Hayflick's (1977) theory that cells can divide a maximum of about 75 to 80 times and that, as we age, our cells become less capable of dividing. Hayflick found that cells extracted from adults in their fifties to seventies divided fewer than 75 to 80 times. Based on the ways cells divide, Hayflick places the upper limit of the human life-span potential at about 120 to 125 years of age.

In the last decade, scientists have tried to fill in a gap in cellular clock theory (Gatza & others, 2006). Hayflick did not know why cells die. The answer may lie at the tips of chromosomes, at *telomeres*, which are DNA sequences that cap chromosomes (Shay & Wright, 2006, 2007).

Each time a cell divides, the telomeres become shorter and shorter (see Figure 15.1). After about 70 or 80 replications, the telomeres are dramatically reduced and the cell no longer can reproduce. Injecting the enzyme *telomerase* into human cells grown in the laboratory can substantially extend the life of the cells beyond the approximately 70 to 80 normal cell divisions (Shay & Wright, 2006). Researchers are currently exploring ways that telomerase can be used to manipulate telomere length and how this cellular engineering might reduce diseases, such as cancer (Shay & Wright, 2007).

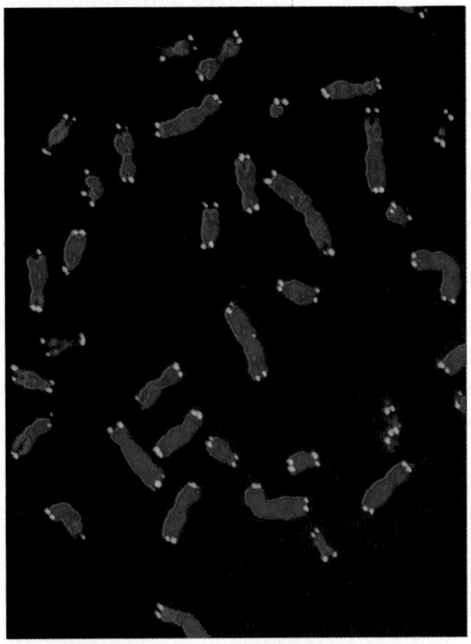

Free–Radical Theory

A second microbiological theory of aging is **free-radical theory**, which states that people age because when cells metabolize energy, the by-products include unstable oxygen molecules known as *free radicals* (Chandel & Budinger, 2007). The free radicals ricochet around the cells, damaging DNA and other cellular structures (Liu & others, 2007). The damage can lead to a range of disorders, including cancer and arthritis (Katakura, 2006). Overeating is linked with an increase in free radicals, and researchers recently have found that calorie restriction—a diet restricted in calories although adequate in proteins, vitamins, and minerals—reduces the oxidative damage created by free radicals (Lopez-Lluch & others, 2006).

Figure 15.1 Telomeres and Aging
The photograph shows actual telomeres lighting up the tips of chromosomes.

Hormonal Stress Theory

The two previous theories of aging attempt to explain aging at the cellular level. In contrast, **hormonal stress theory** argues that aging in the body's hormonal system can lower resistance to stress and increase the likelihood of disease (Finch & Seeman, 1999).

cellular clock theory Leonard Hayflick's theory that the maximum number of times that human cells can divide is about 75 to 80. As we age, our cells have less capability to divide.

free-radical theory A microbiological theory of aging that states that people age because inside their cells normal metabolism produces unstable oxygen molecules known as free radicals. These molecules ricochet around inside cells, damaging DNA and other cellular structures.

hormonal stress theory The theory that aging in the body's hormonal system can lower resilience to stress and increase the likelihood of disease.

Normally, when people experience stressors, the body responds by releasing certain hormones. As people age, the hormones stimulated by stress remain at elevated levels longer than when people were younger (Epel & others, 2006). These prolonged, elevated levels of stress-related hormones are associated with increased risks for many diseases, including cardiovascular disease, cancer, diabetes, and hypertension (Magri & others, 2006).

Which of these biological theories best explains aging? That question has not yet been answered. It might turn out that all of these biological processes contribute to aging.

The Aging Brain

How does the brain change during late adulthood? Does it retain plasticity?

The Shrinking, Slowing Brain

On average, the brain loses 5 to 10 percent of its weight between the ages of 20 and 90. Brain volume also decreases (Enzinger & others, 2005). One recent study found that the volume of the brain was 15 percent less in older adults than younger adults (Shan & others, 2005). Scientists are not sure why these changes occur but believe they might result from a decrease in dendrites, damage to the myelin sheath that covers axons, or simply the death of brain cells.

Some areas shrink more than others. The prefrontal cortex is one area that shrinks with aging, and recent research has linked this shrinkage with a decrease in working memory and other cognitive activities in older adults (Pardo & others, 2007).

A general slowing of function in the brain and spinal cord begins in middle adulthood and accelerates in late adulthood (Birren, 2002). Both physical coordination and intellectual performance are affected. For example, after age 70, many adults no longer show a knee-jerk reflex, and by age 90 most reflexes are much slower (Spence, 1989). The slowing of brain can impair the performance of older adults on intelligence tests, especially timed tests (Birren, Woods, & Williams, 1980).

The Adapting Brain

If the brain were a computer, this description of the aging brain might lead you to think that it could not do much of anything. However, unlike a computer, the brain has remarkable repair capability (Kramer, Fabiani, & Colcombe, 2006). Even in late adulthood, the brain loses only a portion of its ability to function, and the activities older adults engage in can influence the brain's development (Anderton, 2002). For example, in a recent fMRI study, six months of aerobic exercise increased the brain volume of older adults (Colcombe & others, 2006).

Can adults, even aging adults, generate new neurons? Researchers have found that *neurogenesis*, the generation of new neurons, does occur in lower mammalian species, such as mice (Gould & others, 1999). Also, research indicates that exercise and a complex environment can generate new brain cells in mice. It is now accepted that neurogenesis can occur in humans—but at this point, researchers have documented their presence in only two brain regions, the hippocampus, which is involved in memory, and olfactory bulb, which is involved in smell (Elder, De Gasperi, & Gama Sosa, 2006). It also is not known what functions these new brain cells perform, and at this point researchers have documented that they last only for several weeks (Nelson, 2006).

How Would You...? As an educator, how would you use a biological perspective to explain changes in learning as people age?

It does appear that dendritic growth can occur in human adults. One study compared the brains of adults at various ages (Coleman, 1986). From the forties through the seventies, the growth of dendrites increased. However, in people in their nineties, dendritic growth no longer occurred. This dendritic growth might compensate for the possible loss of neurons through the seventies but not in the nineties. Lack of dendritic growth in older adults could be due to a lack of environmental stimulation and activity.

Changes in lateralization may provide one type of adaptation in aging adults (Cabeza, 2002). Recall that lateralization is the specialization of function in one hemisphere of the brain or the other. Using neuroimaging techniques, researchers found that brain activity in the prefrontal cortex is lateralized less in older adults than in younger adults when they are engaging in cognitive tasks (Cabeza, 2002; Rossi & others, 2005). For example, when younger adults are given the task of recognizing words they have previously seen, they process the information primarily in the right hemisphere; older adults are more likely to use both hemispheres (Madden & others, 1999). The decrease in lateralization in older adults might play a compensatory role in the aging brain. That is, using both hemispheres may improve the cognitive functioning of older adults.

The Nun Study

The Nun Study, directed by David Snowdon (2002, 2003), is an intriguing ongoing investigation of aging in 678 nuns, many of whom are from a convent in Mankato, Minnesota. Each of the 678 nuns agreed to participate in annual assessments of their cognitive and physical functioning. They also agreed to donate their brains for scientific research when they die, and they are the largest group of brain donors in the world.

Findings from the Nun Study so far include:

- Idea density, a measure of linguistic ability assessed early in the adult years (age 22), was linked with higher brain weight, fewer incidences of mild cognitive impairment, and fewer characteristics of Alzheimer disease in 75- to 95-year-old nuns (Riley & others, 2005).

- Positive emotions early in adulthood were linked to longevity (Danner, Snowdon, & Friesen, 2001). Handwritten autobiographies from 180 nuns, composed when they were 22 years of age, were scored for emotional content. The nuns whose early writings had higher scores for positive emotional content were more likely to still be alive at 75 to 95 years of age than their counterparts whose early writings were characterized by negative emotional content.

Top: Sister Marcella Zachman (*left*) finally stopped teaching at age 97. Now, at 99, she helps ailing nuns exercise their brains by quizzing them on vocabulary or playing a card game called Skip-Bo, at which she deliberately loses. Sister Mary Esther Boor (*right*), also 99 years of age, is a former teacher who stays alert by doing puzzles and volunteering to work the front desk. *Below:* A Technician holds the brain of a deceased Mankato nun. The nuns donate their brains for research that explores the effects of stimulation on brain growth.

- Sisters who had taught for most of their lives showed more moderate declines in intellectual skills than those who had spent most of their lives in service-based tasks, which supports the notion that stimulating the brain with intellectual activity keeps neurons healthy and alive (Snowdon, 2002).

This and other research provides hope that scientists will discover ways to tap into the brain's capacity to adapt in order to prevent and treat brain diseases (Dobrossy & Dunnett, 2005; Tyas & others, 2007). For example, scientists might learn more effective ways to help older adults recover from strokes. Even when areas of the brain are permanently damaged by stroke, new message routes can be created to get around the blockage or to resume the function of that area, indicating that the brain does adapt.

Physical Development

Physical decline is inevitable if we manage to live to an old age, but the timing of physical problems related to aging is not uniform. Recent research on aging underscores that bodily powers decline slowly and that sometimes even lost function can be restored (Schieber, 2006). What are the main physical changes of late adulthood? To help answer this question, we examine physical appearance and movement, several senses, and circulation and lungs.

Physical Appearance and Movement

In late adulthood, the changes in physical appearance that began occurring during middle age (as discussed in Chapter 13) become more pronounced (McCarter, 2006). Wrinkles and age spots are the most noticeable changes. We also get shorter when we get older. As we saw in Chapter 13, both men and women become shorter in late adulthood because of bone loss in their vertebrae (Hoyer & Roodin, 2003).

Our weight usually drops after we reach 60 years of age. This likely occurs because we lose muscle, which also gives our bodies a "sagging" look (Nair, 2005).

Older adults move slower than young adults, and this slowing occurs for many types of movement with a wide range of difficulty (Shumway-Cook & others, 2007). Even when they perform everyday tasks such as reaching and grasping, moving from one place to another, and continuous movement, older adults tend to move more slowly than when they were young (Newell, Vaillancourt, & Sosnoff, 2006).

The good news is that regular walking decreases the onset of physical disability in older adults (Visser & others, 2005). Also, exercise and appropriate weight lifting can help to reduce the decrease in muscle mass and improve the older person's body appearance (Visser & others, 2005). We will have more to say about the benefits of exercise later in this chapter.

Sensory Development

How do vision, hearing, taste, smell, touch, and pain change in late adulthood?

Vision With aging, visual acuity, color vision, and depth perception decline. Several diseases of the eye also may emerge in aging adults.

In late adulthood, the decline in vision that began for most adults in early or middle adulthood becomes more pronounced (Schieber, 2006). For example, the eye does not adapt as quickly when moving from a well-lighted place to one of semidarkness. The tolerance for glare also diminishes. The area of the visual field becomes smaller, and it's possible that events that occur away from the center of the visual field might not be detected (Fozard & Gordon-Salant, 2001). All these changes may make night driving especially difficult.

Color vision also may also decline as a result of the yellowing of the lens of the eye (Scheiber, 2006). As a result, older adults may have trouble accurately matching closely related colors such as navy socks and black socks.

Depth perception typically declines in late adulthood, which can make it difficult for the older adult to determine how close or far away or how high or low something is (Norman & others, 2006). A decline in depth perception can make steps or street curbs difficult to manage.

Three diseases that can impair the vision of older adults are cataracts, glaucoma, and macular degeneration. **Cataracts** involve a thickening of the lens of the eye that causes vision to become cloudy, opaque, and distorted (Fujikado & others, 2004). By age 70, approximately 30 percent of individuals have cataracts. They are treatable, initially with glasses, and, if necessary, by a simple surgical procedure (Stifer & others, 2004).

Glaucoma involves damage to the optic nerve because of the pressure created by a buildup of fluid in the eye (Coca-Prados & Escribano, 2007). Approximately 1 percent of individuals in their seventies and 10 percent of those in their nineties have glaucoma, which can be treated with eyedrops. If left untreated, glaucoma can ultimately destroy a person's vision.

Macular degeneration is a disease that involves deterioration of the *macula* of the retina. Individuals with macular degeneration may have relatively normal peripheral vision but are unable to see clearly what is directly in front of them. It affects 1 in 25 individuals from 66 to 74 years of age and 1 in 6 of those 75 years old and older. If the disease is detected early, it can be treated with laser surgery (Liscak & Vladyka, 2007). However, macular degeneration is difficult to treat and thus a leading cause of blindness in older adults (Hassell, Lamoureux, & Keeffe, 2006).

Hearing For hearing as for vision, it is important to determine the degree of decline in the aging adult (Stenkley, Vik, & Laukli, 2004). The decline in vision and hearing is much greater in individuals 75 years and older than in individuals 65 to 74 years of age (Charness & Bosman, 1992). Hearing impairment usually does not become much of an impediment until late adulthood, usually due to degeneration of the *cochlea,* the primary neural receptor for hearing in the inner ear (Frisina & Walton, 2006). Even in late adulthood, some, but not all, hearing problems can be corrected by hearing aids (Cook & Hawkins, 2006). Wearing two hearing aids that are balanced to correct the hearing loss in each ear separately can sometimes help hearing-impaired adults.

Smell and Taste Most older adults lose some of their sense of smell or taste, or both (Roberts & Rosenberg, 2006). These losses often begin around 60 years of age (Hawkes, 2006). Healthy older adults experience less decline in smell and

cataracts Involve a thickening of the lens of the eye that causes vision to become cloudy, opaque, and distorted.

glaucoma Damage to the optic nerve because of the pressure created by a buildup of fluid in the eye.

macular degeneration A disease that involves deterioration of the macula of the retina, which corresponds to the focal center of the visual field.

How Would You…? As a health-care professional, how would you respond to an older adult who shows signs of impaired vision but denies, or is unaware of, the problem?

How Would You...?
As an educator, how would you structure your classroom and class activities to accommodate the sensory decline of older adult students?

taste than those who are not as healthy. This decline can reduce enjoyment of food and life satisfaction. Also, a decline in the sense of smell can reduce the ability to detect smoke from a fire. Many older adults compensate for their diminished taste and smell by eating sweeter, spicier, and saltier foods, which can lead to eating more low-nutrient, highly seasoned "junk food" (Hoyer & Roodin, 2003).

Touch and Pain Changes in touch are also associated with aging (Deshpande & others, 2007). One study found that, with aging, individuals could detect touch less in the lower extremities (ankles, knees, and so on) than in the upper extremities (wrists, shoulders, and so on) (Corso, 1977). For most older adults, a decline in touch sensitivity is not problematic (Hoyer & Roodin, 2003).

Older adults are less sensitive to pain and suffer from it less than younger adults (Harkins, Price, & Martinelli, 1986). Although decreased sensitivity to pain can help older adults cope with disease and injury, it can also mask injury and illness that need to be treated.

The Circulatory System and Lungs

Today, most experts on aging recommend that consistent blood pressures above 120/80 should be treated to reduce the risk of heart attack, stroke, or kidney disease (Hawkins & Dunn, 2006). A rise in blood pressure with age can be linked with illness, obesity, anxiety, stiffening of blood vessels, or lack of exercise (Ferinni & Ferrini, 2008). The longer any of these factors persist, the worse the individual's blood pressure gets (Traustadottir, Bosch, & Matt, 2005).

Lung capacity drops 40 percent between the ages of 20 and 80, even without disease (Fozard, 1992). Lungs lose elasticity, the chest shrinks, and the diaphragm weakens (Simpson & others, 2005). The good news, though, is that older adults can improve lung functioning with diaphragm-strengthening exercises. Severe impairments in lung functioning and death can result from smoking.

Sexuality

How Would You...?
As a social worker, how would you advise couples in late adulthood who are concerned that they will no longer be able to have a satisfying sexual relationship due to their age?

In the absence of two circumstances—disease and the belief that old people are or should be asexual—sexuality can be lifelong. Aging, however, does induce some changes in human sexual performance, more so in the male than in the female (Mallis & others, 2006).

Orgasm becomes less frequent in males with age, occurring in every second to third attempt rather than every time. More direct stimulation usually is needed to produce an erection. From 65 to 80 years of age, approximately one out of four men have serious problems getting and/or keeping erections, and after 80 years of age the percentage rises to one out of two men (Butler & Lewis, 2002).

In one study of older adults in their sixties, many were still having sex (Wiley & Bortz, 1996). Women rated kissing as one of the most satisfying sexual activities; Men rated oral sex as the most satisfying.

Health

What types of health problems do adults have in late adulthood, and what can be done to maintain or improve their health and ability to function in everyday life?

Health Problems

As we age, the probability increases that we will have some disease or illness. The majority of adults still alive at 80 years of age or older are likely to have some type of impairment. Chronic diseases (those with a slow onset and a long duration) are rare in early adulthood, increase in middle adulthood, and become more common in late adulthood.

Arthritis is the most common chronic disorder in late adulthood, followed by hypertension. Older women have a higher incidence of arthritis and hypertension and are more likely to have visual problems, but are less likely to have hearing problems, than older men are.

Conflict in relationships has been linked with greater decline in older adults with diabetes or hypertension (Seeman & Chen, 2002). Low income is also strongly related to health problems in late adulthood (Ferraro, 2006). Approximately three times as many poor as non-poor older adults report that chronic disorders limit their activities.

Causes of Death in Older Adults

Nearly three-fourths of all older adults die of heart disease, cancer, or stroke. Chronic lung diseases, pneumonia and influenza, and diabetes round out the six leading causes of death among older adults. If cancer, the second leading cause of death in older adults, were completely eliminated, the average life expectancy would rise by only 1 to 2 years. However, if all cardiovascular and kidney diseases were eradicated, the average life expectancy of older adults would increase by approximately 10 years. This increase in longevity is already under way as the number of strokes among older adults has declined considerably in the last several decades. The decline in strokes is due to improved treatment of high blood pressure, a decrease in smoking, better diet, and an increase in exercise.

Arthritis

Arthritis is an inflammation of the joints accompanied by pain, stiffness, and movement problems. This uncurable disorder can affect hips, knees, ankles, fingers, and vertebrae. Individuals with arthritis often experience difficulty moving about and performing routine daily activities. The symptoms of arthritis can be reduced by drugs, such as aspirin, range-of-motion exercises for the afflicted joints, weight reduction, and, in extreme cases, replacement of the crippled joint with a prosthesis (Issa & Sharma, 2006).

Osteoporosis

Normal aging brings some loss of bone tissue, but for some individuals loss of bone tissue can become severe. **Osteoporosis** involves an extensive loss of bone tissue. Osteoporosis is the main reason many older adults walk with a marked stoop. Women are especially vulnerable to osteoporosis, which is the leading cause of broken bones in women (Kuehn, 2005). Approximately 80 percent of osteoporosis cases in the

arthritis Inflammation of the joints that is accompanied by pain, stiffness, and movement problems; especially common in older adults.

osteoporosis A chronic condition that involves an extensive loss of bone tissue and is the main reason many older adults walk with a marked stoop. Women are especially vulnerable to osteoporosis.

What are the most common chronic conditions in late adulthood?

How Would You...?

As a health-care professional, how would you educate older adults on the range of chronic diseases that are common for this age group?

United States occur in females, 20 percent in males. Almost two-thirds of all women over the age of 60 are affected by osteoporosis. It is more common in non-Latina White, thin, and small-framed women.

Osteoporosis is related to deficiencies in calcium, vitamin D, estrogen, and lack of exercise (Mauck & Clarke, 2006). To prevent osteoporosis, young and middle-aged women should eat foods rich in calcium (such as dairy products, broccoli, turnip greens, and kale), get more exercise, and avoid smoking (Whitehead & others, 2004). A program of regular exercise also has the potential to reduce osteoporosis (Lespessailles & Prouteau, 2006).

Accidents

Accidents are the seventh leading cause of death among older adults. Each year, approximately 200,000 adults over the age of 65 (most of them women) fracture a hip in a fall. Half of these older adults die within 12 months, frequently from pneumonia. In one study, an exercise program reduced the risk of falls in older adults (Province & others, 1995).

Exercise, Nutrition, and Weight

Although we may be in the evening of our lives in late adulthood, we are not meant to live out our remaining years passively. Everything we know about older adults suggests they are healthier and happier the more active they are. Can regular exercise lead to a healthier late adulthood and increase longevity? How does eating a calorie-restricted diet and controlling weight also contribute?

Exercise

In one study, exercise literally meant a difference in life or death for middle-aged and older adults (Blair, 1990). More than 10,000 men and women were divided into categories of low fitness, medium fitness, and high fitness (Blair & others, 1989).

Then they were studied over a period of eight years. As shown in Figure 15.2, sedentary participants (low fitness) were more than twice as likely to die during the eight-year time span of the study than those who were moderately fit and more than three times as likely to die as those who were highly fit. The positive effects of being physically fit occurred for both men and women in this study.

Gerontologists increasingly recommend strength training in addition to aerobic activity and stretching for older adults (Ferrara & others, 2006). Weight lifting can preserve and possibly increase muscle mass in older adults (Sequin & Nelson, 2003). A review of 62 research studies concluded that strength training can improve muscle strength and some aspects of functional limitation, such as gait speed, in older adults (Latham & others, 2004).

Exercise is an excellent way to maintain health (Bradshaw & Klein, 2007). Researchers continue to document its positive effects in older adults (Rizvi, 2007). Exercise helps people to live independent lives with dignity in late adulthood. At 80, 90, and even 100 years of age, exercise

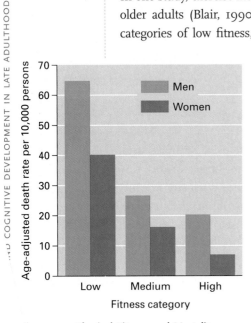

Figure 15.2 Physical Fitness and Mortality
In this study of middle-aged and older adults, being moderately fit or highly fit meant that individuals were less likely to die over a period of eight years than their low-fitness (sedentary) counterparts (Blair & others, 1989).

can help prevent older adults from falling down or even being institutionalized (Villareal & others, 2006). Being physically fit means being able to do the things you want to do, whether you are young or old.

Exercise is linked to increased longevity. Energy expenditure during exercise of at least 1,000 kcal/week reduces mortality by about 30 percent, while 2,000 kcal/week reduces mortality by about 50 percent (Lee & Skerrett, 2001).

Nutrition and Weight

Scientists have accumulated considerable evidence that calorie restriction (CR) in laboratory animals (in most cases rats) can increase the animals' life span (Sinclair & Howitz, 2006). Animals that were fed diets restricted in calories, although adequate in protein, vitamins, and minerals, lived as much as 40 percent longer than animals that were given unlimited access to food (Jolly, 2005). And chronic problems such as kidney disease appear at a later age (Bodkin, Ortmeyer, & Hansen, 2005). CR also delays biochemical alterations such as the age-related rise in cholesterol and triglycerides observed in both humans and animals (Skrha & others, 2005). And recent research indicates that CR may provide protection for an aging central nervous system (Sharma & Kaur, 2005) (see Figure 15.3).

No one knows for certain how CR works to increase the life span of animals. Some scientists believe it might lower the level of free radicals and reduce oxidative stress in cells. For example, one recent study found that calorie restriction slowed the age-related increase in oxidative stress (Ward & others, 2005). Others believe calorie restriction might trigger a state of emergency called "survival mode" in which the body eliminates all unnecessary functions to focus only on staying alive.

Whether similar very low calorie diets can stretch the human life span is not known (Shanley & Kirkwood, 2006). In some instances the animals in these studies ate 40 percent less than normal. In humans, a typical level of calorie restriction involves a 30 percent decrease, which translates into about 1,120 calories a day for the average woman and 1,540 for the average man.

Leaner adults do live longer, healthier lives. In one study of 19,297 Harvard alumni, those weighing the least were less likely to die over the past three decades (Lee & others, 1993).

Figure 15.3 Calorie Restriction in Monkeys
Shown here are two monkeys at the Wisconsin Primate Research Center. Both are 24 years old. The monkey in the top photograph was raised on a calorie-restricted diet, while the monkey in the bottom photograph was raised on a normal diet. Notice that the monkey on the calorie-restricted diet looks younger, he also has lower glucose and insulin levels. The monkey raised on a normal diet has higher triglycerides and more oxidative damage to his cells.

Health Treatment

What is the quality of health treatment that older adults in the United States receive? A recent study of older adults with health problems revealed that they receive the recommended medical care they need only half the time (Wenger & others, 2003). Clearly, the quality of health treatment older adults receive needs to be significantly improved (Gatz, 2006).

Geriatric nurses can be especially helpful in creating a better quality of health treatment. To read about the work of one geriatric nurse, see the Careers in Life-Span Development profile.

CAREERS IN LIFE-SPAN DEVELOPMENT
Sarah Kagan, Geriatric Nurse

Sarah Kagan is a professor of nursing at the University of Pennsylvania School of Nursing. She provides nursing consultation to patients, their families, nurses, and physicians on the complex needs of older adults related to their hospitalization. She also consults on research and the management of patients who have head and neck cancers. Sarah also teaches in the undergraduate nursing program, where she directs the course Nursing Care in the Older Adult. In 2003, she was awarded a MacArthur Fellowship for her work in the field of nursing.

In Sarah's own words:

> I'm lucky to be doing what I love—caring for older adults and families—and learning from them so that I can share this knowledge and develop or investigate better ways of caring. My special interests in the care of older adults who have cancer allow me the intimate privilege of being with patients at the best and worst times of their lives. That intimacy acts as a beacon—it reminds me of the value I and nursing as a profession contribute to society and the rewards offered in return (Kagan, 2007, p. 1).

Geriatric nurses like Sarah Kagan seek to prevent or intervene in the chronic or acute health problems of older adults. They may work in hospitals, nursing homes, schools of

Sarah Kagan with a patient.

nursing, or with geriatric medical specialists or psychiatrists in a medical clinic or in private practice. Like pediatric nurses, geriatric nurses take courses in a school of nursing and obtain a degree in nursing, which takes from two to five years. They complete courses in biological sciences, nursing care, and mental health as well as supervised clinical training in geriatric settings. They also may obtain a master's or doctoral degree in their specialty.

About 3 percent of adults 65 years of age and older in the United States reside in a nursing home at any point in time. As older adults age, however, their probability of being in a nursing home or other extended-care facility increases. Twenty-three percent of adults 85 years of age and older live in nursing homes or other extended-care facilities.

The quality of nursing homes and other extended-care facilities for older adults varies enormously and is a source of continuing national concern (Briesacher & others, 2005; Castle & Engberg, 2005). More than one-third are seriously deficient. Concerns focus on the patient's medical care, right to privacy, access to medical information, safety, and lifestyle freedom within the individual's range of mental and physical capabilities.

Because of the inadequate quality of many nursing homes and the escalating costs for nursing home care, many specialists in the health problems of the aged believe that home health care, day-care centers, and preventive medicine clinics are good alternatives (Castle, 2001). These alternatives are potentially less expensive than hospitals and nursing homes. They also are less likely to engender the

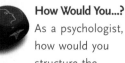

How Would You...?
As a psychologist, how would you structure the environment of a nursing home to produce maximum health and psychological benefits for the residents?

feelings of depersonalization and dependency that occur so often in residents of institutions (Greene & others, 1995). One recent study found that older adults in a community-based long-term care program performed better on cognitive tasks and were less depressed than their counterparts in an institutional-based long-term care facility (Marek & others, 2005).

In a classic study, Judith Rodin and Ellen Langer (1977) found that an important factor related to health, and even survival, in a nursing home is the patient's feelings of control and self-determination. One group was encouraged to make more day-to-day choices and thus feel they had more responsibility for control over their lives. They began to decide such matters as what they ate, when their visitors could come, what movies they saw, and who could come to their rooms. Another group in the same nursing home was told by the administrator how caring the nursing home was and how much the staff wanted to help, but these residents were given no added responsibility over their lives. Eighteen months later, the residents given extra responsibility were more healthy, alert, happy, and active than the residents who did not receive added responsibility. Even more important was the finding that after 18 months only half as many nursing home residents in the "responsibility" group had died as in the "dependent" group (see Figure 15.4). Perceived control over one's environment, then, can literally be a matter of life or death.

How Would You...?
As a health-care professional, how would you use your understanding of development in late adulthood to advocate for improved access to quality medical care for older adults?

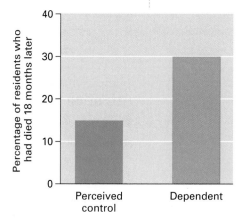

Figure 15.4 Perceived Control and Mortality
In the study by Rodin and Langer (1977), nursing home residents who were encouraged to feel more in control of their lives were more likely to be alive 18 months later than those who were treated to feel more dependent on the nursing home staff.

Cognitive Functioning

At age 76, Anna Mary Robertson Moses, better known as Grandma Moses, took up painting and became internationally famous, staging fifteen one-woman shows throughout Europe. At age 89, the great pianist Arthur Rubinstein gave one of his best performances at New York's Carnegie Hall. When Pablo Casals was 95, a reporter asked him, "Mr. Casals, you are the greatest cellist who ever lived. Why do you still practice six hours a day?" Mr. Casals replied, "Because I feel like I am making progress" (Canfield & Hansen, 1995).

Multidimensionality and Multidirectionality

In thinking about cognitive change in adulthood, it is important to consider that cognition is multidimensional. It is also important to consider that although some dimensions of cognition might decline as we age, others might remain stable or even improve (Salthouse & Baltes, 2006).

Sensory/Motor and Speed-of-Processing Dimensions

It is now well accepted that the speed of processing information declines in late adulthood (Hoyer & Verhaeghen, 2006). Although speed of processing information slows down in late adulthood, there is considerable individual variation in

selective attention Focusing on a specific aspect of experience that is relevant while ignoring others that are irrelevant.

divided attention Concentrating on more than one activity at the same time.

sustained attention The state of readiness to detect and respond to small changes occurring at random times in the environment.

episodic memory The retention of information about the where and when of life's happenings.

this ability (Hartley, 2006). And it is not clear that this slowdown affects our lives in substantial ways. For example, in one experiment, the reaction time and typing skills of typists of varying ages were studied (Salthouse, 1996). The older typists usually had slower reactions, but they actually typed just as fast as the younger typists. Another study suggested this reason for this result: The older typists had learned to look farther ahead, allowing them to type as fast as their younger counterparts.

The decline in processing speed in older adults is likely due to a decline in functioning of the brain and central nervous system (Groth, Gilmore, & Thomas, 2003). Health and exercise may influence how much decline in processing speed occurs (Colcombe & others, 2006).

Attention

Three aspects of attention that have been investigated in older adults are selective attention, divided attention, and sustained attention.

Selective attention is focusing on a specific aspect of experience that is relevant while ignoring others that are irrelevant. An example of selective attention is the ability to focus on one voice among many in a crowded room or a noisy restaurant. Another is making a decision about which stimuli to attend to when making a left turn at an intersection. Generally, older adults are less adept at selective attention than younger adults are (Brown, McKenzie, & Doan, 2005). However, on simple tasks involving search for a feature, such as determining whether a target item is present on a computer screen, age differences are minimal when individuals are given sufficient practice.

Divided attention involves concentrating on more than one activity at the same time. When the two competing tasks are reasonably easy, age differences among adults are minimal or nonexistent. However, the more difficult the competing tasks are, the less effectively older adults divide attention than younger adults (Maciokas & Corgnale, 2003).

Sustained attention is the state of readiness to detect and respond to small changes occurring at random times in the environment. Sometimes sustained attention is referred to as *vigilance*. Researchers have found that older adults perform as well as middle-aged and younger adults on measures of sustained attention (Berardi, Parasuraman, & Haxby, 2001).

Memory

Memory does change during aging, but not all types of memory change with age in the same way (Hoyer & Verhaeghen, 2006). The main dimensions of memory and aging that have been studied include episodic memory and semantic memory, cognitive resources (such as working memory and perceptual speed), explicit and implicit memory, and noncognitive factors such as health, education, and socioeconomic factors (Smith, 1996).

Episodic and Semantic Memory **Episodic memory** is the retention of information about the where and when of life's happenings. For example, what were you doing when you heard that the World Trade Center was attacked on 9/11/2001, or what did you eat for breakfast this morning?

Younger adults have better episodic memory than older adults have (Ronnlund & others, 2005). Also, older adults think that they can remember older events better than more recent events. However, researchers consistently have found that in older adults the older the memory, the less accurate it is (Smith, 1996).

Semantic Memory **Semantic memory** is a person's knowledge about the world. It includes a person's fields of expertise, general academic knowledge of the sort learned in school, and "everyday knowledge" about the meanings of words, important places, and common things. Older adults do often take longer to retrieve semantic information, but usually they can ultimately retrieve it. For the most part, episodic memory declines more in older adults than semantic memory (Ronnlund & others, 2005).

Cognitive Resources: Working Memory and Perceptual Speed Two important cognitive resource mechanisms are working memory and perceptual speed. Recall from Chapter 13 that *working memory* is closely linked to short-term memory but places more emphasis on memory as a place for mental work (Baddeley, 2000). Researchers have found declines in working memory during the late adulthood years (Gazzaley & others, 2005).

Perceptual speed is another cognitive resource that has been studied by researchers on aging. Perceptual speed is the amount of time it takes to perform simple perceptual-motor tasks such as how long it takes to decide whether pairs of two-digit or two-letter strings are the same, or how long it takes someone to step on the brakes when the car directly ahead stops. Perceptual speed shows considerable decline in late adulthood, and it is strongly linked with decline in working memory (Hartley, 2006).

Explicit and Implicit Memory Researchers also have found that aging is linked with changes in explicit memory (Hoyer & Verhaeghen, 2006). **Explicit memory** is memory of facts and experiences that individuals consciously know and can state. Explicit memory also is sometimes called *declarative memory*. Examples of explicit memory include being at a grocery store and remembering what you wanted to buy, or recounting the events of a movie you have seen. **Implicit memory** is memory without conscious recollection; it involves skills and routine procedures that are automatically performed, such as driving a car or typing on a computer keyboard, without having to consciously think about it.

Implicit memory is less likely to be adversely affected by aging than explicit memory (Kessels, Boekhorst, & Postma, 2005). Thus, older adults are more likely to forget what items they wanted to buy at a grocery store than they are to forget how to drive a car. Their perceptual speed might be slower in driving the car, but they remember how to do it.

Conclusions About Memory and Aging Health, education, and socioeconomic status can influence an older adult's performance on memory tasks (Arvanitakis & others, 2006). Although such noncognitive factors as good health are associated with less memory decline in older adults, they do not eliminate memory decline (van Hooren & others, 2007)

semantic memory A person's knowledge about the world—including a person's fields of expertise, general academic knowledge of the sort learned in school, and "everyday knowledge."

explicit memory Memory of facts and experiences that individuals consciously know and can state.

implicit memory Memory without conscious recollection; involves skills and routine procedures that are automatically performed.

Some, but not all, aspects of memory decline in older adults. The decline occurs primarily in episodic and working memory, not in semantic memory or implicit memory. A decline in perceptual speed is associated with memory decline. Successful aging does not mean eliminating memory decline, but reducing it and adapting to it.

Wisdom

Does wisdom, like good wine, improve with age? What is this thing we call "wisdom"? **Wisdom** is expert knowledge about the practical aspects of life that permits excellent judgment about important matters. This practical knowledge involves exceptional insight into human development and life matters, good judgment, and an understanding of how to cope with difficult life problems. Thus, wisdom, more than standard conceptions of intelligence, focuses on life's pragmatic concerns and human conditions (Brugman, 2006; Scheibe, Kunzmann, & Baltes, 2007).

Older adults might not be as quick with their thoughts or behavior as younger people, but wisdom may be an entirely different matter. This older woman shares the wisdom of her experience with a classroom of children. *How is wisdom described by life-span developmentalists?*

In regard to wisdom, research by Baltes and his colleagues (Baltes & Kunzmann, 2004; Baltes, Lindenberger, & Staudinger, 2006) has found the following. (1) High levels of wisdom are rare. Few people, including older adults, attain a high level of wisdom. That only a small percentage of adults show wisdom supports the contention that it requires experience, practice, or complex skills. (2) Factors other than age are critical for wisdom to develop to a high level. For example, certain life experiences, such as being trained and working in a field concerned with difficult life problems and having wisdom-enhancing mentors, contribute to higher levels of wisdom. Also, people higher in wisdom have values that are more likely to consider the welfare of others rather than their own happiness. (3) Personality-related factors, such as openness to experience, generativity, and creativity, are better predictors of wisdom than cognitive factors such as intelligence.

Use It or Lose It

Changes in cognitive activity patterns might result in disuse and consequent atrophy of cognitive skills. This concept is captured in the adage "Use it or lose it." The mental activities that likely benefit the maintenance of cognitive skills in older adults are reading books, doing crossword puzzles, and going to lectures and concerts. These studies support this idea:

- In an analysis of participants in the Victoria Longitudinal Study, when middle-aged and older adults participated in intellectually engaging activities it served to buffer them against cognitive decline (Hultsch & others, 1999). This also was found in another longitudinal study over a 45-year time frame (Arbuckle & others, 1998).

- In a 4½-year longitudinal study of 801 Catholic priests 65 years and older, those who regularly read books, did crossword puzzles, or otherwise exercised their minds were 47 percent less likely to develop Alzheimer disease than the priests who rarely engaged in these activities (Wilson & others, 2002). Shortly, we will have much more to say about Alzheimer disease.

Training Cognitive Skills

If an older adult is losing cognitive skills, can they be retained? Two key conclusions can be derived from research: (1) training can improve the cognitive skills of many older adults; but (2) there is some loss in plasticity in late adulthood, especially in the oldest-old 85 years and older (Baltes, Lindenberger, & Staudinger, 2006).

Evidence of plasticity and the effectiveness of cognitive training comes from the research of Sherry Willis and K. Warner Schaie (1986), who studied approximately 400 adults, most of whom were older adults. Using individualized training, they improved the spatial orientation and reasoning skills of two-thirds of the adults. Nearly 40 percent of those whose abilities had declined returned to a level they had reached 14 years earlier. Further, the effects of training on reasoning lasted up to seven years after training (Saczynski & Willis, 2001). Other research supports the finding that cognitive training interventions can improve the mental functioning and daily functioning of older adults (Boron, Willis, & Schaie, 2007; Levine & others, 2007).

How Would You...?
As a psychologist, how would you design activities and interventions to elicit and maintain cognitive vitality in older adults?

As we discussed earlier in the chapter, researchers are also finding that improving the physical fitness of older adults can improve their cognitive functioning (Kramer, Fabiani, & Colcombe, 2006; Studenski & others, 2006). In sum, the cognitive vitality of older adults can be improved through cognitive and physical fitness training.

Cognitive Neuroscience and Aging

On several occasions in this chapter, we have indicated that certain regions of the brain are involved in links between aging and cognitive functioning. The field of *cognitive neuroscience* has emerged as the major discipline that studies links between brain and cognitive functioning (Kramer, Fabiani, & Colcombe, 2006; Westerman & others, 2007). This field especially relies on brain-imaging techniques, such as fMRI and PET, to reveal the areas of the brain that are activated when individuals are engaging in certain cognitive activities. For example, as an older adult is asked to encode and then retrieve verbal materials or images of scenes, the older adult's brain activity will be monitored by an fMRI brain scan.

Changes in the brain can influence cognitive functioning, and changes in cognitive functioning can influence the brain (Cabeza, Nyberg, & Park, 2005; Nordahl & others, 2006). For example, aging of the brain's prefrontal cortex may produce a decline in working memory. And when older adults do not regularly use their working memory (recall the section on "Use it or Lose it"), neural connections in the prefrontal lobe may atrophy. To reverse this atrophy, cognitive training programs that activate older adults' working memory may increase these neural connections.

Although in its infancy as a field, the cognitive neuroscience of aging is beginning to uncover some important links between aging, the brain, and cognitive functioning (Gordan-Salant & others, 2006; Swick, Senkfor, & van Petten, 2006). We are likely to see increased effort to uncover links between aging, the brain, and cognitive functioning in the next several decades.

Work and Retirement

What percentage of older adults continue to work? How productive are they? Who adjusts best to retirement? These are some of the questions we now examine.

Work

In the beginning of the twenty-first century, the percentage of men over the age of 65 who continue to work full-time is less than at the beginning of the twentieth century. The decline from 1900 to the beginning of the twenty-first century has been as much as 70 percent. An important change in older adults' work patterns is the increase in part-time work after retirement (Hardy, 2006). The percentage of older adults who work part-time postretirement has steadily increased since the 1960s. Some individuals maintain their productivity throughout their lives. Some of these older workers work as many or more hours than younger workers. In the National Longitudinal Survey of Older Men, good health, a strong psychological commitment to work, and a distaste for retirement were the most important characteristics related to continued employment into old age (seventies and eighties) (Parnes & Sommers, 1994). The probability of employment also was positively correlated with educational attainment and being married to a working wife.

Especially important to think about is the large cohort of baby boomers—78 million people who will begin to reach traditional retirement age in 2010. Because this cohort is so large, we are likely to see increasing numbers of older adults continue to work (Louria, 2005; Rogerson & Kim, 2005).

Older workers have lower rates of absenteeism, fewer accidents, and increased job satisfaction, compared with their younger counterparts (Warr, 1994, 2004). This means that the older worker can be of considerable value to a company, above and beyond the older worker's cognitive competence. Changes in federal law now allow individuals over the age of 65 to continue working (Shore & Goldberg, 2005).

An increasing number of middle-aged and older adults are embarking on a second or a third career (Feldman, 2007). In some cases, this is an entirely different type of work or a continuation of previous work but at a reduced level. Many older adults also participate in unpaid work—as volunteers or as active participants in a voluntary association. These options afford older adults opportunities for productive activity, social interaction, and a positive identity.

Ninety-two-year-old Russell "Bob" Harrell (*right*) puts in 12-hour days at Sieco Consulting Engineers in Columbus, Indiana. A highway and bridge engineer, he designs and plans roads. James Rice (age 48), a vice president of client services at Sieco, says that Bob wants to learn something new every day and that James has learned many life lessons from being around him. Bob says he is not planning on retiring. *What are some variations in work and retirement in older adults?*

Adjustment to Retirement

Older adults who adjust best to retirement are healthy, have adequate income, are active, are educated, have an extended social network including both friends and family, and usually were satisfied with their lives before they retired (Moen & Spencer, 2006). Older adults with

How Would You...?

As a psychologist, how would you assist older adults in making appropriate adjustments and preparations for a psychologically satisfying retirement?

inadequate income and poor health, and who must adjust to other stress that occurs at the same time as retirement, such as the death of a spouse, have the most difficult time adjusting to retirement (Reichstadt & others, 2007). A recent study also found that individuals who had difficulty in adjusting to retirement had a strong attachment to work, including full-time jobs and a long work history, lack of control over the transition to retirement, and low self-efficacy (van Solinge & Henkens, 2005).

major depression A mood disorder in which the individual is deeply unhappy, demoralized, self-derogatory, and bored. The person does not feel well, loses stamina easily, has poor appetite, and is listless and unmotivated. Major depression is so widespread that it has been called the "common cold" of psychological disorders.

Mental Health

Although a substantial portion of the population can now look forward to a longer life, that life may unfortunately be hampered by a psychological disorder in old age. This prospect is both troubling to individuals and their families, and costly to society. Psychological disorders make individuals increasingly dependent on the help and care of others. The cost of psychological disorders in older adults is estimated at more than $40 billion per year in the United States. More important than the loss in dollars, though, is the loss of human potential and the suffering. Although psychological disorders in older adults are a major concern, older adults do not have a higher incidence of psychological disorders than younger adults do (Busse & Blazer, 1996).

Depression

Major depression is a mood disorder in which the individual is deeply unhappy, demoralized, self-derogatory, and bored. The person does not feel well, loses stamina easily, has a poor appetite, and is listless and unmotivated. Major depression has been called the "common cold" of psychological disorders. Researchers have found that depressive symptoms vary from less frequent to no more frequent in late adulthood than in middle adulthood (Hybels & Blazer, 2004). One study found that the lower frequency of depressive symptoms in older adults compared with middle-aged adults was linked to fewer economic hardships, fewer negative social interchanges, and increased religiosity (Schieman, van Gundy, & Taylor, 2002). Other research indicates that older adults who engage in physical activity, especially regular exercise, are less likely to be depressed, whereas those who are in poor health and experiencing pain are more likely to be depressed (Kostka & Praczko, 2007; Mavandadi & others, 2007). Depressive symptoms increase in the oldest-old (85 years and older), and this increase is associated with a higher percentage of women in the group, more physical disability, more cognitive impairment, and lower socioeconomic status (Hybels & Blazer, 2004).

What characterizes depression in older adults?

Depression is a treatable condition, not only in young adults but in older adults as well (Berra & Torta, 2007; Ho, 2007). Unfortunately, as many as 80

How Would You...?

As a psychologist, how would you advise families who are dealing with an aging parent suffering from depression?

percent of older adults with depressive symptoms receive no treatment at all. Combinations of medications and psychotherapy produce significant improvement in almost four out of five older adults with depression (Koenig & Blazer, 1996).

Dementia, Alzheimer Disease, and Parkinson Disease

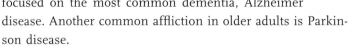

Among the most debilitating of mental disorders in older adults are the dementias (Jellinger & Attems, 2007). In recent years, extensive attention has been focused on the most common dementia, Alzheimer disease. Another common affliction in older adults is Parkinson disease.

Dementia is a global term for any neurological disorder in which the primary symptoms involve a deterioration of mental functioning. Individuals with dementia often lose the ability to care for themselves and can lose the ability to recognize familiar surroundings and people (including family members) (Breitner, 2006). It is estimated that 20 percent of individuals over the age of 80 have some form of dementia.

Alzheimer Disease

One form of dementia is **Alzheimer disease**—a progressive, irreversible brain disorder that is characterized by a gradual deterioration of memory, reasoning, language, and eventually physical function. In 2005, 4.5 million adults in the United States had Alzheimer disease. It is predicted that Alzheimer disease could triple in the next 50 years, as increasing numbers of people live to older ages. Because of the increasing prevalence of Alzheimer disease, researchers have stepped up their efforts to discover the causes of the disease and find more effective ways to treat it (Biswas & others, 2007; Shigeta & Homma, 2007).

Because of differences in onset, Alzheimer also is now described as *early-onset* (initially occurring in individuals younger than 65 years of age) or *late-onset* (which has its initial onset in individuals 65 years of age and older). Early-onset Alzheimer disease is rare (about 10 percent of all cases) and generally affects people 30 to 60 years of age.

Alzheimer disease involves a deficiency in the important brain messenger chemical acetylcholine, which plays an important role in memory (Holzgrabe & others, 2007). Also, as Alzheimer disease progresses, the brain shrinks and deteriorates (see Figure 15.5). The deterioration of the brain in Alzheimer disease is characterized by the formation of *amyloid plaques* (dense deposits of protein that accumulate in the blood vessels) and *neurofibrillary tangles* (twisted fibers that build up in neurons) (Siegel & others, 2007). Researchers are

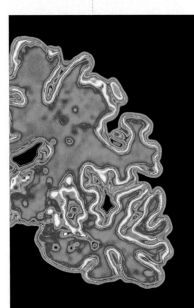

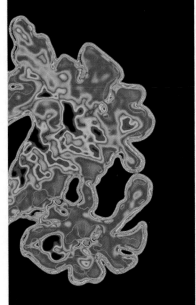

Figure 15.5 Two Brains: Normal Aging and Alzheimer Disease The top computer graphic shows a slice of a normal aging brain, the bottom photograph a slice of a brain ravaged by Alzheimer disease. Notice the deterioration and shrinking in the Alzheimer disease brain.

especially seeking ways to interrupt the progress of amyloid plaques and neurofibrillary tangles in Alzheimer patients (Wenk, 2006).

Although scientists are not certain what causes Alzheimer disease, age is an important risk factor, and genes also likely play an important role (Bertram & others, 2007). The number of individuals with Alzheimer disease doubles every five years after the age of 65. A recent study of almost 12,000 pairs of twins in Sweden found that identical twins were both more likely to develop Alzheimer disease than fraternal twins, suggesting a genetic influence on the disease (Gatz & others, 2006).

Although individuals with a family history of Alzheimer disease are at greater risk, the disease is complex and likely caused by a number of factors, including lifestyles. Scientists are finding that healthy lifestyle factors such as a good diet, exercise, and weight control may lower the risk of Alzheimer disease. Researchers have also revealed older adults with Alzheimer disease are more likely to also have cardiovascular disease than individuals who do not have Alzheimer disease (Razay, Vreugdenhil, & Wilcox, 2007). Autopsies show that brains with the telltale signs of tangles and plaques of Alzheimer patients are three times more common in individuals with cardiovascular disease (Sparks & others, 1990). Recently, more cardiac risk factors have been implicated in Alzheimer disease—obesity, smoking, atherosclerosis, and high cholesterol (Moreira & others, 2006).

Former President Ronald Reagan was diagnosed with Alzheimer disease at age 83.

As with many problems associated with health and aging, exercise may also reduce the risk of Alzheimer disease (Briones, 2006; Stevens & Killeen, 2006). One study of more than 2,000 men 71 to 93 years of age revealed that those who walked less than one-fourth of a mile a day were almost twice as likely to develop Alzheimer disease as their male counterparts who walked more than two miles a day (Abbott & others, 2004).

Early Detection and Drug Treatment Mild cognitive impairment (MCI) represents a transitional state between the cognitive changes of normal aging and very early Alzheimer disease and other dementias (Popovic, Seric, & Demarin, 2007). MCI is increasingly recognized as a risk factor for Alzheimer disease (Maoli & others, 2007).

Deficits in episodic memory appear to be an especially important early indication of risk for subsequent development of Alzheimer disease. Also, special brain scans, such as MRI (magnetic resonance imaging) can detect changes in the brain that are fairly typical of early Alzheimer disease even before symptoms develop (Mimura & Yano, 2006).

Several drugs have been approved by the U.S. Food and Drug Administration to treat Alzheimer disease. Three of these drugs are now widely used: donepezil (Aricept), rivastigmine (Exelon), and galantamine (Razadyne). They are designed to improve memory and other cognitive functions by increasing levels of acetylcholine in the brain (Campanozzi & others, 2007). The drugs have been effective in slowing down the progression of Alzheimer symptoms in mild to moderate stages of the disease, but they have not been approved for advanced stages of Alzheimer disease. Keep in mind, though, that the drugs used to treat Alzheimer

Parkinson disease A chronic, progressive disease characterized by muscle tremors, slowing of movement, and partial facial paralysis.

disease only slow the downward progression of the disease; they do not treat its cause (Shigeta & Homma, 2007).

Caring for Individuals with Alzheimer Disease A special concern is caring for Alzheimer patients (Yaari & Corey-Bloom, 2007). Health-care professionals believe that the family can be an important support system for the Alzheimer patient, but this support can have costs for the family, who can become emotionally and physically drained by the extensive care required for a person with Alzheimer disease (Neri & others, 2007). For example, depression has been reported in 50 percent of family caregivers for Alzheimer patients (Redinbaugh, MacCallum, & Kiecolt-Glaser, 1995). A recent meta-analysis found that female caregivers reported providing more caregiving hours, higher levels of burden and depression, as well as lower levels of well-being and physical health, than male caregivers (Pinquart & Sorensen, 2006).

Respite care (services that provide temporary relief for those who are caring for individuals with disabilities, illnesses, or the elderly) has been developed to help people who have to meet the day-to-day needs of Alzheimer patients. This type of care provides an important break away from the burden of providing chronic care (Garity, 2006).

Parkinson Disease

Another type of dementia is **Parkinson disease**, a chronic, progressive disease characterized by muscle tremors, slowing of movement, and partial facial paralysis. Parkinson disease is triggered by degeneration of neurons that produce dopamine in the brain (Kim, 2007). Dopamine is a neurotransmitter that is necessary for normal brain functioning. Why these neurons degenerate is not known. The main treatment for Parkinson disease involves administering drugs that enhance the effect of dopamine in the disease's earlier stages and later administering the drug L-dopa, which is converted by the brain into dopamine (Androulikakis & others, 2007). However, it is difficult to determine the correct level of dosage of L-dopa, and it loses its efficacy over time (Stocchi, 2006).

Summary

Longevity, Biological Aging, and Physical Development

Life expectancy has dramatically increased; life span has not. An increasing number of individuals live to be 100 or older. On the average, females live about five years longer than males do. The gender difference is likely due to biological and social factors. Three biological theories are cellular clock theory, free-radical theory, and hormonal stress theory. The brain loses weight and volume with age, but older adults can generate new dendritic connections. The aging brain retains considerable plasticity and adaptability. The most obvious signs of aging are wrinkled skin and age spots on the skin. Older adults get shorter, and they may lose weight after age 60 because of loss of muscle. The movement of older adults slows across a wide range of movement tasks. Declines in visual acuity, color vision, and depth perception usually occur in late adulthood. Three diseases that can impair the vision of older adults are cataracts, glaucoma, and macular degeneration. Hearing decline can begin in middle age but usually does not become an impediment until late adulthood. Smell and taste can decline, although the decline is minimal in healthy older adults. Changes in touch sensitivity are associated with aging. Sensitivity to pain decreases in late adulthood. High blood pressure is treated with medication, exercise, and/or a healthy diet. Lung capacity drops with age, but older adults can improve lung functioning with diaphragm-strengthening exercises. Aging in late adulthood does include some changes in sexual performance, more for males than females.

Health

As we age, our probability of disease or illness increases. Chronic disorders are rare in early adulthood, increase in middle adulthood, and become more common in late adulthood. The most common chronic disorder in late adulthood is arthritis. Nearly three-fourths of older adults die of heart disease, cancer, or stroke. Osteoporosis is the main reason many older adults walk with a stoop; women are especially vulnerable. Accidents are usually more debilitating to older than to younger adults. The physical benefits of exercise have clearly been demonstrated in older adults. Calorie restriction in animals can increase the animals' life span, but whether this works with humans is not known. In humans, being overweight is associated with an increased mortality rate. Although only 3 percent of adults over 65 reside in nursing homes, 23 percent of adults 85 and over do. The quality of nursing homes varies enormously. Alternatives to nursing homes are being proposed. Simply giving nursing home residents options for control can change their behavior and improve their health.

Cognitive Functioning

Researchers have found that sensory/motor and speed-of-processing dimensions decline in older adults. Some changes in attention take place in adulthood. For example, in selective attention, older adults fare more poorly than younger adults in general, but when tasks are simple and sufficient practice is given, age differences are minimal. Younger adults have better episodic memory than older adults. Regarding semantic memory, older adults have more difficulty retrieving semantic information, but they usually can eventually retrieve it. Researchers have found declines in working memory and perceptual speed in older adults. Older adults are more likely to show declines in explicit than in implicit memory. Noncognitive factors such as health, education, and socioeconomic status are linked with memory in older adults. Wisdom is expert knowledge about the practical aspects of life that permits excellent judgment about important matters. Researchers are finding that older adults who engage in cognitive activities, especially challenging ones, have higher cognitive functioning that those who don't use their cognitive skills. There has been considerable increased interest in the cognitive neuroscience of aging that focuses on links between aging, the brain, and cognitive functioning. This field relies on fMRI and PET scans to assess brain functioning while individuals are engaging in cognitive tasks.

Work and Retirement

Today, the percentage of men over 65 who continue to work full-time is less than at the beginning of the twentieth century. An important change in older adults' work patterns is the increase in part-time work. Some individuals continue a life of strong work productivity throughout late adulthood. Individuals who are healthy, have adequate income, are active, are better educated, have an extended social network of friends and family, and are satisfied with their lives before they retire adjust best to retirement.

Mental Health

A majority of older adults with depressive symptoms never receive mental health treatment. Dementia is a global term for any neurological disorder in which the primary symptoms involve a deterioration of mental functioning. Alzheimer disease is by far the most common dementia. This predictable, progressive, irreversible disorder is characterized by gradual deterioration of memory, reasoning, language, and eventually physical functioning. Alzheimer disease involves a deficiency in acetylcholine that affects memory. Also, in Alzheimer disease, the brain shrinks and deteriorates as plaques and tangles form. Age and family history are important risk factors. Healthy diet, weight control, and exercise may help to stave off Alzheimer disease. An important concern is caring for Alzheimer patients and the burdens this places on caregivers. Parkinson disease is another type of dementa characterized by a degeneration of neurons that produce dopamine, which is necessary for normal brain functioning.

Key Terms

16

Socioemotional Development in Late Adulthood

Stories of Life-Span Development: Bob Cousy, Adapting to Life as an Older Adult

Bob Cousy was a star player on Boston Celtics teams that won numerous National Basketball Association championships. In recognition of his athletic accomplishments, Cousy was honored by ESPN as one of the top 100 athletes of the twentieth century. After he retired from basketball, he became a college basketball coach and then into his seventies was a broadcaster of Boston Celtics basketball games. Now in his eighties, Cousy has retired from broadcasting but continues to play golf and tennis on a regular basis. He has a number of positive social relationships, including a marriage of more than 50 years, children and grandchildren, and many friends.

As is the case with many famous people, their awards usually reveal little about their personal lives and contributions. Two situations exemplify his humanitarian efforts to help others (McClellan, 2004). When Cousy played for the Boston Celtics, his African American teammate, Chuck Cooper, was refused a room on a road trip because of his race. Cousy expressed anger to his coach about the situation and then accompanied an appreciative Cooper on a train back to Boston. In a second situation, "Today the Bob Cousy Humanitarian Fund honors individuals who have given their lives to using the game of basketball as a medium to help others" (p. 4). The

Humanitarian Fund reflects Cousy's motivation to care for others, be appreciative and giving something back, and make the world less self-centered.

Bob Cousy's active, involved life as an older adult reflects some of the themes of socioemotional development in older adults that we discuss in this chapter. These themes include the important role that being active plays in life satisfaction, adapting to changing skills, and the positive role of close relationships with friends and family in an emotionally fulfilling life.

Our coverage of socioemotional development in late adulthood describes a number of theories of the socioemotional lives of older adults; the older adult's personality and roles in society; the importance of family ties and social relationships; the social contexts of ethnicity, gender, and culture; and the increasing trend of focusing on successful aging. ∎

Bob Cousy, as a Boston Celtics star when he was a young adult (*left*) and as an older adult (*right*). *What are some changes he has made in his life as an older adult?*

Theories of Socioemotional Development

We explore four main theories of socioemotional development that focus on late adulthood: Erikson's theory, activity theory, socioemotional selectivity theory, and selective optimization with compensation theory.

Erikson's Theory

We initially described Erik Erikson's (1968) eight stages of the human life span in Chapter 1, and as we explored different periods of development in this book we examined the stages in more detail. Here we discuss his final stage.

Integrity versus despair is Erikson's eighth and final stage of development, which individuals experience during late adulthood. This stage involves reflecting on the past and either piecing together a positive review or concluding that one's life has not been well spent. Through many different routes, the older adult may have developed a positive outlook in each of the preceding periods. If so, retrospective glances and reminiscences will reveal a picture of a life well spent, and the older adult will be satisfied (integrity). But if the older adult resolved one or more of the earlier stages in a negative way (being socially isolated in early adulthood or stagnated in middle adulthood, for example), retrospective glances about the total worth of his or her life might be negative (despair).

Life review is prominent in Erikson's final stage of integrity versus despair. Life review involves looking back at one's life experiences, evaluating them, interpreting them, and often reinterpreting them. Distinguished aging researcher Robert Butler (1996) argues that the life review is set in motion by looking forward

What characterizes a life review in late adulthood?

CHAPTER 16 SOCIOEMOTIONAL DEVELOPMENT IN LATE ADULTHOOD

406 *What characterizes a life review in late adulthood?*

to death. Sometimes the life review proceeds quietly; at other times it is intense, requiring considerable work to achieve some sense of personality integration. The life review may be observed initially in stray and insignificant thoughts about oneself and one's life history. These thoughts may continue to emerge in brief intermittent spurts or become essentially continuous.

When older adults engage in a life review, they may reevaluate previous experiences and their meaning, often with revision or expanded understanding taking place. This reorganization of the past may provide a more valid picture for the individual, providing new and significant meaning to one's life (Stinson & Kirk, 2006). A life review also may have a positive influence on older adults' mental health (Ando, Tsuda, & Moorey, 2006; Cappeliez & O'Rourke, 2006)

Activity Theory

Activity theory states that the more active and involved older adults are, the more likely they are to be satisfied with their lives. Researchers have found strong support for activity theory, beginning in the 1960s and continuing into the twenty-first century (Haber & Rhodes, 2004; Neugarten, Havighurst, & Tobin, 1968). These researchers have found that when older adults are active, energetic, and productive, they age more successfully and are happier than if they disengage from society.

Activity theory suggests that many individuals will achieve greater life satisfaction if they continue their middle-adulthood roles into late adulthood. If these roles are stripped from them (as in early retirement), it is important for them to find substitute roles that keep them active and involved.

Socioemotional Selectivity Theory

Socioemotional selectivity theory states that older adults become more selective about their social networks. Because they place a high value on emotional satisfaction, older adults spend more time with familiar individuals with whom they have had rewarding relationships. Developed by Laura Carstensen (1998, 2006; Carstensen, Mikels, & Mather, 2006; Löckenhoff & Carstensen, 2007), this theory argues that older adults deliberately withdraw from social contact with individuals peripheral to their lives while they maintain or increase contact with close friends and family members with whom they have had enjoyable relationships. This selective narrowing of social interaction maximizes positive emotional experiences and minimizes emotional risks as individuals become older.

Socioemotional selectivity theory challenges the stereotype that the majority of older adults are in emotional despair because of their social isolation (Carstensen,

Laura Carstensen (right), in a caring relationship with an older adult. *What characterizes Carstensen's socioemotional selectivity theory?*

selective optimization with
compensation theory The
theory that successful aging is
related to three main factors:
selection, optimization, and
compensation.

Mikels, & Mather, 2006; Charles & Carstensen, 2007). Rather, older adults consciously choose to decrease the total number of their social contacts in favor of spending increasing time in emotionally rewarding moments with friends and family. That is, they systematically hone their social networks so that available social partners satisfy their emotional needs.

Is there research evidence to support life-span differences in the composition of social networks? Longitudinal studies reveal far smaller social networks for older adults than for younger adults (Lee & Markides, 1990; Palmore, 1981). In one study of individuals 69 to 104 years of age, the oldest participants had fewer peripheral social contacts than the relatively younger participants but about the same number of close emotional relationships (Lang & Carstensen, 1994).

Socioemotional selectivity theory also focuses on the types of goals that individuals are motivated to achieve (Carstensen, 2006; Carstensen, Mikels, & Mather, 2006). It states that two important classes of goals are (1) knowledge-related and (2) emotion-related. This theory emphasizes that the trajectory of motivation for knowledge-related goals starts relatively high in the early years of life, peaking in adolescence and early adulthood and then declining in middle and late adulthood. The emotion trajectory is high during infancy and early childhood, declines from middle childhood through early adulthood, and increases in middle and late adulthood.

Researchers have found that across diverse samples (Norwegians, Catholic nuns, African Americans, Chinese Americans, and European Americans) older adults report better control of their emotions and fewer negative emotions than younger adults (Mroczek, 2001). Compared with younger adults, the emotional life of older adults is on a more even keel with fewer highs and lows. It may be that although older adults have less extreme joy, they have more contentment, especially when they are connected in positive ways with friends and family.

How Would You...?
As a health-care professional, how would you assess whether an older adult's limited social contacts signal unhealthy social isolation or healthy socioemotional selectivity?

Selective Optimization with Compensation Theory

Selective optimization with compensation theory states that successful aging is linked with three main factors: selection, optimization, and compensation (SOC). The theory describes how people can produce new resources and allocate them effectively to the tasks they want to master (Baltes, Lindenberger, & Staudinger, 2006; Freund, 2006; Riediger, Li, & Lindenberger, 2006). *Selection* is based on the concept that older adults have a reduced capacity and loss of functioning, which require a reduction in performance in most life domains. *Optimization* suggests that it is possible to maintain performance in some areas through continued practice and the use of new technologies. *Compensation* becomes relevant when life tasks require a level of capacity beyond the current level of the older adult's performance potential. Older adults especially need to compensate in circumstances with high mental or physical demands, such as when thinking about and memorizing new material very fast, reacting quickly when driving a car, or running fast. When older adults develop an illness, the need for compensation is obvious.

In Paul Baltes' view (2003; Baltes, Lindenberger, & Staudinger, 2006), the selection of domains and life priorities is an important aspect of development.

25 to 34 Years	35 to 54 Years	55 to 65 Years	70 to 84 Years	85 to 105 Years
Work	Family	Family	Family	Health
Friends	Work	Health	Health	Family
Family	Friends	Friends	Cognitive fitness	Thinking about life
Independence	Cognitive fitness	Cognitive fitness	Friends	Cognitive fitness

Figure 16.1 Degree of Personal Life Investment at Different Points in Life
Shown here are the top four domains of personal life investment at different points in life. The highest degree of investment is listed at the top (for example, work was the highest personal investment from 25 to 34 years of age, family from 35 to 84, and health from 85 to 105).

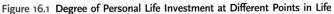

Life goals and personal life investments likely vary across the life course for most people. For many individuals, it is not just the sheer attainment of goals, but rather the attainment of *meaningful* goals, that makes life satisfying. In one cross-sectional study, the personal life investments of 25- to 105-year-olds were assessed (Staudinger, 1996) (see Figure 16.1). From 25 to 34 years of age, participants said that they personally invested more time in work, friends, family, and independence, in that order. From 35 to 54 and 55 to 65 years of age, family became more important than friends to them in terms of their personal investment. Little changed in the rank ordering of persons 70 to 84 years old, but for participants 85 to 105 years old, health became the most important personal investment. Thinking about life showed up for the first time on the most important list for those who were 85 to 105 years old.

Personality and Society

Is personality linked to mortality in older adults? How are older adults perceived and treated by society?

Personality

Might certain personality traits be related to how long older adults live? Researchers have found that some personality traits are associated with the mortality of older adults (Mroczek, Spiro, & Griffin, 2006). We described the big five factors of personality in Chapter 14. Two of the big five factors were linked to older adults' mortality in a recent study with low conscientiousness and high neuroticism predicting earlier death (Wilson & others, 2004).

Affect and outlook on life are also linked to mortality in older adults (Mroczek, Spiro, & Griffin, 2006). Older adults characterized by negative affect don't live as long as those who display more positive affect, and optimistic older adults who have a positive outlook on life live longer than their counterparts who are more pessimistic and have a negative outlook on life (Levy & others, 2002).

Older Adults in Society

Does society negatively stereotype older adults? What are some social policy issues in an aging society? What role does technology play in the lives of older adults?

Stereotyping of Older Adults

Social participation by older adults is often discouraged by **ageism**, which is prejudice against others because of their age, especially prejudice against older adults (Hess, 2006). They are often perceived as incapable of thinking clearly, learning new things, enjoying sex, contributing to the community, or holding responsible jobs. Many older adults face painful discrimination and might be too polite and timid to attack it (Cunningham, 2004). Because of their age, older adults might not be hired for new jobs or might be eased out of old ones; they might be shunned socially; and they might be edged out of their family life.

Ageism is widespread (Reyna, Goodwin, & Ferrari, 2007; Robinson & Umphery, 2006). One recent study found that men were more likely to negatively stereotype older adults than were women (Rupp, Vodanovich, & Crede, 2005). Research indicates that the most frequent form is disrespect for older adults, followed by assumptions about ailments or frailty caused by age (Palmore, 2004). However, the increased number of adults living to an older age has led to active efforts to improve society's image of older adults, obtain better living conditions for older adults, and gain political clout.

Policy Issues in an Aging Society

The aging society and older persons' status in this society raise policy issues about the well-being of older adults. These include the provision of health care, supports for families who care for older adults, and generational inequity, each of which we consider in turn.

An aging society brings with it various problems involving health care (Ferraro, 2006; Moon, 2006). Escalating health-care costs are currently causing considerable concern. One factor that contributes to the surge in health costs is the increasing number of older adults. Older adults have more illnesses than younger adults, despite the fact that many older adults report their health as good. Older adults see doctors more often, are hospitalized more often, and have longer hospital stays. Approximately one-third of the total health bill of the United States is for the care of adults 65 and over, who comprise only about one-eighth of the population. The health-care needs of older adults are reflected in Medicare, the program that provides health-care insurance to adults 65 and over under the Social Security system (Daniel & Malone, 2007).

A special concern is that while many of the health problems of older adults are chronic rather than acute, the medical system is based on a "cure" rather

How Would You...?
As a human development and family studies professional, how would you design a public awareness campaign to reduce ageism?

How Would You...?
As a health-care professional, how would you recommend addressing the medical community's emphasis on 'cure' rather than 'care' when treating chronic illness in older adults?

than a "care" model (Stone, 2006). Chronic illness is long-term, often lifelong, and requires long-term, if not life-term, management (Nutting & others, 2007). The patient's home, rather than a hospital, often becomes the center of managing the patient's chronic illness. In a home-based system, a new type of cooperative relationship between doctors, nurses, patients, family members, and other service providers needs to be developed (Wilkins, 2006). Healthcare personnel need to be trained and be available to provide home services, sharing authority with the patient and perhaps yielding to the patient's authority over the long term.

eldercare Physical and emotional caretaking for older members of the family, whether by giving day-to-day physical assistance or by being responsible for overseeing such care.

Eldercare is the physical and emotional caretaking of older members of the family, whether that care is day-to-day physical assistance or responsibility for arranging and overseeing such care. An important issue involving eldercare is how it can best be provided (Talley & Crews, 2007). With so many women in the labor market, who will replace them as caregivers? An added problem is that many caregivers are in their sixties, and many of them are ill themselves. They may find it especially stressful to be responsible for the care of relatives who are in their eighties or nineties.

The Gray Panthers are actively involved in pressuring Congress on everything from health insurance to housing costs. Along with the American Association for Retired Persons, they have developed a formidable gray lobbying effort in state and national politics. *What are some of the policy issues in an aging society?*

Income

Another concern is older adults who are poor (Holden & Hatcher, 2006). One analysis found that lower health-related quality of life in older adults in the United States was linked with income of $15,000 or less (Centers for Disease Control and Prevention, 2003).

Recent census data suggest that although the overall number of older people living in poverty has declined since the 1960s, the percentage of older persons living in poverty has consistently remained in the 10 to 12 percent range since the early 1980s (U.S. Census Bureau, 2004). More than 25 percent of older women who live alone live in poverty. Also, the number of older single women just above the poverty line remains substantial. Poverty rates among ethnic minorities are two to three times higher than the rate for Whites. Combining gender and ethnicity, 60 percent of older African American women and 50 percent of older Latinas who live alone live in poverty. Also, the oldest-old are the age subgroup of older adults most likely to be living in poverty.

Technology

Another aspect of society that older adults are faced with adapting to is technology (Bunde & others, 2007). How well are older adults keeping up with changes in technology? Older adults are less likely to have a computer in their home and less likely to use the Internet than younger adults, but older adults are the fastest-growing segment of Internet users (Brinthall-Peterson, 2003). A 2003 survey indicated that 32 percent of 65 and older U.S. adults (about 11 million) and 61 percent of 50- to 64-year-olds are online (Harris Interactive, 2003). Older adults log more time on the Internet (an average of 8.3 hours per week), visit more Web sites, and spend more money on the Internet than their younger adult counterparts. They are especially interested in learning to use e-mail and going online for health information. Increasing numbers of older adults use e-mail to communicate with relatives. As with children and younger adults, cautions about the accuracy of information—in areas such as health care—on the Internet need to always be kept in mind (Cutler, 2006).

Families and Social Relationships

Are the close relationships of older adults different from those of younger adults? What are the lifestyles of older adults like? What characterizes the relationships of older adult parents and their adult children? What do friendships and social networks contribute to the lives of older adults? How might older adults' altruism and volunteerism contribute to positive outcomes?

Lifestyle Diversity

The lifestyles of older adults are changing. Formerly, the later years of life were likely to consist of marriage for men and widowhood for women. With demographic shifts toward marital dissolution characterized by divorce, one-third of adults can now expect to marry, divorce, and remarry during their lifetime. Let's now explore some of the diverse lifestyles of older adults, beginning with those who are married or partnered.

Married Older Adults

In 2004, 56 percent of U.S. adults over 65 years of age were married (U.S. Census Bureau, 2006). Individuals who are in a marriage or a partnership in late adulthood are usually happier, are less distressed, and live longer than those who are single (Hagedoorn & others, 2006; Manzoli & others, 2007). One study found that older adults were more satisfied with their marriages than were young and middle-aged adults (Bookwala & Jacobs, 2004). Indeed, the majority of older adults evaluate their marriages as happy or very happy (Huyck, 1995). Marital satisfaction is often greater for women than for men, possibly because women place more emphasis on attaining satisfaction through marriage than men do. However, as more women develop careers, this gender difference may not continue. Also, a recent longitudinal study of adults 75 years of age and older revealed that individuals who were married were less likely to die across a span of seven years (Rasulo, Christensen, & Tomassini, 2005).

What are some characteristics of marriage in late adulthood?

Divorced and Remarried Older Adults

Divorced and separated older adults represented only 8 percent of older adults in 2004 (U.S. Census Bureau, 2006). However, their numbers (2.6 million) have increased considerably since 1990 (1.5 million). Many of these individuals were divorced or separated before they entered late adulthood.

There are social, financial, and physical consequences of divorce for older adults (Jenkins, 2003). Divorce can weaken kinship ties when it occurs in later life, especially in the case of older men (Cooney, 1994). Divorced older women are less likely to have adequate financial resources than married older women, and as earlier in adulthood, divorce is linked to more health problems in older adults (Bennett, 2006).

Rising divorce rates, increased longevity, and better health have led to an increase in remarriage by older adults (Ganong & Coleman, 2006). What happens

How Would You...?

As a psychologist, how would you assist older adults to cope with the unique challenges faced by divorcees at this age?

when an older adult wants to remarry or does remarry? Researchers have found that some older adults perceive negative social pressure about their decision to remarry (McKain, 1972). These negative sanctions range from raised eyebrows to rejection by adult children (Ganong & Coleman, 2006). However, the majority of adult children support the decision of their older adult parents to remarry. Researchers have found that remarried parents and stepparents provide less support to adult stepchildren than parents in first marriages (White, 1992).

Cohabiting Older Adults

An increasing number of older adults cohabit. In 1960, hardly any older adults cohabited (Chevan, 1996). Today, approximately 3 percent of older adults cohabit (U.S. Census Bureau, 2003). In many cases, the cohabiting is more for companionship than for love. In other cases, for example, when one partner faces the potential for expensive care, a couple may decide to maintain their assets separately and thus not marry. One recent study found that older adults who cohabited had a more a more positive, stable relationship than younger adults who cohabited, although cohabiting older adults were less likely to have plans to marry their partner than younger ones (King & Scott, 2005). Recent research also has revealed that middle-aged and older adult cohabiting men and women reported higher levels of depression than their married counterparts (Brown, Lee, & Bulanda, 2006).

Older Adult Parents and Their Adult Children

Approximately 80 percent of older adults have living children, many of whom are middle-aged. About 10 percent of older adults have children who are 65 years or older. Adult children are an important part of the aging parent's social network. Researchers have found that older adults with children have more contacts with relatives than those without children (Johnson & Troll, 1992).

Increasingly, diversity characterizes older adult parents and their adult children. Divorce, cohabitation, and nonmarital childbearing are more common in the history of older adults today than in the past (Pudrovska, Schieman, & Carr, 2006).

Gender plays an important role in relationships involving older adult parents and their children (Ward-Griffin & others, 2007). Adult daughters rather than adult sons are more likely to be involved in the lives of aging parents. For example, adult daughters are three times more likely than are adult sons to give parents assistance with daily living activities (Dwyer & Coward, 1991).

An extremely valuable task that adult children can perform is to coordinate and monitor services for an aging parent (or relative) who becomes disabled (Huyck, Ayalon, & Yoder, 2007). This might involve locating a nursing home and monitoring its quality, procuring medical services, arranging public service assistance, and handling finances. In some cases, adult children provide direct assistance with daily living, including such activities as eating, bathing, and dressing. Even less severely impaired older adults may need help with shopping, housework, transportation, home maintenance, and bill paying.

Friendship

Aging expert Laura Carstensen (2006) concluded that people choose close friends over new friends as they grow older. And as long as they have several close people in their network, they seem content, says Carstensen.

In one study of 128 married older adults, women were more depressed than men if they did not have a best friend, and women who did have a friend reported lower levels of depression (Antonucci, Lansford, & Akiyama, 2001). Similarly, women who did not have a best friend were less satisfied with life than women who did have a best friend.

Two recent studies documented the importance of friendship in older adults:

How Would You...?
As a human development and family studies professional, how would you characterize the importance of friendships for older adults?

- A study of almost 1,700 U.S. adults 60 years and older revealed that friendships were more important than family relationships in predicting mental health (Fiori, Antonucci, & Cortina, 2006). Even when the researchers controlled for health, age, income, and other factors, older adults whose social contacts were mainly restricted to their family members were more likely to have depressive symptoms. Friends likely provide emotional intimacy and companionship, as well as integration into the community.

- A recent longitudinal study of adults 75 years of age and older revealed that individuals with close ties with friends were less likely to die across a seven-year age span (Rasulo, Christensen, & Tomassini, 2005). The findings were stronger for women than men.

Social Support and Social Integration

Social support and social integration play important roles in the physical and mental health of older adults. In the *social convoy* model of social relations, individuals go through life embedded in a personal network of individuals to whom they give, and from whom they receive, social support (Antonucci & Akiyama, 2002). Social support can help individuals of all ages cope more effectively (Griffiths & others, 2007). For older adults, social support is related to their physical and mental health. It is linked with a reduction in symptoms of disease, with the ability to meet one's own health-care needs, and mortality (Lyrra & Heikkinen, 2006; Rook & others, 2007). Social support also decreases the probability that an older adult will be institutionalized and is associated with a lower incidence of depression (Cacioppo & others, 2000).

Social integration also plays an important role in the lives of many older adults (Cavallero, Morino-Abbele, & Bertocci, 2007). Remember from our earlier discussion of socioemotional selectivity theory that many older adults choose to have fewer peripheral social contacts and more emotionally positive contacts with friends and family (Carstensen, 2006). Thus, a decrease in the overall social activity of many older adults may reflect their greater interest in spending more time in the small circle of friends and families where they are less likely to have negative emotional experiences. Researchers have found that a low level of social integration is linked with coronary heart disease in older adults (Loucks & others, 2006). Also, in one study, being part of a social network was related to longevity, especially for men (House, Landis, & Umberson, 1988). And in a longitudinal study, both women and men with more organizational memberships lived longer than their counterparts with low participation in organizations (Tucker & others, 1999).

However, being lonely and socially isolated is a significant health risk factor in older adults (Moren-Cross & Lin, 2006). In one longitudinal study, poor social connections, infrequent participation in social activities, and social disengagement predicted cognitive decline in older adults (Zunzunegui & others, 2003).

What role does social support play in the health of older adults?

How Would You...?
As a health-care professional, how would you advise an older adult patient who states, "I don't really have any friends or family; I rarely talk to anyone."

Altruism and Volunteerism

A common perception is that older adults need to be given help rather than give help themselves. However, researchers have found that when older adults engage in altruistic behavior and volunteering everyone benefits from these activities. One study followed 423 older adult couples for five years (Brown & others, 2003). At the beginning of the study, the couples were asked about the extent to which they had given or received emotional or practical help in the past year. Five years later, those who said they had helped others were half as likely to have died. One possible reason for this finding is that helping others may reduce the output of stress hormones, which improves cardiovascular health and strengthens the immune system.

Researchers also have found that volunteering as an older adult is associated with a number of positive outcomes (George, 2006). An early study of individuals 65 years and older found that volunteer workers compared with nonvolunteers were more satisfied with their lives and were less depressed and anxious (Hunter & Linn, 1980). Another study revealed that being a volunteer as an older adult was associated with more positive affect and less negative affect (Greenfield & Marks, 2004). Among the reasons for the positive outcomes of volunteering are its provision of constructive activities and productive roles, social integration, increased activity level, and enhanced meaningfulness (Tan & others, 2007; Warburton & McLaughlin, 2006).

How Would You...?
As an educator, how would you persuade the school board to sponsor a volunteer program to bring older adults into the school system to work with elementary students?

Edna Wharf, who is retired, volunteers her time as a reading tutor at Claxton Elementary School in Ashville, North Carolina. *What are some of the benefits of volunteering for older adults?*

Ethnicity, Gender, and Culture

How is ethnicity linked to aging? Do gender roles change in late adulthood? What are some of the social aspects of aging in different cultures?

Ethnicity

Of special concern are ethnic minority older adults, especially African Americans and Latinos, who are overrepresented in poverty statistics (Angel & Angel, 2006; Karasik & Hamon, 2007). Comparative information about African Americans, Latinos, and non-Latino Whites indicates a possible double jeopardy for elderly ethnic minority individuals. They face problems related to *both* ageism and racism (Hinrichsen, 2006). One study of more than 4,000 older adults found that African Americans perceived more discrimination than non-Latino Whites (Barnes & others, 2004). Both the wealth and the health of ethnic minority older adults decrease more rapidly than for elderly Whites (Robert & Ruel, 2006; Yee & Chiriboga, 2007). Older ethnic minority individuals are more likely to become ill but less likely to receive treatment (Hinrichsen, 2006). They also are more likely to have a history of less education, unemployment, worse housing conditions, and shorter life expectancies than their older White counterparts (Himes, Hogan, & Eggebeen, 1996). And many ethnic minority workers never enjoy the Social Security and Medicare benefits to which their earnings contribute, because they die before reaching the age of eligibility for benefits.

Despite the stress and discrimination older ethnic minority individuals face, many of these older adults have developed coping mechanisms that allow them to survive in the dominant White world (Markides & Rudkin, 1996). Extension of family networks helps older minority-group individuals cope with the bare essentials of living and gives them a sense of being loved (Karasek & Hamon, 2007). Churches in African American and Latino communities provide avenues for meaningful social participation, feelings of power, and a sense of internal satisfaction (Hill & others, 2005). And residential concentrations of ethnic minority groups give their older members a sense of belonging. Thus, it always is important to consider individual variations in the lives of aging minorities (Whitfield & Baker-Thomas, 1999). To read about one individual who is providing help for aging minorities, see the Careers in Life-Span Development profile.

Gender

Do our gender roles change when we become older adults? Some developmentalists believe there is decreasing femininity in women and decreasing masculinity in men when they reach the late adulthood years (Gutmann, 1975). The evidence suggests that older men do become more feminine—nurturant, sensitive, and so on—but it appears that older women do not necessarily become more masculine—assertive, dominant, and so on (Turner, 1982). Keep in mind that cohort effects are especially important to consider in areas such as gender roles. As sociohistorical changes take place and are assessed more frequently in life-span investigations, what were once perceived to be age effects may turn out to be cohort effects (Schaie, 2007).

Norma Thomas, Social Work Professor and Administrator

Norma Thomas.

Dr. Norma Thomas has worked for more than three decades in the field of aging. She obtained her undergraduate degree in social work from Pennsylvania State University and her doctoral degree in social work from the University of Pennsylvania. Norma's activities are varied. Earlier in her career, as a social work practitioner, she provided services to older adults of color in an effort to improve their lives. She currently is a professor and academic administrator at Widener University in Chester, Pennsylvania, a fellow of the Institute of Aging at the University of Pennsylvania, and the chief executive officer and cofounder of the Center on Ethnic and Minority Aging (CEMA). CEMA was formed to provide research, consultation, training, and services to benefit aging individuals of color, their families, and their communities. Norma has created numerous community service events that benefit older adults of color, especially African Americans and Latinos. She has also been a consultant to various national, regional, and state agencies in her effort to improve the lives of aging adults of color.

Many social workers, such as Norma Thomas, are involved in helping people with social or economic problems. They may investigate, evaluate, and attempt of rectify reported cases of abuse, neglect, endangerment, or domestic disputes. They may intervene in families and provide counseling and referral services to individuals and families. Social workers often work for publicly funded agencies at the city, state, or national level, although increasingly they work in the private sector in areas such as drug rehabilitation and family counseling. Social workers have a minimum of an undergraduate degree from a school of social work that includes coursework in sociology and psychology. Some social workers also have a master's or doctoral degree. For example, medical social workers have a master's degree in social work (MSW) and complete graduate coursework and supervised clinical experiences in medical settings.

A possible double jeopardy also faces many women—the burden of *both* ageism and sexism (Lopata, 1994). The poverty rate for older adult females is almost double that of older adult males.

Not only is it important to be concerned about older women's double jeopardy of ageism and sexism, but special attention also needs to be devoted to female ethnic minority older adults (Locher & others, 2005). They face what could be described as triple jeopardy—ageism, sexism, and racism.

Culture

What factors are associated with whether older adults are accorded a position of high status in a culture? Six factors are most likely to predict high status for older adults in a culture (Sangree, 1989):

- Older persons have valuable knowledge.
- Older persons control key family/community resources.

Cultures vary in the prestige they give to older adults. In the Navajo culture, older adults are especially treated with respect because of their wisdom and extensive life experiences. *What are some other factors that are linked with respect for older adults in a culture?*

- Older persons are permitted to engage in useful and valued functions as long as possible.

- Age-related role changes involve greater responsibility, authority, and advisory capacity.

- The extended family is a common family arrangement in the culture, and the older person is integrated into the extended family.

- In general, respect for older adults is greater in collectivistic cultures (such as China and Japan), than in individualistic cultures (such as the United States). However, some researchers are finding that this collectivistic/individualistic difference in respect for older adults is not as strong as it used to be, and that in some cases older adults in individualistic cultures receive considerable respect (Antonucci, Vandewater, & Lansford, 2000).

Successful Aging

For too long, the positive dimensions of late adulthood were ignored (Ouwehand, de Ridder, & Bensing, 2007; Hendricks & Hatch, 2006). Throughout this book, we have called attention to the positive aspects of aging. There are many robust, healthy older adults (Tafaro & others, 2007). With a proper diet, an active lifestyle, mental stimulation and flexibility, positive coping skills, good social relationships and support, and the absence of disease, many abilities can be maintained or in some cases even improved as we get older (Aldwin, Spiro, & Park, 2006). Even when individuals develop a disease, improvements in medicine mean that increasing numbers of older adults can still lead active, constructive lives (Depp, Glatt, & Jeste, 2007).

Being active is especially important to successful aging (Kramer, Fabiani, & Colcombe, 2006). Older adults who get out and go to meetings, participate in church activities, go on trips, and exercise regularly are more satisfied with their lives than their counterparts who disengage from society (Reichstadt & others, 2007). Older adults who are emotionally selective, optimize their choices, and compensate effectively for losses increase their chances of aging successfully (Baltes, Lindenberger, & Staudinger, 2006).

Successful aging also involves perceived control over the environment (Mroczek, Spiro, & Griffin, 2006). In Chapter 15, we described how perceived control over the environment had a positive effect on nursing home residents' health and longevity. In recent years, the term *self-efficacy* has often been used to describe perceived control over the environment and the ability to produce positive outcomes (Bandura, 2006). Researchers have found that many older adults are quite effective in maintaining a sense of control and have a positive view of themselves (George, 2006; Skaff, 2007). Examining the positive aspects of aging is an important trend in life-span development and is likely to benefit future generations of older adults (Ebner & Freund, 2007; Scheibe, Kunzmann, & Baltes, 2007).

Summary

Theories of Socioemotional Development

Erikson's eighth and final stage of development, called integrity versus despair, involves reflecting on the past and either integrating it positively or concluding that one's life has not been well spent. Life review is an important theme in Erikson's final stage. Activity theory states that the more active and involved older adults are, the more likely they are to be satisfied with their lives. Research strongly supports this theory. Socioemotional selectivity theory states that older adults become more selective about their social networks. Because they place a high value on emotional satisfaction, they are motivated to spend more time with familiar individuals with whom they have had rewarding relationships. Knowledge-related and emotion-related goals change across the life span, with emotion-related goals being more important when individuals get older. Selective optimization with compensation theory states that successful aging is linked with three main factors: (1) selection, (2) optimization, and (3) compensation. These are especially likely to be relevant when mental or physical losses occur.

Personality and Society

Low conscientiousness, high neuroticism, negative affect, pessimism, and a negative outlook on life are related to earlier death in late adulthood. Ageism is prejudice against others because of their age, especially against older adults. Social policy issues in an aging society include the status of the economy and the viability of the Social Security system, the provision of health care, eldercare, and generational inequity. Of special concern are older adults who are in poverty. Poverty rates are especially high among older women who live alone and ethnic minority older adults. Older adults are less likely to have a computer in their home and less likely to use the Internet than younger adults, but they are the fastest-growing age segment of Internet users.

Families and Social Relationships

Married older adults are often happier than single older adults. There are social, financial, and physical consequences of divorce for older adults. More divorced older adults, increased longevity, and better health have led to an increase in remarriage by older adults. An increasing number of older adults cohabit. Approximately 80 percent of older adults have living children, many of whom are middle-aged. Increasingly, diversity characterizes older parents and their adult children. Adult daughters are more likely than adult sons to be involved in the lives of aging parents. An important task that adult children can perform is to coordinate and monitor services for an aging parent who becomes disabled. Ambivalence can characterize the relationships of adult children with their aging parents. Friendship is linked to the mental health and longevity of older adults. Social support is related to improved physical and mental health in older adults. Older adults who participate in more organizations live longer than their counterparts who have low participation rates. Older adults often have fewer peripheral social ties but a strong motivation to spend time in relationships with close friends and family members that are rewarding. Altruism is linked to having a longer life. Volunteering is associated with higher life satisfaction, less depression and anxiety, better physical health, and more positive affect and less negative affect.

Ethnicity, Gender, and Culture

Aging minorities face special burdens, having to cope with the double burden of ageism and racism. Nonetheless, there is considerable variation in aging minorities. There is stronger evidence that men become more feminine (nurturant, sensitive) as older adults than there is that women become more masculine (assertive). Many older women face a double jeopardy of ageism and sexism, and yet others also face a triple jeopardy of ageism, sexism, and racism. Factors that predict high status for the elderly across cultures range from their valuable knowledge to integration into the extended family.

Successful Aging

Increasingly, the positive aspects of older adults are being studied. Factors that are linked with successful aging include an active lifestyle, positive coping skills, good social relationships and support, and the absence of disease.

Key Terms

integrity versus
despair 407
activity theory 407
socioemotional selectivity
theory 407

selective optimization
with compensation
theory 408

ageism 410
eldercare 411

17

Death, Dying, and Grieving

Stories of Life-Span Development: Paige Farley-Hackel and Ruth McCourt, 9/11/2001

Paige Farley-Hackel and her best friend Ruth McCourt teamed up to take McCourt's 4-year-old daughter, Juliana, to Disneyland. They were originally booked on the same flight from Boston to Los Angeles, but McCourt decided to use her frequent flyer miles and go on a different airplane. Both their flights exploded 17 minutes apart after terrorists hijacked them, then rammed them into the twin towers of the World Trade Center in New York City on 9/11/2001.

Forty-six-year-old Farley-Hackel was a writer, motivational speaker, and

spiritual counselor who lived in Newton, Massachusetts. She was looking forward to the airing of the first few episodes of her new radio program, *Spiritually Speaking,* and wanted to eventually be on *The Oprah Winfrey Show,* said her husband, Allan Hackel. Following 9/11, Oprah included a memorial tribute to Farley-Hackel, McCourt, and Juliana.

Forty-five-year-old Ruth McCourt was a homemaker from New London, Connecticut, who met Farley-Hackel at a day spa she used to own in Boston. McCourt gave up the business when

she became married, but the friendship between the two women lasted. They often traveled together and shared their passion for reading, cooking, and learning.

In this chapter, we explore many aspects of death and dying. Among the questions that we will ask are: How can death be defined? How is death viewed in other cultures? How do people face their own death? How do people cope with the death of someone they love?

brain death A neurological definition of death. A person is brain dead when all electrical activity of the brain has ceased for a specified period of time. A flat EEG recording is one criterion of brain death.

Defining Death and Life/Death Issues

Is there one point in the process of dying that is *the* point at which death takes place, or is death a more gradual process? What are some decisions individuals can make about life, death, and health care?

Determining Death

Twenty-five years ago, determining if someone was dead was simpler than it is today. The end of certain biological functions—such as breathing and blood pressure, and the rigidity of the body (rigor mortis)—were considered to be clear signs of death. In the past several decades, defining death has become more complex (Kendall & others, 2007).

Brain death is a neurological definition of death, which states that a person is brain dead when all electrical activity of the brain has ceased for a specified period of time. A flat EEG (electroencephalogram) recording for a specified period of time is one criterion of brain death. The higher portions of the brain often die sooner than the lower portions. Because the brain's lower portions monitor heartbeat and respiration, individuals whose higher brain areas have died may continue breathing and have a heartbeat. The definition of brain death currently followed by most physicians includes the death of both the higher cortical functions and the lower brain stem functions (Joffee & Anton, 2006).

Some medical experts argue that the criteria for death should include only higher cortical functioning. If the cortical death definition were adopted, then physicians could claim a person is dead who has no cortical functioning, even though the lower brain stem is functioning. Supporters of the cortical death policy argue that the functions we associate with being human, such as intelligence and personality, are located in the higher cortical part of the brain. They believe that when these functions are lost, the "human being" is no longer alive.

How Would You...?
As a health-care professional, how would you explain "brain death" to the family of an individual severely injured in an automobile accident?

Decisions Regarding Life, Death, and Health Care

In cases of catastrophic illness or accidents, patients might not be able to respond adequately to participate in decisions about their medical care. To prepare for this situation, some individuals make choices earlier.

Natural Death Act and Advance Directive

For many patients in a coma, it has not been clear what their wishes regarding termination of treatment might be if they still were conscious (Burck & others, 2007). Recognizing that terminally ill patients might prefer to die rather than linger in a painful or vegetative state, the organization "Choice in Dying" created the living will. This document is designed to be filled in while the individual can still think clearly; it expresses the person's desires regarding extraordinary medical procedures that might be used to sustain life when the medical situation becomes hopeless (Wolfson & Morgan, 2007).

Physicians' concerns over malpractice suits and the efforts of people who support the living will concept have produced natural death legislation in many states. For example, California's Natural Death Act permits individuals who have

How Would You...?

As a social worker, how would you explain to terminally ill clients the advantages of preparing a living will?

been diagnosed by two physicians as terminally ill to sign an *advance directive,* which states that life-sustaining procedures shall not be used to prolong their lives when death is imminent (Giger, Davidhizard, & Fordham, 2006). An advance directive must be signed while the individual still is able to think clearly (Teno & others, 2007). Laws in all fifty states now accept advance directives as reflecting an individual's wishes.

euthanasia The act of painlessly ending the lives of persons who are suffering from incurable diseases or severe disabilities; sometimes called "mercy killing."

passive euthanasia The withholding of available treatments, such as life-sustaining devices, allowing the person to die.

active euthanasia Death induced deliberately, as by injecting a lethal dose of a drug.

Euthanasia

Euthanasia ("easy death") is the act of painlessly ending the lives of individuals who are suffering from an incurable disease or severe disability. Sometimes euthansia is called "mercy killing." Distinctions are made between two types of euthanasia: passive and active. **Passive euthanasia** occurs when a person is allowed to die by withholding available treatment, such as withdrawing a life-sustaining device. For example, this might involve turning off a respirator or a heart-lung machine. **Active euthanasia** occurs when death is deliberately induced, as when a lethal dose of a drug is injected.

Technological advances in life-support devices raise the issue of quality of life. Nowhere was this more apparent in the highly publicized case of Terri Schiavo, who suffered severe brain damage related to cardiac arrest and a lack of oxygen to the brain. She went into a coma and spent 15 years in a vegetative state. Across the 15 years, whether passive euthanasia should be implemented, or whether she should be kept in the vegetative state with the hope that her condition might change for the better, was debated between family members and eventually at a number of levels in the judicial system. At one point toward the end of her life in early spring 2005, a judge ordered her feeding tube be removed. However, subsequent appeals led to its reinsertion twice. The feeding tube was removed a third and final time on March 18, 2005, and she died 13 days later. Withholding the life-support system allowed Terri Schiavo to die from passive euthanasia.

Should individuals, like Terri Schiavo, be kept alive in a vegetative state? The trend is toward acceptance of passive euthanasia in the case of terminally ill patients. The inflammatory argument that once equated this practice with suicide rarely is heard today. However, experts do not yet entirely agree on the precise boundaries or the

Terry Schiavo (*right*) shown with her mother in an undated photo. *What issues did the Terry Schiavo case raise?*

exact mechanisms by which treatment decisions should be implemented (Phillips & others, 2005). Can a comatose patient's life-support systems be disconnected when the patient has left no written instructions to that effect? Does the family of a comatose patient have the right to overrule the attending physician's decision to continue life-support systems? These questions have no simple or universally agreed-upon answers (Kelly & McLoughlin, 2002).

The most widely publicized cases of active euthanasia involve "assisted suicide" (Hertogh & others, 2007). Jack Kevorkian, a Michigan physician, has

hospice A program committed to making the end of life as free from pain, anxiety, and depression as possible. The goals of hospice contrast with those of a hospital, which are to cure disease and prolong life.

palliative care Emphasized in hospice care; involves reducing pain and suffering and helping individuals die with dignity.

assisted a number of terminally ill patients to end their lives. After a series of trials, Kevorkian was convicted in the state of Michigan of second-degree murder and given a long prison sentence, which he is still serving.

The law is much better defined for active than for passive euthanasia. Active euthanasia is a crime in most countries and in all states in the United States except one—Oregon (Hedberg, Hopkins, & Kohn, 2003). In 1994, the state of Oregon passed the Death with Dignity Act, which allows active euthanasia under certain conditions. Through 2001, ninety-one individuals were known to have died by active euthanasia in Oregon. Active euthanasia is legal in the Netherlands and Uruguay (Vrakking & others, 2007). In January 2006, the U.S. Supreme Court upheld Oregon's active euthanasia law.

Needed: Better Care for Dying Individuals

Too often, death in America is lonely, prolonged, and painful (Schroepher, 2007). Scientific advances sometimes have made dying harder by delaying the inevitable (Kaufman, 2005). Also, even though painkillers are available, too many people experience severe pain during the last days and months of life (de Graeff & Dean, 2007). Many health-care professionals have not been trained to provide adequate end-of-life care or to understand its importance.

End-of-life care should include respect for the goals, preferences, and choices of the patient and his or her family (International Work Group on Death, Dying, and Bereavement & others, 2006). Many patients who are nearing death want companionship.

Hospice is a program committed to making the end of life as free from pain, anxiety, and depression as possible. Whereas a hospital's goals are to cure illness and prolong life, hospice care emphasizes **palliative care**, which involves reducing pain and suffering and helping individuals die with dignity (Rodriquez, Barnato, & Arnold, 2007). Hospice-care professionals work together to treat the dying person's symptoms, make the individual as comfortable as possible, show interest in the person and the person's family, and help them all cope with death (Dougherty & Long, 2006; Kapo, Morrison, & Liao, 2007).

Today more hospice programs are home-based, a blend of institutional and home care designed to humanize the end-of-life experience for the dying person. To read about the work of a home hospice nurse, see the Careers in Life-Span Development profile.

Death and Sociohistorical Cultural Contexts

When, where, and how people die have changed historically in the United States. Also, attitudes toward death vary across cultures.

Changing Historical Circumstances

We have already described one of the historical changes involving death—the increasing complexity of determining when someone is truly dead. Another historical change involves the age group in which death most often strikes. Two hundred

Kathy McLaughlin, Home Hospice Nurse

Kathy McLaughlin is a home hospice nurse in Alexandria, Virginia. She provides care for individuals with terminal cancer, Alzheimer disease, and other diseases. There currently is a shortage of home hospice nurses in the United States.

Kathy says that she has seen too many people dying in pain, away from home, hooked up to needless machines. In her work as a home hospice nurse, she comments, "I know I'm making a difference. I just feel privileged to get the chance to meet this person who is not going to be around much longer. I want to enjoy the moment with this person. And I want them to enjoy the moment. They have great stories. They are better than novels" (McLaughlin, 2003, p. 1).

Kathy McLaughlin checks the vital signs of Kathryn Francis, 86, who is in an advanced stage of Alzheimer disease.

Hospice nurses, like Kathy McLaughlin, care for terminally ill patients and seek to make their remaining days in life as pain-free and comfortable as possible. They typically spend several hours a day in the terminally ill patient's home, serving not just as a medical caregiver but also as an emotional caregiver. Hospice nurses usually coordinate the patient's care through an advising physician.

Hospice nurses must be registered nurses (RNs) plus be certified as a hospice worker. Educational requirements are an undergraduate degree in nursing; some hospice nurses also have graduate degrees in nursing. To be a certified hospice nurse requires a current license as an RN, a minimum of two years of experience as an RN in hospice-nursing settings, and passing an exam administered by the National Board for the Certification of Hospice Nurses.

years ago, almost one of every two children died before the age of 10, and one parent died before children grew up. Today, death occurs most often among older adults (Lamb, 2003). In the United States, life expectancy has increased from 47 years for a person born in 1900 to 78 years for someone born today (U.S. Census Bureau, 2006). In 1900, most people died at home, cared for by their family. As our population has aged and become more mobile, more older adults die apart from their families. In the United States today, more than 80 percent of all deaths occur in institutions or hospitals. The care of a dying older person has shifted away from the family and minimized our exposure to death and its painful surroundings.

Death in Different Cultures

Cultural variations characterize the experience of death and attitudes about death (Doorenbos, Wilson, & Coenen, 2006). Individuals are more conscious of death in times of war, famine, and plague.

Most societies throughout history have had philosophical or religious beliefs about death, and most societies have a ritual that deals with death (Lobar, Youngblut, & Brooten, 2006) (see Figure 17.1). Death may be seen as a punishment for one's sins, an act of atonement, or a judgment of a just God. For some, death means loneliness; for others, death is a quest for happiness. For still others, death represents redemption, a relief from the trials and tribulations of the earthly world. Some

How Would You...?
As a health-care professional, how do you balance the goals of prolonging life and reducing human suffering?

denial and isolation Kübler-Ross' first stage of dying, in which the dying person denies that she or he is really going to die.

anger Kübler-Ross' second stage of dying, in which the dying person's denial often gives way to anger, resentment, rage, and envy.

embrace death and welcome it; others abhor and fear it. For those who welcome it, death may be seen as the fitting end to a fulfilled life. From this perspective, how we depart from earth is influenced by how we have lived.

In most societies, death is not viewed as the end of existence—though the biological body has died, the spirit is believed to live on (Hedayat, 2006). This religious perspective is favored by most Americans as well (Gowan, 2003). Cultural variations in attitudes toward death include belief in reincarnation, which is an important aspect of the Hindu and Buddhist religions. In the Gond culture of India, death is believed to be caused by magic and demons.

In many ways, we in the United States are death avoiders and death deniers (Norouzieh, 2005). This denial can take many forms: the tendency of the funeral industry to gloss over death and fashion lifelike qualities in the dead; the persistent search for a "fountain of youth"; the rejection and isolation of the aged, who may remind us of death; and the medical community's emphasis on prolonging biological life rather than on diminishing human suffering.

Figure 17.1 A Ritual Associated with Death
Family memorial day at the national cemetery in Seoul, South Korea.

Facing One's Own Death

Most dying individuals want an opportunity to make some decisions regarding their own life and death (Kastenbaum, 2007). Some individuals want to complete unfinished business; they want time to resolve problems and conflicts and to put their affairs in order (Emanuel, Bennett, & Richardson, 2007). Might there be a sequence of stages we go through as we face death?

Kübler-Ross' Stages of Dying

Elisabeth Kübler-Ross (1969) divided the behavior and thinking of dying persons into five stages: denial and isolation, anger, bargaining, depression, and acceptance.

Denial and isolation is Kübler-Ross' first stage of dying, in which the person denies that death is really going to take place. The person may say, "No, it can't be me. It's not possible." This is a common reaction to terminal illness. However, denial is usually only a temporary defense. It is eventually replaced with increased awareness when the person is confronted with such matters as financial considerations, unfinished business, and worry about surviving family members.

Anger is Kübler-Ross' second stage of dying, in which the dying person recognizes that denial can no longer be maintained. Denial often gives way to anger, resentment, rage, and envy. The dying person's question is: "Why me?" At this point, the person becomes increasingly difficult to care for as anger may become displaced and projected onto physicians, nurses, family members, and even God. The realization of loss is great, and those who symbolize life, energy, and competent functioning are especially salient targets of the dying person's resentment and jealousy.

Bargaining is Kübler-Ross' third stage of dying, in which the person develops the hope that death can somehow be postponed or delayed. Some persons enter into a bargaining or negotiation—often with God—as they try to delay their death. Psychologically, the person is saying, "Yes, me, but..." In exchange for a few more days, weeks, or months of life, the person promises to lead a reformed life dedicated to God or to the service of others.

Depression is Kübler-Ross' fourth stage of dying, in which the dying person comes to accept the certainty of death. At this point, a period of depression or preparatory grief may appear. The dying person may become silent, refuse visitors, and spend much of the time crying or grieving. This behavior is normal and is an effort to disconnect the self from love objects. Attempts to cheer up the dying person at this stage should be discouraged, says Kübler-Ross, because the dying person has a need to contemplate impending death.

Acceptance is Kübler-Ross' fifth stage of dying, in which the person develops a sense of peace, an acceptance of one's fate, and in many cases, a desire to be left alone. In this stage, feelings and physical pain may be virtually absent. Kübler-Ross describes this fifth stage as the end of the dying struggle, the final resting stage before death. A summary of Kübler-Ross' dying stages is presented in Figure 17.2.

What is the current evaluation of Kübler-Ross' approach? According to Robert Kastenbaum (2007), there are some problems with Kübler-Ross' approach. For example, the existence of the five-stage sequence has not been demonstrated by either Kübler-Ross or independent research. Also, the stage interpretation neglected the patients' situations, including relationship support, specific effects of illness, family obligations, and institutional climate in which they were interviewed. However, Kübler-Ross' pioneering efforts were important in calling attention to those who are attempting to cope with life-threatening illnesses. She did much to encourage attention to the quality of life for dying persons and their families.

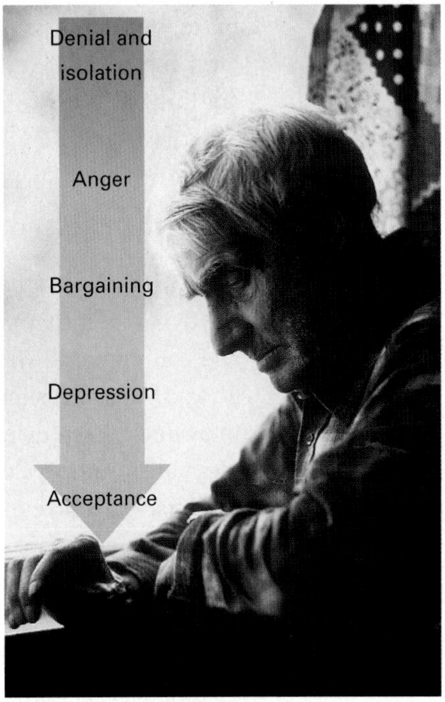

How Would You...?

As a psychologist, how would you prepare a dying individual for the emotional and psychological stages they may go through as they approach death?

bargaining Kübler-Ross' third stage of dying, in which the dying person develops the hope that death can somehow be postponed.

depression Kübler-Ross' fourth stage of dying, in which the dying person comes to accept the certainty of her or his death. A period of depression or preparatory grief may appear.

acceptance Kübler-Ross' fifth stage of dying, in which the dying person develops a sense of peace, an acceptance of her or his fate, and, in many cases, a desire to be left alone.

Figure 17.2 Kübler-Ross' Stages of Dying
According to Elisabeth Kübler-Ross, we go through five stages of dying: denial and isolation, anger, bargaining, depression, and acceptance. *Does everyone go through these stages, or go through them in the same order? Explain.*

Perceived Control and Denial

Perceived control may work as an adaptive strategy for some older adults who face death. When individuals are led to believe they can influence and control events—such as prolonging their lives—they may become more alert and cheerful. Remember from Chapter 15 that giving nursing home residents options for control improved their attitudes and increased their longevity (Rodin & Langer, 1977).

Denial also may be a fruitful way for some individuals to approach death. It can be adaptive or maladaptive. Denial can be used to avoid the destructive impact of shock by delaying the necessity of dealing with one's death. Denial can insulate the individual from having to cope with intense feelings of anger and hurt; however, if denial keeps us from having a life-saving operation, it clearly is maladaptive. Denial is neither good nor bad; its adaptive qualities need to be evaluated on an individual basis.

How Would You...?
As a human development and family studies professional, how would you advise family members to empower dying loved ones to feel they have more control over the end of their lives?

Coping with the Death of Someone Else

Loss can come in many forms in our lives—divorce, a pet's death, loss of a job, loss of a limb—but no loss is greater than that which comes through the death of someone we love and care for—a parent, sibling, spouse, relative, or friend. In the ratings of life's stresses that require the most adjustment, death of a spouse is given the highest number. How should we communicate with a dying individual? How does grieving help us cope with the death of someone we love? How do we make sense of the world when a loved one has passed away? What are the effects on someone after losing a life partner? And what are some forms of mourning and funeral rites?

Communicating with a Dying Person

Most psychologists believe that it is best for dying individuals to know that they are dying, and that significant others know they are dying, so they can interact and communicate with each other on the basis of this mutual knowledge (Banja, 2005). What are some of the advantages of this open awareness for the dying individual? First, dying individuals can close their lives in accord with their own ideas about proper dying. Second, they may be able to complete some plans and projects, can make arrangements for survivors, and can participate in decisions about a funeral and burial. Third, dying individuals have the opportunity to reminisce, to converse with others who have been important in their life, and to end life conscious of what life has been like. And fourth, dying individuals have more understanding of what is happening within their bodies and what the medical staff is doing to them (Kalish, 1981).

In addition to keeping communication open, what are some suggestions for conversing with a dying individual? Some experts believe that conversation should not focus on mental pathology or preparation for death but should focus on strengths of the individual and preparation for the remainder of life. Because external accomplishments are not possible, communication should be directed more at internal growth. Keep in mind also that important support for a dying individual may come not only from mental health professionals, but also from nurses, physicians, a spouse, or intimate friends (DeSpelder & Strickland, 2005).

Effective strategies for communicating with a dying person include these:

1. Establish your presence, be at the same eye level; don't be afraid to touch the dying person—dying individuals are often starved for human touch.

What are some good strategies for communicating with a dying person?

2. Eliminate distraction—for example, ask if it is okay to turn off the TV. Realize that excessive small talk can be a distraction.

3. Dying individuals who are very frail often have little energy. If the dying person you are visiting is very frail, you may want to keep your visit short.

4. Don't insist that the dying person feel acceptance about death if the dying person wants to deny the reality of the situation; on the other hand, don't insist on denial if the dying individual indicates acceptance.

5. Allow the dying person to express guilt or anger; encourage the expression of feelings.

6. Ask the person what the expected outcome for the illness is. Discuss alternatives, unfinished business.

7. Sometimes dying individuals have limited access to other people. Ask the dying person if there is anyone he or she would like to see that you can contact.

8. Encourage the dying individual to reminisce, especially if you have memories in common.

9. Talk with the individual when she or he wishes to talk. If this is impossible, make an appointment for a later time, and keep it.

10. Express your regard for the dying individual. Don't be afraid to express love, and don't be afraid to say good-bye.

Grieving

Our exploration of grief focuses on dimensions of grieving and how coping may vary with the type of death.

Dimensions of Grieving

Grief is the emotional numbness, disbelief, separation anxiety, despair, sadness, and loneliness that accompany the loss of someone we love. Grief is not a simple emotional state but rather a complex, evolving process with multiple dimensions (Maciejewski & others, 2007). In this view, pining for the lost person is one important dimension. Pining or yearning reflects an intermittent, recurrent wish or need to recover the lost person. Another important dimension of grief is separation anxiety, which not only includes pining and preoccupation with thoughts of the deceased person but also focuses on places and things associated with the deceased, as well as crying or sighing. Grief may also involve despair and sadness, which include a sense of hopelessness and defeat, depressive symptoms, apathy, loss of meaning for activities that used to involve the person who is gone, and growing desolation (Ringdal & others, 2001).

These feelings occur repeatedly shortly after a loss (Moules & others, 2004). As time passes, pining and protest over the loss tend to diminish, although episodes of depression and apathy may remain or increase. The sense of separation anxiety and loss may continue to the end of one's life, but most of us emerge from grief's tears, turning our attention once again to productive tasks and regaining a more positive view of life (Carrington & Bogetz, 2004).

The grieving process is more like a roller-coaster ride than an orderly progression of stages with clear-cut time frames. The ups and downs of grief often

grief The emotional numbness, disbelief, separation anxiety, despair, sadness, and loneliness that accompany the loss of someone we love.

involve rapidly changing emotions, meeting the challenges of learning new skills, detecting personal weaknesses and limitations, creating new patterns of behavior, and forming new friendships and relationships (Feldon, 2003). For most individuals, grief becomes more manageable over time, with fewer abrupt highs and lows (Maciejewski & others, 2007). But many grieving spouses report that even though time has brought some healing, they have never gotten over their loss. They have just learned to live with it.

An estimated 80 to 90 percent of survivors experience normal or uncomplicated grief reactions that include sadness and even disbelief or considerable anguish. By six months after their loss, they accept it as a reality, are more optimistic about the future, and function competently in their everyday lives. However, six months after their loss, approximately 10 to 20 percent of survivors have difficulty moving on with their life, feel numb or detached, believe their life is empty without the deceased, and feel that the future has no meaning. Increasingly, the term **complicated grief** is being used to describe this type of grief that involves enduring despair and is still unresolved over an extended period of time. Complicated grief usually has negative consequences for physical and mental health (Piper & others, 2007). Individuals who lose someone they were emotionally dependent on are often at greatest risk for developing complicated grief (Johnson & others, 2007). A recent study found that therapy focused on motivational interviewing, emotion coping, and communication skills was effective in reducing complicated grief (Zuckoff & others, 2006).

Coping and Type of Death

The impact of death on surviving individuals is strongly influenced by the circumstances under which the death occurs (Hanson & Stroebe, 2007; Wortman & Boerner, 2007). Deaths that are sudden, untimely, violent, or traumatic are likely to have more intense and prolonged effects on surviving individuals and make the coping process more difficult for them. Such deaths often are accompanied by post-traumatic stress disorder (PTSD) symptoms, such as intrusive thoughts, flashbacks, nightmares, sleep disturbance, problems in concentrating, and others.

In summary, people grieve in a variety of ways (Hansson, Hayslip, & Stroebe, 2007; Hayes, Yeh, & Eisenberg, 2007). The diverse grieving patterns are culturally embedded practices. Thus, there is no one right, ideal way to grieve. There are many different ways to feel about a deceased person and no set series of stages that the bereaved must pass through to become well adjusted. What is needed is an understanding that healthy coping with the death of a loved one involves growth, flexibility, and appropriateness within a cultural context.

Making Sense of the World

One beneficial aspect of grieving is that it stimulates many individuals to try to make sense of their world (Kalish, 1987). A common occurrence is to go over again and again all of the events that led up to the death. In the days and weeks after the death, the closest family members share experiences with each other, sometimes reminiscing over family experiences. In one study, women who became widowed in midlife were challenged by the crisis of their husband's death to examine meaningful directions for their lives (Danforth & Glass, 2001). Another study found that mourners who expressed positive themes of hope for a positive future showed better adjustment than those who focused on negative themes of pain and suffering (Gamino & Sewell, 2004).

When a death is caused by an accident or a disaster, the effort to make sense of it is pursued more vigorously. As added pieces of news come trickling in, they are integrated into the puzzle. The bereaved want to put the death into a perspective that they can understand—divine intervention, a curse from a neighboring tribe, a logical sequence of cause and effect, or whatever it may be. A recent study of more than 1,000 college students found that making sense was an important factor in their grieving of a violent loss by accident, homicide, or suicide (Currier, Holland, & Neimeyer, 2006).

Losing a Life Partner

Those left behind after the death of an intimate partner often suffer profound grief and often endure financial loss, loneliness, increased physical illness, and psychological disorders, including depression (Zisook & Kendler, 2007). How surviving spouses cope varies con-

Mary Assanful (*front right* with other former restaurant workers) worked at Windows on the World restaurant located in New York's World Trade Center and lost her job when terrorist attacks came. She says that she still in not herself and regularly has nightmares. A Ghana native, Mary is still unemployed. She has joined several other workers who are now planning to return by opening a restaurant near Ground Zero. They hope the new restaurant will honor their co-workers who died and provide a focus and meaning for their still-unsettled lives. Mary says that since they have been working on this new project, her mind has calmed somewhat.

siderably (Ott & others, 2007). In a study that included data from 3 years predeath to 18 months postdeath, nearly half of surviving spouses experienced low levels of distress consistently over the $4^{1}/_{2}$ years (Bonanno, Wortman, & Nesse, 2004). In another study, widowed individuals were more likely to increase their religious and spiritual beliefs following the death of a spouse, and this increase was linked with a lower level of grief (Brown & others, 2004).

Widows outnumber widowers by the ratio of 5 to 1, because women live longer than men, because women tend to marry men older than themselves, and because a widowed man is more likely to remarry. Widowed women are probably the poorest group in America. One study found that most widows in the United States and Germany experienced a decline in living standards in the year following their husband's death, and many fell into poverty when they became widows (Hungerford, 2001). A recent study of Mexican Americans 65 years and older revealed that risk of death linked to widowhood was highest in the first two years following the spouse's death (Stimpson & others, 2007). A study of African American widows found that storytelling was at the heart of widows' description of their bereavement experience (Rodgers, 2004). Six themes were identified in their stories: awareness of death, caregiving, getting through, moving on, changing feelings, and financial security.

Many widows are lonely. The poorer and less educated they are, the lonelier they tend to be. The bereaved are also at increased risk for many health problems (Neimeyer, 2006).

For either widows or widowers, social support helps them adjust to the death of a spouse (Wortman & Boerner, 2007). The Widow-to-Widow program, begun in the 1960s, provides support for newly widowed women. Volunteer widows reach out to other widows, introducing them to others who may have similar problems, leading group discussions, and organizing social activities. The program has been adopted by the American Association of Retired Persons and disseminated throughout the United States as the Widowed Person's Service. The model has since been adopted by numerous community organizations to provide support for those going through a difficult transition.

How Would You...? As a social worker, how would you help a widow or widower to connect with a support group to deal with the death of a loved one?

Forms of Mourning

One decision facing the bereaved is what to do with the body. Approximately 80 percent of corpses are disposed of by burial, the remaining 20 percent by cremation (Cremation Association of America, 2000). Cremation is more popular in the Pacific region of the United States, less popular in the South. Cremation also is more popular in Canada than in the United States and most popular of all in Japan and many other Asian countries.

The funeral is an important aspect of mourning in many cultures. In one study, bereaved individuals who were personally religious derived more psychological benefits from a funeral, participated more actively in the rituals, and adjusted more positively to the loss (Hayslip, Edmondson, & Guarnaccia, 1999).

The funeral industry has been the source of controversy in recent years. Funeral directors and their supporters argue that the funeral provides a form of closure to the relationship with the deceased, especially when there is an open casket. Their critics claim that funeral directors are just trying to make money and that embalming is grotesque. One way to avoid being exploited during bereavement is to purchase funeral arrangements in advance.

A funeral procession of horse-drawn buggies on their way to the burial of five young Amish girls who were murdered in October 2006. A remarkable aspect of their mourning involved the outpouring of support and forgiveness they gave to the widow of the murderer.

The family and the community have important roles in mourning in some cultures. Two of those cultures are the Amish and traditional Judaism (Worthington, 1989). The Amish are a conservative group with approximately 80,000 members in the United States, Ontario, and several small settlements in South and Central America. The Amish live in a family-oriented society in which family and community support are essential for survival. Today, they live at the same unhurried pace as that of their ancestors, using horses instead of cars and facing death with the same steadfast faith as their forebears. At the time of death, close neighbors assume the responsibility of notifying others of the death. The Amish community handles virtually all aspects of the funeral.

The funeral service is held in a barn in warmer months and in a house during colder months. Calm acceptance of death, influenced by a deep religious faith, is an integral part of the Amish culture. Following the funeral, a high level of support is given to the bereaved family for at least a year. Visits to the family, special scrapbooks and handmade items for the family, new work projects started for the widow, and quilting days that combine fellowship and productivity are among the supports given to the bereaved family.

We have arrived at the end of this book. I hope this book and course have been a window to the life span of the human species and a window to your own personal journey in life.

Our study of the human life span has been long and complex. You have read about many physical, cognitive, and socioemotional changes that take place from conception through death. This is a good time to reflect on what you have learned. Which theories, studies, and ideas were especially interesting to you? What did you learn about your own development?

I wish you all the best in the remaining years of your journey through the human life span.

John W. Santrock

Summary

Defining Death and Life/Death Issues

Twenty-five years ago, determining if someone was dead was simpler than it is today. Brain death is a neurological definition of death, which states that a person is brain dead when all electrical activity of the brain has ceased for a specified period of time. Medical experts debate whether this should mean the higher and lower brain functions or just the higher cortical functions. Decisions regarding life, death, and health care can involve whether to sign a living will, to engage in euthanasia, and to have hospice care. Living wills and advanced directives are increasingly used. Euthanasia is the act of painlessly ending the life of a person who is suffering from an incurable disease or disability. Distinctions are made between active and passive euthanasia. Hospice care emphasizes reducing pain and suffering rather than prolonging life.

Death and Sociohistorical, Cultural Contexts

When, where, and why people die have changed historically. Today, death occurs most often among older adults. More than 80 percent of all deaths in the United States now occur in a hospital or another institution; our exposure to death in the family has been minimized. Most societies throughout history have had philosophical or religious beliefs about death, and most societies have rituals that deal with death. Most cultures do not view death as the end of existence—spiritual life is thought to continue. The United States has been described as a death-denying and death-avoiding culture.

Facing One's Own Death

Kübler-Ross proposed five stages: denial and isolation, anger, bargaining, depression, and acceptance. Not all individuals go through the same sequence. Perceived control and denial may work together as an adaptive orientation for the dying individual. Denial can be adaptive or maladaptive, depending on the circumstance.

Coping with the Death of Someone Else

Most psychologists recommend an open communication system with the dying. Communication should not dwell on pathology or preparation for death but should emphasize the dying person's strengths. Grief is the emotional numbness, disbelief, separation, anxiety, despair, sadness, and loneliness that accompany the loss of someone we love. Grief is multidimensional and in some cases may last for years. Complicated grief involves enduring despair and is still unresolved after an extended period of time. Grief and coping vary with the type of death. The grieving process may stimulate individuals to strive to make sense out of their world; each individual may contribute a piece to death's puzzle. Usually the most difficult loss is the death of a spouse. The bereaved are at risk for many health problems, although there are variations in the distress experienced by a surviving spouse. Social support benefits widows and widowers. Forms of mourning vary across cultures. Approximately 80 percent of corpses are disposed of by burial, 20 percent by cremation. An important aspect of mourning in many cultures is the funeral. In recent years, the funeral industry has been the focus of controversy.

Key Terms

brain death 422
euthanasia 423
passive euthanasia 423
active euthanasia 423
hospice 424

palliative care 424
denial and isolation 426
anger 426
bargaining 427
depression 427

acceptance 427
grief 429
complicated grief 430

Glossary

A

A-not-B error (AB error) Occurs when infants make the mistake of selecting the familiar hiding place (A) rather than the new hiding place (not B) as they progress into substage 4 in Piaget's sensorimotor stage. 98

acceptance Kübler-Ross' fifth stage of dying, in which the dying person develops a sense of peace, an acceptance of her or his fate, and, in many cases, a desire to be left alone. 427

accommodation Piagetian concept of adjusting schemes to fit new information and experiences. 95

active euthanasia Death induced deliberately, as by injecting a lethal dose of a drug. 423

activity theory The theory that the more active and involved older adults are, the more likely they are to be satisfied with their lives. 407

adolescent egocentrism The heightened self-consciousness of adolescents. 275

adoption study A study in which investigators seek to discover whether, in behavior and psychological characteristics, adopted children are more like their adoptive parents, who provided a home environment, or more like their biological parents, who contributed to their heredity. Another form of the adoption study is to compare adoptive and biological siblings. 46

aerobic exercise Sustained exercise (such as jogging, swimming, or cycling) that stimulates heart and lung activity. 313

affectionate love In this type of love, also called companionate love, an individual desires to have the other person near and has a deep, caring affection for the other person. 333

ageism Prejudice against other people because of their age, especially prejudice against older adults. 410

Alzheimer disease A progressive, irreversible brain disorder characterized by a gradual deterioration of memory, reasoning, language, and eventually physical function. 400

amygdala The region of the brain that is the seat of emotions. 264

androgyny The presence of positive masculine and feminine characteristics in the same individual. 241

anger Kübler-Ross' second stage of dying, in which the dying person's denial often gives way to anger, resentment, rage, and envy. 426

anger cry A cry similar to the basic cry, with more excess air forced through the vocal cords. 116

animism The belief that inanimate objects have lifelike qualities and are capable of action. 146

anorexia nervosa An eating disorder that involves the relentless pursuit of thinness through starvation. 272

Apgar Scale A widely used assessment of the newborn's health at 1 and 5 minutes after birth. 65

arthritis Inflammation of the joints that is accompanied by pain, stiffness, and movement problems; especially common in older adults. 389

assimilation (culture) The absorption of ethnic minority groups into the dominant group, which often involves the loss of some or virtually all of the behavior and values of the ethnic minority group. 298

assimilation (Piaget) Piagetian concept of the incorporation of new information into existing schemes. 95

attachment A close emotional bond between two people. 123

attachment-related anxiety Involves the extent to which individuals feel secure or insecure about whether a partner will be available, responsive, and attentive. 331

attachment-related avoidance Involves the degree to which individuals feel secure or insecure in relying on others, opening up to them, and being intimate with them. 331

attention The focusing of mental resources. 99

attention deficit hyperactivity disorder (ADHD) A disability in which children consistently show one or more of the following characteristics: (1) inattention, (2) hyperactivity, and (3) impulsivity. 201

authoritarian parenting A restrictive punitive style in which parents exhort the child to follow their directions and to respect work and effort. The authoritarian parent places firm limits and controls on the child and allows little verbal exchange. Authoritarian parenting is associated with children's social incompetence. 175

authoritative parenting A parenting style in which parents encourage their children to be independent but still place limits and controls on their actions. Extensive verbal give-and-take is allowed, and parents are warm and nurturant toward the child. Authoritative parenting is associated with children's social competence. 175

autonomous morality The second stage of moral development in Piaget's theory, displayed by older children (about 10 years of age and older). The child becomes aware that rules and laws are created by people and, in judging an action, one should consider the actor's intentions as well as the consequences. 170

average children Children who receive an average number of both positive and negative nominations from their peers. 254

B

bargaining Kübler-Ross' third stage of dying, in which the dying person develops the hope that death can somehow be postponed. 427

basic cry A rhythmic pattern usually consisting of a cry, a briefer silence, a shorter inspiratory whistle that is higher pitched than the main cry, and then a brief rest before the next cry. 116

behavior genetics The field that seeks to discover the influence of heredity and environment on individual differences in human traits and development. 45

behavioral and social cognitive theories Theories that hold that development can be described in terms of the behaviors learned through interactions with the environment. 21

big five factors of personality Openness to experience, conscientiousness, extraversion, agreeableness, and neuroticism (emotional stability). 370

biological processes Changes in an individual's physical nature. 11

brain death A neurological definition of death. A person is brain dead when all electrical activity of the brain has ceased for a specified period of time. A flat EEG recording is one criterion of brain death. 422

brainstorming A technique in which individuals are encouraged to come up with creative ideas in a group, play off each other's ideas, and say practically whatever comes to mind. 208

Bronfenbrenner's ecological theory Bronfenbrenner's environmental systems theory that focuses on five environmental systems: microsystem, mesosystem, exosystem, macrosystem, and chronosystem. 24

bulimia nervosa An eating disorder in which the individual consistently follows a binge-and-purge pattern. 272

C

care perspective The moral perspective of Carol Gilligan, which views people in terms of their connectedness with others and emphasizes interpersonal communication, relationships with others, and concern for others. 237

case study An in-depth examination of an individual. 27

cataracts Involve a thickening of the lens of the eye that causes vision to become cloudy, opaque, and distorted. 387

cellular clock theory Leonard Hayflick's theory that the maximum number of times that human cells can divide is about 75 to 80. As we age, our cells have less capability to divide. 383

centration The focusing of attention on one characteristic to the exclusion of all others. 147

cephalocaudal pattern The sequence in which the earliest growth always occurs at the top—the head—with physical growth in size, weight, and feature differentiation gradually working from top to bottom. 75

child-centered kindergarten Education that involves the whole child by considering both the child's physical, cognitive, and socioemotional development and the child's needs, interests, and learning styles. 158

child-directed speech Language spoken in a higher pitch than normal with simple words and sentences. 107

chromosomes Threadlike structures made up of deoxyribonucleic acid, or DNA. 39

climacteric The midlife transition in which fertility declines. 350

clique A small group that ranges from 2 to about 12 individuals, averaging about 5 to 6 individuals, and can form because adolescents engage in similar activities. 293

cognitive processes Changes in an individual's thought, intelligence, and language. 11

cohort effects Effects that are due to a subject's time of birth or generation but not age. 32

commitment Marcia's term for the part of identity development in which adolescents show a personal investment in forming an identity. 286

complicated grief Grief that involves enduring despair and is still unresolved over an extended period of time. 430

connectedness Connectedness consists of two dimensions: mutuality (sensitivity to, and respect for, others' views) and permeability (openness to others' views). 287

conservation In Piaget's theory, awareness that altering an object's or a substance's appearance does not change its basic properties. 147

constructive play Play that combines sensorimotor and repetitive activity with symbolic representation of ideas. Constructive play occurs when children engage in self-regulated creation or construction of a product or a problem solution. 190

constructivist approach A learner-centered approach that emphasizes the importance of individuals actively constructing their knowledge and understanding with guidance from the teacher. 249

contemporary life-events approach An approach that emphasizes that how a life event influences the individual's development depends not only on the life event, but also on mediating factors, the individual's adaptation to the life event, the life-stage context, and the sociohistorical context. 366

context The setting in which development occurs that is influenced by historical, economic, social, and cultural factors. 5

continuity-discontinuity issue The debate about the extent to which development involves gradual, cumulative change (continuity) or distinct stages (discontinuity). 15

controversial children Children who are frequently nominated both as someone's best friend and as being disliked. 245

conventional reasoning The second, or intermediate, level in Kohlberg's theory of moral development. At this level, individuals abide by certain standards but they are the standards of others such as parents or the laws of society. 233

convergent thinking Thinking that produces one correct answer and is characteristic of the kind of thinking tested by standardized intelligence tests. 208

corpus callosum The location where fibers connect the brain's left and right hemispheres. 263

correlation coefficient A number based on statistical analysis that is used to describe the degree of association between two variables. 28

correlational research The goal is to describe the strength of the relation between two or more events or characteristics. 28

creative thinking The ability to think in novel and unusual ways and to come up with unique solutions to problems. 209

crisis Marcia's term for a period of identity development during which the adolescent is exploring alternatives. 286

critical thinking Thinking reflectively and productively, as well as evaluating the evidence. 207

cross-cultural studies Comparisons of one culture with one or more other cultures. These provide information about the degree to which children's development is similar, or universal, across cultures, and to the degree to which it is culture-specific. 8

cross-sectional approach A research strategy in which individuals of different ages are compared at one time. 31

crowd A larger group structure than a clique, a crowd is usually formed based on reputation and members may or may not spend much time together. 293

crystallized intelligence Accumulated information and verbal skills, which increase in middle age, according to Horn. 353

cultural-familial retardation Retardation characterized by no evidence of organic brain damage, but the individual's IQ generally is between 50 and 70. 218

culture The behavior patterns, beliefs, and all other products of a group that are passed on from generation to generation. 8

culture-fair tests Tests of intelligence that are designed to be free of cultural bias. 216

cumulative personality model States that with time and age, people become more adept at interacting with their environment in ways that promote the stability of personality. 372

D

date or acquaintance rape Coercive sexual activity directed at someone with whom the perpetrator is at least casually acquainted. 320

deferred imitation Imitation that occurs after a delay of hours or days. 100

dementia A global term for any neurological disorder in which the primary symptoms involve a deterioration of mental functioning. 400

denial and isolation Kübler-Ross' first stage of dying, in which the dying person denies that she or he is really going to die. 426

depression Kübler-Ross' fourth stage of dying, in which the dying person comes to accept the certainty of her or his death. A period of depression or preparatory grief may appear. 427

descriptive research This type of research aims to observe and record behavior. 28

development The pattern of movement or change that starts at conception and continues through the human life span. 3

developmentally appropriate practice Education that focuses on the typical developmental patterns of children (age appropriateness) and the uniqueness of each child (individual appropriateness). 159

difficult child A child who tends to react negatively and cry frequently, who engages in irregular daily routines, and who is slow to accept new experiences. 119

direct instruction approach A structured, teacher-centered approach that is characterized by teacher direction and control, high teacher expectations for students' progress, maximum time spent by students on learning tasks, and efforts by the teacher to keep negative affect to a minimum. 249

dishabituation Recovery of a habituated response after a change in stimulation. 90

divergent thinking Thinking that produces many answers to the same question and is characteristic of creativity. 208

divided attention Concentrating on more than one activity at the same time. 394

DNA A complex molecule with a double helix shape that contains genetic information. 39

Down syndrome A chromosomally transmitted form of mental retardation, caused by the presence of an extra copy of chromosome 21. 43

dynamic systems theory The perspective on motor development that seeks to explain how motor behaviors are assembled for perceiving and acting. 83

dyslexia A category of learning disabilities involving a severe impairment in the ability to read and spell. 201

E

easy child A child who is generally in a positive mood, who quickly establishes regular routines in infancy, and who adapts easily to new experiences. 119

eclectic theoretical orientation An approach that selects and uses whatever is considered the best in many theories. 25

ecological view The view that perception functions to bring us into contact with the environment and to increase adaptation. 89

egocentrism The inability to distinguish between one's own perspective and someone else's (salient feature of the first substage of preoperational thought). 145, 275

elaboration An important strategy that involves engaging in more extensive processing of information. 207

eldercare Physical and emotional caretaking for older members of the family, whether by giving day-to-day physical assistance or by being responsible for overseeing such care. 411

embryonic period The period of prenatal development that occurs two to eight weeks after conception. During the embryonic period, the rate of cell differentiation intensifies, support systems for the cells form, and organs appear. 49

emerging adulthood The transition from adolescence to adulthood (approximately 18 to 25 years of age) that involves experimentation and exploration. 308

emotion Feeling, or affect, that occurs when a person is in a state or interaction that is important to them. Emotion is characterized by behavior that reflects (expresses) the pleasantness or unpleasantness of the state a person is in or the transactions being experienced. 115

empty nest syndrome A term used to indicate a decrease in marital satisfaction after children leave home. 374

epigenetic view Emphasizes that development is the result of an ongoing, bidirectional interchange between heredity and environment. 47

episodic memory The retention of information about the where and when of life's happenings. 394

equilibration A mechanism that Piaget proposed to explain how children shift from one stage of thought to the next. 95

Erikson's theory A psychoanalytic theory in which eight stages of psychosocial development unfold throughout the human life span. Each state consists of a unique developmental task that confronts individuals with a crisis that must be faced. 17

ethnic identity An enduring, basic aspect of the self that includes a sense of membership in an ethnic group and the attitudes and feelings related to that membership. 287

ethnicity A range of characteristics rooted in cultural heritage, including nationality, race, religion, and language. 8

ethology An approach that stresses that behavior is strongly influenced by biology, tied to evolution, and characterized by critical or sensitive periods. 23

euthanasia The act of painlessly ending the lives of persons who are suffering from incurable diseases or severe disabilities; sometimes called "mercy killing." 423

evolutionary psychology Emphasizes the importance of adaptation, reproduction, and "survival of the fittest" in shaping behavior. 37

experiment A carefully regulated procedure in which one or more of the factors believed to influence the behavior being studied is manipulated and all other factors are held constant. Experimental research permits the determination of cause. 29

explicit memory Conscious memory of facts and experiences. 100, 395

F

fetal alcohol syndrome (FAS) A cluster of abnormalities that appears in the offspring of mothers who drink alcohol heavily during pregnancy. 53

fetal period The prenatal period of development that begins two months after conception and lasts for seven months, on the average. 50

fine motor skills Motor skills that involve more finely tuned movements, such as finger dexterity. 89

fluid intelligence The ability to reason abstractly, which steadily declines from middle adulthood on, according to Horn. 353

free-radical theory A microbiological theory of aging that states that people age because inside their cells normal metabolism produces unstable oxygen molecules known as free radicals. These molecules ricochet around inside cells, damaging DNA and other cellular structures. 383

fuzzy trace theory States that memory is best understood by considering two types of memory representations: (1) verbatim memory trace and (2) gist. In this theory, older children's better memory is attributed to the fuzzy traces created by extracting the gist of information. 207

G

games Activities engaged in for pleasure that include rules and often competition with one or more individuals. 190

gender The psychological and sociocultural dimensions of being female or male. 172

gender identity The sense of being male or female, which most children acquire by the time they are 3 years old. 172

gender roles Sets of expectations that prescribe how females or males should think, act, and feel. 171

gender schema theory The theory that gender typing emerges as children gradually develop gender schemas of what is gender-appropriate and gender-inappropriate in their culture. 174

gender stereotypes Broad categories that reflect our impressions and beliefs about females and males. 237

generativity Adults' desires to leave legacies of themselves to the next generation; the positive side of Erikson's generativity versus stagnation middle adulthood stage. 364

genes Units of hereditary information composed of DNA. Genes direct cells to reproduce themselves and manufacture the proteins that maintain life. 39

genotype A person's genetic heritage; the actual genetic material. 41

germinal period The period of prenatal development that takes place in the first two weeks after conception. It includes the creation of the zygote, continued cell division, and the attachment of the zygote to the uterine wall. 49

gifted Having above-average intelligence (an IQ of 130 or higher) and/or superior talent for something. 218

glaucoma Damage to the optic nerve because of the pressure created by a buildup of fluid in the eye. 387

gonads The sex glands—the testes in males and the ovaries in females. 261

goodness of fit Refers to the match between a child's temperament and the environmental demands with which the child must cope. 120

grief The emotional numbness, disbelief, separation anxiety, despair, sadness, and loneliness that accompany the loss of someone we love. 429

gross motor skills Motor skills that involve large-muscle activities, such as walking. 85

H

habituation Decreased responsiveness to a stimulus after repeated presentations of the stimulus. 90

heritability The fraction of variance in a population that is attributed to genetics and is computed using correlational techniques. 214

heteronomous morality (Kohlberg) Kohlberg's first stage in preconventional reasoning in which moral thinking is tied to punishment. 232

heteronomous morality (Piaget) The first stage of moral development in Piaget's theory, occurring from approximately 4 to 7 years of age. Justice and rules are conceived of as unchangeable properties of the world, removed from the control of people. 170

hormonal stress theory The theory that aging in the body's hormonal system can lower resilience to stress and increase the likelihood of disease. 383

hormones Powerful chemical substances secreted by the endocrine glands and carried through the body by the bloodstream. 261

hospice A program committed to making the end of life as free from pain, anxiety, and depression as possible. The goals of hospice contrast with those of a hospital, which are to cure disease and prolong life. 424

hypothalamus A structure in the higher portion of the brain that monitors eating and sex. 261

hypotheses Assertions or predictions, often derived from theories, that can be tested. 16

hypothetical-deductive reasoning Piaget's formal operational concept that adolescents have the cognitive ability to develop hypotheses, or best guesses, about ways to solve problems, such as an algebraic equation. 274

I

identity achievement Marcia's term for adolescents who have undergone a crisis and have made a commitment. 286

identity diffusion Marcia's term for adolescents who have not yet experienced a crisis (explored meaningful alternatives) or made any commitments. 286

identity foreclosure Marcia's term for adolescents who have made a commitment but have not experienced a crisis. 286

identity moratorium Marcia's term for adolescents who are in the midst of a crisis, but their commitments are either absent or vaguely defined. 286

imaginary audience Involves adolescents' belief that others are as interested in them as they themselves are: attention-getting behavior motivated by a desire to be noticed, visible, and "on stage." 275

immanent justice The concept that, if a rule is broken, punishment will be meted out immediately. 170

implicit memory Memory without conscious recollection; involves skills and routine procedures that are automatically performed. 100

inclusion Educating a child with special education needs full-time in the regular classroom. 203

individual differences The stable, consistent ways in which people are different from each other. 210

individualism, instrumental purpose, and exchange The second Kohlberg stage of moral development. At this stage, individuals pursue their own interests but also let others do the same. 233

individuality Individuality consists of two dimensions: self-assertion (the ability to have and communicate a point of view) and separateness (the use of communication patterns to express how one is different from others). 287

individualized education plan (IEP) A written statement that spells out a program tailored to a child with a disability. 203

indulgent parenting A style of parenting in which parents are highly involved with their children but place few demands or controls on them. Indulgent parenting is associated with children's social incompetence, especially a lack of self-control. 175

infinite generativity The ability to produce an endless number of meaningful sentences using a finite set of words and rules. 102

information-processing theory A theory that emphasizes that individuals manipulate information, monitor it, and strategize about it. The processes of memory and thinking are central. 21

insecure avoidant babies Babies that show insecurity by avoiding the caregiver. 125

insecure disorganized babies Babies that show insecurity by being disorganized and disoriented. 126

insecure resistant babies Babies that often cling to the caregiver, then resist her by fighting against the closeness, perhaps by kicking or pushing away. 125

integrity versus despair Erikson's eighth and final stage of development, which individuals experience in late adulthood. This involves reflecting on the past and either piecing together a positive review or concluding that one's life not been well spent. 407

intelligence Problem-solving skills and the ability to learn from, and adapt to, the experiences of everyday life. 210

intelligence quotient (IQ) A person's mental age divided by chronological age, multiplied by 100. 210

intermodal perception The ability to relate and integrate information from two or more sensory modalities, such as vision and hearing. 94

intimacy in friendships Self-disclosure and the sharing of private thoughts. 249

intuitive thought substage Piaget's second substage of preoperational thought, in which children begin to use primitive reasoning and want to know the answers to all sorts of questions (between about 4 and 7 years of age). 146

J

joint attention Occurs when individuals focus on the same object and an ability to track another's behavior is present, one individual directs another's attention, and reciprocal interaction is present. 99

justice perspective A moral perspective that focuses on the rights of the individual; individuals independently make moral decisions. 237

juvenile delinquent An adolescent who breaks the law or engages in behavior that is considered illegal. 299

L

laboratory A controlled setting. 26

language A form of communication, whether spoken, written, or signed, that is based on a system of symbols. 102

language acquisition device (LAD) Chomsky's term that describes a biological endowment that enables the child to detect the features and rules of language. 105

lateralization Specialization of function in one hemisphere of the cerebral cortex or the other. 76

learning disability Includes three components: (1) a minimum IQ level; (2) a significant difficulty in a school-related area (especially reading and/or mathematics); and (3) exclusion of severe emotional disorders, second-language background, sensory disabilities, and/or specific neurological deficits. 200

least restrictive environment (LRE) The concept that a child with a disability must be educated in a setting that is as similar as possible to the one in which

children who do not have a disability are educated. 204

leisure The pleasant times after work when individuals are free to pursue activities and interests of their own choosing. 357

life expectancy The number of years that will probably be lived by the average person born in a particular year. 382

life span The upper boundary of life, the maximum number of years an individual can live. The maximum life span of human beings is about 120 to 125 years of age. 382

life-span perspective The perspective that development is lifelong, multidimensional, multidirectional, plastic, multidisciplinary, and contextual; involves growth, maintenance, and regulation; and is constructed through biological, sociocultural, and individual factors working together. 3

longitudinal approach A research strategy in which the same individuals are studied over a period of time, usually several years or more. 31

long-term memory A relatively permanent type of memory that holds huge amounts of information for a long period of time. 206

M

macular degeneration A disease that involves deterioration of the macula of the retina, which corresponds to the focal center of the visual field. 387

major depression A mood disorder in which the individual is deeply unhappy, demoralized, self-derogatory, and bored. The person does not feel well, loses stamina easily, has poor appetite, and is listless and unmotivated. Major depression is so widespread that it has been called the "common cold" of psychological disorders. 399

meiosis A specialized form of cell division that occurs to form eggs and sperm (or gametes). 400

memory A central feature of cognitive development, pertaining to all situations in which an individual retains information over time. 100

menarche A girl's first menstruation. 260

menopause The complete cessation of a woman's menstruation, which usually occurs in the late forties or early fifties. 350

mental age (MA) Binet's measure of an individual's level of mental development, compared with that of others. 210

mental retardation A condition of limited mental ability in which an individual has a low IQ, usually below 70 on a traditional test of intelligence, and has difficulty adapting to everyday life. 218

metacognition Cognition about cognition, or knowing about knowing. 210

metalinguistic awareness Refers to knowledge about language, such as knowing what a preposition is or the ability to discuss the sounds of a language. 220

middle adulthood The developmental period beginning at approximately 40 years of age and extending to about 60 to 65 years of age. 346

mindset The cognitive view, either fixed or growth, that individuals develop for themselves. 255

mitosis Cellular reproduction in which the cell's nucleus duplicates itself with two new cells being formed, each containing the same DNA as the parent cell, arranged in the same 23 pairs of chromosomes. 40

Montessori approach An educational philosophy in which children are given considerable freedom and spontaneity in choosing activities and are allowed to move from one activity to another as they desire. 158

moral development Development that involves thoughts, feelings, and actions regarding rules and conventions about what people should do in their interactions with other people. 169

morphology Units of meaning involved in word formation. 234

mutual interpersonal expectations, relationships, and interpersonal conformity Kohlberg's third stage of moral development. At this stage, individuals value trust, caring, and loyalty to others as a basis of moral judgments. 233

myelination The process by which the axons are covered and insulated with a layer of fat cells, which increases the speed at which information travels through the nervous system. 139

N

natural childbirth This method attempts to reduce the mother's pain by decreasing her fear through education about childbirth and relaxation techniques during delivery. 64

naturalistic observation Observation that occurs in a real-world setting without an attempt to manipulate the situation. 26

nature-nurture issue The debate about the extent to which development is influenced by nature and by nurture. Nature refers to an organism's biological inheritance, nurture to its environmental experiences. 14

neglected children Children who are infrequently nominated as a best friend but are not disliked by their peers. 245

neglectful parenting A style of parenting in which the parent is very uninvolved in the child's life; it is associated with children's social incompetence, especially a lack of self-control. 175

neo-Piagetians Developmentalists who have elaborated on Piaget's theory, giving more emphasis to how children use attention, memory, and strategies to process information. 205

neuron Nerve cell that handles information processing at the cellular level. 76

nonnormative life events Unusual occurrences that have a major impact on a person's life. The occurrence, pattern, and sequence of these events are not applicable to many individuals. 6

normal distribution A symmetrical distribution with most scores falling in the middle of the possible range of scores and few scores appearing toward the extremes of the range. 210

normative age-graded influences Biological and environmental influences that are similar for individuals in a particular age group. 5

normative history-graded influences Biological and environmental influences that are associated with history. These influences are common to people of a particular generation. 5

O

object permanence The Piagetian term for understanding that objects and events continue to exist, even when they cannot directly be seen, heard, or touched. 97

operations In Piaget's theory, internalized reversible sets of actions that allow children to do mentally what they formerly did physically. 145

organic retardation Mental retardation that involves some physical damage and is caused by a genetic disorder or brain damage. 218

organization Piaget's concept of grouping isolated behaviors into a higher-order, more smoothly functioning cognitive system. 95

organogenesis Organ formation that takes place during the first two months of prenatal development. 49

osteoporosis A chronic condition that involves an extensive loss of bone tissue and is the main reason many older adults walk with a marked stoop. Women are especially vulnerable to osteoporosis. 389

P

pain cry A sudden appearance of loud crying without preliminary moaning, followed by breath holding. 116

palliative care Emphasized in hospice care; involves reducing pain and suffering and helping individuals die with dignity. 424

Parkinson disease A chronic, progressive disease characterized by muscle tremors, slowing of movement, and partial facial paralysis. 402

passive euthanasia The withholding of available treatments, such as life-sustaining devices, allowing the person to die. 423

perception The interpretation of what is sensed. 89

personal fable The part of adolescent egocentrism that involves an adolescent's sense of uniqueness and invincibility (or invulnerability). 275

personality type theory John Holland's view that it is important for individuals to select a career that matches up well with their personality type.

phenotype The way an individual's genotype is expressed in observed and measurable characteristics. 41

phonics approach The idea that reading instruction should teach the basic rules for translating written symbols into sounds. 222

Piaget's theory The theory that children construct their understanding of the world and go through four stages of cognitive development. 19

pituitary gland An important endocrine gland that controls growth and regulates other glands, including the gonads. 261

pluralism The coexistence of distinct ethnic and cultural groups in the same society. Individuals with a pluralistic stance usually advocate that cultural differences be maintained and appreciated. 298

popular children Children who are frequently nominated as a best friend and are rarely disliked by their peers. 245

postconventional reasoning The highest level in Kohlberg's theory of moral development. At this level, the individual recognizes alternative moral courses, explores the options, and then decides on a personal moral code. 233

postformal thought A form of thought that is qualitatively different from Piaget's formal operational thought. It involves understanding that the correct answer to a problem can require reflective thinking, that the correct answer can vary from one situation to another, and that the search for truth is often an ongoing, never-ending process. It also involves the belief that solutions to problems need to be realistic, and that emotion and subjective factors can influence thinking. 322

postpartum period The period after childbirth when the mother adjusts, both physically and psychologically, to the process of childbirth. This period lasts for about six weeks or until her body has completed its adjustment and returned to a near prepregnant state. 69

practice play Play that involves repetition of behavior when new skills are being learned or when physical or mental mastery and coordination of skills are required for games or sports. 189

pragmatics The appropriate use of language in different contexts. 157

preconventional reasoning The lowest level in Kohlberg's theory of moral development. The individual's moral reasoning is controlled primarily by external rewards and punishment. 232

preoperational stage Piaget's second stage, lasting from about 2 to 7 years of age, during which children begin to represent the world with words, images, and drawings, and symbolic thought goes beyond simple connections of sensory information and physical action; stable concepts are formed, mental reasoning emerges, egocentrism is present, and magical beliefs are constructed. 145

prepared childbirth Developed by French obstetrician Ferdinand Lamaze, this childbirth strategy is similar to natural childbirth but includes a special breathing technique to control pushing in the final stages of labor and a more detailed anatomy and physiology course. 64

pretense/symbolic play Play in which the child transforms the physical environment into a symbol. 189

Project Head Start A government-funded program that is designed to provide children from low-income families the opportunity to acquire the skills and experiences important for school success. 160

proximodistal pattern The sequence in which growth starts at the center of the body and moves toward the extremities. 75

psychoanalytic theories Theories that hold that development depends primarily on the unconscious mind and is heavily couched in emotion, that behavior is merely a surface characteristic, that it is important to analyze the symbolic meanings of behavior, and that early experiences are important in development. 16

psychoanalytic theory of gender A theory deriving from Freud's view that the preschool child develops a sexual attraction to the opposite-sex parent, by approximately 5 or 6 years of age renounces this attraction because of anxious feelings, and subsequently identifies with the same-sex parent, unconsciously adopting the same-sex parent's characteristics. 172

puberty A period of rapid physical and sexual maturation that occurs mainly during early adolescence. 259

R

rape Forcible sexual intercourse with a person who does not consent to it. 319

rapport talk The language of conversation; it is a way of establishing connections and negotiating relationships. 342

reciprocal socialization Socialization that is bidirectional; children socialize parents, just as parents socialize children. 129

reflexive smile A smile that does not occur in response to external stimuli. It appears during the first month after birth, usually during sleep. 116

rejected children Children who are infrequently nominated as a best friend and are actively disliked by their peers. 245

report talk Talk that is designed to give information and includes public speaking. 342

rite of passage A ceremony or ritual that marks an individual's transition from one status to another. Most rites of passage focus on the transition to adult status. 297

romantic love Also called passionate love, or eros; romantic love has strong sexual and infatuation components and often predominates in the early period of a love relationship. 333

S

sandwich generation A term used to describe middle-aged adults because of the responsibilities they have for their adolescent and young children on the one hand and their aging parents on the other. 378

scaffolding Parents time interactions so that infants experience turn-taking with the parents. 129

schemes In Piaget's theory, actions or mental representations that organize knowledge. 94

securely attached babies Babies that use the caregiver as a secure base from which to explore the environment. 125

selective attention Focusing on a specific aspect of experience that is relevant while ignoring others that are irrelevant. 394

selective optimization with compensation theory The theory that successful aging is related to three main factors: selection, optimization, and compensation. 408

self-concept Domain-specific evaluations of the self. 228

self-efficacy The belief that one can master a situation and produce favorable outcomes. 230

self-esteem The global evaluative dimension of the self. Self-esteem is also referred to as self-worth or self-image. 228

self-understanding The child's cognitive representation of self, the substance and content of the child's self-conceptions. 197

semantic memory A person's knowledge about the world—including a person's fields of expertise, general academic knowledge of the sort learned in school, and "everyday knowledge." 395

semantics The meaning of words and sentences. 156

sensation The product of the interaction between information and the sensory receptors—the eyes, ears, tongue, nostrils, and skin. 88

sensorimotor play Behavior engaged in by infants to derive pleasure from exercising their existing sensorimotor schemes. 189

sensorimotor stage The first of Piaget's stages, which lasts from birth to about 2 years of age; infants construct an understanding of the world by coordinating sensory experiences with motoric actions. 96

separation protest An infant's distressed crying when the caregiver leaves. 117

seriation The concrete operation that involves ordering stimuli along a quantitative dimension (such as length). 204

service learning A form of education that promotes social responsibility and service to the community. 279

sexually transmitted infections (STIs) Infections contracted primarily through sexual contact, including oral-genital and anal-genital contact. 318

short-term memory The memory component in which individuals retain information for up to 30 seconds, assuming there is no rehearsal of the information. 153

slow-to-warm-up child A child who has a low activity level, is somewhat negative, and displays a low intensity of mood. 119

social clock The timetable according to which individuals are expected to accomplish life's tasks, such as getting married, having children, or establishing themselves in a career. 368

social cognitive theory The theory that behavior, environment, and person/cognitive factors are important in understanding development. 22

social cognitive theory of gender A theory that emphasizes that children's gender development occurs through the observation and imitation of gender behavior and through the rewards and punishments children experience for gender-appropriate and gender-inappropriate behavior. 172

social constructivist approach An approach that emphasizes the social contexts of learning and that knowledge is mutually built and constructed. Vygotsky's theory reflects this approach. 148

social contract or utility and individual rights The fifth Kohlberg stage. At this stage, individuals reason that values, rights, and principles undergird or transcend the law. 234

social play Play that involves social interactions with peers. 190

social policy A national government's course of action designed to promote the welfare of its citizens. 9

social referencing "Reading" emotional cues in others to help determine how to act in a particular situation. 118

social role theory A theory that gender differences result from the contrasting roles of men and women. 172

social smile A smile in response to an external stimulus, which, early in development, typically is a face. 116

social system morality The fourth stage in Kohlberg's theory of moral development. Moral judgments are based on understanding the social order, law, justice, and duty. 233

socioeconomic status (SES) Refers to the conceptual grouping of people with similar occupational, educational, and economic characteristics. 8

socioemotional processes Changes in an individual's relationships with other people, emotions, and personality. 11

socioemotional selectivity theory The theory that older adults become more selective about their social networks. Because they place a high value on emotional satisfaction, older adults often spend more time with familiar individuals with whom they have had rewarding relationships. 407

stability-change issue The debate about the degree to which early traits and characteristics persist through life or change. 15

stagnation Sometimes called "self-absorption"—develops when individuals sense that they have done little or nothing for the next generation; the negative side of Erikson's generativity versus stagnation middle adulthood stage. 364

standardized test A test that is given with uniform procedures for administration and scoring. 27

Strange Situation An observational measure of infant attachment that requires the infant to move through a series of introductions, separations, and reunions with the caregiver and an adult stranger in a prescribed order. 125

stranger anxiety An infant's fear and wariness of strangers; it tends to appear in the second half of the first year of life. 117

strategies Consist of deliberate mental activities to improve the processing of information. 206

sudden infant death syndrome (SIDS) A condition that occurs when an infant stops breathing usually during the night, and suddenly dies without an apparent cause. 79

sustained attention The state of readiness to detect and respond to small changes occurring at random times in the environment. 394

symbolic function substage Piaget's first substage of preoperational thought, in which the child gains the ability to mentally represent an object that is not present (between about 2 and 4 years of age). 145

syntax The ways words are combined to form acceptable phrases and sentences. 156

T

telegraphic speech The use of short and precise words without grammatical markers such as articles, auxiliary verbs, and other connectives. 104

temperament An individual's behavioral style and characteristic way of emotionally responding. 119

teratogen Any agent that can potentially cause a birth defect or negatively alter cognitive and behavioral outcomes. 52

theory A coherent set of ideas that helps to explain data and to make predictions. 16

theory of mind Refers to the awareness of one's own mental processes and the mental processes of others. 154

thinking Manipulating and transforming information in memory. 207

top-dog phenomenon The circumstance of moving from the top position in elementary school to the lowest position in middle or junior high school. 278

transitivity The ability to logically combine relations to understand certain conclusions. 204

triarchic theory of intelligence Sternberg's theory that intelligence consists of analytical intelligence, creative intelligence, and practical intelligence. 212

twin study A study in which the behavioral similarity of identical twins is compared with the behavioral similarity of fraternal twins. 45

U

universal ethical principles The sixth and highest stage in Kohlberg's theory of moral development. Individuals develop a moral standard based on universal human rights. 233

V

visual preference method A method used to determine whether infants can distinguish one stimulus from another by measuring the length of time they attend to different stimuli. 89

Vygotsky's theory A sociocultural cognitive theory that emphasizes how culture and social interaction guide cognitive development. 20

W

whole-language approach An approach to reading instruction based on the idea that instruction should parallel children's natural language learning. Reading materials should be whole and meaningful. 220

wisdom Expert knowledge about the practical aspects of life that permits excellent judgment about important matters. 396

working memory Closely related to short-term memory but places more emphasis on mental work. Working memory is like a mental "workbench" where individuals can manipulate and assemble information when making decisions, solving problems, and comprehending written and spoken language. 355

Z

zone of proximal development (ZPD) Vygotsky's term for tasks too difficult for children to master alone but that can be mastered with assistance. 149

References

A

Aalsma, M., Lapsley, D. K., & Flannery, D. (2006). Narcissism, personal fables, and adolescent adjustment. *Psychology in the Schools, 43,* 481–491

AARP. (2004). *The divorce experience: A study of divorce at midlife and beyond.* Washington, DC: Author.

Abbott, A. (2003). Restless nights, listless days. *Nature, 425,* 896–898.

Abbott, R. D., White, I. R., Ross, G. W., Masaki, K. H., Curb, J. D., & Petrovitch, H. (2004). Walking and dementia in physically capable elderly men. *Journal of the American Medical Association, 292,* 1447–1453.

Abel, E. L. (2006). Fetal alcohol syndrome: A cautionary note. *Current Pharmacy Design, 12,* 1521–1529.

Aber, J. L., Bishop-Josef, S. J., Jones, S. M., McLern, T., & Phillips, D. A. (2006). *Child development and social policy.* Washington, DC: American Psychological Association.

Accornero, V. H., Anthony, J. C., Morrow, C. E., Xue, L., & Bandstra, E. S. (2006). Prenatal cocaine exposure: An examination of childhood externalizing and internalizing behavior problems at age 7 years. *Epidemiology, Psychiatry, and Society, 15,* 20–29.

Adams, K. F., Schatzkin, A., Harris, T. B., Kipnis, V., Mouw, T., Ballard-Barbash, R., Hollenbeck, A., & Leitzmann, M. F. (2006). Overweight, obesity, and mortality in a large prospective cohort of persons 50 to 71 years old. *New England Journal of Medicine, 355,* 763–768.

Adams, R. J. (1989). Newborns' discrimination among mid- and long-wavelength stimuli. *Journal of Experimental Child Psychology, 47,* 130–141.

Adolph, K. E. (1997). Learning in the development of infant locomotion. *Monographs of the Society for Research in Child Development, 62* (3, Serial No. 251).

Adolph, K. E., & Berger, S. E. (2005). Physical and motor development. In M. H. Bornstein & M. E. Lamb (Eds.), *Developmental psychology* (5th ed.). Mahwah, NJ: Earlbaum.

Adolph, K. E., & Berger, S. E. (2006). Motor development. In W. Damon & R. Lerner (eds.). *Handbook of child psychology* (6th ed.). New York: Wiley.

Adolph, K. E., & Joh, A. S. (2007). Motor development: How infants get into the act. In A. Slater & M. Levis (Eds.). *Infant Development* (2nd ed.). New York: Oxford University Press.

Adolph, K. E., & Joh, A. S. (2008, in press). Multiple learning mechanisms in the development of action. In A. Needham & A. Woodward (Eds.), *Learning and the infant mind.* New York: Oxford University Press.

Agahi, N., Ahacic, K., & Parker, M. G. (2006). Continuity of leisure participation from middle age to old age. *Journals of Gerontology B: Psychological Sciences and Social Sciences, 61,* S340–S346.

Agras, W. S., & others. (2004). Report of the National Institutes of Health workshop on overcoming barriers to treatment research in anorexia nervosa. *International Journal of Eating Disorders, 35,* 509–521.

Agviar, A., & Baillargeon, R. (2002). Developments in young infants reasoning about occluded objects. *Cognitive Psychology, 45,* 263–336.

Ah, D. V., Kang, D. H., & Carpenter, J. S. (2007). Stress, optimism, and social support: Impact on immune responses in breast cancer. *Research in Nursing and Health, 30,* 72–83.

Ahrons, C. (2004). *We're still family.* New York: Harper Collins.

Ahrons, C. (2007). Introduction to the special issue on divorce and its aftermath. *Family Process, 46,* 3–6.

Ainsworth, M. D. S. (1979). Infant-mother attachment. *American Psychologist, 34,* 932–937.

Akhter, M., Nishino, Y., Nakaya, N., Kurashima, K., Sato, Y., Kuriyama, S., Tsubono, Y., & Tsuji, I. (2007). Cigarette smoking and the risk of colorectal cancer among men: A prospective study in Japan. *European Journal of Cancer Prevention, 16,* 102–107.

Akiyama, H., & Antonucci, T. C. (1999, November). *Mother-dauhthter dynamics over the life course.* Paper presented at the meeting of the Gerontological Association of America, San Francisco.

Alan Guttmacher Institute. (1998). *Teen sex and pregnancy.* New York: Author.

Aldwin, C. M., & Levenson, M. R. (2001). Stress, coping, and health at midlife: A developmental perspective. In M. E. Lachman (Ed.), *Handbook of midlife development.* New York: John Wiley.

Aldwin, C. M., Spiro, A., & Park, C. L. (2006). Health, behavior, and optimal aging. In J. E. Birren & K. W. Schaie (Eds.), *Handbook of the psychology of aging* (6th d.). San Diego: Academic Press.

Allen, J. P. (2007, March). *A transformational perspective on the attachment system in adolescence.* Paper presented at the meeting of the Society for Research in Child Development, Boston.

Allen, J. P., Marsh, P. A., McFarland, F. C., McElhaney, K. B., Land, D. J., Jodl, K. M., & others (2002). Attachment and autonomy as predictors of the development of social skills and deviance during mid-adolescence. *Journal of Consulting and Clinical Psychology, 70,* 56–66.

Allen, J. P., Philliber, S., Herring, S., & Kuperminc, G. P. (1997). Preventing teen pregnancy and academic failure: Experimental evaluation of a developmentally-based approach. *Child Development, 68,* 729–742.

Allen, M., Brown, P., & Finlay, B. (1992). *Helping children by stengthening families.* Washington, DC: Children's Defense Fund.

Alm, B., Lagercrantz, H., & Wennergren, G. (2006). Stop SIDS—sleeping solitary supine, sucking smoother, stopping smoking substitutes. *Acta Paediatrica, 95,* 260–262.

Almeida, D., & Horn, M. (2004). Is daily life more stressful during middle adulthood? In G. Brim, C. D. Ryff, & R. Kessler (Eds.), *How healthy we are: A national study of well-being in midlife.* Chicago: University of Chicago Press.

Alvarez, A., & Del Rio, P. (2007). Inside and outside the zone of proximal development: An eco-functional reading of Vygotsky. In H. Daniels, J. Wertsch, & M. Cole (Eds.), *The Cambridge companion to Vygotsky.* New York: Cambridge University Press.

Alvik, A., Haldorsen, T., Groholt, B., & Lindemann, R. (2006). Alcohol consumption before and during pregnancy comparing concurrent and retrospective reports. *Alcohol: Clinical and Experimental Research, 30,* 510–515.

Amabile, T. M., & Hennesey, B. A. (1992). The motivation for creativity in children. In A. K. Boggiano & T. S. Pittman (Eds.), *Achievement and motivation.* New York: Cambridge.

Amato, P. R. (2006). Marital discord, divorce, and children's well-being: Results from a 20-year longitudinal study of two generations. In A. Clarke-Stewart & J. Dunn (Eds.), *Families count.* New York: Cambridge University Press.

Amato, P. R., & Booth, A. (1996), A prospective study of divorce and parent-child relationships. *Journal of Marriage and the Family, 58,* 356–365.

Amato, P. R., & Irving, S. (2006). Historical trends in divorce and dissolution. In M. A. Fine & J. H. Harvey (Eds.), *Handbook of divorce and relationship dissolution.* Mahwah, NJ: Erlbaum.

American Academy of Pediatrics Task Force on Infant Positioning and SIDS. (2000). Changing concepts of sudden infant death syndrome. *Pediatrics, 105,* 650–656.

American Association of University Women. (2006). *Drawing the line: Sexual harassment on campus.* Washington, DC: Author.

American Psychological Association. (2003). *Psychology: Scientific problem solvers.* Washington, DC: Author

American Public Health Association. (2006). *Understanding the health culture of recent immigrants to the United States.* Retrieved December, 5, 2006, from www.apha.org/ppp/red/Intro.htm

Amin, A., Monabati, A., Tadayon, A., Attaran, S. Y., & Kumar, P. V. (2006). Testicular fine needle aspiration cytology in male infertility. *Acta Cytologica, 50,* 147–150.

Amsterdam, B. K. (1968). *Mirror behavior in children under two years of age.* Unpublished doctoral dissertation. University of North Carolina, Chapel Hill.

Anastasi, A., & Urbina, S. (1996). *Psychological testing* (7th ed.). Upper Saddle River, NJ: Prentice Hall.

Anderson, C. A. (2007, March). *Violent video games as a risk for aggression: Correlational and experimental evidence.* Paper presented at the meeting of the Society for Research in Child Development, Boston.

Anderson, C. A., & Bushman, B. J. (2001). Effects of violent video games on aggressive behavior, aggressive cognition, aggressive affect, physiological arousal, and presocial behavior: A meta-analytic review of the scientific literature. *Psychological Science, 12,* 353–359.

Anderson, C. A. Gentile, D. A., & Buckle, K. E. (2007). *Violent video game effects on children and adolescents.* New York: Oxford University Press.

Anderson, D. J., & Yoshizawa, T. (2007, in press). Cross-cultural comparisons of the health-related quality of life in Australian and Japanese women: The Australian and Japanese Midlife Women's Health study. *Menopause.*

Anderson, E., Greene, S. M., Heterington, E. M., & Clingempeel, W. G. (1999). The dynamics of parental remarriage. In E. M. Hetherington (Ed.), *Coping with divorce, single parenting, and remarriage.* Mahwah, NJ: Erlbaum.

Anderson, J. E., Santelli, J. S., & Morrow, B. (2006). Trends in adolescent contraceptive use, unprotected and poorly protected sex, 1991–2003. *Journal of Adolescent Health, 38,* 734–739.

Anderson, J. L., Waller, D. K., Canfield, M. A., Shaw, G. M., Watkins, M. L., & Werler, M. M. (2005). Maternal obesity, gestational diabetes, and central nervous system birth defects. *Epidemiology, 16,* 87–92.

Anderson, L. B., Harro, M., Sardinha, L. B., Froberg, K., Ekelund, U., Brage, S., & Anderssen, S. A. (2006). Physical activity and clustered cardiovascular risk in children: A cross-sectional study (The European Youth Heart Study). *Lancet, 368,* 299–304.

Anderson, P. A., (2006). Sex differences that make a difference: Social evolution and reproduction. In K. Dindia & D. J. Canary (Eds.), *Sex differences and similarities in communication.* Mahwah, NJ: Erlbaum.

Anderton, B. H. (2002). Aging of the brain. *Mechanisms of Aging and Development, 123,* 811–817.

Ando, M., Tsuda, A., & Moorey, S. (2006). Preliminary study of reminiscence therapy on depression and self-esteem in cancer patients. *Psychological Reports, 98,* 339–346.

Androulidakis, A. G., & others. (2007). Dopaminergic therapy promotes lateralized motor activity in the subthalamic area in Parkinson's disease. *Brain, 130,* 457–468.

Angel, R. J., & Angel, J. L. (2006). Diversity and aging in the United States. In R. H. Binstock & L. K. George (Eds.), *Handbook of aging and the social sciences (6th ed).* San Diego: Academic Press.

Antai-Otong, D. (2003). Suicide: Life span considerations. *Nursing Clinics of North America, 38,* 137–150.

Antonucci, T. C. & Akiyama, H. (2002). Aging and close relationships over the life span. *International Society for the Study of Behavioural Development Newsletter* (1, Serial No. 41), 2–5.

Antonucci, T. C. (1989). Understanding adult social relationships. In K. Kreppner & R. M. Lerner (Eds.), *Family systems and lifespan development.* Hillsdale, NJ: Erlbaum.

Antonucci, T. C., Lansford, J. E., & Akiyama, H. (2001). The impact of positive and negative aspects of marital relationships and friendships on the well-being of older adults. In J. P. Reinhardt (Ed.), *Negative and positive support.* Mahwah, NJ: Erlbaum.

Antonucci, T. C., Lansford, J. E., & Schaabeg, L., Smith J., Baltes, M., Akiyama, H., Takahashi, K., & Fuhrer, R. (2001). Widowhood and illness: A comparison of social network characteristics in France, Germany, Japan, and the United States. *Psychology and Aging, 16,* 655–665.

Antonucci, T. C., Vandewater, E. A., & Lansford, J. E. (1998). Extended family relationships. In H. S. Friedman (Ed.), *Encyclopedia of mental health* (Vol. 2). San Diego: Academic Press.

Antonucci, T. C., Vandewater, E. A., & Lansford, J. E. (2000). Adulthood and aging: Social processes and development. In A. Kazdin (Ed.), *Encyclopedia of psychology.*

Washington, DC, and New York: American Psychological Association and Oxford University Press.

Antony, A. C. (2007). In utero physiology: Role of folic acid in nutrient delivery and fetal development. *American Journal of Clinical Nutrition, 85 (Suppl),* 598S–603S.

Arbuckle, T. Y., Maag, U., Pushkar, D., & Chaikelsen, J. S. (1998). Individual differences in trajectory of intellectual development over 45 years of adulthood. *Psychology and Aging, 13,* 663–675.

Archibald, A. B., Graeber, J. A., & Brooks-Gunn, J. (1999). Associations among parent-adolescent relationships, pubertal growth, dieting, and body image in young adolescent girls: A short-term longitudinal study. *Journal of Research on Adolescence, 9,* 395–415.

Arenas, A., Bosworth, K., Kwadayi, H. P., & Compare, A. (2006). Civic service through schools: An international perspective. *Journal of Comparative Education, 36,* 23–40.

Arendt, R., Angelopoulos, J., Salvator, A., & Singer, L. (1999). Motor development of cocaine-exposed children at age two years. *Pediatrics, 103,* 86–92.

Ariagno, R. L., Van Liempt, S., & Mirmiran, M. (2006). Fewer spontaneous arousals during prone sleep in preterm infants at 1 and 3 months corrected age. *Journal of Perinatology.*

Ariceli, G., Castro, J., Cesena, J., & Toro, J. (2005). Anorexia nervosa in male adolescents: Body image, eating attitudes, and psychological traits. *Journal of Adolescent Health, 36,* 221–226.

Armstrong, M. L. (1995) Adolescent tattoos: Educating and pontificating. *Pediatric Nursing, 21 (6),* 561–564.

Armstrong, M. L., Caliendo, C., & Roberts, A. E. (2006). Genital piercings: What is known and what people with genital piercings tell us. *Urologic Nursing, 26,* 173–180.

Armstrong, M. L., Roberts, A. E., Owen, D. C., & Koch, J. R. (2004). Contemporary college students and body piercing. *Journal of Adolescent Health, 35,* 58–61.

Arnett, J. J. (1995, March). *Are college students adults?* Paper presented at the meeting of the Society for Research in Child Development, Indianapolis.

Arnett, J. J. (2004). *Emerging adulthood.* New York: Oxford University Press.

Arnett, J. J. (2006). Emerging adulthood: Understanding the new way of coming of age. In J. J. Arnett & J. L. Tanner (Eds.), *Emerging adults in America.* Washington, DC: American Psychological Association.

Arnett, J. J. (2007). Socialization in emerging adulthood. In J. E. Grusec & P. D. Hastings (Eds.), *Handbook of socialization.* New York: Guilford.

Aron, A., Fisher, H., Mashek, D. J., Strdong, G., Li, H., & Brown, L. L. (2005). Reward, motivation, and emotion are associated with early-stage intense romantic love. *Journal of Neurophysiology, 94*, 327–337.

Aronson, E. (1986, August). *Teaching students things they think they already know about: The case of prejudice and desegregation.* Paper presented at the meeting of the American Psychological Association, Washington, DC.

Arpanantikul, M. (2004). Midlife experiences of Thai women. *Journal of Advanced Nursing, 47*, 49–56.

Arredondo, E. M., Elder, J. P., Ayala, G. X., Campbell, N., Baquero, B., & Duerksen, S. (2006). Is parenting style related to children's healthy eating and physical activity in Latino families? *Health Education Research, 21*, 862–871.

Arria, A. M., & others. (2006). Methamphetamine and other substance use during pregnancy: Preliminary estimates from the Infant Development, Environment, and Lifestyle (IDEAL) Study. *Maternal and Child Health Journal, 5*, 1–10.

Arshad, S. H. (2005). Primary prevention of asthma and allergy. *Journal of Allergy and Clinical Immunology, 116*, 3–14.

Arvantitakes, Z., Wilson, R. S., Aggarwad, N. T., & Bennett, D. A. (2006). Diabetes and function in different cognitive systems in older adults without dementia. *Diabetes Care, 29*, 560–565.

Ash, P. (2006). Adolescents in adult court; Does the punishment fit the criminal? *The Journal of the American Academy of Psychiatry and the Law, 34*, 145–149.

Asher, J., & Garcia, R. (1969). The optimal age to learn a foreign language. *Modern Language Journal, 53*, 334–341.

Ashton, D. (2006). Prematurity—infant mortality: The scourge remains. *Ethnicity and Disease, 16 (2 Suppl.)*, S3–S58.

Askham, J., Ferring, D., & Lamura, G. (2007). Personal relationships in later life. In J. Bond, S. Peace, F. Dittman-Kohli, & G. Westerhoff (Eds.), *Aging in society* (3rd ed.). Thousand Oaks, CA: Sage.

Aslin, R. N., Jusczyk, P. W., & Pisoni, D. B. (1998). Speech and auditory processing during infancy: Constraints on and precursors to language. In W. Damon (Ed.), *Handbook of child psychology* (5th ed., Vol. 2). New York: Wiley.

Ateah, C. A. (2005). Maternal use of physical punishment in response to child misbehavior: Implications for child abuse prevention. *Child Abuse and Neglect, 29*, 169–185.

Atiych, G. N., & El-Mohandes, A. (2005) Preventive healthcare of infants in a region of Lebanon: Parental beliefs, attitudes, and behaviors. *Maternal and Child Health Journal 9*, 83–90.

Attie, L., Brooks-Gunn, J. (1989). Development of eating problems in adolescent girls: A longitudinal study. *Developmental Psychology, 25*, 70–79.

Aucoin, K. J., Frick, P. J., & Bodin, S. D. (2006). Corporal punishment and child adjustment. *Journal of Applied Developmental Psychology, 27*, 527–541.

Avgil, M., & Ornoy, A. (2006). Herpes simplex virus and Epstein-Barr virus infections in pregnancy: Consequences of neonatal or intrauterine infection. *Reproductive Toxicology, 21*, 436–445.

Avis, N. E. (1999). Women's health at midlife. In S. L. Willis & J. D. Reid (Eds.), *Life in the middle: Psychological and social development in middle age.* San Diego: Academic Press.

Avis, N. E., Zhao, X., Johannes, C. B., Ory, M., Brockwell, S., & Greendale, G. A. (2005) Correlates of sexual function among multiethnic middle-aged women: Results from the Study of Women's Health Across the Nation (SWAN). *Menopause, 12*, 385–398.

Ayala, G. X., Mickens, L., Galindo, P., & Elder, J. P. (2007). Acculturation and body image perception among Latino youth. *Ethnicity and Health, 12*, 21–41.

Aylott, M. (2006). The neonatal energy triangle. Part 1: Metabolic adaptation. *Pediatric Nursing 18*, 38–42.

Azrin, N. H., Ehle, C. T., & Beaumont, A. L. (2006). Physical exercise as a reinforcer to promote calmness of an ADHD child. *Behavior Modification, 30*, 564–570.

B

B. W., Walton, K. E., & Viechtbauer, W. (2006). Patterns of mean-level change in personality traits across the life course: A meta-analysis of longitudinal studies. *Psychological Bulletin, 132*, 1–25.

Bachman, J. G., O'Malley, P. M., Schulenberg, J., Johnston, L. D., Bryant, A. L., & Merline, A. C. (2002). *The decline of substance abuse in young adulthood.* Mahwah, NJ: Erlbaum.

Baddeley, A. (2000). Short-term and working memory. In E. Tulving & F. I. M. Craik (Eds.), *The Oxford handbook of memory.* New York: Oxford University Press.

Baddeley, A. (2007). *Working memory, thought, and action.* New York: Oxford University Press.

Bahrick, L. E., & Hollich, G. (2008, in press). Intermodal perception. In M. Haith & J. Benson (Eds.), *Encyclopedia of infant and early childhood development.* London: Elsevier.

Bailit, J. L., Love, T. E., & Dawson, N. V. (2006). Quality of obstetric care and risk-adjusted primary cesarean delivery rates. *American Journal of Obstetrics and Gynecology, 194*, 402–407.

Baillargeon, R. (1995). The object concept revisited: New directions in the investigation of infants' physical knowledge. In C. E. Granrud (Ed.), *Visual perception and cognitive in infancy.* Hillsdale, NJ: Erlbaum.

Baillargeon, R. (2004). The acquisition of physical knowledge in infancy: A summary in eight lessons. In U. Goswami (Ed.), *Blackwell handbook of childhood cognitive development.* Malden, MA: Blackwell.

Bakeman, R., & Brown, J. V. (1980). Early interaction: Consequences for social and mental development at three years. *Child Development, 51*, 437–447.

Baker, D. A. (2007). Consequences of herpes simplex virus in pregnancy and their prevention. *Current Opinions in Infectious Diseases, 20*, 73–76.

Baker, S. R. (2006). Towards an idiopathic understanding of the role of social problem solving in daily event, mood, and health experiences: A prospective daily diary approach. *British Journal of Health Psychology, 11*, 513–531.

Baldwin, J. D., & Baldwin, J. I. (1998). Sexual behavior. In H. S. Friedman (Ed.), *Encyclopedia of mental health* (Vol. 3). San Diego: Academic Press.

Baldwin, S., & Hoffiman, J. F. (2002). The dynamics of self-esteem: A growth curve analysis. *Journal of Youth and Adolescence, 31*, 101–113.

Ball, H. (2007). Positive attitudes toward condom use do not equal safe sex among teenagers. *Perspectives on Sexual and Reproductive Health, 39*, 61–62.

Baltes, P. B. (1987). Theoretical propositions of lifespan developmental psychology: On the dynamics between growth and decline. *Developmental Psychology, 23*, 611–626.

Baltes, P. B. (2003). On the incomplete architecture of human ontogeny: Selection, optimization, and compensation as foundation for developmental theory. In U. M. Staudinger & U. Lindenberger (Eds.), *Understanding human development.* Boston: Kluwer,

Baltes, P. B. (2006). *Facing our limits: the very old and the future of aging.* Unpublished manuscript, Max Planck Institute, Berlin.

Baltes, P. B., & Kunzmann, U. (2004). The two faces of wisdom: Wisdom as a general theory of knowledge and judgments about excellence in mind and virtue vs. wisdom as everyday realization in people and products. *Human Development, 47*, 290–299.

Baltes, P. B., & Kunzmann, U. (2007). Wisdom and aging: The road toward excellence in mind and character. In D. C. Park & N. Schwarz (Eds.), *Cognitive aging: A primer* (2nd ed.). Philadelphia Psychology Press.

Baltes, P. B., Lindenberger, U. & Staudinger, U. (2006). Life-span theory in developmental psychology. In W. Damon & R. Lerner (Eds.), *Handbook of child psychology* (6th ed.). New York: Wiley.

Baltes, P. B., & Smith, J. (2003). New frontiers in the future of aging: From successful aging of the young old to the dilemmas of the fourth age. *Gerontology, 49,* 123–135.

Baltes, P. B., Revter-Lorene, P., & Rösler, F. (Eds.) (2006). *Lifespan development and the brain.* New York: (Cambridge University Press.

Bandura, A. (1986). *Social foundations of thought and action: A social cognitive theory.* Englewood Cliffs, NJ: Prentice Hall.

Bandura, A. (1998, August). *Swimming against the mainstream: Accentuating the positive aspects of humanity.* Paper presented at the meeting of the American Psychological Association, San Francisco.

Bandura, A. (2001). Social cognitive theory. *Annual Review of Psychology.* Palo Alto, CA: Annual Reviews.

Bandura, A. (2002). Social cognitive theory. *Annual Review of Psychology.* (Vol. 52) Palo Alto, CA: Annual Reviews.

Bandura, A. (2004, May). *Toward a psychology of human agency.* Paper presented at the meeting of the American Psychological Society, Chicago.

Bandura, A. (2006). Toward a psychology of human agency. *Perspectives on Psychological Science, 1,* 164–180.

Bandura, A. (2007a). Self-efficacy. In S. Clegg & J. Bailey (Eds.), *International encyclopedia of organization studies.* Thousand Oaks, CA: Sage.

Bandura, A. (2007b). Social cognitive theory. In W. Donsbach (Ed.), *International encyclopedia of communication.* Thousand Oaks, CA: Sage.

Banja, J. (2005). Talking to the dying. *Case Manager, 16,* 37–39.

Bank, L., Burraston, B., & Snyder, J. (2004). Sibling conflict and ineffective parenting as predictors of adolescent boys' antisocial behavior and peer difficulties: Additive and interactive effects. *Journal of Research on Adolescence, 14,* 99–125.

Banks, J. A. (2008). *Introduction to multicultural education* (4th ed.). Boston: Allyn & Bacon.

Banks, M. S., & Salapatek, P. (1983). Infant visual perception. In P. H. Mussen (Ed.), *Handbook of child psychology* (4th ed. Vol. 2). New York Wiley.

Bannon, L. (2005). *Gender: psychological perspective* (4th ed.). Boston: Allyn & Bacon.

Barbaresi, W. J., Katusic, S. K., Colligan, R. C., Weaver, A. L., Leibson, C. L., & Jacobsen, S. J. (2006). Long-term stimulant medication treatment of attention-deficit/hyperactivity disorder: Results from a population-based study. *Journal of Developmental and Behavioral Pediatrics, 27,* 1–10.

Barber, B. L. (2006). To have loved and lost….Adolescent romantic relationships and rejection. In A. C. Crouter & A. Booth (Eds.), *Romance and sex in adolescence and emerging adulthood.* Mahwah, NJ: Erlbaum.

Barber, B. L., & Demo, D. (2006). The kids are alright (at least most of them): Links to divorce and dissolution. In M. A. Fine & J. H. Harvey (Eds.), *Handbook of divorce and relationship dissolution.* Mahwah, NJ: Erlbaum.

Barefoot, J. C., Mortensen, E. L., Helms, J., Avlund, K., & Schroll, M. (2001). A longitudinal study of gender differences in depressive symptoms from age 50 to 80. *Psychology and Aging, 16,* 342–345.

Barker, R., & Wright, H. F. (1951). *One boy's day.* New York: Harper & Row.

Barnes, L., L., Mendes de Leon, C. F., Wilson, R. S., Bienias, J. L., Bennett, D. A., & Evans, D. A. (2004). Racial differences in perceived discrimination in a community population of older Blacks and Whites. *Journal of Aging and Health, 16,* 315–317.

Barnet, B., Arroyo, C., Devoe, M., & Duggan, A. K. (2004). Reduced school dropout rates among adolescent mothers receiving school-based prenatal care. *Archives of Pediatric and Adolescent Medicine, 158,* 262–268.

Barnett, R. C. (2001). Work-family balance. In J. Worell (Ed.), *Encyclopedia of women and gender.* San Diego: Academic Press.

Barnett, R. C., Gareis, K. C., James, J. B., & Steele, J. (2001, August). *Planning ahead: College seniors' concerns about work-family conflict.* Paper presented at the meeting of the American Psychological Association, San Francisco.

Baron, N. S. (1992). *Growing up with language.* Reading, MA: Addison-Wesley.

Barr, R., & Hayn, H. (2003). It's not what you know, its who you know: Older siblings facilitate imitation during infancy. *International Journal of Early Years Education, 11,* 7–21.

Barrett, A. E., & Turner, R. J. (2005). Family structure and mental health: The mediating effects of socioeconomic status, family process, and social stress. *Journal of Health and Social Behavior, 46,* 156–169.

Barrett, T. M., Davis, E. F., & Needham, A. (2007). Learning about tools in infancy. *Developmental Psychology, 43,* 352–368.

Bateman, B. T., & Simpson, L. L. (2006). Higher rate of stillbirth at the extremes of reproductive age: A large nationwide sample of deliveries in the United States. *American Journal of Obstetrics and Gynecology, 194,* 840–845.

Bauer, P. J. (2006). Event memory. In W. Damon & R. Lerner (Eds.), *Handbook of child psychology* (6th ed.). New York: Wiley.

Bauer, P. J. (2007). *Remembering the times of four lives.* Mahwah, NJ: Erlbaum.

Bauer, P. J., Wenner, J. A., Dropik, P. I., & Wewerka, S. S. (2000). Parameters of remembering and forgetting in the transition from infancy to early childhood. *Monographs of the Society for Research in Child Development, 65* (4, Serial No. 263).

Baumeister, R. F., & Vohs, K. D. (2002). The pursuit of meaningfulness in life. In C. R. Snyder & S. J. Lopez (Eds.), *Handbook of positive psychology.* New York: Oxford University Press.

Baumeister, R. F., Campbell, J. D., Krueger, J. I., & Vohs, K. D. (2003). Does high self-esteem cause better performance, interpersonal success, happiness, or healthier lifestyles? *Psychological Science in the Public Interest, 4* (No. 1), 1–44.

Baumrind, D. (1971). Current patterns of parental authority. *Developmental Psychology Monographs, 4* (1, Pt. 2).

Baumrind, D., Larzelere, R. E., & Cowan, P. A. (2002). Ordinary physical punishment: Is it harmful? Comment on Gershoff, *Psychological Bulletin, 128,* 590–595.

Bauserman, R. (2002). Child adjustment in joint-custody versus sole-custody arrangements: A meta-analytic review. *Journal of Family Psychology, 16,* 91–102.

Baver, P. J. (2006). Event memory. In W. Damon & R. Lerner (Eds.), *Handbook of child psychology* (6th ed.). New York: Wiley.

Bawks, J. A. (2008). *Introduction to multicultural education* (4th ed.). Boston: Allyn & Bacon.

Bearman, P. S., & Moody, J. (2004). Suicide and friendships among American adolescents. *American Journal of Public Health, 94,* 89–95.

Bearman, S. K., Presnall, K., Martinez, E., & Stice, E. (2006). The skinny on body dissatisfaction: A longitudinal study of adolescent girls and boys. *Journal of Youth and Adolescence, 35,* 217–229.

Bech, B. H., Obel, C., Henriksen, T. B., & Olsen, J. (2007). Effect of reducing caffeine intake on birth weight and length of gestation: Randomized controlled trial. *British Medical Journal, 334,* 409.

Beck, C. T. (2002). Theoretical perspectives of postpartum depression and their treatment implications. *American Journal of Maternal/Child Nursing, 27,* 282–287.

Beck, C. T. (2006). Postpartum depression: It isn't just the blues. *American Journal of Nursing, 106,* 40–50.

Beckmann, M. M., & Garrett, A. J. (2006). Antenatal perineal massage for reducing perineal trauma. *Cochrane Database of Systematic Reviews, 1,* CD005123.

Bednar, R. L., Wells, M. G., & Peterson, S. R. (1995). *Self-esteem* (2nd ed.). Washington, DC: American Psychological Association.

Beech, A. R., Ward, T., & Fisher, D. (2006). The identification of sexual and violent motivations in men who assault women: Implications for treatment. *Journal of Interpersonal Violence, 21,* 1635–1653.

Beeghly, M., Martin, B., Rose-Jacobs, R., Cahral, H., Heeren, T., Augustyn, M., Bellinger, D., & Frank, D. A. (2006). Prenatal cocaine exposure and children's language functioning at 6 and 9.5 years:

moderating effects of child age, birthweight, and gender. *Journal of Pediatric Psychology, 31,* 98–115.

Beehr, T. A., & Bennett, M. M. (2007). Examining retirement from a multi-level perspective. In K. S. Shultz & G. A. Adams (Eds.), *Aging and work in the 21st century.* Mahwah, NJ: Erlbaum.

Belsky, J. (1981). Early human experience: A family perspective. *Developmental Psychology, 17,* 3–23.

Belsky, J., Vandell, D. L., Burchinal, M. Clarke-Stewart, A. K., McCartney, K., Owen, M. T., & the NICHD Early Child Care Research Network. (2007). Are there long term effects of early child care. *Child Development, 78,* 68–701.

Belson, W. (1978). *Television violence and the adolescent boy.* London: Saxon House.

Bender, W. N. (2008). *Learning disabilities* (6th ed.). Boston: Allyn & Bacon.

Bendersky, M., & Sullivan, M. W. (2007). Basic methods in infant research. In A. Slater & M. Lewis (Eds.), *Introduction to infant development* (2nd ed.). New York: Oxford University Press.

Benenson, J. F., Apostolaris, N. H., & Parnass, I. (1997). Age and sex differences in dyadic and group interaction. *Developmental Psychology, 33,* 538–543.

Bengtson, V. L. (1985). Diversity and symbolism in grandparental roles. In V. L. Bengtson & J. Robertson (Eds.), *Grandparenthood.* Newbury Park: CA: Sage.

Bennett, C. I. (2007). *Comprehensive multicultural education* (6th ed.). Boston: Allyn & Bacon.

Bennett, K. M. (2006). Does marital status and marital status change predict physical health in older adults? *Psychological Medicine, 36,* 1313–1320.

Bennett, S. E., & Assefi, N. P. (2005). School-based teenage pregnancy prevention programs: A systematic review of randomized controlled trials. *Journal of Adolescent Health, 36,* 72–81.

Benninghoven, D., Tetsch, N., Kunzendorf, S., & Jantschek, G. (2007). Body image in patients with eating disorders and their mothers, and the role of family functioning. *Comprehensive Psychiatry, 48,* 118–123.

Benson, P. L. (2006). *All kids are our kids* (2nd ed.) San Francisca: Jossey-Bass.

Benson, P. L., Scales, P. C., Hamilton, S. F., & Sesma, A. (2006). Positive youth development. In W. Damon & R. Lerner (Eds.), *Handbook of child psychology* (6th ed.). New York: Wiley.

Berard, A., Azoulay, L., Koren, G., Blais, L., Perreault, S., & Oraichi, D. (2007). Isotretinoin, pregnancies, abortions, and birth defects: A population-based perspective. *British Journal of Pharmacology, 63,* 196–205.

Berardi, A., Parasuraman, R., & Haxby, J. V. (2001). Overall vigilance and sustained attention decrements in healthy aging. *Experimental Aging Research, 27,* 19–39.

Bergens, D. (1988). Stages of play development. In D. Bergen (Ed.), *Play as a medium for learning and development.* Portsmouth, NH: Heinemann.

Berk, L. E. (1994). Why children talk to themselves. *Scientific American, 271* (5), 78–83.

Berk, L. E., & Spuhl, S. T. (1995). Maternal interaction, private speech, and task performance in preschool children. *Early Childhood Research Quarterly, 10,* 145–169.

Berko Gleason, J. (2003). Unpublished review of J. W. Santrack's *Life -span development,* (9th ed.). (New York: McGraw-Hill).

Berko Gleason, J. (2004). Unpublished review of J. W. Santrack's *Life-span development,* 9th ed. (New York: McGraw-Hill).

Berko Gleason, J. (2005), The development of language. In J. Berko Gleason. (Ed.), *The development of language (6th ed.).* Boston: Allyn & Bacon.

Berko, J. (1958). The child's learning of English morphology. *Word, 14,* 150–177.

Berlin, L. J., Ziv, Y., Amaya-Jackson, L., & Greenberg, M. T. (2007). *Enhancing early attachments.* New York: Guilford.

Berlin, L., & Cassidy, J. (2000). Understanding parenting: Contributions of attachment theory and research. In J. D. Osofsky & H. E. Fitzgerald (Eds.), *WAIMH handbook of infant mental health* (Vol. 3). New York: Wiley.

Berlyne, D. E. (1960). *Conflict, arousal, and curiosity.* New York: McGraw-Hill.

Bern, S. L. (1977). On the utility of alternative procedures for assessing psychological androgyny. *Journal of Consulting and Clinical Psychology, 45,* 196–205.

Berndt, T. J. (2002). Friendship quality and social development. *Current Directions in Psychological Science, 11,* 7–10.

Berndt, T. J., & Perry, T. B. (1990). Distinctive features and effects of early adolescent friendships. In R. Montemayor (Ed.), *Advances in adolescent research.* Greenwich, CT: JAI Press.

Berninger, V. W. (2006). Learning disabilities. In W. Damon & R. Lerner (Eds.), *Handbook of child psychology* (6th ed.). New York: Wiley.

Berninger, V. W., & Abbott, R. (2005, April). *Paths leading to reading comprehension in at-risk and normally developing second-grade readers.* Paper presented at the meeting of the Society for Research in Child Development, Atlanta.

Berra, C., & Torta, R. (2007). Therapeutic rationale of antidepressant use in the elderly. *Archives of Gerontology and Geriatrics, 44* (Suppl.), S83–S90.

Berry, J. W. (2007). Acculturation. In J. E. Grusec & P. D. Hastings (Eds.), *Handbook of Socialization.* New York: Guilford.

Bersamin, M. M., Walker, S., Fisher, D. A., & Grube, J. W. (2006). Correlates of oral sex and vaginal intercourse in early and middle adolescence. *Journal of Research on Adolescence, 16,* 59–68.

Berscheid, E. (1988). Some comments on love's anatomy: Or, whatever happened to old-fashioned lust? In R. J. Stemberg (Ed.), *Anatomy of love.* New Haven, CT: Yale University Press.

Berscheid, E. (2000). Attraction. In A. Kazdin (Ed.), *Encyclopedia of psychology.* Washington, DC. and New York: American Psychological Association and Oxford University Press.

Berscheid, E., & Fel, J. (1977). Sexual jealousy and romantic love. In G. Clinton & G. Smith (Eds.), *Sexual Jealousy.* Englewood Cliffs, NJ: Prentice Hall.

Bertram, L., McQueen, M. B., Mullin, K., Blacker, D., & Tanzi, R. E. (2007). Systematic meta-analyses of Alzheimer disease genetic association studies: The AlzGene database. *Nature Genetics, 39,* 17–23.

Bessey, P. Q., Arons, R. R., Dimaggio, C. J., & Yurt, R. W. (2006). The vulnerabilities of age: Burns in children and older adults. *Surgery, 140,* 705–715.

Best, J. M. (2007, in press). Rubella. *Seminars in Fetal and Neonatal Medicine.*

Best, J. W., Kahn, J. V. (2006). *Research in education* (10th ed.). Boston: Allyn & Bacon.

Beutel, M. E., Weidner, W., & Brahler, E. (2006). Epidemiology of sexual dysfunction in the male population. *Andrologia, 38,* 115–121.

Beyene, Y. (1986). Cultural significance and physiological manifestations of menopause: A biocultural analysis. *Culture, Medicine and Psychiatry, 10,* 47–71.

Bhutta, Z. A., Darmstadt, G. L., Hasan, B. S., & Haws, R. A. (2005). Community-based interventions for improving perinatal and neonatal health outcomes in developing countries: A review of the evidence. *Pediatrics, 115,* 519–616.

Bialystok, E. (1993). Metalinguistic awareness: The development of children's representations in language. In C. Pratt & A. Garton (Eds.), *Systems of representation in children.* London: Wiley.

Bialystok, E. (1997). Effects of bilingualism and biliteracy on children's emerging concepts of print. *Developmental Psychology, 33,* 429–440.

Bialystok, E. (1999). Cognitive complexity and attentional control in the bilingual mind. *Child Development, 70,* 537–804.

Bialystok, E. (2001). *Bilingualism in development: Language, literacy, and cognition.* New York: Cambridge University Press.

Bianchi, S. M., & Spani, D. (1986). *American women in transition.* New York: Russell Sage Foundation.

Bierman, K. L. (2004). *Peer rejection*. New York: Guilford.

Bigler, R. S., Averhart, C. J., & Liben, L. S. (2003). Race and the workforce: Occupational status, aspirations, and stereotyping among African American Children. *Developmental Psychology, 19*, 572–580.

Bijur, P. E., Wallston, K. A., Smith, C. A., Lifrak, S., & Friedman, S. B. (1993, August). *Gender differences in turning to religion for coping*. Paper presented at the meeting of the American Psychological Association, Toronto.

Billman, J. (2003). *Observation and participation in early childhood settings: A practicum guide* (2nd ed.). Boston: Allyn & Bacon.

Billy, J. O. G., Rodgers, J. I., & Udry, J. R. (1984). Adolescent sexual behavior and friendship choice. *Social Forces, 62*, 653–678.

Birren, J. E. (2002). Unpublished review of J. W. Santrock's *Life-span development*, (9th ed). New York: McGraw-Hill.

Birren, J. E. (Ed.). (1996). *Encyclopedia of gerontology*, San Diego: Academic Press.

Birren, J. E., Woods, A. M., & Williams, M. V. (1980). Behavioral slowing with age: Causes, organization, & consequences. In L. W. Poon (Ed.), *Aging in the 1980s: Psychological issues*. Washington, DC: American Psychological Association.

Biswas, S. C., Shi, Y., Vonsattel, J. P., Leung, C. L., Troy, C. M., & Greene, L. A. (2007). Bim is elevated in Alzheimer's disease neurons and is required for beta-amyloid-induced neuronal apoptosis. *Journal of Neuroscience, 27*, 893–900.

Bjorklund, D. F. (2006). Mother knows best: Epigenetic inheritance, maternal effects, and the evolution of human intelligence. *Developmental Review, 26*, 213–242.

Bjorklund, D. F. (2007). *Why youth is not wasted on the young*. Malden, MA: Blackwell.

Bjorklund, D. R., & Pellegrinl, A. D. (2002). *The origines of human nature*. New York: Oxford University Press.

Blair, S. N. (1990, January). *Personal communication*. Aerobics Institute, Dallas.

Blair, S. N., Kohl, H. W., Paffenbarger, R. S., Clark, D. G., Cooper, K. H., & Gibbons, L. W. (1989). Physical fitness and all-cause mortality: A prospective study of healthy men and women. *Journal of the American Medical Association, 262*, 2395–2401.

Bloch, M. J., & Basile, J. (2007). Hypertension prevalence increases and hypertension control rates improve in the United States: 2003–2004. *Journal of Clinical Hypertension, 9*, 147–149.

Block, J. (1993). Studying personality the long way. In D. Funder, R. D. Parke, C. Tomlinson-Keasey, & K. Widaman (Ed.), *Studying lives through time*. Washington, DC: American Psychological Association.

Block, J. H., & Block, J. (1980). The role of ego-control and ego-resiliency in the organization of behavior. In W. A. Collins (Ed.), *Minnesota symposium on child psychology* (Vol. 13). Minneapolis: University of Minnesota Press.

Bloom, B. (1985). *Developing talent in young people*. New York: Ballentine.

Bloom, B., & Dev, A. N. (2006). Summary health statistics for U.S. children: National Health Interview survey, 2004. *Vital Health Statistics, 227*, 1–85.

Bloom, L. (1998). Language acquisition in developmental context. In W. Damon (Ed.), *Handbook of child psychology* (5th ed., Vol. 5). New York: Wiley.

Bloom, L., Lifter, K., & Broughton, J. (1985). The convergence of early cognition and language in the second year of life: Problems in conceptualization and measurement. In M. Barrett (Ed.), *Single word speech*. London: Wiley.

Blum, J. W., Beaudoin, C. M., & Caton-Lemos, L. (2005). Physical activity patterns and maternal well-being in postpartum women. *Maternal and Child Health Journal, 8*, 163–169.

Blumenfeld, P. C., Kempler, T. M., & Krajcik, J. S. (2006). Motivation and cognitive engagement in learning environments. In R. K. Sawyer (Ed.), *The Cambridge handbook of the learning sciences*. New York: Cambridge University Press.

Blumenthal, J., Jeffries, N. O., Castellanos, F. X., Liu, H. Zidjdenbos, A., Paus, T., Evans, A. C., Rapoport, J. L., & Gledd, J. N. (1999). Brain development during childhood and adolescence: A longitudinal MRI study. *Nature Neuroscience, 10*, 861–863.

Blurm, R., & Nelson-Mmari, K. (2004). Adolescent health from an international perspective. In R. Lerner & L. Steinberg (Eds.), *Handbook of adolescent psychology*. New York: Wiley.

Blustein, D. L. (2006). *Psychology of working*. Mahwah, NJ: Erlbaum.

Bodkin, N. L., Ortmeyer, H. K., & Hansen, B. (2005). A comment on the comment: Relevance on nonhuman primate dietary restriction to aging in humans. *Journals of Gerontology A: Biological Sciences and Medical Sciences, 60*, 951–952.

Bodrova, E., & Leong, D. J. (2001). *Tools of the mind*. Geneva. Switzerland: International Bureau of Education, UNESCO. Retrieved December 15, 2004, from http://www.ibe.unesco.org/International/Publications/INNODATA Monograph/inno07.pdf

Bodrova, E., & Leong, D. J. (2007). *Tools of the mind* (2nd ed.). Geneva, SWIT: International Bureau of Education, UNESCO.

Bogenschnieder, K. (Ed.) (2006). *Family policy matters*. Mahwah, NJ: Erlbaum.

Bohlin, G., & Hagekull, B. (1993). Stranger wariness and sociability in the early years. *Infant Behavior and Development, 16*, 53–67.

Bonanno, G. A., Wortman, C. B., & Nesse, R. M. (2004). Prospective patterns of resilience and maladjustment during widowhood. *Psychology and Aging, 19*, 260–271.

Bond, L., Butler, H., Thomas, L., Carlin, J., Glover, S., Bowes, G., & Patton, G. (2007). Social and school connectedness in early secondary school as predictors of late teenage substance use, mental health, and academic outcomes. *Journal of Adolescent Health, 40* e9–e18.

Bonvillian, J. (2005). Unpublished review of J. W. Santrock's *Topical life-span development* (3rd ed.). New York: McGraw-Hill.

Bookwala, J. (2005). The role of marital quality in physical health during the mature years. *Journal of Aging and Health, 17*, 85–104.

Bookwala, J., & Jacobs, J. (2004). Age, marital processes, and depressed affect. *The Gerontologist 44*, 328–338.

Booth, M. (2002). Arab adolescents facing the future: Enduring ideals and pressures to change. In B. B. Brown, R. W. Larson $$ & T. S. Saraswathi (Eds.), *The world's youth*. New York: Cambridge University Press.

Bor, W., McGee, T. R., & Fagan, A. A. (2004). Early risk factors for adolescent antisocial behavior: An Australian longitudinal study. *Australian and New Zealand Journal of Psychiatry, 38*, 365–372.

Bornstein, M. H. (2006). Parenting: Science and practice. In W. Damon & R. Lerner (Eds.), *Handbook of child psychology* (6th ed.). New York: Wiley.

Boron, J. B., Willis, S. L., & Schaie, K. W. (2007). Cognitive training gain as a predictor of mental status. *Journals of Gerontology: Psychological Sciences and Social Sciences, 62B*, P45–P52.

Botwinick, J. (1978). *Aging and behavior* (2nd ed.). New York: Springer.

Bouchard, T. J. (1995, August). *Heritability of intelligence*. Paper presented at the meeting of the American Psychological Association, New York.

Bouchard, T. J., Lykken, D. T., McGue, M., Segal, N. L., & Tellegen, A. (1990). Source of human psychological differences. The Minnesota Study of Twins Reared Apart. *Science, 250*, 223–228.

Bower, B. (1985). The left hand of math and verbal talent. *Science News, 127*, 263.

Bowlby, J. (1969). *Attachment and loss* (Vol. 1). London: Hogarth Press.

Bowlby, J. (1989). *Secure and insecure attachment*. New York: Basic Books.

Bowles, T. (1999). Focusing on time orientation to explain adolescent self concept and academic achievement: Part II. Testing a model. *Journal of Applied Health Behaviour, 1*, 1–8.

Boyer, K., & Diamond, A. (1992). Development of memory for temporal order in infants and young children. In A. Diamond (Eds.), *Development and neural bases of higher cognitive function.* New York: New York Academy of Sciences.

Boyle, M. A., & Long, S. (2007). *Personal nutrition* (6th ed.). Belmont, CA: Wadsworth.

Brabeck, M. M. (2000). Kohlberg, Lawrence. In A. Kazdin (Ed.), *Encyclopedia of psychology.* Washington, DC, & New York: American Psychological Association and Oxford University Press.

Bracey, J. R., Bamaca, M. Y., & Umana-Taylor, A. J. (2004). Examining ethnic identity among biracial and monoracial adolescents. *Journal of Youth and Adolescence, 33,* 123–132.

Bracken, M. B., Eskenazi, B., Sachse, K., McSharry, J., Hellenbrand, K., & Leo-Summers, L. (1990). Association of cocaine use with sperm concentration, motility, and morphology. *Fertility and Sterility, 53,* 315–322.

Bradshaw, J., & Klein, W. C. (2007). Health promotion. In J. A. Blackburn & C. N. Dulmas (Eds.), *Handbook of gerontology.* New York: Wiley.

Brainerd, C. J., & Reyna, V. E. (1993). Domains of fuzzy-trace theory. In M. L. Howe & R. Pasnak (Eds.), *Emerging themes in cognitive development.* New York: Springer.

Bransford, J., & others (2006). Learning theories in education. In P. A. Alexander & P. H. Winne (Eds.), *Handbook of educational psychology* (2nd ed.). Mahwah, NJ: Erlbaum.

Bransford, J., Barron, B., Pea, R., Meltzoff, A., Kuhl, P., Bell, P., Stevens, R., Schwartz, D., Vye, N., Reeves, B., Roschelle, J., & Sabelli, N. (2006). Foundations and opportunities for an interdisciplinary science. In R. K. Sawyer (Ed.), *The Cambridge handbook of the learning sciences.* New York: Cambridge University Press.

Bredekamp, S. (1997). NAEYC issues revised position statement on developmentally appropriate practice in early childhood programs. *Young Children, 52,* 34–40.

Brehm, S. S. (2002). *Intimate relationships* (3rd ed.). New York: McGraw-Hill.

Breltner, J. C. (2006). Dementia—epidemiological consideration, nomenclature, and a tacit connseus definition. *Journal of Geriatric Psychiatry and Neurology, 19,* 129–136.

Brenes, G. A., Williamson, J. D., Messier, S. P., Rejeski, W. J., Pahor, M., Ip, E., & Penninx, B. W. (2007). Treatment of minor depression in older adults: A pilot study comparing sertraline and exercise. *Aging and Mental Health, 11,* 61–68.

Brennan, K. A., Clark, C. L., & Shaver. P. R. (1998). Self-report measurement of adult romantic attachment: An integrative overview. In J. A. Simpson & W. S. Rholes (Eds.), *Attachment theory and close relationships* New York: Guilford.

Bretherton, I., Stolberg, U., & Kreye, M. (1981). Engaging strangers in proximal interaction: Infants' social initiative. *Developmental Psychology, 17,* 746–755.

Brewer, J. A. (2007). *Introduction to early childhood education* (6th ed.). Boston: Allyn & Bacon.

Briem, V., Radeborg, K., Salo, I., & Bengtsson, H. (2004). Developmental aspects of children's behavior and safety while cycling. *Journal of Pediatric Psychology, 29,* 369–377.

Briesacher, B. A., Limcangco, M. R., Simoni-Wastilla, L., Doshi, J. A., Levens, S. R., Shea, D. G., & Stuart, B. (2005). The quality of antipsychotic drug prescribing in nursing homes. *Archives of Internal Medicine, 165,* 1280–1285.

Briggs, G. G., & Wan, S. R. (2006). Drug therapy during labor and delivery, part 1. *American Journal of Health-System Pharmacy, 63,* 1038–1047.

Briken, P., Habermann, N., Berner, W., & Hill, A. (2006). XYY chromosome abnormality in sexual homicide perpetrators. *American Journal of Medical Genetics B: Neuropsychiatry and Genetics, 141,* 198–200.

Bril, B. (1999). Dires sur l'enfant selon les cultures, etat des lieux et perspectives. In B. Bril, P. R. Dasen, C. Sabatier, & B. Krewer (Eds.), *Propos sur l'enfant et l'adolescant, Quels enfants pour quelles cultures?* Paris: L'Harmattan.

Brim, O. G. (1999). *The MacArthur Foundation study of midlife development.* Vero Beach, FL: MacArthur Foundation.

Brim, O. G., Ryff, C. D., & Kessler, R. (Eds.). (2004). *How healthy we are: A national study of well-being in midlife.* Chicago: University of Chicago Press.

Brinhall-Peterson, M. (2003). *Older adults are fastest growing Internet audience.* Retrieved November 15, 2003, from www.uwex.edu/news/story.cfm/570.

Briones, T. L. (2006). Environment, physical activity, and neurogenesis: Implications for the treatment of Alzheimer's disease. *Current Alzheimer's Research, 3,* 49–54.

Brock, L. J., & Jennings, G. (2007). Sexuality and intimacy. In J. A. Blackburn & C. N. Dulmas (Eds.), *Handbook of gerontology.* New York: Wiley.

Brockmeyer, S., Treboux, D., & Crowell, J. A. (2005, April). *Parental divorce and adult children's attachment status and marital relationships.* Paper presented at the meeting of the Society for Research in Child Development, Atlanta.

Broderick, R. (2003, July/August). A surgeon's saga. *Minnesota: The magazine of the University of Minnesota Alumni Association,* 26–31.

Brody, N. (2000). Intelligence. In A. Kazdin (Ed.), *Encyclopedia of psychology:* Washington, DC, & New York: American Psychological Association and Oxford University Press.

Brody, N. (2006). Does education influence intelligence? In P. C. Kyllonen, R. D. Roberts, & L. Stankov (Eds.), *Extending intelligence.* Mahwah, NJ: Erlbaum.

Bromage, D. I. (2006). Prenatal diagnosis and selective abortion: A result of the cultural turn? *Medical Humanities, 32,* 38–42.

Bronfenbrenner, U. (1986). Ecology of the family as a context for human development: Research perspectives. *Developmental Psychology, 22,* 723–742.

Bronfenbrenner, U. (2004). *Making human beings human.* Thousand Oaks, CA, Sage.

Bronfenbrenner, U., & Morris, P. (1995). The ecology of developmental processes. In W. Damon (Ed.), *Handbook of child psychology* (5th ed., Vol. 1). New York: Wiley.

Bronfenbrenner, U., & Morris, P. A. (2006) The ecology of human development. In W. Damon & R. Lerner (Eds.), *Handbook of child psychology* (6th ed.) New York: Wiley.

Bronstein, P. (2006). The family environment: Where gender role socialization begins. In J. Worell & C. D. Goodheart (Eds.), *Handbook of girls' and women's psychological health.* New York: Oxford University Press.

Brook, J. S., Brook, D. W., Gordon, A. S., Whiteman, M., & Cohen, P. (1990). The psychological etiology of adolescent drug use: A family interactional approach. *Genetic Psychology Monographs, 116,* (No. 2).

Brooker, R. J., Widmaier, E. P., Graham, L, & Stiling, P. (2008). *Biology.* New York: McGraw-Hill.

Brooks, J. G., & Brooks, M. G. (2001). *The case for constructivist classrooms* (2nd ed.). Upper Saddle River, NJ: Erlbaum.

Brooks, J. S., Ning, Y., Balka, E. B., Brook, D. W., Lubliner, E. H., & Rosenberg, G. (2007). Grandmother and parent influences on self-esteem. *Pediatrics, 119,* e444–e451.

Brooks-Gunn, J. (2003). Do you believe in magic? What we can expect from early childhood programs. Social Policy Report, Society for Research in Child Development, XVII, (No. 1), 1–13.

Brooks-Gunn, J., & Warrens, M. P. (1989). The psychological significance of secondary sexual characteristics in 9- to 11-year-old girls. *Child Development 59,* 161–169.

Brosco, J. P., Mattingly, M., & Sanders, L. M. (2006). Impact of specific medical interventions on reducing the prevalence of mental retardation. *Archives of Pediatric and Adolescent Medicine, 160,* 302–309.

Brower, B. (1985). The left hand of math and verbal talent. *Science News, 127,* 263.

Brown, B. B. (1999). Measuring the peer environment of American adolescents. In S. L. Friedman & T. D. Wachs (Eds.), *Measuring environment across the life span.* Washington, DC: American Psychological Association.

Brown B. B. (2004). Adolescents' relationships with peers. In R. Lerner &

L. Steinberg (Eds.), *Handbook of adolescent Psychology*. New York: Wiley.

Brown, B.B., & Larson, R. W. (2002). The kaleidoscope of adolescence: Experiences of the world's youth at the beginning of the 21st century. In B. B. Brown, R. W. Larson, & T. S. Saraswathi (Eds.), *The world's youth*. New York: Cambridge University Press.

Brown, B. B., & Lohr, M. J. (1987). Peer-group affiliation and adolescent self-esteem: An integration of ego-identity and symbolic-interaction theories. *Journal of Personality and Social Psychology, 52*, 47–55.

Brown, B. V. (Ed.). (2007). *Key indicators of child and youth well-being*. Mahwah, NJ: Erlbaum.

Brown, J. (2005). The compelling nature of romantic love: A psychosocial perspective. *Psychoanalysis, Culture, and Society, 10*, 23–43.

Brown, J. K. (1985). Introduction. In J. K. Brown & V. Kerns (Eds.), *In her prime: A new view of middle-aged women*. South Hadley, MA. Bergin & Garvey.

Brown, L. A., McKenzie, N. C., & Doan, J. B. (2005). Age-dependent differences in the attentional demands of obstacle negotiation. *Journals of Gerontology A: Biological Sciences and Medical Sciences, 60*, 924–927.

Brown, L. S. (1989). New voices, new visions: Toward a lesbian/gay paradigm for psychology. *Psychology of Women Quarterly, 13*, 445–458.

Brown, R. (1958). *Words and things*. Glencoe, IL: Free Press.

Brown, R. (1973). *A first language: The early stages*. Cambridge, MA: Harvard University Press.

Brown, S. L., Nesse, R. M., House, J. S., & Utz, R. L. (2004). Religion and emotional compensation: Results from a prospective study of widowhood. *Personality and Social Psychology Bulletin, 30*, 1165–1174.

Brown, S. L., Nesse, R. M., Vinokur, A. D., & Smith, D. M. (2003). Providing Social Support may be more beneficial than receiving it: Results froma prospective study of mortality. *Psychological Science, 14*, 320–327.

Brownell, K. D., & Cohen, L. R. (1995). Adherence to dietary regimens. *Behavioral Medicine, 20*, 226–242.

Brows, S. L., Lee, G. R., & Bulanda, R. (2006). Cohabitation among elder adults: A national portrait. *Journal of Geneology B: Psychology Science and Social Sciences, 61*, S71–S79.

Bruck, M., & Ceci, S. J. (1999). The suggestibility of children's memory. *Annual Review of Psychology, 50*, 419–439

Bruck, M., Ceci, S. J., & Hembrooke, H. (1998). Reliability and credibility of young children's reports: From research to policy and practice. *American Psychologist, 53 (2)*, 136–151.

Bruck, M., & Melnyk, L. (2004). Individual differences in children's suggestibility: A

review and a synthesis. *Applied Cognitive Psychology, 18*, 947–996.

Brugman, G. M. (2006). Wisdom and aging. In J. E. Birren & K. W. Schaie (Eds.), *Handbook of the psychology of aging* (6th ed.). San Diego: Academic Press.

Bruce, J. M., Olen, K., & Jensen, S. J. (1999, April). *The role of emotion and regulation in social competence*. Paper presented at the meeting of the Society for Research in Child Development, Albuquerque.

Bryant, D. P., Smith, D. D., & Bryant, B. R. (2008). *Teaching students with special needs in inclusive classrooms*. Boston: Allyn & Bacon.

Bryant, J. A. (Ed.) (2007). *The children's television community*. Mahwah, NJ: Erlbaum.

Bryant, J. B. (2005). Language in social contexts: Communicative competence in the preschool years. In J. Berko Gleason (Ed.), *The development of language* (6th ed.). Boston: Allyn & Bacon.

Bugental, D. B., & Grusec, J. E. (2006). Socialization processes. In W. Damon & R. Lerner (Eds.), *Handbook of child psychology* (6th ed.). New York: Wiley.

Buhi, E. R,. & Goodson, P. (2007). Predictors of adolescent sexual behavior and intention: A theory-guided systematic review. *Journal of Adolescent Health, 40*, 4–21.

Buhrmester, D. (1998). Need fulfillment. Interpersonal competence, and the developmental contexts of early adolescent friendship. In W. M. Bukowski & A. F. Newcomb (Eds.), *The company they keep: Friendship in childhood and adolescence*. New York: Cambridge University Press.

Buhrmester, D. (2001, April). *Romantic development: Does age at which romantic involvement start matter?* Paper presented at the meeting of the Society for Research in Child Development, Minneapolis.

Buhrmester, D. (2005, April). *The antecedents of adolescents' competence in close relationships: A six-year-study*. Paper presented at the meeting of the Society for Research in Child Development, Atlanta.

Buhs, E. S., & Ladd, G. W. (2001). Peer rejection as an antecedent of young children's school adjustment: An examination of mediating processes. *Developmental Psychology, 37*, 550–560.

Bukowski, W. M., Brendgen, M., & Vitaro, F. (2007). Peers and socialization: Effects on externalizing and internatlizing problems. In J. E. Grusec & P. D. Hastings (Eds.), *Handbook of socialization*. New York: Guilford.

Bulik, C. M., Berkman, N. D., Brownley, K. A., Sedway, J. A., & Lohr, K. N. (2007, in press). Anorexia nervosa treatment: A systematic review of randomized controlled trials. *International Journal of Eating Disorders*.

Bulik, C. M., Sullivan, P. F., Tozzi, F., Furberg, H., Lichtenstein, P., & Pedersen, N. L. (2006). Prevalence, heritability, and prospective risk factors for anorexia nervosa. *Archives of General Psychiatry, 63*, 305–312.

Buller, D. J. (2005). Evolutionary psychology: The emperor's new paradigm. *Trends in Cognitive Science, 9*, 277–283.

Bumpas, M. R. Crouter, A. C. & McHale, M. (2001). Parental autonomy granting during adolescence: Exploring gender differences in context. *Developmental Psychology, 37*, 163–173.

Bumpass, L., & Aquilino, W. (1994). *A social map of midlife: Family and work over the middle life course*. Center for Demography & Ecology, University of Wisconsin, Madison, WI.

Bunde, M., Suls, J., Martin, R., & Barnett, K. (2007). Online hysterectomy support: Characteristics of website experiences. *Cyberpsychology and Behavior, 10*, 100–107.

Burchinal, M. (2006). Child care subsidies, quality, and preferences among low-income families. In N. Cabera, R. Hutchens, & H. E. Peters (Eds.), *From welfare to childcare*. Mahwah, NJ: Erlbaum.

Burck, J. R., Vena, M., Jolicoeur, M., & Jolicoeur, L. E. (2007). At a threshold: Making decisions when you don't have all the answers. *Physical Medicine and Rehabilitation Clinics of North America, 18*, 1–25.

Bureau of Labor Statistics. U.S. (2005). *People*. Washington, DC: U.S. Department of Labor.

Burgess, E. O. (2004). Sexuality in midlife and later life couples. In J. H. Harvey & A. Wetzel (Eds.), *The handbook of sexuality in close relationships*. Mahwah, NJ: Erlbaum.

Burnett, A. L. (2004). The impact of sildenafil on molecular science and sexual health. *European Urology, 46*, 9–14.

Burrous, E., Crockenberg, S., & Leerkes, E. (2005, April). *Developmental history of care and control, anger and depression: correlates of maternal sensitivity in toddlerhood*, Poster presented at the Biennial Meetings of the Society for Research in Child Development, Atlanta.

Bursuck, W. D., & Damer, M. (2007). *Reading instruction for students who are at risk or have disabilities*. Boston: Allyn & Bacon.

Buss, D. M. (2008). *Evolutionary psychology* (3rd ed.). Boston: Allyn & Bacon.

Buss, D. M. (2004). *Evolutionary psychology* (2nd ed.). Boston: Allyn & Bacon.

Buss, D. M., & Barnes, M. (1986). Preferences in human mate selection. *Journal of Personality and Social Psychology. 50*, 559–570.

Buss, D. M., & others. (1990). International preferences in selecting mates: A study of 37 cultures. *Journal of Cross-Cultural Psychology, 21*, 5–47.

Busse, E. W., & Blazer, D. G. (1996). *The American Psychiatric Press textbook of geriatric psychiatry* (2nd ed.). Washington, DC: American Psychiatric Press.

Bussey, K., & Bandura, A. (1999). Social cognitive theory of gender development and differentiation. *Psychological Review, 106,* 676–713.

Butler, R. N. (1996). Global aging: Challenges and opportunities of the next century. *Ageing International, 21,* 12–32.

Butler, R. N., & Lewis, M. (2002). *The new love and sex after 60.* New York: Ballantine.

Butterworth, G. (2004). Joint visual attention in infancy. In G. Bremner & A. Slater (eds.), *Theories of infant development.* Malden, MA: Blackwell.

Buzwell, S., & Rosenthal, D. (1996). Constructing a sexual self: Adolescents' sexual self-perceptions and sexual risk-taking. *Journal of Research on Adolescence, 6,* 489–513.

Byrnes, J. P. (2005). The development of regulated decision making. In J. E. Jacobs & P. A. Klaczynski (Eds.), *The development of judgment and decision making in children and adolescents.* Mahwah, NJ: Erlbaum.

C

Cabeza, R. (2002). Hemispheric asymmetry reduction in older adults: The HAROLD model. *Psychology and Aging, 17,* 85–100.

Cabeza, R., Nyberg, L., & Park, D. (2005). Cognitive neuroscience of aging: Emergence of a new discipline. In Cabeza, R., Nyberg, L., & Park, D. (Eds.), *Cognitive Neuroscience of aging: Linking cognitive and cerebral aging.* New York: Oxford University Press.

Cacioppo, J. T., Ernst, J. M., Burleson, M. H., McClintock, M. K., Malarkey, W. B., Hawkley, L. C., Kowalewski, R. B., Paulsen, A., Hobson, J. A., Hugdahl, K., Spiegel, D., Berntson, G. G. (2000). Lonely traits and concomitant physiological processes. The McArthur Social Neuro-science studies. *International Journal of Psychophysiology, 35,* 143–154.

Callan, J. E. (2001). Gender development: Psychoanalytic perspectives. In J. Worrel (Ed.). *Encyclopedia of women and gender.* San Diego: Academic Press.

Callaway, L. K., Lust, K., & McIntyre, H. D. (2005). Pregnancy outcomes in women of very advanced maternal age. *Obstetric and Gynecology Survey, 60,* 562–563.

Campanozzi, M. D., Casali, E., Neviani, F., Martini, E., & Neri, M. (2007). Evaluation of the slopes of cognitive impairment and disability in Alzheimer's disease (AD) patients treated with acetylcholinesterase inhibitors (AChEl). *Archives of Gerontology and Geriatrics, 44 (Suppl),* S91–S96.

Campbell, D. A., Lake, M. F., Falk, M., & Backstrand, J. R. (2006). A randomized controlled trial of continuous support by a lay doula. *Journal of Obstetrics and Gynecology: Neonatal Nursing, 35,* 456–464.

Campbell, L., Campbell, B., & Dickinson, D. (2004). *Teaching and learning through multiple intelligence* (3rd ed.). Boston: Allyn & Bacon.

Campbell, S. S., & Murphy P. J. (2007). The nature of spontaneous sleep across audlthood. *Journal of Sleep Research, 16,* 24–32.

Campos, J. J. (2004). Unpublished review of J. W. Santrock's *Life-span development,* 10th ed., New York: McGraw-Hill.

Campos, T. (2005). Unpublished review of J. W. Santrocks. *Life-Span development,* (11th ed.), New York: McGraw-Hill.

Camras, L. A., Oster, H., Campos, J., Campos, R., Ujiie, T., Miyake, K., & others. (1998). Production of emotional facial expressions in European American, Japanese, and Chinese infants. *Developmental Psychology, 34,* 616–628.

Candore, G., & others (2006). Immunogenetics, gender, and longevity. *Annals of the New York Academy of Sciences, 1089,* 516–537.

Canfield, J., & Hansen, M. V. (1995). *A second helping of chicken soup for the soul.* Deerfield Beach, FL: Health Communications.

Canterino, J. C., Ananth, C. V., Smulian, J., Harrigan, J. T., & Vintzileos, A. M. (2004). *Obstetrics and Gynecology Survey, 59,* 649–650. Material age and risk of fetal death in singleton gestation: United States, 1995–2000.

Cappeliez, P., & O'Rourke, N. (2006). Empirical validation of a model of reminiscence and health in later life. *Journals of Gerontology B: Psychological and Social Sciences, 61,* P237-P244.

Carey, S. (1978). The child as word learner. In M. Halle, J. Bresnan, & G. A. Miller (Eds.), *Linguistic theory and psychological reality,* pp. 264–293. Cambridge, MA: MIT Press.

Carlisle, J. F. (2004). Morphological processes that influence learning to read. In C. A. Stone, E. R. Silliman, B. J. Ehren, & K. Apel (Eds.), *Handbook of language and literacy.* New York: Guilford.

Carlo, G. (2006). Care-based and a Ultruistically-based morality. In M. Killen & J. Smetana (Eds.), *Handbook of moral development,* Mahwah, NJ: Erlbaum.

Carnegie Corporation. (1989). *Turning points: Preparing youth for the 21st century.* New York: Author.

Carnegie Corporation. (1996). *Report on education for children 3–10 years of age.* New York: The Carnegie Foundation.

Caron, S. (2007). *Sex matters for college students* (2nd ed.). Upper Saddle River, NJ: Prentice Hall.

Carpendale, J. I., & Chandler, M. J. (1996). On the distinction between false belief understanding and subscribing to an interpretive theory of mind. *Child Development, 67,* 1686–1706.

Carpenter, J., Nagell, K., & Tomasello, M. (1998). Social cognition, joint attention, and communicative competence from 9 to 15 months of age. *Monographs of the Society for Research in Child Development. 70* (1, Serial No. 279).

Carrington, N. A., & Bogetz, J. F. (2004). Normal grief and bereavement. *Journal of Palliative Medicine, 7,* 309–323.

Carroll, J. L. (2007). *Sexuality now* (2nd ed.). Belmont, CA: Wadsworth.

Carroll, J. S., & Doherty, W. J. (2003). Evaluating the effectiveness of premarital prevention programs: A meta-analytic review of outcome research. *Family Relations, 52,* 105–118.

Carskadon, M. A. (2005). Sleep and circadian rhythms in children and adolescents: Relevance for athletic performance of young people. *Clinical Sports Medicine, 24,* 319–328.

Carskadon, M. A. (2006, March). *Too little, too late: Sleep bioregulatory processes across adolescence.* Paper presented at the meeting of the Society for Research on Adolescence, San Francisco.

Carskadon, M. A., Acebo, C., & Jenni, O. G. (2004). Regulation of adolescent sleep: Implications for behavior. *Annals of the New York Academy of Science, 102,* 276–291.

Carskadon, M. A., Mindell, J., & Drake, C. (2006, Septemeber). *Contemporary sleep Patterns in the USA: Results of the 2006 National Sleep Foundation Poll.* Paper presented at the European Sleep Research Society, Innsbruck, Austria.

Carstensen, L. L. (1998). A life-span approach to social motivation. In J. Heckhausen & C. Dweck (Eds.), *Motivation and self-regulation across the life span.* New York: Cambridge University Press.

Carstensen, L. L. (2006) The influence of a sence of time on human development. *Science, 312,* 1913, 1915.

Carstensen, L. L., Mikels, J. A., & Mather, M. (2006). Aging and the intersection of cognition, motivation, and emotion. Doe J. E. Birren, & K. W. Schail (Eds.), *Handbook of the psychology of Aging* (6th ed). An Dieo: Academic Press.

Carter-Saltzman, L. (1980). Biological and sociocultural effects on handedness: Comparison between biological and adoptive families. *Science, 209,* 1263–1265.

Carthenon, M. R., Gulati, M., & Greenland, P. (2005). Prevalence and cardiovascular disease correlates of low cardio respiratory fitness in adolescents and adults. *Journal of the American Medical Association, 294,* 2981–2988.

Carver, K., Joyner, K., & Udry, J. R. (2003). National estimates of romantic relationships. In P. Florsheim (Ed.), *Adolescent romantic relations and sexual behavior.* Mahwah, NJ: Erlbaum.

Case, R. (1999). Conceptual development in the child and the field: A personal view of the Piagetian legacy. In E. K. Skolnick, K. Nelson, S. A. Gelman, & P. H. Miller (Eds.),

Conceptual development. Mahwah, NJ: Erlbaum.

Case, R., & Mueller, M. P. (2001). Differentiation, integration, and covariance mapping as fundamental processes in cognitive and neurological growth. In J. L. McClelland & R. S. Siegler (Eds.), *Mechanisms of cognitive development.* Mahwah, NJ: Erlbaum.

Caspi, A., (1998). Personality development across the life course. In W. Damon (Ed.). *Handbook of child psychology* (Vol. 3). New York: Wiley.

Caspi, A., & Roberts, B. W. (2001). Personality development across the life course: The argument for change and continuity. *Psychological Inquiry, 12,* 49–66.

Caspi, A., & Shiner, R. L. (2006). Personality development. In W. Damon & R. Lerner (Eds.). *Handbook of child psychology* (6th ed.). New York: Wiley.

Castle, N. G. (2001). Innovation in nursing homes. *The Gerontologist, 41 (No. 2),* 161–172.

Castle, N. G., & Engberg, J. (2005). Staff turnover and quality of care in nursing homes. *Medical Care, 43,* 616–626.

Catalano, P. M. (2007). Management of obesity in pregnancy. *Obstetrics and Gynecology, 109,* 419–433.

Cauffman, B. E. (1994, February). *The effects of puberty, dating, and sexual involvement on dieting and disordered eating in young adolescent girls.* Paper presented at the meeting of the Society for Research on Adolescence, San Diego.

Caughey, A. B., Hopkins, L. M., & Norton, M. E. (2006). Chorionic villus sampling compared with amniocentesis and the difference in the rate of pregnancy loss. *Obstetrics and Gynecology, 108,* 612–616.

Cavallero, P., Morino-Addele, F., & Bertocci, B. (2007). The social relations of the elderly. *Archives of Gerontology and Geriatrics, 44,* Suppl. S97–S100.

Ceci, S. J. (2000). Bronfenbrenner, Urie. In A. Kazdin (Ed.). *Encyclopedia of psychology.* Washington, DC. and New York: American Psychological Association and Oxford University Press.

Ceci, S. J., & Gilstrap, L. L. (2000). Determinants of intelligence: Schooling and intelligence. In A. Kazdin (Ed.), *Encyclopedia of Psychology.* Washington, DC, & New York: American Psychological Association and Oxford University Press.

Center for Survey Research at the University of Connecticut. (2000). *Hours on the job.* Storrs: University of Connecticut, Center for Survey Research.

Centers for Disease Control and Prevention (2001). Sexually Transmitted diseases. Attanta: Author.

Centers for Disease Control and Prevention. (2001). *Strategies for stopping smoking.* Atlanta: Author.

Centers for Disease Control and Prevention. (2002). *Adolescent pregnancy.* Atlanta: Author.

Centers for Disease Control and Prevention. (2002). *Cohabitation,* Atlanta, GA: Author.

Centers for Disease Control and Prevention. (2003). Physical activity levels among children aged 9–13—United States, 2002. *Morbidity and Mortality Weekly Report, 52,* 785–788.

Centers for Disease Control and Prevention. (2003). Public health and aging: Health-related quality of life among low-income persons aged 45–64 years—United States. *Morbity and Mortality Weekly Reports, 21,* 1120–1124

Centers for Disease Control and Prevention. (2006). *Health United States 2006.* Atlanta: Author.

Centers for Disease Control and Prevention. (2007). *Body mass index for children and teens.* Atlanta: Author.

Centers for Disease Control and Prevention. (2007). *Death Statistics.* Atlanta: Author.

Chadefaux-Vekemans, B., Rabier, D., Cadoudal, N., Lescoat, A., Chabli, A., Aupetit, J., Dumez, Y., & Oury, J. F. (2006). Prenatal diagnosis of some metabolic diseases using early amniotic fluid samples: Report of a 15 years, experience. *Prenatal Diagnosis, 26,* 814–826.

Chambers, B., Cheung, A. C. K., & Slavin, R. F. (2006). Effective preschool programs for children at risk of school failure: A best-evidence synthesis. In B. Spodek & O. N. Saracho (Eds.), *Handbook of research on the education of young children.* Mahwah, NJ: Erlbaum.

Chandel, N. S., & Budinger, G. R. (2007). The cellular basis for diverse responses to oxygen. *Free Radical Biology and Medicine, 42,* 165–174.

Chang, M. Y., Chen, C. H., & Huang, K. F. (2006). A comparison of massage effects on labor pain using the McGill Pain Questionnaire. *Journal of Nursing Research, 14,* 190–197.

Chao, R., & Tseng, V. (2002). Parenting of Asians. In M. H. Bornstein. *Handbook of parenting* (2nd ed. Vol. 4). Mahwah, NJ: Erlbaum.

Chao, R. (2001). Extending research on the consequences of parenting style for Chinese Americans and European Americans. *Child Development, 72,* 1832–1843.

Chao, R. (2005, April). *The importance of Guan in describing control of immigrant Chinese.* Paper presented at the meeting of the Society for Research in Child Development, Atlanata.

Chao, R. (2007, March). *Research with Asian Americans: Looking back, moving forward.* Paper presented at the meeting of the Society for Research in Child Development, Boston.

Chao, S. Y., Liu, H. Y., Wu, C. Y., Jin, S. F., Chu, T. L., Huang, T. S., & Clark, M. J. (2006). The effects of group reminiscence therapy on depression, self-esteem, and life satisfaction of elderly nursing home residents. *Journal of Nursing Research, 14,* 36–45.

Charles, S. T., & Carstensen, L. L. (2007). Emotion regulation and aging. In J. J. Gross (Ed.), *Handbook of emotion regulation.* New York: Guilford.

Charness, N., & Bosman, E. A. (1992). Human factors and aging. In F. I. M. Craik & T. A. Salthouse (Eds.), *The handbook of aging and cognition.* Hillsdale, NJ: Erlbaum.

Charness, N., Czaja, S., & Sharit, J. (2007). Age and technology for work. In K. A. Schultz & G. A. Adams (Eds.), *Aging and work in the 21st century.* Mahwah, NJ: Erlbuam.

Chattin-McNichols, J. (1992). *The Montessori controversy.* Albany, NY: Delmar.

Chauhuri, J. H., & Williams, P. H. (1999, April). *The contribution of infant temperament and parent emotional availability to toddler attachment.* Paper presented at the meeting of the Society for Research in Child Development. Albuquerque.

Chen, M. Y., Wang, E. K., & Jeng, Y. J. (2006). Adequate sleep among adolescents is positively associated with health status and health-related behaviors. *BMC Public Health, 6,* 59.

Chen, X., Hastings, P.D., Rubin, K. H., Chen, H., Cen, G., & Stewart, S. L. (1998). Child-rearing attitudes and behavioral inhibition in Chinese and Canadian toddlers: A cross-cultural study. *Developmental Psychology, 34,* 677–686.

Chen, X. K., Wen, S. W., Yang, Q., & Walker, M. C. (2007). Adequacy of prenatal care and neonatal mortality in infants born to mothers with and without antenatal high-risk conditions. *Australian and New Zealand Journal of Obstetrics and Gynecology, 47,* 122–127.

Chen, X., Striano, T., & Rakoczy, H. (2004). Auditory-oral matching behaviors in newborns. *Developmental Science, 7,* 42–47.

Cheng, M. H., Lee, S. J., Wang, S. J., Wang, P. H., & Fuh, J. L. (2007, in press). Does menopausal transition affect the quality of life? A longitudinal study of middle-aged women in Kinmen. *Menopause.*

Cherlin, A. J., & Furstenberg, F. F. (1994). Stepfamilies in the United States: A reconsideration. In J. Blake & J. Hagen (Eds.), *Annual review of sociology.* Palo Alto, CA: Annual Reviews.

Chess, S., & Thomas, A. (1977). Temperamental individuality from childhood to adolescence. *Journal of Child Psychiatry, 16,* 218–226.

Chess, S., & Thomas, A. (1987). *Origins and evolution of behavior disorders.* Cambridge, MA: Harvard University Press.

Chevan, A. (1996, August). As cheaply as one: Cohabitation in the older population *Journal of Marriage and the Family, 58*, 656–667.

Chi, M. T. (1978). Knowledge structures and memory development. In R. S. Siegler (Ed.), *Children's thinking: What develops?* Hillsdale, NJ: Erlbaum.

Chia, P., Sellick, K., & Gan, S. (2006). The attitudes and practices of neonatal nurses in the use of kangaroo care. *Australian Journal of Advanced Nursing, 23*, 20–27.

Chifton, R. K., Muir, D. W., Ashmead, D. H., & Clarkson, M. G. (1993). Is visually guided reaching in early infancy a infancy a myth? *Child Development, 64*, 1099–1110.

Child Trends. (2006). *Fast facts et a glance.* Washington, DC: Author.

Child Welfare Information Gateway. (2007). *Child abuse and neglect.* Retrieved April 4, 2007, from www.childwelfare.gov/can/index.cfm

Children's Defense Fund. (2007). *Children's welfare and mental health.* Retrieved January 6, 2007, from www.childrensdefese.org

Chiriboga, D. A. (1982). Adaptation to martial separation in later and earlier life. *Journal of Gerontology, 37*, 109–114.

Chomsky, N. (1957). *Syntactic structures.* The Hague: Mouton.

Christakis, N. A., & Iwashyna, T. J. (2003). The health impact on families of health care: A matched cohort study of hospice use by decedents and mortality outcomes in surviving, widowed spouses. *Social Science and Medicine, 57*(3), 465–475.

Christensen, L. B. (2007). *Experimental methodology* (10th ed.). Boston: Allyn & Bacon.

Christensen, S. L., & Thurlow, M. L. (2004). School dropouts: Prevention, considerations, interventions, and challenges. *Current Directions in Psychological Science, 13*, 36–39.

Christian, P. Jiang, T., Khatry, S. K., LeClerq, S. C., Shrestha, S. R., & West, K. P. (2006). Antenatal supplementation with micronutrients and biochemical indicators of status and subclinical infection in rural Nepal. *American Journal of Clinical Nutrition, 83*, 788–794.

Christie, J. F., Vukellich, C., & Enz, B. J. (2007). *Teaching language and literacy.* Boston: Allyn & Bacon.

Church, D. K., Sleigel, M. A., & Fowler, C. D. (1988). *Growing old in America.* Wylice, TX: Information Aids.

Cichetti, D., & Toth, S. L. (2005). Child maltreatment. *Annual Review of Clinical Psychology, 1.* Palo Alto, CA: Annual Reviews.

Cicchetti, D., & Toth, S. L. (2006). Developmental psychopathology and preventive intervention. In W. Damon & R. Lerner (Eds.), *Handbook of child psychology.* New York: Wiley.

Cicchetti, D., Toth, S. L., & Rogusch, F. A. (2005). *A prevention program for child maltreatment.* Unpublished manuscript, University of Rochester, Rochester, NY.

Cicirelli, V. G. (1991). Sibling relationships in adulthood. *Marriage and Family Review, 16*, 291–310.

Cisneros-Cohernour, E. J., Moreno, R. P., & Cisneros, A. A. (2000). Curriculum reform in Mexico: Kindergarten teacher's challenges and dilemmas. Proceedings of the Lilian Katz Symposium. In D. Rothenberg (Ed.), *Issues in early childhood education: Curriculum reform, teacher education, and dissemination of information.* Urbana-Champaign: University of Illinois.

Clark, E. V. (1993). *The lexicon in acquisition.* New York: Cambridge University Press.

Clarke, E. J., Preston, M., Raksin, J., & Bengtson, V. L. (1999). Types of conflicts and tensions between older adults and adult children. *Gerontologist, 39*, 261–270.

Clarke-Stewart, A. (2006). What have we learned: Proof that families matter, policies for families and children, prospects for future research. In A. Clarke-Stewart & J. Dunn (Eds.), *Families count.* New York: Cambridge University Press.

Clarke-Stewart, A., & Brentano, C. (2006). *Divorce: Causes and consequences.* New Haven, CT: Yale University Press.

Clark-Plaskie, M., & Lachman, M. E. (1999). The sense of control in midlife. In S. L. Willis & J. D. Reid (Eds.), *Life in the middle.* San Diego: Academic Press.

Clausen, J. A. (1993). *American lives.* New York: Free Press.

Clays, E., Leynen, F., De Bacquer, D., Kornitzer, M., Kittle, F., Kraasek, R., De Backer, G. (2007). High job strain and ambulatory blood pressure in middle-aged women from the Belgian Job Stress study. *Journal of Occupational and Environmental Medicine, 49*, 360–367.

Clearfield, M. W., Diedrich, F. J., Smith, L. B., & Thelen, E. (2006). Young infants reach correctly in A-not-B tasks: On the development of stability and perseveration. *Infant Behavior and Development, 29*, 435–444.

Cleveland, J. N., & Lim, A. S. (2007). Employee age and performance in organizations. In K. S. Shultz & G. A. Adams (Eds), *Aging and work in the 21st century.* Mahwah, NJ: Erlbaum.

Clom, K., & Pick, A. D. (2003). Verbal encouragement and joint attention in 18-month-old infants. *Infant Behavior and Development, 26*, 121–131.

Coca-Prados, M., & Escribano, J. (2007, in press). New perspectives in aqueous humor secretion and in glaucoma: The ciliary body as a multifunctional neuroendocrine gland. *Progress in Retinal and Eye Research.*

Cochran, S. D., & Mays, V. M. (1990). Sex, lies, and HIV. *New England Journal of Medicine, 322* (11), 774–775.

Cohen, L. B. (1995). Violent video games: Aggression, arousal, and desensitization in young adolescent boys. Doctoral dissertation, University of Southern California, 1995. *Dissertation Abstracts International, 57*, (2–B), 1463. University Microfilm No. 9616947.

Cohen, L. B., & Cashon, C. H. (2006). Infant cognition. In W. Damon & R. Lerner (Eds.), *Handbook of child psychology* (6th ed.). New York: Wiley.

Cohen, P., Kasen, S., Chen, H., Hartmark, C., & Gordon, K. (2003). Variations in patterns of developmental transitions in the emerging adulthood period. *Developmental Psychology, 39*, 657–669.

Coie, J. (2004). The impact of negative social Experiences on the development of antisocial behavior. In J. B. Kupersmidt & K. A. Dodge (Eds.), *Children's peer relations: from development to intervention.* Washington, DC: American Psychological Association.

Colby, A., Kohlberg, L., Gibbs, J., & Lieberman, M. (1983). A longitudinal study of moral judgment. *Monographs of the Society for Research in Child Development* (Serial No. 201).

Colcombe, S. J., Erickson, K. I., Scalf, P. E., Kim, J. S., Prakash, R., McAuley, E., Elavsky, S., Marquez, D. X., Hu, L., & Kramer, A. F. (2006). Aerobic exercise increases brain volume in aging humans. *Journals of Gerontology: Medical Sciences, 61A*, 1166–1170.

Cole, M. (2006). Culture and cognitive development in phylogenetic, historical, and ontogenetic perspective. In W. Damon & R. Lerner (Eds.), *Handbook of child psychology* (6th ed.). New York: Wiley.

Cole, M., & Gajdamaschko, N. (2007). Vygotsky and culture. In H. Daniels, J. Wertsch, & M. Cole (Eds.), *The Cambridge companion to Vygotsky.* New York: Cambridge University Press.

Cole, P. M., & Tan, P. Z. (2007). Emotion socialization from a cultural perspective. In J. E. Grusec & P. D. Hastings (Eds.), *Handbook of socialization.* New York: Guilford.

Coleman, P. D. (1986, August). *Regulation of dendritic extent: Human aging brain and Alzheimer's disease.* Paper presented at the meeting of the American Psychological Association, Washington, DC.

Coleman, V. H., Erickson, K., Schulkin, J., Zinberg, S., & Sachs, B. P. (2005). Vaginal birth after cesarean delivery: Practice patterns of obstetricians-gynecologists. *Journal of Reproductive Medicine, 50*, 261–266.

Coley, R. (2001). *Differences in the gender gap: Comparisons across racial/ethnic groups in education and work.* Princeton: Educational Testing Service.

Coley, R. L. Li-Grining, & Chase-Lansdale, P. L. (2006). Low-income families' child care experiences. In N. Cabrera, R. Hutchens, H. E. Peters, & L. Peters (Eds.), *From welfare to childcare Mahwah.* NJ: Erlbaum.

Coley, R. L., Morris, J. E., & Hernandez, D. (2004). Out-of-school care and problem behavior trajectories among low-income adolescents: Individual, family, and neighborhood characteristics and added risks. *Child Development, 75*, 948–965.

Collaku, A., Rankinen, T., Rice, T., Leon, A. S. Rao, D. C., Skinner, J. S., Wilmore, J. H., & Bouchard, C. (2004). A genome-wide linkage scan for dietary energy and nutrient intakes. *American Journal of Clinical Nutrition, 79*, 881–886.

Collins, M. (1996, Winter). The job outlook for '96 grads. *Journal of Career Planning*, 51–54.

Collins, R. L., Elliott, M. N., Berry, S. H., Kanocouse, D. E., Kunkel, D., Hunter, S. B., & Miu, A. (2004). Watching sex on television predicts adolescent initiation of sexual behavior. *Pediatrics, 114*, e280–e289.

Collins, W. A., & Steinberg, L. (2006). Adolescent development in interpersonal context. In W. Damon & R. Lerner (Eds.), *Handbook of child psychology* (6th ed). New York: Wiley.

Collins, W. A., & van Dulmen, M. (2006). The significance of middle childhood peer competence for work and relationship in early childhood. In A. C. Huston & M. N. Ripke (Eds.), *Developmental contexts in middle childhood*. New York: Cambridge University Press.

Colombo, J. (2007, March). *The developmental course of attention*. Paper presented at the meeting of the Society for Research in Child Development, Boston.

Comer, J. (1988). Educating poor minority children. *Scientific American, 259*, 42–48.

Comer, J. (2004). *Leave no child behind*. New Haven, CT: Yale University Press.

Comer, J. (2006). Child development: The under-weighted aspect of intelligence. In P. C. Kyllonen, R. D. Roberts, & L. Stankov (Eds.), *Extending intelligence*. Mahwah, NJ: Erlbaum.

Commoner, B. (2002). Unravelling the DNA myth: The spurious foundation of genetic engineering. *Harper's Magazine, 304*, 39–47.

Commons, M. L, & Bresette, L. M. (2006). Illuminating major creative scientific innovators with postformal stages. In C. Hoare (Ed.), *Handbook of adult development and learning*. New York: Oxford University Press.

Comstock, G. & Scharrer, E. (2006). Media and popular culture. In W. Damon & R. Lerner (Eds.), *Handbook of child psychology* (6th ed.). New York: Wiley.

Conduct Problems Prevention Research Group. (2004). The Fast Track experiment: Translating the developmental model into a preventive design. In J. B. Kupersmidt & K. A. Dodge (Eds.), *Children's peer relations: From development to intervention*. Washington, DC: American Psychological Association.

Conger, R. D., & Chao, W. (1996). Adolescent depressed mood. In R. L. Simons (Ed.), *Understanding differences between divorced and intact families: Stress, interaction, and child outcome*. Thousand Oaks, CA: Sage.

Conger, R. D., & Dogan, S. J. (2007). Social class and socialization in families. In J. E. Grusec & P. D. Hastings (Eds.), *Handbook of socialization*. New York: Guilford.

Conner, K. R., Duberstein, P. R., Beckman, A., Helsel, M. J., Hirsch, J. K., Camble, S., & Conwell, N. Y. (2006), Planning of suicide attempts among depressed inpatients aged 50 and over. *Journal of Affective Disorder, 97*, 123–128.

Connors, J. (2007). Casualities of reform. *Phi Delta Kappan, 88*, 518–522.

Conway, K. P., Swendsen, J. D., & Merikangas, K. R. (2003). Alcohol expectancies, alcohol consumption, and problem drinking: The moderating role of family history. *Addictive Behaviors, 28*, 823–836.

Cook, J. A., & Hawkins, D. B. (2006). Hearing loss and hearing aid treatment options. *Mayo Clinic Proceedings, 81*, 234–237.

Coomarasamy, A., Thangaratinam, S., Gee, H., & Khan, K. S. (2006). *European Journal of Obstetrics and Gynecology: Reproductive Biology, 129*, 111–118.

Cooney, T. M. (1994). Young adults' relations with parents: The influence of recent parental divorce. *Journal of Marriage and the Family, 56*, 45–56.

Coontz, S. (2005). *Marriage, history*. New York: Penguin.

Coontz, S. (2007). The origins of modern divorce. *Family Process, 46*, 7–16.

Cooper, C. R. & Grotevat, H. D. (1989, April). *Individuality and connectedness in the family and adolescent's self and relational competence*. Paper presented at the meeting of the Society for Research in Child Development, Kansas City.

Cooper, C. R., Grotevant, H. D., Moore, M. S., & Condon, S. M. (1982, August). *Family support and conflict: Both foster adolescent identity and role taking*. Paper presented at the meeting of the American Psychological Association, Washington, DC.

Corbett, T. (2007). Social indicators as policy tool: Welfare reform as a case study. In B. Brown (Ed.), *Key indicators of child and youth well-being*. Mahwah, NJ: Erlbaum.

Corbin, C. B., Welk, G. J., Corbin, W. R., & Welk, K. A. (2008). *Concepts of fitness and wellness* (7th ed.). New York: McGraw-Hill.

Cornelius, J. R., Clark, D. B., Reynolds, M., Kirisci, L., & Tarter, R. (2006) Early age of first sexual intercourse and affiliation with deviant peers predict development of SUD: A prospective longitudinal study. *Addictive Behavior, 32*, 850–854.

Cornish, K. (2004). The role of cognitive neuroscience in understanding atypical developmental pathways. *Journal of Cognitive Neuroscience, 16*, 4–5.

Corso, J. F. (1977). Auditory perception and communication. In J. E. Birren & K. W. Schaie (Eds.), *Handbook of the psychology of aging* (2nd ed.). New York: Van Nostrand Reinhold.

Costa, P. T., & McCrae, R. R. (1998). Personality assessment. In H. S. Friedman (Ed.), *Encyclopedia of mental health* (Vol. 3). San Diego: Academic Press.

Costa, P. T., & McCrae, R. R. (2000). Contemporary personality psychology. In C. E. Coffey and J. L. Cummings (Eds.), *Textbook of geriatric neuropsychiatry*. Washington, DC: American Psychiatric Press.

Cote, J. E. (2006). Emerging adulthood as an institutionalized moratorium: Risks and benefits to identity formation. In J. J. Arnett & J. L. Tanner (Eds.), *Emerging adults in America*. Washington, DC: American Psychological Association.

Cotten, S. R. (1999). Marital status and mental health revisited: Examining the importance of risk factors and resources. *Family Relations, 48*, 225–233.

Council of Economic Advisers. (2000). *Thomas and their parents in the 21st century. An examination of trends in teen behavior and the role of parent involvement*. Washington; DC: Author.

Courage, M. L., Edison, S. C., & Howe, M. L. (2004). Variability in the early development of visual self-recognition. *Infant Behavior and Development, 27*, 509–532.

Cousineau, T. M., Goldstein, M., & Franco, D. L. (2005). A collaborative approach to nutrition education for college students. *Journal of American College Health, 53*, 79–84.

Cowan, C. P., & Cowan, P. A. (2000). *When partners become parents*. Mahwah, NJ: Erlbaum.

Cowan, P., Cowan, C., Ablow, J., Johnson, V. K., & Measelle, J. (2005) *The family context of parenting in children's adaptation to elementary school*. Mahwah, NJ: Lawrence Erlbaum Associates

Cox, J. (2006). Postnatal depression in fathers. *Lancet, 366*, 982.

Cremation Association of America. (2000). *Fact sheet*. Milwaukee, WI: Author.

Crick, N. R., Ostrov, J. M., & Werner, N. E. (2006). A longitudinal study of relational aggression, physical aggression, and children's social-psychological adjustment. *Journal of Abnormal Child Psychology, 34*, 127–138.

Crockenberg, S. B. (1986). Are temperamental differences in babies associated with predictable differences in caregiving? In J. V. Lerner & R. M. Lerner (eds.), *Temperament and social interaction during infancy and childhood*. San Francisco: Jossey-Bass.

Crockenberg, S. B., Leerkes, E. M., & Lekka, S. K. (2007). Pathways from marital aggression to infant emotion regulation: The development of withdrawal in infancy. *Infant Behavior and development, 30,* 97–113.

Crooks, R. L., & Baur, K. (2008). *Our sexuality* (10th ed.). Belmont, CA: Wadsworth.

Crosby, R. A., & Holtgrave, D. R. (2006). The protective value of social capital against teen pregnancy: A state-level analysis. *Journal of Adolescent Health, 38,* 556–559.

Crossman, A. M., Scullin, M. H., & Melnyk, L. (2004). Individual and developmental differences in suggestibility. *Applied Cognitive Psychology, 18,* 941–945.

Crouter, A. C. (2006). Mothers and fathers at work. In A. Clarke-Stewart & J. Dunn (Eds.), *Families count.* New York: Cambridge University Press.

Crouter, A. C., & McHale, S. (2005). The long arm of the job revisited: Parenting in dual-earner families. In T. Luster & L. Okagaki (Eds.), *Parenting.* Mahwah, NJ: Erlbaum.

Crowley, K., Callahan, M. A., Tenenbaum, H. R., & Allen, E. (2001). Parents explain more to boys than to girls during shared scientific thinking. *Psychological Science, 12,* 258–261.

Csaba, A., Bush, M. C., & Saphier, C. (2006). How painful are amniocentesis and chronic villus sampling? *Prenatal Diagnosis, 26,* 35–38.

Csaja, S. J. (2001). Technological change and the older worker. In J. E. Birren & K. W. Schaie (Eds.), *Handbook of the psychology of aging* (5th ed.). San Diego: Academic Press.

Csikszentmihalyi, M. (1995). *Creativity.* New York: Harper Collins.

Csikszentmihalyi, M. (2000). Creativity: An overview. In A. Kazdin (Ed.), *Encyclopedia of psychology.* Washington, DC, & New York: American Psychological Association and Oxford University Press.

Csikszentmihalyi, M., & Nakamura, J. (2006). Creativity though, the life span from an evolutionary systems perspective. In C. Hoare (Ed.), *Handbook of adult development and learning.* New York: Oxford University Press.

Cuevas, K. D., Silver, D. R., Brooten, D., Youngblut, J. M., & Bobo, C. M. (2005). The cost of prematurity: Hospital charges at birth and frequency of rehospitalization and acute care visits over the first year of life: A comparison of gestational age and birth weight. *American Journal of Nursing, 105,* 56–64.

Cui, X., & Vaillant, G. E. (1996). Antecedents and consequents of negative life events in adulthood: A longitudinal study. *American Journal of Psychiatry, 153,* 123–126.

Cunningham, M. (2004). Old is a three-letter word. *Geriatric Nursing, 25,* 277–280.

Cunningham, W., & Hyson, D. (2006). The skinny on high-protein, low-carbohydrate diets. *Preventive Cardiology, 9,* 166–171.

Curran, K., DuCette, J., Eisenstein, J., & Hyman, I. A. (2001, August). *Statistical analysis of the cross-cultural data: The third year.* Paper presented at the meeting of the American Psychological Association, San Francisco.

Currier, J. M., Holland, J. M., & Neimeyer, R. A. (2006). Sense-making, grief, and the experience of violent loss: Toward a mediational model. *Death Studies, 30,* 403–428.

Cutler, S. J. (2006). Technological change and aging. In R. H. Binstock & I. K. George (Eds.), *Handbook of aging and the social sciences* (6th ed.) San Diego: Academic Press.

D

Dahl, R. E. (2004). Adolescent brain development: A period of vulnerabilities and opportunities. *Annals of the New York Academy of Sciences, 1021,* 1–22.

Dahl, R. E. (2006). Sleeplessness and aggression in youth. *Journal of Adolescent Health, 38,* 641–642.

Dale, P., & Goodman, J. (2004). Commonality and differences in vocabulary growth. In M. Tomasello & D. I. Slobin (Eds.), *Beyond nature-nurture.* Mahwah, NJ: Erlbaum.

Daley, S. E., & Hammen, C. (2002). Depressive symptoms and close relationships during the transition to adulthood: Perspectives from dysphoric women, their best friends, and their romantic partners. *Journal of Consulting and Clinical Psychology, 70,* 129–141.

Dalton, T. C., & Bergenn, V. W. (2007). *Early experience, the brain, and consciousness.* Mahwah, NJ: Erlbaum.

Daly, B. P., Creed, T., Xanthopoulos, M., & Brown, R. T. (2007). Psychosocial treatments for children with attention deficit hyperactivity disorder. *Neuropsychology Review, 17,* 73–89.

Damon, W., & Hart, D. (1992). Self-understanding and its role in social and moral development. In M. H. Bornstein & M. E. Lamb (Eds.), *Developmental psychology: An advanced textbook* (3rd ed.). Hillsdale, NJ: Erlbaum.

Danforth, M. M., & Glass, J. C. (2001). Listen to my words, give meaning to my sorrow: A study in cognitive constructs in middle-aged bereaved windows. *Death Studies, 25,* 513–548.

Daniel, G. W., & Malone, D. C. (2007). Characteristics of older adults who meet the annual prescription drug expenditure threshold for Medicare medication therapy management programs. *Journal of Managed Care Pharmacy, 13,* 142–154.

Daniels, H. (2007). Pedagogy. In H. Daniels, J. Wertsch, & M. Cole (Eds.), *The Cambridge Companion to Vygotsky.* New York: Cambridge University Press.

Daniels, H., Wertsch, J., & Cole, M. (Eds.). (2007). *The Cambridge companion to Vygotsky.* New York: Cambridge University Press.

Daniels, P., Noe, G. F., & Mayberry, R. (2006). Barriers to prenatal care among Black women of low socioeconomic status. *American Journal of Health Behavior, 30,* 188–198.

Daniels, S. R. (2006). The consequences of childhood overweight and obesity. *Future of Children, 16 (No. 1),* 47–67.

Danner, D., Snowdon, D., Friesen, W. (2001). Positive emotions in early life and longevity: Findings from the Nun Study. *Journal of Personality and Social Psychology, 80(5),* 814–813.

Darling-Hammond, L., & Bransford, J. (Eds.). (2005). *Preparing teachers for a changing world.* San Francisco: Jossey-Bass.

Darwin, C. (1859). *On the origin of species.* London: John Murray.

Dasen, P. R. (1977). Are cognitive processes universal? A contribution to cross-cultural Plagetian psychology. In N. Warran (Ed.), *Studies in cross-cultural psychology* (Vol. 1). London: Academic Press.

Datar, A., & Sturm, R. (2004). Childhood overweight and parent- and teacher-reported behavior problems: Evidence from a prospective study of kindergartners. *Archives of Pediatric and Adolescent Medicine, 158,* 804–810.

Dattilio, F. M. (Ed.). (2001). Case studies in couple and family therapy. New York: Guilford.

Daubenmier, J. J., Weidner, G., Sumner, M. D., Mendell, N., Merritt-Worden, T., Studley, J., & Ornish, D. (2007). The contribution of changes in diet, exercise, and stress management to changes in coronary risk in women and men in the multisite cardiac lifestyle intervention program. *Annals of Behavior Medicine, 33,* 57–68.

D'Augelli, A. R. (1991). Gay men in college: Identity processes and adaptations. *Journal of College Student Development, 32,* 140–146.

Davidson, J. (2000). Giftendness. In A. Kazdin (Ed.), *Encyclopedia of psychology.* Washington, DC, & New York: American Psychological Association and Oxford University Press.

Davidson, M. R., London, M. L., & Ladewig, P. A. (2008). *Olds' maternal-newborn nursing and women's health across the lifespan* (8th ed.). Upper Saddle River, NJ: Prentice Hall.

Davidson, R. J., Fox, A., & Kalin, N. H. (2007). Neural basis of emotion regulation in nonhuman primates and humans. *Handbook of emotion regulation.* New York: Guilford.

Davies, J., & Brember, I. (1999). Reading and mathematics attainments and self-esteem in years 2 and 6—an eight-year cross-sectional study. *Educational Studies, 25,* 145–157.

Davies, S. L., DeClemente, R. J. Wingood, G. M., Person, S. D., Dix, E. S., Dix, E. S.,

Harrington, K., Crosby, R. A., & Oh, K. (2006). Predictors of inconsistent contraceptive use among adolescent girls: Findings from a prospective study. *Journal of Adolescent Health, 39,* 43–49.

Davilla, J. S. Steinberg, S. J. (2006). Depression and romantic dysfunction during adolescence. In T. E. Joines, J. S. Brown, & J. Kistner (Eds.). *The interpersonal, cognitive, and social nature of depression.* Mahwah, NJ: Erlbaum.

Davis, A. E., Hyatt, G., & Arrasmith, D. (1998, February). "I Have a Dream" program. *Class One Evaluation Report,* Portland, OR: Northwest Regional Education Laboratory.

Davis, B. E., Moon, R. Y., Saches, M. C., & Ottolini, M. C. (1998). Effects of sleep position on infant motor development. *Pediatrics, 102,* 1135–1140.

Davis, L., & Keyser, J. (1997). *Becoming the parent you want to be: A sourcebook of strategies for the first five years.* New York: Broadway

Davison, G. C., & Neale, J. M. (2007). *Abnormal psychology,* (10th ed.) New York: Wiley.

Davison, K. K., & Birth, L. L. (2001). Weight status, parent reaction, and self-concept in five-year-old girls. *Pediatrics, 107,* 46–53.

Daws, D. (2000). *Through the night.* San Francisco: Free Association Books.

Dawson, D. A., Grant, B. F., & Li, T. K. (2007). Impact of age at first drink on stress-induced drinking. *Alcoholism, Clinical and Experimental Research, 31,* 69–77.

Day, N. L., Goldschmidt, L., & Thomas, C. A. (2006). Prenatal marijuana exposure contributes to the prediction of marijuana use at age 14. *Addition, 101,* 1313–1322.

De Baets, A. J., Bulterys, M., Abrams, E. J., Kankassa, C., & Pazvakavambwa, I. E. (2007). Care and treatment of HIV-infected children in Africa: Issues and challenges at the district hospital level. *Pediatric Infectious Disease Journal, 26,* 163–173.

de Graeff, A., & Dean, M. (2007). Palliative sedation therapy in the last few weeks of life: A literature review and recommendations for standards. *Journal of Palliative Care, 10,* 67–85.

De Litvan, M. A., & Manzano, J. (2005). Intergenerational transmission of psychopathology. *International Journal of Psychoanalysis, 86,* 517–520.

de Luis, D. A., Aller, R., Izaola, O., Gonzales Sagrado, M., Bellioo, D., & Conde, R. (2007). Effects of a low-fat versus a low-carbohydrate diet on adipocytokines in obese adults. *Hormone Research, 67,* 296–300.

de Moraes, Barros, M. C., Guinsburg, R., de Araujo Peres, C., Mitsuhiro, S., Chalem, E., & Laranjeira, R. R. (2006). Exposure to marijuana during pregnancy alters neurobehavior in the early neonatal period. *Journal of Pediatrics, 149,* 781–787.

Deboache, J. S. (2004). Early development of the understanding and use of symbolic artifacts. In U. Goswami (Ed.), *Blackwell Handbook of childhood cognitive development.* Malden, MA: Blackwell.

DeCasper, A. J., & Spence, M. J. (1986). Prenatal maternal speech influences newborn's perception of speech sounds. *Infant Behavior and Development, 9,* 133–150.

Dee, D. L., Ruowei, L, Li-Ching, L., & Grummer-Strawn, L.M. (2007). Associations between breastfeeding practices and young children's language and motor skill development. *Pediatrics, 119 (Suppl.)* S92–S98.

Deeg, D. J. H. (2005). The development of physical and mental health from late midlife to early old age. In S. L. Willis & M. Martin (Eds.), *Middle adulthood.* Thousand Oaks, CA: Sage.

DeGarmo, D. S., & Martinez, C. R. (2006). A culturally informed model of academic well-being for Latino youth: The importance of discriminatory experiences and social support. *Family Relations, 55,* 267–278.

Degutis, L. C., & Greve, M. (2006). Injury prevention. *Emergency Medical Clinics of North America, 24,* 871–888.

Delaunay-El Allam, M., Marlier, L., & Schaal, B. (2006). Learning at the breast: Preference for an artificial scent and its attraction against the odor of maternal milk. *Infant Behavior and Development, 29,* 308–321.

Dempster, F. N. (1981). Memory span: Sources of individual and developmental differences. *Psychological Bulletin, 80,* 63–100.

Denham, S. A. (2006). The emotional basis of learning and development in early childhood education. In B. Spodak & O. N. Saracho (Eds.), *Handbook of research on the education of young children* (2nd ed.). Mahwah, NJ: Erlbaum.

Denham, S. A., Bassett, H. H., & Wyatt, T. (2007). The socialization of emotional competence. In J. E. Grusec & P. D. Hastings (Eds.), *Handbook of Socialization.* New York: Guilford.

Denmark, F. L. Robinowitz, V. C., & Sechzer, J. A. (2005). *Engineering psychology: Women and gender revisited* (2nd ed.) Boston: Allyn & Bacon.

Dennerstein, L., Lehert, P., Koochaki, P. E., Graziottin, A., Leiblum, S., & Alexander, J. L. (2007, in press). A symptomatic approach to understanding women's health expreience: A cross-cultural comparison of women aged 20 to 70 years. *Menopause.*

DePaulo, B. M., & Morris, W. L. (2005). Singles in society and science. *Psychological Inquiry, 16,* 57–83.

Depp, C. A., Glatt, S. J., & Jeste, D. V. (2007). Recent advances in research on successful or healthy aging. *Current Psychiatry Reports, 9,* 7–13.

Derbyshire, E. (2007a). Nutrition in pregnant teenagers: How nurses can help. *British Journal of Nursing, 16,* 144–145.

Derbyshire, E. (2007b). The importance of adequate fluid and fiber intake during pregnancy. *Nursing Standard, 21,* 40–43.

DeRosier, M. E., & Marcus, S. R. (2005). Building friendships and combating bullying: Effectiveness of S. S. Grin at one-year follow-up. *Journal of Clinical Child and Adolescent Psychology, 34,* 140–150.

Deschennes, M. R. (2007, in press). When size really does matter. *Journal of Physiology.*

Deschesnes, M., Fines, P., & Demers, S. (2006). Are tattooing and body piercing indicators of risk-taking behaviors among high school students? *Journal of Adolescence, 29,* 379–393.

Deshpande, N., Metter, E. J., Ling, S., Conwit, R., & Ferruci, L. (2007, in press). Physiological correlates of age-related decline in vibrotactile sensitivity. *Neurobiology of Aging.*

DeSpelder, L. A., & Strickland, A. L. (2005). *The last dance: Encountering death and dying* (7e). NY: McGraw-Hill.

Deutsch, F. M. (1991). Women's lives: The story not told by theories of development. *Contemporary Psychology, 36,* 237–238.

Devos, T. (2006). Implicit bicultural identity among Mexican American and Asian American college students. *Cultural Diversity and Ethnic Minority. Psychology, 12,* 1381–1402.

Diamond, A. D. (1985). Developmental of the ability to use recall to guide action, as indicated by infants' performance on AB. *Child Development, 56,* 868–883.

Diamond, A. D. (2007). Interrelated and interdependent. *Developmental Science, 10,* 152–158.

Diamond, L. (2003). Love matters: Romantic relations among sexual minority youth. In P. Florsheim (Ed.), *Adolescent romantic relations and sexual behavior.* Mahwah, NJ: Erlbaum.

Diamond, L. M. & Lucas, S. (2004). Sexual-minority and heterosexual youths' close relationships: Experiences, expectations, and implications for well-being. *Journal for Research on Adolescence, 14,* 313–340.

Diaz, C. F., Pelletier, C. M., & Provenzo, E. F. (2006). *Touch the future… teach!* Boston: Allyn & Bacon.

Diaz-Rico, L. T. (2008). *A course for teaching English learners.* Boston: Allyn & Bacon.

Dickson, K. L., Fogel, A., & Messinger, D. (1998). The development of emotion from a social process view. In M. F. Mascolo & S. Griffin (Eds.), *What develops in emotional development?* New York: Plenum.

Dindia, K. (2006). Men are from North Dakota, women are from South Dakota. In K. Dindia & D. J. Canary (Eds.), *Sex differences and similarities in communication.* Mahwah, NJ: Erlbaum.

Dittmann - Kohli, F. (2005). Middle age identity in cultural and life span perspective. In S. L. Willis & M. Martin (Eds.), *Middle adulthood,* Thousand Oaks, CA: Sage.

Dixon, L., Browne, K., & Hamilton-Giachritsis, C. (2005). Risk factors of parents abused as children: A mediational analysis of the intergenerational continuity of child maltreatment (Part I). *Journal of Child Psychology and Psychiatry and Allied Disciplines, 46,* 47–57.

Dobrossy, M. D., & Dunnett, S. B. (2005). Optimizing plasticity: Environmental and training associated factors in transplant-mediated brain repair. *Review of Neuroscience, 16,* 1–21.

Dodge, K. A. (1983). Behavioral antecedents of peer social status. *Child Development, 54,* 1386–1399.

Dodge, K. A., Coie, J. D., & Lynam, D. R. (2006). Aggression and antisocial behavior in youth. In W. Damon & R. Lerner (Eds.), *Handbook of child psychology* (6th ed.). New York: Wiley.

Dodge, K. A., & Dishion, T. J. (2006). Deviant peer contagion in interventions and programs: An ecological framework for understanding influence mechanisms. In K. A. Dodge, T. J. Dishion, & J. E. Landsford (Eds.), *Deviant peer influences in programs for youth.* New York: Guilford Press.

Dodge, K. A., & the Conduct Problems Prevention Research Group. (2007, March). *The impact of Fast Track on adolescent conduct disorder.* Paper presented at the meeting of the Society for Research in Child Development, Boston.

Dodge, K. A., Malone, P. S., Lansford, J. E., Miller-Johnson, S., Pettit, G. S., & Bates, J. E. (2006). Toward a dynamic developmental model of the role of parents and peers in early onset substance abuse. In A. Clarke-Stewart & J. Dunn (Eds.), *Families count.* New York: Cambridge University Press.

Doherty, M. (2007). *Theory of mind.* Philadelphia: Psychology Press.

Doherty, T., Chopra, M., Nkonki, L., Jackson, D., & Greiner, T. (2006). Effects of the HIV epidemic on infant feeding in South Africa. "When they see me coming with the tins they laugh at me." *Bulletin of the World Health Organization, 84,* 90–96.

Dohrenwend, B. S., & Dohrenwend, B. P. (1978). Some issues in research on stressful life events. *Journal of Nervous and Mental Disease, 166,* 7–15.

Dohrenwend, B. S., & Shrout, P. E. (1985). "Hassles" in the conceptualization and measurement of life stress variables. *American Psychologist, 40,* 780–785.

Dondi, M., Simion, F., & Caltran, G. (1999). Can newborns discriminate between their own cry and the cry of another newborn infant? *Developmental Psychology, 35(2),* 418–426.

Doorenbos, A. Z., Wilson, S. A., & Coenen, A. (2006). A cross-cultural analysis of dignified dying. *Journal of Nursing Scholarship, 38,* 352–357.

Dorn, L. D., Dahl, R. E., Woodward, H. R., & Biro, F. (2006). Defining the boundaries of early adolescence: A user's guide to assessing pubertal status and pubertal timing in research with adolescents. *Applied Developmental Science, 10,* 30–56.

Dougherty, J., & Long, C. (2006). Seven steps to improving the hospice benefit in dementia. *Caring, 25,* 20–22, 24–26.

Dow, B. J., & Wood, J. (Eds.), (2006) *The Sage handbook of gender and communication.* Thousands Oaks, CA: Sage.

Dowan, M. K. (2006). *Microbiology.* New York: McGraw-Hill.

Dowda, M., Ainsworth, B. E., Addy, C. L., Saunders, R., & Riner, W. (2001). Environmental influences, physical activity, and weight status in 8- to 16-year-olds. *Archives of Pediatric and Adolescent Medicine, 155,* 711–717.

Dowker, A. (2006). What can functional brain imaging studies tell us about typical and atypical cognitive development in children? *Journal of Physiology, Paris, 99,* 333–341.

Driscoll, A., & Nagel, N. G. (2008). *Early childhood education* (4th ed.). Boston: Allyn & Bacon.

Driscoll, J. W. (2006). Postpartum depression: The state of the science. *Journal of Perinatal and Neonatal Nursing, 20,* 40–42.

Driver, J., Tabares, A., Shapiro, A., Nahm, E. Y., & Gottman, J. M. (2003). Interactional patterns in marital success and failure: Gottman laboratory studies. In F. Walsh (Ed.), *Normal family processes* (3rd ed.). New York: Guilford.

Dryfoos, J. G. (1990). Adolescents at risk: *Prevalence or prevention.* New York: Oxford University Press.

Dryfoos, J. G., & Barkin, C. (2006). *Adolescence.* New York: Oxford University Press.

Dubois, J., Dehaene-Lambertz, G., Perrin, M., Mangin, J. F., Cointepas, Y., Ducheesnay, E., Le Bihan, D., & Hertz-Pannier, L. (2007, in press). Asynchrony of the early maturation of white matter bundles in healthy infants: Quantitative landmarks revealed noninvasively by diffusion tensor imaging. *Human Brain Mapping.*

Dubow, E. F., Huesmann, L. R., & Greenwood, D. (2007). Media and youth socialization. In J. E. Grusec & P. D. Hastings (Eds.), *Handbook of socialization.* New York: Guilford.

Duggan, A., Fuddy, L. Burrell, L., Higman, S. M., McFariane E. Windham, A., & Sia, C. (2004). Randomized trial of statewide home visiting program to prevent child abuse: Impact in reducing parental risk factors. *Child Abuse and Neglect, 28,* 623–643.

Dundek, L. H. (2006). Establishment of a Somali doula program at a large metropolitan hospital. *Journal of Perinatal and Neonatal Nursing, 20,* 128–137.

Dunkel Schetter, C., Gurung, R. A. R., Lobel, M., & Wediwa, R. D. (2001), Stress processes in pregnancy and birth. In A. Baum, T. A. Revenson, & J. S. Singer (Eds.), *Handbook of health psychology.* Mahwah, NJ: Erlbaum.

Dunn, J. (1984). Sibling studies and the developmental impact of critical incidents. In P. B. Baltes & O. G. Brim (Eds.), *Life-span development and behavior* (Vol. 6). Orlando, FL: Academic Press.

Dunn, J. (2007). Siblings and socialization. In J. E. Grusec & P. D. Hastings (Eds.), *Handbook of socialization.* New York: Guilford.

Dunn, J., & Kenderick, C. (1992). *Siblings.* Cambridge, MA: Harvard University Press.

Durston, S., & Casey, B. J. (2006). What have we learned about cognitive development from neuroimaging. *Neuropsychologia, 44,* 2149–2157.

Durston, S., Davidson, M. C., Tottenham, N. T., Galvan, A., Spicer, J., Fossella, J. A., & Casey, B. J. (in press). A shift from diffuse to focal cortical activity with development. *Developmental Science.*

Dweck, C. S. (2006). *Mindset.* New York: Random House.

Dwyer, J. W., & Coward, R. T (1991). A multivariate comparison of the involvement of adult sons versus daughters in the care of impaired parents. *Journal of Gerontology: Social Sciences, 46,* S259–S269.

Dyl, J., Kittler, J., Phillips, K. A., & Hunt, J. I. (2006). Body dysmorphic disorder and other clinically significant body image concerns in adolescent psychiatric inpatients: Prevalence and clinical characteristics. *Child Psychiatry and Human Development, 36,* 369–382.

E

Eagly, A. H. (2001). Social role theory of sex differences and similarities. In J. Worrell (Ed.), *Encyclopedia of women and gender.* San Diego: Academic Press.

Eagly, A. H., & Crowley, M. (1986). Gender and helping: A meta-analytic review of the social psychological literature. *Psychological Bulletin, 108,* 233–256.

Eagly, A. H., & Diekman, A. B. (2003). The malleability of sex differences in response to social roles. In L. G. Aspinwell & U. M. Staudinger (Eds.), *A Psychology of human strengths.* Washington, DC: American Psychological Association.

Eagly, A. H., & Steffen, V. J. (1986). Gender and aggressive behavior: A meta-analytic review of the social psychological literature. *Psychological Bulletin, 100,* 309–330.

Eaton, D. K., & others. (2006). Youth risk behavior surveillance—United States, 2005. *MMWR Surveillance Summary, 55*, 1–108.

Ebner, N. C., & Freund, A. M. (2007). Personality theories and successful aging. In J. A. Blackburn & C. N. Dulmus (Eds.), *Handbook of gerontology*. New York: Wiley.

Eccles, J. S. (2007). Families, schools, and developing achievement-related motivations and engagement. In J. E. Grusec & P. D. Hastings (Eds.), *Handbook of socialization*. New York: Guilford.

Eccles, J. S., & Goodman, J. (Eds). (2002). *Community programs to promote youth development*. Washington, DC: National Academy Press.

Echevarria, J., Vogt, M., & Short, D. J. (2008). *Making content comprehensible for English learners* (3rd ed.). Boston: Allyn & Bacon.

Edinburgh, L., Saewye, E., Thao, T., & Levitt, C. (2006). Sexual exploitation of very young Hmong girls. *Journal of Adolescent Health, 39*, 111–118.

Edwards, S. L., & Sarwark, J. F. (2005). Infant and child motor development. *Clinical and Orthopedic Related Research, 434*, 33–39.

Egeland, B., Jacobvitz, D., & Sroufe, L. A. (1988). Breaking the cycle of abuse. *New Directions for Child Development, 11*, 77–92.

Ehey, R. (2005). Language and literacy in two School years. In J. Berko Gleason (Ed.), *The development of language* (6th ed.). Boston: Allen & Bacon.

Eichorn, D. H., Clausen, J. A., Haan, N., Honzik, M. P., & Mussen, P. H. (Eds.). (1981). *Present and past in middle life*. New York: Academic Press.

Eidelman, A. I., & Feldman, R. (2004). Positive effect of human milk on neurobehavioral and cognitive development of premature infants. *Advances in Experimental Medicine and Biology, 554*, 359–364.

Eiferman, R. F. (1971). Social play in childhood. In R. Herron & B. Sutton-Smith (Eds.), *Child's play*. New York: Wiley.

Eilte, D. (2005). The moderating effects of peer substance abuse on the family structure-adolescent substance use association: Quantity versus quality of parenting. *Addictive Behaviors, 30*, 963–980.

Eisenberg, N., Fabes, R. A., Guthrie, I. K., & Reiser, M. (2002). The role of emotionality and regulation in children's social competence and adjustment. In L. Pulkkinen & A. Caspi (Eds.), *Paths to successful development*, New York: Cambridge University Press.

Eisenberg, N., Fabes, R. A., & Spinrad, T. L. (2006). Prosocial development. In W. Damon & R. Lerner (Eds.), *Handbook of child psychology* (6th ed.). New York: Wiley.

Eisenberg, N., Martin, C. L., & Fabes, R. A. (1996). Gender development and gender effects. In D. C. Berliner & R. C. Calfee (Eds.), *Handbook of educational psychology*. New York: Macmillan.

Eisenberg, N., & Morris, A. S. (2004). Moral cognitions and social responding in adolescence. In R. Lerner & L. Steinberg (Eds.), *Handbook of adolescent psychology*. New York: Wiley.

Eisenberg, N., Spinrad, T. L., & Smith, C. L. (2004). Emotion-related regulation: Its conceptualization, relations to social functioning, and socialization. In P. Philippot & R. S. Feldman (Eds.), *The regulation of emotion*. Mahwah, NJ: Erlbaum.

Ekelund, U., Griffin, S. J., & Wareham, N. J. (2007). Physical activity and metabolic risk in individuals with a family history of type 2 diabetes. *Diabetes Care, 30*, 337–342.

Elder, G. A., De Gasperi, R., & Gama Sosa, M. A. (2006). Research update: Neurogenesis in adult brain and neuropsychiatric disorders. *Mt. Sinai Journal of Medicine, 73*, 931–940.

Elder, G. H., & Shanahan, M. J. (2006). The life course and human development. In W. Damon & R. Lerner (Eds.), *Handbook of child psychology* (6th ed.). New York: Wiley.

Eley, T. C., Liang, H., Plomin, R., Sham, P., Sterne, A., Williamson, R., & Purcell, S. (2004). Parental family vulnerability, family environment, and their interactions as predictors of depressive symptoms in adolescents. *Journal of the American Academy of Child and Adolescent Psychiatry, 43*, 298–306.

Elkind, D. (1976). *Child development and education: A Piagetian perspective*. New York: Oxford University Press.

Elliott, V. S. (2004). Methamphetamine use increasing. Retrieved August 15, 2007, www.amaassn.org/amednews/2004/07/26/hlsc0726.htm

Ellis, L., & Ames, M. A. (1987). Neurohormonal functioning and sexual orientation. *Psychological Bulletin, 101*, 233–258.

El-Toukhy, T., Khalaf, Y., & Braude, P. (2006). IVF results: Optimize not maximize. *American Journal of Obstetrics and Gynecology, 194*, 322–331.

Emanuel, L., Bennett, K., & Richardson, V. E. (2007). The dying role. *Journal of Palliative Medicine, 10*, 159–168.

Emde, R. N., Gaensbauer, T. G., & Harmon, R. J. (1976). Emotional expression in infancy: A biobehavioral study. *Psychological Issues: Monograph Series, 10* (37).

Emery, R. E. (1994). *Renegotiating family relationships*. New York: Guilford Press.

Emmers-Sommer, T. M., & Allen, M. (2005). *Safer sex in personal relationships: The role of sexual scripts in HIV infection and prevention*. Mahwah, NJ: Erlbaum.

Eng, P. M., Kawachi, I., Fitzmaurice, G., & Rimm, E. B. (2005). Effects of marital transitions on changes in dietary and other health behaviors in U.S., male health professionals. *Journal of Epidemiology and Community Health, 59*, 56–62.

Engels, R. C., Vermulst, A. A., Dubas, J. S., Bot, S. M., & Gerris, J. (2005). Long-term effects of family functioning and child characteristics on problem drinking in young adulthood. *European Addiction Research, 11*, 32–37.

Ennett, S. T., Bauman, K. E., Hussong, A., Faris, R., Foshee, V. A., & Cai, L. (2006). The peer context of adolescent substance use: Findings from social network analysis. *Journal of Research on Adolescence, 16*, 159–186.

Enzinger, C., Fazekas, F., Matthews, P. M., Ropele, S., Schmidt, H., Smith, S., & Schmidt, R. (2005). Risk factors for progression of brain atrophy in aging: Six-year follow-up of normal subjects. *Neurology, 64*, 1704–1711.

Eogan, M., Daly, L., & O'Herlihy, C. (2006). The effect of regular antenatal perineal massage on postnatal pain and anal sphincter injury: A prospective observational study. *Journal of Maternal-Fetal and Neonatal Medicine, 19*, 225–229.

Epel, E. S., Lin, J., Wilhelm, F. H., Wolkowitz, O. M., Cawthon, R., Adler, N. E., Dolbier, C., Mendes, W. B., & Blackburn, E. H. (2006), Cell aging in relation to stress arousal and cardiovascular disease risk factors. *Psychoneuroimmunology, 31*, 277–287.

Epstein, J. L., & Sheldon, S. B. (2006). Moving forward: Ideas for research on school, family, and community partnerships. In C. F. Conrad & R. Serlin (Eds.), *Sage handbook for research in education*. Thousand Oaks, CA: Sage.

Ercikan, K. (2006). Developments in assessment of student learning. In P. A. Alexander & P. H. Winne (Eds.), *Handbook of educational psychology* (2nd ed.). Mahwah, NJ: Erlbaum.

Erickson, K. I., Colcombe, S. J., Elavsky, S., McAuley, E., Korol, D., Sdalf, P. E., & Kramer, A. F. (2007). Interactive effects of fitness and hormone treatment on brain health in elderly women. *Neurobiology of Aging, 28*, 179–185.

Ericsson, K. A., Charness, N., Feltovich, P. J., & Hoffman, R. R. (Eds.). (2006). *The Cambridge handbook of expertise and expert performance*. New York: Cambridge University Press.

Ericsson, K. A., Krampe, R., & Tesch-Romer, C. (1993). The role of deliberate practice in the acquisition of expert performance. *Psychological Review, 100*, 363–406.

Erikson, E. H. (1950), *Childhood and society*. New York: W.W. Norton.

Erikson, E. H. (1968). *Identity: Youth and crisis*. New York: W. W. Norton.

Eshel, N., Nelson, E. E., Blair, R. J., Pine, D. S., & Ernst, M. (2006). Neural substrates of choice selection in adults and adolescents: Development of the ventrolateral prefrontal and anterior cingulated cortices. *Neuropsychologia. 45,* 1270–1279.

Evans, E., Hawton, K., & Rodham, K. (2005). Suicidal phenomena and abuse in in adolescents: A review of epidemiological studies. *Child Abuse and Neglect, 29,* 45–58.

Evans, G. W., & English, G. W. (2002). The environment of poverty. *Child Development,* 73, 1238–1248

Evert, J., Lawler, E., Bogan, H., & Perls, T. (2003). Morbidity profiles of centenarians: Survivors, delayers, and escapers. *Journal of Gerontology A: Biological Sciences and Medical Sciences, 58,* 232–237.

Evertson, C. M., & Weinstein, C. S. (Eds.), (2006). *Handbook of classroom management.* Mahwah, NJ: Erlbaum.

F

Fagot, B. I., Rodgers, C. S., & Leinbach, M. D. (2000). Theories of gender socialization. In T. Eckes & H. M. Trautner (Eds.), *The developmental social psychology of gender.* Mahwah, NJ: Erlbaum.

Fahey, T. D., Insel, P. M., & Roth, W. T. (2007). *Fit and well brief* (7th ed.). New York: McGraw-Hill.

Falbo, T., & Foston, D. L. (1993). The academic, personality, and physical outcomes of only children in China. *Child Development,* 64, 18–35.

Fallis, W. M., Hamelin, K., Synomds, J., & Wang, X. (2006). Maternal and newborn outcomes related to maternal warming during cesarean delivery. *Journal of Obstetric, Gynecologic, and Neonatal Nursing,* 35, 324–331.

Fanos, J. H., Spangner, K. A., & Musci, T. J. (2006). Attitudes toward prenatal screening and testing for fragile X. *Genetics in Medicine, 8,* 129–133.

Fantz, R. L. (1963). Pattern vision in newborn infants. *Science, 140,* 296–297.

Farrell, M. P., & Rosenberg, S. D. (1981). *Men at mid-life.* Boston: Auburn House.

Fasig, L. (2000). Toddlers' understanding of ownership: Implications for self-concept development. *Social Development, 9,* 370–382.

Fassler, D. (2004, May 8). Commentary in teen brains on trial, *Science News Online,* p. 1.

Favaro, A., Ferrara, S., & Santonastaso, P. (2007). Self-injurious behavior in a community sample of young women: Relationships with childhood abuse and other types of self-damaging behaviors. *Journal of Clinical Psychiatry, 68,* 122–131.

Fear, N. T., Hey, K., Vincent, T., & Murphy, M. (2007). Paternal occupation and neural tube defects: A case-control study based on the Oxford Record Linkage Study register. *Pediatrics and Perinatal Epidemiology, 21,* 163–168.

Feeney, B. C., & Collins, N. L. (2007). Interpersonal safe haven and secure base caregiving processes in adulthood. In W. S. Rholes & J. A. Simpson (Eds.), *Adult attachment.* New York: Guilford.

Feeney, S., Christensen, D., & Moravcik, E. (2006). *Who am I in the lives of children?* (7th ed.). Upper Saddle River, NJ: Prentice Hall.

Fehr, B. (2000). The life cycle of friendships. In C. Hendrick, & S. S. Hendrick (Eds.), *Close relationships.* Thousand Oaks, CA: Sage.

Fein, G. G. (1986). Pretend play. In D. Gorlitz & J. F. Wohlwill (Eds.), *Curiosity, imagination, and play.* Hillsdale, NJ: Erlbaum.

Feinberg, M. E., Button, T. M., Neiderhiser, J. M., Reiss, D., & Hetherington, E. M. (2007). Parenting and antisocial behavior and depression: Evidence of genotype x parenting environment interaction. *Archives of General Psychiatry, 64,* 457–465.

Fekkes, M., Pijpers, F. I., & Verloove-Vanhorick, S. P. (2004). Bullying behavior and associations with psychosomatic complaints and depression in victims. *Journal of Pediatrics, 144,* 17–22.

Feldman, D. C. (2007). Career mobility and career stability among order workers. In K. S. Shultz & G. A. Adams (Eds.), *Aging and work in the 21st century.* Mahwah, NJ: Erlbaum.

Feldman, H. D. (2001, April). *Contemporary developmental theories and the concept of talent.* Paper presented at the meeting of the Society for Research in Child Development, Minneapolis.

Feldman, S. S., & Elliott, G. R. (1990). Progress and promise of research on normal adolescent development. In S. S. Feldman & G. Elliott (Eds.), *At the threshold: The developing adolescent.* Cambridge, MA: Harvard University Press.

Feldman, S. S., Turner, R., & Aruajo, K. (1999). Interpersonal context as an influence on sexual timetables of youths: Gender and ethnic effects. *Journal of Research on Adolescence, 9,* 25–52.

Feldon, J. M. (2003). Grief as a transformative experience: Weaving through different lifeworlds after a loved one has committed suicide. *International Journal of Mental Health Nursing, 12,* 74–85.

Fenix, J. B., Cherlin, E. J., Priegerson, H. G., Johnson-Hurzeler, R., Kasl, S. V., & Bradley, E. H. (2006). Religiousness and major depression among bereaved family caregivers: A 13-month follow-up study. *Journal of Palliative Care, 22,* 286–292.

Fenstermacher, S. K., & Saudino, K. J. (2006). Understanding individual differences in children's imitative behavior. *Developmental Review, 26,* 346–364.

Ferguson, D. M., Harwood, L. J., & Shannon, F. T. (1987). Breastfeeding and subsequent social adjustment in 6- to 8-year-old children. *Journal of Child Psychology and Psychiatry, 28,* 378–386.

Fernandes, O., Sabharwal, M., Smiley, T., Pastuszak, A., Koren, G., & Einarson, T. (1998). Moderate to heavy caffeine consumption during pregnancy and relationship to spontaneous abortion and abnormal fetal growth: A meta-analysis. *Reproductive Toxicology, 12,* 435–444.

Ferrare, C. M., Goldberg, A. P., Ortmeyer, H. K., & Ryan, A. S. (2006). Effects of aerobic and resistive exercise training on glucose disposal and skeletal muscle metabolism in older men. *Journals of Gerontology A: Biological Sciences and Medical Sciences, 61,* 480–487.

Ferraro, K. F. (2006). Health and aging. In R. H. Binstock & L. K. George (Eds.), *Handbook of aging and the social sciences* (6th ed.). San Diego: Academic Press.

Ferrini, A. F., & Ferrini, R. (2008). *Health in the later years* (4th ed.). New York: McGraw-Hill.

Ferris, F. D., & Librach, S. L. (2005). Models, standards, guidelines. *Clinical Geriatric Medicine, 21,* 17–44.

Field, A. E., Cambargo, C. A., Taylor, C. B., Berkey, C. S., Roberts, S. B., & Colditz, G. A. (2001). Peer, parent, and media influences on the development of weight concerns and frequent dieting among preadolescent and adolescent girls and boys. *Pediatrics, 107,* 54–60.

Field, D. (1999). A cross-cultural perspective on continuity and change in social relations in old age: Introduction to a special issue. *International Journal of Aging and Human Development, 48,* 257–262.

Field, T. M. (2001). Massage therapy facilitates weight gain in preterm infants. *Current Directions in Psychological Science, 10,* 51–55.

Field, T. M. (2007). *The amazing infant.* Malden, MA: Blackwell.

Field, T. M., Grizzle, N., Scafidi, F., & Schanberg, S. (1996). Massage and relaxation therapies' effects on depressed adolescent mothers. *Adolescence, 31,* 903–911.

Field, T. M., Hernandez-Reif, M., Feije, L., & Freedman, J. (2006). Prenatal, perinatal, and neonatal stimulation, *Infant Behavior & Development, 29,* 24–31.

Field, T. M., Hernandez-Reif, M., Freedman, J. (2004, Fall). Stimulation programs for preterm infants. *SRCD Social Policy Reports, XVIII* (No. 1), 1–20.

Field, T. M., Schanberg, S. M., Scafidi, F., Bauer, C. R., Vega-Lahr, N., Garcia, R., Nystrom, J., & Kuhn, C. M. (1986). Tactile/kinesthetic stimulation effects on preterm neonates. *Pediatrics, 77,* 654–658.

Fields, M. V., Groth, L., & Spangler, K. (2008). *Let's begin reading right* (6th ed.). Upper Saddle River, NJ: Prentice Hall.

Finch, C. E., & Seeman, T. E. (1999). Stress theories of aging. In V. L. Bengston, & K. W. Schaie (Eds.). *Handbook of theories of aging.* New York: Springer.

Fine, M. A., & Harvey, J. H. (2006). Divorce and relationship dissolution in the United States. In M. A. Fine & J. H. Harvey (Eds.), *Handbook of diverce and relationship dissolution*. Mahwah, NJ: Erlbaum.

Fine, M. A., Ganong, L. H., & Demo, D. H. (2006). Divorce as a family stressor. In P. C. McKenry & S. J. Price (Eds.). *Families and change* (3rd ed.). Thousand Oaks, CA: Sage.

Fingerman, K. L., & Lang, F. R. (2004). Coming together: A perspective on relationships across the life span. In F. R. Lang & K. L. Fingerman (Eds.), *Growing together*. New York: Cambridge University Press.

Finkelstein, L. M., & Farrell, S. K. (2007). An expanded view of age bias in the workplace. In K. S. Shultz & G. A. Adams (Eds.), *Aging and work in the 21st century*. Mahwah, NJ: Erlbaum.

Finn, C. T., & Smoller, J. W. (2006). Genetic counseling in psychiatry. *Harvard Review of Psychiatry, 14*, 109–121.

Finn, Stevenson, M. (2006). What the school of The 21st. Century can teach us about universal preschool. In E. Eigler, W. S. Gilliam, & S. M. Jones (Eds.), *A vision for universal preschool education*. New York: Cambridge University Press.

Fiori, K. L., Antonucci, T. C., & Cortina, K. S. (2006). Social network typologies and mental health among older adults. *Journals of Gerontology B: Psychological Sciences and Social Sciences, 61*, P25–P32.

Fischer, K. W., & Pruyne, E. (2003). Reflective thinking in adulthood: Emergence, development, and variation. In J. Demick & C. Andreoletti (Eds.), *Handbook of adult development*. New York: Kluwer.

Fish, M. (2004). Attachment in infancy and preschool in low socioeconomic status rural Appalachian children: Stability and change and relations to preschool and kindergarten competence. *Developmental Psychopathology, 16*, 293–312.

Fisher, H. E. (2006). Broken hearts: The nature and risks of romantic rejection. In A. C. Crouter & A. Booth (Eds.), *Romance and sex in adolescence and emerging adulthood*. Mahwah, NJ: Erlbaum.

Fisher, S. E., & Marcus, G. F. (2006). The eloquent ape: Genes, brains, and the evolution of language. *Nature Reviews: Genetics, 7*, 9–20.

Fitzgerald, E. F., Hwang, S. A., Lannguth, K., Cayo, M., Yang, B. Z., Bush, S., Worswick, P., & Lauzon, T. (2004). Fish consumption and other environmental exposures and their associations with serum PCB concentrations among Mohawk women at Akwesasne. *Environmental Research, 94*, 160–170.

Fitzgibbon, M. L., Stolley, M. R., Dyer, A. R., VanHorn, L., & Kaufer Chistroffel, K. (2002). A community-based obesity prevention program for minority children:

Rationale and study design for Hip-Hop to Health Jr. *Preventive Medicine, 34*, 289–297.

Fitzgibbon, M. L., Stolley, M. R., Schiffer, L., Van Horn, L., Kaufer Cristoffel, L., & Dyer, A. (2005). Two-year follow-up results for Hip-Hop to Health Jr: A randomized controlled trial for overweight prevention in preschool minority children. *Journal of Pediatrics, 146*, 618–625.

Flannery, D. J., Hussey, D., Biebelhausen, L., & Wester, K. (2003). Crime, delinquency, and youth gangs. In G. Adams & M. Berzonsky (Eds.), *Blackwell handbook of adolescence*. Malden, MA: Blackwell.

Flavell, J. H. (2004). Theory-of-mind development: Retrospect and prospect. *Merrill-Palmer Quarterly, 50*, 274–290.

Flavell, J. H., Friedrichs, A., & Hoyt, J. (1970). Developmental changes in memorization processes. *Cognitive Psychology, 1*, 324–340.

Flavell, J. H., Green, F. L., & Flavell, E. R. (1995). Young children's knowledge about thinking. *Monographs of the Society for Research in Child Development, 60* (1, Serial No. 243).

Flavell, J. H., Green, F. L. & Flavell, E. R. (2000). Development of children's awareness of their own thoughts. *Journal of Cognition and Development, 1*, 97–112.

Flavell, J. H., Miller, P. H., & Miller, S. A. (2002). *Cognitive development* (4th ed.), Upper Saddle River, NJ: Prentice Hall.

Flegal, K. M., Ogden, C. L., & Carroll, M. D. (2004). Prevalence and trends in Mexican-American adults and children. *Nutrition Review, 62*, S144–S148.

Fletcher, A. C., Steinberg, L., & Williams-Wheeler, M. (2004). Parental influences on adolescent problem behavior: Revisiting Stattin and Kerr. *Child Development, 75*, 781–796.

Fletcher, J. M., Lyon, G. R., Fuchs, L. S., & Barnes, M. A. (2007). *Learning disabilities*. New York: Guiford.

Florsheim, P., Moore, D., & Edgington, C. (2003). Romantic relationships among pregant and parenting adolescents. In P. Florsheim (Ed.), *Adolescent romantic relations and sexual behavior*. Mahwah, NJ: Erlbaum.

Florsheim, P., Sumida, E., McCann, C., Winstanley, M., Fukui, R., Seefedlt, T., & Moore, D. (2003). The transition to parenthood among young African American and Latino couples: Relational predictors of risk for parental dysfunction. *Journal of Family Psychology, 17*, 65–79.

Flynn, J. R. (1999). Searching for justice: The discovery of IQ gains over time. *American Psychologist, 54*, 5–20.

Flynn, J. R. (2006). The history of the American mind in the 20th century: A scenario to explain gains over time and a case for the irrelevance of g. In P. C. Kyllonen, R. D. Roberts, & L. Stankov

(Eds.), *Extending intelligence*. Mahwah, NJ: Erlbaum.

Fodor, I. G., & Franks, V. (1990). Women in midlife and beyond. The new prime of life? *Psychology of Women Quarterly, 14*, 445–449.

Follari, L. (2007). *Foundations and best practices in early childhood education*. Upper Saddle River, NJ: Prentice Hall.

Ford, D., & Tower, J. (2006). Genetic manipulation of life span in *Drosophilia melanogaster*. In E. J. Masor & S. N. Austad (Eds.), *Handbook of the biology of aging*. San Diego: Academic Press.

Forrester, M. B. (2007). Oxycodone abuse in Texas, 1998–2004. *Journal of Toxicology and Environmental Health A, 70*, 534–538.

Forrester, M. B., & Merz, R. D. (2007). Risk of selected birth defects with prenatal illicit drug use, Hawaii, 1986–2002. *Journal of Toxicology and Environmental Health A, 70*, 7–18.

Fowler, G. (1999). *As we grow old: How adult children and their parents can face aging with candor and grace*. Valley Forge, PA: Judson Press.

Fox M. K., Pac, S., Devaney, B, & Jankowski, L. (2004). Feeding infants and toddlers study: What foods are infants and toddlers eating? *American Dietetic Association Journal (Suppl), 104*, S22–S30.

Fozard, J. L., & Gordon-Salant, S. (2001). Changes in vision and hearing with aging. In J. E. Birren & K. W. Schaie (Eds.), *Handbook of the psychology of aging* (5th ed.). San Diego: Academic Press.

Fraga, C. G., Motchnik, P. A., Shigenaga, M. K., Helbock, H. J., Jacob, R. A., & Ames, B. N. (1991). Ascorbic acid protects against endogenous oxidative DNA damage in human sperm. *Proceedings of the National Academy of Sciences of the United States, 88*, 11003–11006.

Fraiberg, S. (1959). *The magic years*. New York: Scribner's.

Franc, C. E. (1996). The implications of preschool tempo and motoric activity level for personality decades later. Reported in A. Caspi, Personality development across the life course in W. Damon (Ed.), *Handbook of child psychology* (Vol. 3) New York: Wiley

Frankl, V. (1984). *Man's search for meaning*. New York: Basic Books.

Franks, A., Kelder, S. H., Dino, G. A., Horn, K. A., Gortmaker, S. L., Wiecha, J. L., & Simoes, E. J. (2007). School-based programs: Lessons learned from CATCH, Planet Health, and Not-On-Tobacco. *Preventing Chronic Disease, 4*, A33.

Franks, A., Kelder, S. H., Dino, G. A., Horn, K. A., Gortmaker, S. L., Wiecha, J. L., & Simoes, E. J. (2007). School-based programs: Lessons learned from CATCH, Planet Health, and Not-On-Tobacco. *Preventing Chronic Disease, 4*, A33.

Fraser, S. (Ed.). (1995). *The bell curve wars: Race, intelligence, and the future of America*, New York: Basic Books.

Fraunfelder, F. W., & Fraunfelder, F. T. (2007). Scientific challenges in postmarketing surveillance of ocular adverse drug reactions. *American Journal of Ophthalmology, 143*, 145–149.

Frederikse, M., Lu, A., Aylward, E., Barta, P., Sharma, T., & Perlsons, G. (2000). Sex differences in inferior lobule volume in schizophrenia. *American Journal of Psychiatry, 157*, 422–427.

Freedman, D. S., Mei, Z., Srinivasan, S. R., Berenson, G. S., & Dietz, W. H. (2007). Cardiovascular risk factors and excess adiposity among overweight children and adolescents in the Bogalusa Heart Study. *Journal of Pediatrics, 150*, 12–17.

Freeman, S., & Herron, J. C. (2007). *Evolutionary analysis* (4th ed.). Upper Saddle River, NJ: Prentice-Hall.

Freisthler, B., Merritt, D. H., & LaSacal, E. A. (2006). Understanding the ecology of child maltreatment: for future research. *Child Maltreatment, 11*(3), 263–280.

Freud, S. (1917). *A general introduction to psychoanalysis*. New York: Washington Square Press.

Freund, A. M. (2006). Age-differential motivational consequences of optimization versus compensation focus in younger and older adults. *Psychology and Aging, 21*, 240–252.

Friend, M. (2008). *Special education* (2nd ed.). Boston: Allyn & Bacon.

Frisina, R. D., & Walton, J. P. (2006). Age-related structural and functional changes in the cochlear nucleus. *Hearing Research, 217*, 216–223.

Frost, J. L., Wortham, S. C., Reifel, S., & Contributor, J. Q. (2008). *Play and development* (3rd ed.). Upper Saddle River, NJ: Prentice Hall.

Fry, P. S. (2001). The unique contribution of key existential factors to the prediction of psychological well-being of older adults following spousal loss. *The Gerontologist, 41*, 69–81.

Fujikado, T., Kuroa, T., Maeda, N., Ninomiya, S., Goto, H., Tano, Y., Oshika, T., Hiroshara, Y., & Mihashi, T. (2004). Light scattering and optical aberrations as objective parameters to predict visual deterioration in eyes with cataracts. *Journal of Cataract and Refractive Surgery, 30*, 1198–1208.

Fuligni, A. J., & Fuligni, A. S. (2007). Immigrant families and the educational development of their children. In J. E. Lansford, K. Deater-Deckard, & M. H. Bornstein (Eds.), *Immigrant families in contemporary society*. New York: Guilford.

Fulgini, A. J., & Hardway, C. (2004). Preparing diverse adolescents for the transition to adulthood. *Future of Children, 14*, 99–119.

Fuligni, A. J. & Hardway, C. (2006). Daily variation in adolescents' sleep, activities, and psychological well-being. *Journal of Research on Adolescence, 16*, 353–378.

Fulkerson, J. A., Strauss, J., Neurmark-Sztainer, D., Story, M., & Boutelle, K. (2007). Correlates of psychosocial well-being among overweight adolescents: The role of the family. *Journal of Consulting and Clinical Psychology, 75*, 181–186.

Furman, E. (2005). *Boomerang nation*. New York: Fireside.

Furman, W. C. (2007, March). *The conceptualization of attachment in adolescents' relationships*. Paper presented at the meeting of the Society for Research in Child Development, Boston.

Furman, W., Ho, M., & Low, S. (2005, April). *Adolescent dating experiences and adjustment*. Paper presented at the meeting of the Society for Research in Child Development, Atlanta.

Furth, H. G., & Wachs, H. (1975). *Thinking goes to school*. New York: Oxford University Press.

G

Gable, S., Chang, Y., & Krull, J. L. (2007). Television watching and frequency of family meals are predictive of overweight onset and persistence in a national sample of preschool children. *Journal of the American Dietetic Association, 107*, 53–61.

Galambos, N. L. (2004). Gender and gender role development in adolescence. In R. Lerner & L. Steinberg (Eds.), *Handbook of Adolescence*. New York: Wiley.

Galambos, N. L., & Meggs, J. I. (1989, April). *The afterschool ecology of young adolescents and self-reported behavior*. Paper presented at the biennial meeting of the Society for Research in Child Development, Kansas City.

Galinsky, E., & David, J. (1988). *The preschool years: Family strategies that work—from experts and parents*. New York: Times Books.

Gallo, L. C., Troxel, W. M., Matthews, K. A., & Kuller, L. W. (2003). Marital status and quality in middle-aged women: Associations with levels and trajectories of cardiovascular risk factors. *Health Psychology, 22*, 453–463.

Gallo, W. T., Bradley, E. H., Dubin, J. A., Jones, R. N., Falba, T. A., Teng, H. M., & Kasl, S. V. (2006). The persistence of depressive symptoms in older workers who experience involuntary job loss: Results from the health and retirement survey. *Journals of Gerontology B: Psychological Sciences and Social Sciences, 61*, S221–S228.

Galloway, J. C., & Thelen, E. (2004). Feet first: Object exploration in young infants. *Infant Behavior & Development, 27*, 107–112.

Gallup, G. H. (1987). *The Gallup poll: Public opinion 1986*. Wilmington, DE: Scholarly Resources.

Gamino, L. A., & Sewell, K. W. (2004). Meaning constructs as predictors of bereavement adjustment: A report from the Scott & White grief study. *Death Studies, 28*, 397–421.

Gannon, L. (1998). Menopause. In H. S. Friedman (Ed.), *Encyclopedia of mental health* (Vol. 2). San Diego: Academic Press.

Ganong, L., & Coleman, M. (2006). Obligations to stepparents acquired in later life: Relationship quality and acuity of needs. *Journals of Gerontology B: Psychological Sciences and Social Sciences, 61*, S80–S88.

Ganong, L., Coleman, M., & Hans, J. (2006). Divorce as prelude to stepfamily living and the consequences of re-divorce. In M. A. Fine & J. H. Harvey (Eds.), *Handbook of divorce and relationship dissolution*. Mahwah, NJ: Erlbaum.

Garcia Coll, C. & Pachter, L. M. (2002). Ethnic and minority parenting. In. M. H. Bornstein (Ed.), *Handbook of parenting* (2nd ed., vol. 4). Mahwah, NJ: Erlbaum.

Gardner, H. (1983). *Frames of mind*. New York: Basic Books.

Gardner, H. (1993). *Multiple intelligences*. New York: Basic Books.

Gardner, H. (2002). The pursuit of excellence through education. In M. Ferrari (Ed.), *Learning from extraordinary minds*. Mahwah, NJ: Erlbaum.

Garity, J. (2006). Caring for a family member with Alzheimer's disease: Coping with caregiver burden post-nursing home placement. *Journal of Gerontological Nursing, 32*, 39–48.

Garofalo, R., Wolf, R. C., Wissow, L. S., Woods, E. R., & Goodman, E. (1999). Sexual orientation and risk of suicide attempts among a representative sample of youth. *Archives of Pediatrics and Adolescent Medicine, 153*, 487–493.

Gartner, J., Larson, D. B., & Allen, G. D. (1991). Religious commitment and mental health: A review of the empirical literature. *Journal of Psychology and Theology, 19*, 6–25.

Gate, M. (2006). Mental health and adjustment. In J. E. Birren, & K. W. Schaie (eds.), *Handbook of the psychology of aging* (6th ed.). San Diego: Academic Press.

Gathercole, V. C. M., & Hoff, E. (2007). Input and the acquisition of language: Three questions. In E. Hoff & M. Shatz (Eds.), *Blackwell handbook of language development*. Malden, MA: Blackwell.

Gatz, M., Reynolds, C. A., Fratiglioni, L, Johansson, B., Mortimer, J. A., Berg, S., Fiske, A., & Pedersen, N. L. (2006). Role of genes and environments for explaining Alzheimer's disease. *Archives of General Psychiatry 63*, 168–174.

Gatza, C., Hinkal, G., Moore, L., Dumble, M., & Donehower, L. A. (2006). p53 and mouse aging models. In E. J. Masoro & S. N.

Austad (Eds.), *Handbook of the biology of aging* (6th ed.). San Diego: Academic Press.

Gaudernack, L. C., Forbord, S., & Hole, E. (2006). Acupuncture administered after spontaneous rupture of membranes at term significantly reduces the length of birth and use of oxytocin. *Acta Obstetricia et Gynecologica Scandinavica, 85,* 1348–1353.

Gauvain, M., & Perez, S. M. (2007). The socialization of cognition. In J. E. Grusec & P. D. Hastings (Eds.), *Handbook of socialization.* New York: Guilford.

Gavrilova, L. A., & Gavrilova, N. S. (2006). Reliability theory of aging and longevity. In. E. J. Masoro & S. N. Austad (Eds.). *Handbook of the biology of aging* (6th ed.). San Diego: Academic Press.

Gazzaley, A., Cooney, J. W., Rissman, J., & D'Esposito, M. (2005). *Nature Neuroscience, 8,* 1298–1300.

Gellers, R. J., & Cavanaugh, M. M. (2005). Violence, abuse, and neglect in families and intimate relationships. In P. C. McKenry & S. J. Price (Eds.). *Families and change* (3rd ed.). Thousand Oaks, CA: Sage.

Gelman, R. (1969). Conservation acquisition: A problem of learning to attend to relevant attributes. *Journal of Experimental Child Psychology, 7,* 67–87.

Gelman, R. A., & Opfer, J. E. (2004). Development of the animate-inanimate distinction. In U. Goswami (Ed.), *Blackwell handbook of childhood cognitive development.* Malden, MA: Blackwell.

Gelman, S. A., Heyman, G. D., & Legare, C. H. (2007, in press). Developmental changes in the coherence of essentialist beliefs about psychological characteristics. *Child Development.*

Gelman, S. A., & Kalish, C. W. (2006). Conceptual development. In W. Damon & R. Lerner (Eds.), *Handbook of child psychology* (6th ed.). New York: Wiley.

Gennetian, L. A., & Miller, C. (2002). Children and welfare reform: A view from an experimental welfare reform program in Minnesota. *Child Development, 71,* 601–620.

Gentzler, A. L., & Kerns, K. A. (2004). Associations between insecure attachment and sexual experiences. *Personal Relationships, 11.* 249–266.

George, L. K. (2006). Perceived quality of life. In R. H. Binstock & L. K. George (Eds.), *Handbook of aging and the social sciences* (6th ed.). San Diego: Academic Press.

Gerard, J. M., Landry-Meyer, L., & Roe, J. G. (2006). Grandparents raising grandchildren: The role of social support in coping with caregiving challenges. *International Journal of Aging and Human Development, 62,* 359–383.

Gershoff, E. T. (2002). Corporal punishment by parents and associated child behaviors and experiences: A meta-analysis and

theoretical review. *Psychological Bulletin, 128,* 539–579.

Gessert, C. E., Eliott, B. A., & Haller, I. V. (2003). Mortality patterns in middle and old age. *Journals of Gerontology A: Biological and Medical Science, 58,* B967.

Ghetti, S., & Alexander, K. W. (2004). "If it happened, I would remember it": Strategic use of event memorability in the rejection of false autobiographical events. *Child Development, 75,* 542–561.

Giacomoni, P. U., & Rein, G. (2004). A mechanistic model for the aging of human skin. *Micron, 35,* 179–184.

Giammattei, J., Blix, G., Marshak, H. H., Wollitzer, A. O., & Pettitt, D. J. (2003). Television watching and soft drink consumption: Associations with obesity in 11- to 13-year-old schoolchildren. *Archives of Pediatric and Adolescent Medicine, 157,* 882–886.

Gibbons, J., & Ng, S. H. (2004). Acting bilingual and thinking bilingual. *Journal of Language & Social Psychology, 23,* 4–6.

Gibson, E. J. (1969). *Principles of perceptual learning and development.* New York: Appleton-Century-Crofts.

Gibson, E. J. (1989). Exploratory behavior in the development of perceiving, acting, and the acquiring of knowledge. *Annual Review of Psychology, Vol. 39,* Palo Alto, CA: Annual Reviews.

Gibson, E. J. (2001). *Perceiving the affordances.* Mahwah, NJ: Erlbaum.

Gibson, E. J., & Walk, R. D. (1960). The "visual cliff." *Scientific American, 202,* 64–71.

Gibson, J. H., Harries, M., Mitchell, A., Godfrey, R., Lunt, M., & Reeve, J. (2000). Determinants of bone density and prevalence of osteopenia among female runners in their second to seventh decades of age. *Bone, 26,* 591–598.

Gibson, J. J. (1966). *The senses considered as perceptual systems.* Boston: Houghton Mifflin.

Gibson, J. J. (1979). *The ecological approach to visual perception.* Boston: Houghton Mifflin.

Giedd, J. N., & others (2006). Puberty-related influences on brain development. *Molecular and Cellular Endocrinology, 25,* 154–162.

Giger, J. N., Davidhizar, R. E., & Fordham, P. (2006). Multi-cultural and multiethnic considerations and advanced directives: Developing cultural competency. *Journal of Cultural Diversity, 13,* 3–9.

Gillen, M., Lefkowitz, E., & Shearer, C. (2006). Does body image play a role in risky sexual behavior and attitudes? *Journal of Youth and Adolescence, 35,* 230–242.

Gilligan, C. (1982). *In a different voice.* Cambridge, MA: Harvard University Press.

Gilligan, C. (1982). *In a different voice.* Cambridge, MA: Harvard University Press.

Gilligan, C. (1992, May), *Joining the resistance: Girls' development in adolescence.* Paper presented at the symposium on development and vulnerability in close relationships, Montreal, Quebec.

Gilligan, C. (1996). The centrality of relationships in psychological development: A puzzle, some evidence, and a theory. In G. G. Noam & K. W. Fischer (Eds.), *Development and vulnerability in dose relationships.* Hillsdale, NJ: Erlbaum.

Gilligan, C., Spencer, R., Weinberg, M. K., & Bertsch, T. (2003). On the listening guide: A voice centered relational model. In P. M. Carnie & J. E. Rhodes (Eds.), *Qualitative research in psychology* Washington, DC: American Psychological Association.

Gillum, R. F., & Ingram, D. D. (2007). Frequency of attendance at religious services, hypertension, and blood pressure: The third National Health and Nutrition Examination Survey. *Psychosomatic Medicine, 68,* 382–385.

Gilstrap, L. L., & Ceci, S. J. (2005). Reconceptualizing children's suggestibility: Bidirectional and temporal properties. *Child Development, 76,* 40–53.

Girls, Inc. (1991). *Truth, trusting, and technology: New research on preventing adolescent pregnancy.* Indianapolis: Author.

Glantz, J. C. (2005). Elective induction vs. spontaneous labor associations and outcomes. *Journal of Reproductive Medicine, 50,* 235–240.

Glei, D. A. (1999). Measuring contraceptive use patterns among teenage and adult women. *Family Planning Perspectives, 31,* 73–80.

Gliori, G., Imm, P., Anderson, A., & Knobeloch, L. (2006). Fish consumption and advisory awareness among expectant women. *Wisconsin Medicine Journal, 105,* 41–44.

Gobet, E., & Charness, N. (2006). Expertise in chess. In K. A. Ericsson, N. Charness, P. J. Feltovich, & Hoffman, R. R. (Eds.), *The Cambridge handbook of expertise and expert performance.* New York: Cambridge University Press.

Godding, V., Bonnier, C., Fiasse, L., Michel, M., Longueville, E., Lebecque, P., Robert, A., & Galanti, L. (2004). Does in utero exposure to heavy maternal smoking induce nicotine withdrawal symptoms in neonates? *Pediatric Research, 55,* 645–651.

Goffin, S. G., & Wilson, C. S. (2001). *Curriculum models and early childhood education.* Upper Saddle River, NJ: Prentice Hall.

Golan, M., & Crow, S. (2004). Parents are key players in the prevention and treatment of weight-related problems. *Nutrition Review, 62,* 39–50.

Goldenberg, R. L., & Culhane, J. F. (2007). Low birth weight in the United States. *American Journal of Clinical Nutrition, 85 (Suppl)*, S584–S590.

Goldscheider, F., & Sassler, S. (2006). Creating stepfamilies: Integrating children into the study of union formation. *Journal of Marriage and the Family, 68*, 275–291.

Goldsmith, D. F. (2007). Challenging children's negative internal working models. In D. Oppenheim & D. F. Goldsmith (Eds.), *Attachment theory in clinical work with children*. New York: Guilford.

Goldstein, J. M., Seldman, L. J., Horton, N. J., Makris, N., Kennedy, D. N., Caviness, V. S., Faraone, S. V., & Tsuang, M. T. (2001). Normal sexual dimorphism of the adult human brain assessed by in vivo magnetic resonance imaging. *Cerebral Cortex, 11*, 490–497.

Goldstein, M. H., King, A. P., & West, M. J. (2003). Social interaction shapes babbling: Testing parallels between birdsong and speech. Proceedings of the National Academy of Sciences, 100 (13), 8030–8035.

Gonzales, P., Guzman, J. C., Partelow, L., Pahlke, E., Jocelyn, L., Kastberg, D., & Wiliams, T. (2004). *Highlights from the Trends in International Mathematics and Science Study (TIMSS) 2003*. Washington, DC: U.S. Government Printing Office.

Gonzales, V., Yawkey, T. D., & Minaya-Rowe, L. (2006). *English-as-a-second-language (ESL) teaching and learning*. Boston: Allyn & Bacon.

Gonzalez-del Angel, A. A., Vidal, S., Saldann, Y., del Castillo, V., Angel, M., Macias, M., Luna, P., & Orozco, L. (2000). Molecular diagnosis of the fragile X and FRAXE syndromes in patients with mental retardation of unknown cause in Mexico. *Annals of Genetics, 43*, 29–34.

Gooldner, H., & Strong, M. M. (1987). *Speaking of friendship*. New York: Greenwood Press.

Gooren, L. (2003). Androgen deficiency in the aging male: Benefits and risks of androgen supplementation. *Jouranl of Steroid Biochemistry and Molecular Biology, 85*, 349–355.

Gooren, L. (2006). The biology of human psychosexual differentiation. *Hormones and Behavior, 50*, 589–601.

Gordon-Salant, S., Veni-Komshian, G. H., Fitzgibbons, P. J., S. Barrett, J. (2006). Age related differences in identification and discrimination of temporal cues in speech segments. *Journal of the Asocial Society of America, 129*, 2455–2466.

Gostic, C. L. (2005). The crucial role of exercise and physical activity in weight management and functional improvement for seniors. *Clinical Geriatric Medicine, 21*, 747–756.

Gotesdam, K. G., & Agras, W. S. (1995). General population-based epidemiological survey of eating disorders in Norway.

International Journal of Eating Disorders, 18, 119–126.

Gottlieb, G. (2004). Normally occurring environmental and behavioral influences on gene activity. In C. G. Coll, E. L. Bearer, & R. M. Lerner (Eds.), *Nature and nurture*. Mahwah, NJ: Erlbaum.

Gottlieb, G. (2005). Unpublished review & J. W. Santrock's *Topical life-span development* (3rd ed.). New York: McGraw-Hill.

Gottlieb, G. (2007). Probabalistic epigenesis. *Developmental Science, 10*, 1–11.

Gottlieb, G., Wahlsten, D., & Lickliter, R. (2006). The significance of biology for human development: A developmental psychobiological systems view. In W. Damon & R. Lerner (Eds.), *Handbook of child psychology (6th ed.)*. New York: Wiley.

Gottman, J. M. (1994). *Why marriages succeed or fail*. New York: Simon & Schuster.

Gottman, J. M., & Declaire, J. (1997). *The heart of parenting: Raising an emotionally intelligent child*. New York: Simon & Schuster.

Gottman, J. M., & Levenson, R. W. (2000). The timing of divorce: Predicting when a couple will divorce over a 14-year period. *Journal of Marriage and the Family, 62*, 737–745.

Gottman, J. M., & Notari U.S, C. I. (2000). Decade review: Observing marital interaction. *Journal of Marriage and the Family, 62*, 927–947.

Gottman, J. M., & Parker, J. G. (Eds.). (1987). *Conversations of friends*. New York: Cambridge University Press.

Gottman, J. M., Shapiro, A. F., & Parthemer, J. (2004). Bringing baby home: A preventative intervention program for expectant couples. *International Journal of Childbirth Education, 19*, 28–30.

Gottman, J. M., & Silver, N. (2000). *The seven principles for making marriages work*. New York: Crown.

Gould, E., Reeves, A. J., Graziano, M. S., & Gross, C. G. (1999). Neurogenesis in the neocortex of adult primates, *Science, 286* (1). 548–552.

Gould, S. J. (1981). *The mismeasure of man*. New York: W. W. Norton.

Gove, W. R., Style, C. B., & Hughes, M. (1990). The effect of marriage on the well-being of adults: A theoretical analysis. *Journal of Health and Social Behavior 24*, 122–131.

Gowan, D. E. (2003). Christian beliefs concerning death and life after death. In C. D. Bryant (Ed.), *Handbook of death and dying*. Thousand Oaks, CA: Sage.

Graber, J. A. (2007, in press). Pubertal and neuroendocrine development and risk for depressive disorders. In N. B. Allen, & L. Sheeber (Eds.), *Adolescent emotional development and the emergence of depressive disorders*. New York: Cambridge University Press.

Graber, J. A., & Brooks-Gunn, J. (2001). *Cooccurring eating and depressive problems: An 8-year study of adolescent girls*. Unpublished manuscript, Center for Children and Families, Columbia University.

Graber, J. A., Brooks-Gunn, J., & Warren, M. P. (2006). Pubertal effects on adjustment in girls: Moving from demonstrating effects to identifying pathways. *Journal of Youth and Adolescence, 35*, 391–401.

Graham, S. (2005, February 16). Commentary in *USA Today*, p. 2D.

Grambs, J. D. (1989). *Women over forty* (rev. ed.), New York: Springer.

Grant, J. (1993). *The state of the world's children*. New York: UNICEF and Oxford University Press.

Graven, S. (2006). Sleep and brain development. *Clinical Perinatology, 33*, 693–706.

Graves, M., Juel, C., & Graves, B. (2007). *Teaching reading in the 21st century* (4th ed.). Boston: Allyn & Bacon.

Gray, K. A., Day, N. L., Leech, S., & Richardson, G. A. (2005). Prenatal marijuana exposure: Effect on child depressive symptoms at ten years of age. *Neurotoxicology and Teratology, 27*, 439–448.

Graziano, A. M., & Raulin, M. L. (2007). *Research methods* (6th ed.). Boston: Allyn & Bacon.

Greco, L., Balungi, J., Amono, K., Iriso, R., & Corrado, B. (2006). Effect of low-cost food on the recovery and death rate of malnourished children. *Journal of Pediatric Gastroenterology and Nutrition, 43*, 512–517.

Greene, V. L., Lovely, M. E., Miller, M. D., & Ondrich, J. I. (1995). Reducing nursing home use through community long-term care: An optimization analysis. Journal of Gerontology: Social Sciences, 50B, S259–S268.

Greenfield, L. A., & Marks, N. F. (2004). Formal volunteering as a protective factor for older adults' psychological well-being. *Journal of Gerontology B: Psychological Sciences and Social Sciences, 59*, S258–S264.

Greenfield, P. M. (1966). On culture and conservation. In J. S. Bruner, R. P. Oliver, & P. M. Greenfield (Eds.), *Studies in cognitive growth*. New York: Wiley.

Greenfield, P. M., Trumbull, E., Keller, H., Rothstein-Fisch, Suzuki, L., & Quiroz, B. (2006). Culturral conceptions of learning and development. In P. A. Alexander & P. H. Winne (Eds.), *Handbook of educational psychology* (2nd ed.). Mahwah, NJ: Erlbaum.

Greenough, W. T., Klintsova, A. Y., Irvan, S. A., Galvez, R., Bates, K. E., & Weller, L. J. (2001). Synaptic regulation of protein synthesis and the fragile X protein. *Proceedings of the National Academy of Science, USA, 98*, 7101–7106.

Gregory, R. J. (2007). *Psychological testing* (5th ed.). Boston: Allyn & Bacon.

Greydanus, D. E., Pratt, H. D., & Patel, D. R. (2007). Attention deficit hyperactivity disorder across the lifespan: The child, adolescent, and adult. *Disease-A-Month, 53*, 70–131.

Griffiths, R., Horsfall, J., Moore, M., Lane, D., Kroon, V., & Langdon, R. (2007). Assessment of health, well-being, and social connections: A survey of woman living in western Sydney. *International Journal of Nursing Practice, 13*, 3–13.

Grigorenko, E. (2000). Heritability and intelligence. In R. J. Sternberg (Ed.), *Handbook of intelligence.* New York: Cambridge University Press.

Gringart, E., Helmes, E., & Speelman, C. P. (2005). Exploring attitudes toward older workers among Australia employers: An empirical study. *Journal of Aging and Social Policy, 17*, 85–103.

Grolnick, W. S., Bridges, L. J., & Connell, J. P. (1996). Emotional regulation in two-year-olds: Strategies and emotional expression in four contexts. *Child Development, 67*, 928–941.

Gross, J. J., & Thompson, R. A. (2007). Emotion regulation: Conceptual foundations. In J. J. Gross (Ed.), *Handbook of emotion regulation.* New York: Guilford.

Groth, K. E., Gilmore, G. C., & Thomas, C. W. (2003). Impact of stimulus integrity on age differences in letter matching. *Experimental Aging Research, 29*, 155–172.

Grusec, J. (2006). Development of moral behavior and conscience. In M. Killen & J. G. Smetana (Eds.), *Handbook of moral development.* Mahwah, NJ: Erlbaum.

Grusec, J. E., & Davidov, M. (2007). Socialization in the family: The roles of parents. In J. E. Grusec & P. D. Hastings (Eds.), *Handbook of socialization.* New York: Guilford.

Grusec, J. E., & Hastings, P. D. (Eds.). (2007). *Handbook of socialization.* New York: Guilford.

Guastello, D. D., & Guastello, S. J. (2003). Androgyny, gender role behavior, and emotional intelligence among college students and their parents. *Sex Roles, 49*, 663–673.

Guilford, J. P. (1967). *The structure of intellect.* New York: McGraw-Hill.

Gump, B., & Matthews, K. (2000 March). *Annual vacations, health, and death.* Paper presented at the meeting of American Psychosomatic Society, Savannah, GA.

Gunnar, M. R., & Quevado, K. (2007). The neurobiology of stress and development. *Annual Review of Psychology,* (Vol. 58). Palo Alto, CA: Annual Reviews.

Gunnar, M. R., Malone, S., & Fisch, R. O. (1987). The psychobiology of stress and coping in the human neonate: Studies of the adrenocortical activity in response to stress in the first week of life. In T. Field, P. McCabe, & N. Scheiderman (Eds.), *Stress and coping.* Hillsdale, NJ: Erlbaum.

Gunnar, M., & Quevado, K. (2007). The neurobiology of stress and development. *Annual Review of Psychology, Vol. 58.* Palo Alto, CA: Annual Reviews.

Gur, R. C., Mozley, L. H., Mozley, P. D., Resnick, S. M., Karp, J. S., Alavi, A., Arnold, S. E., & Gur, R. E. (1995). Sex differences in regional cerebral glucose metabolism during a resting state. *Science, 267*, 528–531.

Gurwitch, R. H., Silovksy, J. F., Schultz, S., Kees, M., & Burlingame, S. (2001). *Reactions and guidelines for children following trauma/disaster.* Norman, OK: Department of Pediatrics, University of Oklahoma Health Sciences Center.

Gutmann, D. L. (1975). Parenthood: A key to the comparative study of the life cycle. In N. Datan & L. Ginsberg (Eds), *Life-span developmental psychology: Normative life crises.* New York: Academic Press.

H

Haber, D., & Rhodes, D. (2004). Health contract with sedentary older adults. *Gerontologist, 44*, 827–835.

Hadwin, J., & Perner, J. (1991). Pleased and surprised: Children's cognitive theory of emotion. *British Journal of Developmental Psychology, 9*, 215–234.

Hagedoorn, M., & others (2006). Does marriage protect older people from distress? The role of equity and regency of bereavement. *Psychology and Aging, 21*, 611–620.

Hagestad, G. O. (1985). Continuity and connectedness. In V. L. Bengtson (Ed.), *Grandparenthood.* Beverly Hills, CA: Sage.

Hahn, D. B., Payne, W. A., & Lucas, E. B. (2008). *Focus on health* (8th ed.). New York: McGraw-Hill.

Hahn, W. K. (1987). Cerebral lateralization of function: From infancy through childhood. *Psychological Bulletin, 101*, 376–392.

Hakuta, K. (2005, April). *Bilingalism at the intersection of research and public policy.* Paper reported at the meeting of the Society for Research in Child Development, Atlanta.

Hakuta, K., Butler, Y. G., & Witt, D. (2000). *How long does it take English learners to attain proficiency?* Berkeley, CA: The University of California Linguistic Minority Research Institute Policy Report 2000-1.

Hall, G. S. (1904). *Adolescence* (Vols. 1 & 2). Englewood Cliffs, NJ: Prentice Hall.

Hallahan, D. P., & Kauffman, J. M. (2006). *Exceptional learners* (10th ed.). Boston: Allyn & Bacon.

Halpern, D. (2001). Sex difference research: Cognitive abilities. In J. Worell (Ed.), *Handbook of women and gender.* San Diego: Academic Press.

Halpern, D. F. (2007). The nature and nature of critical thinking. In R. J. Sternberg, H. Roediger, & D. Halpern (Eds.), *Critical thinking in psychology.* New York: Cambridge University Press.

Hankin, B. L., Kassel, J. D., & Abela, J. R. (2005). Adult attachment dimensions and specificity of emotional distress symptoms: Prospective in vestigations of cognitive risk and interpresonal stress generation as mediating mechanisms. *Personality and Social Psychology Bulletin, 31.* 136–151.

Hannish, L. D., & Guerra, N. G. (2004). Aggressive victims, passive victims, and bullies: Developmental continuity or developmental change? *Merrill-Palmer Quarterly, 50*, 17–38.

Hansen, M., Janssen, L., Schiff, A., Zee, P. C., & Dubocovich, M. L. (2005). The impact of school daily schedule on adolescent sleep. *Pediatrics, 115*, 1555–1561.

Hansson, R. O., & Stroebe, M. S. (2007, in press). *Bereavement in late life: Development, coping, and adaptation.* Washington, DC: American Psychological Association.

Hansson, R. O., Hayslip, B., & Stroebe, M. S. (2007). Grief and bereavement. In J. A. Blackburn & C. N. Dulmus (Eds.), *Handbook of gerontology.* New York: Wiley.

Harbosky, J. I., Masheb, R. M., White, M. A., & Grilo, C. M. (2007). Overvaluation of shape and weight in binge eating disorder. *Journal of Consulting and Clinical Psychology, 75*, 175–180.

Hardy, M. (2006). Older workers. In R. H. Binstock & L. K. George (Eds.), *Handbook of aging and the social sciences* (6th ed.). San Diego: Academic Press.

Hargreaves, D. A., & Tiggemann, M. (2004). Idealized media images and adolescent body image: Comparing boys and girls. *Body Image, 1*, 351–361.

Harkins, S. W., Price, D. D., & Martinelli, M. (1986). Effects of age on pain perception. *Journal of Gerontology, 41*, 58–63.

Harkness, S., & Super, C. M. (1995). Culture and parenting. In M. H. Bornstein (Ed.), *Handbook of parenting* (Vol. 3). Hillsdale, NJ: Erlbaum.

Harkness, S., & Super, C. M. (2002). Culture and parenting. In M. H. Bornstein (Ed.), *Handbook of parenting* (2nd ed., vol. 2). Mahwah, NJ: Erlbaum.

Harlow, H. F. (1958). The nature of love. *American Psychologist, 13*, 673–685.

Harman, S. M. (2006). Testosterone in older men after the Institute of Medicine Report: Where do we go from here? *Climacteric, 8*, 124–135.

Harold, R. D., Colarossi, L. G., & Mercier, L. R. (2007). *Smooth sailing or stormy waters: Family transitions through adolescence and their implications for practice and policy.* Mahwah, NJ: Erlbaum.

Harris, C. R. (2002). Sexual and romantic jealousy in heterosexual and homosexual adults. *Psychological Science, 13*, 7–12.

Harris, G., Thomas, A., & Booth, D. A. (1990). Development of salt taste in infancy. *Development Psychology, 26*, 534–538.

Harris Interactive (2003, February 5). *Harris Poll # 8: Adults on the Internet.* Rochester, NY: Author.

Harris, K. M., Gorden-Larsen, P., Chantala, K., & Udry, J. R. (2006). Longitudinal trends in race/ethnic dispartiies in leading health indicators from adolescence to young adulthood. *Archives of Pediatrics and Adolescent Medicine, 160,* 74–81.

Harris, P. L. (2006). Social cognition. In W. Damon & R. Lerner (Eds.), *Handbook of child psychology* (6th ed.). New York: Wiley.

Harris, Y. R., & Graham, J. A. L. (2007). *The African American child.* New York: Springer.

Hart, B., & Risley, T. R. (1995). *Meaningful differences in the everyday experience of young Americans.* Baltimore: Paul H. Brookes.

Hart, C. H., Yang, C., Charlesworth, R., & Burts, D. C. (2003, April). *Early childhood teachers' curriculum beliefs, classroom practices, and children's outcomes: What are the connections?* Paper presented at the biennial meeting of the Society for Research in Child Development, Tampa.

Hart, C. L., Hole, D. J., Lawlor, D. A., Davey Smith, G. (2007). How many cases of type 2 diabetes mellitus are due to overweight in middle age? Evidence from the Midspan prospective cohort studies using mention of diabetes mellitus on hospital death records. *Diabetic Medicine, 24,* 73–80.

Hart, D., Atkins, R., & Donnelly, T. M. (2006). Community service and moral development. In M. Killen & J. Smetana (Eds.), *Handbook of moral development.* Mahwah, NJ: Erlbaum.

Hart, D., & Karmel, M. P. (1996). Self-awareness and self-knowledge in humans, great apes, and monkeys. In A. Russon, K. Bard, & S. Parker (Eds.), *Reaching into thought.* New York: Cambridge University Press.

Harter, S. (2002). Unpublished review of J. W. Santrocks *Child development* (10th ed. New York: McGraw-Hill.

Harter, S. (2006). The Self. In W. Damon & R. Lerner (Eds.), *Handbook of Child Psychology* (6th ed.) New York: Wiley.

Hartley, A. (2006). Changing role of the speed of processing construct in the cognitive psychology of human aging. In J.E. Birren & K. W. Schaie (Eds.), *Handbook of the psychology of aging* (6th ed). San Diego: Academic Press.

Hartshorne, H., & May, M. S. (1928–1930). *Moral studies in the nature of character: Studies in the nature of character.* New York: Macmillan.

Hartup, W. W. (1983). The peer system. In P. H. Mussen (Ed.), *Handbook of child psychology* (4th ed., vol. 4). New York: Wiley.

Hartwell, L. (2008). *Genetics* (3rd ed.). New York: McGraw-Hill.

Harvey, J. H., & Weber, A. L. (2002). *The odyssey of the heart* (2nd ed.). Mahwah, NJ: Erlbaum.

Hasche, L., & Morrow-Howell, N. (2007). Depression. In J. A. Blackburn & C. N. Dulmas (Eds.), *Handbook of gerontology.* New York: Wiley.

Hassell, J. B., Lamoureux, E. L., & Keeffe, J. E. (2006). Impact of age related macular degeneration on quality of life. *British Journal of Ophthalmology, 90,* 593–596.

Hastings, P. D., Utendale, W. T., & Sullivan, C. (2007). The socialization of prosocial development. In J. E. Grusec & P. D. Hastings (eds.), *Handbook of socialization.* New York: Guildford.

Haugaard, J. J., & Hazan, C. (2004). Adoption as a natural experiment. *Developmental Psychopathology, 15,* 909–926.

Hawkes, C. (2006). Olfaction in neurogenerative disorder. *Advances in Otorhinolaryngology, 63,* 133–151.

Hawkins, N. M., & Dunn, F. G. (2006). The management of hypertension in ischemic heart disease. *Current Opinions in Cardiology, 21,* 273–278.

Hayes, J. A., Yeh, Y. J., & Eisenberg, A. (2007). Good grief and not-so-good grief: Counter transference in bereavement therapy. *Journal of Clinical Psychology, 63,* 345–355.

Hayflick, L. (1977). The cellular basis for biological aging. In C. E. Finch & L. Hayflick (Eds.), *Handbook of the biology of aging.* New York: Van Nostrand.

Hayslip, B., Edmondson, R., & Guarnaccia, C. (1999, November). *Religiousness, perceptions of funerals, and bereavement adjustment in adulthood.* Paper presented at the meeting of the Gerontological Society of America, San Francisco.

Hazan, C., Gur-Yaish, N., & Campa, M. (2007). What does it mean to be attached? In W. S. Rholes & J. A. Simpson (Eds.), *Adult attachment.* New York: Guilford.

Hazan, C., & Shaver, P. R. (1987). Romantic love conceptualized as an attachment process. *Journal of Personality and Social Psychology. 52.* 522–524.

Health Management Resources. (2001). *Child health and fitness.* Boston: Author.

Hedayat, K. (2006). When the spirit leaves: Childhood death, grieving, and bereavement in Islam. *Journal of Palliative Medicine, 9,* 1282–1291.

Hedberg, K., Hopkins, D., & Kohn, M. (2003). Five years of legal physician-assisted suicide in Oregon. *New England Journal of Medicine, 348,* 961–964.

Heidi, R. R. (2006). The adaptive response of families to maternal employment. In H. R. Riggio & D. F. Halpern (Eds.), *Changes at the intersection of work and family* (Vol. 2). Thousand Oaks, CA: Sage.

Heiser, P., Friedel, S., Dempfile, A., Kongrad, K., Smidt, J., Grabarkiewicz, J.,

Herpertz-Dahlann, B., Remschmidt, H., & Hebebrand, J. (2004). Molecular genetic aspects of attention deficit/hyperactivity disorder. *Neuroscience and Biobehavioral Reviews, 28,* 625–641.

Hendricks, J., & Hatch, L. R. (2006). Lifestyle and aging. In R. H. Binstock & L. K. George (Eds.), *Handbook of aging and the social sciences* (6th ed.). San Diego: Academic Press.

Hendry, J. (1995). *Understanding Japanese society.* London: Routledge.

Henriksen, T. B., Hjollund, N. H., Jensen, T. K., Bonde, J. P., Andersson, A. M., Kolstad, H., Ernst, E., Giwereman, A., Skakkebaek, N. E., & Olsen, J. (2004). Alcohol consumption at the time of conception and spontaneous abortion. *American Journal of Epidemiology, 160,* 661–667.

Herbst, M. A., Mercer, B. N., Beasley, D., Meyer, N., & Carr, T. (2003). Relationship of prenatal care and perinatal morbidity in low-birth-weight infants. *American Journal of Obstetrics and Gynecology, 189,* 930–933.

Herman, D. R., Harrison, G. G., & Jenks, E. (2006). Choices made by low-income women provided with an economic supplement for fresh fruit and vegetable purchase. *Journal of The American Dietetic Association, 106,* 740–744.

Hermann-Giddens, M. E. (2006). Recent data on pubertal milestones in United States children: The secular trend toward earlier development. *International Journal of Andrology, 29,* 241–246.

Herman-Giddens, M. E. (2007). The decline in the age of menarche in the United States: Should we be concerned? *Journal of Adolescent Health, 40,* 201–203.

Hernandez, D. H. (2007, March). *Children in immigrant families in the 21st century.* Paper presented at the meeting of the Society for Research in Child Development, Boston.

Hernandez, D. J., Denton, N. A., & McCartney, S. E. (2007). Family circumstances of children in immigrant families: Looking to the future of America. In J. E. Lansford, K. Deater-Deckard, & M. H. Bornstein (Eds.), *Immigrant families in contemporary society.* New York: Guilford.

Herrera, V. M., Koss, M. P., Bailey, J., Yuan, N. P., & Lichter, E. L. (2006). Survivors of male violence. In J. Worell & C. D. Goodheart (Eds.), *Handbook of girls' and women's psychological health.* New York: Oxford University Press.

Hertogh, C. M., de Boer, M. E., Droes, R. M., & Eefsting, J. A. (2007). Would we rather lose our life than lose our self? Lessons from the Dutch debate on euthanasia for patients with dementia. *American Journal of Bioethics, 7,* 48–56.

Hertz, R. P., Unger, A. N., & Ferrario, C. M. (2006). Diabetes, hypertension, and dyslipidemia in Mexican Americans and non-Hispanic Whites. *American Journal of Preventive Medicine, 30,* 103–110.

Hess, T. (2006). Attitudes toward aging and their effects on behavior. In J. E. Birren & K. W. Schaie (Eds.), *Handbook of the psychology of aging* (6th). San Diego: Academic Press.

Hetherington, E. M. (1989). Coping with family transitions: Winners, losers, and survivors. *Child Development, 60,* 1–14.

Hetherington, E. M. (1993). An overview of the Virginia Longitudinal Study of Divorce and Remarriage with a focus on early adolescence. *Journal of Family Psychology, 7,* 39–56.

Hetherington, E. M. (2005). Divorce and the adjustment of children. *Pediatrics in Review, 26,* 163–169.

Hetherington, E. M. (2006). The influence of conflict, marital problem solving, and parenting on children's adjustment in nondivorced, divorced, and remarried families. In A. Clarke-Stewart & J. Dunn (Eds.), *Families count.* New York: Oxford University Press.

Hetherington, E. M., & Kelly, J. (2002). *For better or for worse: Divorce reconsidered.* New York: Norton.

Hetherington, E. M., & Stanley-Hagan, M. (2002). Parenting in divorced and remarried families. In M. H. Bornstein (Ed.), *Handbook of parenting* (2nd ed., vol. 3), Mahwah, NJ: Erlbaum.

Hewlett, S. A. (2002). *Creating a life: Professional women and the quest for children.* New York: Talk Miramax Books.

Heyer, W. J., & Verhaeghen, P. (2006). Memory aging. In J. E. Birren & K. W. Schaie (Eds.), *Handbook of the psychology of aging* (6th ed.). San Diego: Academic Press.

Hibell, B., Andersson, B., Bjarnasson, T., & others. (2004), *The ESPAD report 2003: Alcohol and other drug use among students in 35 European Countries.* The Swedish Council for Information on Alcohol and Other Drugs (CAN) and Council of Europe Pompidou Group.

High/Scope Resource. (2005, Spring). The High/Scope Perry Preschool Study and the man who began it. *High/Scope Resource,* p. 9. Ypsilanti, MI: High/Scope Press.

Hijiya, N., & others. (2007). Cumulative incidence of secondary neoplasms as a first event after childhood acute lymphoblastic leukemia. *Journal of the American Medical Association, 297,* 1207–1215.

Hill, C. R. & Stafford, R. E. (1980). Parental care of children: Time diary estimate of quantity, predictability, and variety, *Journal of Human Resources, 15,* 219–239.

Hill, M. A. (2007). Early human development. *Clinical Obstetrics and Gynecology, 50,* 2–9.

Hill, P. C., & Butter, E. M. (1995). The role of religion in promoting physical health. *Journal of Psychology and Christianity, 14,* 141–155.

Hill, P. C., & Pargament, K. I. (2003). Advances in conceptualization and measurement of religion and spirituality: Implications for physical and mental health research. *American Psychologist, 58,* 64–74.

Hill, T. D., Angel, J. L., Ellison, C. G., & Angel, R. J. (2005). Religious attendance and mortality: An 8-year follow-up of older Mexican Americans. *Journals of Gerontology B: Psychological Sciences and Social Sciences, 60,* S102–S109.

Himes, C. L., Hogan, D. P., & Eggebeen, D. J. (1996). Living arrangements of minority elders. *Journal of Gerontology, 51A,* S42–S48.

Hingson, R. W., Heeren, T., & Winter, M. R. (2006). Age at drinking onset and alcohol dependence: Age at onset, duration, and severity. *Archives of Pediatric and Adolescent Medicine, 160,* 739–746.

Hinrichsen, G. A. *(2006).* Why multicultural issues matter for practitioners working with older adults. *Psychology and Aging, 37,* 29–35.

Hirsch, B. J., & Rapkin, B. D. (1987). The transition to junior high school: A longitudinal study of self-esteem, psychological symptomatology, school life, and social support. *Child Development, 58,* 1235–1243.

Hirschhorn, J. N. (2005). Genetic and genomic approaches to studying stature and pubertal timing. *Pediatric Endocrinology Review, 2,* (3. Suppl), 351–354.

Ho, A. P. (2007). A peer counseling program for the elderly with depression living in the community. *Aging and Mental Health, 11,* 69–74.

Hock, R. R. (2007). *Human sexuality.* Upper Saddle River, NJ: Prentice Hall.

Hodapp, R. M., & Dykens, E. M. (2006). Mental retardation. In W. Damon & R. Lerner (Eds.), *Handbook of child psychology.* Mahwah, NJ: Erlbaum.

Hoeger, W. W. K., & Hoeger, S. A. (2008). *Principles and labs for physical fitness* (6th ed.). New York: McGraw-Hill.

Hofer, S. M., & Sliwinski, M. J. (2006). Design and analysis of longitudinal studies on aging. In J. E. Birren & K. W. Schaie (Eds.), *Handbook of the psychology forging* (6th ed.). San Diego: Academic Press.

Hoff, E., & Shatz, M. (Eds.) (2007). *Blackwell handbook of language development.* Malden, MA: Blackwell.

Hoff, E., Laursen, B., & Tardif, T. (2002). Socioeconomic status and parenting. In M. H. Borstein (Ed.), *Handbook of parenting* (2nd ed.). Mahwah, NJ: Erlbaum.

Hofferth, S. L., & Reid, L. (2002). Early childbearing and children's achievement behavior over time. *Perspectives on sexual and reproductive health, 34,* 41–49.

Hoffman, L. W. (1989). Effects of maternal employment in the two-parent family. *American Psychologist, 44,* 283–292.

Hoffman, M. L. (1970). Moral development. In P. H. Mussen (Ed.), *Manual of child psychology* (3rd ed., Vol. 2). New York: Wiley.

Hogan, M. A., Glazebrook, R., Brancato, V., & Rogers, J. (2007). *Maternal-newborn nursing: Review and rationales* (2nd ed.). Upper Saddle River, NJ: Prentice Hall.

Hoimann, M., Strid, K., Smith, L., Tjus, T., Ulvund, S. E., & Mclzoff, A. N. (2006). Exploring the relation between memory, gestural communication, and the emergence of language in infancy: A longitudinal study. *Infant and Child Development, 15,* 233–249.

Holden, K., & Hatcher, C. (2006). Economic status of the aged. In R. H. Binstock & L. K. George (Eds.), *Handbook of aging and the social sciences* (6th ed.). San Diego: Academic Press.

Holland, J. L. (1987). Current status of Holland's theory of careers: Another perspective. *Career Development Quarterly, 36,* 24–30.

Holmes, T. H., & Rahe, R. H. (1967). The social readjustment rating scale. *Journal of Psychosomatic Research, 11,* 213–218.

Holtzen, D. W. (2000). Handedness and professional tennis. *International Journal of Neuroscience, 105,* 101–119.

Holzgrabe, U., Kapkova, P., Alptuzun, V., Scheiber, J., & Kugelmann, E. (2007). Targeting acetylcholinesterase to treat neurodegeneration. *Expert Opinion on Therapeutic Targets, 11,* 161–179.

Horn, J. L., & Donaldson, G. (1980). Cognitive development II: Adulthood development of human abilities. In O. G. Brim & J. Kagan (Eds.), *Constancy and change in human development.* Cambridge, MA: Harvard University Press.

Hornor, G. (2005). Physical abuse: Recognition and reporting. *Journal of Pediatric Health Care, 19,* 4–11.

Horton, D. M. (2001). The disappearing bell curve. *Journal of Secondary Gifted Education, 12,* 185–188.

Horwitz, E. K. (2008). *Becoming a language teacher.* Boston: Allyn & Bacon.

Host, A., & Halken, S. (2005). Primary prevention of food allergy in infants who are at risk. *Current Opinions in Allergy and Clinical Immunology, 5,* 255–259.

House, J. S., Landis, K. R., & Umberson, D. (1988). Social relationships and health. *Science, 241,* 540–545.

Houston-Price, C., Plunkett, K., & Harris, P. (2005). 'Word-learning wizardry' at 1;6. *Journal of Child Language, 32,* 175–189.

Howe, M. J. A. Davidson, J. W., Moore, D. G., & Sloboda, J. A. (1995). Are there early childhood signs of musical ability? *Psychology of Music, 23,* 162–176.

Howell, E. M., Pettit, K. L, & Kingsley, G. T. (2005). Trends in maternal and infant health in poor urban neighborhoods: Good news from the 1990s, but challenges remain. *Public Health Reports, 120,* 409–417.

Hoyer, W. J. & Roodin, P. A. (2003). *Adult development and aging* (5th ed.), New York: McGraw-Hill.

Hoyer, W. J., & Verhaeghen, P. (2006). Memory aging. In J. E. Birren & K. W. Schaie (Eds.), *Handbook of the psychology of aging* (6th ed.). San Diego: Academic Press.

Hoyert, D. L., Mathews, T. J., Menacker, F., Strobino, D. M., & Guyer, B. (2006). Annual summary of vital statistics: 2004 *Pediatrics, 117,* 168–183.

Huang, T., Owolabi, T., Summers, A. M., Meier, C., & Wyatt, P. R. (2005). The identification of risk of spontaneous fetal loss through second-trimester maternal serum screening. *American Journal of Obstetrics and Gynecology, 193,* 395–403.

Huebner, A. M., & Garrod, A. C. (1993). Moral reasoning among Tibetan monks: A study of Buddhist adolescents and young adults in Nepal. *Journal of Cross-Cultural Psychology, 24,* 167–185.

Huerta, M., Cortina, L. M., Pang, J. S., Torges, C. M., & Magley, V. J. (2006). Sex and power in the academy: Modeling sexual harassment in the lives of college women. *Personality and Social Psychology Bulletin, 32,* 616–628.

Huesmann, L. R., Dubow, E. F., Eron, L. D., & Boxer, P. (2006). Middle childhood family—contextual and personal factors as predictors of adult outcomes. In A. C. Huston & M. N. Ripke (Eds.), *Developmental contexts in middle childhood: Bridges to adolescence and adulthood,* New York: Cambridge University Press.

Huesmann, L. R., Moise-Titus, Podolski, C., & Eron, L. D. (2003). Longitudinal relations between exposure to TV violence and their aggressive and violent behavior in young adulthood: 1977–1992. *Developmental Psychology, 39,* 201–221.

Hughes, J. R. (2003). Motivating and helping smokers to stop smoking. *Journal of General Internal Medicine, 18,* 1053–1057.

Hultsch, D. F., Hertzog, C., Small, B. J., & Dixon, R. A. (1999). Use it or lose it: Engaged lifestyle as a buffer cognitive decline in aging? *Psychology and Aging, 14,* 245–263.

Hultsch, D. F., & Plemons, J. K. (1979). Life events and life-span development. In P. B. Baltes & O. G. Brim (Eds.), *Life-span development and behavior.* New York: Academic Press.

Humphreys, C. (2007). A health inequalities perspective on violence against women. *Health and Social Care in the Community, 15,* 120–127.

Hungerford, T. L. (2001). The economic consequences of widowhood on elderly women in the United States and Germany. *The Geronlogist, 41,* 103–110.

Hunter, K. I., & Linn, M. W. (1980). Psychological differences between elderly volunteers and nonvolunteers. *International Journal of Aging and Human Development, 12,* 205–213.

Hurd Clarke, L. (2006). Older women and sexuality: Experiences in marital relationships across the life course. *Canadian Journal of Aging, 25,* 129–140.

Hurt, H., Brodsky, N. L., Roth, H., Malmud, F., & Gianrietta, J. M. (2005). School performance of children with gestational cocaine exposure. *Neurotoxicology and Teratology, 27,* 203–211.

Huston, A. C., & Ripke, M. N. (2006). Experiences in middle childhood and children's development. In A. C. Huston & M. N. Ripke (Eds.), *Developmental contexts in middle childhood.* New York: Cambridge University Press.

Huston, T. L., & Holmes, E. K. (2004). Becoming parents. In A. L. Vangelisti (Ed.), *Handbook of family communication.* Mahwah, NJ: Erlbaum.

Hutchinson, D. M., & Rapee, R. M. (2007, in press). Do friends share similar body image and eating problems? The role of social networks and peer influences in early adolescence. *Behavior Research and Therapy.*

Huttenlocher, P. R., & Dabholkar, A. S. (1997). Regional differences in synaptogenesis in human cerebral cortex. *Journal of Comparative Neurology, 37* (2), 167–178.

Huurre, T., Junkkari, H., & Aro, H. (2006). Long-term psychosocial effects of parental divorce. *European Archives of Psychiatry and Clinical Neuroscience, 256,* 256–263.

Huyck, M. H. (1995). Marriage and close relationships of the marital kind. In R. Blieszner & V. H. Bedford (Eds.), *Handbook of aging and the family,* Westport, CT: Greenwood Press.

Huyck, M. H., Aylaon, L., & Yoder, J. (2007). Using mixed methods to evaluate the use of caregiver strain measure to assess outcomes of a caregiver support program for caregivers of older adults. *International Journal of Geriatrics and Psychiatry, 22,* 160–165.

Hvas, A. M., Nexos, E., & Nielsen, J. B. (2006). Vitamin B(12) and vitamin B(6) supplementation is needed among adults with phenylketonuria (PKU). *Journal of Inherited Metabolic Disorders, 29,* 47–53.

Hybels, C. F., & Blazer, D. G. (2004). Epidemiology of the late-life mental disorders. *Clinical Geriatric Medicine, 19,* 663–696.

Hyde, J. S. (2005). The gender similarities hypothesis. *American Psychologist, 60,* 581–592.

Hyde, J. S. (2007). *Half the human experience* (7th ed.). Bostor: Houghton Mifflin.

Hyde, J. S., & DeLamater, J. D. (2006). *Understanding human sexuality* (9th ed.), New York: McGraw-Hill.

Hyman, L., Kay, B., Tabori, A., Weber, M., Mahon, M., & Cohen, I. (2006). Bullying: Theory, research, and interventions with student victimization. In C. M. Evertson & C. S. Weinstein (Eds.), *Handbook of classroom management.* Mahwah, NJ: Erlbaum.

Hyson, M. (2007). Curriculum. In R. New & M. Cochran (Eds.), *Early childhood education: An international encyclopedia of early childhood education.* New York: Greenwood.

Hyson, M. C., Copple, C., & Jones, J. (2006). Early childhood development and education. In W. Damon & R. Lerner (Eds.). *Handbook of child psychology* (6th ed.). New York: Wiley.

Imada, T., Zhang, Y., Cheour, M., Taulu, S., Ahonen, A., & Kuhl, P. K. (2006). Infant speech perception activates Broca's area: A developmental magnetoencephalography study. *Neuroreport, 17,* 957–962.

Inoff-Germain, G., Arnold, G. S., Nottlemann, E. D., Susman, E. J., Cutler, G. B., & Chrousos, G. P. (1988). Relations between hormone levels and observational measures of aggressive behavior of young adolescents in family interactions. *Developmental Psychology, 24,* 124–139.

Insel P. M., & Roth, W. T. (2008). *Core concepts in health: V, date* (10th ed.) New York: McGraw-Hill.

International Human Genome Sequencing Consortium. (2004). Finishing the euchromatic sequence of the human genome. *Nature, 431,* 931–945.

International Montessori Council. (2007). Much of their success on prime time television. Retrieved February 2, 2007, from www.Montessori.org/enews/barbara_walters.html

Irwin, C. E. (2004). Eating and physical activity during adolescence: Does it make a difference in adult health status? *Journal of Adolescent Health, 34,* 459–460.

Irwin, S. A., Christimon, C. A., Grossman, A. W., Galvez, R., Kim, S. H., DeGrush, B. J., Weiler, I. J., & Greenough, W. T. (2005). Fragile X mental retardation protein levels increase following complex environmental exposure in rat brain regions undergoing active synaptogensis. *Neurobiology, Learning, and Memory, 83,* 180–187.

Issa, S. N., & Sharma, L. (2006). Epidemiology of osteoarthritis: An update, *Current Rheumatological Reports, 8,* 7–15.

Ito, A., Honma, Y., Inamori, E., Yada, Y., Momoi, M. Y., & Nakamura, Y. (2006). Developmental outcome of very low birth weight twins conceived by assisted reproduction techniques. *Journal of Perinatology, 26,* 130–136.

REFERENCES

R-25

Itti, E., Gaw Gonzalo, I. T., Pawlikowska-Haddal, A., Boone, K. B., Mlikotic, A., Itti, L., Mishkin, F. S., & Swerdloff, R. S. (2006). The structural brain correlates of cognitive deficits in adults with Klinefelter's syndrome. *Journal of Clinical Endocrinology and Metabolsim, 91,* 1423–1427.

J

Jabbour, R. A., Hempel, A., Gates, J. R., Zhang, W., & Risse, G. L. (2005). Right hemisphere language mapping in patients with bilateral language. *Epilepsy & Behavior, 6,* 587–592.

Jackson, K. M., & Nazar, A. M. (2006). Breastfeeding, the immune response, and long-term health. *Journal of the American Osteopathic Association, 106,* 203–207.

Jaffee, S., & Hyde, J. S. (2000). Gender differences in moral orientation: A meta analysis. *Psychological Bulletin, 126,* 703–726.

Jahromi, L. B., Putnam, S. P., & Stifter, C. A. (2004). Maternal regulation of infant reactivity from 2 to 6 months. *Developmental Psychology, 40,* 477–487.

Jalongo, M. R. (2007). *Early childhood language arts* (4th ed.), Boston: Allyn & Bacon.

James, D.C., & Dobson, B. (2005). Position of the American Dietetic Association: Promoting and supporting breastfeeding. *Journal of the American Dietetic Association, 105,* 810–818.

James, S. R. (2007). *Nursing care of children* (3rd ed.). London: Elsevier.

James, S. R., & Ashwill, J. (2007). *Nursing care of children* (3rd ed.). London: Elsevier.

James, W. (1890/1950). *The principles of psychology.* New York: Dover.

James, W. H. (2005). Biological and psychosocial determinants of male and female human sexual orientation. *Journal of Biosocial Science, 37,* 555–567.

Jamshidi, Y., Snieder, H., Ge, D., Spector, T. D., & O'Dell, S. D. (2007). The *SH2B* gene is associated with serum leptin and body fat in normal female twins. *Obesity, 15,* 5–9.

Janacek, R. J., Anderson, N., Liu, M., Zheng, S., Yang, O., & Tso, P. (2005). Effects of yo-yo diet, caloric restriction, and olestra on tissue distribution of hexachlorobenzene. *American Journal of Physiology and Gastrointestinal Liver Physiology, 288,* G292–G299.

Jansen, I. (2006). Decision making in childbirth: The influence of traditional structures in a Ghanaian village. *International Nursing Review, 53,* 41–46.

Janssen, I., Craig, W. M., Boyce, W. F., & Picikett, W. (2004). Associations between overweight and obesity with bullying behaviors in school-aged children. *Pediatrics, 113,* 1187–1194.

Janssen, I., Katzmarzyk, P. T., Ross, R., Leon, A. S., Skinner, J. S., Rao, D. C., Wilmore, J. H., Rankinen, T., & Bouchard, C. (2004). Fitness alters the associations of BMI and waist circumference with total and abdominal fat. *Obesity Research, 12,* 525–537.

Jaswal, V. K., & Fernald, A. (2007). Learning to communicate. In A. Slater & M. Lewis (Eds.), *Introduction to infant development* (2nd ed.). New York: Oxford University Press.

Jellinger, K. A., & Attems, J. (2007, in press). Neuropathological evaluation of mixed dementia. *Journal of the Neurological Sciences.*

Jenkins, C. L. (2003). Introduction: Windows and divorcees in later life. *Journal of Women and Aging, 15,* 1–6.

Jenkins, J. M., & Astington, J. W. (1996). Cognitive factors and family structure associated with theory of mind development in young children. *Developmental Psychology, 32,* 70–78.

Ji, B. T., Shu, X. O., Linet, M. S., Zheng, W., Wachoide, S., Gao, Y. T., Ying, D. M., & Jin, F. (1997). Paternal cigarette smoking and the risk of childhood cancer among offspring of nonsmoking mothers. *Journal of the National Cancer Institute, 89,* 238–244.

Jiao, S., Jl, G., & Jing, Q. (1996). Cognitive development of Chinese urban only children and children with siblings. *Child Development, 67,* 387–395.

Joffe, A. R., & Anton, N. (2006). Brain death: Understanding of the conceptual basis by pediatric intensivists in Canada. *Archives of Pediatric and Adolescent Medicine, 160,* 747–752.

Johansson, E. (2006). Children's morality: Perspectives and research. In B. Spodak & N. Saracho (Eds.), *Handbook of research on the education of young children* (2nd ed.). Mahwah, NJ: Erlbaum.

Johnson, A. N. (2005). Kangaroo holding beyond the NICU. *Pediatric Nursing, 31,* 53–56.

Johnson, A. N. (2007). Factors influencing implementation of kangaroo holding in a special care nursery. *MCN American Journal of Maternal Child Nursing, 32,* 25–29.

Johnson, C. L., & Troll, L. E. (1992). Family functioning in late life. *Journals of Gerontology, 47,* S66–S72.

Johnson, G. B. (2008). *The living world* (5th ed.). New York: McGraw-Hill.

Johnson, G. B., & Losos, J. (2008). *Essentials of the living world* (2nd ed.). New York: McGraw-Hill.

Johnson, J. A., Musial, D. L., Hall, G. E., Gollnick, D. M., & Dupuis, V. L. (2008). *Foundations of American education* (14th ed.). Boston: Allyn & Bacon.

Johnson, J. G., Zhang, B., Greer, J. A., & Prigerson, H. G. (2007). Parental control, partner dependency, and complicated grief among widowed adults in the community. *Journal of Nervous and Mental Disease, 195,* 26–30.

Johnson, J. S., & Newport, E. L. (1991). Critical period effects on universal properties of language: The status of subjacency in the acquisition of a second language. *Cognition, 39,* 215–258.

Johnson, M. H. (2005). Developmental neuroscience, psychopathology, and genetics. In M. H. Bornstein & M. E. Lamb (Eds.), *Developmental science.* Mahwah NJ: Erlbaum.

Johnson, M. H. (2007). The social brain in infancy. In D. Coch, K. W. Fischer, & G. Dawson (Eds.), *Human behavior, leaning, and the developing brain.* New York: Guilford.

Johnson, R. S., & Morrison, M. (2007). Toward a resolution of inconsistencies in the phonological deficit theory of reading disorders: Phonological reading difficulties are more severe in high-IQ poor readers. *Journal of Learning Disabilities, 40,* 66–79.

Johnson, W., Bouchard, T. J., Krueger, R. F., McGue, M., & Gottesman, I. I. (2004). Just one g: Consistent results from three test batteries. *Intelligence, 32,* 95–107.

John-Steiner, V. (2007). Vygotsky on thinking and speaking. In H. Daniels, J. Wertsch, & M. Cole (Eds.), *The Cambridge companion to Vygotsky.* New York: Cambridge University Press.

Johnston, L. D., O'Malley, P. M., Bachman, J. G., & Schulenberg, J. E. (2007). *Monitoring the Future national results on adolescent drug use: Overview of key findings, 2006.* Bethesda, MD: National Institute on Drug Abuse.

Jolliffe, C. J., & Hansen, I. (2007). Vascular risks and management of obesity in children and adolescents. *Vascular Health and Risk Management, 2,* 171–187.

Jolly, C. A. (2005). Diet manipulation and prevention of aging, cancer, and autoimmune disease. *Current opinions in Clinical Nutrition and Metabolic Care, 8,* 382–387.

Jones, A., Godfrey, K. M., Wood, P., Osmond, C., Goulden, P., & Phillips, D. I. (2006). Fetal growth and the adrenocortical response to psyychological stress. *Journal of Clinical Endocrinology and Metabolism, 91,* 1868–1871.

Jones, M. C. (1965). Psychological correlates of somatic development. *Child Development, 36,* 899–911.

Jones, S. S. & Hong, H-W. (2005). How some infant smiles get made. *Infant Behavior and Development, 28* (2), 194–205.

Joseph, J. (2004). *The gene illusion.* New York: Algora.

Joseph, J. (2006). *The missing gene.* New York: Algora.

Juffer, F., Bakermans-Kranenburg M. J., & Van Ijzendoom, M. H. (2007). *Promoting positive parenting.* Mahwah, NJ: Erlbaum.

Jung, C., (1993). *Modern man in search of soul*. New York: Harcourt Brace.

Juurlink, D. N., Herrmann, N., Szalai, J. P., Kopp, A., & Redelmier, D. A. (2004). Medical illness and the risk of suicide in the elderly. *Archives of Internal Medicine, 164*, 1179–1184.

K

Kübler-Ross, E. (1969). *On death and dying*. New York: Macmillan.

Kafai, Y. B. (2006). Constructivism. In R. K. Sawyer (Ed.), *The Cambridge handbook of the learning sciences*. New York: Cambridge University Press.

Kagan, J. (1987). Perspectives on infancy. In J. D. Osofsky (Ed.), *Handbook on infant development* (2nd ed.). New York: Wiley.

Kagan, J. (2002). Behavioral inhibition as a temperamental category. In R. J. Davidson, K. R. Scherer, & H. H. Goldsmith (Eds.), *Handbook of affective sciences*. New York: Oxford University Press.

Kagan, J. (2003). Biology, Context, and developmental inquiry. *Annual Review of Psychology, 53*. Palo Alto, CA: Annual Reviews.

Kagan, J. (2004, May 8). Commentary in teen brains on trial, *Science News Online*, p. 2.

Kagan, J. J., Kearsley, R. B., & Zelazo, P. R. (1978). *Infancy: Its place in human development*. Cambridge, MA: Harvard University Press.

Kagan, J., & Fox, N. (2006). Biology, culture, and temperamental biases. In W. Damon & R. Lerner (Eds.), *Handbook of child psychology* (6th ed.). New York: Wiley.

Kagan, J., & Snidman, N. (1991). Infant predictors of inhibited and uninhibited behavioral profiles. *Psychological Science, 2*, 40–44.

Kagan, S. H. (2007). Faculty profile, University of Pennsylvania School of Nursing. Retrieved & March, 3, 2007, from www.nursing.upenn.edu/faculty/profile.asp

Kagan, S. L., & Scott-Little, C. (2004). Early learning standards. *Phi Delta Kappan, 82*, 388–395.

Kagitcibasi, C. (2007). *Family, self, and human development across cultures*. Mahwah, NJ: Erlbaum.

Kaiser Family Foundation. (2006). *The media family: Electronic media in the lives of infants, toddlers, preschoolers, and their parents*. Menlo Park, CA: Author.

Kalant, H. (2004). Adverse effects of cannabis on health: An update of the literature since 1996. *Progress in Neuropsychopharmacology and Biological Psychiatry, 28*, 849–863.

Kaleth, A. S., Chittenden, T. W., Hawkins, B. J., Hargens, T. A., Guill, S. G., Zedalis, D., Gregg, J. M., & Herbert, W. G. (2007). Unique cardiopulmonary exercise test responses in overweight middle-aged adults with obstructive sleep apnea. *Sleep Medicine, 8*, 160–168

Kalichman, S. C., Simbayi, L. C., Jooste, S., Cherry, C., & Cain, D. (2005). Poverty-related stressors and HIV AIDS transmission risks in two South African communities. *Journal of Urban Health, 82*, 237–249.

Kalick, S. M., & Hamilton, T. E. (1986). The matching hypothesis reexamined. *Journal of Personality and Social Psychology, 51*, 673–682.

Kalish, R. A. (1981). *Death, grief, and caring relationships*. Monterey, CA: Brooks/Cole.

Kalish, R. A. (1987). Death. In G. L. Maddox (Ed.), *Encyclopedia of aging*. New York: Springer.

Kamerman, S. B. (1989). Child care, women, work, and the family: An international overview of child-care services and related policies. In J. S. Lande, S. Lande, S. Scarr, & N. Gunzenhauser (Eds.), *Caring for children: Challenge to America*. Hillsdale, NJ: Erlbaum.

Kamerman, S. B. (2000a). Parental leave policies. *Social Policy Report of the Society for Research in Child Development. XIV* (No. 2), 1–15.

Kamerman, S. B. (2000b). From maternity to paternity child leave policies. *Journal of the Medical Women's Association, 55*, 98–99.

Kanaka-Gantenbein, C. (2006). Hormone replacement therapy in Turner syndrome. *Pediatric Endocrinology Review, 3 (Suppl 1)*, 214–218.

Kanner, A. D., Coyne, J. C., Schaefer, C., & Lazarus, R. S. (1981). Comparison of two modes of stress measurement: Daily hassles and uplifts versus major life events. *Journal of Behavioral Medicine, 4* 1–39.

Kapo, J., Morrison, L. J., & Liao, S. (2007). Palliative care for the older adult. *Journal of Palliative Medicine, 10*, 182–183.

Kappor, A., Dunn, E., Kostaki, A., Andrews, M. H., & Matthews, S. G. (2006). Fetal programming of hypothalamo-pituitary-adrenal function: Prenatal stress and glutocorticoids. *Journal of Physiology, 572*, 31–44.

Karniol, R., Grosz, E., & Schorr, I. (2003). Caring, gender-role orientation, and volunteering. *Sex Roles, 49*, 11–19.

Karoly, L. A. & Bigelow, J. A. (2005). *The economics of investing in universal preschool education in California*. Santa Monica, California: The RAND Corporation.

Karp, H. (2002). *The happiest baby on the block*. New York: Bantam.

Karpov, Y. V. (2006). *The neo-Vygotskian approach to child development*. New York: Cambridge University Press.

Karsik, R. J., & Hamon, R. R. (2007). Cultural diversity and aging families. In B. S. Trask & R. R. Hamon (Eds.), *Cultural diversity and families*. Thousand Oaks, CA: Sage.

Kastenbaum, R. J. (2007). *Death, society, and human experience* (ed.). Upper Saddle River, NJ: Prentice Hall.

Katakura, Y. (2006), Molecular basis for the cellular senescence program and its application to anticancer therapy. *Bioscience. Biotechnology, and Biochemistry, 70*, 1076–1081.

Katz, I. E. (1999, April). *Toward a family-based hypervigilance model of childhood aggression: The role of the mother's and the father's meta-emotion philosophy*. Paper presented at the meeting of the Society for Research in Child Development; Albuquerque.

Katz, L. (1999). Curriculum disputes in early childhood education. *ERIC Clearinghouse on Elementary and Early Childhood Education*, Document EDO-PS-99-13.

Kaufman, J. C. (Ed.). (2006). *Creative and reason in development*. New York: Cambridge University Press.

Kaufman, S. R. (2005). *And a time to die*. New York: Scribner.

Kaufman, W., & Groters, S. (2006). Developmental neuropathology in DNT studies–a sensitive tool for the detection and characterizations of developmental neurotoxicants. *Reproductive Toxicology, 22*, 196–223.

Kavanaugh, R. D. (2006). Pretend play. In B. Spodek & O. N. Saracho (Eds.), *Handbook of research on the education of young children* (2nd ed.). Mahwah, NJ: Erlbaum.

Kazdin, A. E., & Benjet, C. (2003). Spanking children: Evidence and issues. *Current Directions in Psychological Science, 12*, 99–103.

Keating, D. P. (1990). Adolescent thinking. In S. S. Feldman & G. R. Elliott (Eds.), *At the threshold: The developing adolescent*. Cambridge, MA: Harvard University Press.

Keating, D. P. (2004). Cognitive and brain development. In R. Lerner & L. Steinberg, (Ed.), *Handbook of Adolescent Psychology*, New York: Wiley.

Keen, R. (2005a). Unpublished review of J. W. Santrock's *Topical life-span development* (3rd ed.) New York: McGraw-Hill.

Keller, A., Ford, L., & Meacham, J. (1978). Dimensions of self-accept in preschool children. *Developmental Psychology, 14*, 483–489

Keller, H. (2007). *Cultures of infancy*. Mahwah, NJ: Erlbaum.

Kellman, P. J., & Arterberry, M. E. (2006). Infant visual perception. In W. Damon & R. Lerner (Eds.), *Handbook of child psychology* (6th ed.) New York: Wiley.

Kelly, B. D., & McLoughlin, D. M. (2002). Euthanasia, assisted suicide, and psychiatry: A Pandora's box. *British Journal of Psychiatry, 181*, 278–279.

Kelly, J. B. (2007). Children's living arrangements following separation and divorce: insights from empirical and clinical research. *Family Process, 46*, 35–42.

Kendall, M., Harris, F., Boyd, K., Sheikh, A., Murray, S. A., Brown, D., Mallinson, I., Kearny, N., & Worth, A. (2007, in press).

Key challenges and ways forward in researching the "good death": Qualitative in-depth interview and focus group study. *British Medical Journal*.

Kennell, J. H. (2006). Randomized controlled trial of skin-to-skin contact from birth versus conventional incubator for physiological stabilization in 1200 g to 2199 g newborns. *Acta Paediatica (Sweden)*, 95, 15–16.

Kennell, J. H., & McGrath, S. K. (1999). Commentary: Practical and humanistic lessons from the third world for perinatal caregivers everywhere. *Birth, 26, 9–10.*

Kenney, C. T., & McLanahan, S. S. (2006). Why are cohabiting relationships more violent than marriages? *Demography, 43, 127–140.*

Kerr, M. (2001). Culture as a context for temperament. In T. D. Wachs & G. A. Kohnstamm (Eds.), *Temperament in context.* Mahwah, NJ: Erlbaum.

Kessels, R. P., Bockhorst, S. T., & Postma, A. (2005). The contribution of implicit and explicit memory to the effects of errorless learning: A comparison between younger and older adults. *Journal of the International Neuropsychological Society, 11, 144–151.*

Killgore, W. D., Gruber, S. A., & Yurgelun-Todd, D. A. (2007, in press). Depressed mood and lateralized prefrontal activity during a Stroop task in adolescent children. *Neuroscience Letters.*

Kilmartin, C., & Allison, J. (2007). *Men's violence against women.* Mahwah, NJ: Erlbaum.

Kim, J., & Cicchetti, D. (2004). A longitudinal study of child maltreatment, mother-child relationship quality and maladjustment: The role of self-esteem and social competence. *Journal of Abnormal Child Psychology, 32, 341–354.*

Kim, S. K. (2007). Common aging pathways in worms, flies, mice, and humans. *Journal of Experimental Biology, 210, 1607–1612.*

Kim, S. U. (2007). Genetically engineered human neural stem cells for brain repair in neurological diseases. *Brain Development, 29, 193–201.*

Kim, S., Hasher, L. (2005). The attraction effect in decision making: Superior performance by older adults. *Quarterly Journal of Experimental Psychology, 58A, 120–133.*

Kimmel, A. J. (2007). *Ethical issues in behavioral research.* Malden, MA: Blackwell.

Kimura, D. (2000). *Sex and cognition.* Cambridge, MA: MIT Press.

Kine, D. W., & Scialfa, C. T. (1996). Visual and auditory aging. In J. E. Birren & K. W. Scahie (Eds.), *Handbook of the psychology of aging* (4th ed.), San Diego: Academic Press.

King, K. M., & Chassin, L. (2007). A prospective study of the effects of age of initiation of alcohol and drug use on young adult substance dependence. *Journal of Studies on Alcohol and Drugs, 68, 256–265.*

King, V., & Scott, M. E. (2005). A comparison of cohabiting relationships among older and younger adults. *Journal of Marriage and the Family, 67, 271–285.*

Kirsch, G., McVey, G., Tweed, S., & Katzman, D. K. (2007). Psychosocial profiles of young adolescent females seeking treatment for an eating disorder. *Journal of Adolescent Health, 40, 351–356.*

Kisilevsky, S., Hains, S. M., Jacquet, A. Y., Granier-Deferre, C., & Lecanuet, J. P. (2005). Maturation of fetal responses to music. *Developmental Science, 7, 550–559.*

Kistner, J., A., David-Ferdon, C. F., Repper, K. K., & Joiner, T. E. (2006). Bias and accuracy of childrens' perceptions of peer acceptance: Prospective associations with depressive symptoms. *Journal of Abnormal Child Psychology, 34, 349–361.*

Kitchener, K. S., King, P. M., & DeLuca, S. (2006). The development of reflective judgemnt in adulthood. In C. Hoare (Ed.), *Handbook of adult development and learning.* New York: Oxford University Press.

Klaczynski, P. (2005). Metacognition and cognitive variability: A two-process model of decision making and its development. In J. Jacobs & P. Klaczynski (Eds.), *The development of decision making: cognitive, sociocultural, and legal perspectives.* Mahwah, NJ: Erlbaum.

Klaczynski, P. A., & Narasimham, G. (1998). Development of scientific reasoning biases: Cognitive versus ego-protective explanations. *Developmental Psychology, 34, 175–187*

Klaus, M., & Kennell, H. H. (1976). *Maternal-infant bonding.* St. Louis: Mosby.

Kling, K. C., Hyde, J. S., Showers, C. J., & Buswell, B. N. (1999). Gender differences in self-esteem: A meta-analysis. *Psychological Bulletin, 125, 470–500.*

Klingman, A. (2006). Children and war trauma. In W. Damon & R. Lerner (Eds.), *Handbook of child psychology* (6th ed.). New York: Wiley.

Kobayashi, K., Tajima, M., Toishi, S., Fujimori, K., Suzuki, Y., & Udagama, H. (2005). Fetal growth restriction associated with measles virus infection during pregnancy. *Journal of Perinatal Medicine, 33, 67–68.*

Koening, H. G., & Blazer, D. G. (1996). Depression. In J. E. Birren (Ed.), *Encyclopedia of gerontology* (Vol. 1). San Diego: Academic Press.

Kohlberg, L. (1958). *The development on modes of moral thinking and choice in the years 10 to 16.* Unpublished doctoral dissertation, University of Chicago.

Kohlberg, L. (1986). A current statement of some theoretical issues. In S. Modgil & C. Modgil (Eds.), *Lawrence Kohlberg.* Philadelphia: Falmer.

Kopp, C. B., & Neufeld, S. J. (2002). Emotional development in infancy. In R. Davidson & K. Scherer (Eds.), *Handbook of effective sciences.* New York: Oxford University Press.

Koppelman, K., & Goodheart, L. (2008). *Understanding human differences* (2nd ed.). Boston: Allyn & Bacon.

Koren-Karie, N., Oppenheim, D., & Goldsmith, D. (2007). Keeping the inner world of the child in mind. In D. Oppenheim & D. Goldsmith (Eds.), *Attachment theory in clinical work with children.* New York: Guilford.

Kosta, T., & Praczko, K. (2007). Interrelationship between physical activity, symptomatology of upper respiratory tract infections, and depression in elderly people. *Gerontology, 53, 187–193.*

Kostelnik, M. J., Soderman, A. K., & Whiren, A. P. (2007). *Developmentally appropriate curriculum* (4th ed.). Upper Saddle River, NJ: Prentice Hall.

Kotre, J. (1984). *Outliving the self: Generativity and the interpretation of lives.* Baltimore: Johns Hopkins University Press.

Kottak, C. P. (2004). *Cultural anthropology* (10th ed.). New York: McGraw-Hill.

Kottak, C. P., & Kozaitis, K. A. (2008). *On being different: Diversity and multiculturalism in the United States* (3rd ed.). New York: McGraw-Hill.

Kozol, J. (2005). *The shame of the nation.* New York: Crown.

Kraebel, K. S., Fable, J., & Gerhardtein, P. (2004). New methodology in infant operant kicking procedures. *Infant Behavior and Development, 127, 1–18.*

Kralisch, S., Bluher, M., Paschke, R., Stumvoll, M., & Fasshauer, M. (2007). Adipokines and adipocyte targets in the future management of obesity and the metabolic syndrome. *Mini Reviews in Medicinal Chemistry, 7, 39–45.*

Kramer, A. F., Fabiani, M., & Colcombe, S. J. (2006) Contributions of cognitive neuroscience to the understanding of behavior and aging. In J. E. Birren & K. W. Schaie (Eds.), *Handbook of the psychology of aging* (6th ed.). San Diego: Academic Press.

Kramer, A. F., Hahn, S., Cohen, N. J., Banich, M. T., McAuley, E., Harrison, C., Chason, J., Vakil, E., Bardell, L., Bolleau, R., & Colcombe, A. (1999, July). Ageing, fitness, and neurocognitive function. *Nature, 400, 418–419.*

Kramer, A. F., & Morrow, D. (2007) Cognitive training and expertise. In D. Park & N. Schmarterz (Eds.), *Cognitive aging: A primer* (2nd Ed.)

Kramer, L. (2006, July 10). Commentary in "How your siblings make you who you are." by Kluger, J. *Time*, pp. 46–55.

Kramer, L., & Perozynski, L. (1999). Parental beliefs about managing sibling conflict. *Developmental Psychology, 35,* 489–499.

Kramer, L., & Radey, C. (1997). Improving sibling relationships among young children: A social skills training model. *Family Relations, 46,* 237–246.

Krause, N. E. (2006). Religion and aging. In J. E. Birren & K. W. Schaie (Eds.), *Handbook of the psychology of aging.* San Diego: Academic Press.

Krebs, N. F. (2007). Food choices to meet nutritional needs of breast-fed infants and toddlers on mixed diets. *Journal of Nutrition, 137,* 511S–517S.

Kreutzer, M., Leonard, C., & Flavell, J. H. (1975). An interview study of children's knowledge about memory. *Monographs of the Society for Research in Child Development, 40* (1, Serial No. 159).

Kristensen, J., Vestergaard, M., Wisborg, I. K., Kesmodel, U., & Secher, N. J. (2005). Pre-pregnancy weight and the risk of stillbirth and neonatal death. *British Journal of Obstetrics and Gynecology, 112,* 403–408.

Kroger, J. (2007). *Identity development: Adolescence through adulthood.* Thousand Oaks, CA: Sage.

Kruger, J., Blanck, H. M., & Gillespie, C. (2006). Dietary and physical activity behaviors among adults successful at weight loss management. *International Journal of Behavioral Nutrition and Physical Activity, 3,* 17.

Ksir, C. J., Chart, C. L., & Ray, O. S. (2008). *Drugs, society, and human behavior* (12th ed.). New York: McGraw-Hill.

Kuebli, J. (1994, March). Young children's understanding of everyday emotions. *Young Children,* pp. 36–48.

Kuehn, B. M. (2005). Better osteoporosis management a priority: Impact predicted to soar with aging population. *Journal of the American Medical Association, 293,* 2453–2458.

Kuhl, P. K. (1993). Infant speech perception: A window on psycholinguistic development. *International Journal of Psycholinguistics, 9,* 33–56.

Kuhl, P. K. (2000). A new view of language acquisition. *Proceedings of the National Academy of Science, 97* (22), 11850–11857.

Kuhl, P. K. (2007). Is speech learning "gated" by the social brain? *Developmental Science, 10,* 110–120.

Kuhl, P. K., Stevens, E., Hayashi, A., Deguchi, T., Kiritani, S., & Iverson, P. (2006). Infants show a facilitation for native language phonetic perception between 6 and 12 months. *Development Science, 9,* F13–F21.

Kuhn, D. (1999). A developmental model of critical thinking. *Educational Researcher, 28,* 16–25.

Kuhn, D., & Franklin, S. (2006). The second decade: What develops (and how)?

In W. Damon & R. Lerner (Eds.), *Handbook of child psychology* (6th ed.). New York: Wiley.

Kumar, R., Gautam, G., Gupta, N. P., Aron, M., Dada, R., Kucheria, K., Gupta, S. K., & Mitra, A. (2006). Role of testicular fine-needle aspiration cytology in infertile men with clinical obstructive azoospermia. *National Medical Journal of India, 19,* 18–20.

Kupermidt, J. B., & Cole, J. D. (1990). Preadolescent peer status, aggression, and school adjustment as predictors of externalizing problems in adolescence. *Child Development, 61,* 1350–1363.

Kupperman, M., Learman, L. A., Gates, E., Gregorich, S. E., Nease, R. F., Lewis, J., & Washington, A. E. (2006). Beyond race or ethnicity and socioeconomic status: Predictors of prenatal testing for Down syndrome. *Obstetrics and Gynecology, 107,* 1087–1097.

Kurdek, L. A. (2006). Differences between partners from heterosexual, gay, and lesbian cohabiting couples. *Journal of Marriage and the Family, 68,* 509–528.

Kurth, T., Everett, B. M., Buring, J. E., Kase, C. S., Ridker, P. M., & Gaziano, J. M. (2007). Lipid levels and the risk of ischemic stroke in women. *Neurology, 68,* 556–562.

Kwan, M. L., Buffler, P. A., Abrams, B., & Kiley, V. A. (2004). Breastfeeding and the risk of childhood leukemia: A meta-analysis. *Public Health Reports, 119,* 521–535.

L

Löckenhoff, C. E., & Carstensen, L. L. (2007). Aging, emotion, and health-related decision strategies: Mutivational manipulation differences. *Psychology and Aging, 22,* 134–146.

La Greca, A. M., & Harrison, H. M. (2005). Adolescent peer relations, friendships, and romantic relationships: Do they predict social anxiety and depression? *Journal of Clinical Child and Adolescent Psychology, 34,* 49–61.

Labouvie-Vief, G. (1986, August). *Modes of knowing and life-span cognition.* Paper presented at the meeting of the American Psychological Association, Washington, DC.

Labouvie-Vief, G. (2006). Emerging structures of adult thought. In J. J. Arnett & J. L. Tanner (Eds.), *Emerging adults in America.* Washington, DC: American Psychological Association.

Labouvie-Vief, G., & Diehl, M. (1999). Self and personality development. In J. C. Kavanaugh & S. K. Whitbourne (Eds.), *Gerontology: An interdisciplinary perspective.* New York: Oxford University Press.

Lachlan, R. F., & Feldman, M. W. (2003). Evolution of cultural communication systems. *Journal of Evolutionary Biology, 16,* 1084–1095.

Lachman, M. E. (2004) Development in midlife. *Annual Review of psychology (Vol. 55)* Palo Alto, CA: Annual Reviews.

Lachman, M. E. (2006). Perceived control over aging-related declines. *Current Directions in Psychological Science, 15,* 282–286.

Lachman, M. E., & Firth, K. (2004). The adaptive value of feeling in control during midlife. In G. O. Brim, C. D. Ruff, & R. C. Kessler (Eds.), *How healthy we are?* Chicago: University of Chicago, Press.

Lachman, M. E., Maier, H., & Budner, R. (2000). *A portrait of midlife.* Unpublished manuscript, Brandeis University, Waltham, MA.

Lachman, M. E., & Weaver, S. L. (1998). Sociodemographic variations in the sense of control by domain: Findings from the MacArthur Study of Midlife. *Psychology and Aging, 13,* 553–562.

Ladd, G. W. (2005). *Peer relationship and social competence of children and adolescents.* New Haven, CT: Yale University Press.

Ladd, G. W., Hearld, S. L., & Andres, R. K. (2006). Young children's peer relations and social competence. In B. Spodek & O. N. Sarancho (Eds.), *Handbook of research on the education of young children.* Mahwah, NJ: Erlbaum.

Laditka, S. B., Laditka, J. N., Bennett, K., J. & Probst, J. C. (2005). Delivery complications associated with prenatal care access for Medicaid-insured mothers in rural and urban hospitals. *Journal of Rural Health, 21,* 158–166.

Laible, D., & Thompson, R. A. (2007). Early socialization: A relationship perspective, In J. E. Grusec & P. D. Hastings (Eds.), *Handbook of socialization.* New York: Guilford.

Laible, D. J., Carolo, G., & Raffaell, M. (2000). The differential relations of parent and peer attachment to adolescent adjustment. *Journal of Youth and Adolescence, 29,* 45–53.

Lamb, C. S., Jackson, L. A., Cassiday, P. B., & Priest, D. J. (1993). Body figure preferences of men and women: A comparison of two generations. *Sex Roles, 28,* 345–358.

Lamb, M. E. (1977). The development of mother-infant and father-infant attachments in the second year of life. *Developmental Psychology, 13,* 637–648.

Lamb, M. E. (1986). *The father's role: Applied perspectives.* New York: Wiley.

Lamb, M. E. (1994). Infant care practices and the application of knowledge. In C. B. Fisher & R. M. Lerner (Eds.), *Applied developmental psychology.* New York: McGraw-Hill.

Lamb, M. E. (2000). The history of research on father involvement: An overview. *Marriage and Family Review, 29,* 23–42.

Lamb, M. E. (2005). Attachments, social networks, and developmental contexts. *Human Development, 48,* 108–112.

Lamb, M. E., & Ahnert, M. E. (2006). Nonparental child care. In W. Damon &

R. Lerner (Eds.), *Handbook of child psychology* (6th ed). New York: Wiley.

Lamb, M. E., Bronskin, M. H., & Teti, D. M. (2002). *Development in infancy* (4th ed.). Mahwah, NJ: Erlbaum.

Lamb, V. L. (2003). Historical and epidemiological trends in mortality in the United States. In C. D. Bryant (Ed.), *Handbook of death and dying*. Thousand Oaks, CA: Sage.

Lamers, W. H. (2007). Defining palliative care, cancer without pain, when to contact hospice, when to treat multiple myeloma, meaning of physical signs, pneumonia at end-of-life. *Journal of Pain and Palliative Care Pharmacology, 21,* 85–90.

Lamont, R. F., & Jaggat, A. N. (2007). Emerging drug therapies for preventing spontaneous labor and preterm birth. *Expert Opinion on Investigational Drugs, 16,* 337–345.

Land, K. C., & Yang, Y. (2006). Morbidity, disability, and mortality. In R. H. Binstock & L. K. George (Eds.), *Handbook of aging and the social sciences* (sixth ed.) San Diego: Academic press.

Lane, H. (1976). *The wild boy of Aveyron.* Cambridge, MA: Harvard University Press.

Lang, F. R., & Carstensen, L. L. (1994). Close emotional relationship in late life: Further support for proactive aging in the social domain. *Psychology and Aging, 9,* 315–324.

Lapsley, D. K., & Narvaez, D. (2006). Character education. In W. Damon & R. Lerner (Eds.), *Handbook of child psychology* (6th ed.). New York: Wiley.

Larson, R. W., & Wilson, S. (2004). Adolescence across place and time: Globalization and the changing pathways to adulthood. In R. Lerner – L. Steinberg (Eds.), *Handbook of adolescent psychology.* New York: Wiley.

Latham, N. K., Bennett, D. A., Stetton, C. M., & Anderson, C. S. (2004). Systematic review of resistance strength training in older adults. *Journals of Geronotology A: Biological Sciences and Medical Sciences, 59,* M48–M61.

Lazarus, R. S., & Folkman, S. (1984). *Stress, appraisal, and coping.* New York: Springer.

Leadbeater, B. J. R., & Way, N. (2001). *Growing up fast.* Mahwah, NJ: Erlbaum.

Leaper, C., & Friedman, C. K. (2007). The socialization of gender. In J. E. Grusec & P. D. Davidson (Eds.), *Handbook of socialization.* New York: Guilford.

Leaper, C., & Smith, T. E. (2004). A meta-analytic review of gender variations in children's language use: Talkativeness, affiliative speech, and assertive speech. *Developmental Psychology, 40,* 993–1027.

LeDoux, J. E. (1998). *The emotional brain: The mysterious underpinnings of emotional life.* New York: Simon & Schuster.

Lee, A., & Chan, S. (2006). Acupuncture and anesthesia. *Best Practices in Research and Clinical Anesthesia, 20,* 303–314.

Lee, D. J., & Markides, K. S. (1990). Activity and mortality among aged persons over an eight-year period. *Journals of Gerontology: Social Sciences, 45,* S39-S42.

Lee, H. Y., Lee, E. L., Pathy, P., & Chan, Y. H. (2005). Anorexia nervosa in Singapore: An eight-year retrospective study. *Singapore Medical Journal, 46,* 275–281.

Lee, I. M., Manson, J. E., Hennekens, C. H., & Paffenbarger, R. S. (1993). Bodyweight and mortality: A 27-year-follow-up. *Journal of the American Medical Association, 270,* 2823–2828.

Lee, I. M., & Skerrett, P. J. (2001). Physical activity and all-cause mortality: What is the dose-response relation? *Medical science and Sports Exercise, 33* (6 Suppl.), S459–S471.

Lee, J., Pommerville, P., Brock, G., Gagnon, R., Mehta, P., Krisdaphongs, M., Chan, M., & Dickson, R. (2006). Physician-rated patient preference and patient rated preference for tadalafil or sildenafil citrate: Results from the Canadian 'Treatment of Erectile Dysfunction' observational study. *British Journal of Urology, 98,* 623–629.

Lee, S., Cho, E., Grodstein, F., Kawachi, I., Hu, F. B., & Colditz, G. A. (2005). Effects of marital transitions on changes in dietary and other health behaviors in U.S. women. *International Journal of Epidemiology, 34,* 69–78.

Lefkowitz, E. S., & Gillen, M. M. (2006). ``Sex is just a normal part of life'': Sexuality in emerging adulthood. In J. J. Arnett & J. L. Tanner (Eds.), *Emerging adults in America.* Washington, DC: American Psychological Association.

Lehman, H. C. (1960). The age decrement in outstanding scientific creativity. *American Psychologist, 15,* 128–134.

Lehr, C. A., Hanson, A., Sinclair, M. F., & Christensen, S. L. (2003). Moving beyond dropout prevention towards school completion. *School Psychology Review, 32,* 342–364.

Leifer, A. D. (1973). *Television and the development of social behavior.* Paper presented at the meeting of the International Society for the Study of Behavioral Development, Ann Arbor, MI.

Leifer, G. (2007). *Introduction to maternity and pediatric nursing* (5th ed.). London: Elsevier.

Lenders, C. M., McBirath, T. F., & Scholl, T. O. (2000). Nutrition in pregnancy. *Current Opinions in Pediatrics. 12,* 291–296.

Leonards, U., Ibanez, V., & Giannakopoulos, P. (2002). The role of stimulus type in age-related changes of visual working memory. *Experimental Brain Research, 146,* 172–183.

Leppanen, J. M., Moulson, M., Vogel-Farley, V. K., & Nelson, C. A. (2007). An ERP study of emotional face processing in the adult and infant brain. *Child Development, 78,* 232–245.

Lerner, H, G. (1989). *The dance of intimacy.* New York: Harper & Row.

Lesaux, N. K., & Siegel, L. S. (2003). The development of reading in children who speak English as a second language. *Developmental Psychology, 39,* 1005–1019.

Lesley, C. (2005). *Burning fence: A Western memoir of fatherhood.* New York: St. Martin's Press.

Lespessailles, E., & Prouteau, S. (2006). Is there a synergy between physical exercise and drug therapies for osteoporosis? *Clinical and Experimental Rheumatology, 24,* 191–195.

Lessow-Hurely, J. (2005). *The foundations of language instruction* (4th ed.). Boston: Allyn & Bacon.

Lester, B. M., Tronick, E. Z., LaGasse, L., Seifer, R., Bauer, C. R., Shankarnan, S., Bada, H. S., Wright, L. L., Smeriglio, V. L., Lu, J., Finnegan, L. P., & Maza, P. L. (2002). The maternal lifestyle study: Effects of substance exposure during pregnancy on neurodevelopmental outcome in 1-month-old infants. *Pediatrics, 110,* 1182–1192.

Levant, R. F. (2002). Men and masculinity. In J. Worell (Ed.), *Encyclopedia of women and gender.* Diego: Academic Press.

LeVay, S. (1991). A difference in the hypothalamic structure between heterosexual and homosexual men. *Science, 253,* 1034–1037.

Levelt, W. J. M. (1989). *Speaking: From intention to articulation.* Cambridge, MA: MIT Press.

Leventhal, A. (1994, February). *Peer conformity during adolescence: An integration of developmental, situational, and individual characteristics.* Paper presented at the meeting of the Society for Research on Adolescence, San Diego.

Levine, B., Stuss, D. T., Winocur, G., Binns, M. A., Fahy, L., Mandic, M., Bridges, K., & Robertson, I. H. (2007). Cognitive rehabilitation in the elderly: Effects on strategic behavior in relation to goal management. *Journal of the International Neuropsychological Society, 13,* 143–152.

LeVine, S. (1979). *Mothers and wives: Gusii women of East Africa.* Chicago: University of Chicago Press.

Levinson, D. J. (1978). *The seasons of man's life.* New York: Knopf.

Levinson, D. J. (1996). *Seasons of a woman's life.* New York: Alfred Knopf.

Levy, B. R. (2002). Longevity increased by positive self-perceptions of aging. *Journal of Personality of personality and Social Psychology, 83,* 261–270.

Lewis, A. C. (2007). Looking beyond NCLB. *Phi Delta Kappan, 88,* 483–484.

Lewis, M. (1997). *Altering fate: Why the past does not predict the future.* New York: Guilford.

Lewis, M. (2001). Issues in the study of personality development. *Psychological Inquiry, 12,* 67–83.

Lewis, M. (2005). Selfhood. In B. Hopkins (Ed.), *The Cambridge Encyclopedia of child development*. Cambridge, UK: Cambridge University Press.

Lewis, M. (2007). Early emotional development. In A. Slater & M. Lewis (Eds.), *Introduction to infant development*. (2nd ed.). New York: Oxford University Press.

Lewis, M., & Brooks-Gunn, J. (1979). *Social cognition and the acquisition of the self*. New York: Plenum.

Lewis, M., Feiring, C., & Rosenthal, S. (2000). Attachment over time. *Child Development, 71*, 707–720.

Lewis, R. (2007). *Human genetics* (7th Ed.). New York. M-Grand-Hill.

Li, C., Ford, E. S., McGuire, L. C., & Mokdad, A. H. (2007). Increasing trends in waist circumference and abdominal obesity among US adults. *Obesity, 15*, 216–224.

Li, C., Goran, M. I., Kauer, H., Nollen, N., & Ahluwalia, J. S. (2007). Developmental trajectories of overweight during childhood: Role of early life factors. *Obesity, 15*, 760–761.

Li, D., Liao, C., Yi, C., & Pan, M. (2006). Amniocentesis for karyotyping prior to induction of abortion at second trimester. *Prenatal Diagnosis, 26*, 192.

Li, D. K., Willinger, M., Petitti, D. B., Odulil, R. K., Liu, L., & Hoffman, H. J. (2006). Use of a dummy (pacifier) during sleep and risk of sudden infant death syndrome (SIDS): Population-based case-control study. *British Medical Journal, 332*, 18–22.

Liben, L. S. (1995). Psychology meets geography: Exploring the gender gap on the national geography bee. *Psychological Science Agenda, 8*, 8–9.

Lie, E., & Newcombe, N. (1999). Elementary school children's explicit and implicit memory for faces of preschool classmates. *Developmental Psychology, 35*, 102–112.

Lieberman, E., Davidson, K., Lee-Parritz, A., & Shearer, E. (2005). Changes in fetal position during labor and their association with epidural analgesia. *Obstetrics and Gynecology, 105*, 974–982.

Liederman, J., Kantrowitz, L., & Flannery, K. (2005). Male vulnerability to reading disability is not likely to be a myth: A call for new data. *Journal of Learning Disabilities, 38*, 109–129.

Limber, S. P. (1997). Preventing violence among school children. *Family Futures, 1*, 27–28.

Limber, S. P. (2004). Implementation of the Olweus Bullying Prevention Program in American schools: Lessons learned from the field. In D. L. Espelage, & S. M. Swearer (Eds.), *Bullying in American schools*. Mahwah, NJ: Erlbaum.

Lin, M., Johnson, J. E., & Johnson, K. M. (2003). Dramatic play in Montessori kindergartens in Taiwan and Mainland China. Unpublished manuscript, Department of Curriculum and Instruction, Pennsylvania State University, University Park, PA.

Lindsay, A. C., Sussner, K. M., Kim, J., & Gortmaker, S. (2006). The role of parents in preventing childhood obesity. *Future of Children, 16 (No. 1)*, 169–186.

Liscak, R., & Vladyka, V. (2007). Radiosurgery in ocular disorders: Clinical applications. *Progress in Neurological Surgery, 20*, 324–339.

Liszkowski, U. (2007, March). *A new look at infant pointing*. Paper presented at the meeting of the Society for Research in Child Development, Boston.

Liu, J., Raine, A., Venables, P. H., Dalais, C., & Mednick, S. A. (2003). Malnutrition at age 3 years and lower cognitive ability at age 11 years: Independence from psychosocial adversity. *Archives of Pediatric and Adolescent Medicine, 157*, 593–600.

Liu, J., Raine, A., Venables, P. H., & Mednick, S. A. (2004). Malnutrition at 3 years and externalizing behavior problems at age 8, 11, and 17 years. *American Journal of Psychiatry, 161*, 2005–2013.

Liu, Q., Xie, F., Rolston, R., Moreira, P. I., Nunomura, A., Zhu, X., Smith, M. A., & Perry, G. (2007). Prevention and treatment of Alzheimer disease and aging: Antioxidants. *Mini Reviews in Medicinal Chemistry, 7*, 171–180.

Liu, Y. J., Xiao, P., Xiong, D. H., Recker, R. R., & Deng, H. W. (2005). Searching for obesity genes: Progress and prospects. *Drugs Today, 41*, 345–362.

Lively, W., & Bromley, D. (1973). *Person perception in childhood and adolescence*. New York: Wiley.

Lobar, S. L., Youngblut, J. M., & Brooten, D. (2006). Cross-cultural beliefs, ceremonies, and rituals surrounding death of a loved one. *Pediatric Nursing, 32*, 44–50.

Locher, J. L., Ritchie, C. S., Roth, D. L., Baker, P. S., Bodner, E. V., & Aliman, R. M. (2005). Social isolation, support, and capital and nutritional risk in an older sample: Ethnic and gender differences. *Social Science Medicine, 60*, 747–761.

Lock, A. (2004). Preverbal communication. In U. Goswami (Ed.), *Blackwell handbook of childhood cognitive development*. Malden, MA: Blackwell.

London, M. L., Ladewig, P. A., Ball, J. W., & Bindler, R. A. (2007). *Maternal and child nursing care (2nd ed.)*. Upper Saddle River, NJ: Prentice Hall.

Lopata, H. Z. (1994). *Circles and settings: Role changes of American women*. Albany State University of New York Press.

Lopez-Liuch, G., & others. (2006). Calorie restriction induces mitochondrial biogenesis and bioenergetic efficiency. *Proceedings of the National Academy of Science USA, 103*, 1768–1773.

Lorenz, K. Z. (1965). *Evolution and the modification of behavior*. Chicago: University of Chicago Press.

Loucks, E. B. & others. (2006). Association of educational level with inflammatory markers in the Framinton Offspring Study. *American Journal of Epidemiology, 163*, 622–628.

Loughlin, K. R. (2007). Urologic radiology during pregnancy. *Urology Clinics of North America, 34*, 23–26.

Louria, D. B. (2005). Extraordinary longevity: Individual and societal issues. *Journal of the American Geriatric Society, 53 (9 Suppl)*. S317–S319.

Lucas, R. E., Clark, A. E., Yannis, G., & Diener, E. (2004). Unemployment alters the setpoint for life satisfaction. *Psychological Science, 15*, 8–13.

Luders, E., Natr, K. L., Thompson, P. M., Rex, D. E., Jancke, L., Steinmetz, H., & Toga, A. W. (2004). Gender differences in cortical complexity. *Native Neuroscience, 1*, 799–800.

Ludington-Hoe, S. M., Lewis, T., Morgan, K., Cong, X., Anderson, L., & Reese, S. (2006). Breast and infant temperatures with twins during kangaroo care. *Journal of Obstetric, Gynecologic, and Neonatal Nursing, 35*, 223–231.

Lundstedt, G., Edlund, B., Engstrom, I., Thurfjell, B., & Marcus, C. (2006). Eating disorder traits in obese children and adolescents. *Eating and Weight Disorders, 11*, 45–50.

Luria, A., & Herzog, E. (1985, April). *Gender segregation across and within settings*. Paper presented at the biennial meeting of the society for Research in Child Development, Toronto.

Lust, R. (2003). *Child language*. New York: Cambridge University Press.

Luyckx, L., Soenens, B., Goosens, L., & Berzonsky, M. D. (2006). Parental control and dimensions of identity formation in emerging adulthood. *Journal of Family Psychology, 42*, 305–318.

Lykken, D. (2001). *Happiness: What studies on twins show us about nature, nurture, and the happiness set point*. New York: Golden Books.

Lyndaker, C., & Hulton, L. (2004). The influence of age on symptoms of perimenopause. *Journal of Obstetric, Gynecological, and Neonatal Nursing, 33*. 340–347.

Lynn, R. (1996). Racial and ethnic differences in intelligence in the U.S. on the Differential Ability Scale. *Personality and Individual Differences, 26*, 271–273.

Lynne, S. D., Graber, J. A., Nichols, T. R., Brooks-Gunn, J., & Botvin, G.J. (2007). Links between pubertal timing, peer influences, and externalizing behaviors among urban students followed through middle school. *Journal of Adolescent Health, 181,* e7–e13.

Lyon, T. D., & Flavell, J. H. (1993). Young children's understanding of forgetting over time. *Child Development, 64,* 789–800.

Lyyra, T. -M., & Heikkinen, R. -L. (2006). Perceived social support and mortality in older people. *Journals of Gerontology B: Psychological Sciences and Social Sciences, 61,* S147–S152.

M

McAdoo, H. P. (2006). *Black Families* (4th ed.). Thousand oaks, CA: Sage.

Maccoby, E. E. (1984). Middle childhood in the context of the family. In *Development during middle childhood.* Washington, DC: National Academy Press.

Maccoby, E. E. (1987, November). Interview with Elizabeth Hall: All in the family. *Psychology Today,* pp. 54–60.

Maccoby, E. E. (1992). The role of parents in the socialization of children: An historical overview. *Developmental Psychology, 28,* 1006–1018.

Maccoby, E. E. (1998). The two sexes: Growing up apart, coming together. Cambridge, MA: Harvard University Press.

Maccoby, E. E. (2002). Gender and group processes. *Current Directions in Psychological Science, 11,* 54–58.

Maccoby, E. E. (2007). Historical overview of socialization research and theory. In J. E. Grusec & P. D. Hastings (Eds.), *Handbook of socialization.* New York: Guilford.

Maccoby, E. E., & Jacklin, C. N. (1974). *The psychology of sex differences,* Palo Alto, CA: Stanford University Press.

Maccoby, E. E., & Martin, J. A. (1983). Socialization in the context of the family: Parent-child interaction. In P. H. Mussen (Ed.), *Handbook of child psychology* (4th ed., Vol. 4). New York: Wiley.

Maccoby, E. E., & Mnookin, R. H. (1992). *Dividing the child: Social and legal dilemmas of custody.* Cambridge, MA: Harvard University Press.

MacFarlane, J. A. (1975). Olfaction in the development of social preferences in the human neonate. In *Parent-infant interaction.* Ciba Foundation Symposium No. 33. Amsterdam: Elsevier.

MacGeorge, E. L. (2003). Gender differences in attributions and emotions in helping contexts. *Sex Roles, 48,* 175–182.

MacGeorge, E. L. (2004). The myth of gender cultures: Similarities outweigh differences in men's and women's provisions of and responses to supportive communication. *Sex Roles, 50,* 143–175.

Maciejewski, P. K., Zhang, B., Block, S. D., & Prigerson, H. G. (2007). *Journal of the American Medical Association, 297,* 716–723.

Maciokas, J. B., & Crognale, M. A. (2003). Cognitive and attentional changes with age: Evidence from attentional blink deficits. *Experimental Aging Research, 29,* 137–153.

Macononchie, N., Doyle, P., Prior, S., & Simmons, R. (2007). Risk factors for first trimester miscarriage—results from a UK-population-based case-control study. *British Journal of Obstetrics and Gynecology, 114,* 170–176.

McAdams, D. P. (2001). Generativity in midlife. In M. E. Lachman (Ed.). *Handbook of midlife development.* New York: Wiley.

Madden, D. J., Gottlob, L. R., Denny, L. L., Turkington, T. G., Provenzale, J. M., Hawk, T. C., & others. (1999). Aging and recognition memory: Changes in regional cerebral blood flow associated with components of reaction time distributions. *Journal of Cognitive Neuroscience, 11,* 511–520.

Mader, S. S. (2008). *Inquiry into life* (12th ed.). New York: McGraw-Hill.

Magnuson, K. A., & Duncan, G. J. (2002). Poverty and parenting. In M. H. Bornstein (Ed.), *Handbook of parenting.* Mahwah, NJ: Erlbaum.

Magrie, F., Cravello, L., Barili, L., Sarra, S., Cinchetti, W., Salmoiraghi, F., Micale, G., & Ferrari, E. (2006). Stress and dementia: The role of the hypothalamic-pituiatary-adrenal axis. *Aging: Clinical and Experimental Research 18,* 167–170.

Main, M. (2000). Attachment theory. In A. Kazdin (Ed.), *Encyclopedia of psychology.* Washington, DC, & New York: American Psychological Association and Oxford University Press.

Mainous, A. G., Majeed, A., Koopman, R. J., Baker, R., Everett, C. J., Tilley, B. C., & Diaz, V. A. (2006). Acculturation and diabetes among Hispanics: Evidence from the 1999–2002 National Health and Nutrition Examination Survey. *Public Health Reports. 121,* 60–66.

Maitland, T. E., Gomez-Marin, O., Weddle, D. O., & Fleming, L. E. (2006). Associations of nationality and race with nutritional status during perimenopause: Implications for public health practice. *Ethnicity and Disease, 16,* 201–216.

Mak, W. W. S., Chen, S. X., Wong, E. C., & Zane, N. W. S. (2005). A psychosocial model of stress-distress relationship among Chinese Americans. *Journal of Social and clinical Psychology, 24,* 422–424.

Makrides, M., Neumann, M., Simmer, K., Pater, J., & Gibson, R. (1995). Are long-chain polyunsaturated fatty acids essential nutrients in infancy? *Lancet, 345,* 1463–1468.

Malamitsi-Puchner, A., & Boutsikou, T. (2006). Adolescent pregnancy and perinatal outcome. *Pediatric Endocrinology Review, 3* (Suppl). 170–171.

Malik, V. S., & Hu, F. B. (2007). Popular weight-loss diets: From evidence to practice. *Nature Clinical Practice. Cardiovascular Medicine, 4,* 34–41.

Mallis, D., Moisidis, K., Kirana, P. S., Papaharitou, S., Simos, G., & Hatzichristou, D. (2006). Moderate and severe erectile dysfunction equally affects life satisfaction. *Journal of Sexual Medicine, 3,* 442–449.

Mandara, J. (2006). The impact of family functioning on African American males' academic achievement: A review and clarification of the empirical literature. *Teachers College Records, 108,* 206–233.

Mandler, J. M. (2004). *The foundations of mind.* New York: Oxford University Press.

Mandler, J. M. (2006). *Jean Mandler.* Retrieved January 5, 2006, from http://cogsci.ucsd.edu/-jean/.

Mandler, J.M., & McDonough, L. (1993). Concept formation in infancy. *Cognitive Development, 8,* 291–318.

Mannessier, L., Alie-Daram, S., Roubinet, F., & Brossard, Y. (2000). Prevention of fetal hemolytic disease: It is time to take action. *Transfusions in Clinical Biology, 7,* 527–532.

Manzoli, L., Villari, P., Pirone, M., & Boccia, A. (2007). Marital status and mortality in the elderly: A systematic review and meta-analysis. *Social Science Medicine, 64,* 77–94.

Maoli, F., & others (2007). Conversion of mild cognitive impairment to dementia in elderly subjects: A preliminary study in a memory and cognitive disorder unit. *Archives of Gerontology and Geriatrics, 44 (Suppl.),* S233–S241.

Marchman, V., & Thal, D. (2005). Words and grammar. In M. Tomasello & D. I. Slobin (Eds.), *Beyond nature-nurture.* Mahwah, NJ: Erlbaum.

Marcia, J. E. (1980). Ego identity development. In J. Adelson (Ed.), *Handbook of adolescent psychology.* New York: Wiley.

Marcia, J. E. (1994). The empirical study of ego. identity. In H. A. Bosma, T. L. G. Grasfsma, H. D. Grotevant, & D. J. De Levits (Eds.), *Identity and development.* Newbury Park, CA: Sage.

Marcia, J. E. (2002). Identity and psychosocial development in adulthood. *Identity, 2,* 7–28.

Marcoen, A., Coleman, P., & O' Hanlon, A. (2007). Psychological aging. In J. Bond, S. Peace, F. Dittman-Kohli, & G. Westerhoff (Eds.), *Aging in society* (3rd ed.). Thousand Oaks, CA: Sage.

Marcon, R. A. (2003). The physical side of development. *Young Children, 58 (No. 1),* 80–87.

Marcovitch, H. (2004). Use of stimulants for attention deficit hyperactivity disorder: AGAINST. *British Medical Journal, 329,* 908–909.

Marek, K. D., Popejoy, L., Petroski, G., Mehr, D., Rantz, M., & Lin, W. C. (2005). Clinical outcomes of aging in place. *Nursing Research, 54*, 202–211.

Markides, K. S., & Rudkin, L. (1996). Race and ethnic diversity, In J. E. Birren (Eds.), *Encyclopedia of gerontology* (Vol. 2). San Diego: Academic Press.

Marsh, H., Ellis, L., & Craven, R. (2002). How do preschool children feel about themselves? Unraveling measurement and multidimensional self-concept structure. *Developmental Psychology, 38*, 376–393.

Marsh-Prelesnik, J. (2006). Midwifery model of care—phase II: Midwife lessons. *Midwifery Today: International Midwife, 77*, 7–9.

Marsiske, M., Klumb, P. L., & Baltes, M. M. (1997). Everyday activity patterns and sensory functioning in old age. *Psychology and Aging, 12*, 444–457.

Martin, C. L., & Ruble, D. N. (2004). Children's search for gender cues. *Current Directions in Psychological Science, 13*, 67–70.

Martin, E. D., & Sher, K. J. (1994). Family history of alcoholism, alcohol use disorders, and the five-factor model of personality. *Journal of Studies in Alcohol, 55*, 81–90.

Martin, H. A., Woodson, A., Christian, C. W., Helfaer, M. A., Rghupathi, R., & Huh, J. W. (2006). Shaken baby syndrome. *Critical Care Nursing Clinics of North America, 18*, 279–286.

Martin, M. T., Emery, R., & Peris, T. S. (2004). Children and parents in single-parent families. In M. Coleman & L. Ganong (Eds.), *Handbook of contemporary families.* Thousand Oaks, CA: Sage.

Mason, W. A., Hitchings, J. E., & Spoth, R. L. (2007). Emergence of delinquency and depressed mood throughout adolescence as predictors of late adolescent problem substance use. *Psychology of Addictive Behaviors, 21*, 13–24.

Masoro, E. J. (2006). Are age-associated diseases an integral part of aging. In E. J. Masoro & S. N. Austad (Eds.), *Handbook of the biology of aging* (6th ed.). San Diego: Academic Press.

Massey, Z., Rising, S. S., & Ickovics, J. (2006). Centering Pregnancy group prenatal care: Promoting relationship-centered care. *Journal of Obstetric, Gynecologic, and Neonatal Nursing, 35*, 286–294.

Masten, A. S., Obradovic, J., & Burt, K. B. (2006). Resilience in emerging adulthood: Developmental perspectives on continuity and transformation. In J. J. Arnett & J. L. Tanner (Eds.), *Emerging adults in America.* Washington, DC: American Psychological Association.

Mastropieri, M. A., & Scruggs, T. E. (2007). *Inclusive classroom* (3rd ed.). Upper Saddle River, NJ: Prentice Hall.

Matijasevich, A., Barros, F. C., Sntos, I. S., & Yemini, A. (2006). Maternal caffeine consumption and fetal death: A case-control study in Uruguay. *Pediatric and Perinatal Epidemiology, 20*, 100–109.

Matlin, M. W. (2004). *The psychology of women* (5th ed.). Belmont, CA: Wadsworth.

Matlin, M. W. (2008). *Psychology of women* (6th ed.). Belmont, CA: Wadsworth.

Matthias, R. F., Lubben, J. E., Atchison, K. A., & Schweitzer, S. O. (1997). Sexual activity and satisfaction among very old adults: Results from a community-dwelling Medicare population survey. *Gerontologist, 37*, 6–14.

Mauck, K. F., & Clarke, B. L. (2006). Diagnosis, screening, prevention, and treatment of osteoporosis. *Mayo Clinic Proceedings, 81*, 662–672.

Maule, M. M., Merietti, F., Pastore, G., Magnani, C., & Richiardi, L. (2007). Effects of maternal age and cohort of birth on incidence time trends of childhood acute lymphoblastic leukemia. *Cancer Epidemiology, Biomarkers, and Prevention, 16*, 347–351.

Maurer, D., & Salapatek, P. (1976). Developmental changes in the scanning of faces by young infants. *Child Development, 47*, 523–527.

Mavandadi, S. & others. (2007). Effects of depression treatment on depressive symptoms in older adulthood: The moderating role of pain. *Journal of the American Geriatrics Association, 55*, 202–211.

Mbonye, A. K., Neema, S., & Magnussen, P. (2006). Treatment-seeking practices for malaria in pregnancy among rural women in Mukono district, Uganda. *Journal of Biosocial Science, 38*, 221–237.

McBurney, D. H., & White, T. L. (2007). *Research methods* (7th ed.). Belmont, CA: Wadsworth.

McCarter, R. J. M. (2006). Differential aging among skeletal muscles. In E. J. Masoro & S. N. Austad (Eds.), *Handbook of the biology of aging* (6th ed.). San Diego: Academic Press.

McCartney, K. (2003, July 16). Interview with Kathleen McCartney In A. Bucuvalas, "Child care and behavior." *HGSE News*, pp. 1–4. Cambridge, MA: Harvard Graduate School of Education.

McClellan, M. D. (2004, February 9). Captain Fantastic: The interview. *Celtic Nation*, pp. 1–9.

McCormick, C. B. (2003). Metacognition and learning. In I. B. Weiner (Ed.), *Handbook of psychology*, Vol. VII. New York: Wiley.

McCrae, R. R., & Costa, P. T. (1990). *Personality in adulthood.* New York: Guilford.

McCraken, M., Jiles, R., & Blanck, H. M. (2007). Health behaviors of the young adult U.S. population: Behavioral risk surveillance system, 2003. *Preventing Chronic Disease, 4*, A25.

McCullough, J. L., & Kelly, K. M. (2006). Prevention and treatment of skin aging. *Annals of the New York Academy of Sciences, 1067*, 323–331.

McCullough, M. E., & Laurenceau, J. P. (2005). Religiousness and the trajectory of self-rated health across adulthood. *Personality and Social Psychology Bulletin, 31*, 560–573.

McDonald, R., & Grych, J. H. (2006). Young children's appraisals of interparental conflict: Measurement and links with adjustment problems. *Journal of Family Psychology, 20*, 88–99.

McDowell, M.A., Brody, D. J., & Hughes, J. P. (2007). Has age at menarche changed? Results from the National Health and Nutrition Examination Survey (NHANES) 1999–2004. *Journal of Adolescent Health, 40*, 227–231.

McGarvey, C., McDonnell, M., Hamiton, K., O'Regan, M., & Matthews, T. (2006). An 8-year study of risk factors for SIDS: Bed-sharing versus non-bed-sharing. *Archives of Disease in Childhood, 91*, 318–323.

McGee, L. M., & Richgels, D. J. (2008). *Literacy's beginnings* (5th ed.). Boston: Allyn & Bacon.

McHale, J. (2007) *Charting the bumpy road of coparenthood.* Washington: Zero to Three Press.

McHale, J. & Sullivan, M. (2007, in press). Family systems. In M. Hersen & A. Gross (Eds.), *Handbook of clinical psychology, Volume II: Children and adolescents.* Hoboken, NJ: John Wiley & Sons.

McHale, J., Johnson, D., & Sinclair, R. (1999). Family dynamics, preschoolers' family representations, and preschool peer relationships. *Early Education and Development, 10*, 373–401.

McHale, J. P., Kuersten-Hogan, R., & Rao, N. (2004). Growing points for coparenting theory and research. *Journal of Adult Development, 11*, 221–234.

McHugh, K. (2007). Renal and adrenal tumors in children. *Cancer Imaging, 7*, 41–51.

McKain, W. C. (1972). A new look at older marriages. *The Family Coordinator, 21*, 61–69.

McLaren, P. (2007). *Life in schools* (5th ed.). Boston: Allyn & Bacon.

McLaughlin, K. (2003, December 30). Commentary in K. Painter, "Nurse dispenses dignity for dying," *USA Today*, Section D. pp. 1–2.

McLean, I. A., Balding, V., & White, C. (2005). Further aspects of male-on-male rape and sexual assault in greater Manchester. *Medical Science and Law, 45*, 225–232.

McLoyd, V. C., Aikens, N. L., & Burton, L. M. (2006). Childhood poverty, policy, and practice. In W. Damon & R. Lerner (Eds.),

Handbook of child psychology (6th ed.). New York: Wiley.

McMillan, J. H. (2007). *Classroom assessment* (4th ed.). Boston: Allyn & Bacon.

McNergney, R. F., & McNergney, J. M. (2007). *Education* (5th ed.). Boston: Allyn & Bacon.

McCrae, R. R., & Costa, P. T. (2003). *Personality in adulthood* (2nd ed.). New York: Guilford.

Meadows, A. T. (2006). Pediatric cancer survivorship: Research and clinical care. *Journal of Clinical Oncology, 24,* 5160–5165.

Meis, P. J., & Peaceman, A. M. (2003). Prevention of recurrent preterm delivery by 17-alpha-hydroxyprogesterone caproate. *New England Journal of Medicine, 348,* 2379–2385.

Melgar-Quinonez, H. R., & Kaiser, L. L. (2004). Relationship of child-feeding practices to overweight in low-income Mexican-American preschool-aged children. *Journal of the American Dietetic Association, 104,* 1110–1119.

Meltzoff, A. N. (1988). Infant imitation and memory: Nine-month-old infants in immediate and deferred tests. *Child Development, 59,* 217–225.

Meltzoff, A. N. (2005). Imitation. In B. Hopkins (Ed.), *Cambridge encyclopedia of child development.* Cambridge: Cambridge University Press.

Meltzoff, A. W., & Brooks, R. (2006). Eyes wide shut: The importance of eyes in infant gaze following and understanding of other minds. In R. Flom, K. Lee, & D. Muir (Eds.), *Gaze following: Its development and significance.* Mahwah, NJ: Erlbaum.

Menias, C. O., Elsayes, K. M., Peterson, C. M., Huete, A., Gratz, B. I., & Bhalla, S. (2007). CT of pregnancy-related complications. *Emergency Radiology, 13,* 299–306.

Menn, L., & Stoel-Gammon, C. (2005). Phonological development: Learning sound and sound patterns. In J. Berko Gleason (Ed.), *The development of language* (6th ed.). Boston: Allyn: Bacan.

Mensah, G. A., & Brown, D. W. (2007). An overview of cardiovascular disease burden in the United States. *Health Affairs, 26,* 38–48.

Menyuk, P., Liebergott, J., & Schultz, M. (1995). *Early language development in full-term and premature infants.* Hillsdale, NJ: Erlbaum.

Meredith, N. V. (1978). Research between 1960 and 1970 on the standing height of young children in different parts of the world. In H. W. Reace & L. P. Lipsitt (Eds.), *Advances in child development and behavior* (Vol. 12). New York: Academic Press.

Merrick, J., Morad, M., Halperin, I., & Kandel, I. (2005). Physical fitness and adolescence. *International Journal of Adolescent Medicine, 17,* 89–91.

Merrill, S. S., & Verbrugge, L. M. (1999). Health and disease in midlife. In S. L. Willis & J. D. Reid (Eds.), *Life in the middle: Psychological and social development in middle age.* San Diego: Academic Press.

Messinger, D. (2007, in press). Smiling. In M. M. Haith & J. B. Benson (Eds.), *Encyclopedia of infant and early childhood development.* London: Elsevier.

Metts, S., & Cupach, W. R. (2007). Responses to relational transgressions. In M. Tafoya & B. H. Spitzberg (Eds.), *The dark side of interpersonal communication.* Mahwah, NJ: Erlbaum.

Meyer, I. H. (2003). Prejudice, social stress, and mental health in gay, lesbian, and bisexual populations: Conceptual issues and research evidence. *Psychological Bulletin, 129,* 674–697.

Michael, R. T., Gagnon, J. H., Laumann, E. O., & Kolata, G. (1994). *Sex in America.* Boston: Little, Brown.

Mikkelsson, L., Kaprio, J., Kautiainen, H., Kujala, U., Mikkelsson, M., & Nupponen, H. (2006). School fitness tests as predictors of adult health related fitness. *American Journal of Human Biology, 18,* 342–349.

Milan, S., Pinderhughes, E. E., & the Conduct Problems Prevention Research Group. (2006). Family instability and child maladjustment trajectories during elementary school. *Journal of Abnormal Child Psychology, 34,* 43–56.

Miles, M. F., & Williams, R. W. (2007). Meta-analysis for microarray studies of the genetics of complex traits. *Trends in Biotechnology, 25,* 45–47.

Miller, C. F., Lurye, L., Zosuls, K., & Ruble, D. N. (2007). *Developmental changes in the accessibility of gender stereotypes.* Unpublished manuscript, Department of Family Resources and Human Development, Arizona State University.

Miller, J. B. (1986). *Toward a new psychlogy of women* (2nd ed.) Boston: Beacon Press.

Miller, J. G. (2006). Insights into moral development from cultural psychology. In M. Killen & J. G. Smetana (Eds.), *Handbook of moral development.* Mahwah, NJ: Erlbaum.

Miller, J. G. (2007). Cultural psychology of moral development. In S. Kitayama & D. Cohen (eds.), *Handbook of cultural psychology.* New York: Guilford.

Miller-Day, M. A. (2004). *Communication among grandmothers, mothers, and adult daughters.* Mahwah, NJ: Erlbaum.

Miller-Perrin, C. L., & Perrin, R. D. (2007). *Child maltreatment* (2nd ed.). Thousand Oaks, CA: Sage.

Milson, A., & Gallo, L. L. (2006). Bullying in middle schools: Prevention and intervention. *Middle School Journal, 37,* 12–19.

Mimura, M., & Yano, M. (2006). Memory impairment and awareness of memory deficits in early-stage Alzheimer's disease. *Review of Neuroscience, 17,* 253–266.

Minino, A. M., Heron, M. P., & Smith, B. L. (2006). Deaths: Preliminary data 2004. *National Vital Statistics Report, 54,* 1–49.

Minuchin, P. (2001). Looking toward the horizon: Present and future in the study of family systems. In J. P. McHale & W. S. Grolnick W. S., & Gurland, S.T. (2001). Mothering: Retrospect and prospect. In J.P. McHale & W.S. Grolnick (eds.).

Minuchin, P. P., & Shapiro, E. K. (1983). The school as a context for social development. In P. H. Mussen (Ed.), *Handbook of child psychology* (4th ed., Vol. 4). New York: Wiley.

Minzenberg, M. J., Poole J. H. Vinogradov, S. (2006). Adult social attachment disturbance is related to childhood maltreatment and current symptoms in borderline personality disorder. *Journal of Nervous and mental Disorders, 194,* 341–348.

Miralles, O., Sanchez, J., Palou, A., & Pico, C. (2006). A physiological role of breast milk leptin in body weight control in developing infants. *Obesity, 14,* 1371–1377.

Mircell, J. J. (2003). Sarcopenia: Causes, consequences, and preventions. *Journal of Gerontology A: Biological and Medical Sciences,* M911–M916.

Mischel, W. (2004). Toward an integrative science of the person. *Annual Review of Psychology* (Vol. 55). Palo Alto, CA: Annual Reviews.

Mitchell, M. L., & Jolley, J. M. (2007). *Research design explained* (6th ed.). Belmont, CA: Wadworth.

Mitchell, R. W. (1993). Mental models of mirror-self-recognition: Two theories. *New Ideas in Psychology, 11,* 295–325.

Mitchell, V., & Helson, R. (1990). Women's prime of life: Is it the 50s? *Psychology of Women Quarterly, 14,* 451–470.

MMWR (2006, June 9). Youth risk behavior surveillance—United States 2005, Vol. 255. Atlanta: Centers for Disease Control and Prevention

Moen, P., & Spencer, D. (2006). Converging divergences in age, gender, health, and well-being: Strategic selection in the third age. In R. H. Binstock & L. K. George (Eds.), *Handbook of aging and the social sciences* (6th ed.). San Diego: Academic Press.

Moise, K. J. (2005). Fetal RhD typing with free DNA I maternal plasma. *American Journal of Obstetrics and Gynecology, 192,* 663–665.

Monsour, M. (2006). Communication and gender among adult friends. In B. J. Dow & J. Wood (Eds.), *The Sage handbook of gender and communication.* Thousand Oaks, CA: Sage.

Montan, S. (2007). Increased risk in the elderly parturient. *Current Opinion in Obstetrics and Gynecology, 19,* 110–112.

Montemayor, R. (1982). The relationship between parent-adolescent conflict and the amount of time adolescents spend with parents, peers, and alone. *Child Development, 53*, 1512–1519.

Moon, M. (2006). Organization and financing of health care. In R. H. Binstock & L. K. George (Eds.), *Handbook of aging and the social sciences* (6th ed.). San Diego: Academic Press.

Mooney, C. G. (2006). *Theories of childhood.* Upper Saddle River, NJ: Prentice Hall.

Moore, D. (2001). *The dependent gene.* New York: W. H. Freeman.

Moos, M. K. (2006). Prenatal care: Limitations and opportunities. *Journal of Obstetric, Gynecologic, and Neonatal Nursing, 35*, 278–285.

Moos, R. H. (1986). Work as a human context. In M. S. Pallack & R. Perloff (Eds.), *Psychology and work: Productivity, change, and employment.* Washington, DC: American Psychological Association.

Moran, S., & Garder, H. (2006). Extraordinary achievements. In W. Damon & R. Lerner (Eds.), *Handbook of child psychology* (6th ed.). New York: Wiley.

Morcno, A., Posada, G. E. & Goldyn, D. T. (2006). Presence and quality of touch influence coregulation in mother-infant dyads. *Infancy, 9*, 1–20.

Morelra, P. L., Zhu, X., Nunomura, A., Smith, M. A., & Perry, G. (2006). Therapeutic options in Alzhelmer's disease. *Expert Reviews in Neurotherapy, 6*, 897–910.

Moren-Cross, J. L., & Lin, N. (2006). Social networks and health. In R. H. Binstock & L. K. George (Eds.), *Handbook of aging and the social sciences* (6th ed.). San Diego: Academic Press.

Morra, S., Gobbo, C., Marini, Z., & Sheese, R. (2007). *Cognitive development: Neo-Piagetian perspectives.* Mahwah, NJ: Erlbaum.

Morrison, G. S. (2008). *Fundamentals of early childhood education* (5th ed.). Upper Saddle River, NJ: Prentice Hall.

Morrow, C. E., Cullbertson, J. L., Accornero, V. H., Xue, I., Anthony, J. C., & Bandstra, E. S. (2006). Learning disabilities and intellectual functioning in school-aged children with prenatal cocaine exposure. *Developmental Neuropsychology.*

Moss, T. J. (2006). Respiratory consequences of preterm birth. *Clinical and Experimental Pharmacology and Physiology, 33*, 280–284.

Moules, N. J., Simonson, K., Prins, M, Angus, P., & Bell, J. M. (2004). Making room for grief. *Nursing Inquiry, 11*, 99–107.

Mounts, N. S. (2002). Parental management of adolescent peer relationships in context: The role of parenting style. *Journal of Family Psychology, 16*, 58–69.

Mraz, M., Padak, N. D., & Rasinski, T. V. (2008). *Evidence-based instruction in reading.* Boston: Allyn & Bacon.

Mroczek, D. K. (2001). Age and emoting in adulthood. *Current Directions in Psychological Science, 10*, 87–90.

Mroczek, D. K., Spiro, A., & Griffin, P. W. (2006). Personality and aging. In J. E. Birren & K. W. Schaie (Eds.), *Handbook of the psychology of aging* (6th ed.). San Diego: Academic Press.

Mullick, S., Beksinksa, M., & Msomi, S. (2005). Treatment for syphilis in antenatal care. *Sexually Transmitted Infections, 81*, 220–222.

Multsch, D. F., Hertzog, C., Small, B. J., & Dixon, R. A. (1999). Use it or lose it: Engaged lifestyle as a buffer of cognitive decline in aging? *Psychology and Aging, 14*, 245–263.

Mumme, D. L., Fernald, A., & Herrera, C. (1996). Infant's responses to facial & emotional signals in a social referencing paradigm. *Child Development, 67*, 3219–3237.

Munakata, Y. (2006). Information processing approaches to development. In W. Damon & R. Lerner (Eds.), *Handbook of child psychology* (6th Ed.). New York: Wiley.

Murphy, M. C. (1996). Stressors on the college campus: A comparison of 1985 and 1993. *Journal of College Student Development, 37*, 20–28.

Murphy-Hoefer, R., Alder, S., & Higbee, C. (2004). Perceptions about cigarette smoking and risks among college students. *Nicotine and Tobacco Research 63. (Suppl. 3)*, S371–S374.

Murray, J. P. (2007). TV violence: Research and controversy. In N. Pecora, J. P. Murray, & E. A. Wartella (Eds.), *Children and television.* Mahwah, NJ: Erlbaum.

Mussen, P. H., Honzik, M., & Eichorn, D. (1982). Early adult antecedents of life satisfaction at age 70. *Journal of Gerontology, 37*, 316–322.

Myers, D. G. (2000). *The American paradox.* New Haven, CT: Yale University Press.

Myers, D. J. (1999). *Excluding violent youths from juvenile court: The effectiveness of legislative waiver.* Doctoral dissertation, University of Maryland, College Park, MD.

Myerson, J., Rank, M. R., Raines, F. Q., & Schnitzler, M. A. (1998). Race and general cognitive ability: The myth of diminishing returns in education. *Psychological Science, 9*, 139–142.

N

Nader, K. (2001). Treatment methods for childhood trauma. In J. P. Wilson, M. J. Friedman, & J. Lindy (Eds.), *Treating psychological trauma and PTSD.* New York: Guilford Press.

Nader, P. R., O'Brien, M., Houts, R., Bradley, R., Belsky, J., Crosnoe, R., Friedman, S., Mei, Z., Susman, E. J., & the National Institute of Health and Human Development Early Childcare Research Network. Identifying risk for obesity in early childhood. *Pediatrics, 118*, e594–e601.

NAEYC (1986). Position statement on developmentally appropriate practice in programs for 4- and 5-year-olds. *Young Children, 41*, 20–29.

NAEYC (2005). *Critical facts about young children and early childhood in the United States.* Washington. DC: Author.

Nair, K. S. (2005). Aging muscle. *American Journal of Clinical Nutrition, 81*, 953–963.

Nansel, T. R., Overpeck, M., Pilla, R. S., Ruan, W. J., Simons-Morton, B., & Scheidt, P. (2001). Bullying behaviors among U.S. youth: Prevalence and association with psychosocial adjustment. *Journal of the American Medical Association, 285*, 2094–2100.

Narkiewicz, K., Phillips, B. S., Kato, M., Hering, D., Bieniaszewski, L., & Somers, V. K. (2005). Gender-selective interaction between aging, blood pressure, and sympathetic nerve activity. *Hypertension, 45*, 522–525.

Narramore, N. (2007). Supporting breastfeeding mothers on children's wards: An overview. *Pediatric Nursing, 19*, 18–21.

Nation, M., & Heflinger, C. A. (2006). Risk factors for serious alcohol and drug use: The role of psychosocial variables in predicting the frequency of substance use among adolescents. *American Journal of Drug and Alcohol Abuse, 31*, 415–433.

National Assessment of Educational Progress. (2000). *The nation's report card.* Washington, DC: National Center for Education Statistics.

National Center for Education Statistics. (2002). *Work during college.* Washington, DC: U.S. Office of Education.

National Center for Education Statistics (2003). *Digest of Education Statistics, Table 52.* Washington, DC: Author.

National Center for Education Statistics. (2003). Dropout rates in the United States: 2003. Washington, DC: U.S. Department of Education.

National Center for Health Statistics. (1999). Current estimates from the National Health Interview Survey, 1996. *Vital and Health Statistics, Series 10* (No. 200). Atlanta: Centers for Disease Control and Prevention.

National Center for Health Statistics. (2000). *Health United States 2000.* Bethesda, MD: U. S. Department of Health and Human Services.

National Center for Health Statistics. (2002). *Sexual behavior and selected health measures: Men and women 15–44 years of age, United States, 2002*, PHS 2003-1250. Atlanta: Centers for Disease Control and Prevention.

National Center for Health Statistics (2004, December 10). *Teens delaying sexual activity.* Atlanta: Centers for Disease Control and Prevention.

National Center for Health Statistics. (2006). *Death statistics.* Atlanta: Center for Disease Control and Prevention.

National Center for Health Statistics. (2006). *Health United States*. Atlanta: Centers for Disease Control and Prevention.

National Center for Juvenile Justice. (2006). *Juvenile offenders and victims: 2006 National report*. Pittsburgh: Author.

National Clearinghouse on Child Abuse and Neglect. (2004). *What is child abuse and neglect?* Washington, DC: U.S. Department of Health and Human Services.

National Council on Aging. (2000, March) *Myths and realities survey results*. Washington. DC: Author.

National Institutes of Health. (2004). *Women's health initiative hormone therapy study*. Bethesda, MD: Author.

National Research Council. (1999). *How people learn*. Washington, DC: National Academy Press.

National Sleep Foundation. (2006). *2006 Sleep in America poll*. Washington, DC: Author.

National Vital Statistics Report. (2004, March 7). Deaths: Leading causes for 2002. Atlanta: Centers for Disease Control and Prevention.

Natsopoulos, D., Kiossroglou, G., Xeraxweritou, A., & Alevrladou, A. (1998). Do the hands talk on the mind's behalf? Differences in language between left- and right-handed children. *Brain and Language, 64,* 182–214.

Needham, A. (2008, in press). Learning in infants' object perception, object-directed action, and tool use. In A. Needham & A. Woodward (Eds.), *Learning and the infant mind*. New York: Oxford University Press.

Needham, A., Barrett, T., & Peterman, K. (2002). A pick-me-up infants' exploratory skills: Early simulated experiences reaching for objects using "sticky mittens" enhances young infants' objects exploration skills. *Infant Behavior and Development, 25,* 279–295.

Neimeyer, R. A. (2006). *Lessons of loss* (2nd ed.). New York: Routledge.

Neisser, U. (2004). Memory development: New questions and old. *Developmental Review, 24,* 154–158.

Neisser, U., Boodoo, G., Bouchard, T. J., Boykin, A. W., Brody, N., Ceci, S. J., Halpern, D. F., Loehlin, J. C., Perioff, R. J., Sternberg, R., & Urbins, S. (1996). Intelligence: Knowns and unknowns. *American Psychologist, 51,* 77–101.

Nelson, C. A. (2003). Neural development and lifelong plasticity. In R. M. Lerner, F. Jacobs, & D. Wertlieb (Eds.), *Handbook of applied developmental science* (Vol. 1). Thousand Oaks, CA: Sage.

Nelson, C. (2007). A developmental congitive neuroscience approach to the study of atypical development. In D. Coch, K. W. Fischer, & G. Dawson (Eds.), *Human behavior, learning, and the developing brain.* New York: Guilford.

Nelson, C. A., Thomas, K. M., & De Haan, M. (2006). Neural bases of Cognitive development. In W. Damon & R. Lerner (Eds.), *Handbook of child Psychology* (6th eds.). New York: Wiley.

Nelson, C. E. (2006). Unpublised review of J. W. Santrock's *Topical life-span development,* (4th ed.), New York: McGraw. Hill.

Nelson, C.A., Zeanah, C., & Fox, N.A. (2007, in press). The effects of early deprivation on brain-behavioral development: The Bucharest Early Intervention Project. In D. Romer & E. Walker (Eds.), *Adolescent psychopathology and the developing brain: Integrating brain and prevention science.* New York: Oxford University Press.

Nelson, M. C., & Gordon-Larsen, P. (2006). Physical activity and sedentary behavior patterns are associated with selected adolescent health risk behaviors. *Pediatrics, 117,* 1281–1290.

Nemund, H. K., & Kolland, F. (2007). Work and retirement. In J. Bond, S. Peace, F. Dittman-Kohli, & G. Westerhoff (Eds.), *Aging in society* (3rd ed.). Thousand Oaks, CA: Sage.

Neri, M., Bonati, P. A., Pinelli, M., Borella, P., Tolve, I., & Nigro, N. (2007). Biological, psychological, and clinical markers of caregiver's stress in impaired elderly with dementia and age-related disease. *Archives of Gerontology and Geriatrics, 44, (Suppl.),* S289-S294.

Ness, A., Dias, T., Damus, K., Burd, I., & Berghella, V. (2006). Impact of recent randomized trials on the use of progesterone to prevent preterm birth: A 2005 follow-up survey. *American Journal of Obstetrics and Gynecology, 195,* 1174–1179.

Neugarten, B. L. (1964). *Personality in middle and late life.* New York: Atherton.

Neugarten, B. L. (1986). The aging society. In A. Pifer & L. Bronte (Eds.), *Our aging society: Paradox and promise.* New York: W. W. Norton.

Neugarten, B. L., & Weinstein, K. K. (1964). The changing American grandparent. *Journal of Marriage and the Family, 26,* 199–204.

Neugarten, B. L., Havighurst, R. J., & Tobin, S. S. (1968). Personality and patterns of aging. In B. L. Neugarten (Ed.), *Middle age and aging.* Chicago: University of Chicago Press.

Neumark-Sztainer, D., Levine, M. P., Paxton, S. J., Smolak, L., Piran, N., & Wertheim, E. H. (2006). Prevention of body dissatisfaction and disordered eating: What next? *Eating Disorders, 14,* 265–285.

Neumark-Sztainer, D., Paxton, S. J., Hannan, P. J., Haines, J., Story M. (2006). Does body satisfaction matter? Five-year longitudinal associations between body satisfaction and health behaviors in adolescent females and males. *Journal of Adolescent Health, 39,* 244–251.

New, R. (2005). The Reggio Emillia approach: Provocations and partnerships with U.S. early childhood educations. In J. I. Roopnarine & J. E. Johnson (Eds.). *Approaches to early childhood education* (4th ed.). Columbus. OH: Merrill/Prentice Hall.

New, R. (2007, in press). Reggio Emilia as cultural activity. *Theory into Practice.*

Newcombe, N. (2007). The development of implicit and explicit memory. In N. Cowan & M. Courage (Eds.), *The development of memory in childhood.* Philadelphia: Psychology Press.

Newell, K., Scully, D. M., McDonald, P. V., & Baillargeon, R. (1989). Task constraints and infant grip configurations. *Development Psychobiology, 22,* 817–832.

Newell, K. M., Vaillancourt, D. E., & Sosnoff, J. J. (2006). Aging, complexity, and motor performance. In J. E. Birren & K. W. Schaie (Eds.), *Handbook of the psychology of aging* (6th ed.). San Diego: Academic Press.

Newman, B. M., & Newman, P. R. (2007). *Theories of human development.* Mahwah, NJ: Erlbaum.

NICHD Early Child Care Research Network. (2001). Nonmaternal care and family factors in early development: An overview of the NICHD study of Early Child Care. *Journal of Applied Developmental Psychology, 22,* 457–492.

NICHD Early Child Care Research Network. (2002). Structure of Process Outcome: Direct and indirect effects of child care quality on young children's development. *Psychological Science, 13,* 199–206.

NICHD Early Child Care Research Network. (2003). Does amount of time spent in child care predict socioemotional adjustment during the transition to kindergarten? *Child Development, 74,* 976–1005.

NICHD Early Child Care Research Network. (2004). Type of child care and children's development at 54 months. *Early Childhood Research Quarterly, 19,* 203–230.

NICHD Early Child Care Research Network. (2005). *Child care and development.* New York: Guilford.

NICHD Early Child Care Research Network. (2005). Predicting individual differences in attention, memory, and planning in first graders from experiences at home, child care, and school. *Developmental Psychology, 41,* 99–114.

NICHD Early Child Care Research Network. (2006). Infant-mother attachment classification: Risk and protection in relation to changing maternal caregiving quality. *Developmental Psychology, 42,* 38–58.

Nielsen, S. J., Siega-Riz, A. M., & Popkin, B. M. (2002). Trends in energy intake in U.S. between 1977 and 1996: Similar shifts seen across age groups. *Obesity Research, 10,* 370–378.

Nieto, S., & Bode, P. (2008). *Affirming diversity* (5th ed.). Boston: Allyn & Bacon.

Nisbett, R. (2003). *The geography of thought,* New York: Free Press.

Noakes, P. S., Thomas, R., Lane, C., Mori, T. A., Barden, A. E., Devadason, S. G., & Prescott S. L. (2007, in press). Maternal smoking is associated with increased infant oxidative stress at 3 months of age. *Thorax*.

Noland, J. S., Singer, L. T., Short, E. J., Minnes, S., Arendt, R. E., Kirchner, H. L., & Bearer, C. (2005). Prenatal drug exposure and selective attention in preschoolers. *Neurotoxicology and Teratology*, 27, 429–438.

Nolen-Hoeksema, S. (2007) *Abnormal psychology* (4th ed.). New York: McGraw-Hill.

Nolen-Hoeksema, S., & Ahrens, C. (2002). Age differences and similarities in correlates of depressive symptoms. *Psychology and Aging*, 17, 116–124.

Nollen, N., Kaur, H., Pulvers, K., Choi, W., Fitzgibbon, M., Li, C., Nazir, N., & Ahluwalia, J. S. (2006). Correlates of ideal body size among Black and White adolescents. *Journal of Youth and Adolescence*, 35, 276–284.

Nordahl, C. W., Ranganath, C., Yonelinas, A. P., Decarti, C., Fletcher, E., & Jagust, W. J. (2006). White matter changes compromise prefrontal cortex function in healthy elderly individuals. *Journal of Cognitive Neuroscience*, 18, 418–429.

Norgard, B., Puho, E., Czeilel, A. E., Skriver, M. V., & Sorensen, H. T. (2006). Aspirin use during early pregnancy and the risk of congenital abnormalities. *American Journal of Obstetrics and Gynecology*, 192, 922–923.

Norman, J. F., Crabtree, C. E., Herrmann, M., Thompson, S. R., Shular, C. F., & Clayton, A. M. (2006). Aging and the perception of 3-D shape from dynamic patterns of binocular disparity. *Perception and Psychophysics*, 68, 94–101.

Norouzieh, K. (2005). Case management of the dying child. *Case Manager*, 16, 54–57.

Nottelmann, E. D., Susman, B. J., Blue, J. H., Inoff-Germain, G., Dorn, L. D., Lorlaux, D. L., Cutler, G. B., & Chrousos, G. P. (1987). Gonadal and adrenal hormone correlates of adjustment in early adolescence. In R. M. Leiner & T. T. Foch (Eds.), *Biological-psychological interactions in early adolescence*. Hillsdale, NJ: Erlbaum.

Nsamenang, A. B. (2002). Adolescence in sub-Saharan Africa: An image constructed from Africa's triple heritage. In B. B. Brown, R. W. Larson, & T. S. Saraswathi (Eds.), *The world's youth*. New York: Cambridge University Press.

Nucci, L. (2006). Education for moral development. In M. Killen & J. Smetana (Eds.), *Handbook of moral development*. Mahwah, NJ: Erlbaum.

Nutting, P. A., Dickinson, W. P., Dickinson, L. M., Nelson, C. C., King, D. K., Crabtree, B. F., & Glasgow, R. E. (2007). Use of chronic care model elements is associated with higher-quality care for diabetes. *Annals of Family Medicine*, 5, 14–20.

O

Oakes, J., & Lipton, M. (2007). *Teaching to change the world* (3rd ed.). New York: McGraw-Hill.

Oakes, L. M., Kannass, K. N., & Shaddy, D. J. (2002). Development changes in endogenous control of attention: The role of target familiarity on infants' distraction latency. *Child Development*, 73, 1644–1655.

Occupational Outlook Handbook. (2006–2007). Washington, DC: U.S. Department of Labor, Bureau of Labor Statistics.

O'Connor, T. G. Ben-Sholomo, Y., Heron, J., Golding, J., Adams, D., & Glover, V. (2005). Prenatal anxiety predicts individual differences in cortisol in pre-adolescent children. *Biological Psychiatry*, 58, 211–217.

O'Donnell, L., O'Donnell, C., Wardlaw, D. M., & Stueve, A. (2004). Risk and resiliency factors influencing suicidality among urban African American and Latino youth. *American Journal of Community Psychology*, 33, 37–49.

Oepkes, D., & others. (2006). Doppler ultrasonography versus amniocentesis to predict fetal anemia. *New England Journal of Medicine*, 355, 156–164.

Offer, D., Ostrov E., Howard, K. I., & Atkinson, R. (1988). *The teenage world: Adolescents' self-image in ten countries*. New York: Plenum.

Ogbu, J. U. (1989, April). *Academic socialization of Black children: An inoculation against future failure?* Paper presented at the meeting of the Society for Research in Child Development, Kansas City.

Ogbu, J., & Stern, P. (2001). Caste status and intellectual development. In R. J. Sternberg & E. L. Grigorenko (Eds.), *Environmental effects on cognitive abilities*. Mahwah, NJ: Erlbaum.

Olson, L. M., Tang, S. F., & Newacheck, P. W. (2005). Children in the United States with discontinuous health insurance coverage. *New England Journal of Medicine*, 353, 418–419.

Oman, D., & Thoresen, C. E. (2006). Do religion and spirituality influence health? In R. F. Paloutzian & C. L. Park (Eds.), *Handbook of the psychology of religion and spirituality*. New York: Guilford.

Onwuegbuzi, A. J., & Dlaey, C. E. (2001). Racial differences in IQ revisited: A synthesis of nearly a century of research. *Journal of Black Psychology*, 27, 209–220.

Oscarsson, M. E., Amer-Wahlin, I., Rydhstroem, H., & Kallen, K. (2006). Outcome in obstetric care related to oxytocin use: A population-based study. *Acta Obstetricia et Gynecologica Scandinavica*, 85, 1094–1098.

Osofsky, J. D. (Ed.). (2007). *Young children and trauma*. New York: Guilford.

Ott, C. H., Lueger, R. J., Kelber, S. T., & Prigerson, H. G. (2007). Spousal bereavement in older adults: Common, resilient, and chronic grief with defining characteristics. *Journal of Nervous and Mental Disease*, 195, 332–341.

Otto, B. W. (2008). *Literacy development in early childhood*. Upper Saddle River, NJ: Prentice Hall.

Ouwehand, C., de Ridder, D. T., & Bensing, J. M. (2007, in press). A review of successful proactive coping as an important additional strategy. *Clinical Psychology Review*.

Overbeek, G., Stattin, H., Vermulst, A., Ha, T., & Engels, R. C. (2007). Parent-child relationships, partner relationships, and emotional adjustment: A birth-to-maturity prospective study. *Developmental Psychology*, 43, 429–437.

Owen, C. J. (2005). The empty nest transition: The relationship between attachment style and women's use of this period as a time for growth and change. *Dissertation Abstracts International, Section B: The Sciences and Engineering*, 65, p. 3747.

Oxford, M. L., Gilchrist, L. D., Gillmore, M. R., & Lohr, M. J. (2006). Predicting variation in the life course of adolescent mothers as they enter adulthood. *Journal of Adolescent Health*, 89, 20–26.

P

Pakpreo, P., Ryan, S., Auinger, P., & Aten, M. (2005). The association between parental lifestyle behaviors and adolescent knowledge, attitudes, intentions, and nutritional and physical activity behaviors. *Journal of Adolescent Health*, 34, 129–130.

Palmer, S. E. (2004). Custody and access issues with children whose parents are separated or divorced. *Canadian Journal of Community Mental Health*, 4 (Suppl.) 25–38.

Palmore, E. (1981). *Social patterns in normal aging: Findings from the Duke Longitudinal Study*. Durham, NC: Duke University Press.

Palmore, E. B. (2004). Research note: Ageism in Canada and the United States. *Journal of Cross Cultural Gerontology*, 19, 41–46.

Paloutzian, R. (2000). *Invitation to the psychology of religion* (3rd ed.). Boston: Allyn & Bacon.

Pals, J. L. (2006). Constructing the "springboard effect": Causal connections, self-making, and growth within the life story. In D. P. McAdams, R. Josselson, & A. Lieblich (Eds.), *Identity and story*. Washington, DC: American Psychological Association.

Parazzini, F., Chatenoud, L., Surace, M., Tozzi, L., Salerio, B., Bettoni, G., & Benzi, G. (2003). Moderate alcohol drinking and risk of preterm birth. *European Journal of Clinical Nutrition*, 57, 1345–1349.

Pardo, J. V. & others (2007, in press). Where the brain grows old: Decline in anterior cigulate and medial prefrontal function with normal aging. *Neuroimage*.

Paris, S. G., & Paris, A. H. (2006). Assessments of early reading. In W. Damon

& R. Lerner (Eds.), *Handbook of child psychology* (6th ed.). New York: Wiley.

Park, D. (2001). Commentary in Restak, R. *The secret life of the brain.* Washington, DC: Joseph Henry Press.

Park, M. J., Mulye, T. P., Adams, S. H., Brindis, C. D., & Irwin, C. E. (2006) The health status of young adults in the United States. *Journal of Adolescent Health, 39,* 305–317.

Park, M. J., Paul Mulye, T., Adams, S. H., Brindis, C. D., & Irwin, C. E. (2006). The health status of young adults in the United States. *Journal of Adolescent Health, 39,* 305–317.

Parke, D., & Schwarte, N. (Eds.) (2007). *Cognitive aging: A primer* (2nd Ed.). Philadelphia: Psychology Press.

Parke, R. D., & Buriel, R. (1998). Socialization in the family. In N. Eisenberg (Ed.), *Handbook of child psychology* (5th ed., Vol. 3). New York: Wiley.

Parke, R. D., & Buriel, R. (2006). Socialization in the family: Ethnic and ecological perspectives. In W. Damon & R. Lerner (Eds.), *Handbook of child psychology* (6th ed.). New York: Wiley.

Parkes, K. R. (2006). Physical activity and self-rated health: Interactive effects of activity in work and leisure domains. *British Journal of Health Psychology, 11,* 533–550.

Parnes, H. S., & Sommers, D. G. (1994). Shunning retirement: Work experiences of men in their seventies and early eighties. *Journal of Gerontology, 49,* S117–S124.

Parten, M. (1932). Social play among preschool children. *Journal of Abnormal Social Psychology, 27,* 243–269.

Partnership for a Drug-Free America. (2005). *Partnership Attitude Tracking Study.* New York: Author.

Pasley, K., & Moorefield, B. S. (2004). Stepfamilies. In M. Coleman & L. Ganong (Eds.), *Handbook of contemporary families.* Thousand Oaks, CA: Sage.

Patterson, C. J. (2004). What differences does a civil union make? Changing public policies and the experiences of same-sex couples: Comment on Solomon, Rothblum, and Balsam (2004). *Journal of Family Psychology, 18,* 287–289.

Patterson, C. J., & Hastings, P. D. (2007). Socialization in the context of family diversity. In J. E. Grusec & P. D. Hastings (Eds.), *Handbook of socialization.* New York: Guilford.

Patton, G. C., Coffey, C., Carlin, J. B., Sawyer, S. M., & Wakefield, M. (2006). Teen smokers reach their mid twenties. *Journal of Adolescent Health, 39,* 214–220.

Paul, E. L., McManus, B., & Hayes, A. (2000). ``Hookups'': Characteristics and correlates of college students' spontaneous and anonymous sexual experiences. *The Journal of Sexual Research, 37,* 76–88.

Paul, P. (2003, Sept/Oct). The PermaParent trap. *Psychology Today, 36(5),* 40–53.

Paxson, C., Donahue, E., Orleans, C. T., & Grisso, J. A. (2006). Introducing the issue. *Future of Children, 16 (No. 1)* 3–17.

Payer, L. (1991). The menopause in various cultures. In H. Burger & M. Boulet (Eds.), *A portrait of the menopause.* Park Ridge, NJ: Parthenon.

Pecora, N., Murray, J. P., & Wartella, E. A. (Eds.). (2007). *Children and television.* Mahwah, NJ: Erlbaum.

Peplau, L. A., & Fingerhut, A. W. (2007). The close relationships of lesbians and gay men. *Annual Review of Psychology (vol. 58).* Palo Alto, CA: Annual Reviews.

Perls, T. T. (2006). The different paths to 100. *American Journal of Clinical Nutrition, 83,* 484S–487S.

Perrig-Chiello, P., & Perren, S. (2005). The impact of past transitions on well-being in middle age. In S. L. Willis & M. Martin (Eds.), *Middle adulthood.* Thousand Oaks, CA: Sage.

Perry, C. M., & Johnson, C. L. (1994). Families and support networks among African American oldest-old. *International Journal of Aging on Human Development, 38,* 41–50.

Perry, W. G. (1999). *Forms of ethical and intellectual development in the college years: A scheme.* San Francisco: Jossey Bass.

Peskin, H. (1967). Pubertal onset and ego functioning. *Journal of Abnormal Psychology, 72,* 1–15.

Petersen, A. C. (1979, January). Can puberty come any faster? *Psychology Today,* pp. 45–56.

Peterson, B. E. (2002). Longitudinal analysis of midlife generativity, intergenerational roles, and caregiving. *Psychology and Aging, 17,* 161–168.

Peterson, B. E., & Stewart, A. J. (1996). Antecedents and contexts of generativity motivation at midlife. *Psychology and Aging, 11,* 21–33.

Peterson, C. C. (1996). The ticking of the social clock: Adults' beliefs about the timing of transition events. *International Journal of Aging and Human Development, 42,* 189–203.

Peterson, C. C. (1999). Grandfathers' and grandmothers' satisfaction with the grandparenting role: Seeking new answers to old questions. *International Journal of Aging and Human Development, 49,* 61–78.

Peterson, K. S. (1997, September 3). In high school, dating is a world into itself. *USA Today,* pp. 1–2D.

Petitto, L. A., Kovelman, I. & Harasymowycz, U. (April 2003). Bilingual language development: Does learning the new damage the old? Presentation at the meeting of the *Society for Research in Child Development,* Tampa, FL.

Phillips, D. (2006). Child care as risk or protection in the context of welfare reform.

In N. Cabrera, R. Hutchens, & H. E. Peters (Eds.), *From welfare to childcare.* Mahwah, NJ: Erlbaum.

Phillips, J. M., Brennan, M., Schwartz, C. E., & Cohen, L. M. (2005). The long-term impact of dialysis discontinuation on families. *Journal of Palliative Medicine, 8,* 79–85.

Phinney, J. S. (2006). Ethnic identity exploration in emerging adulthood. In J. J. Arnett & J. L. Tanner (Eds.), *Emerging adults in America.* Washington, DC: American Psychological Association.

Phinney, J. S., Berry, J. W., Vedder, P. & Liebkind, K. (2006). The acculturation experience: Attitudes, identities, and behaviors of immigrant youth. In J. W. Berry, J. S. Phinney, D. L., Sam, & P. Vedder (Eds.), *Immigrant youth in cultural transition.* Mahwah, NJ: Erlbaum.

Piaget, J. (1932). *The moral judgment of the child.* New York: Harcourt Brace Jovanovich.

Piaget, J. (1952). *The origins of intelligence in children.* (M. Cook, Trans.), New York: International Universities Press.

Piaget, J. (1954). *The construction of reality in the child.* New York: Basic Books.

Piaget, J. (1962). *Thought and language.* Cambridge, MA: MIT Press.

Piaget, J., & Inhelder, B. (1969). *The child's conception of space* (F. J. Langdon & J. L. Lunger, Trans.). New York: W. W. Norton.

Pierce, K. M., Hamm, J. V., & Vandell, D. L. (1997, April). *Experiences in after-school programs and children's adjustment at school and at home.* Paper presented at the meeting of the Society for Research in Child Development, Washington, DC.

Pineda, J. O., & Oberman, L. M. (2006). What goads cigarette smokers to smoke? Neural adaptation and the mirror neuron system. *Brain Research, 1121,* 128–135.

Pinheiro, R. T., Magalhaes, P. V., Horta, B. L., Pinheiro, K. A., da Silva, R. A., & Pinto, R. H. (2006). Is paternal postpartum depression associated with maternal postpartum depression? Population-based study in Brazil. *Acta Psychiatrics Scandinavia, 113,* 230–232.

Pinquart, M., & Sorensen, S. (2006). Gender differences in caregiver stressors, social resources, and health: An updated meta-analysis. *Journals of Gerontology B: Psychological Sciences and Social Sciences, 61,* P33-P45.

Pipe, M. (2007). Children as eye witnesses: Memory in the forensic context. In N. Cowan & M. Courage (Eds.), *The development of memory in childhood* (2nd ed.). Philadelphia: Psychology Press.

Piper, W. E., Ogrodniczuk, J. S., Joyce, A. S., Weideman, R., & Rosie, J. S. (2007). Group composition and group therapy for complicated grief. *Journal of Consulting and Clinical Psychology, 75,* 116–125.

Pipp, S. L., Fischer, K. W., & Jennings, S. L. (1987). The acquisition of self and mother knowledge in infancy. *Developmental Psychology, 23,* 86–96.

Pitkanen, T., Lyyra, A. L., & Pulkkinen, L. (2005). Age of onset of drinking and the use of alcohol in adulthood: A follow-up study from age 8–42 for females and males. *Addiction, 100,* 652–661.

Pitkin, R. M. (2007). Folate and neural tube defects. *American Journal of Clinical Nutrition, 85 (Suppl),* S285–S288.

Pitt-Catsouphes, Kossek, E. E., & Sweet, S. (Eds.). (2006). *The work and family handbook.* Mahwah, NJ: Erlbaum.

Pleck, J. H. (1995). The gender-role strain paradigm. In R. F. Levant & W. S. Pllack (Eds.), *A new psychology of men.* New York Basic Books.

Pliszka, S. R. (2007). Pharmacologic treatment of attention deficit hyperactivity disorder: Efficacy, safety, and mechanisms of action. *Neuropsychology Review, 17,* 61–72.

Plomin, R., & Schalkwyk, L. C. (2007). Microarrays. *Developmental Science, 10* 19–23.

Plomin, R., DeFries, J. C., & Fulker, D. W. (2007). *Nature and nurture during infancy and childhood.* Mahwah, NJ: Erlbaum.

Plomin, R., Reiss, D., Hetherington, E. M., & Howe, G. W. (1994). Nature and nurture: Contributions to measures of the family environment, *Developmental Psychology, 30,* 32–43.

Polanska, K., Hanke, W., Ronchetti, R., Van Den Hazel, P., Zuurbier, M., Koppe, J. G., & Bartonova, A. (2006). Environmental tobacco smoke exposure and children's health. *Acta Pediatrica Supplement, 95,* S86–S92.

Pollack, W. (1999). *Real boys.* New York: Owl Books.

Pollard, I. (2007). Neuropharmacology of drugs and alcohol in mother and fetus. *Seminars in fetal and neonatal medicine, 12,* 106–113.

Pomery, E. A., Gibbons, F. X., Gerrard, M., Cleveland, M. J., Brody, G. H., & Wills, T. A. (2005). Families and risk: Protective analyses of familial and social influences on adolescent substance abuse. *Journal of Family Psychology, 19,* 560–570.

Poole, D. A., & Lindsay, D. S. (1996). *Effects of parents' suggestions, interviewing techniques, and age on young children's event reports.* Paper, presented at the NATO Advanced Study Institute, Porte de Bourgenay, France.

Poponoe, D., & Whitehead, B. (2005). *The state of our unions: 2005.* Piscataway, NJ: The National Marriage Project, Rutgers University.

Poponoe, D., & Whitehead, B. (2006). *The state of our unions 2006.* New Brunswick, NJ: The National Marriage Project, Rutgers University.

Popovic, I. M., Seric, V., & Demarin, V. (2007, in press). Mild cognitive impairment in symptomatic and a symptomatic cerebrovascular disease.

Porath, A. J., & Fried, P. A. (2005). Effects of prenatal cigarette and marijuana exposure on drug use among offspring. *Neurotoxicology and Teratology, 27,* 267–277.

Posner, J. K., & Vandell, D. L. (1994). Low-income children's after-school care: Are there benefits of after-school programs? *Child Development, 65,* 440–456.

Potvin, L., Champagne, F., & Laberge-Nadeau, C. (1988). Mandatory driver training and road safety: The Quebec experience. *American Journal of Public Health, 78,* 1206–1212.

Poulin-Dubois, D., & Graham, S. A. (2007). Cognitive processes in early word learning. In E. Hoff & M. Shatz (Eds.), *Blackwell handbook of language development.* Malden, MA: Blackwell.

Powell, G. N. (2004). *Managing a diverse workforce* (2nd ed.). Thousand Oaks, CA: Sage.

Pratt, M. W., Danse, H. A., Arnold, M. L., Norris, J. E., & Filyer, R. (2001). Adult generativity and the socialization of adolescents. *Journal of Personality, 69,* 89–120.

Pressley, M. (2000). What should comprehension instruction be the instruction of? In M. Kamil (Ed.), *Handbook of reading research.* Mahwah, NJ: Erlbaum.

Pressley, M. (2007). Achieving best practices. In L. B. Bambrell, L. M. Morrow, & M. Pressley (eds.), *Best practices in literacy instruction.* New York: Guilford.

Pressley, M., Billman, A. K., Perry, K. H., Reffitt, K. E., & Reynolds, J. M. (Eds.) (2007). *Shaping literacy achievement.* New York: Guilford.

Pressley, M., Cariligia-Bull, T., Deane, S., & Schneider, W. (1987). Short-term memory, verbal competence, and age as predictors of imagery instructional effectiveness. *Journal of Experimental Child Psychology, 43,* 194–211.

Pressley, M., & Harris, K. (2006). Cognitive strategies instruction. In P. A. Alexander & P. H. Winne (Eds.), *Handbook of educational psychology* (2nd ed.), Mahwah, NJ: Erlbaum.

Pressley, M., & Hilden, K. (2006). Cognitive strategies. In W. Damon & R. Lerner (Eds.), *Handbook of child psychology* (6th ed.). New York: Wiley.

Pressley, M., Raphael, L. Gallagher, D., & DiBella, J. (2004). Providence–St. Mel School: How a school that works for African-American students works. *Journal of Educational Psychology, 96,* 216–235.

Preston, A. M., Rodriguez, C., Rivera, C. E., & Sahai, H. (2003). Influence of environmental tobacco smoke on vitamin C status in children. *American Journal of Clinical Nutrition, 77,* 167–172.

Promislow, D. E. L., Fedeorka, K. K., & Burger, J. M. S. (2006). Evolutionary biology of aging: Future directions. In E. J. Masoro & S. N. Austad (Eds.), *Handbook of the biology of aging* (6th ed.). San Diego: Academic Press.

Province, M. A., Hadley, E. C., Hornbrook, M. C., Lipitz, L. A., Miller, J. P., Mulrow, C. D., Ory, M. G., Sattin, R. W., Tinetti, M. E., & Wolf, S. L. (1995). The effects of exercise on falls in elderly patients. *Journal of the American Medical Association, 273,* 1341–1347.

Pryor, J. H., Hurtado, S., Saenz, V. B., Korn, J. S., Santos, J. L., & Korn, W. S. (2006). *The American freshman: National norms for fall 2006.* Los Angeles: Higher Education Research Institute, UCLA.

Pudrovska, T., Schieman, S., & Carr, D. (2006). Strains of singlehood in later life: Do race and gender matter? *Journals of Gerontology B: Psychological Sciences and Social Sciences, 61,* S315–S322.

Pujol. J., Lopez-Sala, A., Sebastian-Galles, N., Deus, J., Cardoner, N., Soriano-Mas, C., Moreno, A., & Sans, A. (2004). Delayed myelination in children with developmental delay detected by volumetric MRI. *Neuroimage. 22,* 879–903.

Putnam Investments (2006). *Survey of the working retired.* Franklin, MA: Author.

Putnam, S. P., Sanson, A. V., & Rothbart, M. K. (2002). Child temperament and parenting. In M. H. Bornstein (Ed.). *Handbook of parenting* (2nd ed.). Mahwah, NJ: Erlbaum.

Q

Quadrel, M. J., Fischoff, B., & Davis, W. (1993). Adolescent (in) vulnerability. *American Psychologist, 48,* 102–116.

Quinn, P. C. (2007). Categorization. In A. Slater & M. Lewis (Eds.), *Introduction to infant development* (2nd ed.). New York: Oxford University Press.

R

Raffaelli, M., & Ontai, L. L. (2004). Gender socialization in Latino/a families: Results from two retrospective studies. *Sex Roles, 50,* 287–299.

Ramey, C. T., Ramey, S. L., & Lanzi, R. G. (2006). Children's health and education. In W. Damon & R. Lerner (Eds.), *Handbook of child psychology* (6th ed.). New York: Wiley.

Ramey, S. L. (2005). Human developmental science serving children and families: Contributions of the NICHD study of early child care. In NICHD Early Child Care Network (Eds.), *Child care and development.* New York: Guilford.

Raneri, L. G., & Constance, M. W. (2007). Social ecological predictors of repeat adolescent pregnancy. *Perspectives on Sexual and Reproductive Health, 39,* 39–47.

Rapaport, S. (1994, November 28). Interview. *U.S. News & World Report,* p. 94.

Rapkin, A. J. Tsao, J. C., Turk, N., Anderson, M., & Zeltzer, L. K. (2006). Relationships among self-rated Tanner staging, hormones, and psychological factors in healthy female adolescents. *Journal of Pediatric and Adolescent Gynecology, 19,* 181–187.

Rasinski, T. V., & Padak, N. (2008). *From phonics to fluency* (2nd ed.). Boston: Allyn & Bacon.

Rasulo, D., Christensen, K., & Tomasini, C. (2005). The influence of social relations on mortality in later life: A study on elderly Danish twins. *Gerontologist, 45,* 601–608.

Ratey, J. (2006, March 27). Commentary in L. Szabo, "ADHD treatment is getting a workout." *USA Today,* p.6D.

Rathunde, K., & Csikstentmihalyi M. (2006). The developing person: An Experiential perspective. In W. Damon & R. Lerner (eds.), *Handbook & child Psychology* (6th ed.). New York: Wiley

Raymond, F. L., & Tarpey, P. (2006). The genetics of mental retardation. *Human Molecular Genetics, 13 (Special No. 2),* R110–R116.

Razay, G., Vreugdenhil, A., & Wilcock, G. (2007). The metabolic syndrome and Alzheimer disease. *Archives of Neurology, 64,* 93–96.

Redgrave, G. W., Coughlin, J. W., Heinberg, L. J., & Guarda, A. S. (2007). First-degree relative history of alcoholism in eating disorder inpatients: Relationship to eating and substance abuse psychopathology. *Eating Behaviors, 8,* 15–22.

Redinbaugh, E. M., MacCallum, J., & Kiecolt-Glaser, J. K. (1995). Recurrent syndromal depression in caregivers. *Psychology and Aging, 10,* 358–368.

Reed, S. K. (2007). *Cognitive psychology* (7th Ed.). Belmont, CA: Wadsworth.

Regalado, M., Sareen, H., Inkelas, M., Wissow, L. S., & Halfon, N. (2004). Parents' discipline of young children: Results from the National Survey of Early Childhood Health, *Pediatrics, 113* (Suppl.), S1952–S1958.

Regev, R. H., Lusky, A., Dolfin, T., Litmanovitz, I., Arnon, S., Reichman, B., & the Israel Neonatal Network. (2003). Excess mortality and morbidity among small-for-gestational-age premature infants: A population based study. *Journal of Pediatrics, 143,* 186–191.

Reichstadt, J., Depp, C. A., Palinkas, L. A., Folsom, D. P., & Jeste, D. V. (2007). Building blocks of successful aging: A focus group study of older adults' perceived contributors to successful aging. *American Journal of Geriatric Psychiatry, 15,* 194–201.

Reichstadt, J., Depp, C. A., Palinkas, L. A., Folsom, D. P., & Jeste, D. V. (2007). Building blocks of successful aging: A focus group study of older adults' perceived contributors to successful aging. *American Journal of Geriatric Psychiatry, 15,* 194–201.

Reinders, H., & Youniss, J. (2006). School-based required community service and civic

development in adolescence. *Applied Developmental Science, 10,* 2–12.

Religion in America. (1993). Princeton, NJ: Princeton Religious Research Center.

Ressi, A. S. (1989). A life-course approach to gender, aging, and intergenerational relations. In K. W. Schaie & C. Schooler (Eds.), *Social structure and aging.* Hillsdale, NJ: Erlbaum.

Reutzel, D. R., & Cooter, R. B. (2008). *Teaching children to read* (5th ed.). Upper Saddle River, NJ: Prentice Hall.

Revelle, S. P. (2004). High standards high-stakes = high achievement in Massachusetts. *Phi Delta Kappan, 85,* 591–597.

Reyna, C., Goodwin, E. J., & Ferrari, J. R. (2007). Older adult stereotypes among care providers in residential care facilities: Examining the relationship between contact, education, and ageism. *Journal of Gerontological Nursing, 33,* 50–55.

Reyna, V. F. (2004). How people make decisions that involve risk: A dual-process approach. *Current Directions in Psychological Science, 13,* 60–66.

Rholes, W. S., & Simpson, J. A. (2007). Introduction: New directions and emerging issues in adult attachment. In W. S. Rholes & J. A. Simpson (Eds.), *Adult attachment.* New York: Guilford.

Rhule-Louie, D. M., & McMahon, R. J. (2007, in press). Problem behavior and romantic relationships: Assortative mating, behavior contagion, and desistance. *Clinical Child and Family Psychology Review.*

Richardson, C. R., Faulkner, G., McDevitt, J., Skrinar, G. S., Hutchinson, D. S., Piette, J. D. (2005). Integrating physical activity into mental health services for persons with serious mental illness. *Psychiatric Services, 56,* 324–331.

Richardson, G. A., Ryan, C., Willford, J., Day, N. L., & Goldschmidt, L. (2002). Prenatal alcohol and marijuana exposure: Effects on neuropsychological outcomes at 10 years. *Neurotoxiocology and Teratology, 24,* 309–320.

Richardson, V. E. (2007). A dual process model of grief counseling: Findings from the Changing Lives of Older Couples (CLOC) study. *Journal of Gerontological Social Work, 48,* 311–329.

Ridgeway, D., Waters, E., & Kuczaj, S. A. (1985). Acquisition of emotion-descriptive language: Receptive and productive norms for ages 18 months to 6 years. *Developmental Psychology, 21,* 901–908.

Riediger, M., Li, S-C., & Lindenberger, U. (2006). Selection, optimization, and compensation as developmental mechanisms of adaptive resource allocation: Review and preview. In J. E. Birren & K. W. Schaie (Eds.), *Handbook of the psychology of aging* (6th ed.). San Diego: Academic Press.

Riguad, D., Verges, B., Colas-Linhart, N., Petiet, A., Moukkadem, M., Van Wymelbeke,

V., & Brondel, L. (2007, in press). Hormonal and psychological factors linked to the increased thermic effect of food in malnourished fasting anorexia nervosa. *Journal of Clinical Endocrinology and Metabolism.*

Riley, K. P., Snowdon, D. A., Derosiers, M. F., & Markesbery, W. R. (2005). Early life linguistic ability, late life cognitive function, and neuropathology: Findings from the Nun study. *Neurobiology of Aging, 26,* 341–347.

Riley, L. D., & Bown, C. (2005). The sandwich generation: Challenges and coping strategies of multigenerational families. *Family Journal, 13,* 52–58.

Rimsza, M. E., & Kirk, G. M. (2005). Common medical problems of the college student. *Pediatric Clinics of North America, 52,* 9–24.

Ringdal, G. I., Jordhoy, M. S., Ringdal, K., & Kaasa, S. (2001). The first year of grief and bereavement in close family members to individuals who have died of cancer. *Palliative Medicine, 15,* 91–105.

Rizvi, A. A. (2007). Management of diabetes in older adults. *American Journal of Medical Science, 333,* 35–47.

Rizzo, M. S. (1999, May 8). Genetic counseling combines' science with a human touch. *Kansas City Star,* p. 3.

Robbins, G., Powers, D., & Burgess, S. (2008). *A fit way of life.* New York: McGraw-Hill.

Robert, S. A., & Ruel, E. (2006). Racial segregation and health disparities between black and white older adults. *Journals of Gerontology B: Psychological Sciences and Social Sciences, 61,* S203–S211.

Roberts, B. W. (2006). Personality development and organizational dynamics across the life span. In B. M. Staw (Ed.) *Research on organizational behavior.* Elsevier Science/JAI Press.

Roberts, D. F., Hennkson, L., & Foehr, V. G. (2004). Adolescents and the media. In R. Lerner & L. Steinberg (Eds.) *Handbook of adolescent psychology.* New York: Wiley.

Roberts, S. B., & Rosenberg, I. (2006). Nutrition and aging: Changes in the regulation of energy metabolism with aging. *Physiology Review, 86,* 651–667.

Robins, R. W., Trzensiewski, K. H., Tracey, J. L., Potter, J., & Gosling, S. D. (2002). Age differences in self-esteem from age 9 to 90. *Psychology and Aging, 17,* 423–434.

Robins, R. W., Trzesnieswski, K. H., Tracey, J. L., Potter, J., & Gosling, S. D. (2002). Age differences in self-esteem from age 9 to 90. *Psychology and Aging, 17.* 423–434.

Robinson, T., & Umphery, D. (2006). First- and third-person perceptions of images of older people in advertising: An intergenerational evaluation. *International Journal of A ging and Human Development, 62,* 159–173.

Rocha, N. A. C. F., Silva, F. P. S., & Tudella, E. (2006). The impact of object size and rigidity on infant reaching. *Infant Behavior and Development, 29,* 251–261.

Rodaers, L. S. (2004). Meaning of bereavement among older African American widows. *Geriatric Nursing, 25,* 10–16.

Rode, S. S., Chang, P., Fisch, R. O., & Sroufe, L. A. (1981). Attachment patterns of infants separated at birth. *Developmental Psychology, 17,* 188–191.

Rodin, J., & Langer, E. J. (1977). Long-term effects of a control-relevant intervention with the institutionalized aged. *Journal of Personality and Social Psychology, 35,* 397–402.

Rodrigues, A. E., Hall, J. H., & Fincham, F. D. (2006). What predicts divorce and relationship dissolution. In M. A. Fine & J. H. Harvey (Eds.). *Handbook of divorce and relationship dissolution.* Mahwah, NJ: Erlbaum.

Rodriquez, K. L., Barnato, A. E., & Arnold, R. M. (2007). Perceptions and utilization of palliative care services in acute care hospitals. *Journal of Palliative Medicine, 10,* 99–110.

Roemmich, J. N., Epstein, L. H., Raja, S., & Yin, L. (2007). The neighborhood and home environments: Disparate relationships with physical activity and sedentary behaviors in youth. *Annals of Behavioral Medicine, 33,* 29–38.

Roese, N. J., & Summerville, A. (2005). What we regret most…and why. *Personality and Social Psychology Bulletin, 31,* 1273–1285.

Rogerson, P. A., & Kim, D. (2005). Population distribution and redistribution of the baby-boom cohort in the United States: Recent trends and implications. *Proceedings of the National Academy of Science USA, 102,* 15319–15324.

Rogoff, B., Moore, L., Najafi, B., Dexter, A., Correa-Chavez, M., & Solis, J. (2007). Children's development of cultural repertoires through participation in everyday routines and practices. In J. E. Grusec & P. D. Hastings (Eds.), *Handbook of socialization.* New York: Guilford.

Rohrer, J. F., Pierce, J. R., & Blackburn, C. (2005). Lifestyle and mental health. *Preventive Medicine, 40,* 438–443.

Ronnlund, M., Nyberg, L., Backman, L., & Nilsson, L. G. (2005). Stability, growth, and decline in adult life span development of declarative memory: Cross-sectional and longitudinal data from a population-based study. *Psychology and Aging, 20,* 3–18.

Rook, K. S., Mavandadi, S., Sorkin, D. H., & Zettel, L. A. (2007). Optimizing social relationships as a resource for health and well-being in later life. In C. M. Aldwin, C. L. Park, & A. Spiro (Eds.), *Handbook of health psychology and aging.* New York: Guilford.

Roopnarine, J. L., & Metindogan, A. (2006). Early childhood education research in cross-national perspective. In B. Spodek & O. N. Saracho (Eds.), *Handbook of research on the education of young children.* Mahwah, NJ: Erlbaum.

Roring, R. W., Hines, F. G., & Charness, N. (2007). Age differences in identifying words in synthetic speech. *Human Factors, 49,* 25–31.

Rosenberg, M. S., Westling, D. L., & McLeskey, J. (2008). *Special education for today's teachers.* Upper Saddle River, NJ: Prentice Hall.

Rosenthal, C. J., Martin-Matthews, A., & Matthews, S. H. (1996). Caught in the middle? Occupancy in multiple roles and help to parents in a national probability sample of Canadian adults. *Journal of Gerontology: Psychological Sciences and Social Sciences, 51B,* S274–S283.

Roskos, K. A., & Christie, J. F. (Eds.). (2007). *Play and literacy in early childhood* (2nd ed.). Mahwah, NJ: Erlbaum.

Ross, C., & Kirby, G. (2006). Welfare-to-work transitions for parents of infants. In N. Carbera, R. Hutchens, H. E. Peters, & L. Peters (Eds.), *From welfare to childcare.* Mahwah, NJ: Erlbaum.

Ross, M. E. T., & Aday, L. A. (2006). Stress and coping in African American grandparents who are raising their children. *Journal of Family Issues, 27,* 912–932.

Rossi, A. S. (1989). A life-course approach to gender, aging, and intergenerational relations. In K. W. Schaie & C. Schooler (Eds.), *Social structure and aging.* Hillsdale, NJ: Erlbaum.

Rossi, A. S. (2004). The menopausal transition and aging processes. In G. Brim, C. D. Ryff, & R. Kessler (Eds.), *How healthy we are: A national study of well-being in midlife.* Chicago: University of Chicago Press.

Rossi, S., Miniussi, C., Pasqualetti, P., Babiloni, C., Rossini, P. M., & Cappa, S. F. (2005). Age-related functional changes of prefrontal cortex in long-term memory: A repetitive transcranial magnetic stimulation study. *Journal of Neuroscience, 24,* 7939–7944.

Roth, J. L., Books-Gunn, J., Murray, L., & Foster, W. (1998). Promoting healthy adolescents: Synthesis of youth development program evaluations. *Journal of Research on Adolescence, 8,* 423–459.

Rothbart, M. K. & Bates, J. E. (2006). Temperament. In W. Damon & R. Lerner (Eds.), *Handbook of child psychology* (6th ed.). New York: Wiley.

Rothbart, M. K., & Putnam, S. P. (2002). Temperament and socialization. In L. Pulkkinen & A., Caspi (Eds.), *Paths to successful development.* New York: Cambridge University Press.

Rothbaum, F., Poll, M., Azuma, H., Miyake, K., & Weisz, J. (2000). The development of close relationships in Japan and the United States: Paths of symbiotic harmony and generative tension. *Child Development, 71,* 1121–1142.

Rothbaum, F., & Trommsdorff, G. (2007). Do roots and wings complement or oppose one another?: The socialization of relatedness and autonomy in cultural context. In J. E. Grusec & P. D. Hastings (Eds.), *Handbook of Socialization.* New York: Guilford.

Rovee-Collier, C. (1987). Learning and memory in children. In J. D. Osofsky (Ed.), *Handbook of infant development* (2nd ed.). New York: Wiley.

Rovee-Collier, C. (2002). Infant learning and memory. In U. Goswami (Ed.), *Blackwell handbook of childhood cognitive development,* Malden, MA: Blackwell.

Rovee-Collier, C. (2007). The development of infant memory. In N. Cowan & M. Courage (Eds.), *The development of memory in childhood.* Philadelphia: Psychology Press.

Rovee-Collier, C. & Barr, R. (2004). Infant learning and memory. In G. Bremner & A. Fogel (Eds.), *Blackwell handbook of infant development.* Maden, MA: Blackwell.

Roza, S. J., Verburg, B. O., Jaddoe, V. W., Hofman, A., Mackenbach, J. P., Steegers, E. A., Witteman, J. C., Verhulst, F. C., Tiemeir, H. (2007). Effects of maternal smoking in pregnancy on prenatal brain development: The Generation R study. *European Journal of Neuroscience, 25,* 611–627.

Rubin, D. H., Krasilnikoff, P. A., Leventhal, J. M., Weile, B., & Berget, A. (1986, August 23). Effect of passive smoking on birthweight. *The Lancet, 2,* 415–417.

Rubin, K. H., Bukowski, W., & Parker, J. (2006). Peer interactions, relationships, and groups. In W. Damon & R. Lerner (Eds.), *Handbook of child psychology* (6th ed.). New York: Wiley.

Ruble, D. (1983). The development of social comparison processes and their role in achievement-related self-socialization. In E. Higgins, D. Ruble, & W. Hartup (Eds.), *Social cognitive development: A social-cultural perspective.* New York: Cambridge University Press.

Ruble, D. N., Martin, C. L., & Berenbaum, S. (2006). Gender development. In W. Damon & R. Lerner (Eds.), *Handbook of child psychology* (6th ed.). New York: Wiley.

Ruckenhauser, G., Yazdani, F., & Ravaglia, G. (2007). Suicide of Gerontology and Geriatrics, 44 (Suppl.) S355–S358.

Rueter, M. A., & Kwon, H. K. (2005). Developmental trends in adolescent suicide ideation. *Journal of Research on Adolescence, 15,* 205–222.

Ruff, H. A., & Capozzoli, M. C. (2003). Development of attention and distractibility in the first 4 years of life. *Developmental Psychology, 39,* 877–890.

Rumberger, R. W. (1995). Dropping out of middle school: A multilevel analysis of students and schools. *American Education Research Journal, 3,* 583–625.

Runco, M. A. (Ed.). (2006). *Creativity research handbook.* Cresskill, NJ: Hampton Press.

Runquist, J. (2007). Persevering through postpartum fatigue. *Journal of Obstetric, Gynecologic, and Neonatal Nursing, 36,* 28–37.

Rupp, D. E. Jovanovich, S. J., & Crede, M. (2005) The multidimensional nature of ageism: Construct validity and group differences. *Journal of Social Psychology, 145,* 335–362.

Rusbult, C. E., Olsen, N., Davis, J. L., & Hannon, P. A. (2001). Commitment and relationship maintenance mechanisms. In J. H. Harvey & A. Wenzel (Eds.), *Close romantic* NJ: Erlbaum.

Russell, S. T. Jayner, K. (2001). Addescent sexual orientation and suicide risk: Evidence from a national study. *American Journal of Public Health, 91,* 1276–1281.

Rutter, M. (2007). Gene-environment interdependence. *Developmental Science, 10,* 12–18.

Ryan, R. M., Fauth, R. C., & Brooks-Gunn, J. (2006). Childhood poverty: Implications for school readiness and early childhood education. In B. Spodek & O. N. Saracho (Eds.), *Handbook of research on the education of young children.* Mahwah, NJ: Erlbaum.

Ryff, C. D. (1984). Personality development from the inside: The subjective experience of change in adulthood and aging. In P. B. Baltes & O. G. Brim (Eds.), *Life-span development and behavior.* New York: Academic Press.

S

Saarni, C. (1999). *The development of emotional competence.* New York: Guilford.

Saarni, C., Campos, J., Camras, L. A., & Witherington, D. (2006). Emotional development. In W. Damon & R. Lerner (Eds.), *Handbook of child psychology* (6th ed.). New York: Wiley.

Sabol, W. J., Coulton, C. J., & Korbin, J. E. (2004). Building community capacity for violence prevention. *Journal of Interpersonal Violence, 19,* 322–340.

Sacznski, J., & Willis, S. L. (2001). *Cognitive training and maintenance of intervention effects in the elderly.* Unpublished manuscript. University Park, PA: Pennsylvania State University.

Saffran, J. R., Werker, J. F., & Werner, L. A. (2006). The infant's auditory world: Hearing, speech, and the beginnings of language. In W. Damon & R. Lerner (Eds.), *Handbook of child psychology* (6th ed.). New York: Wiley.

Sagi, A., Koren-Karie, N., Gini, M., Ziv, Y., & Joels, T. (2002). Shedding further light on the effects of various types and quality of early child care on infant-mother attachment relationship: The Haifa study of early child care. *Child Development. 73,* 1166–1186.

Sakraida, T. J. (2005). Divorce transition differences of midlife women. *Issues in Mental Health Nursing, 26,* 225–249.

Sallivan, H. S. (1953). *The interpersonal theory of psychiatry.* New York: W. W. Norton.

Salmon, J., Campbell, K. J., & Crawford, D. A. (2006). Television viewing habits associated with obesity risk factors: A survey of Melbourne schoolchildren. *Medical Journal of Australia, 184,* 64–67.

Salthouse, T. A. (1991). *Theoretical perspectives on cognitive aging.* Mahwah, NJ: Erlbaum.

Salthouse, T. A. (1994). The nature of influence of speed on adult age differenes in cognition. *Developmental Psychology, 30,* 240–259.

Salthouse, T. A. (1996). General and specific speed mediation of adult age differences in memory. *Journal of Gerontology, 51A,* P30–P42.

Salthouse, T. A. (2000). Adulthood and aging: Cognitive processes and development. In A. Kazdin (Ed.), *Encyclopedia of psychology.* Washington, DC, and New York: American Psychological Association and Oxford University Press.

Salthouse, T. A., & Balltes, P. R. (2006). Theoretical development in the psychology of aging. In J. E. Birren & K. W. Schaie (Eds.), *Handbook of the psychology of aging.* San Diego: Academic Press.

Salthouse, T. A., & Skovronek, E. (1992). Within-context assessment of working memory. *Journal of Gerontology, 47,* P110–P117.

Sanchez, A., Norman, G. J., Sallis, J.F., Calfas, K. J., Cella, J., & Patrick, K. (2007). Patterns and correlates of physical activity and nutrition behaviors in adolescence. *American Journal of Preventive Medicine, 32,* 124–130.

Sandefur, G. D., & Meier, A. (2007). The family environment: Structure, material resources, and child care. In B. V. Brown (Ed.), *Key indicators of child and youth well-being.* Mahwah, NJ: Erlbaum.

Sandiford, R. (2006). Keeping it natural. *Nursing Times, 102,* 22–23.

Sands, R. G., & Goldberg-Glen, R. S. (2000). Factors associated with stress among grandparents raising their grandchildren. *Family Relations, 49,* 97–105.

Sangree, W. H. (1989). Age and power: Life-course trajectories and age structuring of power relations in East and West Africa. In D. I. Kertzer & K. W. Schaie (Eds.), *Age structuring in comparative perspective.* Hillsdale, NJ: Erlbaum.

Sanson, A., & Rothbart, M. K. (1995). Child temperament and parenting. In M. H. Bornstein (Ed.), *Handbook of parenting* (Vol. 4). Hillsdale, NJ: Erlbaum.

Santelli, J. S., Lindberg, L.D., Finer, L. B., & Singh, S. (2007). Explaining recent declines in adolescent pregnancy in the United States: The contribution of abstinence and improved contraceptive use. *American Journal of Publish Health, 97,* 150–156.

Santelli, J., Ott, M. A., Lyon, M., Rogers, J., Summers, D., & Schleifer, R. (2006). Abstinence and abstinence-only education: A review of U.S. policies and programs. *Journal of Adolescent Health, 38,* 72–81.

Santoro, N., Brockwell, S., J., Crawford, S. L., Gold, E. B., Harlow, S. D., Matthews, K. A., & Sutton-Tyrrell, K. (2007, in press). Helping midlife women predict the onset of the final menses: SWAN, the Study of Women's Health Across the Nation. *Menopause.*

Santrock, J. W., & Warshak, R. A. (1979). Father custody and social development in boys and girls. *Journal of Social Issues, 35,* 112–125.

Santrock, J. W., Sitterle, K. A., & Warshak, R. A. (1988). Parent-child relationships in stepfather families. In P. Bronstein & C. P. Cowan (Eds.), *Fatherhood today: Men's changing roles in the family.* New York: Wiley.

Santrock, J. W., & Halonen, J. (2008). *Your Guide to college success* (5th ed.). New York: Wadsworth.

Savin-Williams, R. C. (2001). *Mom. Dad, I'm gay.* Washington, DC: American Psychological Association.

Savin-Williams, R. C. (2006). *The new gay teenager.* Cambridge, MA: Harvard University Press.

Savin-Williams, R. C., & Diamond, L. (2004). Sex. In R. Lerner & L. Steinberg (Eds.), *Handbook of adolescent psychology.* New York: Wiley.

Sayer, L. C. (2006). Economic aspects of divorce and relationship dissolution. In M. A. Fine & J. H. Harvey (Eds.), *Handbook of divorce and relationship dissolution.* Mahwah, NJ: Erlbaum.

Scafidt, F., & Field, T. M. (1996). Massage therapy improves behavior in neonates born to HIV-positive mothers. *Journal of Pediatric Psychology, 21,* 889–897.

Scarr, S. (1993). Biological and cultural diversity: The legacy of Darwin for development. *Child Development, 64,* 1333–1353.

Scarr, S., & Weinberg, R. A. (1983). The Minnesota adoption studies: Genetic differences and malleability. *Child Development, 54,* 182–259.

Schachter, S. C., & Ransil, B. J. (1996). Handedness distributions in nine professional groups. *Perceptual and Motor Skills, 82,* 51–63.

Schaffer, H. R. (1996). *Social development.* Cambridge, MA: Blackwell.

Schaie, K. W . (1994). The life course of adult intellectual abilities. *American Psychologist, 49,* 304–313.

Schale, K. W. (1996). *Intellectual development in adulthood: The Seattle Longitudinal Study.* New York: Cambridge University Press.

Schaie, K. W. (2000). Unpublished review of J. W. Santrock's *Life-span development,* (8th ed.). New York: McGraw-Hill.

Schaie, K. W. (2007). General differences: The age-cohort period model. In J. E. Birren (Ed.), *Encyclopedia of gerontology* (2nd ed.). Oxford: Elsevier.

Schaie, K. W., & Willis, S. L. (2000). A stage theory model of adult development revisited. In R. Rubinstein, M. Moss, & M. Kleban (Eds.), *The many dimensions of aging:*

Essays in honor of M. Powell Lawton. New York: Springer.

Schattschneider, C., Fletcher, J. M., Francis, D. J., Carlson, C. D., & Foorman, E. R. (2004). Kindergarten prediction of reading skills: A longitudinal comparative analysis. *Journal of Educational Psychology, 96,* 265–282.

Scheibe, S., Freund, A. M., & Baltes, P. B. (2007). Toward a psychology of longings: The optimal (utopian) life. *Developmental Psychology.*

Scheibe, S., Kunzmann, U., & Baltes, P. B. (2007). Wisdom, life longings, and optimal development. In J. A. Blackburn & C. N. Dulmas (Eds.), *Handbook of gerontology.* New York: Wiley.

Schieber, F. (2006). Vision and aging. In J. E. Birren & K. W. Schaie (Eds.), *Handbook of the psychology of aging* (6th ed.). San Diego: Academic Press.

Schieman, van Gundy, K., & Taylor, J. (2004). The relationship between age and depressive Symptoms: A test of competing Explanatory end suppression influences. *Journal of Aging Health, 14,* 260–285.

Schmidt, S., & others. (2006). Cigarette smoking strongly modifies the association of LOC387715 and age-related macular degeneration. *American Journal of Human Genetics, 78,* 852–864.

Schmidt, U. (2003). Aetiology of eating disorders in the 21st century: New answers to old questions. *European Child and Adolescent Psychiatry, 12* (Suppl. 1), 1130–1137.

Schneider, W. (2004). Memory development in childhood. In P. Smith & C. Hart (Eds.), *Blackwell handbook of childhood cognitive development.* Malden, MA: Blackwell.

Schoppe-Sullivan, S. J., Mangelsdorf, S. C., Brown, G. L., & Sokolowski, M. S. (2007). Goodness-of-fit in family context: Infant temperament, marital quality, and early coparenting behavior. *Infant Behavior and Development, 30,* 82–96.

Schroepfer, T. A. (2007). Critical events in the dying process: The potential for physical and psychological suffering. *Journal of Palliative Medicine, 10,* 136–147.

Schulenberg, J. E., O'Malley, P. M., Bachman, J. G., & Johnson, L. D. (2000). "Spread your wings and fly": The course of health and well-being during the transition to young adulthood. In L. Crockett & R. Silbereisen (Eds.), *Negotiating adolescece in times of social change.* New York: Cambridge University Press.

Schulenberg, J. E., & Zarett, N. R. (2006). Mental health during emerging adulthood: Continuity and discontinuity in courses, causes, and functions. In J. J. Arnett & J. L. Tanner (Eds.), *Emerging adults in America.* Washington, DC: American Psychological Association.

Schultz, K. A., & Adams, G. A. (Eds.). (2007). *Aging and work in the 21st century.* Mahwah, NJ: Erlbaum.

Schulz, J. H., & Borowski, A. (2006). Economic security in retirement: Reshaping the public-private pension mix. In R. H. Binstock & L. K. George (Eds.), *Handbook of aging and the social sciences* (6th ed.). San Diego: Academic Press.

Schunk, D. H. (2008). *Learning theories* (5th ed.). Upper Saddle River, NJ: Prentice Hall.

Schunk, D. H., & Zimmerman, B. J. (2006). Competence and control beliefs: Distinguishing the means and ends. In P. A. Alexander & P. H. Winne (Eds.), *Handbook of educational psychology* (2nd ed.). Mahwah, NJ: Erlbaum.

Schwarzer, R., & Schultz, U. (2003). Stressful life events. In I. B. Weiner (Ed.), *Handbook of psychology* Vol. IX New York: Wiley.

Schweinhart, L. J., Montie, J., Xiang, Z. Barnett, W. S., Belfield, C. R., & Nores, M. (2005). *Lifetime effects: The High/Scope Perry Preschool Study Through Age 40.* Ypsilanti, MI: High/Scope Press.

Scialfa, C. T., & Fernie, G. R. (2006). Adaptive technology. In J. E. Birren & K. W. Schaie (Eds.), *Handbook of the psychology of aging* (6th ed.). San Diego: Academic Press.

Scourfield, J., Van den Bree, M., Martin, N., & McGuffin, P. (2004). Conduct problems in children and adolescents: A twin study. *Archives of General Psychiatry, 61,* 489–496.

Sedlak, A. J., Schultz, D., Wells, S. J., Lyons, P., Doueck, H. J., & Gragg, F. (2006). Child protection and justice systems processing of serious abuse and neglect cases. *Child Abuse and Neglect, 30,* 657–677.

Seeman, T. E., & Chen, X. (2002). Risk and protective factors for physical functioning in older adults with and without chronic conditions: MacArthur studies of successful Aging. *Journal of Gerontology: Social Sciences, 57B,* S135-S144.

Seguin, R., & Nelson, M. E. (2003). The benefits of strength training for older adults. *American Journal of Preventive Medicine, 25* (Suppl. 2), 141–149.

Seidenfeld, M. E., Sosin, E., & Rickert, V. I. (2004). Nutrition and eating disorders in adolescents. *Mt. Sinai Journal of Medicine, 71,* 155–161.

Selim, A. J., Fincke, G., Berlowitz, D. R., Miller, D. R., Qian, S. X., Lee, A., Cong, Z., Rogers, W., Sileim, B. J., Ren, X. S., Sppiro. A., Kazis, L. E. (2005). Comprehensive health status assessment of centenarians: Results from the 1999 Large Health Survey of Veteran Enrollees. *Journals of Gerontology: Biological Sciences and Medical Sciences, 60,* 515–519.

Sellers, R. M., Copeland-Linder, N., Martin, P. P., & Lewis, R. L. (2006). Racial identity matters: The relationship between racial discrimination and psychological functioning in African American adolescents. *Journal of Research on Adolescence, 16,* 187–216.

Shafer, V. L., & Garrido-Nag, K. (2007). The neurodevelopmental bases of languge. In E.

Hoff & M. Shatz (Eds.), *Blackwell handbook of language development.* Malden, MA: Blackwell.

Shan, Z. Y., Liu, J. Z., Sahgal, V., Wang, B., & Yue, G. H. (2005). Selective atropohy of left hemisphere and frontal lobe of the brain in older men. *Journals of Gerontology A Biological Sciences and Medical Science, 60,* A165–A174.

Shankaran, S., Lester, B.M., Das, A., Bauer, C. R., Bada, H. S., Lagasse, L., & Higgins, R. (2007). Impact of maternal substance use during pregnancy on childhood outcome. *Seminars in Fetal and Neonatal Medicine, 12,* 143–150.

Shanley, D. P., & Kirkwood, T. B. (2006). Caloric restriction does not enhance longevity in all species and is unlikely to do so in humans. *Biogrontology, 7,* 165–168.

Shapiro, A. F., and Gottman, J. M., (2005). Effects on marriage of a psycho-education intervention with couples undergoing the transition to parenthood, evaluation at 1-year post-intervention. *Journal of Family Communication, 5,* 1–24.

Sharma, B.R. (2007). Sudden infant death syndrome: A subject of microlegal research. *American Journal of Forensic Medicine and Pathology, 28,* 69–72.

Sharma, S., & Kaur, G. (2005). Neuroprotective potential of dietary restriction against kainate-induced excitotoxicity in adult male Wistar rats. *Brain Research Bulletin, 67,* 482–491.

Shastry, B. S. (2007). Assessment of the contribution of the LOC387715 gene polymorphism in a family with oxidative age-related macular generation and heterozygous CFH variant (Y402H). *Journal of Human Genetics, 52,* 384–387.

Shatz, M., & Gelman, R. (1973). The development of communication skills: Modifications in the speech of young children as a function of the listener. *Monographs of the Society for Research in Child Development, 38* (Serial No. 152).

Shaver, P. (1986, August). *Being lonely, falling in love: Perspectives from attachment theory.* Paper presented at the meeting of the American Psychological Association, Washington, DC.

Shaver, P. R., & Mikulincer, M. (2007). Attachment theory and research: Core concepts, basic principles, conceptual bridges. In A. Kruglanski & E. T. Higgins (Eds.), *Social psychology: Handbook of basic principles* (2nd ed.). New York: Guilford.

Shay, J. W., & Wright, W. E. (2006). Telomerase therapeutics for cancer: Challenges and new directions. *Nature Reviews: Drug Discovery, 5,* 577–584.

Shay, J. W., & Wright, W. E. (2007). Hallmarks of telomeres in aging research. *Journal of Pathology, 211,* 114–123.

Shaywitz, B. A., Lyon, G. R., & Shaywitz, S. E. (2006). The role of functional magnetic resonance imaging in understanding reading and dyslexia. *Developmental Neuropsychology,* 30, 613–632.

Shea, A., Walsh, C., MacMillan, H., & Steiner, M. (2005). Child maltreatment and HPA axis dysregulation: Relationship to major depressive disorder and post traumatic stress disorder in females. *Psychoneuroendocrinology,* 30, 162–178.

Sheeber, L. B., Davis, B., Leve, C., Hops, H., & Tildesley, E. (2007). Adolescents' relationships with their mothers and fathers: Association s with depressive disorder and subdiagnostic symptomatology. *Journal of Abnormal Psychology,* 116, 144–154.

Shields, M. (2006). Overweight and obesity among children and youth. *Health Reports,* 17, 27–42.

Shigeta, M., & Homma, A. (2007). Alzheimer's disease. In J. A. Blackburn & C. N. Dulmas (Eds.), *Handbook of gerontology.* New York: Wiley.

Shiner, R. L. (2006). Temperament and personality in childhood. In D. K. Mroczek & T. D. Little (Eds.), *Handbook of personality development,* Mahwah, NJ: Erlbaum.

Shiraer, E., & Levy, D. (2007). *Cross-cultural Psychology* (3rd ed.). Boston: Allyn & Bacon.

Shore, L. M., & Goldberg, C. B. (2005). Age discrimination in the work place. In R. L. Dipobye & A. Colella (Eds.), *Discrimination at work.* Mahwah: NJ: Erlbaum.

Shumway-Cooke, A., Guralnick, J. M., Phillips, C. L., Coppin, A. K., Ciol, M. A., Bandinelli, S., & Ferrucci, L. (2007). Age-associated declines in complex walking task performance: The Walking InCHIANTI toolkit. *Journal of the American Geriatric Society,* 55, 58–65.

Siega-Riz, A. M., Kranz, S., Blanchette, D., Haines, P. S., Guilkey. D. K., & Popkin, B. M. (2004). The effect of participation in the WIC program on preschoolers diets. *Journal of Pediatrics,* 144, 229–234.

Siegel, L. S. (2003). Learning disabilities. In I. B. Weiner (Ed.), *Handbook of psychology,* (Vol. VI). New York: Wiley.

Siegel, S. J., Bieschke, J., Powers, E. T., & Kelly, J. W. (2007). The oxidative stress metabolite 4-hydroxynonenal promotes Alzheimer protofibril formation. *Biochemistry,* 46, 1503–1510.

Siegler, R. S. (2007). Cognitive variability. *Developmental Science,* 10, 104–109.

Siegler, R. S. (2006). Microgenetic analysis of learning. In W. Damon & R. Lerner (Eds.), *Handbook of Child Psychology* (6th Ed.). New York: Wiley.

Siegler, R. S., & Alibali, M. W. (2005). *Children's thinking* (4th ed.). Upper Saddle River, NJ: Prentice Hall.

Silberman, M. (2006). *Teaching actively,* Boston: Allyn & Bacon.

Silva, C. (2005, October 31). When teen dynamo talks, city 1: stems *Boston Globe,* pp. B1, B 4.

Silverstein, M., Gans, D., & Yang, F. M. (2006). Intergenerational support to aging parents. *Journal of Family Issues,* 27, 1068–1084.

Sim, T. N., & Ong, L. P. (2005). Parent punishment and child aggression in a Singapore Chinese preschool sample. *Journal of Marriage and the Family,* 67, 85–99.

Simmons, R. g., & Blyth, D. A. (1987). *Moving into adolescence.* Hawthorne, NY: Aldine.

Simonton, D. K. (1996). Creativity. In J. E. Birren (Ed.), *Encyclopedia of aging.* San Diego: Academic Press.

Simpkin, P., & Bolding, A. (2004). Update on nonpharmacological approaches to relieve labor pain and prevent suffering. *Journal of Midwifery and Women's Health,* 49, 489–504.

Simpkins, S. D., Fredricks, J. A., Davis-Kean, P. E., & Eccles, J. S. (2006). Healthy mind, healthy habits: The influence of activity involvement in middle childhood. In A. C. Huston and M. N. Ripke (Eds.), *Developmental context in middle childhood.* New York: Cambridge University Press.

Simpson, C. F., Punjabi, N. M., Wolfenden, L., Shardell, M., Shade, D. M., & Fried, L. P. (2005). Relationship between lung function and physical performance in disabled older women. *Journals of Gerontology: Biological Sciences and Medical Sciences,* 60, A350–A354.

Simpson, J. A., Collins, W. A., Tran, S., & Haydon, K. C. (2007). Attachment and the experience and expression of emotions in romantic relationships: A developmental perspective. *Journal of Personality and Social Psychology,* 92, 355–367

Simpson, J. A., Rholes, W. S., & Nelligan, J. S. (1992). Support-seeking and support-giving within couple members in an anxiety provoking situation: The role of attachment styles. *Journal of Personality and Social Psychology,* 62, 434–446.

Sinclair, D. A., & Howitz, K. T. (2006). Dietary restrictions, hormesis, and small molecule mimetics. In E. J. Masoro & S. N. Austad (Eds.), *Handbook of the biology of aging* (6th ed.). San Diego: Academic Press.

Singh, S., Wulf, D., Samara, R., & Cuca, Y. P. (2000). Gender differences in the timing of first intercourse: Data from 14 countries. *Internatio nal Family planning Perspectives,* 26, 21–28, 43.

Sinnott, J. D. (2003). Postformal thought and adult development: Living in balance. In J. Demick & C. Andreoletti (Eds.), *Handbook of adult development.* New York: Kluwer.

Skaff, M. M. (2007). Sense of control and health: A dynamic duo in the aging process. In C. M. Aldwin, C. L. Park, & A. Spiro (Eds.), *Handbook of health psychology and aging.* New York: Guilford.

Skinner, B. F. (1938). *The behavior of organism: An experimental analysis.* New York: Appleton-Century-Crofts.

Skinner, B. F. (1957). *Verbal behavior.* New York: Appleton-Century-Crofts.

Skrha, J., Kunesova, M., Hilgertova, J., Weiserova, H., Krizova, J., Kotrlikova, F. (2005). Short-term very low calorie diet reduces oxidative stress in obese type 2 diabetic patients. *Physiological Research,* 54, 33–39.

Slade, E. P. & Wissow, L. S. (2004). Spanking in early childhood and later behavior problems: A prospective study. *Pediatrics,* 113, 1321–1330.

Slater, A., & Lewis, M. (Eds.). (2007). *Introduction to infant development* (2nd ed.). New York: Oxford University Press.

Slater, A., Field, T., & Hernandez-Reif, M. (2007). *The development of the sense.* New York: Oxford University Press.

Sleet, D. A., & Mercy, J. A. (2003). Promotion of safety, security, and well-being. In M. H. Bornstein, L. Davidson, C. L. M., Keyes, & K. A. Moore (Eds.), *Well-being.* Mahwah, NJ: Erlbaum.

Slobin, D. (1972, July). Children and language: They learn the same way around the world. *Psychology Today,* 71–76.

Slomkowski, C., Rende, R., Conger, K. J., Simons, R. L., & Conger, R. D. (2001). Sisters, brothers, and delinquency: Social influence during early and middle adolescence. *Child Development,* 72, 271–283.

Smetana, J. G., Campione-Barr, N., & Metzger, A. (2006). Adolescent development in interpersonal and societal contexts. *Annual Review of Psychology* (Vol. 57). Palo Alto, CA: Annual Reviews.

Smith, A. D. (1996). Memory. In J. E. Birren (Ed.), *Encydopedia of gerontology* (Vol. 2). San Diego: Academic Press.

Smith, L. A., Oyeku, S. O., Homer, C., & Zuckerman, B. (2006). Sickle cell disease: A question of equity and quality. *Pediatrics,* 117, 1763–1770.

Smith, L. M., Chang, L., Yonekura, M. L., Gilbride, K., Kuo, J., Poland, R. E., Walot, I., & Ernst, T. (2001). Brain proton magnetic resonance spectroscopy and imaging in children exposed to cocaine in utero. *Pediatrics,* 107, 227.

Smith, L., Muir, D. W., & Kisilvesky, B. (2001, April). *Preterm infants' responses to auditory stimulation of varying intensity.* Paper presented at the meeting of the Society for Research in Child Development, Minneapolis.

Smith, L. B., & Breazeal, C. (2007). The dynamic lift of developmental processes. *Developmental Science,* 10, 61–68.

Smith, T. E. C., Polloway, E. A., Patton, J. R., & Dowdy, C. A. (2008). *Teaching students with special needs in inclusive settings* (5th ed.). Boston: Allyn & Bacon.

Smoreda, Z., & Licoppe, C. (2000). Gender-specific use of the domestic telephone. *Social Psychology Quarterly,* 63, 238–252.

Snarey, J. (1987, June). A question of morality. *Psychology Today*, pp. 6–8.

Snow, C. (2007, March). *Socializing children for academic success: the power and the limits of language*. Paper presented at the meeting of the Society for Research in Child Development, Boston.

Snow, C. E., & Yang, J. Y. (2006). Becoming bilingual, biliterate, and bicultural. In W. Damon & R. Lerner (Eds.), *Handbook of child psychology* (6th ed.). New York: Wiley.

Snowdon, D. (2002). *Aging with grace: What the Nun study teaches us about leading longer, healthier, and more meaningful lives*. New York: Bantam.

Snowdon, D. A. (2003). Healthy aging and dementia: Findings from the Nun study. *Annals of Internal Medicine, 139*, 450–454.

Soderman, A. K., & Farrell, P. (2008). *Creating literacy-rich preschools and kindergartens*. Boston: Allyn & Bacon.

Soergel, P., Pruggmayer, M., Schwerdtfeger, R., Mulhaus, K., & Scharf, A. (2006). Screening for trisomy 21 with maternal age, fetal nuchal translucency, and maternal serum biochemistry at 11–14 weeks: A regional experience from Germany. *Fetal Diagnosis and Therapy, 21*, 264–268.

Sollod, R. N. (2000). Religious and spiritual practices. In A. Kazdin (Ed.), *Encyclopedia of psychology*. Washington, DC, & New York: American Psychological Association and Oxford University Press.

Solot, D., & Miller, M. (2002). *Unmarried to each other*. New York: Marlowe.

Sophian, C. (1985). Preservation and infants' search: A comparison of two - and three-location tasks. *Developmental Psychology, 21*, 187–194.

Sorof, J. M., Lai, D., Turner, J., Poffenberger, T., & Portman, R. J. (2004). Overweight, ethnicity, and the prevalence of hypertension in school-aged children. *Pediatrics, 113*, 475–482.

Sowell, E. (2004, July). Commentary in M. Beckman, Crime, culpability, and the adolescent brain. *Science Magazine, 305*, p. 599.

Sowell, E. R., Thompson, P. M., Leonard, C. M., Welcome, S. E., Kan, E., & Toga, A. W. (2004). Longitudinal mapping of cortical thickness and brain growth in children. *Journal of Neuroscience, 24*, 8223–8231.

Sparks, D. L., Hunsaker, J. C., Scheff, S. W., Kryscio, R. J., Heuson, H., & Markesbery, W. R. (1990). Cortical senile plaques in coronary artery disease, aging, and Alzheimer's disease. *Neurobiology of Aging, 11*, 601–607.

Spelke, E. I., & Newport, E. I. (1998). Nativism, empiricism, and the development of knowledge. In W. Damon (Ed.), *Handbook of child psychology* (5th ed., Vol. 2). New York: Wiley.

Spelke, E. S. (1991). Physical knowledge in infancy: Reflections on Piaget's theory. In S.

Carey & R. Gelman (Eds.), *The epigenesis of mind: Essays on biology and cognition*. Hillsdale, NJ: Erlbaum.

Spelke, E. S., & Owsley, C. J. (1979). Intermodel exploration and knowledge in infancy. *Infant Behavior and Development, 2*, 13–28.

Spence, A. P. (1989). *Biology of human aging* Englewood Cliffs, NJ: Prentice Hall.

Spence, J. T., & Buchner, C. E. (2000). Instrumental and expressive traits, trait stereotypes, and sexist attitudes: What do they signify? *Psychology of Women Quarterly, 24*, 44–62.

Spence, J. T., & Helmreich, R. (1978). *Masculinity and feminity: Their psychological dimensions*. Austin: University of Texas Press.

Spencer, M. B. (1999). Social and cultural influences on school adjustment: The application of an identity-focused cultural ecological perspective. *Educational Psychologist, 34*, 43–57.

Speranza, M., Corcos, M., Loas, G., Stephan, P., Guilbaud, O., Perez-Diaz, F., Venisse, J. L., Bizouard, P., Halfon, O., Flament, M., & Jeammet, P. (2005). Depressive personality dimensions and alexithymia in eating disorders. *Psychiatry Research, 135*, 153–163.

Spohr, H. L., Willms, J., & Steinhausen, H. C. (2007). Fetal alcohol spectrum disorders in young adulthood. *Journal of Pediatrics, 150*, 175–179.

Sprei, J. E., & Courtois, C. A. (1988). The treatment of women's sexual dysfunctions arising from sexual assault. In R. A. Brown & J. R. Fields (Eds.), *Treatment of sexual problems in individual and group therapy*. Great Neck, NY: PMA.

Spring, J. (2007). *Deculturalization and the struggle for equality* (5th ed.). New York: McGraw-Hill.

Sprinthall, R. C. (2007). *Basic statistical analysis* (8th ed.). Boston: Allyn & Bacon.

Sroufe, L. A. (2007). Commentary: The place of development in developmental psychology. In A. S. Masten (Ed.), *Multilevel dynamics in developmental psychology*. Mahwah, NJ: Erlbaum.

Sroufe, L. A., Egeland, B., Carlson, E., & Collins, W. A. (2005). The place of early attachment in developmental context. In K. E. Grossman, K. Krossman, & E. Waters (Eds.), *The power of longitudinal attachment research: From infancy and childhood to adulthood*. New York: Guilford.

Sroufe, L. A., Waters, E., & Matas, L. (1974). Contextual determinants of infant affectional response. In M. Lewis & L. Rosenblum (Eds.), *Origins of fear*. New York: Wiley.

Stagner, M. W., & Zweig, J. M. (2007). Indicators of youth health and well-being. In B. V. Brown (Ed.), *Key indicators of child and youth well-being*. Mahwah, NJ: Erlbaum.

Stanley, S. M., Amato, P. R., Johnson, C. A., & Markman, H. J. (2006). Premarital

education, marital quality, and marital stability: Findings from a large, household survey. *Journal of Family Pschology, 20*, 117–126.

Stanley, S. M., Rhoades, G. K., & Markman, H. J. (2006). Sliding versus deciding: Intertia and the premarital cohabitation effect. *Family Relations, 55*, 499–509.

Stanner, S. (2006). New thinking about diet and cardiovascular disease. *Journal of Family Health Care, 16*, 71–74.

Staudinger, U. M. (1996). Psychologische Produktivität und Selbstenfaltung im Alter. In M. M. Baltes & L. Montada (Eds.). *Produktives Leben im Alter*. Frankfurt: Campus.

Stebbins, R. A. (2005). Choice and experiential definitions of leisure. *Leisure Sciences, 27*, 349–352.

Steele, J., Waters, E., Crowell, J., & Treboux, D. (1998, June). *Self-report measures of attachment: Secure bonds to other attachment measures and attachment theory*. Paper presented at the meeting of the International Society for the Study of Personal Relationships, Saratoga Springs, NY.

Steele, M., Hodges, J., Kaniuk, J., Steele, H., D'Agostino, D., Blom, I., Hillman, S., & Henderson, K. (2007). Intervening with maltreated children and their families. In D. Oppenheim & D. F. Goldsmith (Eds.), *Attachment theory in clinical work with children*, New York: Guilford.

Stein, D. J., Fan, J., Fossella, J., & Russell, V. A. (2007). Inattention and hyperactivity-impulsivity: Psychobiological and evolutionary underpinnings. *CNS Spectrum, 12*, 190–196.

Stein, M. T., Kennell, J. H., & Fulcher, A. (2004). Benefits of a doula present at the birth of a child. *Journal of Developmental and Behavioral Pediatrics, 25 (Suppl.)*, S89-S92.

Steinberg, L. D. (1986). Latchkey children and susceptibility to peer pressure: An ecological analysis. *Developing Psychology, 22*, 433–439.

Steinberg, L. D. (2007, in press). Risk-taking in adolescence: New perspectives from brain and behavioral science. *Current Directions in Psychological Science*.

Steinberg, L. D., & Silk, J. S. (2002). Parenting adolescents. In M. Bornstein (Ed.), *Handbook of parenting* (2nd ed., Vol. 1). Mahwah, NJ: Erlbaum.

Steiner, J. E. (1979). Human facial expressions in response to taste and smell stimulation. In H. Reese & L. Lipsitt (Eds.), *Advances in child development and behavior* (Vol. 13). New York: Academic Press.

Stenkley, N. C., Vik, O., & Laukli, E. (2004). The aging ear. *Acta Otolaryngology, 124*, 69–76.

Stephan, K. E., Fink, G. R., & Marshall, J. C. (2006, in press). Mechanisms of hemispheric specialization: Insights from analyses of connectivity. *Neuropsychologia*.

Sternberg, R. J. (1986). *Intelligence applied*. San Diego: Harcourt Brace Jovanovich.

Sternberg, R. J. (1988). *The triangle of love*. New York: Basic Books.

Sternberg, R. J. (2002). Intelligence: The triarchic theory of intelligence. In J. W. Gutherie (Ed.), *Encyclopedia of education* (2nd ed.). New York: Macmillan.

Sternberg, R. J. (2004). Individual differences in cognitive development. In U. Goswami (Ed.), *Blackwell handbook of childhood cognitive development.* Malden, MA: Blackwell.

Sternberg, R. J. (2006). *Cognitive psychology* (4th ed.). Belmont, CA: Wadsworth.

Sternberg, R. J. (2007). G, G's, or Jeez: Which is the best model for developing abilities, competence, and expertise? In P. C. Kyllonen, R. D. Roberts, & L. Stankov (Eds.), *Extending intelligence.* Mahwah, NJ: Erlbaum.

Sternberg, R. J. (2008, in press). The triarchic theory of successful intelligence. In N. Salkind (Ed.), *Encyclopedia of educational psychology.* Thousand Oaks, CA: Sage.

Sternberg, R. J., Grigorenko, E. L., & Kidd, K. K. (2005). Intelligence, race, and genetics. *American Psychologist, 60,* 46–59.

Sternberg, R. J., Grigorenko, E. L., & Kidd, K. K. (2006). Racing toward the finish line. *American Psychologist, 61,* 178–179.

Sterns, H., & Huyck, M. H. (2001) The role of work in midlife. In M. Lachman (Ed.), *Handbook of midlife development.* New York: Wiley.

Stetsenko, A. (2002). Adolescents in Russia: Surviving the turmoil and creating a brighter future B. B. Brown, R. W. Larson, & T. S. Saraswathi (Eds.) *The world's youth.* New York: Cambridge University Press.

Steur, F. B., Applefield, J. M., & Smith, R. (1971). Televised aggression and interpersonal aggression of preschool children. *Journal of Experimental Child Psychology, 11,* 442–447.

Stevens, J., & Killeen, M. (2006). A randomized controlled trial testing the impact of exercise on cognitive symptoms and disability of residents with dementia. *Contemporary Nurse, 21,* 32–40.

Stevenson, H. W. (1995). Mathematics achievement of American students: First in the world by 2000? In C. A. Nelson (Ed.), *Basic and applied perspectives in learning, cognition, and development.* Minneapolis: University of Minnesota Press.

Stevenson, H. W. (2000). Middle childhood: Education and schooling. In A. Kazdin (Ed.), *Encyclopedia of psychology.* Washington, DC, & New York: American Psychological Association and Oxford University Press.

Stevenson, H. W., & Hofer, B. K. (1999). Education policy in the United States and abroad: What we can learn from each other. In G. J. Cizek (Ed.), *Handbook of educational policy.* San Diego: Academic Press.

Stevenson, H. W., Lee, S., Chen, C., Stigler, J. W., Hsu, C., & Kitamura, S. (1990). Contexts of achievement, *Monograph of the Society for Research in Child Development, 55* (Serial No. 221).

Stevenson, H. W., Lee, S., & Stigler, J. W. (1986). Mathematics achievement of Chinese, Japanese, and American children. *Science, 231,* 693–699.

Stevenson, H. W., & Newman, R. S. (1986). Longterm prediction of achievement and attitudes in mathematics and reading. *Child Development, 57,* 646–659.

Stevenson, H. W., & Zusho, A. (2002). Adolescence in China and Japan: Adapting to a changing environment. In B. B. Brown, R. W. Larson, & T. S. Saraswathi (Eds.), *The world's youth.* New York: Cambridge University Press.

Stewart, A. J., Ostrove, J. M., & Helson, R. (2001). Middle aging in women: Patterns of personality change from the 30s to the 50s. *Journal of Adult Development, 8,* 23–37.

Stice, E., Presnell, K., Gau, J., & Shaw, H. (2007). Testing mediators of intervention effects in randomized controlled trials: An evaluation of two eating disorder programs. *Journal of Consulting and Clinical Psychology, 75,* 20–32.

Stifer, E., Sacu, S., Weghaupt, H., Konig, F., Richter-Muksch, S., Thaler, A., Velikay-Parel, M., & Radner, W. (2004). Reading performance depending on the type of cataract and its predictability on the visual outcome. *Journal of Cataract and Refractive Surgery, 30,* 1259–1267.

Stiggins, R. (2008). *Introduction to student-involved assessment for learning* (5th ed.). Upper Saddle River, NJ: Prentice Hall.

Stimpson, J. P., Kuos, Y. F., Ray, L. A., Raji, M. A., & Peek, M. K. (2007, in press). Risk of mortality related to widowhood in older Mexican Americans. *Annals of Epidemiology.*

Stinson, C. K., & Kirk, E. (2006). Structured reminiscence: An intervention to decrease depression and increase self-transcendence in older women. *Journal of Clinical Nursing, 15,* 208–218.

Stipek, D. (2004). Head Start: Can't we have our cake and eat it too. *Education Week, 23* (No. 34), 52–53.

Stipek, D. (2005, February 16). Commentary in *USA Today,* p. 1D.

Stocchl, F. (2006). The levodopa wearing-off phenomenon in Parkinson's disease: Pharmacokinetic considerations. *Expert Opinions in Pharmacotherapy, 7,* 1399–1407.

Stocker, C., & Dunn, J. (1990). Sibling relationships in adolescence: Links with friendships and peer relationships. *British Journal of Developmental Psychology, 8,* 227–244.

Stoel-Gammon, C. & Sosa, A. V. (2007). Phonological development. In E. Hoff & M. Shatz (Eds.), *Blackwell handbook of language development.* Malden, MA: Blackwell.

Stolley, M. R., Fitzgibbon, M. L., Dyer, A., Van Horn, L., Kaufer Christoffel, K., & Schiffer, L. (2003). Hip-Hop to Health Jr., an obesity prevention program for minority preschool children: Baseline characteristics of the participants. *Preventive Medicine, 36,* 320–329.

Stone, R. I. (2006). Emerging issues in long-term care. In R. H. Binstock & L. K. George (Eds.), *Handbook of aging and the social sciences* (6th.). San Diego: Academic Press.

Streissguth, A. P., Martin, D. C., Sandman, B. M., Kirchner, G. L., & Darby, B. L. (1984). Intrauterine alcohol and nicotine exposure: Attention and reaction time in four-year-old children. *Developmental Psychology, 20,* 533–543.

Striano, T., Reid, V. M., & Hochl, S. (2006). Neural mechanisms of joint attention in infancy. *European Journal of Neuroscience. 23,* 2819–2823.

Striegel-Moore, R. H., Silberstein, L. R., & Rodin, J. (1993). The social self in bulimia nervosa: Public self-consciousness, social anxiety, and perceived fraudulence. *Journal of Abnormal Psychology, 102,* 297–303.

Stringer, M., Ratcliffe, S. J., Evans, E. C., & Brown, L. P. (2005). The cost of prennatat care attendance and pregnancy outcomes in low-income working women. *Journal of Obstetrical, Gynecologic, and Neonatal Nursing, 34,* 551–560.

Stroebe, M., Schut, H., & Stroebe, W. (2005). Attachment in coping with bereavement: A theoretical integration. *Review of General Psychology, 9,* 48–66.

Strong, B., Yarber, W., Sayad, B., & De Vault, C. (2008). *Human sexuality* (6th ed.). New York: McGraw-Hill.

Strong-Wilson, T., & Ellis, J. (2007, in press). Children and place: Reggio Emilia's environment as a third teacher. *Theory into practice.*

Studenski, S., Carlson, M. C., Fillet, H., Greenough, W. T. Krammer A., & Rebok, G. W. (2006). From bedside to bench: Does mental and physical activity promote cognitive varitality in late life? *Science of Aging, Knowledge, and Environment, 10,* 21.

Sullivan, K., & Sullivan, A. (1980). Adolescent-parent separation. *Developmental Psychology, 16,* 93–99.

Sutte, N. F. (2006). Energy requirements of infants and children. *Nestle Nutrition Workshop Series: Pediatric Program, 58,* 19–32.

Sutterby, J. A., & Frost, J. (2006). Creating play environments for early childhood: Indoors and out. In B. Spodak & O. N. Saracho (Eds.), *Handbook of research on the education of young children* (2nd ed.). Mahwah, NJ: Erlbaum.

Swaab, D. F., Chung, W. C., Kruijver, F. P., Hofman, M. A., & Ishunina, T. A. (2001). Structural and functional sex differences in the huma n hypothalamus. *Hormones and Behavior, 40,* 93–98.

Swain, S. O. (1992). Men's friendships with women. In P. Nard: (Ed.), *Gender in intimate relationships.* Belmont, CA: Wadsworth.

Swick, D., Senkfor, A. J., & Van Patten, C. (2006). Source memory retrieval is affected by aging and prefrontal lesions: Behavioral and ERP evidence. *Brain Research, 1107,* 161–176.

Sykes, C. J. (1995). *Dumbing down our kids: Why American children feel good about themselves but can't read, write, or add.* New York: St. Martin's Press.

T

Tafaro, L., Cicconetti, P., Baratta, A., Brukner, N., Ettorre, E., Marigliano, V., & Cacciafesta, M. (2007). Sleep quality of centenarians: Cognitive and survival implications. *Archives of Gerontology and Geriatrics, 44S,* S385–S389.

Tafoya, M., & Spitzberg, B. H. (2007). The dark side of infidelity. In B. H. Spitzberg and W. R. Cupach (Eds.), *The dark sidde of interpersonal communication.* Mahwah, NJ: Erlbaum.

Takamura, J. (2007). Global challenges for an aging population. In J. A. Blackburn & C. N. Dulmus (Eds.), *Handbook of gerontology.* New York: Wiley.

Talaro, K. P. (2008). *Foundations of microbiology* (6th ed.). New York: McGraw-Hill.

Talge, N. M., Neal, C., Glover, V., and the Early Stress, Translation Research and Prevention Science Network: Fetal and Neonatal Experience on Child and Adolescent Mental Health (2007). Antenatal maternal stress and long-term effects on neurodevelopment: How and why? *Journal of Child Psychology and Psychiatry, 48,* 245–261.

Talley, R. C., & Crews, J. E. (2007). Framing the public health of caregiving. *American Journal of Public Health, 97,* 224–228.

Tamura, T., & Picciano, M. F. (2006). Folate and human reproduction. *American Journal of Human Reproduction, 83,* 993–1016.

Tan, E. J., Xue, Q. L., Li, T., Carlson, M. C., & Fried, L. P. (2007). Volunteering: A physical activity intervention for older adults-the Experience Crops program in Baltimore. *Journal of Urban Health, 83,* 954–969.

Tannen, D. (1990). *You just don't understand: Women and men in conversation.* New York: Ballantine.

Tantillo, M., Kesick, C. M., Hynd, G. W., & Dishman, R. K. (2002). The effects of exercise on children with attention-deficit hyperactivity disorder. *Medical Science and Sports Exercise, 34,* 203–212.

Tappia, P. S., & Gabriel, C. A. (2006). Role of nutrition in the development of the fetal cardiovascular system. *Expert Review of Cardiovascular Therapy, 4,* 211–215.

Tariot, P. N. (2006). Contemporary issues in the treatment of Aleheimer's disease: Tangible benefits of current therapies. *Journal of Chinical Psychiatry, 67,* (3 Suppl.), S15-S22.

Tasker, F. L., and Golombok, S. (1997). *Growing up in a lesbian family: Effects on child development.* New York: Guilford.

Tassell-Baska J. & Stambaugh, T. (2006). *Comprehensive curriculum for gifted learners* (3rd ed.). Boston: Allyn & Bacon.

Taylor, F. M.A., Ko, R., & Pan, M. (1999). Prenatal and reproductive health care. In E. J. Kramer, S. L. Ivey., & Y-W Ying (Eds.), *Immigrant women's health.* San Francisco: Jossey-Bass.

Taylor, R. D., & Lopez, E. I. (2005). Family management practice, school achievement, and problem behavior in African American adolescents: Mediating processes. *Applied Developmental Psychology, 26,* 39–49.

Taylor, S. E. (2006). *Health psychology* (6th ed.). New York: McGraw-Hill.

Taylor, S. E., Stanton, A. L. (2007). Coping resources, coping processes, and mental health. *Annual Review of Clinical Psychology,* (Vol. 3). Palo Alto, CA: Annual Reviews.

Taylor, S. P. (1982). Mental health and successful coping among Black women. In R. C. Manuel (Ed.). *Minority aging Westport,* CT: Greenwood Press.

te Velde, S. J., De Bourdeaudhuij, I., Throsdottir, I., Rasmussen, M., Hagstromer, M., Klepp, K. I., & Brug, J. (2007). Patterns in sedentary and exercise behaviors and associations with overweight in 9–14-year-old boys and girls–a cross-sectional study. *BMC Public Health, 7,* 16.

Teno, J. M., Clarridge, B. R., Casey, V., Welch, L. C., Wetle, T., Shield, R., & Mor, V. (2004). Family perspectives on end-of-life care at the last place of care. *Journal of the American Medical Association, 291,* 88–93.

Teno, J. M., Gruneir, A., Schwartz, Z., Nanda, A., & Wetle, T. (2007). Association between advance directives and quality of end-of-life care: A national study. *Journal of the American Geriatrics Society, 55,* 189–194.

Terman, L. (1925). *Genetic studies of genius. Vol. 1: Mental and physical traits of a thousand gifted children.* Stanford, CA: Stanford University Press.

Terry, W. S. (2001). *Learning and memory* (3rd ed.). Boston: Allyn & Bacon.

Terry, W., Olson, L. G., Ravenscroft, P., Wilss, L., & Boulton-Lewis, G. (2006). Hospice patients' views on research in hospice care. *Internal Medicine Journal, 36,* 406–413.

Teti, D. M. (2001). Retrospect and prospect in the study of sibling relationships. In J. P. McHale & W. S. Grolnick (Eds.), *Retrospect and prospect in the psychological study of families.* Mahwah, NJ: Erlbaum.

Teti, D. M. (2002). Retrospect and prospects in the study of sibling relationships. In J. P. McHale & W. S. Grolnick (Eds.), *Retrospect and prospect in the psychological study of families.* Mahwah, NJ: Erlbuam.

Thaithumyanon, P., Limpongsanurak, S., Praisuwanna, P., & Punnahitanon, S. (2006). Perinatal effects of amphetamine and heroin use during pregnancy on the mother and infant. *Journal of the Medical Associations of Thailand, 88,* 1506–1513.

Thapar, A., Fowler, T., Rice, F., Scourfield, J., Van Den Bree, M., Thomas, S., Harold, G., & Hay, D. (2003). Maternal smoking during pregnancy and attention deficit hyperactivity disorder symptoms in offspring. *American Journal of Psychiatry, 160,* 1985–1989.

Thelen, E., & Smith, L. B. (2006). Dynamic development of action and thought. In W. Damon & R. Lerner (Eds.), *Handbook of child psychology* (6th ed.). New York: Wiley.

Thiessen, E. D., Hill, E. A., & Saffan, J. R. (2005). Infant-directed speech facilitates word segmentation. *Infancy, 7,* 53–71.

Thomas, A., & Chess, S. (1991). Temperament in adolescence and its functional significance. In R. M. Lerner, A. C. Petersen, & J. Brooks-Gunn (Eds.), *Encyclopedia of adolescence* (Vol. 2). New York: Garland.

Thomas, K. (1998, November 4). Teen cyberdating is a new wrinkle for parents, too. *USA Today,* p. 9D.

Thompson, D. R., Obarzanek, E., Franko, D. L., Barton, B. A., Morrison, J., Biro, F. M., Daniels, S. R., & Striegel-Moore, R. H. (2007). Childhood overweight and cardiovascular disease risk factors: The National Heart, Lung, and Blood Institute Growth and Health Study. *Journal of Pediatrics, 150,* 18–25.

Thompson, M. P., Ho, C. H., & Kingree, J. B. (2007). Prospective associations between delinquency and suicidal behaviors in a nationally representative sample. *Journal of Adolescent Health, 40,* 232–237.

Thompson, R., & Murachver, T. (2001) Predicting gender from electronic discourse. *British Journal of Social Psychology, 40,* 193–208.

Thompson, R. A. (2006). The development of the person. In W. Damon & R. Lerner (Eds.), *Handbook of child psychology* (6th ed.). New York: Wiley.

Thompson, R. A., & Goodvin, R. (2005). The individual child: Temperament, emotion, self, and personality. In M. H. Bornstein & M. E. Lamb (Eds.), *Developmental psychology* (5th ed.). Mahwah, NJ: Erlbaum.

Thompson, R. A., Meyer, S., & McGinley, M. (2006). Understanding values in relationships: The development of conscience. In M. Killen & J. Smetana (Eds.), *Handbook of moral development.* Mahwah, NJ: Erlbaum.

Thornton, P. L., Kieffer, E. C., Salbarian-Pena, Y., Odoms-Young, A., Willis, S. K., Kim, H., & Salinas, M. A. (2006). Weight, diet, and physical activity-related health beliefs and practices among pregnant and postpartum Latino women: The role of social support. *Maternal and Child Health Journal, 10,* 95–104.

Thorton, A., & Camburn, D. (1989). Religious participation and sexual behavior and attitudes. *Journal of Marriage and the Family, 49,* 117–128.

Timmer, E., Westerhof, G. J., & Dittmann-Kohli, F. (2005). "When looking back on my past life I regret...": Retrospective regret in the second half of life. *Death Studies, 29,* 625–644.

Toga, A W., Thompson, P.M., & Sowell, E.R. (2006). Mapping brain maturation. *Trends in Neuroscience, 29,* 148-159.

Tomasello, M. (2003). *Constructing a language: A usage-based theory of language acquisition.* Cambridge, MA: Harvard University Press.

Tomasello, M., & Carpenter, M. (2007). Shared intentionality. *Developmental Science, 10,* 121–125.

Tomasello, M., Carpenter, M., & Liszkowski, U. (2007, in press). A new look at infant pointing. *Child Development.*

Tompkins, G. E. (2006). *Literacy for the 21st century* (4th ed.). Upper Saddle River, NJ: Prentice Hall.

Tong, E. K., England, L., & Glantz, S. A. (2005). Changing conclusions on secondhand smoke in a sudden infant death syndrome review funded by the tobacco industry. *Pediatrics, 115,* e356–e366.

Torjesen, I. (2007). Tackling the obesity burden. *Nursing Times, 103,* 23–24.

Tough, S. C., Newburn-Cook, C., Johnston, D. W., Svenson, L. W. Rose, S., & Belik, J. (2002). Delayed childbearing and its impact on population rate changes in lower birth weight, multiple birth, and preterm delivery. *Pediatrics, 109,* 399–403.

Trask, B. S., & Koivur, M. (2007). Trends in marriage and cohabitation. In B. S. Trask & R. R. Hamon (Eds.), *Cultural diversity and families.* Thousand Oaks, CA: Sage.

Traustadottir, T., Bosch, P. R., & Matt, K. S. (2005). The HPA axis response to stress in women: Effects of aging and fitness. *Psychoneuroendocrinology, 30,* 392–402.

Trazesniewski, K. H., Donnellan, M. B., Caspi, A., Moffitt, T. E., Robins, R. W., Poultin, R. (2006). Adolescent low self-esteem is a risk factor for adult poor health, criminal behavior, and limited economic prospects. *Developmental Psychology, 42,* 381–390.

Treffers, P. E., Eskes, M., Kleiverda, G., & van Alten, D. (1990). Home births and minimal medical interventions. *Journal of the American Medical Association, 246,* 2207–2208.

Trehub, S. E., Schneider, B. A., Thorpe, L. A., & Judge, P. (1991). Observational measures of auditory sensitivity in early infancy. *Development Psychology, 27,* 40–49.

Tresaco, B., Bueno, G., Moreno, L. A., Garagorri, J. M., & Bueno, M. (2004). Insulin resistance and impaired glucose intolerance in obese children and adolescents. *Journal of Physiology and Biochemistry, 59,* 217–223.

Tritten, J. (2004). Embracing midwives everywhere. *Practicing Midwife, 7,* 4–5.

Tucker, J. S., Ellickson, P. L., & Klein, M. S. (2003). Predictors of the transition to regular smoking during adolescence and young adulthood. *Journal of Adolescent Health, 32,* 314–324.

Tucker, J. S., Schwartz, J. E., Clark, K. M., & Friedman, H. S. (1999). Age-related changes in the associations of social network ties with mortality risk. *Psychology and Aging, 14,* 564–571.

Turiel, E. (2006). The development of morality. In W. Damon & R. Lerner (Eds.), *Handbook of child psychology* (6th ed.). New York: Wiley.

Turkeltaub, P. E., Gareau, L., Flowers, D. L., Zeffiro, T. A., & Eden, G. F. (2003). Development of neural mechanisms for reading. *Nature Neuroscience, 16,* 765–780.

Turner, B. F. (1982). Sex-related differences in aging. In B. B. Wolman (Eds.), *Handbook of developmental psychology.* Englewood Cliffs, NJ: Prentice Hall.

Turner, J. M. (2006). X-inactivation: Close encounters of the X kind. *Current Biology, 16,* R259–R261.

Turvey, C. L., Carney, C. Arndt, S., & Wallace, R. B. (1999, November). *Conjugal loss and syndromal depression in a sample of elders ages 70 years and older.* Paper presented at the meeting of the Gerontological Society of America, San Francisco.

Tyas, S. L, Salazar, J. C., Snowdon, D. A., Desrosiers, M. F., Riley, K. P., Mendiondo, M. S., & Kryscio, R. J. (2007, in press). Transitions to mild cognitive impairments, dementia, and death: Findings from the Nun study. *American Journal of Epidemiology.*

U

U.S., Census Bureau. (2001). *Statistical abstracts of the United States.* Washington, DC: U.S. Government Printing Office.

U.S. Census Bureau. (2003). *Population statistics* Washington, DC: Author.

U.S. Census Bureau. (2005). *Population Statistics: People* Washington, DC: Author.

U.S. Census Bureau. (2006). *Population Statistics: People,* Washington, DC: Author.

U.S. Department of Education. (1996). *Number and disabilities of children and youth served under IDEA.* Washington, DC: Office of Special Education Programs, Data Analysis System.

U.S. Department of Energy. (2001). *The human genome project.* Washington, DC: Author.

U.S. Department of Health and Human Services. (2005). *Child abuse and neglect statistics.* Washington, DC: Author.

U.S. Food and Drug Administration (2004, March 19). *An important message for pregnant women and women of cildbearing age who may become prgnant about the risk of mercury in fish.* Washington, DC: U.S. Bureau of the Census.

U.S. Surgeon General's Report. (1990). *The health benefits of smoking cessation.* Bethesda,

MD: U.S. Department of Health and Human Services.

Ubell, C. (1992, December 6). We can age successfully. *Parade,* pp. 14–15.

Umana-Taylor, A. J. (2006, March). *Ethnic identity, acculturation, and enculturation: Considerations in methodology and theory.* Paper presented at the meeting of the Society for Research on Adolescence, San Francisco.

Umana-Taylor, A. J., Bhanot, R., & Shin, N. (2006). Ethinic identity formation in adolescence: The critical role of families. *Journal of Family Issues, 27,* 390–414.

UNAIDS. (2006). *2006 report on the global AIDS epidemic.* Geneva, SWIT: Author.

Underwood, M. K. (2004). Gender and peer relations: Are the two cultures really all that different? In J. B. Kupersmidt & K. A. Dodge (Eds.), *Children's peer relations: From development to intervention.* Mahwah, NJ: Erlbaum.

UNICEF (2004). *The state of the world's children 2004.* Geneva, Swit: Author.

UNICEF. (2006). *The state of the world's children 2006.* Geneva, Swit: Author.

UNICEF. (2007). *State of the world's children 2007.* Geneva, Swit: Author.

United Nations. (2002). *Improving the quality of life of girls.* New York: United Nations. Author.

V

Vaillant, G. E. (1977). *Adaptation to life.* Boston: Little, Brown.

Vaillant, G. E. (1992). Is there a natural history of addiction? In C. P. O'Brien & J. H. Jaffe (Eds.), *Addictive states.* Cambridge, MA: Harvard University Press.

Vaillant, G. E. (2002). *Aging well.* Boston: Little, Brown.

Van Beveren, T. T. (2007, January). *Personal conversation.* Richardson, TX: Department of Psychology, University of Texas at Dallas.

Van Buren, E., & Graham, S. (2003). *Redefining ethnic identity: Its relationship to positive and negative school adjustment outcomes for minority youth.* Paper presented at the meeting of the Society for Research in Child Development, Tampa.

van den berg P., Neumark-Sztainer, D., Hannan, P. J., & Haines, J. (2007). Is dieting advice from magazines helpful or harmful? Five-year associations with weight-control behaviors and psychological outcomes in adolescents. *Pediatrics. 119,* e30–e37.

van Hooren, S. A., Valentijn, A. M., Bosma, H., Ponds, R. W., van Boxtel, M. P., & Jolles, J. (2007). Cognitive functioning in healthy older adults aged 64–81: A cohort study into the effects of age, sex, and education. *Neurospsychology, Development, and Cognition B, 14,* 40–54.

Van Hoorn, J., Nourot, P. M., Scales, B., & Alward, K. R. (2007). *Play at the center of the*

REFERENCES

curriculum (4th ed.). Upper Saddle River, NJ: Prentice Hall.

van Jaarsvdeld, C. H., Ranchor, A. V., Kempen, G. I., Coyne, J. C., van Velduisen, D. J., Ormel, J., & Sanderman, R. (2006). Gender-specific risk factors for mortality associated with incident coronary heart disease—a prospective community-based study. *Preventive Medicine, 43,* 361–367.

van Solinge, H., & Henkens, K. (2005). Couples' adjustment to retirement: A multifactor panel study. *Journals of Gerontology B: Psychological Sciences and Social Sciences, 60* S11–S20.

Vandell, D. L. (2004). Early child care: The known and unknown. *Merrill-Palmer Quarterly, 50,* 387–414.

Vandell, D. L., & Wilson, K. S. (1988). Infants' interactions with mother, sibling, and peer: Contrasts and relations between interaction systems. *Child Development, 48,* 176–186.

Venners, S. A., Wang, X., Chen, C., Wang, L., Chen, D., Guang, W., Huang, A., Ryan, L., O'Conner, J., Lasley, B., Overstreet, J., Wilcox, A., & Xu, X. (2005). Paternal smoking and pregnancy loss: A prospective study using a biomarker of pregnancy. *American Journal of Epidemiology, 159,* 993–1001.

Ventura, S. I., Martin, I. A., Curtin, S. C., & Mathews, T. J. (1997, June 10). *Report of final nationality statistics, 1995.* Washington, DC: National Center for Health Statistics.

Verkooijen, K. T., de Vries, N. K., & Nielsen, G. A. (2007). Youth crowds and substance use: The impact of perceived group norm and multiple group identification. *Psychology of Addictive Behaviors, 21,* 55–61.

Verster, J. C., van Duin, D., Volkerts, E. R., Schreueder, A. H., & Verbaten, M. N. (2002). Alcohol hangover effects on memory functioning and vigilance performance after an evening of binge drinking. *Neuropsychopharmacology, 28,* 740–746.

Villareal, T. T., Banks, M., Sinacore, D. R., Siener, C., & Klein, S. (2006). Effect of weight loss and exercise on frailty in obese older adults. *Archives of Internal Medicine, 166,* 860–866.

Visher, E., & Visher, J. (1989). Parenting coalitions after remarriage: Dynamics and therapeutic guidelines *Family Relations, 38,* 65–70.

Visser, M., Simonsick, E. M., Colbert, L. H., Brach, J., Rubin, S. M., Kritchevsky, S. B., Newman, A. B., & Harris, T. B. (2005). Type and intensity of activity and risk of mobility limitation: The mediating role of muscle parameters. *Journal of the American Geriatric Society, 53,* 762–770.

Vogler, G. P. (2006). Behavior genetics and aging. In J. E. Birren & K. W. Schaie (Eds.), *Handbook of the psychology of aging* (6th ed.). San Diego: Academic Press.

Vondra, J., Sysko, H. B., & Belsky, J. (2005). Developmental origins of parenting: Personality and relationship factors. In T.

Luster & L. Okagaki (Eds.), *Parenting (2nd ed.).* Mahwah, NJ: Erlbaum.

Votruba-Drzal, E., Coley, R. L., & Chase-Lansdale, P. L. (2004). Child care and low-income children's development: Direct and moderated effects. *Child Development, 75,* 296–312.

Voydanoff, P. (1990). Economic distress and family relations: A review of the eighties. *Journal of Marriage and the Family, 52,* 1099–1115.

Vrakking, A. M., van der Heid, A., Onwuteaka-Philipsen, B. D., van der Maas, P. J., & van der Wall, G. (2007). Regulating physician-assisted dying for minors in the Netherlands: Views of pediatricians and other physicians. *Acta Pediatrica, 96,* 117–121.

Vukelich, C., Christie, J., & Enz, B. J. (2008). *Helping children learn language and literacy.* Boston: Allyn & Bacon.

Vygotsky, L. S. (1962). *Thought and language.* Cambridge, MA: MIT Press.

W

Wachs, T. D. (1995). Relation of mild-to-moderate malnutrition to human development: Correlational studies. *Journal of Nutrition Supplement. 125,* 2245s–2254s.

Wachs, T. D. (2000). *Necessary but not sufficient.* Washington, DC: American Psychological Association.

Wainryb, C. (2006). Moral development in culture: Diversity, tolerance, and justice. In M. Killen & J. G. Smetana (Eds.), *Handbook of moral development.* Mahwah, NJ: Erlbaum.

Walden, T. (1991). Infant social referencing. In J. Garber & K. Dodge (Eds.), *The development of emotional regulation and dysregulation.* New York: Cambridge University Press.

Waldman, I. D., & Gizer, I. R. (2006). The genetics of attention deficit hyperactivity disorder. *Clinical Psychology Review, 26,* 396–432.

Walker, L. (1982). The sequentiality of Kohlberg's stages of moral development. *Child Development, 53,* 1130–1136.

Walker, L. J. (2006). Gender and morality. In M. Killen & J. G. Smetana (Eds.), *Handbook of moral development.* Mahwah, NJ: Erlbaum.

Wallace Foundation. (2004). *Out-of-school learning: All work and no play.* New York City: Author.

Wallace-Bell, M. (2003). The effects of passive smoking on adult and child health. *Professional Nurse, 19,* 217–219.

Wallerstein, J. S., & Lewis, J. M. (2005). The reality of divorce: Reply to Gordon (2005). *Psychoanalytic Psychology, 22,* 452–454.

Walls, C. (2006). Shaken baby syndrome education: A role for nurse practitioners with families of small children. *Journal of Pediatric Health Care, 20,* 304–310.

Walper, S., & Beckh, K. (2006). Adolescents' development in high-conflict and separated families: Evidence from a German longitudinal study. In A. Clarke-Stewart & J. Dunn (Eds.), *Families count.* New York: Cambridge University Press.

Walsh, D., & Bennett, N. (2004). *WHY do they act that way?: A survival guide to the adolescent brain for you and your teen.* New York: Free Press.

Walsh, L. V. (2006). Beliefs and rituals in traditional birth attendant practice in Guatamala. *Journal of Transcultural Nursing, 17,* 148–154.

Walshaw, C. A., & Owens, J. M. (2006). Low breastfeeding rates and milk insufficiency. *British Journal of General Practice, 56,* 379.

Warburton, J., & McLaughlin, D. (2006). Doing it from your heart: The role of older women as informal volunteers. *Journal of Women and Aging, 18,* 55–72.

Ward, L. M. (2003). Understanding the role of entertainment media in the sexual socialization of American youth: A review of empirical research. *Developmental Review, 23,* 347–388.

Ward, L. M., & Friedman, K. (2006). Using TV as a guide: Associations between television viewing and adolescents' sexual attitudes and behavior. *Journal of Research on Adolescence, 16,* 133–156.

Ward, R. A., & Spitze, G. D. (2004). Marital implications of parent-adult child coresidence: A longitudinal view. *Journals of Gerontology B: Psychological and Social Sciences, 59,* S2–S8.

Ward, W. F., Qi, W., Van Remmen, H., Zackert, W. E., Roberts, L. J., & Richardson, A. (2005). Effects of age and caloric restriction on lipid peroxidation: Measurement of oxidative stress by F–isoprostane levels. *Journals of Gerontology A: Biological Sciences and Medical Sciences, 60,* 847–851.

Ward-Griffin, C., Oudshoorn, A., Clark, K., & Bol, N. (2007). Mother-adult daughter relationships within dementia care: A critical analysis. *Journal of Family Nursing, 13,* 13–32.

Wardlaw, G. M., & Hampl, J. (2007). *Perspectives in nutrition* (7th ed.). New York: McGraw-Hill.

Wark, G. R., & Krebs, D. L. (2000). The construction of moral dilemmas in everyday life. *Journal of Moral Education, 29,* 5–21.

Warr, P. (1994). Age and employment. In M. Dunnette, L. Hough, & H. Triandis (Eds.), *Handbook of industrial and organizational psychology* (Vol. 4), Palo Alto, CA: Consulting Psychologists Press.

Warr, P. (2004). Work, well-being, and mental health. In J. Baring, E. K. Kelloway, & M. R. Frone (Eds.), *Handbook of work stress.* Thousand Oaks, CA: Sage.

Warren, M. P. (2007). Historical perspectives on postmenopausal hormone therapy:

Defining the right does and duration. *Mayo Clinic Proceedings, 82*; 219–226.

Wasserman, M., Bender, D., & Lee, S. Y. (2007). Use of preventive maternal and child health services by Latina women: A review of published intervention studies. *Medical Care Research and Review, 64,* 4–45.

Waterman, A. S. (1985). Identity in the context of adolescent psychology. In A. S. Waterman (ed.), *Identity in adolescence.* thousand Oaks, CA: Sage.

Waterman, A. S. (1992). Identity as an aspect of optimal psychological functioning. In G. R. Adams, T. P. Gullotta, & R. Montemayor (Eds.), *Adolescent identity formation.* Thousand Oaks, CA: Sage.

Waters, E., Corcoran, D., & Anafara, M. (2005). Attachment, other relationships, and the theory that all good things go together. *Human Development, 48,* 85–88.

Wathen, C. N. (2006). Health information seeking in context: How women make decisions regarding hormone replacement therapy. *Journal of Health Communication. 11,* 477–493.

Watson, D. L. & Tharp, R. G. (2007). *Self-directed behavior* (9th ed.). Belmont, CA: Wadsworth.

Watson, J. A., Randolph, S. M., & Lyons, J. L. (2005). African-American grandmothers as health educators in the family. *International Journal of Aging and Human Development, 60,* 343–356.

Watts, C., & Zimmerman, C. (2002). Violence against women: Global scope and magnitude. *Lancet, 359,* 1232–1237.

Waxman, S. R. (2004). Early world-learning and conceptual development. In U. Goswami (Ed.), *Blackwell handbook of infant development.* Malden, MA: Blackwell.

Waxmen, S. R., & Lidz, J. L. (2006). Early word learning. In W. Damon & R. Lerner (Eds.), *Handbook of child psychology* (6th ed.). New York: Wiley.

Weaver, R. F. (2008). *Molecular biology* (4th ed.). New York: McGraw-Hill.

Wechsler, H., Davenport, A., Sowdall, G., Moetykens, B., & Castillo, S. (1994). Health and behavioral consequences of binge drinking in college. *Journal of the American Medical Association, 272,* 1672–1677.

Wechsler, H., Lee, J. E., Kuo, M., Selbring, M., Nelson, T. F., & Lee, H. (2002). Trends in college binge drinking during a period of increased prevention efforts: Findings from 4 Harvard School of Public Health college alcohol study surveys: 1993–2001. *Journal of American College Health, 50,* 203–217.

Wehren, L. E., Hawkes, W. G., Hebel, J. R., Orwig, D. L., & Magaziner, J. (2005). Bone mineral density, soft tissue body composition, strength, and functioning after hip fracture. *Journal of Gerontology: Biological Sciences and Medical Sciences, 60,* A80–A84.

Weikart, D. P. (1993). *Long-term positive effects in the Perry Preschool Head Start Program.* Unpublished data. High Scope Foundation, Ypsilanti, MI.

Weissbluth, M. (2003). *Healthy sleep habits, healthy child.* New York: Fawcett.

Weisz, A. N., & Black, B. M. (2002). Gender and moral reasoning: African American youth respond to dating. *Journal of Human Behavior in the Social Environment, 5,* 35–52.

Wellman, H. M. (2004). Understanding the psychological world: Developing a theory of mind. In U. Goswami (Ed.), *Blackwell handbook of childhood cognitive development.* Malden, MA: Blackwell.

Wellman, H. M., Cross, D., & Watson, J. (2001). Meta-analysis of theory-of-mind development: The truth about false belief. *Child Development, 72,* 655–684.

Wellman, H. M. & Woolley, J. D. (1990). From simple desires to ordinary beliefs: The early development of everyday psychology. *Cognition, 35,* 245–275.

Wenger, N. S., & Others. (2003). The quality of medical care provided to vulnerable community-dwelling older patients. *Annals of Internal Medicine, 139,* 740–747.

Wenk, G. L. (2006). Neuropathology changes in Alzheimer's disease: Potential targets for treatment. *Journal of Clinical Psychiatry, 67* (Suppl), S3–S7.

Wentzel, K. R., & Asher, S. R. (1995). The academic lives of neglected, rejected, popular, and controversial children. *Child Development, 66,* 754–763.

Wentzel, K. R., Barry, C. M., & Caldwell, K. A. (2004). Friendships in middle school: Influences on motivation and school adjustment. *Journal of Educational Psychology, 96,* 195–203.

Wenze, G. T., & Wenze, N. (2004). Helping left-handed children adapt to school experiences. *Childhood Education, 81,* 25–31.

Werth, J. L. (2004). The relationships among clinical depression, suicide, and other actions that may hasten death. *Behavioral Science and the Law, 22,* 627.

Wertsch, J. V. (2007). Mediation. In H. Daniels, J. Wertsch, & M. Cole (Eds.), *The Cambridge companion to Vygotsky.* New York: Cambridge University Press.

Wespes, E., Moncada, I., Schmitt, H., Jungwirth, A., Chan, M., & Varanese, L. (2007). The influence of age on treatment outcomes in men with erectile dysfunction treated with two regimens of tadalafil: Results of the SURE study. *British Jouranl of Urology International, 99,* 121–126.

Westerman, G., Mareschal, D., Johnson, M. H., Sirois, S., Spratling, M. W., & Thomas, M. S. C. (2007). Neurocontructivism. *Developmental Science, 10,* 75–83.

Wethington, E., Kessler, R. C., & Pixley, J. E. (2004). Turning points in adulthood. In O.

G. Brim, C. D. Ryff, & R. C. Kessler (Eds.), *How healthy are we?* Chicago: University of Chicago Press.

Whetstone, L. M., Morrissey, S. L., & Cummings, D. M. (2007). Children at risk: The association between perceived weight status and suicidal thoughts and attempts in middle school youth. *Journal of School Health, 77,* 59–66.

Whiffen, V. (2001). Depression. In J. Worell (Ed.), *Encyclopedia of women and gender.* San Diego: Academic Press.

Whitbourne, S. K. (2001). The physical aging process in middlife: Interactions with psychological and sociocultural factors. In M. E. Lachman (Ed.), *Handbook of midlife development.* New York: John Wiley.

White, C. B., & Catania, J. (1981). Psychoeducational intervention for sexuality with the aged, family members of the aged, and people who work with the aged. *International Journal of Aging and Human Development.*

White, J. W. (2001). Aggression and gender. In J. Worell (Ed.), *Encyclopedia of gender and women.* San Diego: Academic Press.

White, J. W., & Frabutt, J. M. (2006). Violence against girls and women. In J. Worell & C. D. Goodheart (Eds.), *Handbook of girls' and women's psychological health.* New York: Oxford University Press.

White, L. (1992). Stepfamilies over the life course: Social support In A. Booth & J Dunn (Eds.), *Stepfamilies: Who benefits and who does not?* Hillsdale, NJ: Lawrence Erlbaum.

Whitehead, B. D., & Poponoe, D. (2006). *The state of our unions.* Piscataway, NJ: The National Marriage Project, Rutgers University.

Whitehead, D., Keast, J., Montgomery, V., & Hayman, S. (2004). A preventive health education program for osteoporosis. *Journal of Advanced Nursing, 47,* 15–24.

Whitescarver, K. (2006, April). *Montessori rising: Montessori educational in the United States, 1955-present.* Paper presented at the meeting of the American Education Research Association, San Francisco.

Whitfield, K, E., & Baker-Thomas, T. (1999). Individual differences in aging minorities. *International Journal of Aging and Human Development, 48,* 73–79.

Wiesner, M., & Ittel, A. (2002). Relations of pubertal timing and depressing symptoms to substance use in early adolescence. *Journal of Early Adolescence, 22,* 5–23.

Wigfield, A., & Brynes, J. P., & Eccles, J. S. (2006). Development during middle and early adolescence. In P. A. Alexander & P. H. Wynne (Eds.), *Handbook of educational psychology* (2nd ed.). Mahwah, NJ: Erlbaum.

Wight, D., William Son, L., & Henderson, M. (2006). Parental influences on young people's sexual behavior: A longitudinal analysis. *Journal of Adolescence, 29,* 473–494.

Wiley, D., & Bortz, W. M. (1996). Sexuality and aging—usual and successful. *Journal of Gerontology, 51A,* M142–M146.

Wilkins, K. (2006). Government-subsidized home care. *Health Reports, 17,* 39–42.

Willcox, B. J., Willcox, M. D., & Suzuki, M. (2002). *The Okinawa Program.* New York: Crown.

Willcox, D. C., Willcox, B. J., Sokolovsky, J., & Sakihara, S. (2007, in press). The cultural context of "successful aging" among older women weavers in a northern Okinawan village: The role of productive activity. *Journal of Cross Cultural Georontology.*

Wiliams, J. H., & Ross, L. (2007, in press). Consequences of prenatal toxin exposure for mental health in children and adolescents: A systematic review. *European Child and Adolescent Psychiatry.*

Williams, M. H. (2005). *Nutrition for health, fitness, & sport* (7th ed.). New York: McGraw-Hill.

Willis, S. L., & Martin, M. (2005) Preface. In S. L. Willis & M. Martin (Eds.), *Middle adulthood.* Thousand Oaks, CA: Sage.

Willis, S. L., & Schaie, K. W. (1986). Training the elderly on the ability factors of spatial orientation and inductive reasoning. *Psychology and Aging, 1,* 239–247.

Willis, S. L., & Schaie, K. W. (1994). Assessing everyday competence in the elderly. In C. Fisher & R. Lerner (Eds.), *Applied developmental psychology.* Hillsdale, NJ: Erlbaum

Willis. S. L., & Schaie, K. W. (2005). Cognitive trajector in midlife and cognitive functioning in old age. In S. K. Wills & M. Martin (Eds.), *Middle adulthood* Thousand Oaks, CA: Sage.

Wills, T. A., Murry, V. M., Brody, G. H., Gibbons, F. X., Gerrard, M., Walker, C., & Ainett, M. G. (2007). Ethnic pride and self-control related to protective and risk factors: Test of the theoretical model for the strong African American Families program. *Health Psychology, 26,* 50–59.

Wilmoth, J. M., & Chen, P-C. (2003). Immigrant status, living arrangements, and depressive symptoms among middle-aged and older adults. *Journals of Gerontology B: Psychological and Social Sciences, 58,* S305–S313.

Wilson, A. E., Shuey, K. M., & Elder, G. H. (2003). Ambivalence in relationships of adult children to aging parents and in-laws. *Journal of Marriage and the Family, 65,* 1055–1072.

Wilson, R. S., Mendes de Leon, C. F., Barners, L. L., Schneider, J. A., Beinials, J., Evans, D. A., & Bennett, D. A. (2002). Participation in cognitively stimulating activities and risk of incident Alzheimer disease. *Journal of the American Medical Association, 287,* 742–748.

Wilson, R. S., Mendes de Leon, C. F., Bienas, J. L., Evans, D. A., & Bennett, D. A. (2004). Personality and mortality in old age. *Journal of Gerontology: Psychological Sciences, 59B,* 110–116.

Windle, W. F. (1940). *Physiology of the human fetus.* Philadelphia: W. B. Saunders.

Wineberg, H. (1994). Marital reconciliation in the United States: Which couples are successful? *Journal of Marriage and the Family. 56,* 80–83.

Wink, P., & Dillon, M. (2002). Spiritual development across the adult life course: findings from a longitudinal study. *Journal of Adult Development, 9,* 79–94.

Winner, E. (1996). *Gifted children: Myths and realities.* New York: Basic Books.

Winner, E. (2006). Development in the arts. In W. Damen & R. Leiner (Eds.), *Handbook of child psychology (6th ed.).* New York: Wiley.

Winsler, A., Carlton, M. P., & Barry, M. J. (2000). Age-related changes in preschool children's systematic use of private speech in a natural setting. *Journal of Child Language, 27,* 665–687.

Wise, P. M. (2006). Aging of the female reproductive system. In E. J. Masoro & S. N. Austad (Eds.), *Handbook of the biology of aging (6th ed.).* San Diego: Academic Press.

Wiseman, C. V., Sunday, S. R., & Becker, A. E. (2005). Impact of the media on adolescent boy image. *Child and Adolescent Psychiatric Clinics of North America, 14,* 453–471.

Witkin, H. A., Mednick, S. A., Schulsinger, R., Bakkestrom, E., Christiansen, K. O., Goodenbough, D. R., Hirchhorn, K., Lunsteen, C., Owen, D. R., Phillip, J. Ruben, D. S., & Stocking, M. (1976). Criminality in XYY and XXY men. *Science, 193,* 547–555.

Wocadlo, C., & Rieger, I. (2006). Educational and therapeutic resource dependency at early school age in children who were born very preterm. *Early Human Development, 82,* 29–37.

Wolff, J. L., & Kasper, J. D. (2006). Caregivers of frail elders: Updating a national profile. *Gerontologist, 46,* 344–356.

Wolfson, J., & Morgan, R. (2007). Health decisions and directives about the end of life. In J. A. Blackburn & C. N. Dulmus (Eds.), *Handbook of gerontology.* New York: Wiley.

Wong, A. M., Lin, Y. C., Chou, S. W., Tang, F. T., & Wong, P. Y. (2001). Coordination exercise and postural stability in elderly people: Effect of Tai Chi Chuan. *Archives of Physical Medicine & Rehabilitation, 82,* 608–612.

Wood, J. T. (2001). *Gendered lives* (4th ed.). Belmont, CA: Wadsworth.

Wood, M. J., & Atkins, M. (2006). Immersion in another culture: One strategy for increasing cultural competency. *Journal of Cultural Diversity, 13,* 50–54.

Wood, W., & Eagly, A. H. (2007). Social structural origins of sex differences in human mating. In S. W. Gangestad & J. A. Simpson (eds.), *The evolution of mind.* New York: Guilford.

Woodward, A. L., & Markman, E. M. (1998). Early word learning. In D. Kuhn & R. S. Siegler (Eds.), *Handbook of child psychology* (5th ed., Vol. 2). New York: Wiley.

Wooley, S. C., & Garner, D. M. (1991). Obesity treatment: The high cost of false hope. *Journal of the American Dietetic Association, 91,* 1248–1251.

Worell, J., & Goodheart, C. D. (Eds.), (2006). *Handbook of girls' and women's psychological health.* New York: Oxford University Press.

Worku, B., & Kassie, A. (2005). Kangaroo mother care: A randomized controlled trial on effectiveness of early kangaroo care for low birth weight infants in Addis Ababa, Ethiopia. *Journal of Tropical Pediatrics, 51,* 93–97.

World Health Organization. (2000, February 2). *Adolescent health behavior in 28 countries.* Geneva, Swit: Author.

Worthington, E. L. (1989). Religious faith across the life span: Implication for counseling and research. *Counseling Psychologist, 17,* 555–612.

Wortman, C. B., & Boerner, K. (2007). Reactions to the death of a loved one: Beyond the myths of coping with loss. In H. S. Friedman & R. C. Silver (Eds.), *Foundations of health psychology.* New York: Oxford University Press.

Wu, L. T., Pilowsky, D. J., Schlenger, W. E., & Hasin, D. (2007). Alcohol use disorders and the use of treatment services among college-age young adults. *Psychiatric Services, 58,* 192–200.

X

Xu, F., Markowitz, L. E., Gottlieb, S. L., & Berman, S. M. (2007). Seroprevalence of herpes simplex virus types 1 and 2 in pregnant women in the United States. *American Journal of Obstetrics and Gynecology, 196,* e1–e6.

Xu, Y., Cook, T. J., & Knipp, G. T. (2006). Methods for investigating placental fatty acid Transport. *Methods of Molecular Medicine, 122,* 265–284.

Y

Yaari, R., & Corey-Bloom, J. (2007). Alzheimer's disease. *Seminars in Neurology, 27,* 32–41.

Yang, C. K., Kim, J. K., Patel, S. R., & Lee, J. H. (2005). Age-related changes in sleep/wake patterns among Korean teenagers. *Pediatrics, 115* (Suppl 1), S250–S256.

Yang, Q., Wen, S. W., Leader, A., Chen, X. K., Lipson, J. & Walker, M. (2007). Paternal age and birth defects: How strong is the association. *Human Reproduction, 22,* 696–701.

Yang, S., & Sternberg, R. J. (1997). Taiwanese Chinese people's conceptions of intelligence. *Intelligence, 25,* 21–36.

Yang, S. N., Liu, C. A., Chung, M. Y., Huang, H. C., Yeh, G. C., Wong, C. S., Lin, W. W., Yang, C. H., & Tao, P. L. (2006). Alterations of postsynaptic density proteins in the hippocampus of rat offspring from the morphine-addicted mother: Beneficial effects of dextromethorphan. *Hippocampus, 16,* 521–530.

Yang, X. Z., Liu, Y., Mi, J., Tang, C. S., & Du, J. B. (2007). Pre-clinical atherosclerosis evaluated by carotid artery intima-media thickness and the risk factors for children. *China Medical Journal, 120,* 359–362.

Yang, Y. (2006). How does functional disability affect depressive symptoms in late life? The role of perceived support and psychological resources. *Journal of Health and Social Behavior, 47,* 355–372.

Yang, Y., May, Y., Ni, L., Zhao, S., Li, L., Zhang, J., Fan, M., Liang, C., Cao, J., & Xu, L. (2003). Lead exposure through gestation-only caused long-term memory deficits in young adult offspring. *Experimental Neurology, 184,* 489–495.

Yee, B. W. K., & Chiriboga, D. A. (2007). Issues of diversity in health psychology and aging. In C. M. Aldwin, C. L. Park, & A. Spiro (Eds.), *Handbook of health psychology and aging.* New York: Guilford.

Yoo, H. J., Choi, K. M., Ryu, O. H., Suh, S. I., Kim, N. H., Baik, S. H., & Choi, D. S. (2006). Delayed puberty due to pituitary stalk dysgenesis and ectopic neurophyophysis. *Korean Journal of Internal Medicine, 21,* 68–72.

Yoshida, S., Kozu, T., Gotoda, T., & Saito, D. (2006). Detection and treatment of early cancer in high-risk populations. *Best Practice and Research: Clinical Gastroetelogy, 20,* 745–765.

Young, K. T. (1990). American conceptions of infant development from 1955 to 1984: What the experts are telling parents. *Child Development, 61,* 17–28.

Youngblade, L. M., Theokas, C., Schulenberg, J. Curry, L., Huang, I. C., & Novak, M. (2007). Risk and promotive factors in families, schools, and communities: A contextual model of positive youth development in adolescence. *Pediatrics, 119 Suppl 1991,* S47–S53.

Z

Zacker, R. J. (2006). Health-related implications and management of sarcopenia. *Journal of the Academy of Physician Assistancts, 19,* 24–29.

Zangl, R., & Mills, D. L. (2007). Increased brain activity to infant-directed speech in 6- and 13-month-old infants. *Infancy, 11,* 31–62.

Zarit, S. H., & Knight, B. G. (Eds.). (1996). *A guide to psychotherapy and aging.* Washington, DC: American Psychological Association.

Zentall, S. S. (2006). *ADHD and education.* Upper Saddle River, NJ: Prentice Hall.

Zeskind, P. S., Klein, L., & Marshall, T. R. (1992). Adults' perceptions of experimental modifications of durations and expiratory sounds in infant crying. *Developmental Psychology, 28,* 1153–1162.

Zhang, L-F, & Sternberg, R. J. (2008, in press). Learning in cross-cultural perspective. In T. Husen & T. N. Postlethwait (Eds.), *International encyclopedia of education* (3rd ed.). London: Elsevier.

Zigler, E. F., Gilliam, W. S., & Jones, S. M. (2006). *A vision for universal preschool education.* New York: Cambridge University Press.

Zigler, E. F., & Styfco, S. J. (1994). Head Start: Criticisms in a constructive context. *American Psychologists, 49,* 127–132.

Zimmerman, P. (2007, March). *Attachment in adolescence.* Paper presented at the meeting of the Society for Research in Child Development, Boston.

Zimmerman, R. S., Khoury, E., Vega, W. A., Gil, A. G., & Warheit, G. J. (1995). Teacher and student perceptions of behavior problems among a sample of African American, Hispanic, and non-Hispanic White students. *American Journal of Community Psychology, 23,* 181–197.

Zinner, N. (2007). Do food dose and timing affect the efficacy of sildenfil? A radomized placebo-controlled study. *Journal of Sexual Medicine, 4,* 137–144.

Zisook, S., & Kendler, K. S. (2007). Is bereavement-related depression different than non-bereavement-related depression? *Psychological Medicine, 19,* 1–31.

Zittleman, K. (2006, April). *Being a girl and being a boy: The voices of middle schoolers.* Paper presented at the meeting of the American Educational Research Association, San Francisco.

Zuckoff, A., Shear, K., Frank, E., Daley, D. C., Seligman, K., & Silowash, R. (2006). Treating complicated grief and substance use disorders: A pilot study. *Journal of Substance Abuse and Treatment, 30,* 205–211.

Zunzunegui, M., Alvarado, B. E., Del Ser, T., & Vtero, A. (2003). Social networks, social integration, and social engagement determine cognitive decline in communuity-dwelling Spanish older adults. *Journals of Gerontology B: Psychological Sciences and Social Sciences, 58,* S93–S100.

Zverev, Y. P. (2006). Cultural and environmental pressure against left-hand preference in urban and semi-urban Malawi. *Brain and Cognition. 60,* 295–303.

Credits

Text and Line Art Credits

CREDITS

Name Index

NAME INDEX

Subject Index

SUBJECT INDEX

in early childhood, 144
euthanasia and, 423–424
forms of mourning and, 432–433
grieving and, 429–430
historical changes and, 424–425
Kübler-Ross' stages of dying and, 426–427
in late adulthood, 389
of life partner, 431–432
making sense of the world and, 430–431
in middle adulthood, 350
Natural Death Act and, 422–423
perceived control and denial and, 427–428
suicide and, 301–302
type of, coping and, 430
Death with Dignity Act, 424
Debriefing, 32
Deception in research, 32–33
Decision making, 276–277
Deferred imitation, 100
Delivery. See Birth process
Dementia, 400–402
Dendrites, 76, 77
Denial, death and, 427–428
Denial and isolation stage of dying, 426
Dependent variable, 29–30
Depression
in adolescence, 300–301
in late adulthood, 399–400
postpartum, 70
Depression stage of dying, 427
Depth perception
in infancy, 91–92
in late adulthood, 387
Descriptive research, 28
Developing countries, early childhood education in, 162–163
Development. See also specific age groups
age and, concepts of, 13–14
biological, cognitive, and socioemotional processes in, 10–11
as coconstruction of biology, culture, and the individual, 6
contextual nature of, 5–6
continuity-discontinuity issue and, 15–16
definition of, 2
growth, maintenance, and regulation of loss in, 6
lifelong nature of, 4
life-span approach to study of. See Life-span perspective
multidimensional nature of, 4
multidirectional nature of, 4
multidisciplinary nature of, 5
nature-nurture issue and. See Nature-nurture issue
periods of, 11–13
plasticity of, 4–5
stability-change issue and, 15
traditional approach to study of, 3
Developmentally appropriate practice, 159–160
Developmental periods, 11–13
Developmental research. See Research in life-span development
Development theories, 16–25
behavioral and social cognitive, 21–22
cognitive, 19–21
eclectic orientation to, 25
ecological, 24–25
ethological, 23–24
psychoanalytic, 16–19
Diabetes, 44
Diet, maternal, prenatal development and, 56–57
Dieting in early adulthood, 312–313
Difficult children, 119
Direct instruction approach, 249–250

Director of children's services/Head Start, 161
Disabilities in middle and late childhood, 200–203
Disease. See Illness and disease; specific conditions
Disequilibrium in Piaget's theory of cognitive development, 95
Dishabituation, 89–90
Divergent thinking, 208
Diversity, 7–9
Divided attention in late adulthood, 394
Divorce, 337
children and, 183–185
dealing with, 341–342
in middle adulthood, 373–374
older adults and, 412–413
DNA, 38, 39
Dominant genes, 41–42
Dominant-recessive genes principle, 41–42
Doulas, 62–63
Down syndrome, 42, 43, 58
Dropping out, 279
Drugs
for childbirth, 63–64
teratogenetic, 53–54
Dual-career couples, 325–326
Dynamic systems theory, 83–84
Dyslexia, 200

E

Early adulthood, 12, 306–328
careers and work in, 323–326
cognitive development in, 320–323
lifestyles in, 334–338
physical, 310–315
sexual development in, 315–320
socioemotional development in, 329–343
transition from adolescence to, 307–310
transition from childhood to, 330–331
Early childhood, 11, 137–158
brain in, 139
cognitive development in, 144–155
emotional development in, 168–169
families during, 174–187
illness and death in, 143–144
language development in, 155–158
moral development in, 169–171
motor development in, 140–141
nutrition in, 141–143
physical development in, 138–139
socioemotional development in, 165–193
Early childhood education, 158–163
child-centered kindergarten and, 158
controversies in, 161–162
cross-cultural variations in, 162–163
developmentally appropriate and inappropriate, 159–160
for disadvantaged children, 160
Montessori approach to, 158–159
Early identification and intervention for reducing adolescent problems, 303
Easy children, 119
Eating disorders, 272–273
Eating in early adulthood, 312–313
Eclectic theoretical orientation, 25
Ecological theory, 24–25
evaluation of, 25
of perceptual development, 89
Ectoderm, 49
Education, 7. See also College; School(s)
bilingual, 222
for children with disabilities, 202–203
early childhood. See Early childhood education
intelligence and, 215
No Child Left Behind Act and, 203, 250

teaching strategies based on Vygotsky's theory and, 150–151
Education for All Handicapped Children Act of 1975, 202
Effortful control, 119
Eggs, 40
Egocentrism
adolescent, 275–276
in preoperational stage, 145–146
Elaboration to improve memory, 207
Eldercare, 411
Electra complex, 172
Embryo, 49
Embryonic period, 49–50
Emerging adulthood, 307–310
Emotion(s)
definition of, 114
early, 115
maternal, prenatal development and, 57
postpartum fluctuations in, 70–71
regulation of, 118–119, 169
self-conscious, 168
Emotional abuse of children, 179
Emotional development. See also Socioemotional development
biological and environmental influences on, 114–115
child care and, 130–134
in early childhood, 168–169
family and, 128–130
in infancy, 114–119, 127–134
in middle and late childhood, 230–231
social context and, 127–134
Emotional expression, social relationships and, 115–118
Emotion-coaching parents, 168–169
Emotion-dismissing parents, 168–169
Empathy, 169
Employment. See Career entries; Work
Empty nest syndrome, 374–375
Endoderm, 49
Environmental hazards, prenatal development and, 59
Environmental influences
on emotional development, 114–115
on intelligence, 214–215
on language development, 106–110
Epigenetic view, 47–48
Episodic memory in late adulthood, 394–395
Equilibration in Piaget's theory of cognitive development, 95
Erectile dysfunction, 352
Erikson's psychosocial theory, 17–19
early adulthood and, 332
early childhood and, 166
identity and, 285
infancy and, 123, 124
late adulthood and, 406–407
middle adulthood and, 363–364
middle and late childhood and, 230
Estradiol, 261
Estrogen, 261
Ethics in research, 32–33
Ethnic identity, 287–288
Ethnicity, 8. See also Culture; specific groups
academic performance and, 250, 251–253
in adolescence, 297–299
diversity in workplace and, 326
families and, 186–187
immigration and, 298
late adulthood and, 416
life expectancy and, 382
socioeconomic status and, 298–299
Ethological theory, 23–24
evaluation of, 23–24
Ethology, 23
Euthanasia, 423–424

adolescent conflict with, 289–291
adolescent substance use and abuse and, 271
children's weight and, 200
developmental changes in parent-child relationships and, 241–242
emotion-coaching, 168–169
emotion-dismissing, 168–169
empty nest syndrome and, 374–375
gay and lesbian, 185–186
as managers, 242
older adults as, 413–414
working, 182–183, 243–244
Parental leave, 130–131
Parent educators, 340
Parenthood, 340–341
Parenting, 7
context of, 178
coparenting and, 177–178
punishment and, 176–177
styles of, 175–176
temperament and, 120–121
Parietal lobes, 76
Passive euthanasia, 423
Passive genotype-environment correlations, 47
Pastoral counselors, 359
Paternity leave, 130
Pattern perception in infancy, 91
Pediatricians, 82
Peer pressure in adolescence, 292
Peer relations. *See also* Friendships
in adolescence, 291–295, 296–297
adolescent substance use and abuse and, 271
developmental changes and, 244
in early childhood, 169, 188
gender differences and, 173–174
in middle and late childhood, 244–248
sociometric status and, 245–246
Perceived control, death and, 427
Perception, 89
intermodal, 94
Perceptual development
ecological view of, 89
in infancy, 88–94
study of, 89–91
Perceptual speed in late adulthood, 395
Perinatal nurses, 66
Perry Preschool program, 160, 303
Personal control in midlife, 367–368
Personal fables, 275–276
Personality
big five factors of, 370–371
in late adulthood, 409–410
Personality development
child care and, 130–134
family and, 128–130
independence and, 123
in infancy, 121–123, 127–134
life-events approach to, 366–367
in middle adulthood, 363–372
in middle and late adulthood, 227–230
sense of self and, 122–123
social context and, 127–134
stages of adulthood and, 363–366
trust and, 121
Perspective taking, 169
Phenotype, 41
Phenylketonuria (PKU), 44–45
Phonemes, 103
Phonics approach to reading instruction, 221
Phonology, 155
Physical abuse of children, 179
Physical development. *See also* Exercise; Growth; Health; Height; Weight
in early adulthood, 310–315
gender differences in, 237–238

in late adulthood, 386–388
in middle adulthood, 346–353
in middle and late childhood, 195–197
Physical performance in early adulthood, 310
Physiological measures, 28
Piaget's cognitive developmental theory, 19–20
adolescence and, 273–275
early adulthood and, 321–322
early childhood and, 189
evaluation of, 274–275
infancy and, 94–98
middle and late childhood and, 203–205
Pituitary gland, 261
Placenta, 49–50
Play, 188–190
functions of, 188–189
types of, 189–190
Play therapy, 188–189
Pluralism, 298
Polychlorinated biphenyls (PCBs), prenatal development and, 57
Polygenic inheritance, 42
Popular children, 245
Postconventional reasoning, 233
Postformal thought, 322
Postpartum depression, 70
Postpartum period, 69–71
emotional and psychological adjustments in, 70–71
physical adjustments in, 69–70
Poverty. *See also* Socioeconomic status (SES)
in early childhood, 144
early childhood education for disadvantaged children and, 160
in late adulthood, 411
Practical intelligence, 212
Practice play, 189
Pragmatics, 157
Precocity, 219
Preconventional reasoning, 232
Prefrontal cortex, 77
Pregnancy. *See also* Prenatal development
adolescent, 266–268
cultural beliefs about, 60–61
trimesters of, 50
Prenatal care, 59–60
Prenatal development, 48–61
cultural beliefs about pregnancy and, 60–61
in embryonic period, 49–50
in fetal period, 50
in germinal period, 49
hazards to, 52–59
prenatal care and, 59–60
prenatal testing and, 50–51
reproductive technology and, 51–52
Prenatal period, 11
Prenatal tests, 50–51
Preoperational stage, 20, 145–148
centration and, 147–148
intuitive thought substage of, 146
symbolic function substage of, 145–146
Prepared childbirth, 64
Pretense/symbolic play, 190
Preterm infants, 66–67
Primary circular reactions, 96
Private speech, 149
Project Head Start, 160
Prosocial behavior
moral development and, 236–237
television and, 192
Proximodistal pattern, 75
Psychoactive drugs as teratogens, 53
Psychoanalytic theory, 16–19
of Erikson. *See* Erikson's psychosocial theory

evaluation of, 19
of Freud, 17, 123
of gender, 172
Psychological abuse of children, 179
Psychological age, 14
Psychosexual stages, 17
Psychosocial stages, 17–19
Psychosocial theory, 17–19. *See also* Erikson's psychosocial theory
Puberty, 259–263
body image in, 262
early and late maturation and, 263
height and weight and, 260–261
hormonal changes in, 261
sexual maturation and, 160
timing and variations in, 262
Public policy, 9–10
aging society and, 410–411
Punishment in early childhood, 176–177

Q

Questionnaires, 27

R

Random assignment, 3030
Rape, 319–320
Rapid eye movement (REM) sleep, 79
Rapport talk, 342
Raven Progressive Matrices, 216–217
Reading in middle and late childhood, 220–221
Reasoning
conventional, 233
moral, 170
postconventional, 233
preconventional, 232
Recasting, 108
Receptors, sensory, 88
Recessive genes, 41–42
Reciprocal socialization, 129
Referral bias, 200
Reflexes, 84–85
Reflexive smile, 116
Rejected children, 245
Religion
health and, 358–359
in middle adulthood, 357–359
Remarriage, 337–338
older adults and, 412–413
stepfamilies and, 242–243
REM sleep, 79
Report talk, 342
Reproductive technology, 51–52
Research designs, 28–30
Research in behavior genetics, 45–46
Research in life-span development, 25–33
data collection methods for, 26–28
ethics and, 32–33
research designs for, 28–30
time span of, 30–32
Respite care for Alzheimer disease, 402
Retirement, 398–399
Rh factor, 55
RhoGAM, 55
Rites of passage, 297
Roles
gender. *See* Gender roles
social role theory and, 172
Romantic love, 333
Rooming-in, 69
Rooting reflex, 84, 85
Rubella, prenatal development and, 55–56

S

Sandwich generation, 378
Sarcopenia, 348
Scaffolding, 129, 149